## FRANKLIN PARK PUBLIC LIBRARY
## FRANKLIN PARK, ILL.

# Beat Culture

# Editorial Advisors

# Beat Culture

## Icons, Lifestyles, and Impact

Edited by William T. Lawlor,
University of Wisconsin–Stevens Point

A B C ⬤ C L I O

Santa Barbara, California    Denver, Colorado    Oxford, England

Cataloging-in-Publication Data is available from the Library of Congress

08 07 06 05  10 9 8 7 6 5 4 3 2 1

This book is also available on the World Wide Web as an eBook. Visit abc-clio.com for details.

ABC-CLIO, Inc.
130 Cremona Drive, P.O. Box 1911
Santa Barbara, California 93116-1911

This book is printed on acid-free paper ∞.
Manufactured in the United States of America

For Valentina Peguero, who is simply the best!

Permission to quote from *Naked Lunch* (1962) by William Burroughs is granted by Grove/Atlantic, 641 Broadway, New York, New York 10003-4793.

Permission to quote from *Cranial Guitar* by Bob Kaufman is granted by Coffee House Press, 27 N. 4th Street, #400, Minneapolis, MN 55401.

Quotations of copyrighted works of Jack Kerouac reprinted by permission of Sll/sterling Lord Literistic, Inc. Copyright by Jack Kerouac.

Brief excerpts from "Bomb" and "Marriage" from *The Happy Birthday of Death* by Gregory Corso, copyright ©1960 by New Directions Publishing Corp. Reprinted by permission of New Directions Publishing Corp. SALES TERRITORY: World rights.

Excerpt from "Often I Am Permitted to Return to a Meadow" by Robert Duncan from *The Opening of the Field* by Robert Duncan, copyright ©1960 by Robert Duncan. Reprinted by permission of New Directions Publishing Corp. SALES TERRITORY: World rights.

Brief excerpts from "Dog" by Lawrence Ferlinghetti from *A Coney Island of the Mind*, copyright ©1958 by Lawrence Ferlinghetti. Reprinted by permission of New Directions Publishing Corp. SALES TERRITORY: World rights.

Excerpt from "Monet's Lilies Shuddering" by Lawrence Ferlinghetti from *Who Are We Now?* Copyright ©1976 by Lawrence Ferlinghetti. Reprinted by permission of New Directions Publishing Corp. SALES TERRITORY: World rights.

"The Silver Swan: II" by Kenneth Rexroth, from *Flower Wreath Hill*, copyright ©1979 by Kenneth Rexroth. Reprinted by permission of New Directions Publishing Corp. SALES TERRITORY: World rights.

Excerpt from "A Berry Feast" by Gary Snyder from *The Back Country*, copyright ©1968 by Gary Snyder. Reprinted by permission of New Directions Publishing Corp. SALES TERRITORY: World rights.

Brief excerpt from *The Real Work: Interviews and Talks 1964–1979*, copyright ©1980 by Gary Snyder. Reprinted by permission of New Directions Publishing Corp. SALES TERRITORY: World rights.

# Contents

# Contents

Contents

# Thematic Entry List

## People

Adam, Helen
Allen, Donald
Allen, Steve
Amram, David
Apollinaire, Guillaume
Baraka, Amiri
Berman, Wallace
Blackburn, Paul
Blakey, Art
Bowles, Jane
Bowles, Paul
Brautigan, Richard
Bremser, Bonnie
Bremser, Ray
Breton, André
Brooks, Eugene
Brossard, Chandler
Bruce, Lenny
Buckley, Lord
Bukowski, Charles
Burroughs, Ilse Herzfeld
   Klapper
Burroughs, William Seward
Burroughs, William Seward, Jr.
   (III)
Caen, Herb
Cage, John
Cannastra, Bill

Carr, Lucien
Carroll, Paul
Cassady, Carolyn
Cassady, Neal
Charters, Ann
Charters, Sam
Chase, Haldon "Hal"
Clausen, Andy
Coleman, Ornette
Coltrane, John
Conner, Bruce
Corso, Gregory
Cowen, Elise
Creeley, Robert
Cunningham, Merce
de Kooning, Willem
DeFeo, Jay
di Prima, Diane
Duncan, Robert
Dylan, Bob
Ellvins, Kells
Everson, William (Brother
   Antoninus)
Fariña, Richard
Ferlinghetti, Lawrence
Frank, Robert
Gaddis, William
Gaillard, Slim
Genet, Jean

Gillespie, John Brinks
Ginsberg, Allen
Glass, Philip
Goddard, Dwight
Goodrow, Garry
Gordon, Dexter
Gorky, Arshile
Grauerholz, James
Gray, Wardell
Guthrie, Woody
Gysin, Brion
Hawkins, Coleman
Herms, George
Holiday, Billie
Holmes, John Clellon
Huncke, Herbert
Hunt, Tim
Joans, Ted
Johnson, Joyce
Jones, Hettie
Kammerer, David Eames
Kandel, Lenore
Kaufman, Bob
Kenton, Stan
Kerouac, Jack
Kerouac, Jan
Kerouac, Joan Haverty
Kesey, Ken Elton
Kline, Franz

# General Introduction

This encyclopedia of Beat Culture examines the meaning of "beat," the people and writers of the Beat Generation, the participants in artistic movements surrounding the Beats, and the culture and history of the era.

The Beat literary movement, which had its beginnings in New York City in the 1940s and grew in the 1950s through interaction in San Francisco with artists from the San Francisco Literary Renaissance and communication with artists at the Black Mountain School in Black Mountain, North Carolina, is chiefly represented by Allen Ginsberg, Jack Kerouac, and William S. Burroughs, but dozens of other writers are associated with the Beat spirit—a spirit so diverse that the best unifying principles are individuality and intensity of expression.

Perhaps the Beat Generation should be referred to as Jack Kerouac and the Beat Generation. A profound, prolific, and innovative writer, Kerouac was the so-called King of the Beats, the incarnation of the Beat spirit. Kerouac coined the phrase "Beat Generation," and he ultimately became the Suffering Servant who endured personal tragedy, hostility, and misunderstanding. Through his literature, which expressed a broad love for the United States and its ceaseless parade of startling individuals, he sought to redeem and bless the world.

Granted, Kerouac was an alcoholic, and through alcoholism he descended into death. In his final years, he was a political conservative, and he rejected the Beat Generation and the political dissent expressed by Ginsberg, Lawrence Fer-linghetti, Ed Sanders, and others. Even so, the radical Beats never abandoned their admiration for Kerouac, always seeing past intolerance and intoxication to remember the "Great Rememberer." As Ginsberg stood at Kerouac's open casket in Lowell, Massachusetts, in October 1969, he said to Ann Charters, "I think Jack dreamed us all" (quoted in Charters, *Beats and Company*, 24).

Yet Charters herself argues that Ginsberg, not Kerouac, was the source of unity for the Beats. Charters writes that Ginsberg "brought the whole Beat Generation into being with the strength of his vision of himself and his friends as a new beginning—as a new generation. He wove the threads that kept them together, just as he held together the threads that tied his life and his art to the generations of poets before him—Blake, Whitman, Mayakovsky, William Carlos Williams—and to his father and to the memory of his mother Naomi" (Charters, *Beats and Company*, 24). Ginsberg was a master of communications and persuasion, and applying his early experience in marketing, he connected ideas with thinkers, books with readers, and performances with audiences. He was the charismatic person whose personal contacts and public oratory helped the Beats to emerge, flourish, and endure.

Behind the marketing and the spirituality loomed William S. Burroughs, the oldest of the three major Beat writers and the last to die. A Harvard man, Burroughs had the intellectual resources to stimulate diverse reading and conversation among his younger colleagues. At the same time, Burroughs had a taste for the world of petty crime, drugs, and homosexuality. His conventional dress and appearance effectively disguised his readiness to challenge literary and societal conventions. Burroughs acted as an undercover agent bent on breaking down the forces of control. Kerouac admired Burroughs for his intelligence and erudition, and Ginsberg insisted that *Naked Lunch* would "drive everybody mad" ("Howl," dedication page).

The literary movement led by Kerouac, Ginsberg, and Burroughs sprang from many sources and events, but the legendary reading at the 6 Gallery in San Francisco on 7 October 1955, which included Ginsberg's first public reading of "Howl," is often cited as a seminal occurrence, perhaps because the reading led to Lawrence Ferlinghetti's publication of *Howl and Other Poems* and the subsequent "Howl" censorship trial that enhanced sales of the book and generated national publicity. In September 1957, Kerouac's *On the Road,* aided by Gilbert Millstein's prescient and insightful review in the *New York Times,* became a best-seller. With these successes, the Beat literary writers, long an underground and marginalized group, came into public view, provoking unceasing reactions, objections, and cultural transformations.

The "new vision" of the Beat spirit was born as World War II raged toward a nuclear conclusion. While the end of the war led many citizens to seek fulfillment through family, career, and consumerism, the war's end also led to the Korean War, an arms race, the Cold War, the Red Scare, McCarthyism, the military-industrial complex, secret FBI files, and the ongoing threat of the nuclear termination of human civilization. What good were a house with a picket fence, a shiny car, and a washing machine if one had to dig a fallout shelter and be ready to enter it at a moment's notice? What good were a career and social status if society required conformity in dress, language, taste, and thought? What good was a family if divergence from expectations about marriage and parenthood meant that sons and daughters might be committed to institutions for mental health and undergo electroshock treatment?

Even as these pervasive historical and cultural forces antagonized the Beats, artistic activities were inspiring. Spontaneity became the hallmark of creativity as Charlie Parker and other musicians demonstrated their spur-of-the-moment innovation in jazz, as Jackson Pollock made the *act* of painting the focus of artistry, as Merce Cunningham relied on chance for the outcome of his dance, as performance humor thrived on improvisation, as Robert Frank and Alfred Leslie made capturing the moment the object of film, as LeRoi Jones and Diane di Prima made *The Floating Bear* an artistic newsletter of immediacy, as the Living Theatre made drama vibrate with the here and now, and as Neal Cassady's "Joan Anderson Letter" provided a lesson in instantaneous personal exuberance.

Kerouac insisted that American literature was "waiting and bleeding for" the features that writers were systematically revising out of their works (letter to Malcolm Cowley on September 11, 1955, *Selected Letters,* I, 516). "First thought best thought," a phrase attributed to Chögyam Trungpa, stands high in Ginsberg's list of aphorisms and slogans (*Cosmopolitan Greetings,* 13). Burroughs sought an artistic answer to the stagnating forces of control and conformity through cut-ups. Happy with the willful and playful derangement of the senses, Gregory Corso experimented with "goofing," a seemingly nonsensical contortion of language that piqued the imagination with the power of surrealism: "Radio belly! Cat shovel!"; "Telephone snow, ghost parking"; "The top of the Empire State / arrowed in a broccoli field in Sicily" (*The Happy Birthday of Death,* 30, 31, and in the foldout section).

With an emphasis on spontaneity and a desire to dismantle control and conformity, the key themes of the Beat spirit came to the fore. Candor, confession, and honesty—especially about sexuality (including homosexuality)—made the revelation of "secret scatological thought" (Kerouac, *Pull My Daisy,* 23) not only permissible but also desirable. Pretenses and artificiality had to be stripped away; nakedness became the rule not only for the body but also for the soul.

In addition to candor, at the heart of the Beat outlook were sympathy and tenderness. One needed to see others and recognize with imaginative insight their history, backgrounds, values, goals, predicaments, joys, satisfactions, and sorrows. One needed not to intrude but to savor with compassionate appreciation and understanding that reached back to a primordial past and ahead to a heavenly future. Faced with suffering and death, the Beats rejoiced optimistically and innocently in the blessings of life—beatitude. The Beats set out for what Kerouac on *The Steve Allen Show* in 1959 called "pleasure in life," seeking what Ferlinghetti's dog sought by "touching and tasting and testing everything" ("Dog," in *A Coney Island of the Mind,* 68), penetrating the *real* reality. Such experience gave the Beats the means to talk about ontology, eschatology, Dionysian fervor, and religious philosophy. Always aware of the inevitability of suffering and death, the Beats, as Kerouac insisted, were primarily religious (quoted by Holmes, "The Philosophy of the Beat Generation" [67]).

The religious dimensions of the Beats are evident in the boyhood of Kerouac, whose connection to Catholicism especially permeates his novels set in Lowell, Massachusetts, where he was educated in the Catholic schools. Ginsberg's connection to Jewish tradition is apparent in "Kaddish," a poem in honor of Ginsberg's mother written in a scheme parallel to that of Jewish prayers for the dead. Explorations of Eastern religions and meditation are found not only in the works of Kerouac and Ginsberg, but also in the writings of Gary Snyder, Philip Whalen, Joanne Kyger, Lenore Kandel, Diane di Prima, and many others. Zen Buddhism was often a refuge for the Beats, but flexibility and individuality prevailed, with each person discovering the combination of beliefs and practices that yielded the greatest personal satisfaction.

The themes of the Beats could not be expressed in standard metrical cadences, but had to find life in numerous and various literary forms, in the rhythms and accents of natural speech, or in the unpredictable flow of jazz phrasing. The long lines of Walt Whitman, his catalogs of particular details, the imagism of William Carlos Williams and Ezra Pound, and the surrealism of poets and painters were influences. Autobiography was transformed

into personal myth and legend; the journey of life on the road inevitably was metaphoric, drawing allusively on the imaginative flight of Cervantes's Don Quixote, Twain's Huck Finn, Wolfe's Eugene Gant, Bunyan's Christian, and countless figures from the Bible.

Nevertheless, when publicity catapulted the Beats to national attention, the aforementioned themes and artistry went largely unnoticed while a popular, often sensationalized image of the Beats was consolidated. The Beats became associated with the Beat party held at the Beat pad, where liquor and drugs intensified an orgy. Columnist Herb Caen coined the term "beatnik," converting Beat artistry into a caricature of laziness and dirtiness. Feature stories in *Life, Time, Esquire,* and *Playboy,* if they did not make the Beats look like rebels under the flag of foolishness, emphasized hedonism. On TV, Maynard G. Krebs became the American standard for the beatnik. In darker assessments, delinquency and violence were associated with the Beats, who reportedly were angry and rebellious. The stabbing of David Kammerer, the shooting of Joan Vollmer Adams Burroughs, and the arrest of Allen Ginsberg in connection with stolen goods were stories ripe for sensationalism, and journalists exploited this angle to the exclusion of piety, literary innovation, sensitivity, and spontaneity.

Like the sensationalized publicity, literary criticism was initially sour. Despite favorable reviews by Richard Eberhart in the *New York Times Book Review* and Gilbert Millstein in the *New York Times,* Norman Podhoretz, John Ciardi, John Hollander, Diana Trilling, Herbert Gold, Ernest van den Haag, George Will, and others charged that the Beats had no talent and no ideas. To some degree, the negativity, although painful for the Beats to endure, ultimately proved helpful to the Beats because the remarks were vituperative and said more about the critics than about the Beats. Ironically, the scorn of literary critics only heightened the Beat mystique.

The photographic record of the Beats soon became a significant part of their reputation and appeal. In the famous San Francisco Scene issue of *Evergreen Review* (1957), photos of writers by

Harry Redl supplemented the mystique behind Henry Miller, Kenneth Rexroth, Michael McClure, and Allen Ginsberg. In Lawrence Lipton's *The Holy Barbarians* (1959), a sequence of photos revealed the phases of the artistic life in Venice West. *Life* (September 1959) ran a photo spread contrasting "square" life in Hutchinson, Kansas, with "cool" life in Venice, California. The photos made thousands of readers hungry to be cool, not square, and even when *Life* (November 1959) presented a lengthy, derisive article and a satirical photographic impression of the Beats in their pad, the taste for the cool could not be abated. Soon the photos by Fred McDarrah were a dominant part of *The Beat Scene* (1960), an anthology of Beat writings that thrived on images of the scorned and forbidden angels of the cool.

Anthologies soon became the vehicle to unify various emerging streams of writing. Donald Allen's *The New American Poetry* (1960) became the standard for inventive diversity as Allen identified various schools in the innovative wave and unified them in a single volume. Seymor Krim's *The Beats*, Stanley Fisher's *Beat Coast East* (1960), Lawrence Ferlinghetti's *Beatitude Anthology* (1960), and other anthologies pushed forward the Beats with energy, humor, and personal expression. The "generation" that once consisted of a few men engaged in conversation in a Manhattan apartment became a broad, loosely knit association of innumerable writers and artists whose travels ranged from New York to San Francisco, from Lowell to Los Angeles, from Cherry Valley to New Orleans, and from Denver to St. Petersburg. The Beats were globetrotters, visiting Cuba, Nicaragua, Czechoslovakia, England, Tangier, Israel, Cambodia, India, Japan, Peru, France, China, Mexico, and many other places. The lives, creativity, and legend of the Beats became an enduring inspiration throughout the world.

In particular, the Beats inspired the sixties, when goals included civil rights, peace, free speech, women's liberation, gay liberation, liberalization of drug laws, environmental conservation, and heightened consciousness. Beats such as Ginsberg, Ferlinghetti, Gary Snyder, Anne Waldman, Timothy Leary, Ed Sanders, Bob Kaufman, and Hettie Jones fought for these goals. In 1962, Ken Kesey published *One Flew over the Cuckoo's Nest,* creating Randle McMurphy, the Promethean hero determined to resist Nurse Ratched and the oppressive Combine. Kesey turned society's concept of mental illness topsy-turvy. When Neal Cassady joined Kesey and became the driver of *Further,* the bus that carried the Merry Pranksters across America, the challenge to society's control of drugs was on. Leary, Ginsberg, Peter Orlovsky, and others experimented with drugs and founded a psychedelic revolution aimed at the improvement of the world through drugs. Some critics charge that the Beats themselves fell short of their goals because of abuse of drugs, abuse of alcohol, racism, sexism, and misogyny, but in spite of these weaknesses, the Beats were unmistakably forerunners of the social changes of the sixties.

A second generation of the Beats emerged in the East Village in New York City in the mid- and late 1960s. Ed Sanders operated the Peace Eye Bookstore, published *Fuck You: A Magazine of the Arts,* and joined with Ed Weaver and Tuli Kupferberg to form the Fugs, the controversial musical group. Anne Waldman led poetry programs at Saint Mark's in the Bowery for ten years and established Angel Hair Press. Ted Berrigan, who interviewed Jack Kerouac for *Paris Review,* published a little magazine known as *C* and also wrote his *Sonnets* (1964).

The ecological focus of the Beats became especially apparent in *Turtle Island* (1974), by Gary Snyder, which won the Pulitzer Prize for poetry in 1975. Snyder's imagistic poems incorporated Native American traditions and honored the compatibility of native lifestyles with the environment. In "Four Changes," a prose section at the end of *Turtle Island,* Snyder emphasized the need for population control. Similar ideas appeared in the writings of Ferlinghetti and McClure, who resisted the encroachment of corporate development and international exploitation.

When the Vietnam War came to an end and as society addressed, to some degree, the issues of racism and sexism, the Beats—perhaps because the objects of their protests had undergone constructive change—declined in notoriety; indeed, according to William A. Henry in *Time,* when Ginsberg read "Howl" at Columbia University in 1981 on the twenty-fifth anniversary of the poem's publication, the reading created a playful fascination with expressions such as "nowhere Zen New Jersey." The Beats seemed to be a peculiar part of the past.

Ironically, although the place of women was often mentioned in attacks on the Beats, the women of the Beat Generation substantially sustained the Beat movement. Memoirs by Beat women provided new perspectives on Beat history. Joyce Johnson's *Minor Characters* (1983) related her coming of age in New York City with special attention to her love relationship with Jack Kerouac. Hettie Jones, who with LeRoi Jones edited *Yugen,* one of the little magazines that featured the Beats, published *How I Became Hettie Jones* (1990), the story of her love relationship with LeRoi Jones. Carolyn Cassady wrote *Heart Beat* (1976), and later *Off the Road* (1990), to reveal her connection to Neal Cassady, Jack Kerouac, and Allen Ginsberg. Scholarship about the Beats was diligently done by women such as Ann Charters, who edited *The Beats: Literary Bohemians in Postwar America* (1983) and wrote a biography and bibliography of Kerouac. Jennie Skerl, Helen Vendler, Regina Weinreich, Ann Douglas, Hilary Holladay, and many other women did much of the research, editing, reviewing, and writing that kept the Beats alive.

In time, the stamp the Beats had made on history and culture generated recognition and renewed response. In 1982, in Boulder, Colorado, the Naropa Institute hosted a celebration of the twenty-fifth anniversary of the publication of *On the Road.* The celebration was a reunion for dozens of people from the Beat era, and the press coverage was substantial. In succeeding years, conferences on Beat writers and culture became regular events, including symposia held at the University of Massachusetts, Lowell (1995–2003); conferences held at New York University (1994, 1995); international conferences in the Netherlands and in Prague (1998); conferences on popular culture in Albuquerque, New Mexico (2002, 2003); and an interdisciplinary conference on the Age of Spontaneity in Chengdu, China (2004).

Libraries anticipated the growth of Beat studies as extensive collections developed at Columbia University libraries, the New York Public Library, the University of California in Berkeley, Stanford University, the University of Wisconsin–Madison, the State University of New York in Buffalo, and the University of North Carolina–Chapel Hill. Museums honored the Beat tradition and helped to broaden the appreciation of visual arts associated with the Beats with exhibits at the National Gallery in Washington, D.C.; the Whitney Museum in New York; the Walker Art Center in Minneapolis; and the deYoung Memorial Museum in San Francisco.

With honors and recognition accumulating for the Beats, including the Pulitzer Prize, the National Book Award, and several memberships in the National Institute of Arts and Letters, scholarship and editing gained new importance. In the 1990s, various new anthologies of Beat writing appeared, as well as volumes of collected writings by various artists. Ann Charters edited *The Portable Beat Reader* (1992), *The Portable Jack Kerouac* (1995), and two volumes of Kerouac's letters. Volumes of collected and selected letters by Burroughs, Ginsberg, Snyder, Ferlinghetti, Cassady, and many other Beats appeared. Video, audio, and Internet resources became widely available. Critical rejection of the Beats and even hostility toward them persisted, but despite this obstacle, the Beats penetrated the curriculum, meriting references in 258 college catalog descriptions for courses in literature, American studies, history, sociology, religious studies, writing, and political science.

In the twenty-first century, the outlook for the Beats is bright. "Howl," *On the Road,* and *Naked Lunch* continue to be popular, especially on college campuses. With painting, music, photography, drama, and film clearly in the sphere of the Age of Spontaneity, the Beat spirit has a broad base for the future. As war, threats to the environment, materialism, and challenges to personal freedom loom, young people draw inspiration from bohemian predecessors. Young artists seek paths to creativity still to be revealed, and even as members of the Beat Generation die with each passing day, their immortality becomes more certain.

## Bibliographic References

Ann Charters is a prolific editor, bibliographer, biographer, photographer, and scholar on the Beat Generation, and her *Beats and Company,* 1986, features large photos and a compact introduction to principal figures in the movement; Charters is the editor of *Beat Down to Your Soul,* 2001, which gathers various writings that contribute to a definition of Beat life, philosophy, and art; Charters also is the editor of *The Beats: Literary Bohemians in Postwar America,* 1983; *The Portable Beat Reader,* 1992; *The Portable Jack Kerouac,* 1995; and the two-volume collection of *Jack Kerouac: Selected Letters,* 1995 and 1999; Charters's biography *Jack Kerouac,* 1983, complements *A Bibliography of Works by Jack Kerouac, 1939–1975,* 1975. Allen Ginsberg's *Howl and Other Poems,* 1956, is filled with key references to the Beats and people they admire, especially in the dedication of the title poem; *Kaddish and Other Poems,* 1961, includes "Kaddish," which reveals Ginsberg's adaptation of Jewish prayers for the dead; Ginsberg's *Cosmopolitan Greetings,* 1986, incorporates the title poem, which includes the phrase "First thought, best thought." Jack Kerouac, *Good Blonde & Others,* ed. Donald Allen, 1993, includes many of Kerouac's contributions to magazines; Gregory Corso's *The Happy Birthday of Death,* 1960, includes "Marriage" and "Bomb," and these poems include the lines cited earlier as examples of goofing. Jack Kerouac, *Pull My Daisy,* 1960, provides the text for Kerouac's narration of the film and provides photos from the production process; Lawrence Ferlinghetti, *A Coney Island of the Mind,* 1958, includes "Dog," the poem that characterizes the Beat artist as an inquisitive dog. John Clellon Holmes quotes Kerouac about the significance of religion to the Beats in "The Philosophy of the Beat Generation," which appears in *Passionate Opinions,* 1988. Numerous anthologies of the Beats appeared as the movement gained popularity, including Ferlinghetti, ed., *Beatitude Anthology,* 1960; Stanley Fisher, ed., *Beat Coast East,* 1960; Donald Allen, ed., *The New American Poetry,* 1960; Seymour Krim, ed., *The Beats,* 1960; and Elias Wilentz, ed., *The Beat Scene,* 1960; Wilentz's book includes many photos by Fred McDarrah, and a series of early photos is also included in Lawrence Lipton, *The Holy Barbarians,* 1959, and *Evergreen Review* 2 (1957). The coolness of the Beats in Venice Beach is contrasted with traditional Americans in Hutchinson, Kansas, in *Life* 21 September 1959: 31–37, but the Beats are characterized as foolish rebels in Paul O'Neil, "The Only Rebellion Around," in *Life* 30 November 1959: 114–116. One finds early appreciation of the Beats in Richard Eberhart, "West Coast Rhythms," *New York Times Book Review* 2 September 1956: 7 and Gilbert Millstein, "Books of the Times," *New York Times* 5 September 1957: 7, but negative responses are frequent and persistent: see John Hollander, "Poetry Chronicle," *Partisan Review* 24 (Spring 1957): 296–304; Herbert Gold, "Hip, Cool, Beat—and Frantic," *Nation* 16 November 1957: 349–355; Norman Podhoretz, "The Know-Nothing Bohemians," *Partisan Review* 25 (Spring 1958): 305–311; Ernest van den Haag, "Conspicuous Consumption of Self," *National Review* 11 April 1959: 656–658; Diana Trilling, "The Other Night at Columbia: A Report from the Academy," *Partisan Review* 26.2 (Spring 1959): 214–230; John Ciardi, "Epitaph for the Dead Beats," *Saturday Review* 6 February 1960: 11–13; William A. Henry, III, "In New York: 'Howl' Becomes a Hoot," *Time* 7 December 1981: 8; and George Will, "Ginsberg Turned Paranoia into Marketable Commodity," *Rocky Mountain News* 10 April 1997: 56A. Major works that mark the continuation of the counterculture spirit include Ken Kesey's *One Flew over the Cuckoo's Nest,* 1962; Ted Berrigan's *The Sonnets,* 1967; and Gary Snyder's *Turtle Island,* 1974. The importance of women in sustaining the Beats and developing scholarship about them is evident in numerous works: Carolyn Cassady's *Heart Beat,* 1976, and *Off the Road,* 1990, are supplemented by Joyce Johnson's *Minor Characters,* 1983; Jennie Skerl's *William S. Burroughs,* 1985, is complemented by Regina Weinreich's *The Spontaneous Poetics of Jack Kerouac,* 1987; the women's outlook on the Beats is especially clear in Hettie Jones, *How I Became Hettie Jones,* 1990; significant articles by women include Ann Douglas, "On the Road Again," *New York Times Book Review* 9 April 1995: 2, and Helen Vendler, "American X-Rays: Forty Years of Allen Ginsberg's Poetry," *New Yorker* 4 November 1996: 98–102. In "A Compact Guide to Sources for Teaching the Beats," *College Literature* 27.1 (Winter 2000): 232–255, one finds data about the number of college course offerings about the Beats.

# Chronology

| | Beat Lives | Beat Writing and Publication | National Events | Arts News and Events | Taste and Fashion | World Events |
|---|---|---|---|---|---|---|
| 1905 | Naomi Ginsberg, a Russian émigré, arrives in New York City. | | | In Pittsburgh, viewers pay a nickel to see short "moving pictures." | | |
| 1906 | | | Earthquake and fire destroy a large part of San Francisco. | | Kellogg's Corn Flakes appear on the market. The Victrola, an enclosed phonograph, appears on the market. | |
| 1907 | | | Immigration to the United States rises to 1.2 million, with immigrants coming mainly from Europe's southern and eastern nations. | Pablo Picasso: *Les Demoiselles d'Avignon.* | | |
| 1908 | | | Henry Ford introduces the Model T. | Gustav Klimt: *The Kiss.* | | |
| 1909 | | | W. E. B. DuBois founds the NAACP. | | | |
| 1910 | Laura Lee and Mortimer Burroughs marry and move to Detroit. | | | | Instant coffee is available to consumers. | World population reaches 1.5 billion. Of these, 850 million are Asians. |
| 1911 | Gabrielle Levesque (Jack Kerouac's mother) begins work at a shoe factory in Nashua, New Hampshire. | | | | | The Chinese revolution against the Manchu dynasty deposes the emperor. |
| 1912 | | | | Marcel Duchamp: *Nude Descending a Staircase.* | | The *Titanic* sinks. |
| 1913 | | | | Umberto Boccioni: *Unique Forms of Continuity in Space.* | | |
| 1914 | 5 February: Birth of William S. Burroughs. | | The Harrison Act requires individuals to have prescriptions from medical doctors for preparations including narcotics. | | | World War I begins. |

*continues*

| | Beat Lives | Beat Writing and Publication | National Events | Arts News and Events | Taste and Fashion | World Events |
|---|---|---|---|---|---|---|
| 1915 | Kerouac's parents marry. | | The Great Migration of blacks to the North begins. | | | |
| 1916 | | | | | | |
| 1917 | | | The United States enters World War I. | | | The Russian Revolution ousts the czar. |
| 1918 | | | | | | The Spanish influenza epidemic kills 21 million people. |
| 1919 | Birth of Lawrence Ferlinghetti on 24 March. | | Prohibition makes alcoholic beverages illegal. | | | |
| 1920 | | | Women get the right to vote. | | | Bubonic plague strikes India. The League of Nations is established. |
| 1921 | | | | | | |
| 1922 | Birth of Jack Kerouac on 12 March. | | | | | King Tut's tomb is discovered in Egypt. |
| 1923 | | | | | Americans dance the Charleston. Talking movies are invented. | |
| 1924 | | | J. Edgar Hoover becomes the director of the FBI. | | | |
| 1925 | William S. Burroughs attends the John Burroughs School, a private school named after a naturalist. | | The Scopes trial pits the theory of evolution against creationism. | F. Scott Fitzgerald writes *The Great Gatsby*. | Moviegoers see Charlie Chaplin and Harold Lloyd. The "flapper" style is popular. | Hitler publishes *Mein Kampf*. |
| 1926 | Gerard Kerouac, older brother of Jack, dies of rheumatic fever. Allen Ginsberg is born on 3 June. | | | Hemingway publishes *The Sun Also Rises*. *Winnie the Pooh* by A. A. Milne is published. | | |
| 1927 | Kerouac enters school and begins to learn English. A tornado in St. Louis, the home town of William S. Burroughs, kills 300 people. | | | | The pop-up toaster provides new convenience. | Economic collapse in Germany creates a crisis. Trotsky is expelled from the Communist Party. |

*continues*

| | Beat Lives | Beat Writing and Publication | National Events | Arts News and Events | Taste and Fashion | World Events |
|---|---|---|---|---|---|---|
| 1928 | After an accidental explosion involving a chemistry set, William S. Burroughs is treated at a hospital at University City and is given an adult dose of morphine. | | The first scheduled television broadcast occurs in Schenectady, New York. The first color motion picture is shown in Rochester, New York. | D. H. Lawrence publishes *Lady Chatterly's Lover*. Constantin Brancusi: *Bird in Space*. | Bubble gum is invented. | Chiang Kai-Shek is elected president of China. Fleming accidentally discovers penicillin. |
| 1929 | Naomi Ginsberg enters Bloomingdale Sanitarium after a nervous breakdown. Three months before the stock market crash, Mortimer Burroughs, father of William S. Burroughs, sells his remaining shares of the Burroughs Company for $276,000. Burroughs attends Los Alamos Ranch School. | | The stock market collapses and the Great Depression begins. | William Faulkner publishes *The Sound and the Fury*. Ernest Hemingway publishes *A Farewell to Arms*. Erich Masria Remarque publishes *All Quiet on the Western Front*. | The car radio is introduced. | Leon Trotsky is expelled from the Soviet Union. The Nazis win 107 seats in the German Reichstag and win national and international attention. |
| 1930 | | | Boston bans the writings of Trotsky. | Sinclair Lewis wins the Nobel Prize for literature. Charlie Chaplin appears in *City Lights*. | Sliced bread is on store shelves. | |
| 1931 | | | "The Star Spangled Banner" is declared the national anthem. The Empire State Building is completed. | Pearl Buck's *The Good Earth* sells widely. Robert Frost wins the Pulitzer Prize for poetry. Salvador Dali: *The Persistence of Memory*. | | The monument of Christ is mounted in Rio de Janeiro, Brazil. |
| 1932 | Burroughs studies English at Harvard. | | Franklin Delano Roosevelt is elected President. | | Air conditioning is invented. Zippo lighters appeal to smokers. | |
| 1933 | | | FDR begins the New Deal. Prohibition ends in the United States. | Renee Magritte: *The Human Condition*. | Americans eat cheeseburgers for the first time. | Adolf Hitler becomes chancellor of Germany. |
| 1934 | | | John Dillenger is shot by the FBI. The Dust Bowl ruins lives. | Luigi Pirandello wins the Nobel Prize for literature. | | In Venice, Hitler and Mussolini meet. |

*continues*

| | Beat Lives | Beat Writing and Publication | National Events | Arts News and Events | Taste and Fashion | World Events |
|---|---|---|---|---|---|---|
| 1935 | Naomi Ginsberg enters Greystone Sanitarium. | | The United States Social Security Act is signed by Roosevelt. | | | The German Luftwaffe is formed. Germany creates the Nuremberg Laws, which worsen conditions for Jews. |
| 1936 | In Lowell, Massachusetts, the Merrimack River overflows. The flood ruins the printing business of Kerouac's father. Burroughs tours Europe, attends medical school in Vienna, and marries Ilse Klapper. | | The Hoover Dam is completed. | Eugene O'Neill wins the Nobel Prize for literature. The Pulitzer Prize goes to Margaret Mitchell for *Gone with the Wind*. | *Life* magazine begins its run. Americans admire Dale Carnegie for *How to Win Friends and Influence People*. | Hitler and Mussolini declare their alliance. King Edward VIII of England abdicates. The Spanish Civil War begins. |
| 1937 | Naomi Ginsberg attempts suicide. | | The Golden Gate Bridge opens for traffic. | John Steinbeck publishes *Of Mice and Men*. | | Italy withdraws from the League of Nations. Chiang Kai-Shek, Mao Tse-Tung, and Chao En-Lai resist Japanese aggression. Amelia Earhart disappears on a Pacific flight. |
| 1938 | Kerouac falls in love with Mary Carney. His best friend is Sebastian Sampas. Burroughs studies anthropology at Harvard. | | The Supreme Court rules that the University of Missouri Law School must admit blacks. | Orson Welles surprises America with *War of the Worlds*. Thomas Wolfe dies. Pearl Buck wins the Nobel Prize for literature. Thornton Wilder publishes *Our Town*. | Benny Goodman's style of jazz gains popularity. | Hitler and Mussolini meet in Rome. The United States and Germany withdraw ambassadors. Hitler annexes Austria. |
| 1939 | Kerouac graduates from Lowell High School and enrolls at Horace Mann School for Boys in Manhattan. | | | James Joyce publishes *Finnegan's Wake*. For *The Grapes of Wrath*, John Steinbeck wins the Pulitzer Prize. | | Hitler invades Poland. World War II begins. *Mein Kampf* is translated into English. Refugees on the *St. Louis* are refused entry to any country. |

*continues*

| | Beat Lives | Beat Writing and Publication | National Events | Arts News and Events | Taste and Fashion | World Events |
|---|---|---|---|---|---|---|
| 1940 | With a football scholarship, Kerouac attends Columbia University. During a practice, he suffers a broken leg. | | FDR wins a third term. Mount Rushmore is completed. The Manhattan Project begins. | Slim Gaillard, jazz musician, gains national fame. Charlie Parker's first known recordings are made at a Wichita radio station. Hemingway publishes *For Whom the Bell Tolls*; Richard Wright publishes *Native Son*; Thomas Wolfe's *You Can't Go Home Again* is published after the author's death. | Nylon stockings enter the marketplace. | World War II rages in Europe. Trotsky is assassinated in Mexico. |
| 1941 | Kerouac reenters Columbia but soon drops out. | | | Louis Armstrong appears in the film *Birth of the Blues*. In Harlem clubs, one can hear Lester Young, Dizzy Gillespie, Thelonious Monk, and Charlie Christian. | | The Japanese bomb Pearl Harbor. The United States declares war on Japan, Germany, and Italy. Wilhelm Reich sends an orgone energy accumulator to Albert Einstein. Einstein dismisses the idea as foolishness. |
| 1942 | As a merchant seaman, Kerouac sails to Greenland. Late in the year, he enlists in the navy. | | Japanese Americans are interned. | | | |
| 1943 | Lucien Carr attempts suicide and is subsequently hospitalized in Cook County Hospital. Later he registers for classes at Columbia University. William Burroughs begins residence in New York. Jack Kerouac is honorably discharged from the U.S. Navy despite difficulties with his mental health during his time of service. As a merchant seaman, he sails to Liverpool. | At home in Lowell, Massachusetts, Jack Kerouac writes *The Sea Is My Brother*. | Rationing limits supplies of canned goods, meat, cheese, butter, and shoes. A Supreme Court decision affirms the right of schoolchildren not to salute the flag if their religion proscribes such saluting. The Young Communist League in the United States, by its own proclamation, comes to an end. | *Lady Chatterley's Lover* survives a censorship trial. *Oklahoma* by Rodgers and Hammerstein shines on Broadway. | European influence over women's fashions declines as the war inhibits trade. Americans dance the Jitterbug to jive music. | Hitler pursues a "scorched earth" policy in Europe. The Casablanca Conference plots strategy against the Axis forces. Eisenhower assumes leadership over Allied forces in Europe. In the Warsaw Ghetto, an uprising challenges German authority. |

*continues*

| Beat Lives | Beat Writing and Publication | National Events | Arts News and Events | Taste and Fashion | World Events |
|---|---|---|---|---|---|
| Edie Parker introduces Jack Kerouac to Lucien Carr. Allen Ginsberg meets Lucien Carr. Carr later connects William Burroughs and David Kammerer with Ginsberg. | | | | | Allied forces land in Normandy. German occupation in Paris and Brussels ends as Allied forces arrive. Germans enhance their firepower with a huge missile (1,600 pounds), which has a firing range of 200 miles. |
| **1944** February: David Kammerer introduces Burroughs to Kerouac. Spring: Lucien Carr introduces Kerouac and Ginsberg. 14 August: Angered by unwanted sexual advances, Lucien Carr stabs to death David Kammerer. Kerouac and Burroughs become material witnesses. After a trial for manslaughter (6 October), Lucien Carr begins a jail term at Elmira Reformatory. 22 August: Kerouac marries Edie Parker and they move to Grosse Point, Michigan. Philip Lamantia works at *View* magazine. At 419 West 115th Street in Manhattan, Edie Parker and Joan Vollmer establish a communal apartment. | Kerouac, Carr, and Ginsberg debate and formulate their New Vision, including candor and psychic experimentation. George Leite publishes *Circle*, a small literary magazine that features Henry Miller, Robert Duncan, William Everson, and Kenneth Rexroth. Burroughs and Kerouac collaborate on "And the Hippos Were Boiled in Their Tanks." | Citizens in the United States no longer have to endure the rationing of meat. Consumer goods return to the marketplace. The Communist Political Association replaces the Communist Party. The Supreme Court rules against the denial of voting rights based on race. Franklin D. Roosevelt is elected to a fourth term. At Harvard, a huge but functional computer is developed. | Billy Eckstein's band includes Dexter Gordon, Charlie Parker, and Sarah Vaughan. Duke Ellington plays at Carnegie Hall. Tennessee Williams writes *The Glass Menagerie*. Jean Paul Sartre writes *No Exit*. In Waldport, Oregon, the Civilian Public Service Camp for conscientious objectors provides a productive and interdisciplinary environment for artists. Americans see *Appalachian Spring* by Aaron Copland on Broadway. | In the movies, the stars are Bing Crosby, Gary Cooper, Bob Hope, Betty Grable, Spencer Tracy, Greer Garson, Humphrey Bogart, Abbot and Costello, Cary Grant, and Bette Davis. Censorship embroils Lillian Smith, author of *Strange Fruit*, and Kathleen Winsor, author of *Forever Amber*. Both books are best-sellers. Because of shortages of materials during the war, some publishers offer paperback editions. The "football player look" emphasizes oversize shoulders and jutting lapels. Ball-point pens are marketed. | |

*continues*

| | Beat Lives | Beat Writing and Publication | National Events | Arts News and Events | Taste and Fashion | World Events |
|---|---|---|---|---|---|---|
| 1945 | Authorities at Columbia University determine that Ginsberg, a resident in a university dormitory, has harbored Kerouac in the dorm and has written vulgar and racist words in the dust on a window. The university authorities suspend Ginsberg for twelve months, and Ginsberg takes up residence at the apartment at 419 West 115th Street. 1 August: Neal Cassady marries LuAnne Henderson. August: After a stay at his home in St. Louis, Burroughs returns to New York. Ginsberg spends four months in the Merchant Marine Academy. Kerouac is hospitalized for thrombophlebitis—a result of his use of amphetamines. | In the apartment at 419 West 115th Street, conversations culminate in the Night of the Wolfeans, with Kerouac and Hal Chase taking the Wolfean side and Ginsberg and Burroughs taking the non-Wolfean side. | | In Open City, Roberto Rosselini makes the docudrama reveal the atrocities of the Nazis committed against Italian Catholics. Miles Davis and Charlie Parker record together. George Orwell writes Animal Farm. | The marketing of Tupperware begins. Paperback books sell well. The new sound in jazz is "bebop." | About 7.2 million U.S. soldiers are active; 292,000 soldiers are recorded as dead in battle; 613,611 are recorded wounded. U.S. Marines achieve victory on Iwo Jima after thirty-six days of hard fighting. Hitler commits suicide. Germany surrenders on the Italian front. VE (Victory in Europe) established on 8 May. The United Nations begins in San Francisco. The U.S. Senate firmly approves the United Nations Charter (89–2). Atomic bombs devastate Hiroshima and Nagasaki. Japan surrenders. |
| 1946 | Burroughs, under the influence of Herbert Huncke, becomes an addict. Burroughs lives at Joan Vollmer's communal apartment. Burroughs is arrested for trying to use a falsified prescription and is left under his family's supervision in St. Louis. The communal apartment ceases in the summer. Vollmer suffers from | Kerouac begins The Town and the City. | The Atomic Energy Commission is created. Frances X. Cabrini becomes the first U.S. citizen to be declared a saint by the Roman Catholic Church. In Mississippi, blacks vote in primary elections for the first time. | Charged with treason, Ezra Pound begins a twelve-year commitment to St. Elizabeth's sanitarium. Herman Hesse wins the Nobel Prize in literature. John Hersey writes Hiroshima. | Ranch and split-level homes dominate new home construction. Las Vegas competes for leadership in entertainment. Parents show confidence in Dr. Spock's The Common Sense Book of Baby and Child Care. The bikini becomes available. | John D. Rockefeller's gift makes possible the construction of the headquarters for the United Nations in New York City. In Vietnam, the French engage in a military conflict. Fourteen Nazis are convicted as war criminals at the Nuremberg trials. Churchill makes current the phrase "Iron Curtain" during a speech in Fulton, Missouri. He refers to the barrier separating the Soviet Union from the rest of the world. |

*continues*

| | Beat Lives | Beat Writing and Publication | National Events | Arts News and Events | Taste and Fashion | World Events |
|---|---|---|---|---|---|---|
| | drug-induced illusions and is sent to Bellevue for treatment. Burroughs returns to New York to get Vollmer out of the hospital. William Burroughs III is conceived, and the couple moves to New Waverly, Texas, where they plan to grow a crop of marijuana. Kerouac annuls his marriage to Edie Parker and lives at home.<br><br>Leo Kerouac, Jack Kerouac's father, dies of stomach cancer.<br><br>Ginsberg is at sea as a merchant marine.<br><br>December: Cassady arrives in New York with LuAnne Henderson and meets Kerouac and Ginsberg. | | | | | |
| 1947 | At the San Remo, a bar in New York City, avant-garde artists gather to socialize and exchange ideas.<br><br>Gregory Corso enters Clinton State Prison and pursues reading and the writing of poetry.<br><br>Herbert Huncke joins Joan Vollmer and William Burroughs in New Waverly, Texas. Burroughs develops an interest in the work of psychologist Wilhelm Reich. A bond forms between Neal Cassady and Allen Ginsberg. | | The plan to "contain" Soviet expansion is declared by Truman, and the policy is known as the Truman Doctrine.<br><br>Charged with abuses, unions face limitations under the Taft-Hartley Bill.<br><br>Jackie Robinson signs a contract to play major-league baseball for the Brooklyn Dodgers.<br><br>The House Un-American Activities Committee seeks out those who have associations with communist activities; blacklisting of individuals | Americans see *A Streetcar Named Desire* by Tennessee Williams. The play wins a Pulitzer. | For $1,700, one can fly around the world on Pan American Airlines.<br><br>Polaroid cameras make instant photography possible.<br><br>People compete to blow the best bubbles with bubble gum.<br><br>Women adopt "the New Look," accenting a narrow waist and salient breasts.<br><br>Many Americans follow Oral Roberts, a faith healer.<br><br>*Kraft Television Theater* successfully markets cheese products, affirming the power of television to sell. | The Marshall Plan, led by Secretary of State George Marshall, offers help to devastated nations in Europe.<br><br>India and Pakistan become independent nations.<br><br>On the raft named *Kon-Tiki*, Thor Heyerdahl sets sail to demonstrate the possibility of early trans-Pacific migration.<br><br>The Dead Sea Scrolls are discovered. |

*continues*

| Beat Lives | Beat Writing and Publication | National Events | Arts News and Events | Taste and Fashion | World Events |
|---|---|---|---|---|---|
| On 4 March, Cassady departs from New York. In the weeks that follow, he meets Carolyn Robinson and begins a relationship with her in Denver. Ginsberg joins Cassady in Denver. On 21 July, William Burroughs III is born. Ginsberg and Cassady join Burroughs in New Waverly, Texas. Gary Snyder begins formal work at Reed College in Oregon. Ginsberg sails for Dakar as a merchant seaman aboard the *John Blair*. Burroughs, Huncke, and Cassady fail in their efforts to transport marijuana to New York for sale and profit. Charlie Parker recuperates from addiction at Camarillo State Hospital. | | makes employment in Hollywood and other areas very difficult. | | The arts enjoy financial support from big businesses, such as Chrysler, Pepsi-Cola, and others. | |
| **1948** Neal Cassady marries Carolyn Robinson on 1 April. Ginsberg has a vision of William Blake in an uptown Manhattan apartment, and the vision inspires Ginsberg for many years. On Christmas Eve, William Everson has a vision that transforms | Kerouac completes a draft of *On the Road.* In May, Kerouac completes his first version of *The Town and the City.* | In a spy trial, Alger Hiss is accused of giving secrets to communist spies. The Supreme Court rules that New York's obscenity law, including its suppression of Edmund Wilson's *Memoirs of Hecate County,* is appropriate. The Supreme Court finds | The long-playing record is developed. George Balanchine and Lincoln Kirstein are the first directors of the New York City Ballet. Jean Genet avoids life imprisonment when fellow writers rise in his support. T. S. Eliot wins the Nobel Prize in literature. | Television features *Howdy Doody* and *Meet the Press.* | Mahatma Gandhi is the victim of assassination in India. Israel achieves nationhood. Tensions between the United States and the Soviet Union are referred to as the "Cold War." |

*continues*

*continues*

| | Beat Lives | Beat Writing and Publication | National Events | Arts News and Events | Taste and Fashion | World Events |
|---|---|---|---|---|---|---|
| | his religious outlook. He becomes the Dominican monk known as Brother Antoninus. In Rocky Mount, North Carolina, Cassady, LuAnne Henderson, and Al Hinkle visit Kerouac at the home of his sister. Kerouac takes his first trip with Cassady. Burroughs takes the cure for addiction in Lexington, Kentucky, and moves to Algiers, Louisiana. | | that in public schools religious education is a violation of the First Amendment. Harry Truman is elected President. Alfred Kinsey publishes *Sexual Behavior in the Human Male*. | Norman Mailer writes *The Naked and the Dead*. W. H. Auden wins the Pulitzer for "The Age of Anxiety." | | |
| 1949 | Kerouac, Cassady, LuAnne Henderson, and Al Hinkle begin a transcontinental journey, including a visit to Burroughs in Louisiana. After arriving in San Francisco, Kerouac and Cassady go separate ways, with Kerouac eventually riding the bus back to New York. Huncke makes Ginsberg's New York apartment a site for storage of stolen goods. Huncke's accomplices are Vicki Russell and Little Jack Melody. While driving in a car loaded with stolen goods, Allen Ginsberg, Vicki Russell, and Little Jack Melody are arrested for thievery. | Barney Rosset establishes Grove Press. On 29 March Harcourt Brace pays an advance of $1,000 to Kerouac for *The Town and the City*. In a conversation with John Clellon Holmes, Kerouac uses the term *Beat Generation*. | Cortisone becomes a source of relief for rheumatoid arthritis. Cigarette smoking is linked to cancer, according to the American Cancer Society and the National Cancer Institute. | George Orwell's *1984* appears. *Death of a Salesman* by Arthur Miller debuts on Broadway and the play wins the Pulitzer. Miles Davis and the Modern Jazz Quartet make cool jazz a new art form. | On television, *I Remember Mama* and *The Goldbergs* prove to be successful. The post–World War II baby boom slows. Women wear bikinis to the beach. | European nations and the United States found the North Atlantic Treaty Organization. Apartheid makes the separation of blacks and whites in South Africa the rule of law. China becomes a communist nation. The Soviets have the atomic bomb. |

| | Beat Lives | Beat Writing and Publication | National Events | Arts News and Events | Taste and Fashion | World Events |
|---|---|---|---|---|---|---|
| 1950 | Burroughs is arrested on drug charges in Louisiana. Kerouac moves to Denver and sets up residence with his mother. In response to Ginsberg's arrest, authorities decide to send him to the Columbia Psychiatric Institute. There Ginsberg meets Carl Solomon, to whom Ginsberg later dedicates "Howl." Ginsberg spends time in Paterson, New Jersey, with his family. Ginsberg meets William Carlos Williams. Burroughs and Joan Vollmer move to Mexico City. Near the end of the year, Carl Solomon leaves Columbia Psychiatric Institute. Robert Duncan and Jess Collins begin a homosexual partnership. Lawrence Ferlinghetti, then known as Lawrence Ferling, arrives in San Francisco. Gary Snyder discovers friendship with Philip Whalen and Lew Welch at Reed College. 27 February: Allen Ginsberg is formally discharged from the Columbia Psychiatric Institute. Ginsberg hears William Carlos Williams at the Guggenheim and begins a correspondence with him. | Burroughs begins work on the manuscript later to be titled *Junky* and sends the manuscript to Ginsberg. Kerouac is inspired by the spontaneity and freshness in Neal Cassady's letter to Kerouac, now known as the Joan Anderson Letter. Harcourt Brace publishes Kerouac's *The Town and the City*. Gershon Legman and Jay Landesman edit *Neurotica*, a magazine that features writers who are later associated with the Beats, including | Senator Joseph McCarthy of Wisconsin stirs controversy with accusations against the State Department, which he says is under the influence of communists. The McCarran Act, also known as the Internal Security Act, calls for the registration of communists and their organizations. McCarthyism leads to blacklisting. Among others, Gypsy Rose Lee, Arthur Miller, Pete Seeger, Zero Mostel, Howard K. Smith, and Orson Welles face blacklisting. Doctors successfully | The Dave Brubeck Quartet popularizes jazz. Jackson Pollock paints *Lavender Mist*. The painting initiates Pollock's series of action paintings. | Responding to the nuclear threat, Americans construct family bomb shelters. *Peanuts* debuts as a comic strip. The United States is 97 percent literate. Sociologist David Riesman's *The Lonely Crowd* draws widespread attention. According to *Life* magazine, teens admire Louisa May Alcott, Joe DiMaggio, Franklin Delano Roosevelt, Abraham Lincoln, Roy Rogers, General Douglas MacArthur, Clara Barton, Doris Day, Sister | According to the United Nations, 450 million of the world's 800 million children suffer from undernourishment. The United States invades North Korea. President Truman directs the Atomic Energy Commission to develop the hydrogen bomb. |

*continues*

continues

| | Beat Lives | Beat Writing and Publication | National Events | Arts News and Events | Taste and Fashion | World Events |
|---|---|---|---|---|---|---|
| | Ginsberg and Corso meet in Greenwich Village. Neal Cassady, while still married to Carolyn Cassady, marries Diana Hansen, who is pregnant with his child. Lucien Carr visits William Burroughs and Jane Vollmer in Mexico City. On 17 November, Kerouac marries Joan Haverty. After the marriage, Kerouac goes to Denver with Cassady and then visits Burroughs in Mexico City. | Carl Solomon, who writes "Report from the Asylum" under the pen name Carl Goy. | transplant kidneys and aortas. Alger Hiss is convicted of perjury. In Los Angeles, the Mattachine Society is established to work for homosexual rights. | | Elizabeth Kenny, Babe Ruth, and Florence Nightingale. Dress emphasizes casual comfort, with short hair and dungarees. The modern credit card is introduced. | |
| 1951 | Gary Snyder graduates from Reed College. Burroughs seeks the drug *yagé* in Ecuador. Ginsberg and Carr visit Joan Vollmer in Mexico City. On 6 September, Burroughs accidentally shoots Joan Vollmer in Mexico City. The shooting occurs when Burroughs fails to shoot a glass off her head and instead shoots a bullet into her forehead. Burroughs is imprisoned. On 8 December, officially declared "a pernicious foreigner," Burroughs leaves Mexico. Kerouac meets Corso in New York. Kerouac pursues studies of Buddhism. | Cassady starts *The First Third*, his autobiography. Holmes shares the manuscript for the autobiographical novel entitled *Go* with Kerouac. Cid Corman initiates publication of *Origin*. In April, Kerouac engages in a legendary three-week typing marathon that results in the scroll of *On the Road*. Kerouac associates himself with "spontaneous prose" and "bop prosody." Monologist Lord Buckley records the routines that become selections on the LP records *The Best of Lord Buckley*. | Julius and Ethel Rosenberg are convicted of conspiracy involving the passing of secret documents to the Soviet Union. American Telephone and Telegraph sets a new record as a widely held stock with more than 1 million shareholders. A mass-produced computer, the UNIVAC I, enters the U.S. market. Images and sound are recorded on magnetic tape by means of a video camera. Television signals are broadcast across the nation for the first time; the broadcast occurs between New York and San Francisco. The United States detonates the first hydrogen bomb. | | Psychological therapy, thanks to Carl Rogers, places emphasis on the patient. Television reinforces the trend toward relaxed styles in dress. Color television becomes available. | North Korea participates in talks to declare a truce in the Korean conflict. |

| | Beat Lives | Beat Writing and Publication | National Events | Arts News and Events | Taste and Fashion | World Events |
|---|---|---|---|---|---|---|
| 1952 | Jan Kerouac is born in New York, but Jack Kerouac refuses to acknowledge paternity and tries not to pay for child support. Ginsberg takes peyote. | Kerouac completes a manuscript later to be published as *Visions of Cody.* During a stay with Burroughs, Kerouac composes *Dr. Sax.* Burroughs writes *Queer.* Burroughs accepts an advance of $1,000 from Ace Books for the publication of *Junkie.* Holmes makes Kerouac envious when Holmes gets a $20,000 advance for *Go.* 16 November: In the *New York Times Magazine,* Holmes contributes "This Is the Beat Generation." Peter Martin edits the magazine *City Lights* in San Francisco. | DNA is revealed to be the genetic basis of viruses. Republicans Eisenhower and Nixon take control of the White House; Republicans dominate Congress as well. The Supreme Court allows schools to refuse to hire "subversives" as teachers. When a strike threatens to halt production in steel mills, the president orders that the mills be seized; the Supreme Court finds that such a seizure is in violation of the Constitution. George Jorgensen becomes Christine Jorgensen through sex-change surgery. Tests begin to determine if Thorazine can help patients with schizophrenia. | The success of Samuel Beckett's *Waiting for Godot* draws attention to the theater of the absurd. *Invisible Man* by Ralph Ellison appears. | *Mad* debuts. On television, viewers see *I've Got a Secret, The Adventures of Ozzie and Harriet, Dragnet,* and *The Today Show.* Panty raids become a special sport on college campuses. 3-D movies briefly capture national attention. Additions to the dictionary: *hot rod, miniaturization, globalist, Pentagonese, telethon, psycholinguistics, hack.* Car seat belts are introduced | Jonas Salk refines an effective vaccine to prevent polio. |
| 1953 | In Central and South America, Burroughs resumes his quest for *yagé.* Snyder ascends Sourdough Mountain to serve as a fire lookout. Snyder studies Oriental languages at the University of California, Berkeley. Burroughs visits Ginsberg in New York and briefly they are lovers. Burroughs visits Venice, Italy, and then begins residence in Tangier. | Ace Books publishes *Junkie* by William Burroughs, and the paperback, printed together with *The Narcotics Agent* by Morris Helbrant, sells more than 100,000 copies. City Lights Bookstore, under the direction of Peter Martin and Lawrence Ferlinghetti, opens in San Francisco. The store is perhaps the first bookstore to sell | The Rosenbergs are executed. Earl Warren becomes chief justice of the Supreme Court. The U.S. Communist Party is compelled by the Justice Department to register itself as an organization under the direction of the Soviet Union. The Department of Health, Education, and Welfare is founded. General Electric declares | Gerry Mulligan and Chet Baker create the West Coast sound in jazz. The first Newport Jazz Festival is staged. Hemingway wins the Nobel Prize in literature. *On the Waterfront,* starring Marlon Brando, wins an Academy Award. | Comic books achieve wide popularity. TV dinners sell well. Hugh Hefner initiates publication of *Playboy.* American activities are reflected in language such as *cookout, drag strip, split-level,* and *girlie magazine.* | After losing more than 25,000 soldiers, the United States agrees to end the war in Korea. Edmund Hillary and Tenzing Norkay ascend Mount Everest. Stalin dies; Khrushchev assumes leadership in the Soviet Union. Queen Elizabeth II is crowned. |

*continues*

continues

| | Beat Lives | Beat Writing and Publication | National Events | Arts News and Events | Taste and Fashion | World Events |
|---|---|---|---|---|---|---|
| | Kerouac has an affair with Alene Lee. | only paperback books. Kerouac writes "Essentials of Spontaneous Prose." Kerouac writes *The Subterraneans* and *Maggie Cassidy*. Burroughs writes "Roosevelt After Inauguration," his first routine. He also starts to write *Naked Lunch*. | that all communist employees will be dismissed from the company's payroll. *Sexual Behavior in the Human Female* by Alfred Charles Kinsey is published. B. F. Skinner publishes *Science of Human Behavior*. | | | |
| 1954 | Bob Kaufman begins life in San Francisco. Michael McClure meets Robert Duncan at the San Francisco State University. Kerouac tutors Ginsberg about Buddhism. The Cassadys are inspired by the writings of Edgar Cayce. Ginsberg spends the first half of the year in Mexico City. Kerouac visits the Cassadys in San Jose. In March, Robert Creeley joins Black Mountain College in North Carolina. He teaches and also edits *Black Mountain Review*. Ginsberg lives with the Cassadys briefly and then ventures into San Francisco. | *Black Mountain Review* begins its run. | In *Brown v. Board of Education*, the Supreme Court rules that segregation of schools by race is against the Constitution. The stock market reaches its highest level since 1929. Senator McCarthy faces the Army-McCarthy hearings and is eventually censured for conduct unbecoming a senator. Plastic contact lenses prove to be effective. Communists, fascists, and Ku Klux Klan members are barred from the U.S. Steelworkers Union. The Salk vaccine turns the tide in the struggle against polio. | | On television, *The Wonderful World of Disney* is shown for the first time. Juvenile delinquency stirs controversy. Coffee, beer, wine, and liquor are popular beverages; almost half of all Americans smoke twenty cigarettes a day. The Cold War and the atomic bomb prove to be hot topics for book sales. *Davy Crockett* is a smash hit on TV and the theme music is marketed broadly. | |

*continues*

| | Beat Lives | Beat Writing and Publication | National Events | Arts News and Events | Taste and Fashion | World Events |
|---|---|---|---|---|---|---|
| 1955 | In the milieu at Black Mountain College are Robert Duncan and John Wieners. September: Kerouac joins Ginsberg, Snyder, and Whelen in San Francisco. Kerouac lives in Mexico City. Ginsberg, in Berkeley as a graduate student, meets Robert La Vigne and Peter Orlovsky. Ginsberg's analyst tells Ginsberg to be himself, move in with Orlovsky, and be a poet. With Snyder, Kerouac goes mountain climbing and discusses Buddhism. Kerouac returns to North Carolina to be with his mother, sister, and brother-in-law. | Kerouac's "Jazz of the Beat Generation," a selection from *On the Road*, appears in *New World Writing*. On 7 October, the 6 Gallery in San Francisco is the scene for a legendary reading hosted by Kenneth Rexroth and featuring Lamantia, McClure, Snyder, Whalen, and Ginsberg. The reading of material from "Howl" proves especially provocative. Corso publishes *The Vestal Lady on Brattle*. Ferlinghetti publishes *Pictures of the Gone World* as the first title in the Pocket Poets Series by City Lights Books. Ginsberg continues the writing of "Howl," composing the initial and final portions. Kenneth Patchen publishes *Poems of Humor and Protest*. In Mexico City, Kerouac writes *Mexico City Blues* and begins *Tristessa*. Snyder works on translations of Han Shan. | In Montgomery, Alabama, blacks refuse to ride on segregated buses. Martin Luther King gains recognition as a leader of passive resistance. Marian Anderson is the first African American to sing at the Metropolitan Opera; Arthur Mitchell is the first black person to dance with the New York City Ballet. The Presbyterian Church allows the ordination of women. In San Francisco, the Daughters of Bilitis organizes to fight for lesbian rights. | James Dean dies in a car crash. Charlie Parker dies. Tennessee Williams wins the Pulitzer Prize for *Cat on a Hot Tin Roof*. | Juvenile delinquency is associated with rock-and-roll music. Reserpine and thorazine are approved for use as prescription medications for the treatment of schizophrenia. Disneyland opens in Anaheim, California. Americans begin their fascination with pizza. Lawrence Welk brings his style of music to television. The first McDonald's restaurant opens. | Winston Churchill resigns as prime minister in Britain. Juan Peron resigns the presidency of Argentina. |

continues

| | Beat Lives | Beat Writing and Publication | National Events | Arts News and Events | Taste and Fashion | World Events |
|---|---|---|---|---|---|---|
| 1956 | Creeley joins Kerouac and Ginsberg in San Francisco. Kerouac spends sixty days on Desolation Peak as a fire lookout. 5 May: Gary Snyder departs for Japan. 9 June: Naomi Ginsberg dies. | Kerouac writes Visions of Gerard, The Scripture of the Golden Eternity; he starts Desolation Angels and The Dharma Bums. James Harmon and Michael McClure edit Ark II/ Moby 1, another little magazine drawing together several schools of writers. McClure publishes Passages. City Lights publishes Ginsberg's Howl and Other Poems. Viking accepts On the Road for publication. | Eisenhower is reelected. Eleven arrests in Montgomery, Alabama, mark the struggle to desegregate the bus lines. The transatlantic telephone cable becomes operational. The suspension of Autherine Lucy, the first black student on the campus of the University of Alabama, prompts violence. Eventually Lucy is expelled. Lung cancer is clearly attributed to cigarette smoking. The CIO disassociates itself from James Hoffa and the Teamsters. In Michigan, the world's longest suspension bridge carries traffic. The Devil Outside, a book by John Howard Griffith whose sale had led to the arrest of a bookseller in Michigan, is declared acceptable reading material by the Supreme Court. Venereal disease becomes more prevalent, reversing trends established since 1948. Eisenhower sends soldiers to Little Rock, Arkansas, to guarantee the right of blacks to attend Little Rock Central High School. Medications enable many long-term patients in mental hospitals to leave them. Congress passes new civil rights legislation, the first such legislation since 1872. | Under the direction of architect Frank Lloyd Wright, workers begin construction of the Guggenheim Museum in New York City. Following the successful run of My Fair Lady on Broadway, women adopt the "Edwardian Look"; men prefer the "Madison Avenue Look." Dizzy Gillespie, sponsored by the U.S. State Department, begins a series of jazz performances. Britain's "angry young men" are reflected in John Osbourne's play Look Back in Anger. John Coltrane joins the Miles Davis Group. Peyton Place is a best-seller. Richard Hamilton: Just What Is It That Makes Today's Homes So Different, So Appealing? | Teens dress as "weenies" or "greasers." Ed Sullivan features Elvis Presley on national TV and Elvis subsequently dominates the pop charts. In Minnesota, Southdale establishes the trend toward shopping malls. Americans see movies at the drive-in theater. Suburbia proves attractive to the lower middle class. The police are called the fuzz; a psychiatrist is a headshrinker or shrink; a wonderful person is the most. One in eight new cars sold is a station wagon. | Jordan and Israel accept United Nations truce proposals. Pakistan becomes an Islamic republic. Citizens rebel against communist rule in Hungary. |

| | Beat Lives | Beat Writing and Publication | National Events | Arts News and Events | Taste and Fashion | World Events |
|---|---|---|---|---|---|---|
| 1957 | After traveling by sea to Tangier, Kerouac assists Burroughs by typing the manuscript and providing the title for *Naked Lunch*. On the return trip, Kerouac visits Paris and London. Ginsberg, Peter Orlovsky, and Alan Ansen arrive in Tangier and contribute to the editing of *Naked Lunch*. In San Francisco, U.S. Customs authorities seize copies of Ginsberg's *Howl and Other Poems*, which City Lights had contracted to a British printer. Customs authorities deem the material obscene but, when challenged by the ACLU, they later release the books. At City Lights Books, Ferlinghetti and Shig Murao are arrested by San Francisco authorities, who press for convictions on obscenity charges. Nevertheless, Judge Clayton Horn on 3 October clears the accused of charges. The publicity of the trial makes the poetry book sell well. LeRoi Jones and Hettie Jones begin their literary activities in Greenwich Village. Ginsberg and Orlovsky live in Paris at the "Beat Hotel" (9 rue Git-le-Coeur). Kerouac travels with his mother to San Francisco, | The Cellar proves to be a venue for combining jazz and poetry, as revealed by the appearances of Ferlinghetti and Rexroth. In *Dissent*, Norman Mailer's essay "The White Negro" appears. City Lights Books republishes the essay. *Black Mountain Review*'s last issue, coedited by Creeley and Ginsberg, features Beat and Black Mountain writers. Kerouac's *On the Road*, favorably reviewed in the *New York Times*, sells well. Barney Rosset begins publication of *Evergreen Review*. The second issue, which focuses on the "San Francisco Scene," gathers Beat and West Coast writers. Ginsberg begins "Kaddish" in Paris. Kerouac completes *The Dharma Bums*. | NASA is founded. | Videotape is applied in the production of television programming for *Truth or Consequences*. Juvenile delinquency becomes a topic for the Broadway show *West Side Story*. Elvis Presley acquires Graceland. Albert Camus wins the Nobel Prize in Literature. Eugene O'Neill wins the Pulitzer Prize for *Long Day's Journey into Night*. Dizzy Gillespie and Stan Getz record together. | In *Mademoiselle*, public attention is drawn to artists in the San Francisco Renaissance. Americans are fascinated by TV game shows and the prizes they award. The "sack dress" is a prominent fashion. At the movies, America sees Rock Hudson, John Wayne, Pat Boone, Elvis Presley, Frank Sinatra, Gary Cooper, William Holden, James Stewart, Jerry Lewis, and Yul Brynner. Many American women style their hair in a "bouffant." Children enjoy silly putty. Dick Clark's *American Bandstand* proves popular. | With the launching of Sputnik I and Sputnik II, the Soviet Union challenges the United States to venture into space. In Britain, the Wolfenden Report comments on homosexuality and prostitution. |

*continues*

*continues*

| | Beat Lives | Beat Writing and Publication | National Events | Arts News and Events | Taste and Fashion | World Events |
|---|---|---|---|---|---|---|
| | where he meets Whalen and Cassady. Kerouac meets Joyce Glassman in New York. | | | | | |
| 1958 | Kerouac moves to Northport, Long Island. Welch moves to the East-West House in San Francisco and studies Zen with Snyder. Neal Cassady is arrested for possession of marijuana and is sentenced to five years to life at San Quentin. | Viking publishes Kerouac's *The Dharma Bums*. Through Grove Press, Kerouac publishes *The Subterraneans*. In *Chicago Review*, an excerpt from *Naked Lunch* prompts calls for censorship. LeRoi and Hettie Jones initiate the publication of *Yugen*, an avant-garde small magazine. Random House publishes Holmes's *The Horn*. Diane di Prima publishes *This Kind of Bird Flies Backwards*. Corso publishes *Bomb* and *Gasoline*. Ferlinghetti publishes *A Coney Island of the Mind*. Robert Frank and Alfred Leslie produce the film *Pull My Daisy*, including Kerouac as narrator and Ginsberg, Orlovsky, Corso, David Amram, and Larry Rivers as actors. John Wieners publishers *The Hotel Wentley Poems*. | The John Birch Society establishes its highly conservative principles in Joseph Welch's *The Blue Book of the John Birch Society*. The copying machine is introduced to business by Xerox. *The Daily Worker*, the newspaper of the Communist Party, ceases to publish. Elvis Presley registers for the military draft. Serial murderer Charles Starkweather and Carol Fugate, his teenage girlfriend, face prosecution. America responds to Sputnik with Explorer 1, America's first satellite. | *Lolita* by Vladimir Nabokov is successful and controversial. The phrase *pop art* first appears in the writing of Lawrence Alloway. Dexter Gordon and Jackie McLean record for the Blue Note label. Miles Davis and Gil Evans record *Porgy and Bess and Sketches of Spain*. Boris Pasternak, author of *Dr. Zhivago*, wins the Nobel Prize. | Membership at Catholic and Protestant churches rises. Hula hoops become a craze. Ford Motors debuts the Edsel. Barbie dolls appear on the market. | Fidel Castro resists Batista in Cuba. Charles De Gaulle is elected president of France. |

| | Beat Lives | Beat Writing and Publication | National Events | Arts News and Events | Taste and Fashion | World Events |
|---|---|---|---|---|---|---|
| 1959 | When *Chicago Review* faces censorship, Ginsberg and Corso help raise funds to defend the magazine. Welch drives Kerouac from San Francisco to New York. Snyder returns to Japan for a five-year stay. | In Paris, Olympia Press publishes *The Naked Lunch*. In *Big Table*, Burroughs's "In Quest of Yage" is included, and the Post Office tries to prevent distribution through the mail. In San Francisco, *Beatitude* begins its run. New Directions publishes a segment from Kerouac's *Visions of Cody*; Kerouac publishes *Dr. Sax* through Grove Press; through Avon Books he publishes *Maggie Cassidy*; through Grove Weidenfeld he publishes *Mexico City Blues*. On the Fantasy record label, Ginsberg records *Howl and Other Poems*. Newly inspired, he resumes the composition of "Kaddish." Robert Frank publishes *The Americans*, a collection of photos. Kerouac writes the introduction. For Hanover records, Kerouac and Steve Allen record *Poetry for the Beat Generation*. Jack Kerouac appears on the *Steve Allen Show*. City Lights releases Bob Kaufman's "Abomunist Manifesto" as a broadside. Snyder publishes *Riprap*. McClure publishes *Hymns to St. Geryon*. | Seven American astronauts prepare for space travel. Nikita Khrushchev visits the United States. A quiz show scandal unfolds; Charles Van Doren, a successful participant, is the informer. In Greensboro, North Carolina, nonviolent demonstrations end segregation at lunch counters. | *A Raisin in the Sun* by Lorraine Hansberry succeeds on Broadway. Motown Records opens for business under the direction of Berry Gordy. In film, French New Wave cinema proves influential. Miles Davis makes the album *Kind of Blue*. Dizzy Gillespie and Duke Ellington record together. Gunter Grass's *The Tin Drum* appears. | Televisions are in 86 percent of American homes. On television, *The Many Loves of Dobie Gillis* makes Maynard G. Krebs a popular caricature of the Beat male. Movies strain to compete with television. Albert Zugsmith's *The Beat Generation* distorts and trivializes Beat life. Articles in *Life* and the *New York Post* bring Beats to wide public attention. According to the pop charts, Americans like these songs: "The Battle of New Orleans," "Stagger Lee," and "He's Got the Whole World in His Hands." A plane crash kills Buddy Holly, Richie Valens, and the Big Bopper ("the day the music died"). | Castro assumes power in Cuba. |

*continues*

| | Beat Lives | Beat Writing and Publication | National Events | Arts News and Events | Taste and Fashion | World Events |
|---|---|---|---|---|---|---|
| 1960 | Ginsberg experiments with *yagé* in Peru. Judge Hoffman clears *Big Table* of obscenity charges. Neal Cassady leaves San Quentin on Independence Day after serving two years. Jack Kerouac stays at Ferlinghetti's cabin near Big Sur. He sees Ferlinghetti, the McClures, Lew Welch, Philip Whalen, and Lenore Kandel. Kerouac experiences a psychological crisis. Ginsberg and Timothy Leary experiment with mushrooms and conclude that the best hope for humankind's future is drugs. Ginsberg takes LSD at Harvard. Welch lives with Lenore Kandel at the East-West House. | Donald M. Allen's anthology *The New American Poetry: 1945–1960* presents various schools of contemporary poetry together for a general audience. Other anthologies include *Beat Coast East*, ed. Stanley Fisher; *The Beat Scene*, ed. Elias Wilentz; *The Beats*, ed. Seymour Krim (with photos by Fred McDarrah); *Beatitude Anthology*, ed. Lawrence Ferlinghetti. Corso publishes *The Happy Birthday of Death* through New Directions. Robert Duncan publishes *The Opening of the Field*. Brion Cysin, William Burroughs, Gregory Corso, and Sinclair Beiles collaborate on *Minutes to Go*, an experimental work revealing the cut-up technique. In *Evergreen Review*, "Deposition: Testimony Concerning a Sickness" is published. | Television gains a central influence in national politics with the broadcast of the Nixon-Kennedy debates. The Southern Presbyterian Church allows that sex within marriage without the intent to have children is morally acceptable. Kennedy and Johnson win the presidential election. The payola scandal emerges, involving Alan Freed and others in bribery charges. Civil rights advocates stage sit-ins at segregated dining areas in the South. | John Coltrane releases *Village Blues*. Ornette Coleman leads "Free jazz." For *To Kill a Mockingbird*, Harper Lee wins the Pulitzer Prize. | Americans listen to Chubby Checker and do the "twist." Compact cars dominate new car sales. | |
| 1961 | Diane di Prima and LeRoi Jones found the New American Theater | Diane di Prima and LeRoi Jones publish *Floating Bear*. | Freedom Riders resist segregation on public buses. | Joseph Heller publishes *Catch 22*. | | The American invasion at the Bay of Pigs proves insufficient to depose Castro. |

*continues*

| | Beat Lives | Beat Writing and Publication | National Events | Arts News and Events | Taste and Fashion | World Events |
|---|---|---|---|---|---|---|
| | for Poets. The Post Office seizes *Floating Bear #9.* Ginsberg travels to the Near and Far East, where he meets Buber, Swami Shivananda, and the Dalai Lama. | Ginsberg publishes *Kaddish and Other Poems* through City Lights. McClure, Ferlinghetti, Meltzer, and Snyder edit *The Journal for the Protection of All Beings.* Thomas Parkinson edits *A Casebook on the Beat.* City Lights publishes Kerouac's *Book of Dreams.* | | | | The Berlin Wall goes up. Moscow closes synagogues. |
| 1962 | Dexter Gordon leaves the United States for Europe. At the International Writers Conference in Edinburgh, Mary McCarthy and Norman Mailer praise the works of William Burroughs. Kerouac lives in Northport, Long Island, with his mother. Stanley Twardowicz becomes Kerouac's friend. Joan Haverty's lawsuit obliges Kerouac to acknowledge paternity of Jan Kerouac, for whom he must pay child support. Welch breaks with Kandel and leaves San Francisco. | The U.S. edition of *Naked Lunch* appears; in Paris, Olympia Press publishes Burroughs's *The Ticket That Exploded.* Kerouac publishes *Big Sur.* Kesey publishes *One Flew over the Cuckoo's Nest.* | | | The Bossa Nova dance craze begins. | |
| 1963 | *Naked Lunch* is banned in Boston. A trial follows. Kerouac paints with Sanley Twardowicz in Northport, Long Island. | City Lights publishes *The Yage Letters* by Burroughs and Ginsberg. LeRoi Jones edits | John F. Kennedy is shot dead. Martin Luther King delivers his "I Have a Dream" speech. | | | |

*continues*

*continues*

| | Beat Lives | Beat Writing and Publication | National Events | Arts News and Events | Taste and Fashion | World Events |
|---|---|---|---|---|---|---|
| 1964 | Kerouac's sister Nin dies of a heart attack at age forty-five. With Neal Cassady as driver, Ken Kesey and the Merry Pranksters travel across the nation in the bus known as "Further." Kerouac sees Cassady for the last time at a party for the Merry Pranksters in New York. Kerouac lives with his mother in Tampa, Florida. Snyder returns to the United States, where he teaches at the University of California, Berkeley. Welch returns to San Francisco and begins a relationship with Magda Craig. | *The Moderns* and publishes *Blues People.* Kerouac publishes *Visions of Gerard.* Burroughs publishes *Nova Express.* Dr. Timothy Leary publishes *The Psychedelic Experience.* LeRoi Jones publishes *Dutchman* and *The Slave.* He also publishes *The Dead Lecturer. Dutchman* wins an Obie Award. | Johnson defeats Goldwater and becomes president. Martin Luther King wins the Nobel Peace Prize. Involvement of the United States in the Vietnam War increases. | In addition to Miles Davis, the Miles Davis Quintet features Wayne Shorter, Herbie Hancock, Rony Carter, and Tony Williams. The Beatles tour the United States. Cassius Clay wins the heavyweight boxing championship and becomes Muhammad Ali. | The World's Fair shines in New York. | |
| 1965 | Burroughs lives in the United States for about a year. His father dies. Ginsberg travels to Cuba. He also travels to Prague, where he is proclaimed King of May. Ginsberg is outspokenly against the war in Vietnam. Kerouac travels to France. Welch teaches at the extension of the | In Florida, Kerouac writes *Satori in Paris.* He publishes *Desolation Angels.* Michael McClure publishes *The Beard.* Bob Kaufman publishes *Solitudes Crowded with Loneliness.* Joanne Kyger publishes *The Tapestry and the Web.* | United States troops in Vietnam double in number. In Harlem, Malcolm X is assassinated. An antiwar movement grows in the Unites States. A giant blackout leaves much of the East Coast without power. | Norman Mailer publishes *An American Dream.* Robert Lowell publishes *For the Union Dead.* | Ralph Nader publishes *Unsafe at Any Speed.* | |

| | Beat Lives | Beat Writing and Publication | National Events | Arts News and Events | Taste and Fashion | World Events |
|---|---|---|---|---|---|---|
| | University of California in San Francisco. Snyder returns to Japan. He ends his marriage with Joanne Kyger. | | | | | Indira Gandhi becomes prime minister of India. |
| 1966 | Burroughs settles in London. *Naked Lunch* is cleared of obscenity charges in the United States. Kerouac and his mother move to Cape Cod. Kerouac's mother suffers a stroke, and Kerouac marries Stella Sampas. The family returns to Lowell. Snyder does literary readings in the United States. Whalen lives in Japan. LeRoi Jones moves to New York and founds Spirit House. | Lenore Kandel publishes *The Love Book.* Kerouac publishes *Satori in Paris.* The Beats become a topic for *Monarch Notes,* a series of study guides for students. | | | Catholics are given permission to eat meat on Fridays. *Quotations from Chairman Mao Tse-tung* becomes available in bookstores in the United States. | |
| 1967 | The Human Be-In occurs in San Francisco and includes Ginsberg, Snyder, Ferlinghetti, McClure, and Kandel. Snyder returns to Japan, lives at Banyam Ashram, and marries Masa Uehara. Jan Kerouac visits Jack in Lowell. | Ann Charters, in cooperation with Kerouac, compiles *A Bibliography of Works by Jack Kerouac.* In Lowell, Kerouac writes *Vanity of Duluoz.* Holmes's *Nothing More to Declare* contributes to the development of the Beat essay. | Thurgood Marshall takes a seat on the Supreme Court. | Dustin Hoffman stars in *The Graduate.* | | The United States bombs Hanoi. France launches a nuclear submarine. The People's Republic of China develops a hydrogen bomb. |
| 1968 | Cassady dies in Mexico. Burroughs and Ginsberg observe the Democratic National Convention in | Kerouac publishes *Vanity of Duluoz.* Janine Pommy Vega publishes *Poems to* | Robert F. Kennedy is assassinated. Martin Luther King is assassinated. | | | |

*continues*

*continues*

| | Beat Lives | Beat Writing and Publication | National Events | Arts News and Events | Taste and Fashion | World Events |
|---|---|---|---|---|---|---|
| | Chicago and report on it for *Esquire*. They see Kerouac for the last time. Kerouac moves to St. Petersburg, Florida. Snyder returns to the United States. LeRoi Jones becomes Amiri Baraka. | *Fernando.* Gary Snyder publishes *The Back Country.* Tom Wolfe publishes *The Electric Kool-Aid Acid Test.* | Riots plague the Democratic National Convention in Chicago. Promising to end the war, Nixon wins the presidential election. | | | |
| 1969 | Kerouac dies in Florida and is buried in Lowell, Massachusetts. Allen Ginsberg participates in the trial of the Chicago Seven, who allegedly provoked people to riot at the Democratic Convention. | Diane di Prima publishes *Memoirs of a Beatnik.* Gary Snyder publishes *Earth House Hold.* Bonnie Bremser publishes *Troia: Mexican Memoirs.* | Eisenhower dies. Woodstock immortalizes three days of peace and love. The Chicago Eight go to trial. Judge Hoffman decides to separate Bobby Seale's case from the case of the seven other defendants, who become known as the Chicago Seven. | Duke Ellington wins the Presidential Medal of Freedom. Samuel Beckett wins the Nobel Prize for literature. | | |
| 1970 | Ginsberg and Chögyam Trungpa meet. Ginsberg travels to India and West Bengal and views the effects of flooding. Burroughs's mother dies. | With *Scenes Along the Road,* Ann Charters adds to the growing photographic record of the Beats. Corso publishes *Elegiac Feelings American.* Daniel Oldier publishes *The Job: Interviews with W. S. Burroughs.* | National Guard troops shoot students at Kent State University, Kent, Ohio. The first Earth Day is celebrated. | The Beatles dissolve. | | Aswan High Dam is finished in Egypt. |
| 1971 | | City Lights publishes Neal Cassady's autobiography *The First Third.* Bruce Cook's *The Beat Generation* develops the journalistic view of the Beats in book form. | The antiwar march on Washington draws national attention. | | | |

| | Beat Lives | Beat Writing and Publication | National Events | Arts News and Events | Taste and Fashion | World Events |
|---|---|---|---|---|---|---|
| 1972 | | *Scattered Poems* by Kerouac is published. Allen Ginsberg publishes *The Fall of America*. The book eventually wins the National Book Award. John Wieners publishes *Selected Poems*. | The Watergate scandal begins to unfold. | | | Terrorists attack and kill athletes at the Olympics in Munich, West Germany. The Strategic Arms Limitation Treaty (SALT) is signed by the United States and the Soviet Union. |
| 1973 | | Ann Charters publishes her biography of Kerouac. The full run of *Floating Bear* is reprinted in one large volume. The complete version of *Visions of Cody* goes to press. *Ring of Bone* by Lew Welch is published. | Abortion is legalized in the United States. The United States withdraws from Vietnam. The Arab Oil Embargo cuts supplies of fuel in the United States. | | Phillips, a Dutch electronics manufacturer, markets a video compact cassette recorder. Though expensive and unreliable, this invention marks the beginning of the home video age. | |
| 1974 | With Anne Waldman and Chögyam Trungpa, Allen Ginsberg founds the Jack Kerouac School of Disembodied Poetics in Boulder, Colorado. Burroughs resumes residence in New York. | Gary Snyder publishes *Turtle Island*. The book eventually wins the Pulitzer Prize. Ferlinghetti publishes *City Lights Anthology*. | Nixon resigns as president of the United States. The country endures an economic recession. Ford becomes president. | | Mikhail Baryshnikov defects from the Soviet Union to the United States. | The Terra Cotta army is discovered in China. |
| 1975 | | Ed Sanders publishes *Tales of Beatnik Glory*. Anne Waldman publishes *Fast Talking Woman*. *Love Is the Silence* by Stuart Perkoff is published. Diane di Prima publishes *Selected Poems: 1956–1975*. | Microsoft is founded. | | | The United Nations declares the International Year of the Woman. |

*continues*

*continues*

| | Beat Lives | Beat Writing and Publication | National Events | Arts News and Events | Taste and Fashion | World Events |
|---|---|---|---|---|---|---|
| 1976 | Louis Ginsberg, the father of Allen Ginsberg, dies at eighty years of age. At a retreat near Snowmass, Colorado, W. S. Merwin and his companion, Dana Naone, are denied their preference not to participate in a nude Halloween party. Chögyam Trungpa directs several party people to compel Merwin and Naone to be at the party and stripped of their garments. The incident proves a lingering embarrassment and source of tension. | Carolyn Cassady contributes to the development of the Beat memoir with *Heart Beat*. John Tytell publishes his critical study *Naked Angels*. | The nation celebrates its 200th year of independence. | | | |
| 1977 | | Gordon Ball edits the journals of Allen Ginsberg, and Creative Arts Books publishes the correspondence between Ginsberg and Cassady. | | Elvis Presley dies. *Star Wars* is a successful film. | | |
| 1978 | | Ray Bremser publishes *Blowing Mouth: The Jazz Poems*. Barry Gifford and Lawrence Lee publish *Jack's Book*, an oral history of Kerouac and his times. Arthur Winfield Knight and Kit Knight publish *The Beat Journey*. Anne Waldman and Marilyn Webb edit *Talking Poetics from Naropa Institute*. | The first test-tube baby is born. Love Canal is evacuated. | | | Jim Jones leads a mass suicide in Guyana. |

| | Beat Lives | Beat Writing and Publication | National Events | Arts News and Events | Taste and Fashion | World Events |
|---|---|---|---|---|---|---|
| 1979 | Ginsberg, Corso, and Orlovsky give readings in Europe. Burroughs moves to Lawrence, Kansas. | Neeli Cherkovski publishes a biography of Ferlinghetti. Dennis McNally writes a biography of Kerouac and a history of the Beats. Aram Saroyan writes *Genesis Angels*. | At Three Mile Island a nuclear accident occurs. | | Sony offers the Walkman. | Iran takes Americans hostage. |
| 1980 | | Ginsberg publishes *Composed on the Tongue*. Huncke publishes *The Evening Sun Turned Crimson*. Snyder publishes *The Real Work: Interviews and Talks 1964–1979*. | | John Lennon is assassinated in New York. Pink Floyd releases *The Wall*. | Rubik's Cube is popular. Americans read Carl Sagan's *Cosmos*. College freshmen exceed their predecessors in a desire for power, status, and wealth. Many enter business management. | |
| 1981 | Ginsberg takes up residence in Boulder, Colorado. Ginsberg visits Nicaragua. William Burroughs III dies. | *The Beats: Essays in Criticism*, ed. Lee Bartlett, presents a variety of views of the Beats. Tim Hunt's *Kerouac's Crooked Road* analyzes the sequence of composition of Kerouac's works. Bob Kaufman's *The Ancient Rain: Poems 1956–1978* appears. | President Reagan survives an assassination attempt. AIDS becomes a plague. IBM introduces personal computers. | | Pac-Man is popular. Millions see the wedding of Prince Charles and Lady Diana on TV. | The Pope survives an assassination attempt. |
| 1982 | At the Naropa Institute in Boulder, Colorado, and at the University of Colorado in Boulder, the twenty-fifth anniversary of the publication of *On the Road* inspires a celebration. In attendance are Burroughs, Corso, Orlovsky, Ferlinghetti, McClure, di Prima, Kesey, Berrigan, Huncke, Leary, Ginsberg, and many others. | Michael McClure's *Scratching the Beat Surface* assesses the formation of the Beat spirit. Burroughs's *Letters to Allen Ginsberg* appears. | | Michael Jackson's *Thriller* is a success. | *E.T.* is a popular film. | Argentina invades the Falkland Islands. |

*continues*

| Beat Lives | Beat Writing and Publication | National Events | Arts News and Events | Taste and Fashion | World Events |
|---|---|---|---|---|---|
| **1983** | Ann Charters edits *The Beats: Literary Bohemians in Postwar America.* Gerald Nicosia's lengthy biography of Kerouac, *Memory Babe,* appears. | President Reagan announces a defense system called Star Wars. | | Cabbage Patch Kids dominate the toy market. *Flashdance* succeeds at the box office and influences fashions. | Terrorists bomb the U.S. embassy in Beirut, Lebanon. |
| **1984** With Toni Morrison, Gary Snyder, and William Gass, Ginsberg travels to China. | Joyce Johnson publishes *Minor Characters.* Lewis Hyde edits *On the Poetry of Allen Ginsberg,* a collection of articles about Ginsberg. | The Vietnam War Memorial opens in Washington. | | | A very large leak of poison gas occurs in Bhopal, India, at the Union Carbide plant. 2000 people die, and 200,000 others suffer permanent harm. |
| **1985** | John Antonelli's biographical film, *Kerouac,* is released. Howard Brookner's biographical film, *Burroughs,* is released. Rudi Horemans edits *Beat Indeed!* Fred McDarrah gathers photos and other materials in *Kerouac and Friends.* Jennie Skerl publishes *William S. Burroughs.* | | Rock Hudson dies of AIDS. Crack cocaine leads to a rise in imprisonments and violent crimes. | The New Coke is marketed. Bruce Springsteen releases "Born in the U.S.A." | A hole is discovered in the ozone layer of the atmosphere. Mikhail Gorbachev pursues the policy of *Glasnost* and *Perestroika.* |
| **1986** Ginsberg accepts a post as distinguished professor at Brooklyn College of the City University of New York. | Ann Charters's *Beats and Company* presents a collection of photos related to the Beats. Warren French publishes *Jack Kerouac.* Allen Ginsberg publishes *Howl: Original Draft Facsimile.* | The *Challenger* space shuttle explodes. The Iran-Contra scandal captures headlines. | | | A nuclear accident occurs in Russia at the Chernobyl plant. The United States bombs Libya. |

*continues*

| | Beat Lives | Beat Writing and Publication | National Events | Arts News and Events | Taste and Fashion | World Events |
|---|---|---|---|---|---|---|
| 1987 | Chögyam Trungpa dies. | 11 April 1987 is proclaimed Bob Kaufman Day in San Francisco. A street is named in Kaufman's honor. *Displaced Person: The Travel Essays* by John Clellon Holmes is published. Park Honan edits *The Beats: An Anthology of Beat Writing.* Huncke publishes *Guilty of Everything.* Regina Weinreich publishes *The Spontaneous Prose of Jack Kerouac.* | Black Monday is the occasion for a drastic drop in prices at the New York Stock Exchange. DNA proves effective for identification of criminals. | Americans read *Cultural Literacy* by E. D. Hirsch and *The Closing of the American Mind* by Allan Bloom. | | Nazi Klaus Barbie is sentenced to life in prison. |
| 1988 | | *Passionate Opinions and Representative Men* by Holmes are published. Arthur and Kit Knight publish *Kerouac and the Beats: A Primary Sourcebook.* Ted Morgan publishes *Literary Outlaw: The Life and Times of William S. Burroughs.* Jack Kerouac Alley is established in San Francisco. Jack Kerouac Park is dedicated in Lowell, Massachusetts. | Funding is created for the Human Genome Project. | | | Pan Am Flight 103 explodes over Scotland. The United States shoots down an Iranian airbus. |
| 1989 | Ginsberg meets Tibetan Lama Gelek Rinpoche. | Corso's *Mindfield* appears as a set of collected poems. Michael Davidson publishes *The San Francisco Renaissance.* Barry Miles publishes | The Alaskan coast is damaged by the spill of millions of gallons of oil from the *Exxon Valdez.* | | | The Berlin Wall comes down. Students are massacred in Tiananmen Square in China. |

*continues*

continues

| Beat Lives | Beat Writing and Publication | National Events | Arts News and Events | Taste and Fashion | World Events |
|---|---|---|---|---|---|
| | *Ginsberg: A Biography.* Gregory Stephenson publishes *The Daybreak Boys*, a collection of essays on the Beats, and *Exiled Angel*, a study of Gregory Corso. | | | | |
| 1990 | Carolyn Cassady writes *Off the Road.* Diane di Prima publishes *Pieces of a Song.* Allen Ginsberg's *Photographs* presents black and white photos of the Beats in an oversize format. *The Jack Kerouac Collection* appears on tape and on CD. Hettie Jones publishes *How I Became Hettie Jones.* John Arthur Maynard publishes *Venice West.* Ed Sanders publishes an enlarged version of *Tales of Beatnik Glory.* Rebecca Solnit's *Secret Exhibition* examines visual arts related to the Beat Generation. | The Hubble Telescope is positioned in space. | *Dances with Wolves* is named best picture | The grunge look becomes a popular style of dress among young people. Hip Hop music becomes broadly popular. | Nelson Mandela is freed from prison. |
| 1991 | Amiri Baraka publishes *The LeRoi Jones/Amiri Baraka Reader.* Ann Charters edits *The Portable Beat Reader.* Ed Foster publishes *Understanding the Beats.* Jon Halper edits *Gary Snyder,* a collection of articles and commentaries. | Anita Hill accuses Clarence Thomas of sexual harassment. Citizens view live coverage of the Gulf War on CNN. | | | The Soviet Union collapses. South Africa ends Apartheid. The United States launches Operation Desert Storm in Kuwait. |

continues

continues

| Beat Lives | Beat Writing and Publication | National Events | Arts News and Events | Taste and Fashion | World Events |
|---|---|---|---|---|---|
| | Jennie Skerl and Robin Lydenbert edit *William Burroughs at the Front*, a collection of essays about Burroughs. | | | | |
| 1992 | A set of tapes, *The Beat Generation*, offers a re-creation of the mood and spirit of the Beats. Burroughs publishes *Nova Express, Port of Saints,* and *The Wild Boys.* Charter's *The Portable Beat Reader* appears in paperback. Patrick Murphy publishes *Understanding Gary Snyder.* Michael Schumacher writes *Dharma Lion.* | The verdict in the Rodney King case leads to riots. | | | The Cold War ends. World Wide Web is initiated. |
| 1993 | Oliver Harris edits *Burroughs, Letters 1945–1959.* Ginsberg's *Snapshot Poetics* contributes to the photographic history of the Beats. *Howls, Raps, and Roars,* compiled by Ann Charters, offers recordings of numerous Beats in performance. Ferlinghetti publishes *These Are My Rivers,* a set of new and collected poems. Kerouac's *Good Blonde and Others* and *Old Angel Midnight* are published. | A raid on a cult group in Waco, Texas, leads to fire and death. The World Trade Center is bombed. | Toni Morrison wins the Nobel Prize for Literature. *Schindler's List* is named best picture | | Users of the Internet grow much more numerous. |

| | Beat Lives | Beat Writing and Publication | National Events | Arts News and Events | Taste and Fashion | World Events |
|---|---|---|---|---|---|---|
| 1994 | Ginsberg sells his archives to Stanford University for 1 million dollars. He purchases loft space in Manhattan. | In honor of Lawrence Ferlinghetti, *Via Ferlinghetti* is established in San Francisco. Ginsberg publishes *Cosmopolitan Greetings*. Ginsberg's *Holy Soul Jelly Roll: Poems and Songs 1949–1993* offers a rich selection of Ginsberg's recordings. | Lorena Bobbit cuts off the penis of her husband. O. J. Simpson is arrested for an alleged double murder. | *Forrest Gump* wins the Oscar for best picture | | A tunnel beneath the English Channel connects France and Britain. Genocide in Rwanda begins. Nelson Mandela becomes president of South Africa. |
| 1995 | | Burroughs publishes *My Education*. Charters edits *The Portable Jack Kerouac*. *A Jack Kerouac Romnibus* offers diverse materials in the format of a CD ROM. Carol Tonkinson edits *Big Sky Mind: Buddhism and the Beat Generation*. | The Oklahoma City bombing shocks the nation. | | | The Ebola virus affects Zaire. Poison gas is spread by terrorists in the subways of Tokyo. |
| 1996 | | Ginsberg publishes *Selected Poems 1947–1995*. Brenda Knight edits *Women of the Beat Generation*. A. Robert Lee edits *The Beat Generation Writers*, a collection of articles on the Beats. Fred McDarrah and Gloria McDarrah publish in an oversize format numerous photos of the Beats in | The Unabomber is arrested. | | | Mad cow disease affects Britain. |

*continues*

| Year | Beat Lives | Beat Writing and Publication | National Events | Arts News and Events | Taste and Fashion | World Events |
|---|---|---|---|---|---|---|
| | | Beat Generation: Glory Days in Greenwich Village. Ashleigh Talbot publishes Beat Speak: An Illustrated Beat Glossary circa 1956–1959. Lisa Phillips edits Beat Culture and the New America: 1950–1965. Snyder publishes Mountains and Rivers without End. Waldman edits The Beat Book. Chuck Workman releases The Source, a film on the development of the Beat Generation. | | | | |
| 1997 | 5 April: Allen Ginsberg dies. 2 August: William Burroughs dies. | Ferlinghetti publishes A Far Rockaway of the Heart. Kerouac's Some of the Dharma is published in a facsimile format. Bill Morgan authors The Beat Generation in New York: A Walking Tour of Jack Kerouac's City. Richard Peabody edits A Different Beat: Writings by Women of the Beat Generation. Ben Shafer edits The Herbert Huncke Reader. | | | | Hong Kong is unified with China. Princess Diana dies in a car crash. Scientists produce a cloned sheep. The tallest building in the world rises in Kuala Lumpur. |
| 1998 | | Burroughs's collected writings appear in | President Clinton is impeached. Viagra is marketed. | | Titanic proves to be the most successful movie | India and Pakistan develop nuclear capabilities. |

continues

| Beat Lives | Beat Writing and Publication | National Events | Arts News and Events | Taste and Fashion | World Events |
|---|---|---|---|---|---|
|  | *Word Virus*, edited by James Grauerholz and Ira Silverberg. Steven Clay and Rodney Phillips publish *A Secret Location on the Lower East Side*, a study of the small press and little literary magazines. David Sterritt publishes *Mad to Be Saved*, a study of films related to the Beats. Ferlinghetti is named first Poet Laureate of San Francisco. |  |  | ever. 98 percent of homes in the United States have televisions. 74 percent are connected to cable television. | 100 million people have access to the World Wide Web. |
| 1999 | Charters edits the second volume of *Jack Kerouac: Selected Letters*. Holly George Warren edits *The Rolling Stone Book of the Beats*. Ginsberg's *Death and Fame* is published. Kerouac's *Atop an Underwood* presents Kerouac's short prose. George Plimpton edits *Beat Writers at Work*, a collection of interviews from *Paris Review*. Snyder's *The Gary Snyder Reader* appears. | Students murder their fellow students in Columbine High School. John F. Kennedy Jr. dies in a plane crash. | Günter Grass wins the Nobel Prize. | The fear of the Y2K Bug dominates the news. | NATO attacks Serbia. The Panama Canal is placed under Panamanian authority. |

*continues*

| Beat Lives | Beat Writing and Publication | National Events | Arts News and Events | Taste and Fashion | World Events |
|---|---|---|---|---|---|
| 2000 | Ginsberg's *Deliberate Prose*, a collection of essays, is published. James Grauerholz edits *Last Words: The Final Journals of William S. Burroughs*. Ed Sanders publishes *America: A History in Verse* and *The Poetry and Life of Allen Ginsberg: A Narrative Poem*. *Teaching Beat Literature*, a special issue of *College Literature*, offers articles on teaching the Beats. | *Timothy McVeigh is executed for the Oklahoma City Bombing.* Vermont is the first state to allow same-sex marriages. The Supreme Court declares George Bush president. | Eminem wins two Grammy awards. After eighteen years on Broadway, *Cats* closes. | A federal court thwarts the downloading of music from the Internet by shutting down Napster. Kids enjoy collapsible scooters. | Violence between Palestinians and Israelis intensifies. U.S. Navy destroyer *Cole* is the object of a terrorist attack. |
| 2001 | | Enron goes bankrupt and leaves employees without retirement benefits. | George Harrison, an original Beatle, dies of cancer. | 50% of homes in the U.S. have access to the Internet. | Terrorists hijack airliners and crash into the World Trade Center and the Pentagon. The United States invades Afghanistan. |
| 2003 | City Lights Books celebrates its fiftieth anniversary in San Francisco. | | | | SARS breaks out in China, stalling tourism. The United States invades Iraq. |
| 2004 | The scroll of *On the Road* begins a road trip to libraries and museums across the country. | | | | On December 26, a tsunami devastates portions of Indonesia, Sri Lanka, Thailand, and South India, causing approximately 300,000 deaths. |
| 2005 | Beat enthusiasts note the fiftieth anniversary of the 6 Gallery reading. | | Clint Eastwood's *Million Dollar Baby* wins various Oscars, including best picture. | | A barrel of crude oil sells for a record price—$56 |
| 2006 | Readers celebrate the fiftieth anniversary of the publication of Ginsberg's *Howl and Other Poems* | | | | |
| 2007 | Readers celebrate the fiftieth anniversary of the publication of *On the Road*. | | | | |

## Adam, Helen (1909–1992)

Poet, playwright, actor, and performance artist. Born in Glasgow, Scotland, in 1909, but raised in Dundee, where she gained fame as a child prodigy because of her ability to speak spontaneously in verse. Her first book, *The Elfin Pedlar* (1923), was published when she was fourteen and was a collection of 120 ballads. Throughout her life she maintained an interest in magic and spells, and these interests recur in her ballads and plays.

With her sister and mother, Helen Adam came to Hartford, Connecticut, in 1939, but soon relocated to New York City. After seven years, the trio moved to San Francisco, where Helen became a friend of Robert Duncan and a significant artist in the San Francisco Renaissance. Helen Adam attended the poetry workshops led by Duncan, participated in Jack Spicer's Magic Workshop, and established in 1957 a group dedicated to poetry performance called The Maidens, which included Madeline Gleason, Duncan, James Broughton, and others.

Adam's play *San Francisco's Burning* premiered in March of 1962 at Broughton's theater space, The Playhouse. Broughton revised the play, making it a musical, and these revisions irked Duncan, who felt that the spirit of the original verse play was lost.

Despite the dispute among friends, the play ran successfully for twelve weeks. With a grant from the Merrill Foundation (which came as a result of Duncan's support), Helen and her sister traveled to New York in 1964, hopeful about bringing the play to Broadway. *San Francisco's Burning* was staged in an off-Broadway production in 1964 but never rose to the heights of a full Broadway production.

In 1975, Helen Adam read at the Naropa Institute, where she was introduced by Allen Ginsberg, who acknowledged her subtle influence on the Beat writers.

—*William Lawlor*

### Principal Works

Helen Adam's early works include *The Elfin Pedlar*, 1923; *Tales Told by Pixie Pool*, 1923; and *Charms and Dreams from the Elfin Pedlar's Pack*, 1924; *San Francisco's Burning*, 1963, was reprinted by Hanging Loose Press in 1985; other works by Helen Adam are found in *Selected Poems and Ballads*, 1974, and *Stone Cold Gothic*, 1984.

### Bibliographical References

The Poetry/Rare Books Collection, State University of New York, Buffalo, houses the Helen Adam Archive; see Brenda Knight, "Helen Adam: Bardic Matriarch" in *Women of the Beat Generation*, ed. Brenda Knight, 1996; Kristin Prevallet, "The Worm King Emerges: Helen Adam and the Forgotten Ballad Tradition" in *Girls Who Wore Black*, eds. Ronna Johnson and Nancy Grace, 2002, provides ample recognition of Helen Adam's artistic gifts.

*See also* Duncan, Robert; San Francisco Renaissance; Spicer, Jack.

## Algiers, Louisiana

A small community across the Mississippi River from New Orleans; William S. Burroughs (1914–1997) resided there from June 1948 to April 1949. In May 1948, Burroughs moved his family—his common-law wife Joan Vollmer (1923–1951), her daughter Julie, and their infant son Bill, Jr.—to New Orleans. They stayed first in a small house on US Highway 61, in Harahan Junction west of Metairie, but in August Burroughs purchased the one-story "shotgun"-style house at 509 Wagner Street in Algiers, on the "Right Bank" of the river.

Algiers at that time had a population of less than 27,000 and was mostly quiet and residential. The nearby Canal Street Ferry landing gave Burroughs easy access to the hotspots of the French Quarter. As recounted in his autobiographical book, *Junky* (1953), he looked into the queer scene in the Quarter but was mostly repelled by the southern queens' style. He had been off junk only four months when he met a forty-three-year-old junky, Joe Ricks, who introduced him to the local drug scene, quickly readdicting him and involving him in a complex new social scene.

Burroughs dabbled in real estate: in October he bought a tract of "swamp land" near Highway 61 in the Airline Park neighborhood and told Allen Ginsberg he wanted to build a house there. He feuded with his Italian American neighbors in Algiers; then in January he and Joan received visitors arriving from New York on a cross-country road trip: Neal Cassady; his then-wife, LuAnne Henderson; one of Neal's Denver friends and his new wife, Al and Helen Hinkle; and Jack Kerouac, who described the visit in his 1957 novel, *On the Road*, including a visit to the horse races.

On 4 March 1949, three days after Mardi Gras that year, Burroughs suddenly listed his Algiers home for sale; evidently his parents visited him and Vollmer in Algiers during Mardi Gras week and found the house unsuitable for their son. His father Mortimer selected 1128–30 Burgundy in the French Quarter and contracted to buy the house. A few weeks later Burroughs was arrested on 5 April 1949, in a car with two older junkies (Ricks and Horace Guidry) and a young merchant seaman (Alan Cowie). The ensuing events are minutely described in *Junky*: Burroughs's Algiers house was searched, and he was charged, questioned, and held for further interrogation while an agonizing withdrawal syndrome began. Within two days Burroughs's lawyer secured his release, on bail, to Charity Hospital with a quick transfer to Touro Infirmary.

Eight days later, Burroughs was released to his wife, "AMA"—against medical advice. By 27 May Burroughs and Vollmer and their children were living again in Pharr, Texas, on the Mexican border, contemplating an ominous New Orleans court appearance five months away, 27 October. Burroughs's father took over the Burgundy house purchase, and the Wagner Street house sold in late July; the "swamp land" was sold at sheriff's auction the following spring. Burroughs visited Mexico City in August 1949. Two months later that city became his little family's next home, when he fled the United States rather than face his court date.

—*James Grauerholz*

### Bibliographical References

For information on Algiers and the Beats, see Ted Morgan, *Literary Outlaw: The Life and Times of William S. Burroughs*, 1988; Oliver Harris, ed., *The Letters of William S. Burroughs, 1945–1959*, 1993; and Carolyn Cassady, *Off the Road: My Years with Cassady, Kerouac, and Ginsberg*, 1990. The fictional development of Algiers in Beat literature is revealed in William S. Burroughs, *Junky*, 1953, and Jack Kerouac, *On the Road*, 1957.

***See also*** Burroughs, William Seward

## Allen, Donald (1912-2004)

Don Allen was the most important editor and publisher of poetry during the counterculture period that included the Beats and the hippie movement. Allen was born in 1912 and educated in the Midwest. As a young man, he was interested in theater as much as poetry and later translated the plays of Eugene Ionesco. He served in the U.S. Navy as an intelligence officer and translator during World War II on the Pacific front. After getting a master's degree at the University of California, Berkeley, in the late 1940s, he moved to New York and worked for New Directions on a number of projects, including a collection of stories by Dylan Thomas. In the mid-1950s he went to work for Grove Press and founded *Evergreen Review* with coeditor and Grove publisher Barney Rosset. Allen edited the "San Francisco Scene" issue of *Evergreen Review* and then expanded that project into a full-scale anthology published in 1960, *The New American Poetry.* Allen subsequently moved to San Francisco and then to Bolinas, where he began publishing poetry under his own imprints, Four Seasons and Gray Fox. He continued to edit other books, most notably the *Collected Poems* of Lew Welch, and several posthumous collections of Frank O'Hara's poetry. Allen also published and edited or coedited books of interviews with Philip Whalen and Allen Ginsberg and published early novels by Richard Brautigan. In 1973 Allen coedited *The Poetics of the New American Poetry,* and in 1982 he coedited an updated version of *New American Poetry, The Postmoderns.* In 1998 the University of California Press reprinted the original edition of *New American Poetry.*

—*Bill Mohr*

### Principal Projects as Editor or Co-Editor
*Evergreen Review,* 1957–1960; *New American Poetry,* 1960; *The Poetics of the New American Poetry,* 1973; *The Collected Poems of Frank O'Hara,* 1971; *The Selected Poems of Frank O'Hara,* 1974; *The Postmoderns: The New American Poetry Revised,* 1982.

### Bibliographical References
Donald Allen's role in the emergence of the Beat Generation and the shift toward postmodern poetry remains a virtually unexamined field. His editorial archives are at the University of California, San Diego. He makes furtive appearances in a biography of Frank O'Hara, *City Poet,* 1993, as well as Tom Clark's biography, *Charles Olson,* 1991, but plays a more prominent role in Lewis Ellingham and Kevin Killian, *Poet Be Like God,* 1998, which is a biography of Jack Spicer.

***See also*** Little Magazines

## Allen, Steve (1921–2000)

Author, composer, comedian, musician, and television talk-show host. He originated and hosted NBC's *Tonight Show* (1954–1957) and was the star of *The Steve Allen Show* (1956–1960) and many other television shows known by the same title (1960–1976). Steve Allen's connection to the Beat Generation is immortal because of the memorable appearance of Jack Kerouac on Allen's show: Kerouac did a poignant reading of selections from *Visions of Cody* and *On the Road* while Allen improvised on piano. Kerouac later combined with Allen on a long-playing record. On the video *The Beat Generation: An American Dream,* one can view selections from Kerouac's appearance on the Allen show and hear Allen's comments about his connection to Kerouac.

—*William Lawlor*

Steve Allen hosted a memorable reading by Jack Kerouac on the *Steve Allen Show* in 1959. (Bettmann/Corbis)

**Bibliographical References**

For background on Steve Allen, see Gerald Nachman, *Seriously Funny: The Rebel Comedians of the 1950's and the 1960's*, 2003, and Bernard Timberg and Bob Erler, *Television Talk: A History of the TV Talk Show*, 2002.

*See also* Performance Humor

## Amram, David (1930–)

David Amram is a musician and composer who has worked with numerous jazz greats, including Charlie Parker, Dizzy Gillespie, Sonny Rollins, Charles Mingus, and George Barrow. Amram's music celebrates music and culture from around the world. He has traveled to Kenya, Central America, the Middle East, China, and Cuba, and he brings both the music and the instruments of diverse cultures, including Native American cultures, to his performances. He is best known to admirers of the Beat Generation for his work with Jack Kerouac in the first jazz-poetry concert at the Brata Art Gallery in New York in 1957 and for his appearance with Allen Ginsberg, Gregory Corso, and Larry Rivers in *Pull My Daisy*, a film created by Robert Frank and Alfred Leslie. Kerouac narrated the film, and Amram composed an original musical score.

—*William Lawlor*

**Principal Works**

See *Offbeat: Collaborating with Kerouac*, 2002, which is a memoir of Amram's life, times, and art. An earlier autobiographical text is *Vibrations: The Adventures and Musical Times of David Amram*, 1968.

*See also* Music; First Poetry-Jazz Concert; Film

## Anarchy, Christian

Initially, there may seem to be little connection between the Christian Anarchist movement and beatnik hipsters of the 1950s and 1960s. On the surface, these two groups seem contradictory, and one might consider any relationship between the two to be an inconsistency either of Christian ideals or of the Beats' self-styled Eastern spirituality. On closer examination, however, a direct link can be established between the Beats and radical Christians of the Roman Catholic Church. According to John Clellon Holmes in his essay "The Philosophy of the Beat Generation," which appears in *Passionate Opinions* (1988), Jack Kerouac (often considered the King of the Beats) once stated that "the Beat Generation is basically a religious generation." In Kerouac's mind, the Beats were on a mystic spiritual quest to find truth through a Buddha, and in Kerouac's case through awareness of Christ. In a confusing postwar America where hypocrisy seemed to reign supreme as an acceptable way to deal with the terror and the pain brought on by the bombings of Hiroshima and Nagasaki in 1945, Kerouac and many other members of the Beat Generation looked for new answers that could only be found through profound spiritual search well beyond the intellect and art.

The connection between Beats and contemporary Christian Anarchists can be directly traced to one of the most organized of all formal religions by way of the Catholic Worker movement. Aside from the fact that Jack Kerouac had been raised a Catholic (serving as an altar boy in Lowell, Massachusetts) and that he insisted on being buried with his rosary in his hands, much of Kerouac's writings also make apparent that he lived a spiritual life torn between his Catholic beliefs and his newly found devotion to Zen Buddhism. Still, these facts do not connect the Beats to Christian Anarchists.

Specific historical incidents demonstrate that the Beats, indeed, had some ties to traditional religion through the radical Catholic left. The direct connection between radical Christianity and the Beats comes through the Catholic Worker movement founded in the early 1930s in New York City by former communist, anarchist, and Catholic convert Dorothy Day and by Peter Maurin, who had been raised a peasant in France by the liberal Christian Brothers order. Maurin and Day based their new organization on what they understood to be anarchist Catholicism. According to Fred Boehrer, this basis meant they subscribed to a "persona list" philosophy that "the lack of rules and clearly defined expectations created an environment which permitted individuals to freely express their own views—sometimes consistent, other times incompatible with views of other community members" (104). The Catholic Worker movement was Christian and communitarian, but it was never Marxist or even liberal in the common definition of that term. In this way, these ideals fit with the ideals of many Beats, especially Jack Kerouac, who never saw himself as a liberal, a left-wing agitator, an anti-American protestor, or a radical. With this distaste for externally imposed rules as a basic philosophy and common ground, these two seemingly different groups connected. Although Catholic Workers were radically left, they also had a strong belief in traditional Roman Catholicism. This belief may seem an impossible pairing, but the Catholic Worker movement remains to this day heavily involved in secular, left-wing politics and important social issues as part of the Catholic Church's teachings on social justice (i.e., dignity of the human person, the concept of common good, and the rights of workers to organize and be treated fairly by employers). Dorothy Day had strong commitments to doing the work of mercy to serve society's poor and downtrodden. In addition, Day and others in the movement had a sincere desire to eliminate war, poverty, and the overall hypocrisy of postwar America. These very acts and beliefs drew members of the Beat Generation into various levels of engagement with the Catholic Workers.

Whether Jack Kerouac ever actually interacted with Dorothy Day and the Catholic Workers is not known, but Allen Ginsberg in fact did first read his famous long poem "Kaddish" in its entirety in 1960 at the office of the *Catholic Worker* newspaper. This location for Ginsberg's reading is interesting because it places Ginsberg in a clearly religious (albeit left-wing) venue reading a kaddish (a Jewish prayer-poem that may have seemed heretical to many orthodox Jews) in front of an audience filled with radical Catholics (Dickstein 5).

Another famous incident that directly ties the Beats to the Catholic Worker movement is that several members of the Beat Generation lived, for a time, at Dorothy Day's Catholic Worker House in the Bowery on the Lower East Side of New York

City. In 1962, Dorothy Day was so offended and enraged at Ed Sanders (founder of the Fugs and a younger member of the Beat Generation) for his local literary publication *Fuck You: A Magazine of the Arts* that she angrily cleared the Catholic Worker House of all who had published in and associated with the magazine. This act became known throughout the Lower East Side as the "Dorothy Day Stomp." Day felt the literature published in *Fuck You* was pornographic and not helpful to the Anarchist resolutions to end violence and poverty and to address other serious issues of the 1960s; from Day's perspective, these young radicals and bohemians abused drugs and misused sex. She felt that they were not only endangering their own lives, but that their childish actions were jeopardizing the antiwar efforts of the radical left, keeping the Christian Anarchists from being taken more seriously by the community as a whole. For Day, these Beats were more nihilistic than revolutionary.

Ed Sanders responded in his magazine with this statement: "Several staff members of the *Catholic Worker* were stomped off the *Worker* set as a result of publishing in *Fuck You: A Magazine of the Arts* or as a result of continued association with its editor (Sanders): the head stomper (Day) at the *CW* has succumbed to Jansenist dialectic and flicked 4 people off the set there. This outburst of Calvinistic directives seems to us not in the spirit of anarchy, nonviolence, and the view of Christ in every man. However, we understand the need of the grand old lady of pacifism for a closed metaphysical system where there are no disturbances" (Miller 484–485). However, long before Day's death in 1980, Dorothy and Ed Sanders had settled their differences from the early 1960s.

This incident was not the last connection between the Beat Generation or the subsequent hippie movement and the Catholic Worker movement, which went on to lead the way for many latter-day Beats and hippies in the anti–Vietnam War movement of the 1960s and 1970s. Day, along with two brothers, Catholic priests Daniel and Philip Berrigan, *Catholic Worker* editor Tom Cornell, and many other Christian Anarchists, played a major role in the antiwar movement. In fact, Tom Cornell and David Miller, representatives from the *Catholic Worker*, were among the first arrested and imprisoned for burning their draft cards in public as an act of defiance against America's unjust and immoral war in Southeast Asia. Although the Beats and the Christian Anarchists had, at times, radically different agendas and moral beliefs, in many other areas they were in complete agreement. Both the Beats and Christian Anarchists believed in the principles of freedom and liberty for all.

—*M. L. Liebler*

## Bibliographical References

Insider views of Christian Anarchy are found in Dorothy Day, *The Long Loneliness: The Autobiography of Dorothy Day*, 1952, and Ammon Hennacy, *Autobiography of a Catholic Anarchist*, 1954. For a general view of Christian Anarchy and its context, see Peter Maurin, *Catholic Radicalism: Phrased Essays for a Green Revolution*, 1949; Mel Piehl, *Breaking Bread: The Catholic Worker and the Origin of Catholic Radicalism in America*, 1982; William D. Miller, *Dorothy Day: A Biography*, 1982; and William Thorn, with Phillip Runkel and Susan Mountain, eds., *Dorothy Day & the Catholic Worker Movement: Centenary Essays*, 2001. The edition by Thorn, Runkel, and Mountain includes Fred Boehrer's essay, "Diversity, Plurality, and Ambiguity: Anarchism and the Catholic Worker Movement." On page 5 of Morris Dickstein, *Gates of Edne: American Culture in the Sixites*, 1978, one finds the description involving Ginsberg's reading of "Kaddish" at the office of the *Catholic Worker*.

*See also* Religion, The Beats and

## Anderson, Joan, Letter about

Written by Neal Cassady to Jack Kerouac and reportedly dated December 17, 1950, the Joan Anderson letter is a long, uninhibited, effusive, and digressive description of personal feelings and sexual adventures. Originally much longer than the surviving fragment, the letter inspired spontaneity in the writings of Kerouac and Allen Ginsberg. Cassady describes his meetings with Joan Anderson shortly after her suicide attempt and relates the conflict between their feelings of sexual excitement and the conservative mood of the nurse and the married couple who care for Joan. Cassady abruptly shifts to an account of a madcap meeting with "Cherry Mary." Once again, sexual energy between Cassady and his partner is disrupted by the arrival of a conservative person, in this case the mother of a child for whom Cherry Mary is babysitting. Nude in the bathroom and engaged in sexual preliminaries, Cassady is obliged to hide while Mary diverts the visitor and gathers Cassady's clothes from another room. Cassady slips through a tiny bathroom window and avoids discovery. Freezing outside, he eventually gets some of his clothes back from Mary and is on his way. These descriptions of Cassady's sexual episodes are interspersed with his regrets, reflections, and memories. He relates his pool hall background; he admits his alcoholism and his sentence at hard labor in the New Mexico State Reformatory. He makes silly jokes and recalls his confrontation with police, who try to charge him with statutory rape and burglary.

For Kerouac, the letter's verve and frank treatment of personal moments were inspiring. Kerouac wrote to Cassady that that the letter was a brilliant piece combining the best of Dostoyevsky, Joyce, Celine, and Proust. Seeing Cassady's letter as the basis for a new American literature, Kerouac began his legendary three-week composition of *On the Road* in April 1951.

For Ginsberg, the letter was also inspiring, but mindful of marketability, he was not able to accept the spontaneous composition as a finished work ready for publication. Ginsberg urged Cassady to revise, improve structure, and design an appropriate ending.

For Cassady, the responses of Kerouac and Ginsberg were encouraging, but Cassady soon found himself stalled as a writer. He fell into self-doubt and all but abandoned writing endeavors.

—*William Lawlor*

## Bibliographical References

The remaining fragment of the original letter is in Neal Cassady, *The First Third*, 1981. Brief commentaries on the letter appear in Ann Charters, *The Portable Beat Reader*, 1992, and Michael Schumacher, *Dharma Lion*, 1992; see

Dave Moore, ed. *Neal Cassady: Collected Letters, 1944–1967*, 2004.

*See also* Cassady, Neal; Kerouac, Jack; Ginsberg, Allen; Spontaneity, The Beat Generation and the Culture of

## Aphorisms and Slogans

Pithy, meaningful expressions characteristic of the Beat Generation. In part, these phrases reflect the Buddhist outlook—a confidence in succinct truth, especially as expressed in koans. In addition, the aphorisms and slogans have a hip attraction and serve as markers of the cool.

Jack Kerouac's "Belief & Technique for Modern Prose" is a "List of Essentials" that economically expresses key ideas and makes them memorable. For example, Kerouac writes, "Be in love with yr life," "Be crazy dumbsaint of the mind," "You're a Genius all the time," and "Believe in the holy contour of life." Such phrases buoy the spirit and set the imagination to work. To establish a writing method, Kerouac writes, "Remove literary, grammatical, and syntactical inhibition," "Don't think of words when you stop but to see picture better," and "Struggle to sketch the flow that already exists intact in mind."

Allen Ginsberg's Mindwriting Slogans have a similar effect. He takes heart from phrases such as, "Candor ends paranoia" and "First thought, best thought." To establish a frame of mind for thinking, he tells himself, "Notice what you notice," and "Catch yourself thinking." In selecting slogans, Ginsberg borrows from others, crediting Ezra Pound for the slogan "Only emotion endures," citing Percy Bysshe Shelley for "Poets are the unacknowledged legislators of the world," and acknowledging Chögyam Trunpa for "First thought, best thought."

In *The Dharma Bums* by Jack Kerouac, Japhy Ryder shares many aphoristic expressions with Ray Smith. While mountain climbing, Ray remembers the famous Zen expression, "When you get to the top of a mountain, keep climbing" (83–84). Watching Japhy descend the mountain in twenty-foot strides, Ray realizes that "it's impossible to fall off mountains" (85). Alvah Goldbook, in a saying that counteracts the optimism of these Zen expressions, says, "It all ends in tears anyway" (216).

Lawrence Ferlinghetti offers variations on familiar or memorable phrases. A news reporter may speak of the Freedom of Information Act, but Ferlinghetti wants to have a Freedom of the Imagination Act. In *Minor Characters*, Joyce Johnson recalls that at the time of her split with Kerouac, Jack remarked, "Unrequited love's a bore." In all, the Beats are always ready to make pithy language into memorable expressions of life's most complicated ideas.

—*William Lawlor*

### Bibliographical References

See Jack Kerouac, "Essentials of Spontaneous Prose," in Ann Charters, ed., *The Portable Beat Reader*, 1992. Compare Allen Ginsberg, *Cosmopolitan Greetings*, 1994, and Jack Kerouac, *The Dharma Bums*, 1958.

## Apollinaire, Guillaume (born Guillelmus Apollinaris de Kostrowitsky, 1880–1918)

Like many of the artists of his generation, Guillaume Apollinaire fought in the First World War; he died in France in the great influenza epidemic that followed the war. An influential poet and critic, he was known for his experimentation with modernist poetic forms and his psychological analyses of modern painting. Perhaps his best-known works today are *Meditations esthetiques: les peintres cubists* (1913), which brought attention to the Cubist movement, and *Alcools* (1913), his first widely recognized book of poetry. A precursor of the Surrealist school of poetry, Apollinaire was influential among Beat poets such as Allen Ginsberg, who found that the concept of regulating the line according to the breath was a concept "implicit in Apollinaire" (*Spontaneous Mind*, 146).

—*David Arnold*

### Bibliographical References

For a general impression of Apollinaire, see LeRoy C. Breunig, *Guillaume Apollinaire*, 1969. The

Beat connection to Apollinaire is expressed in Allen Ginsberg, *Spontaneous Mind: Selected Interviews 1958–1996*, ed. David Carter, 2001.

## Apomorphine Treatment

In "Deposition: Testimony Concerning a Sickness," an essay appended to *Naked Lunch*, William Burroughs praises the apomorphine treatment, which he maintains is a cure for addiction to drugs. Having developed a costly and dangerous habit, Burroughs traveled to England, where he underwent the apomorphine treatment. According to Burroughs in "Deposition," apomorphine, a compound created by boiling morphine with hydrochloric acid, "acts on the back brain to regulate the metabolism and normalize the blood stream in such a way that the enzyme system of addiction is destroyed over a period of four or five days" (203). Burroughs notes that he had tried many other methods of ending addiction without much success, but the apomorphine treatment, and treatments that may be developed through future refinements, offer the best solution to the problem of drug addiction.

—*William Lawlor*

**Bibliographical Reference**

Burroughs's respect for the apomorphine treatment is in "Deposition: Testimony Concerning a Sickness," in *Naked Lunch: The Restored Text*, ed. James Grauerholz and Barry Miles, 2001.

***See also*** Burroughs, William Seward

## Atomic Era

An era of developing, testing, and deploying of nuclear weapons that led to an international arms race and a society that lived in fear of devastation on one hand and in denial of the nuclear threat on the other.

On July 13, 1942, with World War II in progress, the United States undertook the Manhattan Project for the development of a nuclear weapon. On July 16, 1945, in Alamogordo, New Mexico, it successfully detonated an atomic bomb. With a tangible nuclear threat at its disposal, the United States

A mushroom cloud towers 20,000 feet above Nagasaki, Japan, following a second nuclear attack by the United States on August 9, 1945. The bombing—which took place three days after the first nuclear attack on Hiroshima—was followed by Japan's surrender on August 14, bringing an end to World War II. (Bettmann/Corbis)

sought surrender from the Japanese, but the Japanese emperor refused. On August 6, 1945, a U.S. B-29 bomber dropped the Little Boy bomb on Hiroshima, Japan, unleashing the devastating force of fifteen kilotons of explosives. Three days later, another U.S. B-29 bomber dropped the 22-kiloton Fat Man bomb on Nagasaki, Japan. The two atomic bombings led to the surrender of Japan and the end of World War II.

The ensuing Cold War led to an arms race between the United States and the Soviet Union. The Soviets tested their own atomic bomb in 1949; the United States then entered the age of thermonuclear weapons on November 1, 1952, with the detonation of a bomb named "Mike." Exploded at Eniwetok Atoll in the Pacific Ocean, this bomb was five hundred times more powerful than the bomb tested in Alamogordo, New Mexico. The Soviet Union soon tested its own thermonuclear weapon, and soon England, France, and other nations developed nuclear arsenals as well.

With nuclear attack from a foreign nation a possibility, U.S. strategists spoke of a "missile gap" and the need to develop missiles in silos, missiles in roving submarines, and a large squadron of B-52 bombers with nuclear arms.

Nuclear war could be avoided, some strategists suggested, if a "nuclear deterrent" could be established so that no nation would attack the United States or its allies because U.S. response would be catastrophic. Furthermore, the supremacy of the United States in nuclear weaponry would solidify the connections of western European nations to the United States rather than to the Soviet Union. Ironically, the possibility of nuclear catastrophe was so frightening that the United States came to view the nuclear alternative as an undesirable last resort; thus, the massive development of weapons was based on the idea that such weapons should never be used.

The psychological effects of the nuclear era were powerful. Citizens went on with their normal working lives, but within themselves they feared that all could be lost in a sudden flash of light and heat. Although citizens feared the nuclear holocaust, they reconciled themselves to the fact that the nation's resources were substantially dedicated toward making nuclear devastation a reality. Citizens imagined that normal life could go on after a nuclear attack and built bomb shelters and rehearsed "duck and cover" drills in schools.

Among the Beats, the nuclear era provoked various responses. Near the end of *On the Road,* when Sal and Dean visit Mexico, Sal notices the innocence of the Native Americans, who reach out to Sal and Dean for some sample of civilization. Sal sees that the natives do not realize that civilization now offers a bomb that can leave all in ruin. In "Howl," Allen Ginsberg recreates society's trepidation about the possibility of sudden nuclear destruction when he refers to those who are "listening to the crack of doom on the hydrogen jukebox" (11). In "Bomb," Gregory Corso playfully personifies the bomb itself, treating it as a potential lover, but bemoaning humankind's love affair with weapons of all kinds. The poem itself is shaped like a mushroom cloud.

The Beat lifestyle, which is dedicated to experience and pleasure in life, is largely a response to the nuclear threat. If the world can end at any moment, then the person who dedicates himself or herself to unsatisfying work for mere material rewards is grossly misguided. Instead, one should do things before the chance to do them is lost. One should travel, hear music, see nature's wonders, appreciate resourceful and inventive people, and take pleasure in intimacy. One should strive to find "It" before all striving becomes impossible.

In particular, the nuclear age shaped the outlook of Lawrence Ferlinghetti, whose role in the U.S. Navy during World War II afforded him the opportunity to visit Japan after the devastation of the nuclear bombs. Having seen the effects of atomic weapons only weeks after the bombings, Ferlinghetti dedicated himself to peace.

—*William Lawlor*

## Bibliographic References

*The Nuclear Age: Power, Proliferation, and the Arms Race,* 1984, is a government document on nuclear weapons and energy and discusses the arms race, the antinuclear movement, and nuclear disarmament. In *The Future of Immortality and Other Essays for the Nuclear Age,* 1987, Robert J. Lifton explores the psychological and sociological aspects of the nuclear age. Ira Chermus, *Nuclear Madness: Religion and the Psychology of the Nuclear Age,* 1991, further explores the effects of the nuclear age on the human outlook. Gregory Corso's "Bomb" is available as a broadside from City Lights, but one also finds it in *The Happy Birthday of Death,* 1960. See also Jack Kerouac, *On the Road,* 1957, and Allen Ginsberg, *Howl and Other Poems,* 1956.

# B

## Baraka, Amiri (LeRoi Jones) (1934–)

Formerly known as LeRoi Jones; a poet, editor, playwright, musical critic, and social activist. In the late 1950s, Jones had bohemian beginnings in New York City, associating with writers often connected to the Beat literary movement. With Hettie Jones, LeRoi Jones was the editor of *Yugen,* a little magazine that featured many writers of the Beat Generation. With Diane di Prima, Jones edited *Floating Bear,* a mimeographed poetry newsletter that flourished because of its spontaneity and immediacy.

With the assassination of Malcolm X in 1965, Jones underwent changes that led to a separation from the Beats. In the mid-1960s, Jones became a prominent voice in the Black Arts movement, founded the Black Arts Repertory Theater-School, and participated in the rise of Black Cultural Nationalism, taking the name Imamu (spiritual leader) Ameer (prince) Baraka (blessed) in 1967; he subsequently dropped the spiritual title and revised the spelling, making himself Amiri Baraka. In 1974, Baraka renounced Black Nationalism and declared himself a Marxist-Leninist. Although this activist prefers the name Amiri Baraka, a slash is often presented as part of his name, making him LeRoi Jones/Amiri Baraka.

Jones's parents were Coyette LeRoy Jones, a postal worker, and Anna Lois Jones, a social worker. After being raised in an integrated neighborhood, Jones graduated with honors in 1951 at age sixteen from Barringer High School in Newark, New Jersey. He attended Rutgers University in Newark on a scholarship but later transferred to Howard University, where he did not complete a degree. Jones was a sergeant in the air force; in 1957, he was discharged from military service and began an artistic life in Greenwich Village.

In 1958, Jones and Hettie Cohen wed. As coeditors of *Yugen,* an avant-garde literary magazine, Jones and his wife published Beat writers, including Jack Kerouac and Allen Ginsberg. With Diane di Prima, Jones coedited *Floating Bear,* a mimeo magazine delivered by mail. By quickly editing and printing issues of the magazine, Jones and di Prima capitalized on the currency of material.

In 1965, Jones left Hettie and the Beat milieu, and a year later he married Sylvia Robinson (now known as Amina Baraka). During the marriage with Hettie, two children were born: Kellie and Lisa. The marriage with Amina has led to five children: Obalaji, Ras, Shani, Amiri Jr., and Ahi.

Gifted with a flair for drama, Amiri Baraka can convert a meeting in an auditorium into a theatrical event. In an antagonistic style, Baraka condemns academics, established authorities, Jews, gays, whites, and middle-class blacks. He ridicules hypocrisy, ignorance, or oppressive conduct. If the object of ridicule reacts, then his or her guilt is evident; if the object of ridicule remains calm, then the person's implacability suggests that the charges are unfounded. Even as Baraka stings his target, which is often part of his own audience, he does so with wit, often winning the enthusiasm of an audience that, in large measure, is also the object of his derision.

Jones's first collection of poems, *Preface to a Twenty Volume Suicide Note* (1961), reveals the author's early connection to the Beats. John Wieners, Michael McClure, Gary Snyder, and Allen Ginsberg are all referred to in dedications. The Projectivist approach of Charles Olson is an influence on Jones, but he keeps his poems lively with references to comic-book heroes and pop-culture figures and surrealistic imagery. The title suggests the suddenness of suicide, but the suicide is absurdly deferred because the business at hand is a preface, and twenty volumes of work remain to be done before the suicide can occur. Stanzas and patterns of rhyme are absent, but at work are word play; inventive spelling, capitalization, and punctuation; and imaginative images. Jones's wife and daughter are the topic of some poems, but he often turns to literary, social, and political subjects.

*Dutchman* (1964) is perhaps Jones's most well-known work, and Clay, a main character in the play, may be Jones's look back at himself as a youthful Beat poet. In *Dutchman*, which opened at the Cherry Lane Theater in New York City on March 24, 1964, Lula, "a thirty-year-old white woman," antagonizes Clay, a "twenty-year-old Negro." On a hot summer night in the subway, Lula taunts Clay, who responds with sexual interest but is maneuvered into clumsiness. With racial insults, Lula provokes Clay, who finally explodes in anger. Angrily insisting that black musicians have always mocked whites by exploiting a secret musical code in their music, Clay enjoys a momentary triumph; however, Lula suddenly stabs Clay and commands the others on the train to dispose of his body. Lula records her victory, and the cycle of torment and death begins anew when another young Negro appears—Lula's next victim.

Although Baraka's career led him away from the Beats, he has found his way into renewed contact with them. He appeared with Allen Ginsberg at the 92nd Street Y in New York City and spent time at the Naropa Institute in Boulder, Colorado. With Lawrence Ferlinghetti, he appeared for a radio interview in Denver.

In the 1970s, Baraka dedicated himself to political activities, especially the campaign of Kenneth Gibson for mayor of Newark, New Jersey; in 1984 Baraka published his autobiography. He became the Poet Laureate of New Jersey in 2001, yet "Somebody Blew Up America," his poem written in the aftermath of the events of September 11, 2001, embroiled him in controversy, which led to calls for his dismissal. Today Baraka maintains his diverse work as a lecturer, teacher, and activist.

—*William Lawlor*

## Principal Works

*Preface to a Twenty Volume Suicide Note*, 1961, and *The Dead Lecturer*, 1964, are collections of poems; *Dutchman*, 1964, won an Obie Award; an experimental novel is *The System of Dante's Hell*, 1965; his collection of essays is *Home: Social Essays* (1966); his collection of short stories is *Tales*, 1967; to carry forward the work of *Blues People*, a historical and cultural interpretation of black music, Baraka offers *Black Music*, 1968; with Lary Neal, Baraka is the editor of an anthology of black writers titled *Black Fire*, 1968; the collection of poetry reflecting his participation in Black Cultural Nationalism is *Black Magic*, 1969. For convenience, one might consult *The LeRoi Jones/Amiri Baraka Reader*, ed. William Harris, 1991, which includes most of the material mentioned here; *Transbluency*, ed. Paul Vangelisti, 1995, offers selections from ten previous volumes of poetry.

## Bibliographical References

Studies of Baraka include Jerry Gafio Watts, *Amiri Baraka: The Politics and Art of a Black Intellectual*, 2001; Kimberly Benston, *Baraka: The Renegade and the Mask*, 1976, and Werner Sollors, *Amiri Baraka/ LeRoi Jones: The Quest for a "Populist Modernism,"* 1978.

*See also* Censorship; Theater; Little Magazines; Jones, Hettie; Communism and the Workers' Movement

## Beat and Beatnik

If someone has to ask what "Beat" is, then he or she is probably hopelessly conventional, but that conventionality has not stopped an ongoing discussion of the meaning of Beat, Beat Generation, and beatnik.

Jazz musicians in the 1940s used the term "Beat" to express poverty and desperation. According to Allen Ginsberg, Herbert Huncke, a Times Square hustler who conversed with William Burroughs, Jack Kerouac, and other young New York writers, used the word to express "exhausted, at the bottom of the world, looking up or out, sleepless, wide-eyed, perceptive, rejected by society, on your own, streetwise" (quoted in Charters, *Portable Beat Reader*, xviii). Relentlessly asked about the meaning of "Beat," Kerouac became more resourceful, telling Steve Allen that "sympathetic" is a synonym for beat and even transforming the word with references to beatitude and beatific.

According to John Clellon Holmes in "The Name of the Game," which appears in *Passionate Opinions* (1988), in a Manhattan apartment in November 1948, Holmes and Jack Kerouac had a conversation during which they tried to characterize their generation. According to Holmes, Kerouac perceived "a sort of furtiveness" in his contemporaries, "a weariness with all the forms, all the conventions of the world" (54). Kerouac concluded, "I guess you might say we're a beat generation" (55).

Holmes incorporated this characterization in his novel *Go* (1952), inspiring Gilbert Millstein, a writer for the *New York Times*, to assign to Holmes an article that ran in the *New York Times Magazine* on Sunday, 16 November 1952. The article's title, "This Is the Beat Generation," brought Kerouac's idea to a broad audience and initiated the animated discussion of Beat, Beat Generation, and beatniks that continues to this day.

Considering the successes and notoriety of Ginsberg and Kerouac, one might assume that their works became the central focus of the attention paid to them. Unfortunately, journalists and reviewers often chose to emphasize what it means to be Beat and what the Beat Generation is all about. Instead of asking Kerouac about spontaneous prose based on bop and jazz, journalists pursued the idea of frantic, angry delinquents relentlessly seeking kicks through sex orgies, highway adven-

*San Francisco Chronicle* columnist Herb Caen coined the term "beatnik." (AP Photo/HO, Columbia University)

tures, passionate jazz, and unrestricted drugs and alcohol. Instead of asking Ginsberg about the tradition of Walt Whitman and the inventiveness of William Carlos Williams, writers mocked the dress and idiom of the Beats, reducing literary artistry to berets, shades, and bongos, betraying literary language with "like," "cool," and "hip."

Herb Caen, a writer for the *San Francisco Chronicle*, adapted the suffix from *Sputnik*, the newly launched Soviet satellite, and coined the word "beatnik" in his column dated 2 April 1958, half a year after the Russians launched *Sputnik*, establishing the caricature of the Beats as lazy, indulgent, and probably communist weirdos. "Beatnik" caught on, and the Beats themselves often used the term, perpetuating the confusion between authentic artists and the derisive caricature established by Caen. Maynard G. Krebs, a character on the television program *The Many Loves of Dobie Gillis*, reinforced the caricature, but Bob Denver played the role with such charm that thousands of viewers loved the beatniks.

—*William Lawlor*

## Bibliographical References
See Ann Charters's Introduction to *The Portable Beat Reader*, 1992, for Huncke's role in the

development of "Beat." John Clellon Holmes, "The Name of the Game," in *Passionate Opinions*, 1988, discusses the origin of "Beat Generation." Caen's column, titled "Pocketful of Notes," appears in the *San Francisco Chronicle*, 2 April 1958. Jesse Hamlin reviews Caen's coining of "beatnik" in "How Herb Caen Named a Generation" in the *San Francisco Chronicle*, 26 November 1995: 28.

*See also* Krebs, Maynard G.

## Beat Conferences, University of Massachusetts, Lowell

The University of Massachusetts, Lowell's Beat Literature Symposium was founded in 1995, with Ann Charters as the inaugural keynote speaker. Subsequent keynote speakers for the annual symposium have been Albert Gelpi, Ann Douglas, Jay Wright, Janine Pommy Vega, Robert Creeley, Omar Swartz, and Regina Weinreich. Other speakers included David Amram, Ronna Johnson, Matt Theado, Douglas Brinkley, and Nancy Grace.

In 1999, the Beat Literature Symposium was renamed the Beat Attitudes Conference. That year, John Sampas became a conference benefactor. Because the growing conference required extensive advance planning, Professor Hilary Holladay, the founding director of the conference, scheduled the meeting biennially rather than annually. The next conference, therefore, was held in 2001.

The 2003 conference was the Jack Kerouac Conference on Beat Literature and the meeting focused mostly on poetry of the Beat movement. In other years, panels have struck a balance between senior and junior scholars speaking on Kerouac, Ginsberg, Burroughs, and the female Beats, among others. Beat writers who typically receive less attention than the three most famous Beats are highlighted; papers on Herbert Huncke and Bob Kaufman, for instance, have been given their due attention.

The conference is held the same weekend (traditionally the first weekend in October) as Lowell Celebrates Kerouac! (LCK!; a community-based activity) so that out-of-town visitors can participate in both events. In addition to Beat literature schol-ars from across the United States and beyond, audience members typically include University of Massachusetts students and faculty, visitors in town for LCK!, students and faculty from other colleges in the region, and area residents with an abiding interest in Kerouac and the Beats. The Kerouac Conference is free and open to the public.

—*William Lawlor*

### Bibliographical Reference

The website is http://www.uml.edu/KerouacConference.

## Beatitude

An aspect of the definition of "Beat" suggesting the religious devotion and blessed state of the "Beat angels." Jack Kerouac faced relentless questioning from journalists about the meaning of "Beat," and journalists were predisposed toward answers involving rebellion, anger, delinquency, promiscuity, and wildness. Kerouac counteracted such ideas by turning to the Bible's Sermon on the Mount, especially the portion often referred to as the Beatitudes (Matthew 5: 1–12). Jesus explains who is blessed and why. Kerouac argues that Beat involves the pursuit of beatitude—the state of being blessed.

—*William Lawlor*

### Bibliographical Reference

In "Beatific: The Origins of the Beat Generation," which originally appeared in *Playboy* (June 1959) and is reprinted in *The Portable Jack Kerouac*, ed. Ann Charters, 1995, Kerouac explains his connection between Beat and beatitude.

## Be-In

On 14 January 1967 on a mild and bright day in San Francisco's Golden Gate Park, approximately 25,000 people formed "A Gathering of the Tribes for a Human Be-In," a meeting intended to bring together activists and flower children for the start of a new age of joy and enlightenment. Timothy Leary, Michael McClure, Jerry Rubin, Lenore Kandel,

Lawrence Ferlinghetti, Gary Snyder, Dick Gregory, and Allen Ginsberg read poetry or gave speeches, and the Grateful Dead, Jefferson Airplane, and Quicksilver Messenger Service played music. The Diggers distributed free food (including sandwiches laced with LSD), and bikers from the Hell's Angels helped rejoin parents and small children who became separated. The spirit that arose from the Be-In was infectious, and the event became a touchstone for many similar gatherings during the "summer of love" and afterwards.

During the Be-In itself, all parties were peaceful, and there were no arrests; however, as the day turned to night and some congregants refused to disperse, police took action to break up the crowd. This police action solidified the adversarial relationship between young people in the street and the police.

—*William Lawlor*

**Bibliographical References**
See Michael Schumacher, *Dharma Lion*, 1992, and Jane Kramer, *Allen Ginsberg in America*, 1969; compare Derek Taylor, *It Was Twenty Years Ago Today*, 1987, and Helen Perry, *The Human Be-In*, 1968.

*See also* Ginsberg, Allen

# Berman, Wallace (1926–1976)

Central figure in California Assemblage movement, a group of artists dedicated to gathering abandoned materials or scrap and sculpting with such material. Berman is also known for artwork for books and literary magazines, especially *Semina,* which included various Beat writers.

Born in New York City in 1926, Berman moved with his family to Los Angeles. As a teen he involved himself with jazz performances on the West Coast, and he briefly attended the Jepson Art School and Chouinard Art School.

Berman persistently displayed interdisciplinary interests. Produced on an early version of the copy machine, Berman's "verifax collages" displayed subtle brown tones. *Semina* was a literary magazine without conventional design or contents: Berman

presented material in envelopes of different sizes and included experimental writers such as Michael McClure, Philip Lamantia, and David Meltzer. Berman himself adopted the pen name Pantale Xantos when he wrote poetry for *Semina.*

In Los Angeles in 1957, Berman installed an exhibit of art at Ferus, a gallery established by Walter Hopps and Edward Kienholz. Because a drawing or sculpture in the show represented copulation, Berman faced charges of obscenity. He was convicted and fined, and this confrontation with the authorities led Berman to leave Los Angeles for San Francisco. So troublesome was this experience with censorship that Berman thereafter strove to maintain a low profile.

—*William Lawlor*

**Bibliographic References**
Rebecca Solnit, "Historical Constellations: Notes on California, 1946–1961," in *Beat Culture and the New America 1950–1965,* ed. Lisa Phillips, 1995, comments on Berman's role in the Assemblage movement; see also Richard Candida Smith, *Utopia and Dissent: Art, Poetry, and Politics in California,* 1995, and John Maynard, *Venice West,* 1991.

*See also* Painting

# Big Sur

Between San Francisco and Los Angeles along California's coastal Highway 1, a ninety-mile scenic and rocky region whose name is derived from the Spanish "El Sur Grande," which means "The Big South."

For the Beats, Big Sur was especially connected with Bixby Canyon, where Lawrence Ferlinghetti owns a small and rustic cabin. In 1960, Ferlinghetti and Jack Kerouac planned a retreat for Kerouac, who was to stay at Ferlinghetti's cabin to enjoy scenic splendor and private study. Unfortunately, Kerouac did not follow the plans for a secret retreat; instead, he arrived in San Francisco and began an alcoholic binge. When Kerouac finally got to Bixby Canyon, he tried to settle into a routine of writing, but the foggy and ominous environment proved

The Bixby Bridge crosses a canyon along the coast of Big Sur, California. Lawrence Ferlinghetti's cabin in the canyon is the setting for Jack Kerouac's *Big Sur*. (Craig Lovell/Corbis)

Ferlinghetti attempted to arrange a meeting of Kerouac and Miller, but Kerouac got drunk and failed to attend. Miller was the author of an introduction for Kerouac's *The Subterraneans* and agreed to meet with Kerouac in Carmel, California. However, when Kerouac went out with Neal Cassady and other friends, he got drunk and missed the meeting.

—*Valentina Peguero*

**Bibliographic References**

Warren French, *Jack Kerouac*, 1986, offers a concise explanation of Kerouac's experience in Big Sur and his development of the experience in *Big Sur*, 1962; although fiction, *Big Sur* is often seen as the work that shows his most faithful reproduction of the events of his own life; Barry Silesky's *Ferlinghetti: The Artist in His Time*, 1990, reveals Ferlinghetti's unsuccessful efforts to make Kerouac's experience in Bixby Canyon worthwhile and to arrange a meeting with Henry Miller. In Chris Felver's video *The Coney Island of Lawrence Ferlinghetti*, one can see Ferlinghetti at his cabin in Bixby Canyon.

more maddening than soothing. Instead of establishing productive privacy, Kerouac brought friends and acquaintances to the remote cabin. Affected by excessive drinking, Kerouac suffered a nervous breakdown.

Kerouac's experience in Bixby Canyon is recorded in his novel *Big Sur* (1962). The novel establishes an extraordinary narrator who looks back on his mental deterioration and chronicles it with clarity, frankness, and specificity. This insightful and disturbing prose is accompanied by a concluding sound poem, "Sea," the subtitle of which is "Sounds of the Pacific Ocean at Big Sur." While some readers find this poem to be nothing more than senseless raving, other readers recognize Kerouac's peculiar innovation.

Other literary figures connected to Big Sur include Henry Miller (1891–1980), an author whose influence on the Beats is immeasurable. Miller visited Big Sur in 1944 and fell in love with the peaceful and inspiring environment. He bought a home on Partington Ridge and lived in the Big Sur region until 1962, writing productively.

# Black Mountain, North Carolina, and Black Mountain College

Established in 1933 in the mountains near Asheville, North Carolina, Black Mountain College operated until 1957. The college featured a progressive educational philosophy designed to be enacted both inside and outside the classroom. The school's founders envisioned an experimental program that encompassed academics as well as the practical knowledge needed for a holistic life. The school attracted distinctive teachers and students, including some associated with the Beat movement: Charles Olson, Robert Creeley, and Robert Duncan. From 1954 until 1957, Olson and Creeley published an important literary journal, *Black Mountain Review*. Contributors to the *Black Mountain Review* included Allen Ginsberg, Jack Kerouac, William Burroughs, Gary Snyder, Michael McClure, Philip Whalen, and Jonathan Williams.

John Andrew Rice, a classics teacher, founded Black Mountain College after he left Rollins College in Florida following a dispute over educational philosophies. Influenced by John Dewey's progressive principles of education, Rice sought to create a cohesive union of liberal arts and fine arts that would teach the whole student on a campus where students and faculty alike would engage in physical work, typically by farming or maintaining the school's infrastructure. With several former members of the Rollins College faculty, he moved to the Blue Ridge Mountains to carry out his ideas. Rice soon attracted a distinguished faculty, including Josef Albers, a German artist and designer, and his wife, Anni, a textile designer, both significant figures from the Bauhaus school who arrived in 1933. Although many Black Mountain College faculty members taught sporadically or only for short periods, Josef and Anni Albers were fixtures at the school until 1949. Other significant teachers over the years included Walter Gropius, Willem de Kooning, Robert Motherwell, John Cage, Merce Cunningham, and R. Buckminster Fuller. Albert Einstein and William Carlos Williams served for a time on the board of directors.

For its first eight years, the college leased buildings from the Blue Ridge Assembly, but in 1941 the college established its own campus at nearby Lake Eden, where its main classroom building and most of its lodges and cabins still stand. Due in large part to Josef and Anni Albers's presence on the faculty, the college earned early renown in the fields of art and design. Through the ensuing three decades of its existence, the school also developed strong reputations for its study and production of music and literature.

Black Mountain College students were not divided into the typical four-year classifications and were not graduated based solely on the number of courses completed. Instead of required courses, students set up plans with their advisors that satisfied the university's goal of providing a comprehensive education. Teachers did not give grades; students were graduated only after undergoing comprehensive written and oral exams rendered by outside professors. Despite the unconventional nature of the curriculum, students typically matriculated easily into graduate programs at other schools.

The beautiful mountain setting combined with the progressive educational atmosphere lured strong faculty members who were willing to forego more lucrative positions elsewhere. While faculty salaries at the school were never high, lodging and food, much of which was grown on the school's farm, were provided. Charles Olson first taught poetry at Black Mountain College in 1948; in 1951, he became the final rector of the college. During his tenure, the college completed its transition from being known primarily for art to being best known for literature. Indeed, one of the groundbreaking poetry movements in the middle 1950s came to be known as the Black Mountain Poets. This group included Robert Creeley (a graduate of Black Mountain College) and Robert Duncan, who taught at the college, as well as unaffiliated poets Denise Levertov, Paul Blackburn, Larry Eigner, and Paul Carroll. Young poets were attracted to the college as students; Ed Dorn, Joel Oppenheimer, Jonathan Williams, and John Wieners were students of Olson at the college and went on to notable literary careers. Dorn, who attended Black Mountain College when he was in his twenties, later recalled that the school featured famous artists and painters during the summers, but the winters could be hard and oppressing. Dorn notes that during his time, the school offered an eclectic although not a thorough education. Dorn was strongly influenced by other faculty members, but Olson had the most lasting impact, and Dorn decided to dedicate his life to poetry.

Charles Olson was an imposing figure. He was a big man, physically, and a robust presence in literature who is best known for his three-volume *Maximus Poems* that employs his conjectures on poetic forms. His theories of "projective" verse challenged the conventional structures of poetry in the 1950s, and many poets reacted to the publication of his essay "Projective Verse" in 1950. He urged poets to pay less attention to received forms for poetry and more attention to their own natural voices. Olson encouraged his students to avoid distractions over subject matter and meaning and instead to center their attention on the use and dynamics of language. The meaning of poetry, for Olson, rises in emotion and imagination, while adherence to "closed" or fixed forms limits the poet's range of expression. Olson drew on ideas of earlier poets, including Walt Whitman, William Carlos Williams, and e. e. cummings, to determine a rationale for "open" verse forms. Robert Creeley was particularly receptive to Olson's ideas, and in 1954, Olson invited Creeley to teach at Black Mountain College and edit the *Black Mountain Review*. Creeley had experience as a literary editor from his work on *Origin* with Cid Corman. Although only seven issues were published between 1954 and 1957, the *Black Mountain Review* became one of the most important little magazines of the 1950s. Four rebellious literary movements came to the fore in the 1950s: the Beat Generation, the San Francisco Poets, the New York School, and the Black Mountain Poets. The various groups overlapped; the *Black Mountain Review* and *Yugen,* LeRoi Jones/Amiri Baraka's New York School magazine, are examples of little magazines that published poets from the different groups.

The experimental college had run its course by the middle 1950s. Many of the faculty and students had departed for San Francisco and New York, and few of the remaining participants showed strong interest in the original impulses of the program, particularly the farming and maintenance. In response to the financial difficulties that developed for the school, some members were willing to allow the school to adopt a more conventional structure. Even though Olson continued to suggest new ideas, the school finally closed in the spring of 1957. The final issue of the *Black Mountain Review* appeared that fall, and Black Mountain College became history, a significant and influential development in American experimental education.

—*Matt Theado*

## Bibliographical References

A thorough treatment of the Black Mountain experience is Martin Duberman, *Black Mountain: An Exploration in Community,* 1972; Duberman's work is brought up to date by Mary Emma Harris, *The Arts at Black Mountain College,* 1987 (reprinted 2002), and Martin Brody, Robert Creeley, and Kevin Power, *Black Mountain College: Experiment in Art,* 2003. Individual recollections are gathered in Mervin Lane, *Black Mountain College: Sprouted Seeds: An Anthology of Personal Accounts,* 1990. See also Katherine C. Reynolds, *Visions and Vanities: John Andrew Rice of Black Mountain College,* 1998.

***See also*** Little Magazines; De Kooning, Willem; Motherwell, Robert; Cage, John; Cunningham, Merce; Williams, William Carlos; Olson, Charles; Blackburn, Paul; Creeley, Robert; Duncan, Robert; Carroll, Paul; Dorn, Ed; Wieners, John; Influences

## Blackburn, Paul (1926–1971)

Paul Blackburn is noted not just as a poet, but also as a translator. His involvement with the Beats was primarily through his role as editor and his enormous networking abilities. He was responsible for organizing many of the readings in which Beat writers participated during the 50s and 60s in New York City.

Blackburn was born November 24, 1926, in Vermont. When he was three, his parents separated. He was primarily raised by his maternal grandparents until the age of fourteen when he and his mother moved to Greenwich Village. From his mother's encouragement, he began to explore himself through poetry and discovered not only an aptitude for writing it, but a deep love of the form.

Blackburn enrolled in New York University (NYU) in 1945, only to enter the service shortly thereafter. Upon discharge in 1947, he returned to NYU, but transferred to the University of Wisconsin, Madison, in 1949. At Madison he began writing to Ezra Pound and soon began visiting him at the hospital in Washington, D.C. Pound served as an early mentor to Blackburn and helped guide and encourage his development as a poet. Beyond that, it was through his association with Pound that Blackburn met many other influential poets, including Charles Olson.

Olson and Blackburn found a shared vision of poetry that led to Blackburn's participation in Olson's literary endeavors. However, although he was involved in the first two issues of Olson's *Black Mountain Review,* Blackburn is not properly categorized as a Black Mountain poet, having never taught or studied at the college. Blackburn stressed repeatedly that he was generally opposed to casting poets into "schools" of thought and actively resisted any such categorization for himself. Blackburn came into the popular consciousness as a poet through his inclusion in Donald Allen's influential anthology *The New American Poetry: 1945–1960* (1960), a position that has often caused him to be cast in with any number of avant-garde or bohemian categorizations.

Blackburn's poetry is often inspired by his early apprenticeship with Pound. Blackburn was also deeply moved by Provençal poetry (a body of literary work), which he read in response to Pound's advice. He began exploring it early in his career, and sustained this interest throughout his life. He published thirteen books while alive, and another nine were issued posthumously. Although no single volume can be said to have captured the popular imagination, Blackburn was always a well-respected poet. Blackburn was also a well-recognized translator, working often from Spanish to English. Two of his most notable translations are his version of the Spanish epic *El Cid* and his work on a collection of Picasso's poetry. Blackburn also translated works from French, including Provençal poetry and French troubadour poets.

Furthermore, Blackburn helped build alliances and networks between poets. He helped to organize a number of readings and events that brought together Beats, Black Mountain poets, Deep Imagists, and many others. He continued to produce poetry, teach, and work with other writers until his death in 1971.

—*John M. Carey*

## Principal Works

*The Dissolving Fabric,* 1955; *Poem of The Cid* (translation), 1966; Picasso's *Hunk of Skin* (translation), and *The Reardon Poems,* 1967. *The Collected Poems of Paul Blackburn* was issued in 1985. *Selected Poems of Paul Blackburn* followed in 1989. Transcripts and tapes of many of the readings Blackburn organized are available in the Special Collections Archive of University of California, San Diego.

***See also*** Little Magazines; Black Mountain, North Carolina, and Black Mountain College

## Blakey, Art (1919–1990; aka Abdullah Ibn Buhaina)

Originally a pianist, Art Blakey reputedly switched to drums when the drummer for the band in which he was playing called in sick. He became widely known during the forties as the drummer behind such acts as the Fletcher Henderson orchestra and Billy Eckstein's ensemble (which featured talents such as Dizzy Gillespie, Miles Davis, and Charlie Parker, whom Allen Ginsberg dubbed the "Secret Heroes" of the Beat poets). In 1955, Blakey formed the Jazz Messengers and helped develop the style known as hard bop, a derivation of bebop that contrasted with the mellow West Coast "cool jazz" sound. In his own groups and as a popular sideman, he was a regular fixture at the Birdland Monday sessions throughout 1954.

—*David Arnold*

### Bibliographical References

For a general view of Blakey's life and career, see Leslie Gourse, *Art Blakey: Jazz Messenger,* 2002. In *Spontaneous Mind: Selected Interviews 1958–1996,* ed. Allen Ginsberg and David Carter, 2001, one can catch connections between Blakey and the Beats.

***See also*** Music

## Bohemian Movements: Predecessors of the Beats

Although the Beat movement has had a singular and continuing effect on American culture and literature, the Beats' attitudes toward the political and economic forces shaping mainstream American society and toward the role of the radical artist within that society has some precedents among earlier groups of writers and artists—in particular, among the radical naturalists who were prominent at the turn of the century, among the Jazz Age writers and the postwar expatriates, among the "proletarian" writers of the Depression era, and among the African American poets of the Harlem Renaissance and beyond.

It has often been noted that the works of Stephen Crane, Frank Norris, Jack London, and the other American naturalists include romantic elements that distinguish them from their models in the works of Émile Zola and the European naturalists. Certainly the Americans' acceptance of determinism and social Darwinism was tempered by their belief in the social efficacy of radical, progressive politics and by their conception of the writer as something more than just a vivid documenter of social realities—the writer was a herald and even an agent of social progress. In these attitudes and in their roving adventurousness, the radical naturalists were clearly as influenced by the French bohemians as by the naturalists.

After the First World War shattered faith in Western institutions, American writers who had survived the war expressed their rejection of seemingly bankrupt social norms by embracing the vibrant subversiveness of the Jazz Age and becoming expatriates in Europe. The "Lost Generation" found its voice in the rhythms of African American music and in the fractured forms created by the most radically experimental writers and artists of Europe. After the war, bootleg booze became a metaphor for an exhausted culture bracing itself for the collapse of a false prosperity that represented a squandering of the last of its illusions. Interestingly, following what James Jones, in *World War II: A Chronicle of Soldiering* (1975), describes as the corporatization of conflict in the Second World War (222), he and other American writers of his generation were drawn to Paris much as Hemingway's generation and, earlier, as European bohemians had been drawn to the city, seeing it as a haven for subversive thought or, at least, as a reprieve from conformity.

In the 1930s, radical politics became somewhat normalized in the face of an economic catastrophe that was almost impossible to explain as anything other than an unprecedented failure of American democracy and speculative capitalism. A whole generation grew into maturity with a visceral sympathy for, if not a deep belief in, leftist political ideals. When these leanings were declared "un-American" in the early years of the Cold War, it was predictable that they would become a fixed feature of the political and cultural "underground" that attempted to express what had been repressed within the mainstream.

Contemporaries of the proletarians, Robinson Jeffers and Henry Miller were so idiosyncratic in their rejection of conventional American attitudes and behavioral norms that they inevitably attracted devotees and imitators. As a result, their unconventional attitudes became, paradoxically, more commonplace, and ultimately they became something akin to "patron saints" among the Beats and counterculturalists of the 1960s and 1970s. Likewise, in the work of Langston Hughes and associated African American writers, there was a deliberate fusion of music and poetry, of popular and high culture, that established a basis for the mainstreaming of African American culture that occurred during the Beat era and beyond.

—*Martin Kich*

### Bibliographical References

See Maxwell Geismar, *Rebels and Ancestors: The American Novel, 1890–1915: Frank Norris, Stephen Crane, Jack London, Ellen Glasgow, and Theodore Dreiser*, 1953. Later influences on the Beats can be seen in Noel Riley Fitch, *Sylvia Beach and the Lost Generation: A History of Literary Paris in the Twenties and Thirties*, 1983, and Gerald J. Kennedy, *Imagining Paris: Exiles, Writing, and American Identity*, 1993. The special influence of jazz is elucidated in Art Lange and Nathaniel Mackey, eds., *Moment's Notice: Jazz in Poetry and Prose*, 1993.

*See also* Influences

## Bowles, Jane (1917–1973)

Experimental writer, novelist, and playwright, Bowles was well known and respected in avant-garde artistic groups in New York, Mexico, and Paris. She is the author of the novel *Two Serious Ladies* (1943) and the play *In the Summer House* (1947). Although not connected directly to the Beat milieu, her approach to art and life, which includes a focus on alienation, guilt, isolation, and absurdity, connects her with them.

Born Jane Auer, she married composer and author Paul Bowles in 1938. She had difficulties with alcoholism and suffered a stroke in 1957. Despite a limited public response to her work during her lifetime, Jane Bowles's work has endured and drawn scholarly interest.

—*William Lawlor*

**Bibliographical References**

Millicent Dillon, ed., *The Portable Paul and Jane Bowles,* 1994, offers a broad selection of work by Jane Bowles. In Jennie Skerl, ed., *A Tawdry Place of Salvation: The Art of Jane Bowles,* 1997, one finds a collection of diverse essays on Jane Bowles.

*See also* Bowles, Paul

## Bowles, Paul (1910–1999)

Paul Bowles, composer, musicologist, novelist, short-story writer, travel writer, translator, poet, painter, and memoirist, cannot technically be called a Beat, but his influence on and affinity with the Beat Generation should not be underestimated. Inspired by Bowles's novels *The Sheltering Sky* and *Let It Come Down,* William S. Burroughs decided to go to Tangier in 1954. Burroughs felt a great attraction to Bowles and introduced him to the Beats who visited Tangier. Allen Ginsberg found Bowles's wife, Jane, to be very similar to Joan Vollmer, Burroughs's deceased wife, and suggested that Bowles publish *A Hundred Camels in the Courtyard,* stories based around the use of the drug *kif,* with Lawrence Ferlinghetti's City Lights Books. Bowles encouraged Burroughs, Ginsberg, Peter Orlovsky, and Gregory Corso to experiment with the Moroccan drugs *majoun* and *kif.* Like many of the Beats, and Jack Kerouac in particular, Bowles promoted the unleashing of conscious control when writing poetry (although Bowles preferred craftsmanship when it came to prose). He also experimented as early as 1956 with tape recordings—something with which Beats, especially Kerouac and Burroughs, were fascinated.

Bowles, the only child of a dentist father and schoolteacher mother, was born in New York City on 30 December 1910. His first poems were published by *Transition* in France when he was only a

Paul Bowles, seated with manuscript, ca. 1947. (Condé Nast Archive/Corbis)

teenager. Intrigued that Edgar Allan Poe had gone to the University of Virginia, Bowles studied there before going to Paris. Studying music composition with Aaron Copland and Virgil Thomson, Bowles later wrote the scores for *South Pacific* (1943), *The Glass Menagerie* (1945), and *Sweet Bird of Youth* (1956). He married Jane Auer on 21 February 1938 and was inspired by her to start writing short stories. Both Bowles and his wife were bisexual. His friends Gertrude Stein, who did not like Bowles's surrealistic poetry, and Alice B. Toklas suggested that Tangier was the place for his creative flowering; they were right. He first went to Morocco with Aaron Copland in 1931, and this city later became his greatest source of inspiration. His literary masterpiece, *The Sheltering Sky* (1948), depicts a godless world where Westerners are ill equipped to master the indifferent and brutal African desert. The film *The Sheltering Sky* (1990) includes narration by Bowles and stars John Malkovich and Debra Winger.

Bowles found it difficult to write after his wife suffered a stroke in 1957 and began to physically deteriorate. Jane Bowles died in a sanatorium in Málaga, Spain, in 1973. Bowles successfully returned to writing and received an American Book Award nomination in 1980 for *Collected Stories of Paul Bowles, 1939–1976*. Bowles died of a heart attack in a Tangier hospital on 18 November 1999.

—*Kurt Hemmer*

## Principal Works

Poetry: *Two Poems,* 1933; *Scenes,* 1968; *The Thicket of Spring: Poems 1926–1969,* 1972; *Next to Nothing: Collected Poems, 1926–1977,* 1981.

Prose: *The Sheltering Sky,* 1948; *The Delicate Prey and Other Stories,* 1950; *Let It Come Down,* 1952; *The Spider's House,* 1955; *A Hundred Camels in the Courtyard,* 1962; *Up above the World: A Novel,* 1966; *Without Stopping: An Autobiography,* 1972; *The Collected Stories,* 1979; *Days: Tangier Journal, 1987–1989,* 1991; *Too Far from Home: The Selected Writings of Paul Bowles,* 1993.

## Bibliographical References

Queer theory is applied to both Bowles and Burroughs in Greg Mullins, *Colonial Affairs: Bowles, Burroughs, and Chester Write Tangier,* 2002; Millicent Dillon, *You Are Not I: A Portrait of Paul Bowles,* 1998, is an informative biography; letters to Ginsberg, Orlovsky, Corso, Kerouac, Burroughs, and Ferlinghetti can be found in *In Touch: The Letters of Paul Bowles,* 1994; see also Gena Dagel Caponi, *Paul Bowles: Romantic Savage,* 1994; Gena Dagel Caponi, ed., *Conversations with Paul Bowles,* 1993; the relationship between Bowles and the Beats is discussed in detail in Michelle Green, *The Dream at the End of the World: Paul Bowles and the Literary Renegades of Tangier,* 1991; Christopher Sawyer Laucanno, *An Invisible Spectator: A Biography of Paul Bowles,* 1990, offers another view.

***See also*** Tangier; Technology, Beats and; Bowles, Jane

## Brautigan, Richard (1935–1984)

Richard Brautigan was a whimsical minimalist poet and experimental novelist who served his literary apprenticeship as a young writer in San Francisco in the aftermath of the Beat Generation's initial rise to prominence. He became an almost iconic figure to the hippie generation and its followers.

Richard Brautigan helped foster the Beat spirit in the hippie movement. (Library of Congress)

Brautigan was born in Tacoma, Washington, on 30 January 1935, but little is known of his upbringing outside of hints of impoverishment and familial chaos. He had limited contact with his biological father, and an uncle was killed early in World War II. He was already writing poems when he moved to San Francisco in the mid-1950s and encountered the brief confluence of Beat writers in that city. His first significant publication was in a small anthology of poets published by Inferno Press in 1957. Small editions of other poetry collections followed, including one by White Rabbit Press, but Brautigan was making little headway in terms of literary recognition. Between 1961 and 1964, he wrote three novels, which eventually became his most famous and popular works: *Trout Fishing in America, A Confederate General in Big Sur,* and *In Watermelon Sugar.* By his thirtieth birthday, however, only *A Confederate General in Big Sur* had been published, and it sold so poorly that Grove Press remaindered it.

In 1967, Don Allen's Four Seasons Press published *Trout Fishing in America*. Despite the fact that the novel was rooted in the fifties, Brautigan's book flourished within the influential hippie crowd and became a literary password in the same manner that the previous generation had enunciated "Howl" and *On the Road. Trout Fishing* ran through four printings before Allen sold it to a New York publishing house. In 1968, Brautigan got a writing grant from the National Endowment for the Arts, and Allen published both *In Watermelon Sugar*, the final novel from his most prolific period, and *The Pill versus the Springhill Mine Disaster*. Only a small proportion of Brautigan's poetry found its way into contemporary anthologies.

Brautigan moved to Montana in the early 1970s, but a collection of his short stories, *Revenge of the Lawn*, and all of his subsequent novels faltered in terms of critical response, and interest never surpassed the original burst of enthusiasm. Brautigan's reputation was largely built on word-of-mouth among readers. In his later work, the tone shifted from counterculture charm to grim parody of a variety of genres, including the detective novel. Brautigan continued to write poetry, but little of it appeared in the underground poetry magazines favored by Beat writers and the rapidly expanding small-press movement. In 1976, Simon and Schuster published *Gathering Mercury with a Pitchfork*, a selection of his poems from the earlier, out-of-print book as well as new work. Brautigan visited Japan, but not to study Zen Buddhism as other Beat writers did. His poetic model seemed to be Issa, to whom he dedicated a poem which he wrote in a bar. Brautigan eventually moved to Bolinas, California, a beach town favored by New York expatriate poets, where he committed suicide in mid-October 1984. His body was discovered on 25 October.

—*Bill Mohr*

## Principal Works

Poetry: *The Pill versus the Springhill Mine Disaster*, 1968; *Rommel Drives on Deep into Egypt*, 1970; *Loading Mercury with a Pitchfork*, 1975; *June 30th, June 30th*, 1978.

Prose: *A Confederate General from Big Sur*, 1964; *Trout Fishing in America*, 1967; *In Watermelon Sugar*, 1968; *The Abortion: An Historical Romance 1966*, 1971; *The Hawkline Monster*, 1974; *Willard and His Bowling Trophies*, 1975; *Sombrero Fallout*, 1976; *Dreaming of Babylon*, 1977; *The Tokyo-Montana Express*, 1980; *So the Wind Won't Blow It All Away*, 1982.

## Bibliographical References

John F. Barber's *Richard Brautigan: An Annotated Bibliography*, 1990, provides a substantial review of his life and work along with a personal account of Brautigan. Another partial biography is Keith Abbott's memoir of his friendship with Brautigan, *Downstream from "Trout Fishing in America,"* 1989. Terence Malley, 1972, Edward Halsey Foster, 1983, Marc Chenetier, 1983, and Jay Boyer, 1987, have all published critical studies titled *Richard Brautigan*. Claudia Grossman provides a German critique in *Richard Brautigan: Pounding at the Gates of American Literature*, 1986.

# Bremser, Bonnie (Brenda Frazer) (1939–)

Bremser is the author of *Troia: Mexican Memoirs*. Bremser married Beat "jailhouse" poet Ray Bremser in 1959. Shortly after they married, Ray was incarcerated on narcotics charges. The couple had a child together, and after Ray's release from prison, the young family moved to Mexico. In Mexico, Bonnie Bremser worked as a prostitute and panhandled to support the family and their drug habits. The couple eventually returned to New York, and their daughter, Rachel, was given up for adoption. Bremser later spent time at Allen Ginsberg's Cherry Valley farm in upstate New York. Bremser has reassumed her given name, Brenda Frazer.

Bremser's memoir, *Troia: Mexican Memoirs*, recounts her journey to Mexico and describes the ensuing hardships she and her family faced. *Troia* captures the gritty drug lifestyle of Mexico in a spontaneous prose style inspired by Beat writer Jack Kerouac. Two selections of previously unpublished memoirs, "Poets and Oddfellows" and "The Village Scene," are found in *Beat Down to Your Soul*, edited by Ann Charters. Like *Troia*, these selections evoke the Beat experience of constant mobility, poverty, and a life dedicated to art.

—*Jessica Lyn VanSlooten*

### Bibliographical References

See Bonnie Bremser, *Troia: Mexican Memoirs*, 1969. In Ann Charters, ed., *Beat Down to Your Soul: What Was the Beat Generation?*, 2001, see "Poets and Oddfellows" and "The Village Scene." For background on Bonnie Bremser, see Brenda Knight, *Women of the Beat Generation: The Writers, Artists and Muses at the Heart of a Revolution*, 1996.

***See also*** Cherry Valley, New York; Bremser, Ray

## Bremser, Ray (1934–1998)

Poet Charles Plymell claimed that Ray Bremser was more "Beat" than Allen Ginsberg. Although this hyperbolism seems like it can easily be dismissed, there is something astute about Plymell's remark. Unlike Ginsberg and Jack Kerouac, and more like Gregory Corso, Bremser is a poet of jails and rough streets. He is more "Beat" in Herbert Huncke's sense of "beaten down" than in Kerouac's sense of "beatific," although his poetry is also characterized by whimsical humor. For a time, he was one of Bob Dylan's favorite poets, appearing in Dylan's liner notes to *Highway 61 Revisited*, and Dylan also provided the often-indigent Bremser with some financial support in the 70s.

Bremser was born in Jersey City, New Jersey, on 22 February 1934 to a mother who inspected condoms and a pianist father, who supposedly was part of the band on the ship *Orizaba* from which Hart Crane leaped to his death in April 1932. Joining the U.S. Air Force in 1951, Bremser went AWOL after four days, yet eventually received an honorable discharge. While the Beat Generation was blossoming, Bremser was in Bordentown Reformatory from April 1952 to November 1958 for armed robbery.

Like Corso, Bremser became a self-taught poet while incarcerated. He finished his high school ed-ucation, read Shakespeare and Jean Genet, corresponded with Ezra Pound, and sent poems to Corso and Ginsberg in Paris. LeRoi Jones (Amiri Baraka) first published Bremser in the journal *Yugen*. After his release, Bremser was introduced to the inner circle of the New York Beat community, Jones became his guardian, and Kerouac was one of his favorite drinking buddies. Three weeks after meeting Bonnie Frazer at a poetry reading in Washington, D.C., he married her on 21 March 1959.

In November 1959, Bremser made the mistake of promoting the legalization of marijuana on Ralph Collier's Philadelphia talk show. This behavior possibly prompted the New Jersey authorities to book him for violating his parole by marrying Bonnie without permission. A letter from William Carlos Williams helped get Bremser released from Trenton State after he had served six months. After being accused of a robbery he claimed not to have committed, Bremser, his wife, and their child Rachel fled to Mexico in December 1960 with the help of money borrowed from Elaine de Kooning. In Mexico Bonnie became a prostitute to support her family. Her experiences were later published as *Troia: Mexican Memoirs* (1969). Sent to Laredo after being apprehended in Mexico, Bremser was bailed out with the help of Elaine de Kooning's friends in Texas. After giving their child up for adoption, the Bremsers returned to Mexico where they lived briefly with Philip Lamantia. Meanwhile, Bremser had been published in Donald Allen's *The New American Poetry*.

After a split with Bonnie, Bremser arrived in New York in April 1961 and became acquainted with John Coltrane. Bonnie joined him in New York in July, but Bremser was busted for marijuana possession shortly after. Corso bailed him out, but Bremser was considered a fugitive from justice. He gave himself up and eventually spent time in both Trenton State and Rahway prisons from 1961 to late 1965. His first volume of poetry, *Poems of Madness*, was published with an introduction by Ginsberg while Bremser was still in prison. His second book, *Angel* (1967), had an introduction by Lawrence Ferlinghetti. The Bremsers lived in

Guatemala and had a second daughter, Georgia, before splitting again. In the early 70s Bremser lived at Ginsberg's farm in Cherry Valley, New York. He had a son, Jesse Dylan Bremser, with poet Judy Johnson and eventually moved to Utica.

At the end of his life, Bremser appeared as a mysterious, mythical, and revered outlaw figure of the Beat past, reading at such events as The Writings of Jack Kerouac conference in 1995 at New York University. He died in Utica, New York from lung cancer on 3 November 1998.

—*Kurt Hemmer*

**Principal Works**

Poetry: *Poems of Madness*, 1965; *Angel*, 1967; *Drive Suite*, 1968; *Black Is Black Blues*, 1971; *Blowing Mouth/The Jazz Poems, 1958–1970*, 1978; *Born Again*, 1985; *The Conquerors*, 1989; *The Dying of Children*, 1999.

**Bibliographical References**

There is not much written about Ray Bremser. He appears in anecdotes in some of the biographies of the more famous Beat writers. The essay by Arnold Moodnik and Mikhail Horowitz in *Dictionary of Literary Biography, Volume 16: The Beats: Literary Bohemians in Postwar America*, ed. Ann Charters, 1983, provides some basic information, but there is certainly a need for more critical work to be done on Bremser.

*See also* Bremser, Bonnie; Cherry Valley, New York

# Breton, André (1896–1966)

A medical doctor by profession, André Breton was an influential French writer and editor, who together with Louis Aragon and Philip Soupault founded the French magazine *Literature* in 1919. A Dadaist, Breton helped to establish Surrealism through his *Manifesto of Surrealism* (1924) and subsequent versions of that manifesto. Breton favored the free flight of the imagination and longed for artistic expression uninhibited by rational frameworks. Breton, Aragon, and Eluard joined the Communist Party in 1927 and sought to make Surrealism contribute to world revolution. Breton's

André Breton's dadaism and surrealism influenced the Beats. (Library of Congress)

endeavors with Surrealism influenced various Beat writers, especially Philip Lamantia.

—*William Lawlor*

**Bibliographical References**

See Mary Ann Caws, *André Breton*, 1996, and Anna Elizabeth Balakian and Rudolf E. Kuenzli, *André Breton Today*, 1989.

*See also* Influences; Lamantia, Philip; Joans, Ted.

# Brooks, Eugene (Eugene Brooks Ginsberg) (1921–)

Elder brother of Allen Ginsberg, Eugene Brooks, named for Eugene Debs, is a poet, but he is also a successful attorney. Whereas Allen Ginsberg had some of the physical characteristics of his mother, Eugene looked more like his father, especially because of Eugene's thin build and medium height. Allen Ginsberg wrote "Kaddish" in memory of his mother; Eugene wrote "To My Mother," a poem published in the *New York Times*.

—*William Lawlor*

**Bibliographic References**

See Michael Schumacher, *Dharma Lion,* 1992. *The Life and Times of Allen Ginsberg,* 1993, a video by Jerry Aronson, includes several segments that feature Eugene Brooks.

*See also* Ginsberg, Allen

## Brossard, Chandler (1922–1993)

Chandler Brossard, also known as Daniel Harper and Iris-Marie Brossard, was a novelist, playwright, and journalist. *Who Walk in Darkness* (1952) is the work that connects Brossard, perhaps mistakenly, to the Beats because the novel relates the experiences of Blake Williams in Greenwich Village in New York City during one month in the summer of 1948. Williams observes those who drink, indulge in drugs, and pursue gratification as they ramble about New York City, but Williams himself seeks a cleaner life—a life free from lies. Henry Porter serves as a foil to Blake Williams, as Porter fails to establish any degree of authenticity. By meeting Grace and falling in love, Blake Williams separates himself from the misguided life that surrounds him. The novel is narrated in matter-of-fact language, with power generated from understatement rather than sensationalism.

Born in Idaho Falls, Idaho, and raised in Washington, D.C., Brossard pursued a career in journalism, working for the *Washington Post, Time,* and the *New Yorker.* Although *Who Walk in Darkness* links Brossard to the Beats, he disavowed any parallels between his work and that of the Beats.

—*William Lawlor*

**Bibliographical References**

See *Review of Contemporary Fiction* 7.1 (Spring 1987). This issue is dedicated to Brossard and his writing career. *Who Walk in Darkness,* 1952, rpt. 2000, is of special interest to those exploring the Beats, but those who want to know Brossard in general may consult *The Unknown Chandler Brossard: Collected Works 1971–1991,* 2002.

*See also* New York City

## Bruce, Lenny (1926–1966)

Lenny Bruce (Leonard Alfred Schneider) was a nightclub performer and comedian who tested the bounds of propriety in the early 1960s by challenging social values and norms and by making free use of vulgarities. After a performance at Cafe au Go-Go in Greenwich Village, police officers who secretly attended the show charged Bruce with the use of "obscene" language. In State Supreme Court in Manhattan, Bruce was convicted of giving an obscene performance and was sentenced to four months on Rikers Island. In the appeal process, Bruce attempted to defend himself without legal counsel and was never successful in overturning his conviction. With his career destroyed by the con-

Lenny Bruce relentlessly challenged censorship of his comedy routines. (Library of Congress)

viction, Bruce turned to drugs, and he died of an overdose in 1966.

The play *Lenny* (1971) by Julian Bary was later produced as a film *Lenny* (1974), in which Dustin Hoffman played Bruce and earned an Academy Award nomination. On 23 December 2003, thirty-seven years after Bruce's death, New York Governor George A. Pataki pardoned Bruce in an effort to uphold First Amendment rights.

—*William Lawlor*

## Bibliographical References

Bruce's autobiography is *How to Talk Dirty and Influence People*, 1965; see William Karl Thomas, *Lenny Bruce: The Making of a Prophet*, 1989, and Frank Kofsky, *The Comedian as Social Critic and Secular Moralist*, 1974.

*See also* Performance Humor; Buckley, Lord

## Buckley, Lord (1906–1960)

Richard Buckley, "his Royal Hipness," developed the bebop slang of black jazzmen into a series of standup routines that embodied the apotheosis of hip coolness, influencing both Lenny Bruce and Bob Dylan. He began in Chicago speakeasies, in the 1920s and 1930s, developing a novelty act in which he, a white man, performed jive versions of Shakespeare, "Willie the Shake," the Bible, including treatments of "the Naz" (Jesus of Nazareth), and famous set speeches such as the Gettysburg Address. He later appeared on the Ed Sullivan and Red Skelton shows. Sporting white tie and tails with his signature waxed mustache, he combined the diction and rhythms of the hipster with the manner of a ham Shakespearean actor.

—*Thomas L. Cooksey*

## Selected Discography

*Hipsters, Flipsters, and Finger-Poppin' Daddies, Knock Me Your Lobes*, 1955; *Way Out Humor*, 1959; *The Best of Lord Buckley*, 1963; *The Parabolic Revelations of the Late Lord Buckley: A Collection of Six Lessons by the "Hip Messiah,"* 1963; *Lord Buckley: Blowing His Mind (and Yours Too)*, 1966; *Bad-Rapping of the Marquis de Sade*, 1969; *A Most Immaculately Hip Aristocrat*, 1970; *His Royal Hipness, Lord Buckley*, 1992; *Dig Infinity! The Life and Art of Lord Buckley*, 2002.

## Bibliographic References

Roy Carr, Brian Cox, and Fred Deller, *The Hip: Hipsters, Jazz and the Beat Generation*, 1986, offers a good treatment of Buckley in relation to the black hipsters. An insightful review of Buckley and his art is Albert Goldman, *Freakshow: The Rocksoulbluesjazzsickjewblackhumoursexpoppsych Gig and Other Scenes from the Counter-Culture*, 1971. Essentially an undigested collection of quotes and commentary, arranged chronologically without an index, Oliver Trager, *Dig Infinity! The Life and Art of Lord Buckley*, 1971, is difficult to use but is the only book on Buckley. It does include a CD that provides samples of Buckley's best routines and an interview with Studs Terkel.

*See also* Performance Humor; Bruce, Lenny

## Bukowski, Charles (1920–1994)

Charles Bukowski was a poet, fiction writer, screenwriter, editor, and voluble correspondent whose work as a whole constitutes a crucial tangent to the Beat generation. Few direct links exist between Bukowski and the best-known Beats: Bukowski's encounter with Neal Cassady shortly before Cassady collapsed and died in Mexico is a one-way street; none of the major Beats associated with the San Francisco Renaissance has written of any pas de deux with their underground cousin to the south. Furthermore, in contrast to the peripatetic Beats, Bukowski lived almost all of his life as a writer in Los Angeles, a city for which he had an affection that belied his cantankerous persona. This endearment probably made him seem all the more unlikely to Kerouac and company as a genuine member of any literary avant-garde. Bukowski's writing, however, continues to tantalize young writers and students of the Beat movement, and their reading of this period frequently juxtaposes the Beats and Bukowski as brothers-in-arms reflecting each other's defiance of easy respectability and conventional prosody. Bukowski's free verse seems almost impertinent in its casual approach to line breaks, but the apparent ease with which it can be read masks the bittersweet layers of its ironic, profane sincerity. Through its very divergence and contrast in poetics and subject matter, Bukowski's writing therefore demarcates and reinforces the Beat critique.

Bukowski was born in Germany in 1920 and brought to America at age two. He grew up in Los Angeles, attended City College, and began writing stories. He briefly published and then began wandering the United States, taking on a series of low-paying jobs and living in boarding houses, not so much a *poet maudit* as a man who was both self-destructive and a cunning survivor. In the mid-fifties, his long alcoholic spree concluded with him on the verge of death in a public hospital. When he finally recovered, he started writing poetry and, undeterred by his close call, resumed drinking. The two activities kept him going for nearly another forty years. Bukowski's emergence from the small-press publishing underground was a much slower process for him than the younger set of poets of the Beat generation. Although by the early 1960s, Bukowski's work appeared more than once alongside poets such as Ginsberg, Corso, and Ferlinghetti, his poetry seemed more doggedly existential in his alienation than the writing of the Beats, who were notorious for their scorn of work. Bukowski had a job; maybe he was surly about it, but he went to work. In the end, this employment proved to be the basis for his way out of drudgery. An aspiring small-press publisher in Los Angeles, John Martin, gambled on Bukowski's capacity for generating mounds of poems in hopes that he could be equally prolific as a fiction writer and offered to subsidize him while he produced a novel. *Post Office,* a picaresque account of Bukowksi's only sustained job, appeared in 1971, and in 1972 Bukowski won a creative writing grant from the National Endowment for the Arts. Martin went on to reprint his first two major collections of poetry, *It Catches My Heart in Its Hands* and *Crucifix in a Deathhand,* in a combined collection titled *Burning in Water, Drowning in Flame.*

Bukowski wrote a column for the Los Angeles *Free Press,* "Notes of a Dirty Old Man," collected in 1969 in a volume published by City Lights Books.

City Lights also published *Erections, Ejaculations, and Other Tales of Ordinary Madness* in 1972, making Bukowski the only writer during his lifetime to gain that spectrum of West Coast imprints. Black Sparrow Press, however, continued to be his primary publisher, churning out almost a volume of his writing every year. By the late seventies, much of his work became overly self-conscious, with the author spending considerable time mulling over his predicaments as a writer who was becoming increasingly famous, especially in Europe.

Bukowski also worked as a little magazine editor, including one he founded in Los Angeles with Neeli Cherri, *Laugh Literary and Man the Humping Guns* in 1969. Perhaps Bukowski's attenuated relationship with the Beats is most visible in the poets he chose for the three issues he published, Harold Norse, Jack Micheline, and Doug Blazek, or his inclusion of Stuart Perkoff and John Thomas in the *Anthology of L.A. Poets,* which Bukowski coedited. His preference for literary company leaned toward those who could not be easily assimilated into any public group. In a similar manner, when Penguin books issued a series of small volumes in the late 1960s each containing a trio of poets, Bukowksi's work was accompanied by Philip Lamantia and Norse.

Bukowski was also a successful screenwriter. His script for *Barfly,* an account of his youthful alcoholic sojourn, was made into a successful film by Barbet Schroeder in 1987. Bukowski found himself acknowledged as a primary influence on the Southern California school known as Stand Up poetry and continued to pour out poems and short stories until his death in Los Angeles in 1994.

—Bill Mohr

## Principal Works

Poetry: *The Roominghouse Madrigals: Early Poems 1946–1966,* 1988; *Burning in Water, Drowning in Flame, Poems 1955–1973,* 1973; *War All the Time: Poems 1981–1984,* 1984; *The Last Night of the Earth,* 1992; *Bone Palace Ballet,* 1997.

Fiction and Prose: *Notes of a Dirty Old Man,* 1969; *Post Office,* 1971; *Factotum,* 1975; *Women,* 1978; *Ham on Rye,* 1982; *Hot Water Music,* 1983; and two volumes of selected letters, *Screams from the*

*Balcony*, 1993, and *Living on Luck*, 1995, both edited by Seamus Cooney.

**Bibliographical References**

Three major biographies, *Bukowski: A Life*, by Neeli Cherkovski, 1997; *Charles Bukowski*, by Gay Brewer, 1997, and *Charles Bukowski: Locked in the Arms of a Crazy Life*, by Howard Sounes are complemented by several shorter accounts by poets who knew him, including *Charles Bukowski: A Sure Bet*, by Gerald Locklin, 1996; *Spinning Off Bukowski*, by Steve Richmond, 1992; *Bathing with Bukowski*, by John Thomas, 1997; *Drinking with Bukowski: Recollections of the Poet Laureate of Skid Row*, edited by Daniel Weizman, 2000. Analysis of his work includes *Miller, Bukowski and Their Enemies: Essays on Contemporary Culture* by William Joyce, 1996; *Against the American Dream: Essays on Charles Bukowski*, edited by Russell Harrison, 1994.

*See also* Norse, Harold; Micheline, Jack; Perkoff, Stuart Z.

## Burroughs, Ilse Herzfeld Klapper (1900–1982)

First wife of William S. Burroughs. Born 19 April 1900 in Hamburg, Germany, into a wealthy Jewish family who owned a department store. In 1920s Berlin, she associated with prominent Weimar-era personalities such as Konrad Veidt, Marlene Dietrich, Kurt Weill, Ludwig Marcuse, Hermann Kesten, and members of the Thomas Mann family. She married a German physician named Klapper, but by 1933 she was separated from her husband and living in Dubrovnik, Croatia, where she met the twenty-two-year-old Burroughs, in summer 1936. He married her 2 August 1937 at the U.S. Consulate in Athens, Greece, so she could emigrate to the United States and avoid Nazi persecution; the marriage was never consummated.

Finally arriving in New York in 1938, Ilse was secretary to the German Socialist playwright Ernst Toller (1893–1939) until his suicide 22 May 1939 and then was secretary to Vienna-born actor Kurt Kasznar (1913–1979) in the early 1940s. Burroughs continued to see Ilse socially in New York until she returned to Europe in 1945; in St. Louis in 1946,

he arranged an uncontested divorce from her. Burroughs saw Herzfeld for the last time in New York in 1965. At the time of her death in August 1982, she was living in Ascona, in southern Switzerland.

—*James Grauerholz*

**Bibliographical References**

Basic background is offered in Ted Morgan, *Literary Outlaw: The Life and Times of William S. Burroughs*, 1988. One can examine Ted Morgan's papers at the Arizona State University Special Collections. See also Harold von Hofe, ed., *Briefe von and an Ludwig Marcuse*, 1975.

*See also* Burroughs, William Seward

## Burroughs, William Seward (1914–1997)

William Seward Burroughs was, alongside Allen Ginsberg and Jack Kerouac, one of the founders and central figures of the Beat Generation. The three writers emerged during the 1950s to form a troika of distinctly individual identities but shared countercultural status and international fame. Burroughs's relationship to the Beat movement was always anomalous, however; if his image has remained essential to the popularity of the Beats—which it has—it is for the paradoxical reason that he never was completely there and never quite belonged.

Even though Burroughs played a key role in the early Beat scene of the 1940s, his life and work always placed him at one remove from the center of Beat activity, and this separation was the case quite literally from 1950 onward. To escape his criminalization as a drug user and a homosexual, Burroughs left Cold War America at that time, beginning twenty-five years as a writer-in-exile, first moving to Mexico, then South America, North Africa, and finally Europe. In his absence, Burroughs's initial reputation in the United States was promoted by Ginsberg and Kerouac, who conjured him as a vividly ambiguous figure, their mysterious and vaguely sinister master. As he developed into one of the most innovative and influential cultural figures of the late twentieth century, however, Burroughs, unlike Ginsberg and Kerouac, created a reputation

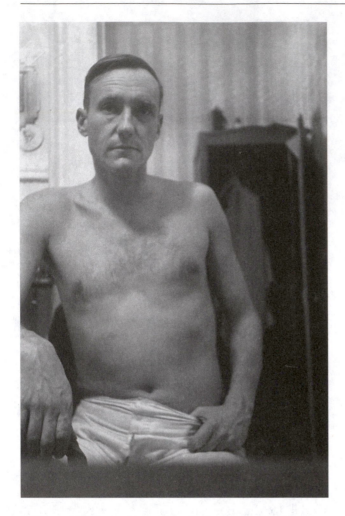

William S. Burroughs in New York City in 1953. (Allen Ginsberg/Corbis)

and a body of work that lost any meaningful relation to the history and features of a Beat identity. Burroughs now exists through the circulation of a whole series of defining images and iconic cult figures, as the "Holy Monster" of the Beat Generation (Cook 165) was succeeded by the *eminence grise* of 1960s counterculture, the avant-garde mapmaker of inner space, the guerrilla leader of the electronic revolution, the shaman of queer magic, and the godfather of cyberpunk.

It is no longer possible to claim, as Jennie Skerl did in 1983 in one of the first detailed biographical accounts, that "the significance of Burroughs' work must also be judged according to the significance of the Beat movement" (1983, 67). Indeed, more

recent critical study of Burroughs has downplayed his work's relation to the Beats, even when dealing with his novels of the 1950s, the period in which his writing, like that of Ginsberg and Kerouac, was directly and visibly shaped by his autobiography. Steering a path between these opposed approaches, one finds that it is more accurate to acknowledge that the fifties were the one decade in which Burroughs's personal and creative relationships with Ginsberg and Kerouac were of real material importance, and to recognize that any biographical account of Burroughs in a Beat context should properly focus in most detail on those years.

All biographical approaches to Burroughs must contend with the special difficulties that he has posed for the biographical enterprise itself. The first of these difficulties is, in fact, central to Skerl's claim for Burroughs's affinity to Ginsberg and Kerouac: "All three," she argued, "fictionalized their lives in their art and thus created an autobiographical myth" (1983, 56). In the case of Burroughs, his legendary status has made the life and work inseparable in the public imagination. However, the simultaneous importance and difficulty of biography is further complicated by the particular part that his fellow writers, especially Kerouac, played in constructing that very legend. Before Burroughs could fictionalize his life, beginning with *Junky* (published as *Junkie* in 1953; the title was changed for the reedited 1977 edition), Kerouac did it for him in his own debut novel, *The Town and the City* (1950), and darkly enigmatic portraits in Kerouac's following novels ensured that a mythic version of Burroughs achieved recognition ahead of his own work. In this way, the earliest representations of Burroughs not only tied him to a Beat context but invested his biography with the quality of fiction, one that the more sensational facts of Burroughs's actual life, especially in the 1940s and 1950s, did nothing to dispel. Fact and fiction have been a revolving door for Burroughs's biographers.

The second major difficulty that biographers of Burroughs have faced derives from his own attitude toward the basic premises and purposes of biography. The aims of traditional literary biography are essentially twofold: to gain insights into the inner life from an evocation of external events and to explain the creative process by relating the artist to his artifacts. Each aim assumes the possibility of uncovering a coherent identity, one that emerges through a chronological and factual narrative of causes and consequences. Long before postmodern critical theory threw such values into doubt, Burroughs actively subverted the possibility that biography could reveal the essential person and narrate his creative development over time.

Burroughs made this subversion an explicit project in late 1959, shortly after publication of his most famous work, *Naked Lunch*. "I have no past life at all," he announced in what he referred to as a "Biographical Note," insisting to Ginsberg, "and that is not a malapropism" (1993, 431). And so, although *Naked Lunch,* together with Ginsberg's poem "Howl" (1956) and Kerouac's novel *On the Road* (1957), was hailed as the third key text written by the Holy Trinity of Beat writers, its publication marked a break in Burroughs's close personal and creative associations with the Beats. For Burroughs, 1959 was a watershed year, and his claim to deny history and identity launched the "cut-up" project, a range of experimental practices that developed the radical antinarrative potentials of the novel he had just published, as described by Greg Mullins: "*Naked Lunch* exposes the fictitiousness of all narratives, especially those narratives that constitute what is thought of as reality. The novel overflows with stories, but each story is a 'cover story' " (77).

Biographies of Burroughs have therefore had to contend not only with the mediation of his identity through the fictional work of others and with his own fictional use of autobiography—versions of the truth that add up to a series of "cover stories"— but with his active hostility to the very possibility of reconstructing the facts and fixing a stable identity. "The past only exists in some record of it," he once insisted to an interviewer; "There are no facts" (Malanga 302). Unsurprisingly, the received version of Burroughs's life and creative history has had to be revised over time, but false accounts remain common because the mystifying force of legend still largely persists. The final paradox is that Bur-

roughs not only contributed to such mystification but highlighted it repeatedly.

Most pointedly, he drew attention to the staged and therefore highly suspect quality of his literary biography in his essay, "The Name Is Burroughs," which appears in *The Adding Machine* (1985): "I can divide my literary production into sets: where, when and under what circumstances produced. The first set is a street of red brick three-story houses with slate roofs, lawns in front and large back yards" (1985b, 2). Turning the most objective of facts into features on a "set," Burroughs manages to cast a shadow of doubt over the very time and place of his birth.

William Seward Burroughs II was born on 5 February 1914 in the family house in the central West End of St. Louis. The younger of two sons, he was a child of privilege, modest wealth, and social status. On both sides, he was heir to the traditions of two very different upper-middle-class families that played significant parts in the modernization of corporate America. His paternal grandfather and namesake was a northern inventor who, in the late 1880s, perfected the modern adding machine. The international company that bore the Burroughs name later became a key player in pioneering the computer age, although the last family connection to the firm was broken in 1929, when, just before the great crash, his son, Mortimer, sold the inherited stock and so ensured his own son's financial security. William Burroughs's mother, Laura Lee, was the daughter of a circuit-riding Southern Methodist minister. Whereas Mortimer was a remote and diffident father, the young William's mother doted on her youngest son. Laura Lee's brother, Ivy, also achieved national fame—or rather notoriety; as one of the pioneers of public relations, he earned the nickname "Poison Ivy," and counted John D. Rockefeller, his image bloodstained by the Ludlow Massacre of 1914, among his dubious clients.

Although William Burroughs did not fictionalize the era of his youth until the late 1960s and 1970s, all his work later showed the influence of his family inheritance. In fact, his oeuvre is legible as a sustained project to subvert the traditions of American capitalism represented by the Burroughs-Lee partnership. It is no coincidence that for his first two novels Burroughs adopted, and was initially published under, the name William Lee; this move simultaneously acknowledged his family origins and, given the subject matter of *Junky* and *Queer* (1985; written 1952), opened them to devastating critique. This filial revolt remained implicit in his first autobiographical account, published as the prologue to *Junky*, in which Burroughs presented his life as a heroin addict and petty criminal as the career path taken by a terminally "disaffected insider" (Skerl 1983, 47).

In a highly selective account of Burroughs's early years, the prologue to *Junky* invites readers to connect the youth, alienated from his haute bourgeois environment and repressed by its values, with the adult addict, and to conclude that, far from representing a fall from grace, the loss of a Midwestern idyll, his life of addiction and crime offered a more interesting alternative world. The key to this other world is given, far from coincidentally, as another memoir read by the disenchanted adolescent: "At this time I was greatly impressed by an autobiography of a burglar, called *You Can't Win*" (2003, xxxvi).

This memoir, which has become a cult classic through its association with Burroughs, vividly documented another, more alluring lost world: not the fading, country-club suburban society set of the 1920s, but, from a generation earlier and several social classes lower, what Burroughs later called the "underworld of seedy rooming-houses, pool parlors, cat houses and opium dens, of bull pens and cat-burglars and hobo jungles" (1988, v). In retrospect, it is clear that the criminal milieu of *Junky*, based closely on Burroughs's experiences during the 1940s, allowed him to explore and dramatize an equivalent world of colorful social outcasts unconstrained by the empty promises and ethics of official culture.

Burroughs, however, appeared to follow the route expected of him when, after attending Los Alamos Ranch School for Boys in New Mexico, he entered Harvard University in 1932, the proper training ground for a man of his class. But Burroughs knew he did not belong, and he cultivated the eccentricities of a loner and a dandy. On graduation in the summer of 1936, he joined what he called "the international queer set" (2003, xxxvii) on a European tour that took him through Germany and Austria. He stayed on in Vienna for six months to study medicine, and, in his boldest break from the family that still supported him financially through a monthly stipend, married Ilse Klapper, a German Jew, to help her escape the Nazi occupation. (They separated on arrival in New York.)

From the mid-1930s, Burroughs effectively drifted for a decade without clear direction—the term "drift" appears repeatedly in the account given in his prologue to *Junky*—and during this time he took psychology classes at Columbia University, returned to study anthropology at Harvard, and made there his first mature effort at writing. This was "Twilight's Last Gleaming," a comic sketch based on the sinkings of the *Morro Castle* and *Titanic*, featuring the debut of Dr. Benway, one of Burroughs's most potent characters. Years later, Ginsberg identified this passage as "the whole key to all his work, like the sinking of America" (285), but Burroughs recognized its significance in terms of the creative process itself. For "Twilight's Last Gleaming" came about as a dramatic collaboration acted out with one of the key figures in his early life, Kells Elvins, so setting a pattern of collaborative creativity that recurred throughout Burroughs's career. In fact, the scene of collaboration with Elvins in 1938 was effectively duplicated with Kerouac seven years later, when they cowrote a novella that also involved the acting out of fictional scenes. Neither effort succeeded, however, and Burroughs—unlike Kerouac or Ginsberg—had no sense of vocation, of his destiny as a writer.

In late summer 1939, Burroughs moved to Chicago to attend lectures given by Alfred Korzybski, one of the (now largely neglected) founders of language theory. Then, in the fall, having moved back to New York to take anthropology classes at Columbia, he began an obsessive relationship that made visible the extreme pathological factors that drove his personal—and to some degree his creative—life. The details of Burroughs's infatuation with the young man, Jack Anderson, have become familiar because he used their relationship as the basis for two of his earliest short stories: "Driving Lesson" and, most significantly, "The Finger" (both published in *Interzone*). A macabre tale of masochistic desire, "The Finger" narrates the traumatic episode when Burroughs severed a finger joint to offer as a token to Anderson, and then his subsequent commitment to Bellevue, that took place in April 1940. Burroughs's psychoanalytic treatment, which continued for the next twenty years, began as a condition imposed by his anxious parents, who continued to financially support their increasingly wayward youngest son.

Moving back and forth between Chicago and New York during the early 1940s, Burroughs failed to enlist in officer training programs, while avoiding being drafted into the regular army on the basis of his psychiatric record. Instead, he took on odd jobs—private detective, bug exterminator, bartender—seemingly to live out roles that suited his anthropological interest, and increasing involvement, in a world of criminal characters and escapades.

In spring 1943, Burroughs returned to New York and joined a Greenwich Village circle based around the relationship between Lucien Carr and David Kammerer, two old friends from St. Louis. Through Carr he soon met first Allen Ginsberg and then Jack Kerouac, one a current, the other a former student at Columbia, and together they began to form a still larger circle made up of students, street criminals, and would-be artists. Over the next two years, the center of gravity shifted between the Lower East Side and Times Square before settling on the Upper West Side, where two Barnard students, Joan Vollmer Adams and Frankie Edie Parker, turned their 115th Street apartment into a bohemian salon. Burroughs found an immediate intellectual rapport with Joan and, despite his homosexuality, they shared a common-law marriage. With constant repetition over time, this formation of the original Beat Generation scene has become one of the most familiar episodes in American literary history and popular culture. Its duration was actually quite brief—Burroughs's involvement lasted less than three years—but it was packed with personal drama and cultural significance and, in different ways, marked a turning point in the lives of all those involved.

A dozen years older than Ginsberg and eight older than Kerouac, Burroughs immediately assumed the role of a mentor, while offering a true alternative to the instruction either had at Columbia. Burroughs not only possessed the classical education of a man of his generation and social status with the unorthodox interests of an intellectual adventurer, he also combined literary taste and philosophical rigor with a cool, sardonic disregard for human pieties. Kerouac and Ginsberg were fascinated. Significantly, Kerouac constantly fictionalized Burroughs's tutoring role in his novels, but always ambivalently, with a hint of menace or snake oil, as though both attracted and repelled by his power. Burroughs himself only came close to participating in the autobiographical group mythmaking that typified Beat writing once, in the summer of 1945, when he and Kerouac cowrote "And the Hippos Were Boiled in Their Tanks" (part of which is published in *Word Virus*), based on the most dramatic event of the early Beat scene, Lucien Carr's killing of Dave Kammerer, which took place in August 1944.

In April 1946, Burroughs was arrested for forging a narcotics prescription and, to meet the terms of a suspended sentence, had to return home. From St. Louis he moved to Texas, buying some land near Pharr, to be with his old friend Kells Elvins. It is by no means clear that Burroughs intended to return to New York and resume his relationship with Joan; but he did, rescuing her from Bellevue, after a breakdown that summer. He brought Joan (and Julie, her infant daughter by a previous relationship) back to Texas, where they settled in New Waverly, near Houston, and established a curious scene of rural domesticity on a ninety-nine-acre farm. Burroughs began to raise crops, to build an orgone accumulator (his characteristically practical response to reading the theories of Wilhelm Reich), and supported an on-off heroin habit. Joan became addicted to Benzedrine, bore their son, Billy, born in July 1947, and started to lose her health.

In 1948, after a spell in the "narcotic farm" at Lexington, Kentucky, which he described in particular detail in *Junky*, Burroughs relocated his family to New Orleans, settling in a small house across the Mississippi in Algiers. There, in January 1949, they received a visit from Kerouac and Neal Cassady that later became a famous episode in the cross-country travels narrated in *On the Road*. Burroughs was soon forced to move on again, this time after an arrest for possession of firearms and drugs, again described at length in *Junky*. That September, Burroughs visited Mexico City and began the process of outrunning an inevitable prison sentence, returning to Louisiana only to bring his family back with him. At first, Mexico City appeared the promised land. Burroughs enrolled for courses at Mexico City College, explored the local drug and homosexual underworlds, found himself at home in the expatriate community, and tried to acquire Mexican citizenship. In the first months of 1950, he also began work on a book he called "Junk," his first sustained—and eventually successful—literary effort.

It was certainly more than chance that Burroughs's writing career should have coincided with his expatriation, but his precise motivation was unclear. According to one account, he was encouraged to document his past experiences by Kells Elvins; according to Ginsberg, it emerged in the course of their long-distance correspondence; the publication of Kerouac's first novel, *The Town and the City*, in March 1950, probably inspired him to take his own writing more seriously. Burroughs denied there was any particular motivation, but by the end of the year he had managed to complete a 150-page manuscript. It would take another eighteen months and the tireless promotional efforts of Ginsberg before the manuscript was accepted by Ace Books, one of the new paperback publishers, and another year before a revised version finally appeared. It did so under Burroughs's pen name, William Lee, with numerous cuts and even a new title chosen by his editors (*Junkie: Confessions of an Unredeemed Drug Addict*), a sensationally lurid cover, and, as protection against controversy, bound back-to-back with a reprint of the memoirs of a federal narcotics agent. It took two further editions and fifty years to restore the text of Burroughs's original design, but the fact of publication confirmed his identity as a writer.

*Junky* has always had an anomalous status within the Burroughs oeuvre. It is by a long way the most autobiographical and most conventionally linear or realist narrative he would ever write. Its narrator's voice is almost always coolly detached, apparently objective: "Here are the facts" (2003, 15). Compared with the uncompromisingly experimental fiction that would follow it, *Junky* places few demands on the reader. Yet although its apparently straightforward, first-person, documentary style disarms close analysis, critical approaches have found in the novel both a trenchant political agenda and clear signs of Burroughs's more characteristic literary practices. It has been seen as both an exception to the rule of the Burroughs oeuvre and as the "blueprint" for it, and there is a measure of truth in both verdicts.

*Junky* has most often been read as one of the first works of Beat literature, and in this context it has been taken as fictionalized autobiography: a roman à clef. Because the novel is a highly selective version of events and its narrating protagonist such a radically reduced version of its author, however, the biographical approach has relied very heavily on reading the novel in terms of what is absent from it. Equally, *Junky* lacks all the hallmarks of Beat writing, especially a communal utopian desire and the value of expressive spontaneity: whereas Kerouac and Ginsberg so often idealized the bonds of intimate friendship, *Junky* has a hauntingly detached, solitary quality. Beat readings of the novel have also had to ignore the conspicuous absences of Burroughs's encounters in New York with Kerouac and Ginsberg from an account that begins in precisely that place and period. If biography has been of dubious value to reading *Junky*, so, too, the value of *Junky* to biography.

The bulk of *Junky* narrates a series of episodes in the criminal subcultures and nighttime social underworlds of America during the late 1940s, ending with a shorter section set in Mexico. Its architecture follows the plot of Burroughs's own experience, and many of the descriptions match actual events. In this sense, it functions as an authentic documentation and detailed critique of Cold War America, seen in the dark mirror of its most demonized subgroups.

The final quarter of *Junky*, set in Mexico, was written during 1952, as Burroughs began work on a sequel, *Queer*, and awaited news of publication plans from Ginsberg, who now acted as his amateur literary agent in New York. It was completed, therefore, after the catastrophic evening of 6 September 1951, when, in what has become the most notorious episode in Burroughs's biography, he shot and killed his wife during a drunken game of William Tell. Until recently, the precise sequence of events, and how to interpret them, remained uncertain, mainly because of Burroughs's reluctance to give a clear or consistent account; since the publication in 1985 of his introduction to *Queer*, however, biographers and critics have been enabled—even encouraged—to speculate.

For here Burroughs set out in the most dramatic fashion his own "appalling conclusion": that it was the shooting of his wife that "motivated and formulated" his writing by bringing him in contact with an evil, possessing force he called Control or, more vividly, "the Ugly Spirit" (1985, xxii). So traumatic an event can only be seen as a turning point in Burroughs's biography, but its role in his literary history is much less obvious, and most commentators have, rightly, suspected Burroughs's own conclusion. On the other hand, the location and timing of Burroughs's account—in the introduction to *Queer* on its long-delayed publication—has made the shooting appear the key factor that accounts for the sudden and startling transformation in Burroughs's writing from his first novel to his second.

*Queer* was begun in March 1952, but its genesis goes back to the previous year when all the events it fictionalizes took place. During the spring of 1951, Burroughs had started to pursue a young American ex-serviceman, Lewis Marker, whom he knew from the expatriate bar scene in Mexico City. That summer, they traveled together through Central America, ostensibly in Burroughs's quest to discover *yagé*, a drug used by native Indians for its hallucinatory and telepathic properties, but the relationship with Marker broke down badly. These events comprise the minimal plot of *Queer*, the main narrative of which ends just before the point at which Burroughs returned—alone—to Mexico

City, just a few days before the fateful shooting of his wife. The shooting appears to play a curiously circular role, then, in the history of *Queer*: Burroughs started writing the novel after the incident, while the events fictionalized in the novel led up toward the shooting. The emphatic focus of biography on Joan's death, however, has had the effect of displacing attention from Burroughs's relationship with Marker, even though that story of impossible desire is the substance of *Queer*.

From one point of view, *Queer* is a natural pair to *Junky*. Taken together, these two novels can be seen as consecutive chapters of Burroughs's life, presented under the name William Lee and turned into blasts against the political and moral order of Cold War America. The obvious stylistic differences make them actually a very odd pair, however. Whereas *Junky* is a sustained, first-person, realist narrative, composed in a superficially neutral register, *Queer* is a fragmentary story told in the third person that, through Lee's numerous monologues, breaks into the hyperbolic fantasy mode that Burroughs called "routines." These virtuoso performances of Burroughs's distinctively visceral black humor are the crucial creative development that divides *Junky* from *Queer*, and they are also the key to the second novel's equally distinctive political force. The importance of *Queer* in the Burroughs oeuvre is that, unlike *Junky*, it already modeled the creativity and politics that would culminate in Burroughs's seminal work, *Naked Lunch*.

Although a slighter work than *Junky*, *Queer* achieved a dramatic politicization of Burroughs's writing by investing his own persona with a disturbing new identity. The cool neutrality of Lee in *Junky* is replaced by a desperate, hysterical persona, whose verbal routines dramatize an ugly, compulsive drive to possess the reluctant object of his desire, Eugene Allerton. At the same time, the sadistic and obscene humor of these routines is consistently tied to Lee's national identity, so that, through constant allusions to Cold War politics, his fantasies of control act out a nightmare version of the Ugly American. It is as though, rather than trying to resist or escape his own class and culture, Burroughs sought to exorcise it by exaggerating its worst features to a point of horrific excess. Because, too, Lee's imperial fantasies together with his identity as a queer, the result is a profoundly ambiguous and disturbing politicization of homosexuality.

The creativity and political force of *Queer*'s routines derive from Burroughs's doomed pursuit of Lewis Marker. Significantly, Burroughs wrote this material in spring 1952, sending it to Marker as a way to reestablish that relationship through correspondence with his absent lover. Indeed, he explained to Ginsberg that he "wrote *Queer* for Marker" (1993, 138). It was also at this point, in April 1952, that Burroughs wrote the first draft of "The Finger," the story based on his earlier masochistic desire for Jack Anderson. Burroughs was forcing himself to confront the deepest pathological features of his own biography, and to use them as the source of his writing. However traumatic, the shooting of his wife does not directly relate to the striking discontinuity that separates *Queer* from *Junky*.

With a smart lawyer and his family's support, Burroughs had escaped a prison sentence for the manslaughter of his wife. Nevertheless, he was classed as a "pernicious foreigner" (*Letters* 97), had lost his own family (the children were taken back to the United States), and knew it was time to move on yet again. Kerouac visited him in the summer, writing *Doctor Sax* while Burroughs worked on *Queer*, and then he left Mexico and set out, alone, on a second quest southward through the Americas in search of *yagé*. From January to July 1953, he traveled from Panama to Peru on this quasi-anthropological mission, aided by an encounter with Dr. Richard Evans Schultes, the preeminent ethnobotanist and *yagé* expert. Burroughs's experiences with the hallucinogen comprise a vivid but brief field report in "In Search of Yage," the section of *The Yage Letters* (1963) written in 1953. The rest is, like *Queer* rather than *Junky*, another curious narrative fragment.

"Yage" is presented in the form of a series of epistolary bulletins sent out by William Lee, in which he largely reports on the political corruption and unrealized human potentials he witnesses in South American colonial societies. Although some of this material overlaps closely with the actual letters that Burroughs wrote to Ginsberg during the first six months of 1953, most of it does not; contrary to appearances, "William" and "Allen" are fictional correspondents, and the letters were largely fabricated from journal notes that Burroughs kept on his travels. "Yage" introduced to the West firsthand information about an important psychotropic drug, but it has had only a marginal position within the Burroughs oeuvre.

Burroughs traveled to escape from social oppressions and he sought consciousness-changing drugs to escape from himself, but in fall 1953, he returned to New York with only the publication of his first novel to offset a catalog of personal disasters. He moved into Ginsberg's Lower East Side apartment and worked with him on the rough manuscripts of *Queer* and "In Search of Yage." Kerouac immediately fictionalized this three-month period of reunion in his novel *The Subterraneans* but did not focus on the real drama. Burroughs and Ginsberg had not seen each other for over six years. Having maintained a regular long-distance correspondence, however, Burroughs was now drawn toward Ginsberg and pressured him into an affair. The emotional strain on the former relationship of mentor and student was too great for Ginsberg, and, after a painful separation, in December 1953 Burroughs set out yet again on foreign travels, this time leaving for Europe.

After a short visit to Rome, in January 1954 Burroughs reached Tangier, the North African port city that became his headquarters for the next four years. Tangier, then an International Zone administered by colonial powers, drew Burroughs because of its image as an exotic no man's land and haven for outcasts, a reputation he knew from the Moroccan-set, existential thrillers of Paul Bowles, particularly *Let It Come Down* (1952). Taking advantage of the legal protection granted American citizens, Burroughs was able to live freely as a drug addict and homosexual, but the social license of Tangier did not compensate for his new isolation or bouts of drug-fueled paranoia and despair. Venturing out from his room in the old medina, he did meet Bowles, a permanent member of the expatriate artistic community, and the painter Brion Gysin, but befriended neither at this time. As his heroin addiction worsened, Burroughs turned again to Ginsberg and came to depend increasingly on the relationship constructed by their correspondence.

During 1954, Burroughs worked on fragmentary writing projects—short stories, routines, journal notes, magazine articles, episodes of a novel—in a make-or-break attempt to establish a literary career. Much of his creativity was structured by the long and regular letters he wrote to Ginsberg, an investment of energy that developed still further the process that had resulted in the routines of *Queer*. As Burroughs realized, however, these pieces did not add up to the sustained writing of a novel, and their chief effect was to lure Burroughs back to the United States in fall 1954 in another attempt to fulfill his desire for Ginsberg. After receiving a blunt rebuff by letter, and knowing he could not live in the United States, Burroughs returned to Tangier in December.

Throughout 1955, Burroughs worked on the novel he now called "Interzone." He tried vainly to reconcile the spontaneous, fragmentary, typically obscene fantasies of his routines, such as "The Talking Asshole," written that February, with plans for a coherent and structured narrative. Meanwhile, his addiction reached a critical point, and in spring 1956, he left for London to take the apomorphine cure, a treatment he would often champion. When he returned to Tangier, after a trip through Scandinavia, Burroughs no longer oriented himself via Ginsberg and entered a new phase of writing.

In early 1957, Kerouac, Ginsberg, his new lover, Peter Orlovsky, and Alan Ansen all visited Tangier to help Burroughs type up and organize the chaotic manuscripts that now went under the name *Naked Lunch*, a title that Kerouac had given him several years earlier. Although Burroughs continued to work on the manuscript for two more years, right up until the point of publication in Paris, the reputation and reception of *Naked Lunch* was always closely associated, in both the popular imagination and in critical accounts, with the story of its creation in Tangier. David Cronenberg's film version (1991) is only an extreme example of the general

trend: it fictionalized the creative process rather than *Naked Lunch* itself, turning Tangier into Interzone and the novel into a hallucinatory version of Burroughs's biography.

*Naked Lunch* does invite autobiographical readings, principally through the introduction that Burroughs added after the first edition, which explained the novel in terms of his experience of addiction. Yet even when it accepts the truth of Burroughs's own account, criticism has nevertheless shown how reductive this approach is to the text as a whole. It requires taking the intermittent presence of William Lee, and the general scenario of drug addiction and withdrawal, as the basis in reality to a world of dreams and fantasies. At first sight, this approach seems to confirm Burroughs's own conception of the novel in late 1955: based on Tangier, interzone is "the prognostic pulse of the world, like a dream extending from past into the future, a frontier between dream and reality—the reality of both called into question" (1993, 302). However, the deconstructive logic of the final phrasing warns against reading *Naked Lunch* through Burroughs's biography, because it is not only William Lee's "reality" that is called into question but his own. This questioning of reality is one reason Burroughs flaunted the idiom and persona of the conman, the huckster, the charlatan, even in his supposedly factual introduction. In *Naked Lunch*, telling is equated with selling, appearance with deception, authority with power.

Although *Naked Lunch* can be contextualized generally by reference to past literary traditions, contemporary experimental art forms, and indeed Burroughs's own previous novels—it recycles parts of all three—it retains the stunning force of a remarkably singular reading experience. Despite a mass of interpretations, the novel as a whole seems destined, if not actually designed, to elude the critical grasp. Individual parts, however, are much more readily understood as potent satirical assaults on the economic, moral, and political order of America and, by extension, of Western capitalism and modernity. Both shockingly funny and obscene, it works through a range of fictional forms, cultural narratives, and generic voices to make a thoroughgoing attack on the "reality" of both the world and the individual subject, a reality that is seen to structure and perpetuate exploitative and repressive relations of power. Predictably, the addict and the homosexual are identified as exemplary subjects caught up in the manipulation of need and desire. Whereas *Junky* and *Queer* document more or less contemporary worlds, however, *Naked Lunch* visibly exceeds its own historical points of reference and, through the modes of fantasy and science fiction, does indeed aim to take the "prognostic pulse of the world."

Inevitably, publication was not straightforward. First Maurice Girodias of Olympia Press in Paris and then Lawrence Ferlinghetti at the newly established City Lights in San Francisco turned the manuscript down. Only a censorship controversy, caused by the appearance of selected episodes in U.S. magazines, persuaded an opportunistic, if also adventurous Girodias to change his mind. *The Naked Lunch* duly appeared in July 1959 (the article was cut from the title for U.S. editions), but another six years passed before a decision in the Massachusetts Supreme Court, reversing an earlier verdict, allowed it to go on sale in the United States. As usual, the effect of being banned in Boston was to fuel public interest, and Burroughs's own absence overseas helped generate the mysterious aura of underground notoriety.

Eighteen months before publication, Burroughs had left Tangier and moved to Paris. Here he resumed psychoanalysis and met up again with Ginsberg, Peter Orlovsky, and Gregory Corso. They stayed at the so-called Beat Hotel, a Left Bank international rendezvous for artists and hipsters. But it was here that the axis of Burroughs's world began to shift, as his longstanding relationship with Ginsberg yielded to the influence of another hotel resident, Brion Gysin. Burroughs settled in Europe and, together with Gysin, embarked on a collective experimental venture that was of an entirely different order to the loose creative affiliations of the Beat movement in the United States: the cut-up project.

Burroughs's new methods of textual production belonged to a tradition, pioneered by the Dada and Surrealist movements, of aesthetic and magical practices based on chance operations and collage practices. The methods were, as he often insisted, "experimental in the sense of being *something to do*" (1978, 31), and he would spend the whole decade doing a great range of activities based on that principle: three novel-length works, hundreds of short texts, dozens of scrapbook collages, photomontages, tape-recorder experiments, and, with Anthony Balch, several cut-up films. Nevertheless, Burroughs's immediate enthusiasm was a remarkable act of brinkmanship that risked his future career and alienated former supporters: Gregory Corso even inserted a retraction in *Minutes to Go* (1960), the collaborative launching manual and manifesto of the first cut-up methods, objecting to "uninspired machine-poetry" (63).

In keeping with the logic of a true experiment, Burroughs revised his cut-up methods over time based on results, not only expanding their application from one medium to another but also reediting his trilogy of novels: *The Soft Machine* was published in three distinct editions (1961, 1966, 1968), and *The Ticket That Exploded* in two (1962, 1967); only *Nova Express* (1964) remained unrevised. The narrative of this trilogy is minimally structured by the Nova conspiracy, a science fiction mythology based on a war between alien powers of control and guerilla forces of human resistance. Formally, they are highly complex, unique adventures in experimental prose that produce an extraordinary and paradoxical reading experience: shocking, boring, lyrical, disturbing, uncanny. Although Burroughs had high expectations, they never won a wide readership, and he turned increasingly to the dissemination of shorter pieces in avant-garde journals, little magazines, and underground presses.

During the 1960s, Burroughs made London his headquarters, taking brief trips back to New York and Tangier. While his public profile was boosted by his appearance at the Edinburgh Writers conference in 1962 and, the following year, a controversy in the *Times Literary Supplement,* Burroughs was steadily acquiring an international underground reputation. In London, however, he actually lived in a very small circle, featuring Gysin and other close collaborators Ian Sommerville and Anthony Balch. Burroughs didn't publish another novel-length book until *The Wild Boys* in 1971, an anarchic, utopian queer fantasy that marked the beginning of a return to narrative form and that featured, for the first time, a boyish hero based on his own childhood. As Leon Lewis observes in *American Novelists Since World War II* (1995), this novel was "the first unit in what might be seen as the second half of his oeuvre" (26). That this was a period of transition is in fact clear from *The Job* (1970), a book begun as a series of interviews and then expanded by Burroughs with articles, polemics, and short fictional texts. Giving explicit form to artistic and political views developed over the previous decade, the book proved one of the most valuable resources until the essays collected in *The Adding Machine* appeared in 1985. On the other hand, although Burroughs's attitude is typically revisionist—rewriting his understanding of a decade devoted to cut-up experiments—little in *The Job* indicates the kind of creative directions he would next take. Critics and readers have mined the book for Burroughs's clearest statements on a wide range of subjects, but in many ways it reflects his position at a specific and limited point in time.

While Burroughs also produced several very interesting shorter experimental and polemical works in the early 1970s, it was clear that London no longer nourished him personally or creatively. Having advanced on many fronts, the cut-up project had finally run into a dead end, and Burroughs himself was drinking heavily, increasingly isolated, and beset by acute financial problems. After raising money by selling a huge archive of manuscript materials in 1973, Burroughs took up an invitation from Ginsberg to return to New York in spring 1974 for a semester's teaching in the English Department of City College. Whether or not he realized it, on the eve of his sixtieth birthday, Burroughs had come to the end of his quarter-of-a-century as an expatriate artist.

Based in New York, Burroughs spent the rest of the 1970s reinventing his cult reputation for a new generation. He began to move in celebrity avant-garde and rock music circles while acquiring new audiences through reading tours. Coinciding with the belated publication of *The Third Mind* (a major volume of cut-up collage and theory, originally put together with Brion Gysin in the mid-1960s), in December 1978 the Nova Convention was held in Burroughs's honor, and he was feted by a wide range of luminaries, from Laurie Anderson and Frank Zappa to John Cage and Timothy Leary. With close editorial and practical support from his new aide, James Grauerholz, Burroughs saw his first full-length novel for a decade, *Cities of the Red Night,* published in early 1981; its significant success was overshadowed, however, by the death that March of his son, Billy, after chronic alcohol problems led to liver failure.

In the winter, to escape the New York social scene and a heroin habit, Burroughs moved with Grauerholz to Lawrence, Kansas, and the Midwest town became his permanent home. There, Grauerholz established William Burroughs Communications to manage more professionally Burroughs's increasingly varied creative projects. He even launched a new career as a visual artist, starting with his "shotgun paintings," although Burroughs did not exhibit publicly until after the death of his longtime collaborator Brion Gysin in July 1986. In 1984, he published the second novel of a final trilogy, *The Place of Dead Roads*, an experimental Western narrative that featured, as Grauerholz pointed out, "the first elderly, self-referential protagonist in all Burroughs' work" (409).

Burroughs's critical profile had long been higher in Europe than America (the first full-length studies were published during the mid-1970s in England and France), but in 1983, he was made a member of the Academy and Institute of Arts and Letters, and he now enjoyed both popular and critical recognition, as well as, for the first time in his life, financial security. The first full-scale biographies, dozens of interviews and articles, several dedicated academic works, and a collection of his critical reception appeared. On the other hand, Burroughs's place in the larger canon of American literature still remained deeply contentious, and this failure to fit in unequivocally suited Burroughs's sense of his own singularity. "Twenty years ago, they were saying I belonged in jail," he said after his induction into the Academy; "Now they're saying I belong in their club. I didn't listen to them then, and I don't listen to them now" (quoted in Morgan, 13).

In his last decade, Burroughs continued to expand his range of creative collaborations, working with the likes of Kurt Cobain, Keith Haring, and Tom Waits, while one musical or artistic counterculture group after another anointed him their patron saint. Burroughs's final novel, *The Western Lands*, a literary meditation on immortality named after the Egyptian land of the dead, was published in 1987. The novel's preoccupation with death

William S. Burroughs in 1990. (William Coupon/Corbis)

would feature in Burroughs's final two books, *My Education: A Book of Dreams* (1995) and *Last Words: The Final Journals of William S. Burroughs* (2000). Although these edited collections of material from dream diaries and journal notes possess an undiminished vitriol, directed at Burroughs's longstanding targets, they also suggest a fading and rather narrowed imaginative power. This impression is only emphasized by the appearance shortly before this period of important, previously unpublished work from the 1950s, his first decade as a writer: *Queer* in 1985, the *Interzone* collection in 1987, his *Letters, 1945–1959* in 1993. That much of this early material had also been written in the form of dream diaries and journal notes only underscored the sense that Burroughs's career as a writer was coming to an end. The death in April 1997 of his old Beat comrade and lifelong friend Allen Ginsberg, a full dozen years his junior, foreshadowed Burroughs's own, just three months later, in the Lawrence Memorial Hospital on 2 August 1997. As Grauerholz observed, he had already lived "far longer than anyone might have expected, in view of the dangers he courted throughout his life" (in Burroughs 1998, 528). Those "dangers," as much a part of Burroughs's creative life as his personal one, would invite his obituaries to headline all the clichéd epithets: Beat Generation Guru, Wife Killer, Master Addict, Queer Avant-Gardist, Postmodern Icon. While Burroughs remains the face that does not fit, those dangers have ensured the enduring fascination of his image, and maybe his immortality as a writer.

## A Chronology of the Life and Career of William S. Burroughs

| | |
|---|---|
| 1914 | Born 5 February in St. Louis, Missouri |
| 1929 | Attends Los Alamos Ranch School, New Mexico |
| 1932–36 | Majors in English at Harvard University |
| 1936–37 | Tour of Europe; attends medical school in Vienna; marries Ilse Klapper |
| 1938 | Studies anthropology at Harvard; with Kells Elvins writes "Twilight's Last Gleaming" |
| 1939 | In Chicago attends lectures by Korzybski; cuts off a finger joint to impress a lover |
| 1940–43 | Odd jobs in Chicago and New York |
| 1943 | Moves to New York, where he meets Ginsberg and Kerouac |
| 1944–45 | Carr–Kammerer murder; Burroughs and Kerouac cowrite "And the Hippos Were Boiled in Their Tanks" based on the case |
| 1945–46 | Moves in with Joan Vollmer; meets Herbert Huncke and enters the drug underground scene |
| 1946–47 | Relocates to Texas with Joan and her daughter; their son, William Jr., born on 21 July 1947 |
| 1948–49 | Settles in New Orleans |
| 1950 | Moves with family to Mexico City; begins work on "Junk" |
| 1951 | Travels through Central America with Lewis Marker; 6 September, kills wife in William Tell shooting accident |
| 1952 | Writes *Queer* manuscript |
| 1953 | January to July, travels through Central and South America looking for *yagé*; April, *Junkie* published by Ace Books; Burroughs returns to New York in the fall; affair with Ginsberg ends with Burroughs's departure for Europe |
| 1954–57 | In Tangier, addiction worsens; Burroughs writes fragmentary materials, mainly via his correspondence with Ginsberg; in spring 1956, takes the apomorphine cure in London |
| 1957 | Visit to Tangier by Ginsberg and Kerouac to work on *Naked Lunch* manuscripts |
| 1958 | Moves to Paris, staying at so-called Beat Hotel |
| 1959 | In July, *The Naked Lunch* published by Olympia Press; begins collaborations with Brion Gysin, developing the first "cut-up" methods |

| | |
|---|---|
| 1960 | *Minutes to Go* and *The Exterminator* include first cut-up texts; moves to London |
| 1961 | *The Soft Machine* (1st edition) published |
| 1962 | Edinburgh Writer's Conference; *The Ticket That Exploded* (1st edition) published |
| 1963 | *The Yage Letters* published |
| 1964 | *Nova Express* published; stays in New York |
| 1965 | Father dies; Boston trial of *Naked Lunch* |
| 1966 | *Naked Lunch* declared not obscene; *The Soft Machine* (2nd edition) published |
| 1967 | *The Ticket That Exploded* (2nd edition) published |
| 1968 | Covers Chicago Democratic Convention for *Esquire* |
| 1970 | Mother dies; *The Job* expanded interviews published |
| 1971 | *The Wild Boys* published |
| 1974 | Moves from London to New York; meets James Grauerholz |
| 1977 | *Junky* (reedited edition of *Junkie*) published |
| 1978 | *The Third Mind* published; Nova Convention in New York |
| 1979 | Moves to Lawrence, Kansas |
| 1981 | Son dies; *Cities of the Red Night* published |
| 1983 | Inducted into American Academy of Arts and Letters |
| 1984 | *The Place of Dead Roads* and *The Burroughs File* collection of short texts published |
| 1985 | *Queer* and *The Adding Machine* essays published |
| 1986 | Brion Gysin dies |
| 1987 | *The Western Lands* published; first painting exhibition in New York |
| 1989 | *Interzone* collection of early material published |
| 1992 | David Cronenberg's film of *Naked Lunch* released |
| 1993 | *The Letters of William S. Burroughs, 1945–59* published |
| 1995 | *Ghost of Chance* and *My Education* published |
| 1996 | *Ports of Entry* art exhibition and catalog publication |
| 1997 | Dies 2 August |
| 2000 | *Last Words* journal entries published |
| 2003 | New editions of *Junky* and *Naked Lunch* published on fiftieth anniversary of his literary career |

—Oliver Harris

## Principal Works

*Junkie: Confessions of an Unredeemed Drug Addict*, 1953; republished as *Junky*, 1977; republished as *Junky: The Definitive Text of "Junk,"* 2003; *The Naked Lunch*, 1959; republished as *Naked Lunch*, 1962; republished as *Naked Lunch: The Restored Text*, eds. James Grauerholz and Barry Miles, 2001; with Brion Gysin, Sinclair Beiles, and Gregory Corso, Burroughs is the author of *Minutes to Go*, 1960; *The Soft Machine*, 1961, 2nd ed.,1966, 3rd ed.,1968; *The Ticket That Exploded*, 1962, 2nd ed., 1967; *The Yage Letters*, 1963, *Nova Express*, 1964; *The Wild Boys*, 1971; with Brion Gysin, *The Third Mind*, 1978; *Cities of the Red Night*, 1981; *The Place of Dead Roads*, 1983; *Queer*, 1985; *The Adding Machine*, 1985; *The Western Lands*, 1987; Foreword in *You Can't Win* by Jack Black,1988; *Interzone*, ed. James Grauerholz, 1989; *The Letters of William S. Burroughs 1945–1959*, ed. Oliver Harris, 1993; *Word Virus: The William S. Burroughs Reader*, ed. James Grauerholz and Ira Silverberg, 1998.

## Bibliographical References

Bruce Cook includes commentary on Burroughs in *The Beat Generation*, 1971, which was republished in 1994. Allen Ginsberg refers to Burroughs in an interview with Thomas Clark in *Paris Review Interviews*, 3rd series, ed. George Plimpton, 1967. In *Word Virus*, James Grauerholz is the author of "The Red Night Trilogy" and "Epilogue," 1998. Leon Lewis contributes "William S. Burroughs" to *American Novelists Since World War II*, 4th series, *The Dictionary of Literary Biography*, eds. Wanda H. Giles and James R. Giles, 1995. Gerald Malanga's "An Interview with William Burroughs" in *Burroughs*

*Live: The Collected Interviews of William S. Burroughs 1960–1997,* ed. Sylvère Lotringer, 2001, offers Burroughs's own perspective on his work. A quick review of Burroughs is available in Jennie Skerl, "William S. Burroughs," in *The Beats: Literary Bohemians in Postwar America,* 16, *The Dictionary of Literary Biography,* ed. Ann Charters, 1983; a comprehensive critical biography is Ted Morgan, *Literary Outlaw: The Life and Times of William S. Burroughs, 1988.* Perhaps the most current critical interpretation is Oliver Harris, *William Burroughs and the Secret of Fascination,* 2003. One should also consult Robin Lydenberg, *Word Cultures: Radical Theory and Practice in William S. Burroughs' Fiction,* 1987; Barry Miles, *William Burroughs: El Hombre Invisible,* 1992; Timothy Murphy, *Wising Up the Marks: The Amodern William Burroughs,* 1997; Jamie Russell, *Queer Burroughs,* 2001; Jennie Skerl, *William S. Burroughs,* 1985; Jennie Skerl and Robin Lydenberg, eds. *William S. Burroughs at the Front: Critical Reception, 1959–1989,* 1991; and Robert Sobieszek, *Ports of Entry: William S. Burroughs and the Arts,* 1996.

**See also** Burroughs, Ilse Herzfeld Klapper; Vollmer Adams Burroughs, Joan; Burroughs, William Seward, Jr.; Apomorphine Treatment; Algiers, Louisiana; Kerouac, Jack; Ginsberg, Allen; Drugs; Kammerer, David Eames; New York City; Reich, Wilhelm; Lexington, Kentucky; Mexico City; Painting; Elvins, Kells

# Burroughs, William Seward, Jr. (III) (1947–1981)

Only son of William S. Burroughs II (1914–1997) and author of two autobiographical books, *Speed* (1970) and *Kentucky Ham* (1973). Born 25 July 1947 in Conroe, Texas, to Burroughs and his common-law second wife, Joan Vollmer (1924–1951). The family included Julie, born August 1944, Vollmer's daughter from her previous marriage to Paul Adams. During 1947–1951, they lived in rural east Texas (while also operating a cotton farm with Kells Elvins in south Texas), and then from June 1948 to May 1949 in New Orleans, where Burroughs was arrested for drugs, causing him to move with his wife and children to Mexico City in September 1949. On 6 September 1951, William Burroughs fatally shot Joan Vollmer while drunk, after they had dared each other to a "William Tell act." Julie's grandparents took her home to New York State, and Burroughs's aged parents took Billy home to St. Louis, Missouri, then moved with him to Palm Beach, Florida, in spring 1952.

After an unsuccessful six months with his father in Tangier, Morocco, Billy returned to Florida in late 1963. His grandfather died in January 1965; Billy, then seventeen, ran away to New York and was involved in the Lower East Side Methedrine scene before being arrested and brought home. He was treated at the federal Lexington Narcotics Hospital in Kentucky, and then his father sent him to the Green Valley School near Orange, Florida, in hopes of taming him. In 1968, he married a classmate, Karen Beth Perry, and they lived in her hometown of Savannah, Georgia, while he wrote *Speed,* about his New York escapade. Restlessly traveling through Georgia, Florida, Colorado, and the Yucatán while Billy's drinking escalated, the couple separated by 1974. Nevertheless, Billy had completed *Kentucky Ham,* dealing with his childhood and his time at Green Valley.

While visiting the Naropa Institute in Boulder, Colorado, with his loyal girlfriend, Georgette Larrouy, in August 1976 for a reading, Billy suddenly suffered a complete liver failure, and received one of the first two hundred transplanted livers in the United States. He spent many months at Denver General Hospital and for four years thereafter lived despairingly in Denver or Boulder, where Allen Ginsberg and the Naropa group offered him support, even though he resumed drinking and taking drugs. His father resided mostly in Boulder during 1976–1978 to be near him.

In January 1981, in dire physical straits, Billy went back to Palm Beach on the invitation of another Green Valley classmate, Teina DeBakey, who had long carried a torch for him. Shocked at his condition, she set him up in an apartment, but the next month he went to DeLand, Florida, for a reunion with his Green Valley headmaster, George von Hilsheimer, whose reception was ambivalent. His anti-rejection drugs abandoned, his new liver collapsing, and almost all his friends expended, Billy was found in a ditch and taken to West Volusia Hospital, where he died on 3 March 1981.

Billy had called his last book project (written 1975–1980) "Prakriti Junction"; it was unfinished when he died, but from his unpublished writings and interviews with friends and family, a posthumous volume, *Cursed from Birth: The Short, Unhappy Life of William S. Burroughs, Jr.,* was edited by David Ohle and set for publication in 2001.

—*James Grauerholz*

## Bibliographical Sources

William S. Burroughs, Jr., wrote *Speed,* 1970, and *Kentucky Ham,* 1973. Details of Burroughs's life are included in Ted Morgan's thorough study of Burroughs's father: *Literary Outlaw: The Life and Times of William S. Burroughs,* 1988. Jennie Skerl is the author of an entry on William S. Burroughs, Jr., in Ann Charters, ed., *The Beats: Literary Bohemians in Postwar America,* Part 1, 1983.

***See also*** Burroughs, William Seward; Vollmer Adams Burroughs, Joan

# C

## Caen, Herb (1916–1997)

Columnist for *San Francisco Chronicle* who coined the term "beatnik." The term found instant acceptance in the media and has been confused with "Beat" ever since. According to Jesse Hamlin, the Beats responded humorously to Caen, posting a sign at the Co-Existence Bagel Shop in San Francisco: "We feature separate toilet facilities for HERB CAEN." In Norman Mailer's *Advertisements for Myself,* a footnote indicates that "beatnik" is a "word coined by an idiot columnist in San Francisco."

—*William Lawlor*

### Bibliographical References

See Herb Caen and Barnaby Conrad, *The World of Herb Caen: San Francisco 1938–1997,* 1999; Jesse Hamlin sums up the coining of "beatnik" in "How Herb Caen Named a Generation" in *the San Francisco Chronicle* 26 November 1995, p. 28.

*See also* Beat and Beatnik; News Media and Publicity, The Beats and

## Cage, John (1912–1992)

Composer, writer, poet, and visual artist, most famous for his experimental approach to musical composition and performance. Cage believed that music can be expressed through means other than musical instruments—music may incorporate sounds, noises, or silence and may even involve the stillness and movement of dance. Although not a Beat artist, Cage was appreciated by the Beats because of his experimental and collaborative approach to art. Like the Beats, Cage found that the artistic milieu at Black Mountain College was a touchstone to subsequent creativity.

For Cage, communication is not the reason for composition. Too often, the intended message is received with an unintended understanding. Music, for Cage, can be indeterminate and does not have to be recorded on scores.

Cage was a lifetime collaborator with Merce Cunningham. At Black Mountain College, with Charles Olson, Robert Rauschenberg, Merce Cunningham, and David Tudor, Cage prompted the first "happening," an experimental presentation of simultaneous dance, poetry, visual art, piano, and victrola playing.

At Town Hall in New York City in 1958, Émile de Antonio, Jasper Johns, and Robert Rauschenberg honored Cage, celebrating a quarter century of creativity.

—*William Lawlor*

### Bibliographical References

See David Nicholls, ed., *The Cambridge Companion to John Cage,* 2002; a biographical study is David Revill, *The Roaring Silence: John Cage: A Life,* 1993. Cage's own "Autobiographical Statement," originally published in *Southwest Review,* 1991, is a compact and lively review of Cage's life and productivity.

*See also* Music; Cunningham, Merce; Rauschenberg, Robert; Black Mountain, North Carolina; and Black Mountain College

## Cannastra, Bill (1921-1950)

Outrageous, daring, no-fear friend of Kerouac and other Beats in Manhattan. Friend of Joan Haverty, who married Kerouac on November 17, 1950, only weeks after Cannastra's shocking death on October 12, 1950, when he tried to leave a subway car through a window as the train left the Bleecker Street station. He could not complete his exit or return to the car before the impact with the subway tunnel killed him.

Cannastra is a recurrent figure in Beat literature. In "Howl," Allen Ginsberg recalls Cannastra's death in the subway window and his outrageous antics, including a jump into the polluted Passaic River (17). In *Visions of Cody*, Kerouac incorporates Cannastra in the Legend of Duluoz as Finistra. In *Go*, John Clellon Holmes fits Cannastra into his roman à clef as Agatson.

Although Cannastra was a graduate of Harvard Law School and brilliant in many ways, he also had a problem with alcohol and was apparently affected by a death wish. Stories about him include his teetering at the edge of a building seventy feet above the pavement, his wet kissing of unknown and burly men in taverns, and his lying down in streets with heavy traffic. Cannastra's death is variously referred to as a prank gone sour, an accident, or a suicide.

—*William Lawlor*

### Bibliographical References

The basic details of Cannastra's connection to the Beats and the circumstances of his death are in Dennis McNally, *Desolate Angel*, 1978, and Michael Schumacher, *Dharma Lion*, 1992. An obituary in the *New York Times* 13 October 1950, p. 19, misspells Cannastra's name and apparently misstates his age, but supplies the details of his death. See Jack Kerouac, *Visions of Cody*, 1972; John Clellon Holmes, *Go*, 1952; and Allen Ginsberg, "Howl," in *Howl and Other Poems*, 1956.

*See also* Ginsberg, Allen; Kerouac, Jack; Kerouac, Joan Haverty

## Carr, Lucien (1925-2005)

Youthful catalyst of the formative Beat Generation, during 1943–1946. Born 1 March 1925 in New York City, Carr was raised in St. Louis, Missouri, after his hard-drinking father, Russell Carr, deserted his mother, Marian Gratz, around 1930. The Carrs were a founding family of St. Louis, and the Gratzes of New York were wealthy in business. In his early teens in St. Louis, Carr met David Kammerer (1911–1944), a youth-group leader who became a father figure and literary icon for him. Kammerer, who was homosexual, was progressively more obsessed with Carr and visited him at his private schools in Massachusetts and Maine, eventually following him to the University of Chicago in 1942. A personal crisis at finals time resulted in Carr transferring to Columbia University in fall 1943, and at the same time Kammerer and his close friend William Burroughs also moved to New York.

The Kammerer-Carr affair continued, intensifying but never consummated, to such a point that on 13 August 1944, during a struggle with Kammerer on the banks of the Hudson River on the Upper West Side, Carr fatally stabbed his older friend. A day later, after involving Jack Kerouac and William Burroughs as accessories after the fact, Carr turned himself in and eventually served two years at Elmira Reformatory in New York State for manslaughter. The case gained such notoriety that fictionalized versions of it can be recognized in published writings by Jack Kerouac, Chandler Brossard, Alan Harrington, and James Baldwin; Kerouac, Burroughs, and Allen Ginsberg also wrote still-unpublished versions.

Carr remained in touch with his New York friends and after his release found work at United Press International. With Ginsberg he visited Joan Vollmer Burroughs in Mexico City just two weeks before her accidental death at Burroughs's hand. His "Beat" friends eventually became famous writers, and Kerouac based characters on him in several works: "Kenneth Wood" in *The Town and the City*, "Damion" in *On the Road*, "Sam Vedder" in *The Subterraneans*, "Julian" in *Big Sur*, and "Claude de Maubris" in *Vanity of Duluoz*. Carr shied away from the publicity attracted by the Beats, however, and although flattered by Ginsberg's 1956 dedication of "Howl" to him, he asked that his name be removed from later editions. When Carr retired from UPI in the 1980s, he had been married twice and fathered three sons: Simon, Caleb, and Ethan. Caleb became a celebrated author in the 1990s. Lucien Carr lived in quiet seclusion in the District of Columbia until his death in 2005.

—James Grauerholz

**Bibliographical References**

One can find background on Lucien Carr in Ted Morgan, *Literary Outlaw: The Life and Times of William S. Burroughs,* 1988; Barry Gifford and Lawrence Lee, *Jack's Book: An Oral Biography of Jack Kerouac,* 1978; and Barry Miles, *Ginsberg: A Biography,* 1989. James Grauerholz conducted an interview with Lucien Carr on 11 October 1999, but that interview remains unpublished.

*See also* Kerouac, Jack; Burroughs, William Seward; Ginsberg, Allen; Kammerer, David; Vollmer Adams Burroughs, Joan

## Carroll, Paul (1927–1996)

Critic, editor, poet, and teacher, born in Chicago, 1927, died 1996. Carroll's poetry combines iconoclastic, unconventional irregularity with lyrical passion. Supportive of new Beat prose and verse writers, he edited *The Chicago Review,* cofounded *Big Table* when censorship of Beat writers in *Chicago Review* became a problem, and compiled influential anthologies, *The Young American Poets* (1968), and *Earthquake on Ada Street* (1979). A popular pedagogue, who insisted on contemporary poetry's expressive capacities, Carroll reached full professorship at the University of Illinois, Chicago, before a midlife decline. His poetry volumes include *Odes* (1969), *The Luke Poems* (1971), and *Poems* (1988); his major critical work is *The Poem in Its Skin* (1968).

—Kevin De Ornellas

**Bibliographical References**

A tribute to Carroll is Paul Hoover, "The Poet in His Skin: Remembering Paul Carroll," *The Chicago Review,* 44 (1), 1998; Carroll's discussion of Ginsberg's "Wichita Vortex Sutra" appears in Lewis Hyde, ed., *On the Poetry of Allen Ginsberg,* 1984.

*See also* Censorship; Little Magazines

## Cassady, Carolyn (1923–)

Memoirist and homemaker, Carolyn Cassady entered the Beat Generation through her relationships with pivotal Beat figures Neal Cassady, Jack Kerouac, and Allen Ginsberg. Perhaps the most enduring of the women married into the Beat Generation, Cassady remains important for the stability she maintained as wife, mother, and muse as well as for the insight her memoir provides into the lives of such major figures as Neal Cassady and Jack Kerouac. Her position places her as a unique hybrid figure between the 1950s ideal housewife role and the countercultural Beat chick.

Carolyn Cassady was born Carolyn Robinson on April 28, 1923, in East Lansing, Michigan. The daughter of two educators, she was reared in an intellectual atmosphere that encouraged curiosity and creativity. She attended Bennington College on a scholarship and earned a bachelor's degree in drama while also studying painting, drawing, and sculpture. In 1947, she moved to Denver, Colorado, to pursue her master of fine arts degree at the University of Denver. It was there during March 1947 that she was introduced to Neal Cassady.

In her initial meeting with Neal, Carolyn was charmed by his good looks and engaging manner, but stopped short of pursuing her interest upon learning he was already married. She consented to have dinner with his friends, however, whom Neal invited back to her apartment to celebrate his return to Denver. Neal showed up with his wife clinging to his arm, then left with her only to return to Carolyn's apartment in the middle of the night, seeking a place to stay, telling her he had left his wife. The unconventional interactions of that first evening became a precursor to their relationship. In this night, Cassady unwittingly took her place as the provider of a stable home for Neal, just as Gabrielle Kerouac did for her son Jack.

Cassady believed Neal's assurances that his marriage to LuAnne Henderson would be annulled, and she consented, against her upbringing, to live with Neal until they could be married. She was convinced that they were destined to be together. Neal soon introduced Cassady to his writer friends from New York, Allen Ginsberg and Jack Kerouac. Sexual tension tied the Cassadys together for the rest of their lives.

Although three years older than Neal, Cassady remained innocent of the countercultural Beat lifestyle, and she was ignorant not only of Neal's continued sexual relationship with LuAnne, but also his sexual relationship with Ginsberg. When introduced to Ginsberg, she assumed friendship accounted for his closeness to her husband, but her assumptions were shattered when, on the morning she planned to leave Denver for Hollywood, she found Neal in bed between Allen and LuAnne, all naked.

Cassady fled Neal and the Beat scene by moving to Los Angeles and then to San Francisco, but she could not resist Neal when he wrote with apologies and explanations, begging her to reunite with him. He arrived in San Francisco in October 1947. Cassady soon became pregnant with their first child and the couple was married 1 April 1948, an event that failed to provide the stable family life that Cassady sought.

To meet the family's financial needs, and knowing Neal's wanderlust prevented his remaining in one place long, Cassady took a job as a receptionist for a doctor's office to support herself and her daughter. Without the steady presence or income from her husband, Cassady gained an independence and resourcefulness that sustained her through Neal's absences and gave her the safety net of self-reliance that allowed her to take Neal back after each absence.

Cassady remained faithful to Neal, despite his bigamous marriage to model Diana Hansen in 1950, the same year of her second daughter's birth. Cassady granted Neal a divorce; however, he was back on her doorstep begging for forgiveness the day after he married the already-pregnant Hansen. For the next few months, Cassady provided a sometime home for Neal as he drifted between his two families.

The Cassady family grew by a son in 1951 and then incorporated Jack Kerouac in 1952 when he came to live in their attic to finish *On the Road*. The sexual tension returned to the household, and this time Carolyn Cassady succumbed. She consummated an affair with Kerouac with Neal's knowledge. For a few months, she adopted Neal's former role as the partner with two devoted lovers, but the strain between Neal and Kerouac became too great, and Cassady eventually chose to remain with Neal.

Cassady did not remain immune to the spiritual seeking being done by Beat writers, and in 1954, she and Neal became engrossed by the work of Edgar Cayce when they moved from San Francisco to Los Gatos. That same year, Cassady threw Ginsberg out of her house after walking in on him and Neal sexually engaged.

Cassady continued to provide a stable home for Neal, choosing not to move abroad while he was in prison in 1958 because he could not be released without a home to go to. She supported her family, accepting Neal's wanderlust and inconstancy, and as the 1950s ended, she returned to her painting and writing. When Neal died in Mexico in 1968, Cassady began her memoir *Off the Road*, a version of which became the screenplay for the movie *Heart Beat*. In 1984, Cassady moved to London where she continues to write and paint portraits.

—*Jennifer Love*

## Principal Works

Prose: *Heart Beat: My Life with Jack and Neal*, 1976; *Off the Road: My Years with Cassady, Kerouac, and Ginsberg*, 1990.

## Bibliographical References

Her memoir *Off the Road*, 1990, provides the most intimate biographical material on Carolyn Cassady; Brenda Knight also provides biographical material in *Women of the Beat Generation*, 1996; in *The Birth of the Beat Generation*, 1995, Steven Watson includes Cassady in his study of Neal Cassady, Kerouac, and Ginsberg; in her anthology *Beat Down to Your Soul*, 2001, Ann Charters includes Carolyn Cassady's comments during the Panel Discussion with Women Writers of the Beat Generation, held at NYU in 1994.

**See also** Cassady, Neal; Film; Denver, Colorado

## Cassady, Neal (1926–1968)

After enduring a difficult childhood, Neal Cassady hoped to become a writer by learning from the writers who eventually formed the Beat Generation, but inspiration actually flowed in the opposite direction. Recognizing the intensity, frankness, and free expression of Cassady, Jack Kerouac and Allen Ginsberg strove to make their writing as uninhibited as Cassady's letters. Cassady attempted to write his autobiography, and *The First Third* (1971; revised edition 1981) is the fragment he produced; nevertheless, Cassady is immortal as a member of the Beat Generation because he is the real-life model for the mythic figure developed in *Go* by John Clellon Holmes; *On the Road, Visions of Cody, Big Sur,* and other works by Jack Kerouac; "The Green Automobile," "Howl," and "Elegy for Neal Cassady" by Allen Ginsberg; *The Electric Kool-Aid Acid Test* by Tom Wolfe; and *Over the Border* and "The Day after Superman Died" by Ken Kesey.

Neal Cassady was born in Salt Lake City on February 8, 1926. Because his parents were traveling to Hollywood, where Neal's father planned to open a barber shop, Neal was, as the story goes, "born on the road." Any romance connected with Neal's birth lasted a very short time, and his parents divorced when Neal was six years old. Neal remained in the care of his alcoholic father, who initiated Neal to a life among conmen, hustlers, and alcoholics on Larimer Street in Denver, Colorado. Neal involved himself in a life of stealing cars and chasing women. When law enforcement intervened, Neal spent time in reform schools.

Despite this troubled start in life, Neal Cassady developed an interest in literature and philosophy. High school counselor Justin Brierly encouraged Neal to pursue his reading, and when Hal Chase, a student from Columbia University, returned to his home in Denver, Cassady befriended him. After Chase returned to New York City, Cassady established a correspondence with him. Chase showed Cassady's lively letters to others in a group of young writers near Columbia University, including Jack Kerouac, Allen Ginsberg, and William Burroughs.

In 1946, now married to LuAnne Henderson, who was only fifteen years old, Cassady traveled to New York, where he met Kerouac, Ginsberg, and many others. Kerouac recognized Cassady as a conman and tried to stay at a distance, but Ginsberg was less cautious, commencing an intense sexual relationship.

In 1947, having received encouragement to be a writer from Kerouac and Ginsberg, Cassady embarked for Denver. On 7 March 1947, he wrote to Kerouac from Kansas City the "Great Sex Letter," which was the first of two letters that profoundly influenced Kerouac. Cassady's writing was uninhibited, free flowing, and explicit, and Kerouac discovered in the letter the spirit of the spontaneous prose he wanted to write.

In Denver, Cassady's romantic life took on new heights of extravagance. He met Carolyn Robinson, and after annulling the marriage to LuAnne Henderson, he married Carolyn, who was pregnant, in 1948. To support his family, Neal worked on the Southern Pacific Railroad but was later laid off. He went back and forth between Carolyn and LuAnne and journeyed to and from New York, Denver, and San Francisco. In New York, he met Diana Hansen, bigamously married her, and then went back to Carolyn and his job on the railroad.

In December 1950, when Kerouac was struggling to write a road book, Cassady sent the "Joan Anderson Letter," a 23,000-word account of girlfriends and madcap sexual adventures. Inspired again, Kerouac strove to write with full frankness and bright intensity his road book about his own experiences with Neal, as if Kerouac were addressing his wife.

In 1958, Cassady was arrested for possession of marijuana and served two years in San Quentin. Troubled by this setback, Cassady wrote frequently to Carolyn to express his sorrow, and these letters were eventually collected as *Grace Beats Karma: Letters from Prison, 1958–1960.*

In 1960, Cassady attempted to put his family life on firm footing, but the attempt was not successful, and the marriage of Carolyn and Neal ended in divorce in 1963. Neal Cassady spent the next five years with Ken Kesey and the Merry Pranksters. Although Cassady became known as "Speed Limit" and although the travels on the bus, made famous

In San Francisco in 1955, Neal Cassady studies a selection of used cars. (Allen Ginsberg/Corbis)

by Tom Wolfe's *Electric Kool-Aid Acid Test* (1968), involved abundant drugs and craziness, Cassady drove the bus from coast to coast without a traffic accident.

In 1968, while walking the railroad tracks on the way to Mexico, a heavily intoxicated Neal Cassady collapsed and died of exposure, but his death cannot diminish his importance in the literature of the Beat Generation. In *Go* (1952) by John Clellon Holmes, Neal Cassady is rendered as Hart Kennedy, a character who combines the characteristics of a conman, hustler, hedonist, and liar with the traits of exuberance, energy, and pleasant wildness.

In *On the Road*, Jack Kerouac uses Neal Cassady as the model for Dean Moriarty. While Dean is spontaneous and sensual, he is also tricky and disloyal. Dean is Sal's lost brother and is the "Holy Goof"; Dean has the sensitivity to recognize intuitively the inner lives of others, yet he draws criticism from women around him, who charge that he is selfish and irresponsible. Perhaps the strongest association made with Dean is his connection to the spirit of the American West; he is a cowboy born after the time of the cowboys; he is a trailblazer born in a time when all the trails have already been blazed. He expresses the openness and energy that all Americans have within them but few can bring to the surface in their lives.

Kerouac draws from Cassady in various other works, including *Visions of Cody, Book of Dreams, Pull My Daisy, The Dharma Bums, Desolation Angels,* and *Big Sur.* In *Visions of Cody,* the psychological background of Cody Pomeray is rendered through scenes from his life, especially in the novel's treatment of Cody's childhood and adolescence. In *Pull My Daisy,* Milo is the working railroad man with wife and child; yet he is also part of an artistic community. In *Big Sur,* Cody is still the friend of Jack Duluoz, but Cody has been released from jail and needs to show order and responsibility, especially with his wife and child.

Ginsberg's connection to Cassady is evident because Ginsberg makes Cassady one of the persons mentioned on the dedication page of "Howl." In the poem itself, Cassady is referred to as "cocksman and Adonis of Denver" (14). In "The Green Automobile," which is included in *Reality Sandwiches: 1953–1960,* Ginsberg fulfills his need for a loving connection with Neal Cassady through a flight of the imagination: Ginsberg and Neal are freed from their commitments and responsibilities to enjoy the spirit of an earlier and more pleasant time in their lives. In "Elegy for Neal Cassady," which is included in *The Fall of America,* Ginsberg recalls the same tender connection to Cassady on the occasion of Cassady's death.

In Tom Wolfe's *The Electric Kool-Aid Acid Test,* the myth of Neal Cassady is carried to special heights. Because Cassady connects Kesey's revolutionary antics with the Beats who preceded Kesey, Wolfe assigns mythic qualities to Cassady in a work that is supposed to be nonfiction. Cassady is the extraordinary driver who is beyond the ordinary process of thinking. All human beings function with a delay—perhaps a thirtieth of a second—between a sensory impression and the reception of the impression in the mind, but Cassady minimizes the lag and naturally is especially in contact with the moment at hand.

Kesey's short story "The Day after Superman Died" pays special tribute to "Sir Speed" Houlihan, who mystifies Devlin Deboree because Houlihan's last words are "Sixty-four thousand nine hundred and twenty eight." Deboree is disappointed to think that Houlihan's life ended in senselessness and fears that Houlihan's whole life was similarly devoid of meaning. However, Deboree learns that Houlihan, intoxicated beyond measure, set off walking down a railroad track, determined to count the ties. The act of counting is fully rational, and Deboree's confidence in Houlihan is restored.

—*Kit Knight*

## Principal Works

Cassady's autobiography is *The First Third,* eds. Lawrence Ferlinghetti and Nancy J. Peters, 1981; Cassady's correspondence is in *As Ever: The Collected Correspondence of Allen Ginsberg and Neal Cassady,* 1977, and *Grace Beats Karma: Letters from Prison, 1958–1960.* These collections are surpassed by Dave Moore, ed., *Neal Cassady: Collected Letters, 1944–1967,* which features highly informative notes and an introduction by Carolyn Cassady. The "Great Sex Letter" and the remaining fragment of the "Joan Anderson Letter" are reprinted in Ann Charters, ed., *The Portable Beat Reader,* 1992.

## Bibliographical References

The only biography of Neal Cassady is William Plummer, *The Holy Goof,* 1981; however, Carolyn Cassady's memoir *Off the Road* offers biographical information, too. In Steven Watson, *The Birth of the Beat Generation,* 1995, one finds a short biography; in Gregory Stephenson, *The Daybreak Boys,* one finds a chapter on treatments of Neal Cassady in numerous examples of Beat literature. Oliver Harris reviews the correspondence in "Old War Correspondents: Ginsberg, Kerouac, Cassady, and the Political

Economy of Beat Letters," in *Twentieth-Century Literature* 46.2 (summer 2000): 171–192.

***See also*** Chase, Haldon "Hal"; Kerouac, Jack; Ginsberg, Allen; Anderson, Joan, Letter about; Cassady, Carolyn; Kesey, Ken Elton; Merry Pranksters; Furthur/Further; Denver, Colorado; Drugs

## Censorship

An obstacle for the publication and distribution of Beat books, magazines, and performances, but ultimately a favorable force, as controversy and publicity brought Beat works to public attention. The Beats' frank and frequent references to sex led to efforts to censor Beat poems, plays, and readings, but political statements were also problematic. Although the Beats often prevailed in legal battles and thereby strengthened freedom of expression, the fight against censorship remained a priority for Beats.

The Comstock Law, also known as the Federal Anti-Obscenity Act (1873), was the basis for many efforts to ban the written word because the law made illegal the mailing of obscene materials. Although not regularly enforced now, the Comstock Law remains in effect.

A key breakthrough in struggles against modern censorship was the decision by Justice John M. Woolsey on 6 December 1933 to lift the ban on *Ulysses* (1922) by James Joyce. In his decision, Woolsey found that the book "did not tend to incite sexual impulses or lustful thoughts" but instead noted that Joyce's book was "a powerful commentary on the inner lives of men and women" (in James Joyce, *Ulysses,* xi).

In 1956, when Lawrence Ferlinghetti published *Howl and Other Poems* by Allen Ginsberg, the Beats dramatically entered the national controversy over censorship. Printed in England, the second shipment of *Howl and Other Poems* was not allowed to pass U.S. Customs on 25 March 1957, when Collector of Customs Chester MacPhee declared that the book was obscene. However, when the U.S. attorney in San Francisco declined to proceed against Ginsberg's collection of poems, customs released the 520 seized copies on 29 May 1957.

Lawrence Ferlinghetti and Shig Murao at the censorship trial for *Howl and Other Poems*. (Time Life Pictures/Getty Images)

Nevertheless, the city of San Francisco decided to press charges. Captain William Hanrahan of the San Francisco Police found that *Howl and Other Poems* and another book sold at City Lights Bookstore were inappropriate for juveniles and arrested Ferlinghetti and Shig Murao, for whom the American Civil Liberties Union (ACLU) provided bail and legal counsel. Deputy District Attorney Ralph McIntosh was the prosecutor, but defense attorneys invoked the precedent of *Roth vs. U.S.* (1957), which established that a work that has "redeeming social value" cannot be found obscene. After numerous literary experts testified about the worth of "Howl," Judge Clayton Horn determined on October 3, 1957, that despite objections from witnesses for the prosecution, "Howl" had social value and therefore was not obscene.

The trial received national attention, including a feature article in *Life*. Ginsberg's *Howl and Other Poems*, which might have languished in obscurity, sold widely and became an enduring work of literature.

Despite the success of the defendants in the censorship trial for *Howl and Other Poems,* problems with censorship persisted for the Beats and other artists. In Los Angeles in 1957, Wallace Berman, an Assemblage artist, was convicted of obscenity and fined when a show he installed at Ferus, an art gallery, included artwork that revealed copulation.

At the University of Chicago, Irving Rosenthal became the editor of *Chicago Review* in 1958, and in three consecutive issues, Rosenthal provided a forum for the Beats. In the issue for spring 1958, Ferlinghetti, Ginsberg, Lamantia, McClure, Kerouac, Burroughs, and others were included. The summer 1958 issue took on a Zen theme, including contributions from Alan Watts and Gary Snyder. In the autumn 1958 issue, Rosenthal featured selections from *Naked Lunch* by Burroughs. *Chicago Daily News* writer Jack Mabley wrote a column to object to the writing in *Chicago Review*, prompting university authorities to prevent the publication of another Beat issue, which was already scheduled to include Kerouac's "Old Angel Midnight" and more of *Naked Lunch*. Rather than comply with the censorship that the university intended to impose, Irving Rosenthal and Paul Carroll decided to create a new, independent magazine: *Big Table*. A benefit reading for *Big Table* held in Chicago drew a large and enthusiastic audience, but press coverage in Chicago newspapers and *Time* ignored the turnout and responded negatively to the performers. When *Big Table* was ready to be mailed to ten thousand subscribers in April, the Post Office denied the editors a mailing permit. Within a month, Judge Julius Hoffman ordered that the mailing be executed. *Big Table* ran for five issues and established the openness necessary for Beat writings, but eventually a lack of financial support made the continuation of publication impossible.

In New York City, LeRoi Jones and Diane di Prima published *Floating Bear*, a mimeo magazine that was distributed through the mail to subscribers. When one subscriber was sent his copy of issue nine of *Floating Bear* while he was in jail, the publication was intercepted by a prison censor, who objected, di Prima supposes, to *The System of Dante's Hell* by Jones and "Roosevelt after Inauguration" by William Burroughs. On 18 October 1961, Jones was arrested at his apartment for mailing obscene material. Later that day, di Prima and Stanley Faulkner, who was Jones's attorney, appeared at the courthouse. Before the day was done, the editors were released with no requirement for bail.

On the advice of Faulkner, Jones demanded that a grand jury be convened, and, testifying with eloquence, he cited many examples of well-established works of literature and demonstrated how inclusions in *Floating Bear* were consistent in quality with time-proven literature. In addition, letters from literary experts attested to the literary merit of material in *Floating Bear*. The grand jury refused to refer the case for prosecution.

William Burroughs was a key figure in the censorship controversy, and in 1959 *The Naked Lunch* was published in Paris, France. Publishing and selling Burroughs's novel in the United States, however, involved numerous obstacles.

The first was that Barney Rosset, who planned to make *Naked Lunch* available in the United States, was embroiled in censorship problems involving Henry Miller's *Tropic of Cancer*. Published in France in 1934, *Tropic of Cancer* was not published in the United States until April 1961, and promptly numerous booksellers around the nation faced charges of selling obscene material. Rosset had pledged to defend these booksellers, and legal costs soon were a challenge. Not wanting to overextend himself, Rosset delayed the release of *Naked Lunch* even though he had 10,000 copies ready for sale. Finally, Rosset was victorious in the *Tropic of Cancer* case in Chicago, and when a case in Florida in June 1964 went to the Supreme Court, the outcome was favorable.

With *Tropic of Cancer* in the clear, Rosset shipped *Naked Lunch* to bookstores. By November 1962, sales were good, but censorship became an issue in Boston, where Theodore Mavrikos, a bookseller with various previous arrests on obscenity charges, was arrested for selling *Naked Lunch*. Boston was a challenging location for a trial, but Rosset hired Edward De Grazia, a First Amendment specialist, who managed to establish the trial as an examination of the book, not the bookseller. De Grazia considered bringing Burroughs himself as a witness, but decided to drop that idea when De Grazia recalled the fact that Burroughs had shot and killed his wife in Mexico.

The trial began in Boston Superior Court on January 12, 1965. Despite the testimony of various literary experts on the literary merits of *Naked Lunch*, on 23 March 1965, Judge Eugene A. Hudson accepted the prosecutor's arguments that *Naked Lunch* lacked redeeming social value, appealed to prurient interests, and was patently offensive. The judge ruled that *Naked Lunch* was obscene.

On appeal, the case went to the Massachusetts Supreme Court on 8 October 1965. The decision in the appeal hinged on deliberations of the U.S.

Supreme Court, which on 21 March 1966 ruled that to be obscene, a work had to meet three requirements:

1. The central purpose and theme of the work must be to appeal to the prurient interests of the reader.
2. Judging by contemporary community standards, one must find that the work in question is patently offensive.
3. The work must have no redeeming social value.

Using these standards, Justice William J. Brennan wrote the opinion that reflected the Supreme Court's decision that *The Memoirs of a Woman of Pleasure, or Fanny Hill* (1749) was not obscene. In Massachusetts, knowing the view of the High Court, the Massachusetts Supreme Court ruled on 7 July 1966, that *Naked Lunch* was not obscene.

In 1962 in New York City, Ed Sanders published a mimeo magazine titled *Fuck You: A Magazine of the Arts.* The first issue was produced at the office of the *Catholic Worker,* but Dorothy Day, the founder of the newspaper, disapproved of *Fuck You* and insisted that Sanders and his collaborators leave.

In late 1964, Sanders opened the Peace Eye Bookstore in what was once a kosher butcher shop on the Lower East Side in Manhattan. This location immediately became the secret production site for *Fuck You* and other literary works, including *Bugger: An Anthology of Buttockry, Despair, Poems for Marilyn,* and *Marijuana Newsletter.* New York City police raided the Peace Eye Bookstore in 1966, charging Sanders with purveying obscene materials, but the ACLU successfully defended Sanders.

When the publisher of the Italian translation of Jack Kerouac's *The Subterraneans* faced legal problems in 1963, Kerouac enlisted the help of Grove Press and Barney Rosset, who had published the book in English in 1960. Kerouac, with advice from legal representatives at Grove Press, wrote an open letter to the Italian judge in the case, and Rosset published the letter in the fall 1963 edition of *Evergreen Review.* Kerouac referred to his Catholic boyhood and the responsibility of the person who goes to confession to be completely honest. Kerouac asked the Italian court to allow such completeness, yet conceded that for some readers the publication of uninhibited confession might not be appropriate. The influence of Kerouac's letter cannot be ascertained, but in a letter dated 18 November 1963, Kerouac wrote to Philip Whalen that censorship problems in Italy regarding the translation of *The Subterraneans* were solved.

In 1966 in San Francisco, Jay Thelin and Allen Cohen at the Psychedelic Shop and Robert Muszalski at City Lights Bookshop were arrested on obscenity charges for selling *The Love Book* (1966) by Lenore Kandel. A five-week trial ended in a guilty verdict, but on appeal, the guilty verdict did not stand.

*The Beard* (1967), a play by Michael McClure, was staged at the Actor's Workshop in San Francisco in 1965 and also in Berkeley, but objecting to sexual references, police harassed and arrested performers. Although the ACLU defended the right to produce *The Beard,* problems persisted. Efforts to stage the play at the University of California, Fullerton, spurred objections in newspapers, and a committee from the state senate opened an investigation. Unable to work normally, actors eventually chose not to go on with the play.

In 1990, an amended version of The National Foundation on the Arts and Humanities Act required the Chairperson of the National Endowment for the Arts (NEA) to provide for review of applications for "general standards of decency." Four artists sued, and initially a trial judge ruled in favor of the artists because the decency clause was both unconstitutionally vague and overbroad. This decision was affirmed in the U.S. Court of Appeals for the 9th Circuit, which found that the decency clause was vague and a violation of the First Amendment. Nevertheless, on 25 June 1998, the Supreme Court, in a decision written by Justice Sandra Day O'Connor, determined that the law requiring the NEA to consider "general standards of decency and respect for the diverse beliefs and values of the American public" does not violate the

First Amendment and thereby overturned previous decisions. Because the issue of "decency" has a bearing on Beat writing and art, this decision was a setback for grant support for Beat artists.

In 1988, in Federal Court the ACLU brought suit on behalf of Allen Ginsberg and Pen Club to challenge the Federal Communications Commission (FCC) regulation prohibiting the broadcast of "indecent" language from 6:00 A.M. to midnight. The court ruled in favor of Ginsberg, declaring that programming for the general public could not be reduced to the level of children's programming unless proof could be adduced to show that particular hours of programming affected children. Despite the court's ruling, Senator Jesse Helms introduced a bill that made indecency unacceptable twenty-four hours a day. The bill passed, and President Ronald Reagan signed it into law. Pacifica Radio, which previously broadcast readings of Ginsberg's "Howl" and other literary works, desisted in such broadcasts. Helms's law had a chilling effect not because Pacifica felt it could not win a legal fight, but because a successful legal fight would be prohibitively expensive.

Helms's law did not survive the test of its constitutionality, and in 1992, Congress gave instructions to the FCC to provide hours for programming that might be deemed indecent. Before the rules for hours could be put in effect, the rules were called up for judicial review, but finally on 28 August 1995, regulation of broadcast indecency between 6:00 A.M. and 10:00 P.M. went into effect with the intent to protect children.

The problem that arises in this control of indecency is that no clear distinction is made between literature that includes potentially offensive language and "shock-jock routines" that have no literary significance. With substantial fines looming for violators of the indecency rules, broadcasters who might want to offer literary programming feel the chilling effect of the law.

On 19 September 2002, at the Geraldine R. Dodge Poetry Festival in Waterloo Village in Stanhope, New Jersey, Amiri Baraka, formerly known as LeRoi Jones, read his poem "Somebody Blew Up America." Jewish groups charged that the poem, which poses a question about foreknowledge by Israelis of the terrorist attacks on the World Trade Center on September 11, 2001, is anti-Semitic. Baraka denied charges of anti-Semitism and in response insisted that if Israel has faults one should not shield Israel from examination by raising the issue of anti-Semitism.

As poet laureate of New Jersey, Baraka faced a particular controversy after reading his poem. New Jersey governor James McGreevey called for Baraka's resignation, but Baraka refused. New Jersey law did not provide for the removal of a poet laureate, but McGreevey froze funding for Baraka's $10,000 stipend, and in cooperation with the state legislature eliminated the position of poet laureate.

A debate followed on the issue of censorship, with some insisting that Baraka had been denied free speech. Others replied that Baraka had full freedom to speak but because of his poem could not be the representative of New Jersey.

In January 2003, First Lady Laura Bush cancelled a poetry forum at the White House when poets revealed intentions to speak against the U.S. government's intentions to invade Iraq. A White House spokeswoman said Mrs. Bush respected the free speech of poets, but viewed the forum, which was scheduled for 12 February 2003, as an occasion for poetry, not political protest. Poet Sam Hamill chose not to accept his invitation and called on poets to send him antiwar poems and asked poets in attendance at the forum to protest war. Among the contributors to Hamill's collection was Lawrence Ferlinghetti.

Ferlinghetti finds that the most insidious form of censorship is self-censorship. According to Ferlinghetti, an alarming preoccupation with political correctness stifles expression, and mocking the oft-cited Freedom of Information Act, Ferlinghetti suggests that the nation needs a Freedom of Imagination Act.

Some scholars charge that the estate of Jack Kerouac has imposed a voluntary censorship over the writings of Kerouac, permitting the publication of only selections from his letters and journals. Whereas Kerouac may have insisted on complete honesty, the managers of his unpublished works prefer to use their judgment in timing the release of the full collection of Kerouac's writings

—*William Lawlor*
*Diane De Rooy*

**Bibliographic References**

See Judge Woolsey's statement in James Joyce, *Ulysses*, 1961; the language in Allen Ginsberg, *Howl and Other Poems*, 1956, made the poem controversial; Lawrence Ferlinghetti, "Horn on Howl," in *The Portable Beat Reader*, ed. Ann Charters, 1992, explains the history of the trial; compare "Big Day for Bards at Bay: Trial over *Howl and Other Poems*," *Life* 9 September 1957: 105–108; Rebecca Solnit, "Heretical Constellations: Notes on California, 1946–1961," in *Beat Culture and the New America 1950–1965*, ed. Lisa Phillips, 1995, refers to Wallace Berman's problem with censorship in Los Angeles; Dennis McNally, *Desolate Angel*, 1979, reviews the details of the case of *The Chicago Review* and *Big Table*; Ted Morgan, *Literary Outlaw*, 1988, reviews the details of the censorship trial of *Naked Lunch; The Floating Bear*, ed. Diane di Prima and LeRoi Jones, 1973, is a bound collection of all the issues of *The Floating Bear*, and di Prima's introduction reviews this censorship incident; Jack Kerouac, *Selected Letters 1957–1969*, ed. Ann Charters, 1999, includes Kerouac's reference to the end of censorship problems for the Italian version of *The Subterraneans*.

***See also*** Ginsberg, Allen; Burroughs, William Seward; Berman, Wallace; Ferlinghetti, Lawrence; Kerouac, Jack; Little Magazines; Anarchy, Christian

Sam and Ann Charters have written extensively about Beat literature and music. (Christopher Felver/Corbis)

*Kerouac*, 1995; and two volumes of *Jack Kerouac: Selected Letters*, 1995 and 1999.

***See also*** Scholarship and Critical Appreciation, A Survey of

# Charters, Ann (1936–)

Prolific biographer, bibliographer, editor, photographer, and scholar, especially on Jack Kerouac, but also on the Beats in general, modern and contemporary literature, and literature in general.

**Bibliographic References**

*Kerouac*, 1973, was reprinted in 1987; *The Beats: Literary Bohemians in Postwar America*, 1983, is a two-volume study of major figures in the Beat Generation. Her many other works include *The Portable Beat Reader*, 1992; *The Portable Jack*

# Charters, Sam (1929–)

Ethnomusicologist, novelist, blues and jazz historian, poet and translator. Charters's *Some Poems, Poets: Studies in Underground Poetry Since 1945*, 1971, is a groundbreaking work in the study of the Beats.

**Bibliographic References**

In addition to a dozen books of poetry and various novels, Samuel Charters has written *The Roots of the Blues*, 1980; *Jazz: New Orleans, 1885–1963*, 1963; and *The Bluesmen*, 1967.

## Chase, Haldon "Hal" (1923–)

Anthropologist who was part of the first Beat circle in New York City, 1944–1945. Born around 1923 in Colorado, Chase was a graduate student in anthropology at Columbia University when he met Joan Vollmer and shared her apartments (with, at various times, Edie Parker, Jack Kerouac, John Kingsland, William Burroughs, and Allen Ginsberg) at 421 W. 118th St. (1943–1944) and at 419 W. 115th St. (1945–1946) in New York.

Chase's friendship with fellow Coloradoan Frank Jeffries played a key role in the 1947 arrival in New York of their Denver friend Neal Cassady (1926–1968), who became Kerouac's primary muse and went on to join Ken Kesey's psychedelic adventures in California in the mid-1960s. (Kerouac fictionalized Chase in *On the Road* as "Chad King.") Chase later drifted apart from the Beats, of whose hard-partying lifestyle he did not approve. He conducted important archaeological research at Trinidad, Colorado, in 1949, and in 1951, when Burroughs and Vollmer were living in Mexico City, Chase was studying the Zapotecan language at Mexico City College. He appears in fictional form as "Winston Moor" in Burroughs's *Queer*. Chase was distinctly unimpressed with Burroughs's "cowboy act," and after Vollmer's death in 1951, he distanced himself from Burroughs. He returned to

Hal Chase, Jack Kerouac, Allen Ginsberg, and William Burroughs (left to right) walk together near Columbia University in Manhattan in 1944. (Allen Ginsberg/Corbis)

the United States in 1956 and eventually retired to a hermit's existence in rural California.

—James Grauerholz

## Bibliographical Sources

For background information, see Ted Morgan, *Literary Outlaw: The Life and Times of William S. Burroughs*, 1988, and Bill Morgan, *The Beat Generation in New York: A Walking Tour of Jack Kerouac's City*, 1997. Howard Campbell, "Beat Mexico: Bohemia, Anthropology, and 'the Other'" in *Critique of Anthropology*, 23. 2 (June 2003) offers additional detail.

***See also*** Mexico City; Kerouac, Jack

## Cherry Valley, New York

Cherry Valley is a small town near the center of New York state, at the edge of the Mohawk Valley, on the original road to the West; it was first settled in 1740. Sixteen miles from the larger Cooperstown, Cherry Valley is surrounded mainly by dairy farms and hills rising some two thousand feet.

In 1968, Allen Ginsberg (through his nonprofit foundation Committee on Poetry [C.O.P.], Inc.) purchased an old farm house and seventy acres ("East Hill Farm") five miles from town. He intended the farm to serve as a retreat from urban woes for fellow poets and friends. For several years, Ginsberg (when not on reading tours to support the farm) and others (including Peter and Julius Orlovsky and Gordon Ball) lived and farmed there; numerous guests (including Corso, Creeley, Huncke, Ferlinghetti, Bremser, Brenda Frazer, Gary Snyder, Charles Plymell, Andy Clausen, John Giorno, and Barry Miles) came for varying spells.

While at the farm, Ginsberg composed much of his music for William Blake's *Songs of Innocence and of Experience*, as well as numerous poems, including "In a Moonlit Hermit's Cabin," "Death on All Fronts," "Ecologue," and "Returning to the Country for a Brief Visit." Orlovsky wrote "Don't Bite Please" and such songs as "Skip to My Farm Sweet Worm Manure," "All around the Garden," and "Feeding Them Rassberries to Grow." Bremser completed several poems there; Miles began his bi-

ography of Ginsberg, and Ball shot his movie *Farm Diary* on East Hill. Reminiscences of Cherry Valley are found in Plymell's *Hand on the Doorknob: A Charles Plymell Reader* and Miles's *In the Sixties*. Frazer is writing a memoir of her Cherry Valley years, and Ball has recently completed his *East Hill Farm: Seasons with Allen Ginsberg*.

Ultimately the farm's remoteness (no electricity) and typically harsh winters proved too much for continuous residence. The site (today referred to as "The Committee") is now used for occasional mild weather retreats by C.O.P. Ginsberg's presence brought a number of visitors to the area, some of whom took up residence in Cherry Valley: poet Charles Plymell and writer Carl Waldman, among others, live there today. Latter-day arts events have included an East Hill memorial service for Bremser in 1998, and two festivals, in 1998 and 2002, centering on Ginsberg and the Beats. Plymell's Cherry Valley Editions (started in 1974) has featured Huncke, Janine Pommy Vega, Burroughs, Ginsberg, and others, and continues publishing today.

—Gordon Ball

## Bibliographical References

Michael Schumacher on page 522 of *Dharma Lion*, 1992, describes the farm in Cherry Valley; Ann Charters includes several large color photographs of the farm in Cherry Valley on pages 113–115 in *Beats and Company*, 1986.

***See also*** Ginsberg, Allen; Bremser, Bonnie; Bremser, Ray

## China, Beats in

Acceptance of the Beat Generation in mainland China has developed slowly since the 1950s.

In the early 1950s, the *Reference News* (an official daily newspaper published by Xinhua News Agency, which was affiliated with the government's propaganda department) used the Chinese phrase "kua diao yi dai" to describe the Beats. However, "kua diao" is a derogatory term suggesting "good for nothing, decadent, rotten, degenerate, depraved, corrupted"; if personalized, the term is associated with English words such as "gangster, swindler, hustler, criminal." The Beat Generation did not conform to communist values, in particular in the Cold War period, when China and the United States were hostile to each other, and therefore the Beats were demonized in China. Regrettably this language is still applied to the Beats today in China. In the 1950s, several articles in officially controlled mass media rejected and denounced the Beats.

The translation of Beat writings did not appear until 1962 when the first Chinese abridged version of *On the Road* was published as part of the Grey Cover Series together with J. D. Salinger's *The Catcher in the Rye*. These works were seen as examples of the vicious nature of Western capitalism and were not for sale. Such works could only be read by selected communist officials. However, later in the cultural revolution of the early 1960s to middle 1970s, the books were smuggled, read, and secretly distributed among some of the Red Guards and young intellectuals who were sent to the countryside by Mao to be re-educated by peasants. These young readers saw in *On the Road* something thrilling, entirely new, and encouraging. The readers identified with the American Beats, who felt the pressure of McCarthyism in the dull years of Eisenhower. The readers savored individuality, daring spiritual adventure, and bohemian freedom because these pleasures were absent in the era of Mao. *On the Road*, together with other Grey Cover Series Western literary books, inspired Chinese young people to seek a new life. The new spirit was revealed in the first generation of the Chinese *New Poetry Wave* or *Underground Poetry* during the Cultural Revolution; subsequently, the spirit showed in the *School of Obscurity* represented by Baidao, a renowned poet who now resides in the United States. In later years, the Beat spirit was revealed in poetry publications such as *Manghan* and *Feifei*.

Thanks to Deng Xiaoping's reforms and his openness to the world outside China, especially the normalization of Sino-America relations, the study and translation of Western literature and art began to boom, resulting in what was known as an "emancipation of ideology" that stimulated "cultural

zest." Several Chinese versions of "Howl" by Allen Ginsberg came out around 1984; excerpts of the Chinese version *On The Road* were included in a then widely read volume *An Anthology of Western Modernism;* another shortened Chinese version of *On the Road* was published in 1990. Despite mistranslation, average readers for the first time had access to Beat writings.

Allen Ginsberg's trip to China in 1984 as a member of a delegation of American writers, which included Gary Snyder and others, further aroused the enthusiasm for the Beats in China. During a month-long stay, Ginsberg gave lectures and readings in Beijing and Shanghai; in Baoding Ginsberg composed poems that were published in *White Shroud* (1986), including "I Love Old Whitman So," "Written in My Dream by W. C. Williams," "One Morning I Took a Walk in China," and "Reading Bai Juiyi."

Chinese scholars such as Zao Yifan of the Chinese Academy of Social Sciences and Wen Chu-an of Sichuan University began to examine the Beats and their writings with objective and reasonable academic arguments that contrasted with official criticism, exploring the social and literary value of the Beats, foreseeing the upcoming Chinese academic re-evaluation of the Beats in following years.

Influences upon Chinese literature in this period can be seen in *Pizi Literature* as represented by Wang Shuo, who is seen by Western critics as "China's Kerouac," and a host of young writers, poets, artists, and musicians known as the Chinese Vanguard School. In the late 1980s, one could see the rise of a Chinese subculture with nonofficial writing, jazz, and rock-and-roll music that displayed the affinities and differences between the American Beats and their Chinese followers.

China's steady economic progress, its participation in the international community, and its loosened political control led to a free climate for the introduction and translation of Beat literature. Translations of Jack Kerouac's *On the Road*, Allen Ginsberg's *Kaddish and Other Poems*, and John Tytell's *Naked Angels* appeared in the 1990s. Ou Hong wrote a doctoral dissertation entitled *Gary Snyder and Chinese Culture* in English.

In the twenty-first century in China, one sees the spirit of the Beats in "linglei," a term connected to young female writers born in the 1970s such as Wei Hui, the author of the novel *Shanghai Baby*, and Mianmian, who wrote the novel *Sugar*. These writers declared that they were indebted to the Beats for characteristics of their writing: first-person narration and love stories involving urban, marginalized individuals or free professionals. The characters were sensitive, lonely, and desperately burning with emotion. The most striking feature was the combination of sex with psychological description and the lifestyle the authors associated with the early Beats of the 1950s, including drug use. Positively, such writing broke through the literary norm; perhaps the authors failed to get into the core of the Beat vision—the spiritual quest rather than materialistic comfort and sensual indulgence.

In general, interest in Beat writings in China is growing among scholars and students, whose articles and dissertations about the Beats are more numerous than before. Scholars analyze not only Kerouac and Ginsberg but also Burroughs, Corso, and even later Beats. The influence of the Beats now affects social life. For instance, "bohemian life" or the "rucksack revolution" are now in China very current terms among youngsters. The striking feature now is the open re-evaluation of the Beats in China, overthrowing to some extent the bad name "kua diao."

—*Wen Chu-an*

### Bibliographical References

One can review Allen Ginsberg's trip to China in Michael Schumacher, *Dharma Lion*, 1992: 681–684; see also Harrison E. Salisbury, "On the Literary Road: American Writers in China," *New York Times Book Review* 20 Jan 1985: 3–4.

*See also* Snyder, Gary; Ginsberg, Allen; Travel: The Beats as Globetrotters

## Clausen, Andy (1943–)

Poet, teacher, and editor. Clausen was born in Belgium during World War II and came as a child to the United States, where he grew up in Oakland, California. Influenced by Jack Kerouac, Allen Ginsberg, and Gregory Corso, he often writes about his connection to Beat authors. Clausen has taught creative writing at Naropa Institute and in the New York City public schools.

—*William Lawlor*

### Principal Works

Clausen's poetry includes *Extreme Unction*, 1974; *Austin, Texas, Austin, Texas*, 1981; *Without Doubt*, 1991; *Trek to the Top of the World*, 1996; *Fortieth Century Man: Selected Verse, 1966–1996*, 1997. Clausen is editor, with Allen Ginsberg and Eliot Katz, of *Poems for the Nation: A Collection of Contemporary Political Poems*, 1999. He and Jack Micheline perform on a video entitled *Recent Readings/NY, Volume 14: Micheline-Clausen*, 1996.

### Bibliographic Reference

An entry on Clausen appears in Ann Charters, ed., *The Beats: Literary Bohemians in Postwar America*, 1983.

## Cold War

An international struggle following World War II between the United States and its allies and the Soviet Union and allied communist nations. The term "Cold War," coined in a speech delivered on 16 April 1947 by financier Bernard Baruch at the South Carolina state legislature and repeated by Baruch in his address to the Senate's Special Committee Investigating the National Defense Program on 24 October 1947, suggests strategic moves and political tensions that fall short of the heat of actual battle; however, such a suggestion is inaccurate because the Cold War became hot in various locations, including Asia, Africa, Southeast Asia, and Central America, as struggling nations became surrogates for world powers in international conflicts. Beat writers, who were disturbed by irrational fears of communism, an ominous arms race, a misguided use of resources, and waves of propaganda, bemoaned the leaders and the policies that made the Cold War the chief factor in world history in the second half of the twentieth century.

When World War II ended, the Soviet Union, conscious of the grievous losses it had suffered because of Nazi attacks, sought to strengthen defenses against any future attack from the West by dominating Eastern Europe. The United States favored self-determination for Eastern European nations and feared the expansion of communism into Western Europe, charging that the Soviets had erected an "Iron Curtain"—a phrase coined by Winston Churchill in a speech delivered at Westminster College in Fulton, Missouri, on 5 March 1946.

Tensions developed over the political alignment of Greece, Turkey, and Germany. In 1947, the Marshall Plan assisted economic recovery in Western Europe, including West Germany, but communist forces took power in Czechoslovakia, and Soviet authorities closed off Western access to Berlin. In response, the West supplied West Berlin via air freight. In 1949, the North Atlantic Treaty Organization (NATO) was formed in opposition to a mounting Soviet threat in Eastern Europe.

With the establishment of communist authority in China under Mao Tse-Tung in 1949, Asia became another theater for the Cold War, with the Korean War (1950–1953) a key boiling point. With Chinese troops bolstering the North Koreans, the United States could not achieve a clear victory, and Americans as a whole developed a dim view of all communist governments.

The United States pursued a policy of containment, whereby Soviet efforts to expand communism would meet resistance. George Kennan, a United States diplomat, coined the term "containment" in his "Long Telegram" sent from Moscow on 22 February 1946; Dean Acheson, secretary of state (1949–1953), advocated the policy, insisting on enhancement of NATO's strength. John Foster Dulles, who succeeded Acheson as secretary of state (1953–1960), carried the policy forward with a determination to provide economic and military support to any nation facing a communist threat. To organize the opposition to communism, Dulles cultivated new alliances such as the Southeast Asian Treaty Organization and the Central Treaty Organization.

Under Nikita Khrushchev, the Soviets expanded aid to nations such as Ghana, Egypt, India, and Indonesia and encouraged communist uprisings wherever possible. In Guatemala and Cuba, where communists were already in power, the Soviets extended friendship and economic support. In Germany, the Soviets renewed efforts to drive Western influence from Berlin. These Cold War tensions culminated in the Berlin Crisis of 1961 and the Cuban Missile Crisis of 1962.

With the Nuclear Test Ban Treaty of 1963, the conversion of the Cold War into a nuclear disaster seemed less likely. Despite this progress, conflicts between communist and Western spheres continued many years, as shown in Vietnam, Afghanistan, and Nicaragua. Negotiations between East and West improved through détente, and the Strategic Arms Limitation Talks led to positive agreements in 1972 and 1974. Under Ronald Reagan, however, the United States announced intentions to develop the Strategic Defense Initiative, also known as Star Wars, whereby the United States would be impervious to nuclear attack.

In 1985, Mikhail Gorbachev assumed leadership in the USSR and pursued improved relations with the West. In 1989, the Cold War apparently ended with the dismantling of the Berlin Wall and the dissolution of the Soviet Union in 1990.

The Beats felt disconnected and disgruntled about mainstream political views. These writers had inherited a modernist sensibility that denied them the comfort of empire, religion, or a sense of socially valuable progress. They seemed to strike an immediate chord in this generation, leading Paul Goodman in *Growing Up Absurd* to describe them as a small group with large influence made possible in the years following World War II and the Korean War; to Goodman, the Beats were on the margins of society and did not have enthusiasm for society's factories, markets, and social fabric (170). Most of the writers who came to be associated with this phenomenon were engaged with political issues, but indirectly, and often in a confusing and contradictory fashion; one could more easily describe what the Beats were against than what they were for. Old Bull Lee in Jack Kerouac's *On the Road,* for example, detests the political system in Washington and recalls a bygone age when one could get morphine in a local drugstore without a doctor's written consent (144). In "America," which appears in *Howl and Other Poems*, Ginsberg, too, is sentimental about what America has lost, including Wobblies, communists, and Trotskyites (39–43). This antiauthoritarianism, indeed this antipolitics, was appropriated and assimilated into struggles in the late '60s against the increasingly nefarious effects of Cold War policies and a growing sense that America had lost its way. Denise Levertov writes in Part I of "To Stay Alive" that she is in favor of revolution, even an unplanned revolution, because the alternative is the ending of life (137). In "April Fool Birthday Poem for Grandpa," which is included in *Pieces of a Song* (1990), Diane di Prima also perceives a rising tide of social change (69). Despite these references to revolution, there is no blueprint, and certainly no single "Beat" politic; in fact, many of those most frequently associated with the Beat Generation were neither comfortable with the Beat label, nor in agreement about prevailing literary or social issues. In 1958, Robert Brustein published "The Cult of Unthink" (now reprinted in Ann Charters, *Beat Down to Your Soul*) in which he accused William Burroughs, Jack Kerouac, Michael McClure, Michael Rumaker, and other Beats of creating a hero who is disconnected from culture, society, and even himself (50).

Nevertheless, against a backdrop of mainstream politics and government policies aimed at promoting Cold War conformity, the Beat Generation's rebellious figures proposed an array of spontaneous carnivalesque performances of topsy-turvydom, inspiring road trips of the mind and the body, word viruses, howls of self-expression, Buddhist and Zen reflection, to resist what Diane di Prima in "Rant," which is included in *Pieces of a Song* (1990), saw as a war against the creative mind (159–160).

There is also a resistance in the Beat corpus to harnessing the power of science or mathematics to inhuman ends such as destruction and firepower. References to the space race, to Einstein's theories, and to the bomb, which are scattered throughout the Beat writing, relate to issues of progress, ultimate annihilation, the uses of technology, and the the buildup of weapons, which are all by-words of the Cold War mentality. Resistance to this kind of thinking took a range of forms, including, most notoriously, Gregory Corso's suggestion that we embrace the bomb, an idea recorded in his 1958 poem "Bomb," a poem included in *The Happy Birthday of Death* (1960) in which Corso speaks of courting and seducing the bomb as if it were a woman (foldout without pagination).

Most of the overtly political statements in Beat writing tend to verge on the Dadaist, the surrealist, the clowning of the disenfranchised. In 1957, before the publication of either "Howl" or *On the Road*, Kenneth Rexroth in *New World Writing* (included in *Protest: The Beat Generation and the Angry Young Men*) wrote about Beat Generation disconnection from society and the joy of hearing audiences applaud and approve of Allen Ginsberg (337), who in *Journals Early Fifties Early Sixties* showed himself to be a revolutionary poet (153–154) by mocking the Republican Convention, Postmaster General Summerfield, President Eisenhower, and *Newsweek*.

This Beat Generation's corpus of work and performances, which eventually gave impetus to student revolt, the New Left, and a libertarian counterculture, was at the outset a mostly literary phenomenon, with precursors among the British, Irish, French, or Americans who were raucous, rebellious and liberated on their own terms. Auden, Artaud, Blake, Baudelaire, Byron, Céline, Cummings, Dostoyevsky, Eliot, Genet, Lawrence, Mallarmé, Pound, Rimbaud, Rexroth, Sade, Verlaine, Whitman, Williams, and Wolfe were important inspirations and fellow travelers to the Beat writers, who had far-ranging literary interests and remarkable literary knowledge. The Beats also had a range of artistic friends and fellow travelers in their resistance to the Cold War sterile thinking, including Joan Baez, Bob Dylan, Mitchell Goodman, Denise Levertov, Federico García Lorca, Norman Mailer, and Henry Miller, who in their own ways celebrated the sexuality, deviance, rebellion, and openendedness that are evident in the Beat corpus. The Beats in turn inspired and were inspired by a host of social thinkers who joined them in various forms of rebellion against the Cold War ethos, which at times brought them into contact with such icons as

Noam Chomsky, Abbie Hoffman, Herbert Marcuse, Wilhelm Reich, Jerry Rubin, and Howard Zinn.

The transition toward more political engagement among Beat writers and those associated with them took hold with the U.S. involvement in Vietnam, which began when the communist leader of the Viet Minh, Ho Chi Minh, proclaimed Vietnam independent of France in 1945 and proceeded in earnest when France was defeated by the Viet Minh in 1954. President Eisenhower feared that free elections in Vietnam, scheduled to be held in 1956, would result in a landslide victory for Ho Chi Minh over Ngo Dinh Diem, in the newly established independent South Vietnam, and pledged his support for Diem in the Civil War that followed. Lawrence Ferlinghetti responded with a little booklet published in 1958 called *Tentative Description of a Dinner Given to Promote the Impeachment of President Eisenhower* (included in *The Beat Scene*), which ends with the president's resignation after a host of realizations, including the determination that the Voice of America failed to listen to the rest of the world and in particular that the president turned a deaf ear to Third World protests against worldwide pollution (135).

In a letter to Peter Orlovsky from Paris in 1958 Allen Ginsberg declared the Cold War over, with a new "love generation" to take over in its place. In 1963, at a conference at the University of British Columbia, he reiterated the same idea, suggesting that all we have to do is "love one another." And Frank Barron watched Ginsberg try to call Russian leader Nikita Khrushchev on the telephone from a Boston apartment in 1960 to "get the love flowing on the electric Bell-Telephone network." Ginsberg never reached Khrushchev that evening, but according to Michael Schumacher in *Dharma Lion*, Ginsberg did end up having a lengthy conversation with Jack Kerouac (345–346). In his travels, Ginsberg managed to connect with, and generally raise the ire of, government leaders, and his work records encounters with officials in the Eastern Bloc, Europe, Cuba, Latin America, and, of course, the United States.

—*Robert F. Barsky*

**Bibliographical References**

See James Campbell, *This Is the Beat Generation*, 1999; Ann Charters, ed., Beat *Down to Your Soul*, 2001; Gregory Corso, *The Happy Birthday of Death*, 1960; Gene Feldman and Max Gartenberg, eds., *Protest: The Beat Generation and the Angry Young Men*, 1959; Diane di Prima, *Pieces of a Song*, 1990; Denise Levertov, *Poems 1968–1972*, 1987; Allen Ginsberg, *Journals Early Fifties Early Sixties*, ed. Gordon Ball, 1977; Paul Goodman, *Growing Up Absurd: Problems of Youth in the Organized System*, 1960; Jack Kerouac, *On the Road*, 2000; Brenda Knight, ed., *Women of the Beat Generation*, 1998; Lawrence Lipton, *The Holy Barbarians*, 1959; Dennis McNally, *Desolate Angel: Jack Kerouac, the Beat Generation and America*, 1979; Michael Schumacher, *Dharma Lion: A Critical Biography of Allen Ginsberg*, 1992; Elias Wilentz, ed., *The Beat Scene*, 1960.

*See also* Red Scare; Communism and the Workers Movement; Atomic Era

## Coleman, Ornette (1930–)

Beginning on alto saxophone and switching to tenor at age sixteen, Coleman spent several years moving between New Orleans, Los Angeles, and his hometown of Fort Worth, Texas, playing for rhythm and blues bands. Settling in Los Angeles in the late 50s, he worked as an elevator operator and studied music theory, developing a revolutionary approach to harmonics that drew jazz beyond the experimental chord patterns and improvisation of bebop. In 1959, he attended the School of Jazz in Lennox, Massachusetts, and released his debut album, *Something Else*, which ushered in the era of free jazz, a challenging and, to many, an obscure take on composition that influenced later works of Beat poets such as Ted Joans.

—*David Arnold*

**Bibliographical References**

Peter Niklas Wilson, *Ornette Coleman: His Life and Music*, trans. Robert Dobbin, 1999; Allen Ginsberg, *Spontaneous Mind: Selected Interviews 1958–1996*, ed. David Carter, 2001.

*See also* Music

## Coltrane, John (1926–1967)

Born in Hamlet, North Carolina, Coltrane experimented with several instruments before settling on tenor saxophone. After moving to Philadelphia he was inducted into the navy in 1945 and played alto saxophone with the navy band. Throughout the late 40s he played with Dizzy Gillespie's band and returned to Philadelphia in 1950 to study music at Granoff Studios and the Ornstein School of Music. He played regularly around New York City during the 50s with musicians such as Miles Davis and Thelonious Monk. Associated with bebop, the improvisational jazz tradition that inspired Jack Kerouac and Allen Ginsberg, Coltrane sought to extend the range of the saxophone, blowing at times almost savagely and reeling off strings of notes that some critics found pointless and others mesmerizing.

—*David Arnold*

### Bibliographical References

Bill Cole, *John Coltrane,* 1976; Allen Ginsberg, *Spontaneous Mind: Selected Interviews 1958–1996,* ed. David Carter, 2001.

*See also* Music

## Communism and the Workers' Movement

A political system conceived by Karl Marx and Friederich Engels, who authored *The Communist Manifesto* (1848), and applied by V. I. Lenin and Leon Trotsky, who spearheaded the Bolshevik Revolution (1917) that made Russia a communist state. With ideals such as a harmonious, classless society offering rights and benefits for workers, communism—especially as manifested by the Workers Party in the United States—appealed to some Beats; however, as totalitarianism and violations of human rights marked the communist governments in Russia, Eastern Europe, China, Cuba, and other nations, the Beats doubted and resisted communism as much as any other abusive governmental authority.

According to *The Communist Manifesto*, society faces a struggle between capitalistic employers (the bourgeoisie) and workers (the proletariat). Through revolution, the workers overcome the capitalistic employers and establish an egalitarian system.

In the struggle to establish a new order following the Russian Revolution, the Bolsheviks contended with the Mensheviks. Mensheviks were willing to accept transitional phases in a movement toward communism, but Bolsheviks, under Lenin and Trotsky, sought immediate rule by workers and peasants. The Bolsheviks prevailed and established a strict system to guarantee that a world revolution would proceed. Under Lenin, Trotsky became commisar of war (1918–1925) and organized the Red Army. The Bolsheviks collectivized agriculture and industry, but human rights were not preserved.

With the death of Lenin in 1924, Stalin came to power, and Trotsky, Stalin's opponent, lost sway and eventually went into exile. Stalin's rule, marked by brutal tactics against Bolsheviks, the Red Army, and the general citizenry, endured until Stalin's death in 1953.

In exile, Trotsky wrote many works, including *The Revolution Betrayed* (1937). Viewed as a threat to Stalin's rule, Trotsky was assassinated in Mexico in 1940.

In 1923 in the United States, communism surfaced as the Workers (Communist) Party led by Charles E. Ruthenberg. Communism in the United States was disunified, with socialists, unionists, and Marxists struggling to establish direction. In 1929, the party was renamed the Communist Party USA (CPUSA), and under Earl Browder's leadership, party membership grew tenfold and focused on opposition to Nazis and fascists. In 1939, the party had 75,000 members and many other supporters in socalled front organizations. Browder sought to make the party a uniquely American organization despite efforts by Communist International (Comintern) to exert influence. The Cold War, McCarthyism, and the House Un-American Activities Committee made affiliation with communism difficult, and members of the communist movement in the United States either disassociated themselves from the party or went underground.

The Beat Generation had some connections to the Communist movement in the United States; in fact, newspaper columnist Herb Caen coined the term "beatnik" to associate the Beats with communism by applying the suffix "nik" to "beat," creating a verbal parallel to *Sputnik*, the Soviet satellite launched in 1957.

Allen Ginsberg's mother was a Russian émigré and was affiliated with the Communist Party in the United States. In "America," a poem included in *Howl and Other Poems* (1956), Ginsberg refers to the party meetings he attended with his mother and describes party members as warm, friendly people (42). Drawing ideas and ideals from such people, Ginsberg intended to become a labor lawyer. Ginsberg also refers to Trotskyites in "America" (39), revealing nostalgia for communist goals prior to Stalin and noting the vast proportions of Trotsky's legacy. In "Howl," Ginsberg refers to the distribution of communist brochures at Union Square in New York City (13).

Gary Snyder was involved in the union movements for loggers in Washington and was later refused employment with the U.S. Forest Service because of perceived communist associations. Disgusted by such blacklisting, Snyder eventually left the United States for Japan.

Despite previous connections to communism, Ginsberg clashed with communist authorities when he traveled to various communist nations. In Cuba in 1965, Ginsberg objected to the failure of the government to protect the rights of homosexuals. Driven from Cuba, Ginsberg won popular support in Czechoslovakia and was named King of May in 1965. Nevertheless, communist authorities seized his notebook, and, viewing Ginsberg as a dangerous agitator, the authorities expelled him from the country.

In 1982, during a visit to Nicaragua, Ginsberg sought to avoid the controversies of 1965 and in a meeting with Daniel Ortega expressed concerns that both communists and capitalists might exploit Ginsberg's visit for the purposes of propaganda. Ginsberg questioned freedom of the press in Nicaragua because a newspaper opposed to the government had been silenced. Learning that this newspaper was an arm of the U.S. Central Intelligence Agency, Ginsberg subsequently accepted the actions against the paper. Joining with Yevgeny Yev-

tushenko and Ernesto Cardenal, who were in Nicaragua as part of an international poetry meeting, Ginsberg contributed to "Declaration of Three" (1982), which supported the Nicaraguan government and questioned the tactics of the United States in opposition to the Sandinistas.

In 1984, Ginsberg visited China as part of a special visit for a group of American writers, including Gary Snyder, Toni Morrison, and William Least Heat Moon. Ginsberg extended his visit by arranging to teach, and through many conversations he learned about the hardships of the Cultural Revolution and restrictions on sexual freedom in the People's Republic. He questioned such limitations on freedom and found that communist China had two levels of freedom, the first in the public sector, where expression was limited, and the second in the home, where personal views might be shared with confidence.

Lawrence Ferlinghetti was receptive to communism as an alternative to capitalism but refused to be blind to the faults of communism. In January 1959, Ferlinghetti and Ginsberg, at the invitation of the communist party in Chile, attended a writers conference at the University of Concepción and appreciated presentations about communism. Ferlinghetti visited Cuba in December 1960 and found that the redistribution of wealth was an improvement of Cuban society, an improvement not in evidence in other Caribbean nations. In his journal, Ferlinghetti describes the beauty and peacefulness in Havana and in Cuba as a whole. In 1967, Ferlinghetti visited Germany, where he planned to read with Russian poet Andrei Voznesenski at a colloquium. The Berlin Wall depressed Ferlinghetti, and life in the eastern sector seemed devoid of zest and spirit. Voznesenski facilitated a visit to the Soviet Union, and after a brief visit to Moscow, Ferlinghetti began a journey on the Trans-Siberian Railway, a journey that fell far short of his expectations and ultimately necessitated his return to the United States so that he could recover from pneumonia. In 1984, in Nicaragua, Ferlinghetti tried to be open to the Sandinistas, but was concerned about communist leaders who dressed elegantly, had servants, and lived in relative luxury. Nevertheless, he participated in an international poetry gathering and enjoyed contact with Ernesto Cardenal and Daniel Ortega. Back in the United States, Ferlinghetti compiled an account of this visit to Nicaragua and published it through City Lights under the title *Seven Days in Nicaragua Libre* (1984). Ferlinghetti made a second visit to Nicaragua with his son in 1989 and reaffirmed his positive view of the Sandinista regime.

In 1960, LeRoi Jones visited Castro's Cuba, and artists there challenged Jones to make his art a vehicle for political activism. Subsequently, Jones disconnected himself from the Beats and pursued black nationalism, but around 1974, LeRoi Jones/Amiri Baraka began to feel that the movement for black nationalism was flawed. He sought a new design for art, and, returning to ideas first suggested to him in Cuba, he advocated through his art the destruction of the capitalist system and the development of a socialist system. He expressed his preference for socialism in the poetry collection *Hard Facts* (1975) and in the play *What Was the Relationship of the Lone Ranger and the Means of Production?* (1978). *Daggers and Javelins* (1984), a collection of essays, also advocated Marxism.

Of all the Beat writers, Jack Kerouac had the least taste for communism. He disassociated himself from the protests and radicalism in which some Beats participated, distrusting challenges to the nation he loved. He declared that his family had always voted for the Republican Party.

—*James E. Lawlor*

## Bibliographical References

For a review of events related to the rise of communism in Russia, see Robert Service, *A History of Twentieth-Century Russia,* 1998; compare John Paxton, ed., *Encyclopedia of Russian History,* 1993; for information on the Communist Party in the United States, see F. M. Ottanelli, *The Communist Party of the United States from the Depression to World War II,* 1991, and J. E. Haynes and H. Klehr, *The American Communist Movement,* 1992; Barry Silesky, *Ferlinghetti: The Artist in His Time,* 1990, covers the details of Ferlinghetti's visits to communist countries; Michael Schumacher, *Dharma Lion,* 1992, offers the details of Ginsberg's visits to communist nations; for information on the connection of LeRoi Jones/Amiri Baraka to communism, see William J. Harris, ed., *The LeRoi Jones/Amiri Baraka Reader,* 1991.

*See also* Ginsberg, Allen; Ferlinghetti, Lawrence; Baraka, Amiri

# Confession

Confessional literature is raw, highly personal, and emotional. It often takes on taboo subject matter, such as mental illness, suicide, homosexuality, and drug use. As the label suggests, confessional poetry gives the reader a sense of knowing intimate details about the writer. Brutal honesty and frankness, as well as intimacy, are inherent in the genre.

The writer of the confessional poem often feels a sense of release, having shared intimate secrets with a willing and sympathetic audience. Like a sinner confessing to a priest, the poet feels a sense of weight being lifted, and the reader can help to carry that weight simply by understanding, by responding to the poem in a positive way. Under the right circumstances, the reader may even feel that the poet speaks for him or her in some way. Confessional poetry can, then, provide emotional cleansing and release for both the writer and the reader.

In the extended narrative of Part II of "Kaddish," which is published in *Collected Poems: 1947–1980* (1984), Allen Ginsberg describes his journey with his mentally disturbed mother to find a rest home in New Jersey. Only twelve years old, Allen must assist his mother despite her delusions and irrational fears. Allen succeeds in getting his mother into the rest home, and he returns to the family's residence. This episode is intensified when Naomi goes mad in the middle of the night and young Allen must witness Louis Ginsberg, Allen's father, who receives a frightening phone call at two in the morning and must set out to take care of Naomi and bring her to a mental hospital.

Ginsberg also confesses in Part II of "Kaddish" the horrible moments of his mother's illness when her excretory functions rage out of control and she vomits blood into the toilet. He recalls her dreamy recollection of an afternoon spent with God, whom she sees as a helpless and lonely figure. Ginsberg even confesses that his mother's behavior is at times grossly erotic, making him contemplate an incestuous union.

In Part IV of "Kaddish," Ginsberg addresses his dead mother, recalling her agony and unfolding the agony he experienced in response to his mother's illness. In particular, Ginsberg focuses on his mother's eyes as he lists horrors and a few moments of tender pleasure. At the end of this reading, the reader's emotions are drained.

Two other well-known Beat writers who fall under the category of confessional poets of the Beat Generation are Diane di Prima and Jack Kerouac. Di Prima's poetry possesses a unique combination of strength and vulnerability. Her words feel like an extension of herself, particularly in poems included in *Pieces of a Song* (1990), such as "Song for Baby-O, Unborn," "Rant," and "Poem of Refusals." Di Prima's poem "Brass Furnace Going Out," which is included in Ann Charters, ed., *The Portable Beat Reader* (1992), is a woman's confession about her experience with abortion. It is divided into twelve numbered sections, each section expressing a new difficult and emotionally charged reaction to the abortion. In "Brass Furnace," di Prima speaks of sending the fetus in a bottle to the father with an extended letter. Not every stanza, however, is an example of horror. Even though the child is aborted, di Prima imagines that the child is somehow alive and expresses motherly concern, tenderness, and generosity toward it. In all, the poem gathers images that reflect the range of emotions of a woman who has experienced an abortion and gives voice to the feelings that many writers could never be frank enough to reveal.

Like Ginsberg and di Prima, Jack Kerouac is powerfully confessional in his writing. In *The Subterraneans* (1958), he acknowledges that the act of writing may not purge his pain and may, in fact, intensify his agony, but he aims to achieve some dignity for his pain through his candid prose. In a surge of emotion, Kerouac recounts the sorrow of a love affair ruined by disloyalty.

Two other confessional novels by Kerouac are *Visions of Gerard,* in which the reader watches as the young narrator loses his saintly brother to rheumatic fever and *Desolation Angels,* in which the reader encounters the narrator's literal and figurative sense of isolation and solitude, as well as his introspective self-examination, as he tells his story from a lonely mountain top. Other confessional Beat poets include, but are certainly not limited to, Philip Whalen, LeRoi Jones/Amiri Baraka, Elise Cowen, Lawrence Ferlinghetti, and Michael McClure.

—*Beth Lagaron*

**Bibliographical References**

One finds "Kaddish" in Allen Ginsberg, *Collected Poems 1947–1980,* 1984; Diane di Prima, "Brass Furnace Going Out: Song, after an Abortion," appears in Ann Charters, ed., *The Portable Beat Reader,* 1992, and with short introductory remarks from the editor; Diane di Prima, *Pieces of a Song,* 1990, offers a full range of confessional poems; Jack Kerouac, *The Subterraneans,* 1958; *Visions of Gerard,* 1963, and *Desolation Angels,* 1965, are prime examples of Kerouac writing in the confessional mode; Robert Phillips in *The Confessional Poets,* 1973, intentionally leaves Ginsberg out of his discussion, but Phillips explains his decision in the introduction.

***See also*** Ginsberg, Allen; di Prima, Diane; Kerouac, Jack; Whalen, Philip; Baraka, Amiri; Cowen, Elise; Ferlinghetti, Lawrence; McClure, Michael

# Conformity

Uniformity of behavior, goals, values, and attitudes associated with the post–World War II environment in the United States, particularly in suburban areas.

In the Eisenhower years, many people of similar ages had similar backgrounds; these people pursued marriage, family, home ownership, and material gratification. Though not all of post–World War II America participated in such behavior, a pattern of conformity did emerge, and the Beat Generation, with its emphasis on individuality, rebelled against oppressive and limiting standards for work, dress, daily life, success, and artistic expression.

Soldiers returned from war, and anxious to set the hardships and sacrifices of the past behind

Conformity at midcentury is revealed in Levittown, where thousands of identical homes were constructed. (Bettmann/Corbis)

them, young men and women got married and started families. These families soon needed homes, and in some cases land developers, such as the Levitt family, met the need for housing by building many identical homes in sprawling suburban projects. For example, in 1946 the Levitts converted 4,000 acres of potato fields in a sector within commuting distance of Manhattan into a development of more than 17,000 identical four-bedroom, Cape Cod–style houses. Soon more than 80,000 people occupied the development.

The Federal Housing Authority and Veterans Administration provided home mortgage loans to many returning military personnel, with loan practices often contributing to racial uniformity in occupancy. Zoning ordinances further contributed to uniformity by preventing the intrusion of industry

or other development. Federal funds were dedicated to the development of highways, leaving private money to steer community development. The result was suburbia, a community in which people were substantially alike.

Reinforcing patterns of conformity were trends in communications and politics. Television centralized news coverage, reducing the effect of diverse local newspapers. Dwight Eisenhower dominated national politics, and his landslide election and re-election demonstrated that Americans, to a significant degree, were thinking as one.

If homes, cars, televisions, and clothing seem to be superficial indications of the direction of a society, one should consider what William H. Whyte, the author of *The Organization Man* (1956), noticed about careers at midcentury. According to Whyte, citizens accepted the idea that they were valuable insofar as they could contribute to the progress of a group or organization. Citizens thought about their immediate surroundings and circumstances, leaving issues of morality and social progress to the organization. Even if citizens disagreed with the organization and rejected it, ultimately they returned to it or connected themselves to another group or organization.

The Beats turned a creatively critical eye on a society they felt was slipping into unhealthy conformity. Gregory Corso in "Marriage," which is included in *The Happy Birthday of Death* (1960), envisions various scenarios for marriage, including one involving the husband who returns from work to sit in a big chair by the fire while his wife, the ecstatic homemaker, prepares (and burns!) his dinner. Corso imagines a community with lawnmowers, picket fences, daily milk deliveries, and concerned citizens collecting for charity. Fearful of losing his freedom, Corso finds that he cannot commit to marriage and its requirements for health insurance, payments of bills, and community organizations (29–32). In *Big Sur* (1962), Jack Kerouac mocks the conformity of Americans on vacation as they travel in their station wagons and wear carefully pressed clothing. Children in the backseat shout and bicker. A travel service has planned and mapped the whole trip in standard fashion, and no hope for spontaneous exploration exists (44–45).

In Jack Kerouac's *The Dharma Bums* (1959), Ray Smith bemoans the sad pattern of conformity in neighborhoods near college campuses. People view the same programs at scheduled times and experience a uniform response to the broadcasts (39). Instead of enjoying individual conversations, people silently bathe in the blue light of TV (104). Ray's friend, Japhy Ryder, distinguishes himself from the world of work and consumerism that imprisons people and makes them demand senseless products that soon become senseless trash (97). When Ray stops in Independence, Missouri, on his way to Rocky Mount, North Carolina, he looks out his window in the morning and sees energetic young men dressed in the formal style that their office jobs require—all the men are hurrying to be successful on the national scene (131).

Perhaps the biggest rebellion against conformity occurs in *Junky* (1953) by William Burroughs. In the prologue to the novel, although William Lee, the narrator, refers to an era prior to the late forties and early fifties, he nevertheless comments on the stifling conventionality of middle-class life in the Midwest. The lawn, the garden, and the home surrounded by a fence are comfortable but oddly unsatisfying (xxxv). After reading the autobiography of a burglar who winds up in jail for most of his adulthood, Lee remarks that jail seems more interesting than living in a lifeless suburb (xxxvi). Lee goes on to narrate his descent into crime and drug addiction.

Despite the negative views of suburbia and conformity, the overall effect of such a lifestyle is not so clear. Herbert Gans in *The Levittowners* (1967) notes that some analysts theorize that a commuting father, a homogeneous community, and a dull environment create depression and even madness, but Gans insists that families are in fact unified, happy, and productive (220).

—*James E. Lawlor*

**Bibliographical References**
One can get information about the rise of suburban conformity in Kenneth T. Jackson, *Crabgrass Frontier: The Suburbanization of the United States*, 1985; Herbert Gans, *The Levittowners: Life and Politics in a New Suburban Community*, 1967; David Halberstam, *The Fifties*, 1993; and William H. Whyte, *The Organization Man*, 1956. The Beat response to this trend in society is clear in Gregory Corso, *The Happy Birthday of Death*, 1960; Jack Kerouac, *Big Sur*, 1962; *The Dharma Bums*, 1959; and William S. Burroughs, *Junky*, 1953.

***See also*** Styles of Dress, The Beats and; Materialism; Marriage; Sexual Attitudes and Behavior; Cold War

## Conner, Bruce (1933–)
Assemblage artist and filmmaker; photographer and producer of light shows. Instrumental in the Assemblage movement in San Francisco that flowered in 1957.

Born in McPherson, Kansas, Conner attended high school with Michael McClure. Conner earned a bachelor of fine arts from the University of Nebraska in 1956 and arrived in San Francisco in 1957, where he met Wallace Berman and the group of artists associated with him.

In assemblages, Conner brings together waste and scrap materials and often includes wax and nylon stockings. "Child" (1959), now in the collection at the Museum of Modern Art in New York City, displays a charred, waxy baby that is shrouded in nylon and fastened in a high chair. "Couch" (1963), now part of the collection at the Norton Simon Museum in Pasadena, California, appears to be a once dignified daybed made wretched through wear and tear and an accumulation of paint. "Portrait of Allen Ginsberg" (c. 1960–1961) is a profoundly abstract gathering of debris, wax, and paint. Large images of these assemblages are shown in *Beat Culture and the New America 1950–1965*, ed. Lisa Phillips (1995) the book that serves as a record of an exhibition at the Whitney Museum in 1995.

Conner's films include *A Movie* (1958), which presents portions of previously made films edited so as to create a subliminal commentary on the original films. *Marilyn Times Five* (1973) similarly interweaves selections from Marilyn Monroe's various films.

Conner laments that his work, which was sometimes sold in an unfinished state, has been modified or "repaired" by subsequent owners or gallery directors.

—*William Lawlor*

## Bibliographical References

See Kristina McKenna, "Bruce Conner in the Cultural Breach," *Los Angeles Times*, 10 June 1990; Rebecca Solnit, "Historical Constellations: Notes on California, 1946–1961," in *Beat Culture and the New America 1950–1965*, ed. Lisa Phillips, 1995, comments on Conner's role in the Assemblage movement.

*See also* Painting; Film; Berman, Wallace; DeFeo, Jay; McClure, Michael

## Corso, Gregory (1930–2001)

Throughout the early years of the Beat movement, the poet Gregory Corso was a popular literary figure, characterized by a talent for irreverent humor, surrealistic imagination, and a rebellion against society's standard traditions and conventions. When the Beat Generation finally erupted into public consciousness in the late 1950s, the mass media focused its attention on three major figures as representatives of the group: Jack Kerouac, Allen Ginsberg, and Gregory Corso. In part, this focus was because of the willingness of this trio to take on the task of challenging the social and literary mores of the time, but the central role of this trio of writers was also a result of their ability to capture the rebellious spirit of the Beats.

Corso, in particular, was able to captivate the media's fascination with the outré: his unconventional behavior and surrealistic comments, more than the quality and nature of his writing, of which many of the correspondents seemed unaware, vaulted him onto a platform of prominence, and Corso delighted in generating outrage, in daring to snap a wet towel at society's buttocks—and the media smiled in indulgent patronization of his antics. *Time* magazine published an article on the "Beatniks" of California's Venice West and North Beach and quoted a passage from his poem "Bomb," even titling the article "Bang Bong Bing," an altered version of a passage from the poem, and including a photograph of one of the Beat writers—Corso. *Newsweek* provided an article on a 1959 symposium in New York City on the Beats, including one photograph, again of Corso. In the same year, *Mademoiselle* featured an article on the Beats and included one poem: Corso's "The Shakedown." In addition, a 1963 *Time* article on the gentrification of the Beats focused on Corso's first marriage, without even mentioning his most famous poem, "Marriage."

Gregory Corso was born in Greenwich Village, New York, on 26 March 1930. His mother abandoned the family before he was a year old, and Corso spent much of his childhood and early adolescence in a variety of foster homes (briefly returning to live with his father when the latter remarried), orphanages, and Catholic Boys' homes, attending school only to the sixth grade. In 1942, charged with theft, he was sent to a Youth Home for

Beatnik poet Gregory Corso reading his work at a party. (Time Life Pictures/Getty Images)

four months, and then spent three months in the children's observation ward of Bellevue Hospital. He spent most of the next few years living on the streets of New York, and in 1946 he organized a robbery heist of $21,000 and fled to Florida. Arrested, he was sentenced in 1947 to Clinton Prison in Dannemora, New York, where he was incarcerated for three years. Although this experience was traumatic for the young man, he also discovered the delights of classic literature, especially the works of Percy Bysshe Shelley, in the prison library and began writing his own poetry. Released in 1950, Corso found work doing manual labor in New York's garment district, and in the Pony Stable, a Greenwich Village bar, he met Allen Ginsberg, who

later introduced him to Jack Kerouac, William S. Burroughs, and John Clellon Holmes. After itinerant jobs as a cub reporter for the *Los Angeles Examiner,* a door-to-door salesman of tract homes in Fort Lauderdale, Florida, and a merchant seaman on a Norwegian ship, he moved to Cambridge, Massachusetts, where he was a drop-in at Harvard University. Here he published poems in local periodicals and wrote a brief play, which was performed by the Harvard Dramatic Workshop in 1955. The same year, a group of local subscribers funded the publication of his first collection of poems, *The Vestal Lady on Brattle and Other Poems,* an apprentice work with some flashes of real, if stumbling, brilliance.

In the summer of 1956, he joined Ginsberg in San Francisco, where Corso gave a reading at San Francisco State College, which led to an invitation by the critic and poet Randall Jarrell to Washington, D.C. Corso traveled first to Mexico City and then, after a brief stay with Jarrell, went to New York before leaving for Europe in 1957 for an extended stay, living primarily in Paris for several years. By 1958, he had begun taking heroin, and during the 1960s his addiction had significantly affected his poetic output. He returned to the United States at the end of 1958 and participated in a number of readings and performances with Ginsberg, including a benefit for *Big Table* and a presentation at Columbia University, before returning to Western Europe in mid-1959, spending the following years wandering back and forth across the Atlantic. In January 1965, he taught a course on Shelley at the State University of New York at Buffalo but was dismissed for declining to sign a certificate declaring nonaffiliation with communism required of New York teachers by the 1949 Feinberg law. Beginning in 1975, he taught sporadically during summers at the Naropa Institute (now Naropa University) in Boulder, Colorado.

In 1958, Lawrence Ferlinghetti published Corso's *Gasoline* in the City Lights Pocket Poets Series. This volume, although containing such overindulgent exercises as "Ode to Coit Tower" and "Sun," showcases some of the poet's brilliant short works, including "Italian Extravaganza," "Birthplace Revisited," "This Was My Meal," and "Last

Night I Drove a Car." These and other brief poems in the volume reveal tight control of tone, telling imagery, and canny wit. Later in the same year, Ferlinghetti published as a broadside Corso's "Bomb," a longer poem with a visual motif of a mushroom cloud. This surreal poem caused a minor sensation because of its celebration of the bomb in a transhistorical and transgeographic setting.

In 1960, Corso published his remarkable collection *The Happy Birthday of Death*. This volume proclaims the poet as a major talent and contains many of Corso's most important poems, including his most famous poem, "Marriage," a whimsical and humorous exploration of the social conventions and clichés of courtship, wedding, honeymoon, cohabitation, and parenthood. The poem dances back and forth between the attractions of commitment and social integration and the threats of loss of individuality and the sacrifice of imaginative integrity. In addition, in an innovative publishing feat, "Bomb" was included as a central foldout in the collection.

In 1961, Corso published *The American Express*, an experimental fabulist novel featuring a cast of unconventional and discontented characters with parallels to the Beat writers of the 1950s. The following year saw the publication of *Long Live Man*, a disparate collection of homily-like poems lacking the control of his previous volume of poetry.

His 1970 collection *Elegiac Feelings American* primarily included poems that had appeared in periodicals between 1956 and 1963. Most noteworthy are a number of newer long poems, including "The Geometric Poem," whose holographic pages reveal Corso's revisions, and several poems that examine the poet's complex feelings toward America, attitudes especially evident in his elegies for John F. Kennedy ("Lines Written Nov. 22, 23—1963—in Discord") and for Jack Kerouac ("Elegiac Feelings American"). Also notable in this volume is "Mutation of the Spirit" (originally published in 1964 as a sheaf of nine poem pages, which Corso designed to be read in chance order), a remarkable testimony to the strength and persistence of the human spirit.

Corso's next collection, *Herald of the Autochthonic Spirit*, was more than ten years later, in 1981. The opening poem, "Columbia U Poesy Reading—1975," directly addresses Corso's Beat connections and his drug dependency, as well as the latter's effect on his poetic production, with defensiveness, lack of conviction, and ambiguous apology. However, many of the poems—especially "For Homer," "I Gave Away . . . ," and "The Whole Mess . . . Almost"—recapture the power, humor, and skill of his strongest earlier work.

Corso's last volume, *Mindfield*, appeared in 1989 and included poems selected from his earlier books, previously uncollected poems, and several new poems. One of the new poems, "Field Report," an apparent pastiche of poetic fragments, has a tone and quality of literary farewell.

Corso died of prostate cancer on 17 January 2001 after extended illness, leaving behind a body of work that is singular in its contributions to humor in poetry, its experimental use of language and imagery, and its passionate celebration of imagination and individuality in the midst of stifling convention. His ashes were buried at the foot of Shelley's grave in the Protestant Cemetery of Rome, Italy.

—Michael Skau

## Principal Works

Poetry: *The Vestal Lady on Brattle and Other Poems*, 1955; *Gasoline*, 1958; *Bomb* (broadside), 1958; *The Happy Birthday of Death*, 1960; *Selected Poems*, 1962; *Long Live Man*, 1962; *The Mutation of the Spirit: A Shuffle Poem*, 1964; *Elegiac Feelings American*, 1970; *Herald of the Autochthonic Spirit*, 1981; *Wings, Wands, Windows*, 1982; *Mindfield*, 1989.
Novel: *The American Express*, 1961.
Film: *Pull My Daisy*, 1959.
Recording: *Die on Me*, 2002.
Letters: *An Accidental Autobiography: The Selected Letters of Gregory Corso*, 2003.

## Bibliographical References

Corso's early autobiographical summary can be found in Donald Allen and George F. Butterick, eds., *The Postmoderns: The New American Poetry Revised*, 1982; other biographical materials can be found in Carolyn Gaiser's "Gregory Corso: A Poet the Beat Way," in Thomas Parkinson, ed., *A Casebook on the Beat*, 1961, 266–75; Bruce Cook's chapter "An Urchin Shelley," in his *The Beat Generation*, 1971;

Thomas McClanahan's entry in *American Poets since World War II,* Vol. 5, Part 1 of *Dictionary of Literary Biography,* 1980, and Marilyn Schwartz's fine entry in *The Beats: Literary Bohemians in Postwar America,* Vol. 16, Part 1 of the same dictionary, 1983, and Neeli Cherkovski's more personal "Revolutionary of the Spirit: Gregory Corso," in his *Whitman's Wild Children,* 1988; critical analysis of Corso's works appears in Gregory Stephenson's *Exiled Angel: A Study of the Works of Gregory Corso,* 1989; Michael Skau's *"A Clown in a Grave": Complexities and Tensions in the Works of Gregory Corso* (which also includes a thorough bibliography of Corso's own publications), 1999; and Kirby Olson's *Gregory Corso: Doubting Thomist,* 2002; important, and often very personal, interviews of Corso appear with Allen Ginsberg in *Journal for the Protection of All Beings* 1 (1961): 79–83; with Michael Andre in *Unmuzzled Ox* 2.1–2 (1973): n. p.; with Robert King in Arthur and Kit Knight, eds., *The Beat Diary,* 1977: 4–24; and with Gavin Selerie in *The Riverside Interviews: 3—Gregory Corso,* 1982.

*See also* Atomic Era; Cold War; Conformity; Film; Marriage; Native American Cultures; Paris, The Beats in

## Cowen, Elise (1933–1962)

Poet; last girlfriend of Allen Ginsberg and typist for the manuscript of "Kaddish"; friend of Joyce Johnson, who records Cowen's life and tragic decline in *Come and Join the Dance* (1962) and *Minor Characters* (1983).

Born on Long Island in 1933, Cowen was the daughter of well-to-do Jewish parents. The family took an apartment on Bennett Avenue in the Washington Heights area of Manhattan, and Cowen, accepted at Barnard College, began her university studies in the spring of 1952. While at Barnard, Cowen met Joyce Johnson and Leo Skir; she also began an affair with philosophy professor Alex Greer, and through Greer, Cowen met Allen Ginsberg, whom she dated in 1953. Cowen developed an unshakable desire for Ginsberg, and even after Ginsberg declared his homosexual desires for Peter Orlovsky, Cowen persisted in her efforts to be connected with Ginsberg. In *Desolation Angels* (1965), Jack Kerouac describes the problematic re-

lationship between Ginsberg and Cowen, referring to Ginsberg as Irwin Garden and Cowen as Barbara Lipp.

Cowen's mother and father wanted the capstone of their success to be the flowering of their daughter, but Cowen never met their expectations. She had recurring problems with depression and mental illness; she did not perform consistently at the university; she fell in with friends who were homosexuals and drug users.

Despite her mental distress, Cowen was an active intellectual. She studied French so that she could read Arthur Rimbaud in the original. The books she favored included *The Oxford Anthology of Greek Poetry, The Poems of Dylan Thomas,* Ezra Pound's *Pisan Cantos,* Freud's *Introductory Lectures,* and Voltaire's *Candide.* For a university assignment, she attempted to fully explicate T. S. Eliot's *Four Quartets.* She completed a degree at Barnard in 1956.

After treatment at Bellevue for depression, Cowen returned to her parents' home on Bennett Avenue. Her parents had plans for a trip to Florida to facilitate Cowen's recuperation, but on 1 February 1962, Cowen leapt to her death from the window of her parents' apartment.

Tormented by the suicide and displeased by the references to drugs and sex in Cowen's writings, Cowen's parents destroyed all of her works in their possession; however, Leo Skir retained a collection of poems and fragments at his home. Those poems are the surviving record of Elise Cowen's artistic production.

—*William Lawlor*

### Bibliographical References

See Joyce Johnson, *Minor Characters,* 1983, and Joyce Glassman (Joyce Johnson) *Come and Join the Dance,* 1962. See also Leo Skir, *Boychick,* 1971; Herbert Huncke, *Guilty of Everything: The Autobiography of Herbert Huncke,* 1990: 127–143; Herbert Huncke, *The Evening Sun Turned Crimson,* 1980: 183–194; a compact treatment of Cowen's life and anguish is Leo Skir, "Elise Cowen: A Brief Memoir of the Fifties," in Brenda Knight, ed., *Women of the Beat Generation,* 1996. Knight's collection also includes a biographical discussion of Elise Cowen, selections of Cowen's writings, and bibliographical references to little magazines in which Cowen's poetry appears. Additional samples of Cowen's poetry are in Richard Peabody, ed., *A Different Beat*, 1997. Allen Ginsberg refers to Elise Cowen in his *Journals: Early Fifties, Early Sixties*, ed. Gordon Ball, 1977; Jack Kerouac gives his fictional interpretation of Elise Cowen in *Desolation Angels*, 1965.

*See also* Johnson, Joyce; Mental Illness

## Creeley, Robert (1926–2005)

Robert Creeley, one of the Black Mountain Poets, is known for minimalist poetry that is explicitly self-conscious and that, incorporating rhythms and phrasings of speech, demands to be read aloud for full effect. In the 1950s, Creeley was invited by poet Charles Olson, rector of Black Mountain College, an experimental school in North Carolina, to join the faculty of writers and artists. There Creeley developed his poetic style while also editing the prestigious *Black Mountain Review*. He later established a close relationship with such Beat writers as Allen Ginsberg and Jack Kerouac in San Francisco. In his poetry, Creeley attempted to locate the essence of the present moment as he experienced it, a paring away that led to minimalism in wording and structure. He helped to divert poetry from its past grounding in traditional conventions in favor of a self-conscious examination of the poet's immediate thoughts and feelings. He also contributed to the growing sense of poetry as performance that marked some of the most innovative poetry of the 1950s and 1960s, including the work of Ginsberg, Lawrence Ferlinghetti, and Gary Snyder.

Robert Creeley was born on 21 May 1926 in Arlington, Massachusetts, and enrolled at Harvard University in 1943. World War II intervened, and Creeley left Harvard for wartime duty, driving ambulances for the American Field Service in India and Burma. He later returned to Harvard but did not complete a degree.

The defining period for Creeley as a poet occurred in 1950 when, with a friend, Jacob Leed, he embarked on a plan to begin a poetry magazine. That project led to correspondence with a number of poets, including Charles Olson. Although the magazine failed to materialize, Creeley continued a voluminous exchange of letters with Olson that was said by Creeley to occupy as much as eight hours per day at its peak (published in *Charles Olson and Robert Creeley: The Complete Correspondence*, in nine volumes, 1980–90). The aspiring poet was invited by Olson to join the Black Mountain College faculty in 1954, where he joined such poets as Denise Levertov and Ed Dorn. To ensure Creeley's academic qualifications, Olson awarded him an undergraduate degree from the college. Creeley continued his academic studies at the University of New Mexico, where he earned a master of arts degree in 1960.

Creeley collaborated with Olson in exploring a new approach to poetry while also editing the *Black Mountain Review*. Both broke with traditional conventions and models while emphasizing what they called "projective verse," poetry in which the form of a poem is a projection of the poet's self-consciously personal subject matter.

Throughout the 1960s and 1970s, Creeley continued to explore his intimate relationship with the moment, seeking the minimal essence of an experience, an approach that yielded a corresponding minimalism in structure and wording. Many of his poems consist of short lines with a high percentage of monosyllabic words. Interacting with the Beat poets, including Allen Ginsberg, encouraged attention to performance-based poetry, with reading aloud required for a full appreciation of many of Creeley's poems. Subtle reflections of the rhythms of the spoken word, along with muted rhyming easily missed when silently reading the words on paper, became prominent characteristics of his poetry. At the same time, he usually avoided such traditional devices as metaphor, irony, and inherited stanzaic forms. His poetry, both then and later, is often domestic, addressing important relationships with family and friends.

Donald Allen's influential anthology *The New American Poetry: 1945–1960* (1960) included a selection of Creeley's poetry. Creeley's first major volume, *For Love: Poems 1950–1960*, appeared in 1962 and was followed in 1967 by an expanded edition of

*Words,* first published two years earlier. Other important volumes of poetry throughout the 1960s and 1970s included *Pieces* (1968), expanded and rereleased in 1969; *Thirty Things* (1974); *Selected Poems* (1976); and *Hello: A Journal, February 29–May 3, 1976* (1978). A more inclusive collection of poetry from these decades is *The Collected Poems of Robert Creeley, 1945–1975* (1982). He also published a novel, *The Island* (1963); the collection of short stories *The Gold Diggers and Other Stories* (1965); and a play, *Listen,* first produced in London in 1972 and published the same year.

The 1979 volume *Later* marked a change in Creeley's approach. Departing from an almost exclusive focus on the present moment, he turned increasingly to the past and a reliance on memory. The fact of aging informs much of the poetry from the late 1970s onward, drawing the poet into the process of looking backward while growing older in order to understand one's life as a whole. This expanded perspective continues in subsequent collections, among them *Mirrors* (1983), *Memory Gardens* (1986), *Windows* (1990), *Echoes* (1994), *Life & Death* (1998), and *Just in Time: Poems 1984–1994* (2001). The titles of some of these later collections are evocative of the poet's growing sense of mortality and the shortness of time.

By the end of the twentieth century, Creeley had published more than sixty collections of poetry along with several volumes of fiction and a wide range of critical nonfiction. Many of his essays were gathered in *Collected Essays* (1989). He also published an account of his own life, *Autobiography* (1990). His editorial efforts included *Whitman: Selected Poems* (1973), *The Essential Burns* (1989), and Charles Olson's *Selected Poems* (1993). In addition, he influenced generations of students through his teaching. After Black Mountain College, which he left in 1955, he taught at a school for boys in Albuquerque, New Mexico; the University of British Columbia, Vancouver; the University of New Mexico; and, from 1965 on, the State University of New York at Buffalo. At Buffalo, he held several positions of increasing honor, culminating in that of Samuel P. Capen Professor of Poetry and Humanities in 1989. He also was New York State

Poet (1989–1991) and a chancellor of the Academy of American Poets (1999–2002).

—*Edward J. Rielly*

## Bibliographical References

Tom Clark, *Robert Creeley and the Genius of the American Common Place*, 1993; Cynthia Edelberg, *Robert Creeley's Poetry: A Critical Introduction*, 1978: Ekbert Faas, with Maria Trombacco, *Robert Creeley: A Biography*, 2001; Willard Fox, *Robert Creeley, Edward Dorn, and Robert Duncan: A Reference Guide*, 1989.

*See also* Black Mountain, North Carolina, and Black Mountain College; Little Magazines

## Cunningham, Merce

Dancer and choreographer noted for spontaneous and collaborative performances. Although not a Beat artist, his experimental approach to dance corresponds in various ways to the experimentations of the Beats in writing and other forms.

Born in Centralia, Washington, on 16 April 1919, the son of Clifford Cunningham, a lawyer, and Marion Cunningham, Merce Cunningham, according to his mother's recollection, danced down the aisle of his family's church at age four. At age eight, he began lessons in tap dance. In high school, Cunningham studied with Maud Barret, who opened Cunningham's mind to the possibility of dropping rules and conventions.

Cunningham spent a year at the University of Washington in Seattle in 1937 but transferred to the Cornish School for Performing and Visual Arts. He studied with Bonnie Bird, who taught the techniques of Martha Graham. He met John Cage, a musician and composer, and began a lifelong partnership in the arts. He spent summers at Mills College in Oakland, California, where he was able to study under Martha Graham. From 1939 to 1945, he participated in Graham's dance company in New York City.

In 1944, Cunningham gave his first solo dance concert in New York. In 1947, he wrote a work for the New York Ballet.

In 1953, he joined Black Mountain College and founded a company of six dancers. For this company,

John Cage and David Tudor were musicians. Robert Rauschenberg served as a set designer. In 1954, Cunningham's dance company gave its first New York performance, but the performance was not reviewed.

In 1954, Cunningham won a Guggenheim fellowship. Despite this award, financial struggles always imposed limits on productions and performances. He relied on the support of fellow artists often.

In 1964, Cunningham and his company began a world tour, and from 1965 to 1968, the company performed many times, both abroad and in the United States.

Cunningham did not try to steer the thinking of his audience. He sought dance that was beyond intention and aimed at discovery in the moment, in the act of dance. The conventional structures of dance, including conflict and resolution, or cause and effect, did not suit Cunningham. He expected dancers not to play roles but to be themselves.

*Winterbranch* (1963) was based on the motion of falling. The production included lights, but they were not coordinated to highlight particular portions of the dance. La Monte Young prepared an experimental musical score of loud tape-recorded sounds.

*Story* (1963) allowed dancers to approach a pile of clothing and make a selection; each dancer had to invent a dance based on the selected clothing.

*Field Dances* (1963) gave dancers the options of performing or not performing. Dancers chose their own gestures and movements.

*Variations* V (1965) included sensors as part of the set; when dancers moved, they tripped sensors, which cued musicians to make sound. The set was experimental and included a TV, film images, a bicycle, a gym mat, plastic plants, and furniture.

*How to Pass, Kick, Fall, and Run* (1965) presented readings of stories by John Cage. Dancers responded to sports images.

During his career, Cunningham made collaboration a prominent part of his work. Jasper Johns, Frank Stella, Andy Warhol, Marcel Duchamp, and Robert Morris all worked in conjunction with Cunningham.

*Canfield* (1969) was based on the card game known as solitaire. The duration of the performance was not fixed and ranged from twenty minutes to almost two hours. The background was reflective, as were the dancers' costumes. The outcome was unpredictable.

Cunningham showed that dance could be anything. A dancer could stand still, ride a bike, or engage in any locomotion. Cunningham revolutionized the concept of dance as he moved dance from the stage to gymnasiums and even Grand Central Station.

By the 1980s, Cunningham had entered the mainstream. His company offered a regular summer season of performances.

—*William Lawlor*

**Bibliographical References**
James Klosty, ed., *Merce Cunningham,* 1975, includes an introductory chapter and contributions by fellow dancers and collaborators, including John Cage. In *The Dancer and the Dance: Merce Cunningham in Conversation with Jacqueline Lesschaeve,* 1985, one finds an interview with Cunningham, who comments on his own choreography. Ricard Kostelanetz, ed., *Merce Cunningham: Dancing in Space and Time,* 1992, includes contributions by Cunningham's friends and colleagues, with selections representing each stage in Cunningham's career.

*See also* Dance; Black Mountain, North Carolina, and Black Mountain College; Cage, John

# Curriculum, Beats in the

Once excluded from university and high school curricula, the Beats are now present in diverse courses in literature, history, political science, sociology, religious studies, music, film, painting, photography, dance, women's studies, and many other subjects. A computer search based on the key words "Beat Generation" and "syllabus" yields more than four thousand items, many of them syllabi for classes dedicated, in whole or in part, to the artistry and cultural influences of the Beat Generation.

The proliferation of courses on the Beat Generation is ironic because in the 1950s neither teachers nor the Beats themselves wanted the Beats in the curriculum. Skeptical about the merit of *Howl*

Cadets at the Virginia Military Institute read *Howl and Other Poems* by Allen Ginsberg. (Photo by Gordon Ball)

*and Other Poems* (1956), *On the Road* (1957), and *Naked Lunch* (1959), professors and academics dismissed such works as insubstantial material that was part of a passing fad. The Beats themselves rejected boring academics who too often stood by as hypocrisy, injustice, and militarism went forward. If being part of the curriculum meant being part of courses taught by such academics, then exclusion from the curriculum was preferable.

Nevertheless, neither the academics nor the Beats kept Beats out of the classroom. John Tytell, who has taught classes on the Beat Generation since the 1960s at Queens College of the City University of New York, states that enrollment for courses on the Beats has always exceeded expectations. Despite demand for the classes, course proposals have faced some obstacles because the checkered reputation of the Beats has sparked re-

sistance from academics interested in rigor, discipline, and the established canon.

Questions about the reputation of the Beats persist despite distinctions such as the Pulitzer Prize, the National Book Award, and membership in the American Academy of Arts and Letters. During the 1970s the study of the Beats occurred less frequently in literature classes and more frequently in courses on sociology, history, and American studies. However, as the 1980s drew to a close, a substantial revival of interest in the Beats occurred, and sales of their books were impressive, particularly on college campuses. In the 1990s, New York University hosted two major conferences on the Beat Generation, and then the National Gallery and the Whitney Museum had exhibitions that brought to light the diverse, interdisciplinary aspects of the Beat movement.

Several key questions are central to the study of the Beat Generation. The first is the issue of whether a Beat Generation actually exists. If the Beat Generation consists of Kerouac, Ginsberg, Burroughs, and a few others, then the Beat Generation does not exist because a generation cannot be based on just a few people. On the other hand, if the Beat Generation includes dozens and dozens of artists, including not only writers but also dancers, painters, sculptors, musicians, then the Beat Generation does not exist because the concept is too loose, too vague.

If one accepts that the Beat Generation exists, then the definition of "Beat," "beatnik," "beatitude," and "Beat Generation" must be explored; indeed, the history and evolution of these terms bears consideration. Once such terms are defined, one can proceed to distinguish fact from legend, artistry from pop-culture impressions.

Perhaps the greatest teacher of the Beat Generation was Allen Ginsberg. At Brooklyn College and the Naropa Institute, Ginsberg often gave classes on Beat literary history. He loved to collaborate with others in the teaching process, and to make ideas rich and clear, he invited speakers and formed panels to discuss topics such as censorship and the significance of particular writers. Students had the chance to hear about the Beats not only from Ginsberg, but also from Herbert Huncke, Michael McClure, William S. Burroughs, and dozens of other friends who answered Ginsberg's call for assistance. Ginsberg gave bibliographical assignments to his students, guiding them toward an understanding of the achievements of individual authors. Always conscious of the preservation of his teaching activities for the future, Ginsberg arranged for video and audio recordings and compiled many files of documents. These recordings and files are now part of the Ginsberg archive housed at Stanford University.

Numerous other figures from the Beat Generation have also taught about the Beats. Anne Waldman, Diane di Prima, Gary Snyder, David Meltzer, and many others have offered classes. This core of teachers is now greatly expanded. In 2000, a study of college catalogs revealed 269 courses with specific references to the Beats in the course descriptions. These data, however, represent only the tip of the iceberg because numerous classes that do not refer to Beats in their catalog descriptions, such as "Contemporary Literature" or "Themes in Literature," nevertheless treat the Beats substantially in many cases.

—*William Lawlor*

## Bibliographical References

*College Literature* 27.1 (Winter 2000) is a special issue dedicated to the theme of teaching Beat literature. To that issue, William Lawlor contributes "A Compact Guide for Sources for Teaching the Beats." A more thorough treatment of teaching the Beats is Lawlor's *The Beat Generation: A Bibliographical Teaching Guide*, 1998.

**See also** Whitney Museum Exhibition: Beat Culture and the New America 1950–1965; New York University Conferences on Beat Culture; Tytell, John; Beat and Beatnik; Beatitude; Library Holdings

# D

## Dance

Avant-garde dance in the second half of the twentieth century, like the Beat movement, was a reaction to established patterns and an exploration of new possibilities in movement and presentation. Although avant-garde dancers are not usually seen as representatives of the Beat movement, underlying theories of creativity, including the abandonment of conventional continuity and an emphasis on chance and responses to the moment at hand, establish clear parallels. Avant-garde dancers came of age in a bohemian era cultivated by the Beats; the art of William S. Burroughs influenced dancers, and the interdisciplinary interests of Diane di Prima created interaction among Beat poets, Beat dramatists, and avant-garde dancers.

In the late 1920s, dance was primarily theatrical, and movements in dance were symmetrical and delicate. The repertoire of movements for such performances proved unsatisfactory for a new group of dancers, many of whom studied under Martha Graham, Doris Humphrey, and Charles Weidman. The new dancers expressed social protest and psychological complexities through distortions of ordinary motion; the dancers' method was parallel to the work of abstract painters who distorted the human form in their work to express emotions.

Eventually, however, the expression of emotion—or social commentary—lost its appeal, yet the new repertoire of movements retained value. Dancers sought to make motion itself the primary

consideration. Like the writers of the Beat Generation, who set aside rules for form and trusted the subconscious and spontaneous creativity, avant-garde dancers refused to let logic dominate movement. Drawing from the same Black Mountain teachings that influenced the Beats, avant-garde dancers sought to follow the edict of Charles Olson in his essay "Projective Verse," which appeared in *Human Universe* (1951): "One perception must immediately and directly lead to a further perception."

Merce Cunningham was significant in advancing the principles of avant-garde dance. He studied anatomy and the motions associated with each body part. Once he developed an inventory of movements, he experimented with simultaneous presentations of ordinary and extraordinary motions. To determine the direction and duration for motion, Cunningham relied on chance. He also was open to motionlessness as part of dance.

Like Cunningham, Katherine Litz and Sybil Shearer juxtaposed typical and atypical bodily movements; however, as these dancers made their juxtaposed movements into part of a passage through a dance space, the atypical movements became less pronounced. Alwin Nikolais, like Cunningham, studied motions associated with particular actions; by removing the motions from their standard contexts, Nikolais isolated motion and made it the focus of art. Paul Taylor allowed time and space to influence his style of motion: a dancer might begin movement across a dance space with common motion and

Merce Cunningham, the founder of the Merce Cunningham Dance Company and a pioneer in modern dance, rehearses with his dance group, 1957. (Charles E. Rotkin/Corbis)

shift to uncommon motion after a particular duration or upon reaching a particular point in the dance space.

George Balanchine carried avant-garde dance forward with his resourceful invention of new movements, but Balanchine coordinated his gestures with musical scores. In response to Balanchine, Merle Marsicano sought to reduce the authority of music over dance by choosing music that downplayed emotion and did not draw attention to itself. The disconnection of music from choreography was furthered when Merce Cunningham combined with composer John Cage. Agreeing on a particular duration for a collaborative work, Cage conceived music independently while Cunningham worked out movement. In performance, music combined with dance only by chance, and rules of continuity went unobserved.

In the summer of 1962 at the Judson Memorial Church in Greenwich Village, New York, avant-garde dance entered a new phase. The rise of the Beat culture in the United States gave new emphasis to the bohemian lifestyle in Greenwich Village, and this atmosphere created new possibilities in dance. Happenings were occurring, and Pop Art was on the rise. Influenced by the collaboration of Cunningham and Cage, avant-garde dancers turned away from music and toward dance concerts. Chance was allowed to rule, and everyday activity became the dancer's point of focus.

Communication with James Waring led to interaction among avant-garde dancers, members of the Living Theater, and people involved with Diane di Prima and Alan Marlowe in the New York Poets Theater. In *The Floating Bear,* a mimeographed journal published by di Prima and LeRoi Jones, reviews of avant-garde dance concerts appeared often.

These interactions reinforced and carried forward ideas. Dancers intended not to tell a story, not to express emotion. The audience was important, but gratifying the expectations of the audience was not. Instead of trying to make movement "mean" something, movement itself was the object of art. Even the absence of movement could be considered dance. Both William Burroughs and avant-garde dancers took inspiration from the Dadaists, and avant-garde dancers found that Burroughs's *Naked Lunch* demonstrated possibilities for an antinovel that could help a dancer arrive at an antidance. Charlie Parker's improvisational jazz style also suggested to dancers that art could be discovered in the midst of performance.

In March 1962, a Poets Festival was held at the Maidman Playhouse on 42nd Street in Manhattan. The program included music, happenings, films, and dance concerts. The event was reviewed in various newspapers and journals, with one reviewer noting the presence of beatniks, another expressing distaste, and another revealing openness to the experimentation.

From these beginnings one may trace the performances of Yvonne Rainer, who creates a dialectical combination of grotesque and ordinary movements; the work of Steve Paxton, who emphasizes quotidian activities, such as walking or eating; and the efforts of Robert Morris, whose use of props connected history and dance.

—*William Lawlor*

## Bibliographical References

For a review of the founders of the avant-garde in dance, see Selma Jeanne Cohen, "Avant-garde Choreography," *Criticism* 3 (Winter 1961): 16–35; this article reappeared in *Dance Magazine* as a three-part study published in 1962 in the June, July, and August issues. The development of avant-garde dance in the Judson Dance Theater is explained in Sally Banes, *Democracy's Body,* 1983. *Merce Cunningham* (1975), ed. James Klosty, includes an introductory chapter and contributions from fellow dancers and collaborators, including John Cage.

*See also* Cunningham, Merce; Black Mountain, North Carolina, and Black Mountain College; Cage, John

# de Kooning, Willem (1904–1997)

Painter and sculptor, pioneer of Abstract Expressionism, and influential as a forerunner of Pop Art, de Kooning, along with Jackson Pollock, was one of the leading avant-garde artists whose reputation and influence helped to make New York the center of artistic innovation after World War II.

Born in Rotterdam and formally trained as a commercial artist and designer, de Kooning emigrated to the United States and settled in New York in 1927. From the 1920s to the 1940s, he created experimental and abstract still lifes. He worked for the Federal Art Project from 1935 to 1937 and had his first one-man show at age forty-four in 1948. Best known for his *Women* series, of the 1950s, de Kooning's impressionistic style was influenced by Cubism and Surrealism, and his own work influenced leading artists such as Jasper Johns and Robert Rauschenberg. De Kooning died of natural causes in East Hampton, New York, on 19 March 1997, following a long bout with Alzheimer's disease.

—*Gary Kerley*

## Bibliographical References

Sally Yard, *Willem de Kooning,* 1997; Diane Waldman, *Willem de Kooning,* 1988; George Scrivani, ed., *The Collected Writings of Willem de Kooning,* 1988; Harry F. Gaugh, *Willem de Kooning,* 1983; T. B. Hess, *Willem de Kooning,* 1959.

*See also* Rauschenberg, Robert; Painting

## DeFeo, Jay (1929-1989)

Avant-garde painter in San Francisco noteworthy especially for *The Rose*, a long-term project begun in 1958 and continued until 1966, when DeFeo was compelled to vacate her apartment and had to remove the massive work. When *The Rose* was displayed at the Whitney Museum in New York City in 1995, specifications indicated that through years of accumulated painting and embedding, DeFeo had created an abstract assemblage eleven inches thick, about eleven feet tall, and around eight feet wide. The painting (or sculpture) weighed about a ton.

DeFeo was born Joan DeFeo on 31 March 1929. She attended the University of California, Berkeley (1946–1950), and with a Sigmund Martin Heller Traveling Fellowship (1951–1952) from Berkeley, she traveled to Florence, Italy, and Paris, France, where she studied and experienced numerous works of art. She was married to fellow artist Wally Hedrick.

DeFeo's apartment at 2332 Fillmore Street in San Francisco was a gathering point for various artists, including Joan Brown, Bruce Conner, Michael McClure, Joanna McClure, Jack Spicer, and Ed Moses.

In 1954, she exhibited her work at The Place in San Francisco. In 1957, she showed her work at the Ferus Gallery in Los Angeles. In 1959, her work (and the work of Wally Hedrick) was displayed alongside the works of Jasper Johns, Robert Rauschenberg, and Frank Stella at the Museum of Modern Art in New York as part of an exhibit titled "16 Americans."

After her death from cancer in Oakland, California, on 11 November 1989, the Whitney Museum hosted exhibitions (1995 and 2003). In 2004, at the San Francisco Museum of Modern Art, a symposium titled "Jay DeFeo: Myth and Reality" included a screening of Bruce Conner's film *The White Rose* (1967), which documented the removal of *The Rose* from the Fillmore Street apartment.

—*William Lawlor*

### Bibliographical References

See *Jay DeFeo and* The Rose, eds. Jane Green and Leah Levy, 2003; Michael Kimmelman's "An Obsession: Now Excavated," which summarizes the career and personality of DeFeo, appears in the *New York Times,* 10 October, 2003; Rebecca Solnit, "Heretical Constellations: Notes on California 1946–1961" in *Beat Culture and the New America 1950–1965,* ed. Lisa Phillips, 1995, includes commentary on DeFeo's work and career and features a large photo of "The Rose."

*See also* Whitney Museum Exhibition: Beat Culture and the New America 1950–1965; Conner, Bruce; San Francisco; Painting

## Denver, Colorado

In 1947, a year after Jack Kerouac and Neal Cassady met in New York City, Kerouac and Allen Ginsberg decided to spend the summer with Cassady in Denver. Although Cassady had been born in Salt Lake City, he had grown up in the Curtis Park neighborhood in Denver. For Kerouac and Ginsberg, Cassady himself was enough of a reason to spend a few months in Denver. Kerouac was, of course, fascinated by the Beat prototype that he recognized in Cassady, and even though Cassady was married to his first wife, LuAnne Henderson, and had just become romantically involved with Carolyn Robinson, who would become his second wife, Ginsberg made no secret of his own sexual attraction to Cassady.

Denver was an interesting place and convenient base for the Beats for other reasons as well. They spent most of their time in Denver in the Larimer Street district of the city, a skid-row area that over the past several decades has gradually been razed until almost nothing now remains of it. When they were in Denver, however, it was a colorfully seedy area full of eccentric characters and idiosyncratic establishments. Nearby was the Five Points district. Long a predominantly African American neighborhood, it included the well-known Rossonian Hotel, as well as a number of smaller clubs that featured live jazz performances.

Moreover, as the Beat writers established themselves in New York and San Francisco, Denver became a natural stopover in their transcontinental jaunts and a base for their journeys south to visit William S. Burroughs in Mexico. Kerouac was so enamored of Denver that he used his advance for

*The Town and the City* to buy a modest home on West Center Avenue in Lakewood, a town just west of Denver. When he attempted to relocate, however, his family felt more dislocated than at home, and Kerouac soon gave up the idea of using the city as a more permanent base.

Finally, in the 1940s and 1950s, Denver was home to a number of vibrant small presses, most notably Alan Swallow's independent publishing company. These book publishers and literary journals were receptive to the work of new writers, including the Beats—with Swallow, for instance, publishing the work of Harold Norse and the first studies of Kenneth Patchen's work.

—Martin Kich

## Bibliographical References
The experiences of the Beats in Denver have been chronicled in Neal Cassady, *The First Third,* 1971 (rev. ed. 1981); in Kerouac's *On the Road,* 1957, and *Visions of Cody,* 1972, and in Ginsberg's *Howl and Other Poems,* 1956, and "Denver Doldrums." A virtual "Beat Tour" of the city is available at *http://www.denvergov.org/AboutDenver/today_driving_beat.asp*

**See also** Cassady, Carolyn; Cassady, Neal; Ginsberg, Allen; Kerouac, Jack

## Desolation Peak
A mountaintop in the state of Washington where Jack Kerouac spent sixty-three days in solitude in the summer of 1956 as a fire lookout for the U.S. Agriculture Department. At an elevation of more than 6,000 feet, Kerouac lived in a small cabin that offered panoramic views of surrounding mountains and bodies of water, including Mount Hozomeen (8,080 feet) and Ross Lake. The names of surrounding mountains are sometimes innocuous, as in Jack Mountain or Golden Horn, but names such as Mount Terror, Mount Fury, Mount Despair, and Mount Challenger reveal the demands of the environment. Kerouac's experience impressed him so deeply that he referred substantially to Desolation Peak in four books: *The Dharma Bums* (1958), *Desolation Angels* (1965), *Book of Blues* (1995), and *Lonesome Traveler* (1960). Shortly after Ker-

ouac's descent from Desolation Peak, a review of *On the Road* (1957) in the *New York Times* made Kerouac famous overnight.

—William Lawlor

## Bibliographic References
See James Jones, *Jack Kerouac's Nine Lives,* 2001; John Suiter, *Poets on the Peaks,* 2002.

**See also** Mountains, Beats in the

## di Prima, Diane (1934–)
Prolific writer, founder of the Poets Press, and coeditor of *The Floating Bear,* Diane di Prima defied the expectations of family, friends, and society—she pursued the path of a woman writer during a time when that was an anomaly, and she is thus considered the archetypal Beat woman. During her connection with the Beat movement, di Prima clearly struggled within the confines of that male-dominated ideology: she at times was slighted for having children and often was not invited to poetry readings with her male counterparts, even though she published alongside them, simply because of her status as a woman writer. Yet di Prima never sacrificed her identity. She survives as a working writer, one whose bibliography includes poetry, memoirs, and drama. By writing about personal experiences, whether symbolically or overtly, di Prima has created a body of literature that exudes an ardor toward the transgression of limits. Her oeuvre stands as a testament to the provocative nature of the Beat Generation.

Born on 6 August 1934 in Brooklyn, New York, di Prima is a second-generation Italian American. Domenico Malozzi, her maternal grandfather, was an anarchist and atheist, and di Prima spent the early years of her life listening to Italian opera and reading Dante with him. She grew up during World War II and went to Catholic school at St. Mary's until age thirteen.

Di Prima attended Manhattan's all-girls Hunter High School; while there she studied French and Latin, read Nietzsche and Wolfe, and ran the literary magazine. She discovered the English Romantics, and with a passion for Keats at age fourteen, she vowed to be a poet. During the summer months, she took typing classes and studied at Washington Irving High School. She then attended Swarthmore College in Pennsylvania. After a year and a half, she and some friends dropped out and headed for New York City's Greenwich Village. By the spring of 1953, di Prima had her own apartment on the Lower East Side and continued her education, taking courses at various schools and beginning her life as a working writer.

Along with Keats, Ezra Pound had a great influence on di Prima. During the midfifties, she established correspondence with Pound, visiting him a few times during his stay at St. Elizabeth's Hospital in Washington, D.C. Di Prima also exchanged letters with Kenneth Patchen. By 1956, she began corresponding with Lawrence Ferlinghetti and Allen Ginsberg as well, and a year later she met Ginsberg, Peter Orlovsky, Gregory Corso, and Jack Kerouac in New York. The same year, 1957, she had her first

Diane di Prima is a poet, prose writer, playwright, and editor. (Christopher Felver/Corbis)

child, for whom di Prima, a single mother, assumed responsibility.

Di Prima published her first book of poems, *This Kind of Bird Flies Backward,* in 1958, only a year after Kerouac's *On The Road* introduced readers to the Beat milieu. She published this collection of poems with LeRoi and Hettie Jones's Totem Press, and the work includes an introduction by Lawrence Ferlinghetti. The writing and publishing of *This Kind of Bird Flies Backward,* simultaneous with the publication of "Howl" and *On The Road,* marks di Prima as a Beat writer not because of her connection with Ginsberg and Kerouac, but because of the new bohemian vision she shared with them. *This Kind of Bird Flies Backward* thematically focuses on identities of the self as defined through the discourses of love, birth, and death; di Prima weaves her words between the identities of single mother and hip Village poet.

*This Kind of Bird Flies Backward* subtly gestures toward what di Prima's next publication, *Dinner and Nightmares* (1961), more clearly accomplishes: a prosaic presentation of the humor and horror prevalent in the domestic spaces of struggling artists and writers. *Dinners and Nightmares,* one of di Prima's more famous publications, explores the creativity that lies within the life of the Beat artist. In this work, she plainly places domesticity and femininity into Beat poetry; thus *Dinners and Nightmares* can be considered the highlight of di Prima's publications as Beat woman writer because it successfully works alongside, yet so unashamedly transcends, the masculine values of the Beat aesthetic.

Along with the publication of *Dinners and Nightmares* in 1961, di Prima cofounded the New York Poets Theatre with LeRoi Jones and other artists. She also began editing *The Floating Bear* with Jones. *The Floating Bear* published works by writers such as William Burroughs and Gary Snyder. As editors of that free literary newsletter, di Prima and Jones were arrested and charged with obscenity (although this case was thrown out by a grand jury). During this time, di Prima and Jones broke off the intimate affair they began years earlier; Jones is the father of di Prima's second child.

Also in the sixties, di Prima began studying Zen Buddhism and lived for a while at Timothy Leary's farm in Millbrook, New York. By 1968, di Prima moved to San Francisco and began work with the Diggers, an anarchist street theater group. During this time, she wrote *Revolutionary Letters,* a sequence of poems later published by City Lights Books.

Olympia Press published *Memoirs of a Beatnik* in 1969. In this memoir, di Prima celebrates Beat existence through a female lens. Chronicling her encounters with lovers and describing her 1957 introduction to Ginsberg, Orlovsky, Corso, and Kerouac, *Memoirs of a Beatnik* aptly describes the game of "cool" Beat women were expected to play. Although it is certainly a (s)exploitation of di Prima's writing abilities and a parody of the clichéd image of a beatnik, *Memoirs of a Beatnik* brilliantly captures bohemian living for the reader.

*Loba,* di Prima's epic poem that began in 1971, shows di Prima as one who has survived the struggling essence of a woman writer and who is thus prepared to examine the universal experience of a multilayered female life-principle. Although *Loba* is surely well beyond di Prima's existence as Beat writer, its exploration into feminine mythology stands as a reminder of the Beat Generation's dedication to spiritual investigation.

Di Prima has been a teacher of many and has carried the Beat torch of community and experience into the millennium. She continues to share her works with others in print and performance and often offers writing workshops in the San Francisco area.

—*Dawn M. Janke*

## Principal Works

Poetry: *This Kind of Bird Flies Backward,* 1958; *Dinners and Nightmares,* 1961; *The New Handbook of Heaven,* 1963; *Earthsong,* 1968; *Kerhonkson Journal 1966,* 1971; *Revolutionary Letters,* 1971; *The Calculus of Variation,* 1972; *Freddie Poems,* 1974; *Selected Poems: 1956–1975,* 1975; *Brass Furnace Going Out: Song after an Abortion,* 1975; *Pieces of a Song: Selected Poems,* 1990; *Seminary Poems,* 1991; *Loba* (Parts 1–16: Books I and II), 1998; *Dinners and Nightmares* (expanded edition), 1998.

Translation: *Seven Love Poems from the Middle Latin,* 1965.
Memoirs: *Memoirs of a Beatnik,* 1969; *Memoirs of a Beatnik* (revised edition), 1988; *Recollections of My Life as a Woman: The New York Years,* 2001.
Drama: *Zip Code: The Collected Plays of Diane di Prima,* 1992.

## Bibliographical References

George F. Butterick provides a biography of di Prima in *The Beats: Literary Bohemians in Postwar America,* Vol. 16, Parts 1 and 2 of *Dictionary of Literary Biography,* edited by Ann Charters, 1983; Michael Davidson analyzes the poetry of di Prima and other San Francisco writers in his book, *The San Francisco Renaissance: Poetics and Community at Mid-Century,* 1989; *Girls Who Wore Black: Women Writing the Beat Generation,* 2002, includes an article by Anthony Libby, "Diane di Prima: 'Nothing Is Lost; It Shines in Our Eyes,'" which discusses a range of works from di Prima's oeuvre; Brenda Knight's *Women of the Beat Generation: The Writers, Artists, and Muses at the Heart of a Revolution,* 1996, devotes a section to di Prima and her writing, titled "Diane di Prima, Poet Priestess"; David Meltzer, Marina Lazzara, and James Brook published an in-depth interview with di Prima in the book *San Francisco Beat: Talking with the Poets,* 2001; Ann Charters analyzes *Loba* in an article titled "Diane di Prima and the Loba Poems: Poetic Archetype as Spirit Double," published in *Beat Indeed!* 1985, and Peter Warshall interviewed di Prima regarding her writing of *Loba* in "The Tapestry of Possibility," published in *Whole Earth* 98 (Fall 1999): 20–22; Amy L. Friedman's "'Being here as hard as I could': The Beat Generation Women Writers," published in *Discourse* 20.1 and 2 (Winter and Spring 1998): 229–244, offers insight into di Prima's role as woman writer of that milieu, as does Alix Kates Shulman's "Women Writers in the Beat Generation" published in *Moody Street Irregulars* 28 (Fall 1994): 3–9; Joyce Johnson's "Beat Queens: Women in Flux" and Hettie Jones's "Babes in Boyland," both published in *The Rolling Stone Book of the Beats: The Beat Generation and American Culture,* 1999, also offer commentary on the role women played in the Beat movement.

***See also*** Censorship; Baraka, Amiri; Little Magazines; Jones, Hettie

## Dorn, Edward (1929–1999)

One of the most significant Black Mountain poets, Edward Dorn is distinguished among his contemporaries as a strikingly political voice. He was born in Villa Grove, Illinois, on 2 April 1929. He spent some time at the University of Illinois, Urbana, and had a brief stay at Eastern Illinois University, where he met Ray Obermayr, a professor who told him about Black Mountain College in North Carolina.

Partly in an effort to avoid being sent to Korea, Dorn, who was interested in painting, went to Black Mountain College in 1951, before Charles Olson became the rector. Dorn left after a short time, but returned in the fall of 1954, studying with Olson and becoming one of the few people to take a degree from the college. Robert Creeley was his outside examiner.

When Dorn moved to San Francisco in 1956, Kenneth Rexroth became his mentor, and Dorn met Allen Ginsberg and Jack Kerouac. Like Ginsberg, he was a baggage clerk at the Greyhound Bus Terminal. Unfortunately, Dorn became involved in the controversy surrounding Robert Creeley's affair with Marthe Rexroth. Dorn was also a player in the Merwin incident at Naropa in 1977. He was close to LeRoi Jones, who published Dorn's first collection of poems. Jones (now Amiri Baraka) thought of Dorn as one of the most intelligent men he had ever met and one of the few white men who understood him. Although they continued to correspond, they had a falling out over one of Dorn's poems. Dorn taught at Idaho State University at Pocatello, the University of Essex, the University of California at Riverside and at La Jolla, and the University of Colorado. His comic epic poem *Gunslinger*, which he started writing as a visiting professor at Essex and wrote over several years, is one of the neglected masterpieces of twentieth-century poetry. Dorn died in Denver, Colorado, on 10 December 1999 after losing his battle with pancreatic cancer.

—*Kurt Hemmer*

### Principal Works

Poetry: *The Newly Fallen*, 1961; *Hands Up!*, 1964; *Recollections of Gran Apacheria*, 1974; *Slinger*, 1975 (republished as *Gunslinger*, 1989); *Collected Poems: 1956–1974*, 1975; *Hello, La Jolla*, 1978.
Prose: *The Shoshoneans*, 1966; *The Rites of Passage*, 1965 (republished as *By the Sound*, 1971); *Some Business Recently Transacted in the White World*, 1971; *The Poet, the People, the Spirit*, 1976; *Way West: Stories, Essays & Verse Accounts, 1963–1993*, 1993.

### Bibliographical References

The most recent biography is Tom Clark, *Edward Dorn: A World of Difference*, 2002; a short biography is William McPheron, *Edward Dorn*, 1988; an excellent discussion of *Gunslinger* is James K. Elmborg, "A Pageant of Its Time": *Edward Dorn's "Slinger" and the Sixties*, 1998.

*See also* Black Mountain, North Carolina, and Black Mountain College

## Drugs

More than any other community of American writers, the Beats used various drugs to attain spiritual enlightenment and to gain aesthetic inspiration. Their receptiveness to drug experimentation derived from their interest in African American jazz culture and the hipster culture of underground, urban America. Although the Beat writers had various opinions regarding drug use as it pertained to their artistic endeavors, and although not all the writers associated with the Beats believed in its importance, drug use was seminal to the Beat movement. William S. Burroughs, Allen Ginsberg, and Jack Kerouac used drugs to inspire their artistic output. Their most inspirational works, *Naked Lunch*, "Howl," and *On the Road*, respectively, can be read as the products of drug-induced states. As the Beat movement became more of a West Coast phenomenon in the late 1950s and early 1960s, hallucinogens replaced marijuana, Benzedrine, and heroin as the drugs of choice. Timothy Leary and Ken Kesey, figures closely associated with and inspired by the Beats, attempted to promote hallucinogens, with the support of Ginsberg, for social change. Although there were drug casualties among them, some of the Beats continued their adherence to the benefit of drug-induced mind alteration well into old age.

African American jazz culture and the Times Square hipster culture (introduced to the Beats by Herbert Huncke) provided the Beats with access to drug scenes that were prevalent in these environments. The jazz genius Charlie Parker, who was one of the great artistic inspirations for Kerouac, was a notorious drug user. Another catalyst for the Beats' involvement with drugs was Rimbaud's belief in the systematic derangement of the senses as a method to escape the confines of society's ideological chains. This attitude posited that ideologies established by the dominant culture could control the senses, and that what was required to dismantle this control was the breakdown of the body's perceptions manufactured by society. This dismantling was done in an effort to confront the reality the manufactured senses concealed. Drugs were used as tools to break through to a higher, more profound consciousness. The drugs of choice for the Beats living in New York City in the 1940s were marijuana, Benzedrine, and heroin. Hallucinogens became more prevalent as the hub of the Beat scene became established on the West Coast in the late 1950s.

The Beats generally believed society's fear of illicit drug use was both hypocritical and calculated. Those against the free use of drugs had no moral ground as long as they continued to accept the sale and distribution of harmful legal drugs. A conspiracy theory was conceived by some of those in the counterculture. Certain drugs were prohibited from the masses, they believed, not because of the government's concern over the well-being of its citizens, but because of the government's fear over losing control over citizens' thoughts and lifestyles if certain illegal drugs were consumed. In reaction to the containment culture, the Beats saw experimentation with drugs as a necessary attempt to avoid what they considered to be the mental shackles of society.

The most notorious Beat drug user was William S. Burroughs. Burroughs's first experiments with hard drugs can be traced back to his meeting Herbert Huncke in the mid-40s. Huncke was a crucial figure in influencing the Beats' attitudes toward drugs. A Times Square hustler and habitual drug user, Huncke was not only intelligent, but genuinely kind. Huncke became the model for the downtrodden, underground figure wrongly rejected by society that the Beats chose to champion. He confirmed for the Beats that kindness of soul did not necessarily correspond to conformist attitudes. Desiring to enter into the criminal world already inhabited by Huncke, Burroughs was inspired to try one of the stolen morphine tartrate Syrettes he had tried to sell Huncke during their first encounter. Burroughs's early experiences as a junky were used as the basis for his first novel, *Junky* (1953), originally published as *Junkie* under the pseudonym William Lee by Ace Books. Subtitled *Confessions of an Unredeemed Drug Addict*, it was sold as part of "two books in one" with the reprint of Maurice Helbrant's *Narcotics Agent*. Although drug use provided the material for *Junky,* it was not until Burroughs began the writings that became his most famous novel, *Naked Lunch* (1959), that drug use had a profound influence on Burroughs's creative process. Burroughs's drug use gave him the freedom finally to find his own voice. Unhindered by aesthetic and moral constraints while writing certain sections of what would become the novel, Burroughs explored, via drugs, the intriguing and often horrifying images that had previously been hidden in his unconscious. The result was one of the most astonishing and disturbing books of the twentieth century.

Although *Naked Lunch* can be read as a book arguing against the use of addictive drugs, it has probably inspired as much drug experimentation as it has deterred. With the publication of *Naked Lunch* and its ensuing censorship trials, Burroughs became a famous junky. His face was on the cover of the Beatles' *Sgt. Pepper's Lonely Hearts Club Band* album and he was invited to Mick Jagger's wedding to Bianca. In the 70s, when Burroughs lived in the apartment known as the Bunker, he became the grandfather of the new punk movement as musicians, such as Lou Reed, Iggy Pop, David Bowie, and Deborah Harry, came to pay homage. Unfortunately, many fans also wanted to use drugs with Burroughs. As heroin prices plummeted on the streets of New York in 1979, Burroughs renewed a habit that he would not kick until just before he left to live in Lawrence, Kansas in 1981. Even while in Kansas, Burroughs received visits by drug enthusiasts. Kurt Cobain visited Burroughs in 1993, and the following year committed suicide after taking a large dose of heroin. It is arguable that Burroughs became such an important countercultural icon as much for his drug use as his writings. The irony is that Burroughs spent his life trying to fight against being controlled. This effort ultimately led to his experimentation with drugs and his addiction. His addiction helped him theorize about the concept of control, but it also pigeonholed him as a gentleman junky to many of his admirers and detractors. Some say that Burroughs would not have become a writer had it not been for the encouragement of Ginsberg and Kerouac. Burroughs himself wrote that he would not have become a writer had it not been for his accidental shooting of his wife Joan in Mexico in 1951. Yet another argument can be made that Burroughs would not have become a writer had it not been for his drug use.

Burroughs is arguably the junky par excellence, but Allen Ginsberg was the leading Beat proponent of drug use as a means of establishing a new mass consciousness. Although Burroughs's addiction to heroin eventually led him to see the horrors of control, Ginsberg's extensive drug experimentation inspired him to imagine a new collective consciousness. In 1948, he experienced his Blake visions, a series of auditory and mystical sensations that convinced him to pursue the elimination of his ordinary consciousness in an effort to embrace a spiritual consciousness through drug use. This pursuit dominated the next fifteen years of his life. The major works of Ginsberg's career were partially influenced by his belief in the creative benefits of drugs. Part II of "Howl" was inspired by the horrifying experiences Ginsberg had with Peter Orlovsky while on peyote. Using a combination of heroin, liquid Methedrine, and Dexedrine tablets, Ginsberg began composing "Kaddish." The success of his poetic skills while on various substances convinced Ginsberg that he was on the right path.

In 1961, Ginsberg, having complete faith in his own drug experiences, started to conceive of a psychedelic revolution with Timothy Leary. Leary was a Harvard professor who had experimented with psychedelic mushrooms in 1960 and experimented successfully with psilocybin, the active ingredient in the mushrooms, on prison inmates. Ginsberg and Leary, whose mantra was "Turn On, Tune In, Drop Out," organized a series of drug experiments with psilocybin pills in an effort to gain support in the artistic community for the public use of hallucinogens. Willem de Kooning, Franz Kline, Dizzy Gillespie, and Thelonious Monk were the first to partake in the experiment and were later joined by Robert Lowell, Charles Olson, Barney Rosset, Burroughs, and Kerouac. Resolute in his opinion that hallucinogens were not the answer, Kerouac quipped, "Walking on water wasn't built in a day," a phrase he later included in *Satori in Paris* (108).

A decade earlier, Kerouac's use of alcohol, marijuana, and Benzedrine helped create a good portion of his own work. Some scholars have speculated that the famous 1951 scroll draft of *On the Road*, composed in a manic three-week burst, was the result of Kerouac's own experimentation with drugs. Supposedly, he slept rarely, typed continuously, and went through dozens of sweat-soaked T-shirts. This description suggests, as many believe, that Kerouac's novel was written while he was using Benzedrine. The Sampas family, heirs and promoters of the Kerouac estate, steadfastly deny that Kerouac used anything stronger than coffee when producing the text. Whether or not this claim is true, Kerouac was not the drug advocate that some of his acolytes became. By the end of the 1960s, with the help of Leary and Ginsberg, millions of Americans had experimented with LSD. It was not until 1963 while in India that Ginsberg, inspired by the advice of various gurus, decided to give up on his attempt to reproduce the Blake visions, and Buddhism eventually replaced drug use as Ginsberg's source for attaining universal harmony.

Leary, considered the "High Priest" of LSD, continued to administer drug experiments in order to attain spiritual enlightenment. While Leary revered drug use as a religious experience, Ken Kesey and the Merry Pranksters, who took off across America with Neal Cassady, an amphetamines user with interest in hallucinogens, at the wheel in 1964, brought their own twist to the psychedelic revolution. Kesey had volunteered for drug experiments while working as a night attendant on the psychiatric ward of a hospital in 1959. His first novel, *One Flew Over the Cuckoo's Nest* (1962), was inspired by a peyote vision. Rather than being awed by the spiritual dimensions of hallucinogens, the Merry Pranksters embraced the comic absurdity of drug use in an effort to tear down the serious façade that they saw as stifling the American imagination. For Kesey, LSD could only open a new door for its user, and this door, once entered, could not be entered again. As the 60s came to a close, and an increasing number of people became statistics of illicit drug use, it became increasingly difficult to promote seriously the use of drugs as life enhancing. Many of the Beat writers suffered the consequences of their often naïve experiments. Perhaps the Beat experiment with drugs was a necessary failure—a warning for generations to come. Yet the price for this failure was extremely high. Kerouac was plagued with thrombophlebitis caused by excessive Benzedrine use from the mid-40s. Some scholars claim that Gregory Corso failed to achieve his full poetic promise because of his drug use. Other critics say that drug use explains Kesey's lack of output throughout his career. Cassady died from a lethal mix of alcohol and barbiturates on the railroad tracks of Mexico, just shy of his forty-second birthday. Dozens of minor characters associated with the Beats also became the casualties of drugs. Nonetheless, Burroughs, Huncke, and Leary continued to use various drugs until their deaths at ripe old ages.

—*Kurt Hemmer*

**Bibliographical References**

Tom Wolfe, *The Electric Kool-Aid Acid Test*, 1968; Gerald Nicosia, *Memory Babe: A Critical Biography of Jack Kerouac*, 1983; Ted Morgan, *Literary Outlaw: The Life and Times of William S. Burroughs*, 1988; Barry Miles, *Ginsberg: A Biography*, 1989; references to Artaud, Lenny Bruce, Burroughs, and Leary can be found in Richard Rudgley, *The Encyclopaedia of Psychoactive Substances*, 1999.

*See also* Cassady, Neal; Ginsberg, Allen; Leary, Timothy; Kerouac, Jack; Burroughs, William Seward

# Duncan, Robert (1919–1988)

Poet; political and literary activist. In San Francisco, Robert Duncan established a literary circle that inspired several Beats. Recognizing Duncan's importance, Lawrence Ferlinghetti published Duncan's *Selected Poems* (1959) as a City Lights title; Donald Allen, aware of Duncan's connection to both Black Mountain College and the San Francisco Renaissance, made Duncan a significant contributor to *The New American Poetry* (1960).

Born in Oakland, California, Duncan was the adopted child of Theosophists Edwin Joseph Symmes, an architect, and Minnehaha Harris, who together stimulated Duncan's interest in the occult. Edward Howard Duncan and Marguerite Pearl Carpenter were Duncan's biological parents, but Duncan's mother died in giving birth, and Duncan's father did not have the resources to raise his child; therefore, the father surrendered his son for adoption. At age three, Duncan suffered an injury to his eyes that left him with double vision, and this injury, in addition to Duncan's fascination with the occult, influenced the formation of Duncan's poetic outlook.

In 1938, Duncan traveled to New York, where various movements in art, including Abstract Expressionism, Modernism, and Surrealism, were interacting. With Sanders Russell, Duncan published *Experimental Review*, which featured works from writers such as Henry Miller, Anais Nin, and Kenneth Patchen. Around this time Duncan also worked in connection with James Cooney, whose publication *The Phoenix* was produced at a commune in Woodstock, New York.

In 1941, Duncan was drafted for military service, but he soon declared his homosexuality and received a psychiatric discharge. Despite this declaration, Duncan married Marjorie McKee in 1943, but the marriage quickly ended. In 1944, in *Politics*, Duncan published his essay "The Homosexual in Society."

In San Francisco in the mid 1940s, Duncan came under several important influences. Kenneth Rexroth, who organized literary gatherings in his home, spurred Duncan's interest in the writings of H. D., who became the focus of many of Duncan's subsequent efforts in literary criticism. Jack Spicer and Robin Blaser experimented with forms based on recurring images, and subsequently Duncan conceived poetry based on the techniques of collage. Charles Olson and Duncan met in 1947, and this relationship led to the maturation of Duncan's theory of poetics and to Duncan's involvement at Black Mountain College in the 1950s, including Duncan's association with Robert Creeley.

Duncan's first book, *Heavenly City, Earthly City*, was published in 1947, but the poem that was the touchstone for many of his subsequent writings was "The Venice Poem" (1948). The poem gained form through recurrent themes and mythic references.

In 1951, Duncan forged a lasting relationship with Jess Collins, a visual artist with special interests in collage. Collins and Duncan collaborated on many books, with Duncan adapting the techniques of collage to his writing.

In 1952, Duncan's poems began to appear in Cid Corman's *Origin* and in *Black Mountain Review*, the publication of Black Mountain College, where Duncan became a member of the faculty in 1956.

Duncan emerged as a major writer in the 1960s. In *The Opening of the Field* (1960), he wrote of a pastoral place that is a product of his thought but also a possession of his soul—a place that lasts and shines forever and generates its own form. In *Roots and Branches* (1964) and *Bending the Bow* (1968), he further established his characteristic experimental style. As the Vietnam war progressed, Duncan often expressed his opposition to the war.

Duncan won a Guggenheim Fellowship in 1963 and received writing fellowships from the National Endowment for the Arts three times. He won the National Poetry Award in 1985.

In San Francisco in 1988, Duncan died after a long struggle with renal disease.

—*William Lawlor*

### Principal Works

*Heavenly City, Earthly City*, 1947; *Poems 1948–49*, 1949; *Medieval Scenes*, 1950; *Fragments of a Disordered Devotion*, 1952; *Caesar's Gate Poems 1949–1950 with Collages by Jess Collins*, 1955; reprinted as *Caesar's Gate Poems 1949–1950 with Paste-Ups by Jess*, 1972; *Letters Poems*

*MCMLIII–MCMLVI*, 1958; *Selected Poems*, 1959; *The Opening of the Field*, 1960; *Unkingd by Affection*, 1963; *Writing, Writing*, 1964; *Roots and Branches*, 1964; *Passages 22–27 of the War*, 1966; *The Years as Catches First Poems (1939–1946)*, 1966; *A Book of Resemblances: Poems 1950–1953*, 1966; *Names of the People*, *Bending the Bow*, 1968; *The First Decade Selected Poems 1940–1950*, 1969; *Derivations Selected from 1950–1956*, 1969; *Achilles' Song*, 1969; *Play Time Pseudo Stein*, 1969; *Tribunals Passages 31–35*, 1970; *Ground Work*, 1971; *Poems from the Margins of Thom Gunn's Moly*, 1972; *A Seventeenth Century Suite in Homage to the Metaphysical Genius in English Poetry 1590/1690: Being Imitations, Derivations & Variations Upon Certain Conceits and Findings Made Among Strong Lines*, 1973; *An Ode and Arcadia* (with Jack Spicer), 1974; *Dante*, 1974; *The Venice Poem*, 1975; *Ground Work: Before the War*, 1983; *Ground Work II: In the Dark*, 1987

### Bibliographical References

See Michael Davidson, *The San Francisco Renaissance*, 1989: 125–149; Ekbert Faas, *Young Robert Duncan: Portrait of the Poet as Homosexual in Society*, 1983, is a biography that covers the period through age thirty. Mark Andrew Johnson, *Robert Duncan*, 1988, serves as a clear introduction, and *Robert Duncan: Scales of the Marvelous*, eds. Robert Bertholf and Ian W. Reid, 1979, is a collection of essays. Nathaniel Mackey's "The World-Poem in Microcosm: Robert Duncan's 'The Continent,'" *ELH* 47 (1980): 595–618, interprets Duncan's method; Steven Watson, "Robert Duncan," in *The Birth of the Beat Generation*, 1995, provides a quick review.

***See also*** San Francisco Renaissance; Influences; Spicer, Jack

## Dylan, Bob (1941–)

Preeminent singer-songwriter of his generation, harbinger of social change and role model for restless youth, Bob Dylan was inspired and empowered by the somewhat older Beats. An original lyricist, conceptual visionary, and creative interpreter of folk, blues, rock, pop, jazz, and other idioms, he expanded on Beat consciousness through musical performance and recording, often in a Woody

Guthrie–style voice that has been much imitated and satirized. A pop "legend," he has maintained a life so private that biographers debate the number of women he has married. An important admirer and ally of Allen Ginsberg, Dylan also inspired the older man.

Grandson of Russian-Jewish immigrants, Bob Dylan was born Robert Allen Zimmerman, 24 May 1941, in Duluth, Minnesota. His father, Abram, was employed by Standard Oil until crippled by polio. In 1947, the Zimmermans moved to the northern Minnesota "iron ore capital" of Hibbing, childhood home of Robert's mother, Beatrice.

As a teenager, "Bobby," a rhythm and blues enthusiast who most emulated Little Richard, played piano and sang in several rock-and-roll bands. After his 1959 graduation from Hibbing High School, he attended the University of Minnesota, Minneapolis, where he embraced folk music and acoustic guitar.

In his sophomore year, now calling himself "Bob Dylan"—a name that revealed his respect for the poet Dylan Thomas—the young musician left college for New York City to meet his idol, Woody Guthrie. Dylan was soon established as a Greenwich Village–based folk singer and songwriter. The single, "Blowin' in the Wind," as sung by folk-trio Peter, Paul, and Mary, remains his most popular composition. Romantic and professional involvement with folk "queen" Joan Baez advanced Dylan's writing and performing career.

In 1965, Dylan's abrupt conversion to an electrified accompaniment, surreal lyrics, and a rock-and-roll persona, as revealed at the Newport Folk Festival, dismayed folk purists. Inventive and personal lyrics from this period of greatest verbal genius make up the albums *Bringing It All Back Home*, *Highway 61 Revisited*, and *Blonde on Blonde* and found greatest popular acceptance on the single "Like a Rolling Stone." A "fab" Dylan is depicted in the D. A. Pennebaker documentary, *Don't Look Back*, which includes a version of "Subterranean Homesick Blues," considered by many to be the first "rock video."

The pressures of public scrutiny, intense adulation, and drug usage appeared to threaten the pop

Bob Dylan plays guitar in 1965. (Library of Congress)

idol's equilibrium. Following a 1966 one-motorcycle accident, he lived in relative seclusion near Woodstock, New York, with wife, Sara, children Jesse, Jakob, Samuel, and Anna, and Sara's daughter, Maria, whom Dylan adopted. Here, Dylan wrote the quietly allegorical *John Wesley Harding* and, with The Band, the louder and light-hearted songs collected later as *The Basement Tapes*. Both stood in marked contrast to then-current psychedelia. Negative criticism of efforts following the 1969 *Nashville Skyline* was relieved by the popularity of "Knockin' on Heaven's Door" from the movie *Pat Garrett and Billy the Kid*, in which Dylan played the bit part of "Alias."

Dylan's much-anticipated "novel," *Tarantula*, was published reluctantly in 1971, as a response to widespread bootlegging. In 1975, Dylan resumed public performance with his Rolling Thunder Revue, playing small venues while accompanied by an entourage of musicians, poets, and playwrights. Extensive filming of the tour resulted in his self-directed, fictional, four-hour feature, *Renaldo and Clara.*

The 1975 album *Blood on the Tracks,* viewed as a passionate reaction to the end of his marriage to Sara, was a critical and popular success. "Hurricane," a 1976 single, received significant airplay and was aimed at the release of imprisoned boxer, Rubin Carter.

After the 1979 conversion of Jewish-born Dylan, several factions of fans fled Christian-themed concerts and rejected albums such as *Slow Train Coming.* Now widely viewed by critics as a figure in decline, Dylan garnered his first Grammy award for vocals on the single, "Gotta Serve Somebody." The 1985 multiple-set album *Biograph,* released after the waning of his overt proselytizing, confirmed recognition of Dylan's contribution to American music.

Since the late 1980s, Dylan has undertaken a "Never Ending Tour," that began after tours with rock groups such as Tom Petty and the Heartbreakers and The Grateful Dead. Together with Petty, Beatle George Harrison, Jeff Lynne, and Roy Orbison, Dylan helped write and record as the "Traveling Wilburys." He contributed several songs to *Hearts of Fire,* a failed 1987 film in which Dylan's portrayal of the retired and reclusive rock star Billy Parker demonstrated an awkward but affecting charisma. Renditions of folk-blues on *Good As I Been to You* (1992) and *World Gone Wrong* (1993) confirmed Dylan's ability to ignore the usual commercial forces and invited comparison with similar material performed more than thirty years earlier.

By the time he emerged from a life-threatening attack of histoplasmosis in May 1997, Dylan's place in rock history was secure, and he had become an ironic and uneasy establishment figure. The aptly stark dignity of the September 1997 album *Time Out of Mind* brought critical acclaim rivaling that of his "genius" period of the 1960s.

As his generation and that following it ascended to power in the 1990s, Dylan's honors multiplied with a Grammy Lifetime Achievement Award, his Thirtieth Anniversary Concert Celebration, an appearance before Pope John Paul II, Kennedy Center Honors, and an Academy Award for the single, "Things Have Changed." Throughout, the neo-beatnik poet himself remained an enigmatic and romantic figure, what was once a baby face now a sagging, deeply lined countenance adorned with a pencil-thin mustache.

Dylan was exposed in 1958–1959 to elements of Beatness with visits to James Reese, aka Jim Dandy, a black disc jockey in nearby Virginia, Minnesota, who shared an extensive collection of jazz and blues. While of high school age and later as a college student, Dylan frequented a bohemian locale adjacent to the University of Minnesota named Dinkytown, where "beatniks" such as Dave Morton and Dave Whitaker introduced left-wing politics, marijuana, folk music, and the Beat classics *A Coney Island of the Mind,* "Howl," and *On the Road.* The spontaneous bop prosody of Kerouac's *Mexico City Blues,* according to Allen Ginsberg in *Spontaneous Mind,* "blew [Dylan's] mind" (393). The connection between music and poetry made by Kerouac, Kenneth Patchen, Kenneth Rexroth, and Lawrence Ferlinghetti, who were primarily writers, would be continued through Dylan, a musician who is sometimes called a poet. Dylan has also acknowledged early familiarity with Gary Snyder, Philip Whalen, Gregory Corso, and Frank O'Hara. Ginsberg's "city poetry," he said, helped shape his own "city songs" such as "Desolation Row" (McGregor).

Noted for his ability to assimilate and transform styles, in his surrealistic songs such as "Subterranean Homesick Blues" and albums such as *Highway 61 Revisited* Dylan borrowed terms, attitude, and general bop-ness from Ginsberg and Ferlinghetti. The seemingly spontaneous prose passages in Dylan's novella *Tarantula* borrowed from the fiction of Kerouac, the "cut-ups" of William Burroughs, and the *Journal of Albion Moonlight* by Kenneth Patchen.

In 1965, a well-circulated set of photos by Larry Keenan meant for the *Blonde on Blonde* cover showed Dylan, Robbie Robertson, Michael McClure, and Allen Ginsberg posing in an alley behind Ferlinghetti's City Lights Books. Ginsberg reported that Dylan's "chains of flashing images" of the period were a stylistic debt to Kerouac (*Screaming with Joy*). Dylan began to tout Ginsberg as a poet, mentor, and friend.

Besides absorbing Beat ideas, in his early years, Dylan favored a "beatnik" lifestyle of apparent rootlessness and poor hygiene. He indulged in an excess of wine, marijuana, and cigarettes. Eccentric appearance and sarcastic interviews exuded a Beat scorn of the hip for the square. He was often photographed wearing sunglasses.

Dylan's "finger-pointing" protest songs, such as "Blowin' in the Wind," "A Hard Rain's a-Gonna Fall," and "The Times They Are a-Changin'" brought him to the attention of Ginsberg. After a meeting at a party and an invitation from Dylan to a concert at Princeton, the clean-shaven and top-hatted author of "Howl" subsequently showed up on the sleeve of the Dylan album *Bringing It All Back Home*.

Ginsberg's unreciprocated sexual attraction for the heterosexual Dylan did not interfere with a life-long professional and personal relationship that ranged from Ginsberg escorting Dylan's children trick-or-treating and Dylan teaching Ginsberg a chord sequence, allowing him to progress into musical accompaniment of his voice. In 1965, Ginsberg toured the United States composing a poem on an expensive tape recorder that Dylan paid for. Ginsberg appeared in the 1967 documentary *Don't Look Back* and visited Dylan at Woodstock after the singer's motorcycle accident.

In 1971, with Dylan's accompaniment on piano, organ, and guitar, Ginsberg, at his expense, recorded "September on Jessore Road" and other material, later included on *Holy Soul Jelly Roll – Poems and Songs (1949–1993)*. He was an active participant in the Rolling Thunder Revue and in the resulting movie, *Renaldo and Clara*. Among other scenes, he and Dylan, in Lowell, Massachusetts, stood at Kerouac's grave, read from *Mexico City Blues*, and improvised a song.

According to Ginsberg's biographer Barry Miles, who visited John Lennon in Manhattan in 1976, Lennon said that hearing Ginsberg reading "Kaddish" for a radio program made Lennon think of Dylan's voice. The experience prompted Lennon to say he understood how much Ginsberg had influenced Dylan and how close their styles were.

—*Dave Engel*

**Principal Works**

Selected Albums: *The Freewheelin' Bob Dylan*, 1963; *Bringing It All Back Home*, 1965; *Highway 61 Revisited*, 1965; *Blonde on Blonde*, 1966; *Blood on the Tracks*, 1975; *Desire*, 1976; *Slow Train Coming*, 1979; *Biograph*, 1985; *Time Out of Mind*, 1997.

Books: Bob Dylan, *Tarantula*, 1971; *Chronicles Volume I*, 2004.

Movies: *Don't Look Back*, 1967; *Renaldo and Clara*, 1976; *Hearts of Fire*, 1987; *Masked and Anonymous*, 2003.

**Bibliographical References**

Graham Caveney, *Screaming with Joy: The Life of Allen Ginsberg*, 1999; Dave Engel, *Just Like Bob Zimmerman's Blues: Dylan in Minnesota*, 1997; Allen Ginsberg, *Spontaneous Mind: Selected Interviews, 1958–1996*, 2001; Michael Gray, *Song and Dance Man: The Art of Bob Dylan*, 1981; Clinton Heylin, *Bob Dylan: Behind the Shades Revisited*, 2001; *The Rolling Stone Book of the Beats: The Beat Generation and American Culture*, ed. Holly George-Warren, 1999; Robert Shelton, *No Direction Home: The Life and Music of Bob Dylan*, 1986; Howard Sounes, *Down the Highway: The Life of Bob Dylan*, 2001.

***See also*** Music; Ginsberg, Allen; Fariña, Richard

# E

## Eastern Culture

The Beat Generation actively explored Eastern cultures and the religions associated with them. This exploration affected the spiritual lives of the Beats and was manifested in their artistic productivity.

Jack Kerouac, whom Allen Ginsberg in the dedication to "Howl" called the "New Buddha of American prose" (5), dedicated himself to understanding the Eastern outlook through composition of *Some of the Dharma*, which he intended as a guidebook to Buddhism for Allen Ginsberg but later claimed for himself as a sacred personal text.

In *Some of the Dharma,* Kerouac explores Buddhism's Four Noble Truths and the Eight-Fold Path, but he also reflects on contrasts between East and West. Kerouac remarks that people of the West know nothing of enlightenment and cannot make spiritual connections that involve Nirvana. Kerouac compares the Westerner to an investigator relentlessly struggling to develop an original type of sorrow (79). Interested in bringing enlightenment to himself and to Western society in general, Kerouac proposes a practical way of living that involves the purchase of a used truck (117). This truck should become a mobile monastery, which may be located on seacoasts, in the mountains, or outside Mexican villages. Properly equipped with materials for eating, writing, studying, camping, and seeing by night (117), the enlightened man can maintain his bearings toward what is pure (117).

In "A Vision of Joy," which is included in *Some of the Dharma* (127), Kerouac creates an Eastern world adapted for Western circumstances. He pictures himself in California or Mexico, with his beard grown for four months, his supplies of water ample and varied, and his schedule uncluttered. He reads his Buddhist books and contemplates as he wishes. At night under the stars, he enters a state of meditation and prayer that allows him to know enlightenment and set aside material possessions (127).

On December 27, 1955, in Rocky Mount, North Carolina, Kerouac in *Some of the Dharma* announces the start of his work on *Visions of Gerard*, the novel about Kerouac's brother, who died of rheumatic fever. Kerouac invokes the help of God, praying to God for dedication to spiritual tasks and for immersion in the power of holy language (367).

When Kerouac connected with Gary Snyder, the Beat link to the East gained strength. Whereas Kerouac was self-taught, Snyder at Berkeley was a formal student of Eastern languages and literatures. To a significant extent, Snyder tutored Kerouac and refined his understanding of Buddhist writers and their texts. Snyder's skills in mountaineering drew Kerouac into serving as a fire lookout, which afforded solitude and profound awareness of nature. The Eastern consciousness explored by Snyder and Kerouac is a memorable part of *The Dharma Bums* (1958) as Japhy Ryder and Ray Smith exchange ideas on Eastern poetry and thought.

In Snyder's writings, the appreciation of Eastern culture, philosophy, and literature is present in almost every work, but *Earth House Hold* (1969), which includes "Buddhism and the Coming Revolution" (90–93), is a concise discussion of Snyder's views of various forms of Buddhism and their contrasts to Western political and religious systems. Snyder discusses the general Buddhist view that all life is suffering and that suffering is caused by senseless craving (90). Snyder concedes that Mahayana Buddhism faces the question of the salvation of all people but sees Buddhism in general as a means to overcome the traps of a person's own mind and the habits established by culture (90). Institutional Buddhism, which makes too many compromises with civil authority, can extinguish Buddhism (90). In Snyder's view, Avatamsaka (Kegon) Buddhism is based on the interconnection of all things: he insists that the predatory bird, its downward flight, and the prey it seeks are one (92). Returning to a general view of Buddhism, Snyder indicates that wisdom, meditation, and morality (the three components in the dharma path) apply not only to the Buddhist pursuit of self-knowledge, but also to the Western pursuit of social justice (93).

Snyder's outlook on Eastern thinking and its application to the improvement of Western civilization is humorously developed in "Smokey the Bear Sutra," which is included in *The Portable Beat Reader*, edited by Ann Charters (1992). The Great Sun Buddha discusses enlightenment in the world (569). In the future the Sun Buddha will return as Smokey the Bear, whose gestures and dress will reveal that he is Buddha. He will require the world's inhabitants to live responsibly in the universe and to serve as caretakers for the planet. Those who will not live responsibly will incur Smokey's wrath; those who learn the sutra and put its ideas into practice will enjoy a pleasant and enlightened life (571).

Snyder intensified his association with Eastern ideas when he traveled to Japan to formalize his studies of Zen. For twelve years, Snyder participated in Zen studies in Japan. Ruth Fuller Sasaki, the widow of Sokei-an, introduced Snyder to Zen Master Muira Isshu, who later became Snyder's teacher at the Shokoku Temple.

Just as the travels of Snyder led to an awareness of Eastern cultures, the travels of Allen Ginsberg connected him to the East. In India in 1962, Ginsberg saw widespread poverty and disease, but in 1963, he was able to take the counsel of Bankey Behari and Kali Pado Gaha Roy. These thinkers gave new outlooks to Ginsberg, and the trip itself eventually led to *Indian Journals* (1970).

In Cambodia, Allen visited Angkor Wat, the ruins of a twelfth-century temple which had been the center of Hinduism for six hundred years. This experience proved influential and led to the long poem "Angkor Wat." Ginsberg's travels to the East ended with his reunion with Gary Snyder in Japan. Ginsberg became involved in extended meditation, control of breathing, and chanting. By the end of this third leg of the journey, Ginsberg was fully impressed with Eastern culture.

Back in the United States, Ginsberg's open disposition toward Eastern culture and Buddhism was shown in his affiliation with Tibetan Chögyam Trungpa Rinpoche. Trungpa founded the Naropa Institute with "crazy wisdom" and tried to establish the end of "spiritual materialism." Anne Waldman and Allen Ginsberg founded the Jack Kerouac School of Disembodied Poetics at Naropa, and the Beat-East connection was solidified in Boulder, Colorado.

Although Kerouac, Snyder, and Ginsberg were all drawn to Eastern cultures, William S. Burroughs never embraced them. He took part in a Buddhist retreat on one occasion; on the whole, however, he showed no enthusiasm because he insisted he was a writer, not a Buddhist. In fact, Burroughs distrusted Chögyam Trungpa, whose thirst for liquor and appetite for women made Buddhist asceticism seem remote from Trungpa's daily ways.

A key figure in the Beat connection to the East is Alan Watts, who fostered an appreciation of Zen and Eastern thinking through his lectures and writings. "Beat Zen, Square Zen, and Zen" is the essay that connects Watts most directly to the Beats, but Watts also offered a critical examination of *The Dharma Bums*, declaring that the novel transformed Zen's original sense of "anything goes."

Philip Whalen, one of the readers at the 6 Gallery on 7 October 1955, established formal connections to Eastern culture through his visits to Japan in 1967 and 1969–1971. A resident of the San Francisco Zen Center in 1972, Whalen was ordained as a Zen Buddhist monk in 1973. In 1991, Whalen was installed as Abbot at the Hartford Street Zen Center in San Francisco.

—*William Lawlor*

## Bibliographical References

*Some of the Dharma*, 1997, is published in an oversize format to recreate the feel of Kerouac's diverse entries. On Eastern topics, the book is rambling and repetitive, but the intensity of personal comments saves the book. *The Dharma Bums*, 1958, emerges as a shorter and more positive revelation of Kerouac's interpretation of Eastern ideas. Gary Snyder's interest in Eastern thinking is a major theme throughout his writing, but *Earth House Hold*, 1969, and "Smokey the Bear Sutra" are accessible and brief entry points. By examining *Indian Journals*, 1970, and "Angkor Wat," 1968, one sees Ginsberg's view of the East through both prose and poetry. Ginsberg's travels in the East are described by Michael Schumacher in *Dharma Lion*, 1992. To learn about a writer and speaker who made Eastern thinking available to many Western readers and listeners, see Alan Watts, "Beat Zen, Square Zen, and Zen," which appears in *The Portable Beat Reader*, ed. Ann Charters, 1992. Philip Whalen's *Overtime*, 1999, reveals Whalen's progress toward immersion in Eastern consciousness.

*See also* Kerouac, Jack; Snyder, Gary; Ginsberg, Allen; Watts, Alan; Whalen, Philip; Naropa Institute; Trungpa, Chögyam

## Elvins, Kells (1913–1961)

Kells Elvins was a lifelong friend of William S. Burroughs. Elvins lived near Burroughs on Price Road in St. Louis, and they met in their early teens. It was Elvins's father, Politte, who famously described the teenage Burroughs as looking "like a sheep-killing dog." Elvins, on the other hand, was handsome and athletic, and Burroughs had an early crush on him; however, according to Burroughs, their relationship was never a physical one over the years.

Both Burroughs and Elvins attended Harvard as undergraduates in the early 1930s and later, in 1938, as graduate students. There at Harvard, Elvins and Burroughs collaborated on Burroughs's first serious piece of writing, titled "Twilight's Last Gleaming" (1938), which they unsuccessfully tried to sell to *Esquire* magazine. The next year, Burroughs visited Elvins in Huntsville, Texas, where Elvins was working as a prison psychiatrist and researching a master's thesis in psychology titled "Forty-Four Incestuous Fathers of Texas." Elvins joined the Marines during World War II, earning a Purple Heart. Following the war, he moved to Pharr, Texas, to oversee the citrus farm he inherited from his father, who died in an automobile accident in 1943.

When Burroughs was forced to leave New York City because of a drug conviction in 1946, Elvins suggested Burroughs buy some land and join him in south Texas. The two were "gentlemen farmers" together from 1946 to 1949. Elvins introduced "Billy" to a crowd of south Texas "Beats" including "Tiger" Terry, Ted Marak, Walter Benson, and Obie Dobbs. Burroughs describes his life among this crowd and his experiences as a farmer in *Junky*, in which Elvins is called "Evans." (Elvins also appears briefly in *Queer*, and he is "K. E." in *Naked Lunch*.)

Neither Burroughs nor Elvins, however, was successful as a farmer, and Burroughs, Joan, and the two children moved to Mexico City in September 1949. Elvins and Marianne Standing arrived in January 1951 and were living there when Burroughs accidentally shot his wife, Joan, although Elvins was apparently not present at the fatal party. Burroughs and Elvins saw each other often over the next ten years—in Mexico, Tangier, and, most significantly, in Copenhagen, where Kells was living with his third wife, the actress Mimi Heinrich. Burroughs says that his trip to Denmark was the catalyst for writing the important "Freeland" section of *Naked Lunch*. Elvins died in 1961 in a hotel in New York City, where his wife was promoting her fashion line. He is buried in McAllen, Texas.

James Grauerholz has compared Elvins's relationship with Burroughs to Neal Cassady's relationship with Jack Kerouac: like Cassady, Elvins was a charismatic, larger-than-life character ("the alcoholic 'Playboy of the Western World,'" according to his son Peter), and Burroughs followed him around to be in on the action and to see what would happen next. Elvins thus played a key role in Burroughs's development as a writer. In fact, Kells suggested to Burroughs that he write down a "factual" account of his days as a drug addict in New York, leading to the publication of *Junkie* (1953), Burroughs's first book. Kells was probably Burroughs's closest friend, and Burroughs was reportedly able to be himself around Elvins in a way he couldn't with anyone else. Burroughs continued to write about Elvins up to the end of his life, in the dream book *My Education* as well as in *Last Words.* Elvins's letters to Burroughs are currently unpublished, as is a collection of short stories that Elvins wrote during the 1950s.

—*Rob Johnson*

### Bibliographical References
See Ted Morgan, *Literary Outlaw: The Life and Times of William S. Burroughs,* 1988; Rob Johnson, "William S. Burroughs: South Texas Farmer, Junky, and Queer," in *Southwestern American Literature* (Spring 2001); Rob Johnson and Juan Ochoa, "The South Texas Beats" in *Beat Scene* (Spring 2003).

*See also* Burroughs, William Seward

## Environmentalism

With Ralph Waldo Emerson and Henry David Thoreau as forefathers, and Eastern philosophies and Native American and multiple mythologies in their backgrounds, several of the Beat writers carried forth an abiding concern for the environment and ecological well-being through their writings. Nature, to the Beat writers, should be appreciated and protected; human beings should not destroy it and should learn to live with it, according to the visions of Gary Snyder, Jack Kerouac, Allen Ginsberg, and Michael McClure. These writers are advocates for the natural world, celebrate it, express an understanding of it, and feel compassion for it.

In Gary Snyder's *Turtle Island* (1974), environmental activism stands out clearly. In "Facts," Snyder converts a context that calls for a poem into an opportunity to present a numbered list of environmental considerations. For example, only six of every one hundred people in the world live in the United States, but these people use thirty percent of the energy (31). Snyder further predicts that the list of basic materials is short, but by the start of the twenty-first century the United States will rely on imports for all of the raw materials except phosphorous (31). "Facts" takes a political turn when Snyder identifies big oil companies as the enemy (31).

In "Mother Earth: Her Whales," which is also in *Turtle Island,* Snyder indicts nations that fail to protect the world's ecology. Japan, for example, rationalizes continued whale hunting and violates its Buddhist traditions by polluting the sea with heavy metals (47); China, in its quest for progress, forsakes its wildlife to create parking areas for thousands of trucks (48).

Snyder's integration of world cultures and ecological history helps the reader to reach into cultural memories and long lovingly for a better, purer time. The environment has been damaged, but not irrecoverably. Those who love the world can redeem it.

At the end of *Turtle Island,* Snyder includes "Plain Talk," and the environmental message is made directly. The first issue is population, and as a caretaker of the earth, each human must aim to cut the population of the world in half (91). The actions to bring about this end include abortions, vasectomies, and sterilizations. If the Catholic Church opposes these actions, then it must be opposed for its thoughtlessness about its role in the world (92). A second issue is pollution, which includes chemical poisons in the air and water, nuclear waste, and food additives. Snyder insists that society must dedicate itself to efficiency (95). Society cannot forge ahead with nuclear power and fossil fuels because no system is in place to deal effectively with the consequences.

Snyder adds humor to his environmental message in "Smokey the Bear Sutra," which is included in *The Portable Beat Reader,* edited by Ann Charters (1992). The poem, the author declares, may be redistributed for free forever. The figure from the announcements of the U.S. Forest Service is given voice in the poem, and the individual characteristics of the Buddha are humorously aligned with the characteristics of Smokey the Bear. Smokey has a worldview of ecology and knowledge of ecological history. The great geological features, such as the Grand Canyon and the Columbia River, are named for reverence and protection. If opponents to the plan of preservation and conservation come forward, then the advocates of the environment must "CRUSH THEIR BUTTS" (571).

Like Snyder, Allen Ginsberg recognizes the threat to the world's environment and uses his writing as a means to end the threat. In "Birdbrain!" (1980), which appears in *Collected Poems 1947–1980*, Ginsberg creates an inventory of social, political, and ecological abuses; the abuses to natural resources are especially clear when Ginsberg bemoans the construction of the World Trade Center without consideration for the effects of the sewage it will generate and when he notes the destruction of the Amazon Rainforest so that wood pulp can be manufactured on the banks of the river. In "Ballad of Poisons" (1978), which also appears in *Collected Poems*, Ginsberg's catalog of ecological shamefulness is more extensive. He mentions nuclear waste, pesticides, contamination of foods, heavy metals in plants, and raw sewage in the seas (692). In "Garden State" (1979), Ginsberg contrasts New Jersey's trash deposited in wetlands with the flowering bushes and trees of a previous generation (718). He sees a proliferation of television antennas and recalls rustic cemeteries adjacent to churches (718).

These complaints about the deterioration of the environment are counterbalanced by other poems. Ginsberg in "Homework," which is included in *Collected Poems* (731), adopts an apparently happier tone as he makes the act of doing laundry a metaphor for the renewal of the environment. If Ginsberg could clean up the world in the way a person does a load of wash, Ginsberg would cleanse the Amazon, restore wildlife to natural habitats, and rid the world of nuclear contamination. The ecstasy that Ginsberg discovers in the en-

vironment is clearest in "Wales Visitation," also included in *Collected Poems* (480–482), a poem he composed in London in 1967 while on LSD. Ginsberg's description of clouds, mist, grass, ferns, and flowers reveals enchantment and delight.

Like Ginsberg and Snyder, Michael McClure has a profound concern for ecology, and this concern is evident in "For the Death of 100 Whales," a poem he read at the 6 Gallery reading on 7 October 1955. According to a report in *Time* in April 1954, soldiers stationed at a NATO base in Iceland rounded up a pod of killer whales and exterminated them with rifle fire. McClure's poem is a tribute to the natural wolf-like spirit of the whales and an indictment of those who participated in a shameful execution.

McClure's writings express closeness to nature and its underlying spirit. In "Point Lobos: Animism," which McClure also read at the 6 Gallery, McClure describes an intense communion with the environment and indicates that the spirit of the forest and wildlife is more important than human disease and death. In "Ghost Tantras," McClure develops "Beast language," an idiom of growls, roars, and moans, and on several occasions McClure voiced this language to animals in zoos—eliciting responses! In *Scratching the Beat Surface*, McClure includes "A Mammal Gallery," which sets forth McClure's vision of the interconnectedness of all creatures in Nature, especially mammals. He hears the words of a man and wife arguing over a trivial detail, and closing his eyes, McClure hears the words only as sounds—as an example of a mammalian rite.

Like Snyder, Ginsberg, and McClure, Lawrence Ferlinghetti is a staunch defender of the environment. "In Goya's Greatest Scenes," a poem included in *A Coney Island of the Mind* (1958), Ferlinghetti describes the horrors and atrocities Goya reveals in his paintings, but Ferlinghetti then turns to the misery of the twentieth century, referring to the uncontrolled development of highways and the visual pollution created by mindless billboards. In his newspaper column, Ferlinghetti refers to the coming apocalypse caused by multiplying automobiles, which pollute the air, kill millions, and inspire madness behind the wheel. In Ferlinghetti's view, the key factor threatening the environment is overpopulation. Runaway development and exploitation of resources can be traced to demands created by the growing population, and to save the world, people must bring population growth under control.

For many members of the Beat Generation, the question of defending the environment is a longstanding concern. Publications such as *Journal for the Protection of All Beings*, edited by Ferlinghetti, David Meltzer, Snyder, and McClure, and *City Lights Review*, edited by Nancy Peters, provide discussion of ecological issues and present creative writing with environmental themes.

—*Maura Gage*

### Bibliographical References

Among many other works, Snyder's *Earth House Hold: Technical Notes & Queries to Fellow Dharma Revolutionaries*, 1969; and *Turtle Island*, 1974; are keys to his ecological outlook. "Smokey the Bear Sutra" can be found in *The Portable Beat Reader*, ed. Ann Charters, 1992, or *The Gary Snyder Reader*, 1999. For analysis, see Patrick Murphy, ed., *Critical Essays on Gary Snyder*, 1991; and Rod Phillips, *"Forest Beatniks" and "Urban Thoreaus": Gary Snyder, Jack Kerouac, Lew Welch, and Michael McClure*, 2001; Nick Selby discusses Snyder's ecological awareness in "Poem as Work-place: Gary Snyder's Ecological Poetics," *Sycamore* 14 (Winter 1997). *Allen Ginsberg's Collected Poems 1947–1980*, 1984, contains most of the poems in which Ginsberg comments on the environment. Michael McClure's "For the Death of 100 Whales" appeared originally in *Hymn to St. Geryon*, 1959; and additional commentary by McClure can be found in *Scratching the Beat Surface*, 1982. Ferlinghetti's "In Goya's Greatest Scenes" is the first poem in *A Coney Island of the Mind*, 1958. Ferlinghetti continues his commentary on automobiles and other threats to the environment in his newspaper columns, one of which is "Poetry and Autogeddon," *San Francisco Chronicle*, 13 August 2000.

*See also* Snyder, Gary; Ginsberg, Allen; Ferlinghetti, Lawrence; McClure, Michael

## Europe, Bohemian Movements Related to the Beat Movement in

Concurrent with the emergence of the Beat Generation in the United States, after the Second World War in Europe and other parts of the world, literary movements appeared whose members to varying degrees lived a bohemian life and shared other characteristics with the Beats. Most of these movements do not actually owe their existence to the Beats, but in several cases the poetry and fiction they produced reveal affinity with the Beat movement and at times showed the influence of its writers.

That affinity and influence are hardly to be found in the work of a group of British writers who were briefly seen as the English equivalent of the Beats, the Angry Young Men. On the whole writers like John Braine, Kingsley Amis, and John Wain were primarily concerned with Britain's political and social reality, while the interests of the Beats focussed on the transcendental and the art of writing. Only in the 1960s, under the influence of the Beats, a more poetical and also more bohemian literary movement emerged in England, including poets like Adrian Henri and Roger McGough.

In post–World War II France the major bohemian movement was that of the Existentialists. Although the rather grim notions of their spiritual leader, the philosopher Jean-Paul Sartre, clash with the inherent optimism of the Beat Generation, the antiauthoritarian stance of the Existentialists, as well as their interest in jazz and colorful writing, suggest some striking similarities with the Beats.

Other bohemians in Europe that are reminiscent of the Beats are the Dutch "Fiftiers" and the so-called Wiener Gruppe in Austria. The Fiftiers had their origins in the art world of postwar Amsterdam, among the painters who became part of the internationally known Cobra movement. Reacting against the conformity and restraints of both postwar Dutch society and literature, the Fiftiers used open forms and spontaneous writing to explore "the space of complete living," as poet Lucebert put it. Through Fiftier poet and novelist Simon Vinkenoog, Allen Ginsberg's Dutch translator, the Beats also exerted some influence on the Provo movement of the 1960s.

In post-1945 Austria, the Wiener Gruppe rebelled against their country's conservatism and materialism. This group of writers (H. C. Artmann, Gerhard Rühm, Konrad Bayer, Oswald Wiener, and Friedrich Achleitner) largely lacked the Beats' interest in religion but shared their obsession with language. To liberate language and man, the Wiener Gruppe looked back to Expressionism, Dadaism, and Surrealism, but a later publication, Wiener's novel *Die Verbesserung von Mitteleuropa*, also refers to Kerouac and Burroughs.

In Germany and Italy, individual writers such as Rolf Dieter Brinkmann and Pier Vittorio Tondelli helped to spread the influence of the Beat Generation. Elsewhere in the world various literary movements show affinity with the Beats. Postwar Japan spawned a new Lost Generation with Beat characteristics, which included novelist Osamu Dazai and the young Yukio Mishima. An even closer tie exists between the Beats and India's Hungry Generation, introduced to the West by Allen Ginsberg. In the end, however, the Beats left their mark on individuals rather than groups.

—*Jaap van der Bent*

## Bibliographical References

Gene Feldman and Max Gartenberg edited *The Beat Generation and the Angry Young Men*, 1958, a classic anthology whose introduction and texts collate Beat and Beat-related writing with that of the Angry Young Men. A substantial anthology of antiacademic British poetry is *Children of Albion: Poetry of the Underground in Britain*, 1969, ed. Michael Horovitz, who added a long, informative afterword. James Campbell wrote a lively account of post–World War II artistic activity in Paris, which also pays attention to the contribution of the Beats and other expatriates: *Exiled in Paris: Richard Wright, James Baldwin, Samuel Beckett, and Others on the Left Bank*, 1995. Peter Glassgold edited *Living Space: Poems of the Dutch "Fiftiers,"* 1979, an anthology of poetry by a revolutionary group of Dutch poets, whose work is compared with that of the Beats and poets like Charles Olson and Robert Duncan. Peter Weiber

put together *Die Wiener Gruppe/The Vienna Group: A Moment of Modernity 1954–1960*, 1997, a huge overview, also available on the internet, which focuses on the Vienna Group's visual works and actions but also pays attention to its writings.

*See also* Bohemian Movements: Predecessors of the Beats

# Everson, William (Brother Antoninus) (1912–1994)

Poet, professor, monk, Jeffers scholar, William Everson is a key representative and defender of the spiritual, mystical, religious, and intellectually revolutionary elements of the Beats and the San Francisco Renaissance. Everson began his poetic work early in his life and remained an active author until his death. Everson provided a crucial and necessary defense of the Beats through a series of letters and through his scholarly work, demonstrating their connection to the Dionysian elements in literature and their subsequent place within an intellectual and literary tradition of rebellion. Everson also displayed the Beats' awareness of their similarities and differences with moderns through his scholarly work on Robinson Jeffers, whom Everson credits for his poetic awakening at the age of twenty-three.

Everson was born in Sacramento, California, on 12 September 1912 at home. His father was a Norwegian immigrant, and his mother was from a German-Irish farming family. His mother was raised as a Catholic but converted to Christian Science when she married. He finished high school in Selma, California, and began attending Fresno State in 1931, but he dropped out of college the following year. In 1934, Everson returned to Fresno and began studying Robinson Jeffers. As a consequence of Jeffers's influence on Everson's intellectual life, Everson began working on his own poetry and published his first book of poems *These Are the Ravens* in 1934. In 1946 in San Francisco, Everson began his affiliation with other Bay writers, including Kenneth Rexroth, Robert Duncan, Philip Whalen, and Philip Lamantia. By the 1950s, Everson had written a dozen books of poetry, was awarded a Guggenheim Fellowship, had served as the director of the Fine Arts Project at Waldport, and had helped to establish the Untide Press. In 1948, Everson converted to Catholicism at Christmas mass at St. Mary's Cathedral in San Francisco. Everson was accepted as a lay brother in the Dominican Order at St. Albert's in Oakland and received the name Brother Antoninus. In 1969 at a poetry reading at the University of California, Davis, Everson publicly announced his decision to leave the brotherhood after reading "Tendril in the Mesh" and declared his intention to marry Susanna Rickson.

Everson's poetry can be regarded in three distinct phases that also correspond to collected versions published by Black Sparrow Press: *The Residual Years: Poems 1934–1948*, *The Veritable Years: Poems 1949–1966*, and *The Integral Years: Poems 1966–1994*. These are the definitive collections and offer excellent introductions and notes, including an introduction by Kenneth Rexroth in *The Residual Years*. The phases correspond to his preconversion years, his Catholic years, and his post-Catholic years. Although these periods coincide with Everson's connection to or estrangement from Catholicism, his poetry retains certain thematic qualities throughout all of these phases. Everson was predominantly interested in the Beats' fascination with mysticism and spiritual questing. The poems that garner the most attention include "Year's End" and "The Raid" from his early period, which describes the malaise of a post-WWII world; "The Poet Is Dead," which is a tribute to Robinson Jeffers; "Tendril in the Mesh," which describes his passionate break from the brotherhood; "The Man Fate," which describes his post-brotherhood life; and "Runoff," which reveals his later interest in ecological concerns.

Arguably as important as his poetry was his defense of the Beats as part of a Dionysian tradition,

articulated in a series of letters to Lee Bartlett that were first published in *Fresco* in 1959, later in *Earth Poetry* in 1980, and most recently in *Beat Down to Your Soul* in 2001. These letters explain the reemergence of a Dionysian sensibility in the twentieth century that Everson claims as the basis of Beat literature. Everson displays a keen scholarly insight and convincing prose that emphasizes the ecstatic, spontaneous, and subconscious elements that many Beat writers claimed as goals within their works and as methods of production. Everson also explains the importance of Rexroth as a guiding light for the early Beats, and he outlines the writers before the Beats who could also be regarded as part of a Dionysian tradition.

—Pat Connelly

## Principal Works

*The Residual Years: Poems 1934–1948: Volume I of the Collected Poems; The Veritable Years: Poems 1949–1966: Volume II of the Collected Poems; The Integral Years: Poems 1966–1994: Volume III of the Collected Poems.* These collections encompass all of his publications during these years and include excellent introductions and notes.

## Bibliographical References

Lee Bartlett, *Benchmark & Blaze: The Emergence of William Everson*, 1979; Lee Bartlett, *On Writing the Waterbirds and Other Presentations: Collected Forewords and Afterwords 1935–1981*, 1983; Robert Duncan, *Single Source: The Early Poems of William Everson, 1934–1940*, 1966; Kenneth Rexroth, "Introduction," in William Everson, *The Residual Years: Poems 1934–1948: The Pre-Catholic Poetry of Brother Antoninus*, 1968; William E. Stafford, ed., *The Achievement of Brother Antoninus: A Comprehensive Selection of His Poems with a Critical Introduction*, 2001.

*See also* Religion, The Beats and

# F

## Fariña, Richard (1937–1966)

The novelist, poet, and songwriter who linked the Beats and the Age of Aquarius, Richard Fariña died at the age of twenty-nine, two days after the publication of his novel *Been Down So Long It Looks Like Up to Me* (1966). The accidental death curtailed the development of an ambitious and eclectic body of journalism, short fiction, poetry, and song. David Hadju's *Positively Fourth Street* (2001) argues the significance of Fariña's role in the urban folk music revival of the early to mid-1960s. Less clearly defined is Fariña's literary legacy. The body of his literary work is slender—aside from his novel, his work is represented only by the collection *Long Time Coming and a Long Time Gone* (1969) and a number of uncollected poems, stories, essays, and an unpublished play, *The Shelter.* Despite the brevity of his career, Fariña's work identifies him as a young writer whose depiction of bohemian culture of the late 1950s in *Been Down So Long* augured cultural upheaval in the 1960s in much the same manner as the better known and earlier work of Kerouac, Ginsberg, and Burroughs. With Kesey, Brautigan, and others, Fariña stands as a link between Beat literature of the 1950s and the counterculture of the 1960s.

Born 8 March 1937 in Brooklyn to an Irish mother and a Cuban father, Fariña cultivated a strong identity with both his Celtic and Caribbean roots and traveled to Ireland and Cuba in his youth. He attended Catholic elementary school and the competitive Brooklyn Technical High School, from which he matriculated to Cornell on a scholarship as an engineering major in 1955. Having switched his major to English in his sophomore year, Fariña won Cornell's undergraduate short story writing competition in early 1958. "With a Copy of Dylan under My Arm" recounts the experience of a young American in Belfast and displays evidence of Fariña's debt to both Dylan Thomas and Ernest Hemingway. The story is among the earliest work of Fariña reprinted in *Long Time Coming.* Fariña, who had traveled to Ireland in the summer of 1955, asserted in later accounts that relatives there were members of the IRA and alluded to participation in an IRA bombing that resulted in the death of five members of the Royal Navy. While the veracity of this story is undetermined, one of Fariña's stronger stories, "An End to a Young Man" (*Long Time Coming*) recounts a similar incident. Fariña traveled to Cuba twice in the first half of 1958, reconnecting his ethnic ties and allegedly pursuing connections with Fidel Castro. These episodes play out in climactic chapters of *Been Down So Long* and precipitated the story "The Passing of Various Lives" (*Long Time Coming*).

Fariña left Cornell in 1959 without receiving his degree, having established a strong friendship with fellow undergraduate Thomas Pynchon, who later dedicated *Gravity's Rainbow* to Fariña. Fariña took a position in Manhattan with the advertising agency J. Walter Thompson in spring 1959. In 1960, Fariña married popular folksinger Carolyn Hester, whom he had met at the White Horse Tavern earlier that year. Through engagement in Hester's career, Fariña took up the dulcimer and began to write songs. His poetry meanwhile reached a national audience in 1961 with publications in the *Atlantic Monthly* and the *Transatlantic Review,* and a story, "The Vision of Brother Francis," was later published in 1962 in *Prairie Schooner.* Fariña spent much of 1962 on the road in Europe with and without Hester. According to Hester, he began seriously to draft *Been Down So Long* in London that year (Unterberger 241). He later recorded an album of traditional folk songs with Eric Von Schmidt in London in early 1963, accompanied by Bob Dylan. Fariña separated from Hester in 1962 and married Mimi Baez, whom he had met in Paris, the following year.

Publishing the poem "The Field Near the Cathedral at Chartres" and several essays in *Mademoiselle* from 1963 to 1964, Fariña's engagement with the burgeoning folk music movement intensified, at least partially due to his relationship with Bob Dylan, and much of his productive effort focused on songwriting. On the basis of a five-song demo recorded by sister-in-law Joan Baez in November 1963, Fariña was signed to a publishing contract with Vanguard Records shortly thereafter. Richard and Mimi Fariña debuted as a duo at the Big Sur Folk Festival in June 1964, mixing guitar and dulcimer instrumentals with allegorical ballads ("The Falcon") and topical songs of social protest ("Birmingham Sunday"). Their first album *Celebrations for a Grey Day* was recorded in Manhattan in autumn 1964 and was followed with the late 1965 release of a second LP, *Reflections in a Crystal Wind,* which was noted by the *New York Times* as one of ten best folk albums of the year. Richard and Mimi's year was highlighted by a memorable performance in a drenching downpour at the Newport Folk Festival.

In between recordings and performances with Mimi, Fariña had by early 1965 finished *Been Down So Long It Looks Like Up to Me* in the cabin the couple shared in Carmel, California. Fariña's *bildungsroman,* featuring his alter ego Gnossos Pappadopoulis and set in a college town much like Cornell's Ithaca in the late 1950s, was scheduled for an early 1966 publishing by Random House. Pynchon had preceded Fariña in publication with his own novel *V.* and promised endorsement of

Fariña's novel. Fariña's frank treatment of sexual episodes in the novel caused some concern, and according to Hadju, some of the more ribald episodes were struck from the narrative (271).

On 30 April 1966, Fariña attended a book-signing party in Carmel Valley for his just-released novel. Later that evening, in the midst of a surprise twenty-first birthday party that he had arranged for Mimi, he departed on the back of an acquaintance's motorcycle for a brief ride. Returning to the party shortly thereafter, driver Willie Hinds failed to negotiate a turn, and he and Fariña were thrown from the bike. Hinds escaped with minor scrapes. Fariña died instantly of a blow to the head.

Mimi Fariña was to release one more LP of prior recorded songs (*Memories*), which included Fariña's send up of Bob Dylan, "Morgan the Pirate." Aside from the posthumous collection *Long Time Coming and a Long Time Gone,* Fariña's "Ringing Out the Old Year in Havana" ran in *Esquire* (September 1969). An underdistributed film of Fariña's novel followed, as did a 1970s New York musical production *Richard Fariña: Long Time Coming and a Long Time Gone,* starring Richard Gere. *Been Down So Long It Looks Like Up to Me,* reprinted in 1983 with an introduction by Thomas Pynchon, remains in print in the Penguin Twentieth Century Classics series.

—*Tracy Santa*

## Bibliographical References

Douglas Cooke, "The Richard & Mimi Fariña Website" at http://www.richardandmimi.com; David Hajdu, *Positively 4th Street: The Lives and Times of Joan Baez, Bob Dylan, Mimi Baez Fariña, and Richard Fariña,* 2001; Thomas Pynchon, "Introduction" to *Been Down So Long It Looks Like Up to Me,* 1983 (rpt.1996); Richie Unterberger, "Richard and Mimi Fariña" in *Urban Spacemen and Wayfaring Strangers: Overlooked Innovators and Eccentric Visionaries of '60s Rock,* 2000.

*See also* Music

## Fellaheen

Fellaheen, or fellahin, is the term Jack Kerouac uses to describe the world's poor. Kerouac admires the fellaheen because their poverty reduces them to the basic essentials of life, giving them unfailing insight about life and death.

The *Oxford English Dictionary* explains that "fellah" refers to a peasant in a nation where Arabic is spoken, particularly Egypt. The plural can be fellahs, fellahin, or fellaheen. The *OED* notes that the word may be used figuratively, and perhaps Kerouac intends a figurative association when he capitalizes the word.

In *On the Road* (1957), Sal and Dean travel to Mexico, and when Dean finally sleeps, Sal takes over the wheel (279–280). Sal contemplates the Indians and thinks of the Fellahin, whom he describes as the poor people who inhabit the equatorial regions of the world. These people are the source of life and know life with silent wisdom. Sal insists that when the world reaches the next apocalyptic moment, all people will view the world with the knowing eyes of the Fellahin.

In *Lonesome Traveler* (1960), Kerouac includes "Mexico Fellaheen" (21–36), and this travel essay refers to the outlook of the fellaheen—a happiness that arises when people do not preoccupy themselves with broad considerations of culture and society. Kerouac believes this outlook is noticeable in Latin America, Morocco, and Dakar.

—*William Lawlor*

**Bibliographical References**

Jack Kerouac, *On the Road*, 1957; Jack Kerouac, *Lonesome Traveler*, 1960.

*See also* Mexico City

# Ferlinghetti, Lawrence (1919–)

Writer, founder of the City Lights Bookstore in San Francisco, promoter of the Beats, and publisher of some of their key books, Lawrence Ferlinghetti is a central figure in the Beat literary movement of the fifties. Not usually associated with the beginnings of the Beat Generation in New York City following World War II, he nevertheless added great force, energy, spirit, and determination to the movement as it arrived on the West Coast, and is the pivotal figure in the San Francisco Literary Renaissance.

His industry as a writer, his inventiveness in combining poetry and jazz, his success in establishing the first bookstore to sell only paperbacks, and his uncompromising efforts in publishing works that tested the limits of law and social acceptance make him not only an important figure in the bohemian struggle, but also a major figure in his own right.

Ferlinghetti was born in Yonkers, New York, on 24 March 1919. His childhood was a disrupted one: his father died before he was born, and shortly afterward his mother entered a state hospital, leaving her five sons in desperate circumstances. His mother's aunt, Emily Mendes-Monsanto, took Lawrence to France for five years, but on their return to New York, her marital problems forced her to place Ferlinghetti briefly in an orphanage. Seven

Lawrence Ferlinghetti reads his poetry. (Time Life Pictures/ Getty Images)

months later, he was reclaimed, and with the support of two affluent families, his upbringing and education were finally arranged.

In 1933, Ferlinghetti began high school at Mount Hermon, a private school in Massachusetts, where he developed an early interest in Thomas Wolfe. In 1937, probably deliberately following the path of Wolfe, who had made the same choice of university, he began college at Chapel Hill, North Carolina, where the program made it possible for Ferlinghetti to meet major artists, including Carl Sandburg, Edgar Lee Masters, and Vachel Lindsay. After a four-year tour in the navy, Ferlinghetti settled in New York City, where he studied for a master's degree at Columbia and mixed with intellectuals in Greenwich Village. In 1947, he went to Paris, completing his doctoral degree at the Sorbonne two years later. It was after this, in the early 1950s, that he made the crucial move to San Francisco, where, initially, he struggled to find artistic direction. Soon, however, his friendships with Kenneth Rexroth and Peter Martin spurred the development of his writing and encouraged him to take up his pivotal role in bookselling and publishing.

Shortly after founding the City Lights publishing company, Ferlinghetti launched the Pocket Poets Series with a volume of his own, *Pictures of the Gone World* (1955). The poems reveal international sophistication and surreal sensuality, but, in contrast, a common theme is the quiet struggle of ordinary people. The unusual distribution of lines on the page, and the inventiveness with word play and rhyme, show Ferlinghetti's sense of freedom, itself a key notion in his work. The Pocket Poets Series continued with works by Rexroth and Kenneth Patchen, but the publication of Allen Ginsberg's *Howl and Other Poems* (1956), following the famous reading at the 6 Gallery (1955), brought Ferlinghetti's publishing house to national attention. Ginsberg's book faced problems with U.S. Customs when an edition printed in England arrived in San Francisco in 1957, and the problems continued when the San Francisco Police arrested Ferlinghetti and his partner, charging that they had sold an obscene book. The American Civil Liberties Union defended *Howl and Other Poems*, bringing

numerous recognized artists and literary authorities to testify to the poem's merit and worth. "It is not the poet but what he observes which is revealed as obscene," Ferlinghetti said in the poem's defense. "The great obscene wastes of *Howl* are the sad wastes of the mechanized world, lost among atom bombs and insane nationalisms" (quoted in Silesky, 70, from a column by Ferlinghetti published in the *San Francisco Chronicle* on 19 May 1956). The court's decision vindicated Ferlinghetti: *Howl and Other Poems* became a best seller, and the Beat movement became associated with freedom of expression, with Ferlinghetti acknowledged as a key player in the making of that freedom.

*A Coney Island of the Mind* (1958) is Ferlinghetti's most perennially popular book. The volume includes poems selected from *Pictures of the Gone World* and a special series of poems intended for oral presentation with jazz accompaniment. The title of the selection represents what Ferlinghetti calls "a kind of circus of the soul" (8). The voice in these poems is personal and richly allusive, yet the poems also reveal surrealism and social commentary.

Although *A Coney Island of the Mind* is Ferlinghetti's most enduring work, his novels, plays, poetry, travel journals, and other writings demonstrate his continuing productivity. *These Are My Rivers: New and Selected Poems 1955–1993* (1994) reveals his characteristic combination of old and new work in successive publications.

After being named the first Poet Laureate of San Francisco in 1998, Ferlinghetti compiled *San Francisco Poems* (1998), which gathers from his career the poems that take San Francisco as their subject.

A painter as well as a poet, Ferlinghetti has displayed his paintings at various galleries in Europe and the United States. He creates an interdisciplinary effect in his works because his paintings often incorporate words and phrases and his poems make references to the act of painting. *How to Paint Sunlight* (2001) refers frequently with a painter's eye to the effect of light falling on the city, and *Life Studies, Life Stories* (2003) presents many of Ferlinghetti's drawings, some in color, some in black and white.

In *Americus, Book I* (2004), Ferlinghetti renews his discussion of America and the nation's politics. In characteristic style, he modifies and weaves strands of language from the history of culture and literature, generating humor, satire, and sensitive reflection.

With a career of more than a half-century behind him, Ferlinghetti is the recipient of numerous honors. In San Francisco, an alley was officially designated as Via Ferlinghetti in 1994. As Poet Laureate he began to write columns for the *San Francisco Chronicle*, commenting on art, literature, politics, and life. In 2003, he received the Robert Frost Memorial Medal, was presented the Authors Guild Lifetime Achievement Award, and was made a member of the American Academy of Arts and Letters.

—*William Lawlor*

## Principal Works

Poetry: *Pictures of the Gone World*, 1955; *A Coney Island of the Mind*, 1958; *Starting from San Francisco*, 1961; *The Secret Meaning of Things*, 1969; *Open Eye, Open Heart*, 1973; *Who Are We Now?*, 1976; *Landscapes of Living and Dying*, 1979; *Endless Life: Selected Poems*, 1981; *These Are My Rivers: New and Selected Poems*, 1994; *Pictures of the Gone World* (revised with eighteen new poems), 1995; *San Francisco Poems*, 1998; *How to Paint Sunlight*, 2001; *Americus, Book I*, 2004.

Prose: *Her*, 1966; *Tyranus Nix?*, 1969; *The Mexican Night*, 1970; *Back Roads to Far Places*, 1971; *Literary San Francisco: A Pictorial History from Its Beginnings to the Present Day*, 1980; *A Trip to Italy and France*, 1980; *Love in the Days of Rage*, 1988.

Drama: *Unfair Arguments with Existence*, 1963; *Routines*, 1964.

Art: *Life Studies, Life Stories*, 2003.

## Bibliographical References

The most recent biography is Barry Silesky, *Ferlinghetti: The Artist in His Time*, 1990; another biography is Neeli Cherkovski, *Ferlinghetti: A Biography*, 1979; a general review of Ferlinghetti's writings may be found in Larry Smith, *Lawrence Ferlinghetti: Poet-at-Large*, 1983; and in Michael Skau, *Constantly Risking Absurdity*, 1989; in *Six San Francisco Poets*, David Kherdian presents a chapter "Lawrence Ferlinghetti" that describes a day in the life of the poet and publisher; in *Golden Gate: Interviews with Five San Francisco Poets*, 1971, David Meltzer presents an extended interview with Ferlinghetti; in Gregory Stephenson, *The Daybreak Boys: Essays on the Literature of the Beat Generation* (1990), a chapter, "The 'Spiritual Optics' of Lawrence Ferlinghetti," presents a general view of Ferlinghetti's writings; in *A Casebook on the Beat*, 1961, Thomas Parkinson includes his essay titled "Phenomenon or Generation"; Crale D. Hopkins, "The Poetry of Lawrence Ferlinghetti: A Reconsideration," *Italian Americana* (1974): 59–76; and L. A. Ianni, "Lawrence Ferlinghetti's Fourth Person Singular and the Theory of Relativity," *Wisconsin Studies in Contemporary Literature* 8 (1967): 392–406 are valuable studies.

*See also* Censorship; Publishers; San Francisco; Atomic Era; Big Sur; Sea, Beats at

# Film

During the Beat era, independent filmmakers found outlets for their creativity and expression, producing films with innovative techniques, spontaneous design, and social commentary. Although the Beats themselves played roles in several of these independent films, the clearest view of the Beats emerges in numerous documentaries. Biographical and historical in their approaches, these documentaries present the Beats in performance and offer commentaries from artists and family members. Because of the notoriety of the Beats, Hollywood film producers pursued the Beats as a point of focus, but with few exceptions, the Hollywood films reinforced stereotypes, suffered from abominable scripts and poor acting, and distorted the literature and personalities in question.

The film movement that most intersects with the Beat movement in literature is called the New York Underground Cinema movement. Although independent films were being shown in New York beginning in the 1930s, New York Underground Cinema usually refers to the independent film movement of the late 1940s through the 1960s. The Underground Cinema began to develop with the opening of Cinema 16 by Amos and Marcia Vogel in 1947. This film society exhibited experimental films and presented annual Creative Cinema Awards for documentaries and avant-garde films. Then, Maya Deren, herself an experimental filmmaker, organized the Film Artists Society, which became the Independent Film Makers Association, in 1953. This organization met monthly to discuss the developments of the Underground Cinema movement. Deren also founded the Creative Film Foundation, which wrote grants for independent filmmakers. An important periodical of the New York Underground, *Film Culture: America's Independent Motion Picture Magazine*, was founded in 1955. The *Village Voice* also commented on the movement in a weekly column beginning in 1958. The most notorious organization of the New York Underground Cinema, the Film-Makers' Cooperative, was founded in 1962 and, unlike the previous organizations, accepted any films submitted for screening and distribution. This film association cemented the Underground Cinema movement by showing independent films regularly at local theaters and by making independent films more widely available for rental.

The filmmakers of the New York Underground Cinema operated independently of Hollywood probably because Hollywood studios would have refused to produce or distribute their films. These filmmakers utilized both formal innovation and controversial subject matter, and the filmmakers valued originality and novelty over narrative plot and standard film conventions. Many works of this movement are more accurately described as film poems than movies. Stan Brakhage, for instance, worked directly with the film stock, scratching it, dying it, painting it, even gluing moth wings to it, to create unusual images. New York Underground films are frequently similar in style to the European avant-garde films of the 1920s, exhibiting elements of impressionism, surrealism, and expressionism. Filmmakers, most famously Andy Warhol, often interacted with and borrowed images from pop culture, simultaneously parodying and paying homage to popular icons and mass culture. The films created as a result of the Underground Cinema movement represented protest about social, political, and sexual issues. The primary influences of this film movement were Pop Art, performance and dance, minimalism, rock-and-roll music, comic books, and Beat literature itself.

Jonas Mekas (b. 1922) was a significant figure in the New York Underground culture. Born in Lithuania, he came to New York City as a refugee in 1949. He began watching screenings at Cinema 16 and making his own films. By serving on the editorial board of *Film Culture* and writing a weekly column for the *Village Voice*, Mekas became a crucial voice for and promoter of the movement. As a critic, Mekas sustained the Beat notions of spontaneity and originality as standards of authenticity. In addition, he was instrumental to the formation of the Film-Makers' Cooperative. He directed and produced his own film, *Guns of the Trees*, in 1961. *Guns of the Trees* is the story of two young New York couples living under the threat of an atomic bombing. Allen Ginsberg wrote and recited poetry as part of the soundtrack for this film. *Guns of the Trees* won the first prize at the Second International Free Cinema Festival in Italy in 1962. Mekas went on to create other films and also to cofound the Anthology Film Archives, a film museum devoted to art films, in 1970. He has continued to work for the Anthology up until the present day.

Robert Frank (b. 1924), another immigrant to the United States, was first a photographer and then a filmmaker during the New York Underground Cinema movement. After emigrating from Switzerland, he was given a Guggenheim Fellowship to travel cross-country by car and photograph American life and geography in 1955. With the photographs that he acquired on this journey, he published a picture book titled *The Americans*. Jack Kerouac wrote the introduction to this book and later asked Frank to collaborate on a film with him. Their film, produced in 1959, became *Pull My Daisy*. Kerouac narrated; Ginsberg, Peter Orlovsky, Larry Rivers, David Amram, Gregory Corso, and others acted; and Frank and Alfred Leslie codirected this film. *Pull My Daisy* is based on the last act of an unpublished three-act play written by Kerouac. It was filmed in an improvisational style, although it was completely scripted. The film is based on an encounter between a group of Beats and a bishop that occurred at Neal Cassady's home. It won the Independent Film Award presented by *Film Culture* in 1960. After *Pull My Daisy*, Frank returned to his career as a photographer.

Today *Pull My Daisy* is an enduring artifact of the Beat Generation. One sees Ginsberg, Corso, Orlovsky, Amram, and Rivers in their playful youth, and the extended narration of Jack Kerouac may be the best surviving example of sustained expressive reading by Kerouac. Music composed by David Amram enlivens the film with its title song and the soundtrack as a whole.

The codirector of *Pull My Daisy* was Alfred Leslie (b. 1927). He collaborated with Frank and Kerouac for this project and later went on to make other films as well. Leslie's primary works, however, are paintings, drawings, and prints. He had his first art exhibition in New York in 1951. His first work is considered Abstract Expressionism, but in the late 1950s, he turned to Realism. He is most well known for his stark representations of both female and male nudes.

Another experimental filmmaker is Anthony Balch, whose work is done in collaboration with William S. Burroughs and Brion Gysin. *Ghosts at No. 9* (1962) features a soundtrack by Burroughs and, according to the video package, is "from the archives of Psychic TV." A collection of other experimental works by Balch is *Towers Open Fire, The Cut-Ups, Bill and Tony,* and *William Buys a Parrot* (1962–1972). These works abandon conventional narratives to present experimental loops and sequences.

Another New York Underground Cinema filmmaker was John Cassavetes (1929–1989). Cassavetes began his film career in 1959 by starring in the television program *Johnny Staccato*. In this series, he played an average urban character with vague Beat culture connections. In 1957, Cassavetes filmed *Shadows* on the streets of New York. He did not utilize a script, and the film falls somewhere between the categories of documentary and improvisation. *Shadows* has three plot lines, with each revealing issues of race and identity. *Shadows* received the first Independent Film Award in 1959. Cassavetes went on to work as a filmmaker for the rest of his life, directing such films as *Faces*

(1968), *A Woman under the Influence* (1974), *The Killing of a Chinese Bookie* (1976), and *Opening Night* (1977).

Documentaries about the Beat Generation are numerous and offer a rich background for the study of Beat art. Perhaps the single most important documentary is John Antonelli's *Kerouac* (1984), which has been released under various titles, including *On the Road with Jack Kerouac* (1990). Now the film is also available as a DVD. Antonelli's film dramatizes Kerouac's upbringing in Lowell, Massachusetts, and recreates scenes from Kerouac's writings with selected passages as part of the soundtrack. Antonelli provides commentaries from the people who surrounded Kerouac, including William S. Burroughs, Allen Ginsberg, John Clellon Holmes, Joyce Johnson, and Stanley Twardowicz. Especially significant are scenes from Jack Kerouac's appearances on *The Steve Allen Show* (1959) and William F. Buckley's *Firing Line* in 1968. Although brief, Kerouac's reading of the closing lines from *On the Road* with Steve Allen on piano may be the quintessential artifact of the Beat Generation. The film's musical soundtrack includes selections from key jazz artists.

Scenes from Kerouac's appearance on *The Steve Allen Show* and *Firing Line* are also available on *What Happened to Kerouac?* (1985). This film includes commentaries from Beat Generation personalities, especially Gregory Corso. The film emphasizes Kerouac's problem with fame and decline into alcoholism.

A third documentary on Kerouac is *Jack Kerouac's Road: A Franco-American Odyssey* (1987). This film, produced by the National Film Board of Canada, emphasizes the Franco-American background of Kerouac and features an interview of Kerouac conducted in French and presented with subtitles in English.

Special coverage of the 1982 conference on the twenty-fifth anniversary of the publication of *On the Road* is available in the third portion of *Go Moan for Man* (2000). The first two parts systematically cover the life and career of Kerouac and provide scenes from locations where Kerouac lived and traveled.

To get a strong background about Kerouac's experience in the mountains, one may turn to a program originally produced by the BBC but subsequently shown on the Bravo television channel as a Bravo Profile. John Suiter and Tom Clark comment on Kerouac's experience on Desolation Peak, and the film reveals the hardships and solitude of Kerouac during his time as a fire lookout. Upon his descent from Desolation Peak, Kerouac soon became famous, and in this Bravo Profile Joyce Johnson comments on the tragic changes in his life.

Ginsberg's life is unfolded in a decade-by-decade fashion in *The Life and Times of Allen Ginsberg* (1993). The film provides generous samples of readings by Ginsberg; comments from his brother and stepmother enrich the viewer's understanding of the family background and the significance of Allen's mother, Naomi.

*Allen Ginsberg: Literary Video* ((1989), a production of the Lannan Foundation, combines Lewis MacAdams's interview of Ginsberg with readings by Ginsberg. *Beat Legends: Allen Ginsberg* (1994) offers readings of poems other than "Howl" and "Kaddish" and presents Ginsberg before a live audience.

To learn more about William S. Burroughs, one may view *Burroughs: The Movie* (1983). The film provides biographical background, as well as interviews and performances. *Commissioner of Sewers* (1995) does not systematically cover the life of Burroughs, but readings and interviews reveal his personality and style of performance.

Other major figures in the Beat Generation are also viewable in documentaries. *The Coney Island of Lawrence Ferlinghetti* (1996) reveals Ferlinghetti's biography, literary career, interest in painting, and political activism. Gregory Corso is the subject of *Beat Legends: Gregory Corso* (1994). In this film, Corso reads at New York University. *Gary Snyder: Literary Video* (1989) presents readings by Snyder and an interview conducted by Lewis MacAdams.

Other documentaries, instead of selecting individual personalities, treat the Beat Generation as a movement. The rise of the Beats on the West Coast is the focus of *West Coast Beat and Beyond* (1984) and *The Beats: An Existential Comedy* (n.d.). In

the latter of these two works, a feminist perspective supplements the examination of male artists. In *Gang of Souls* (1988) and *Fried Shoes Cooked Diamonds* (1989), one sees the Beats at Naropa Institute. The social and cultural context for the Beat Generation is well shown in *The Beat Generation: An American Dream* (1986). *The Atomic Café* (1982) does not focus specifically on the Beats but does show the cultural context with respect to the rise and acceptance of nuclear weaponry.

Chuck Workman's *The Source* (1999) presents the Beats as the inspiration for the countercultural movements of the 1960s and subsequent alternative outlooks. *The Source* features film highlights of the Beats themselves, but also features appearances by Johnny Depp, Dennis Hopper, and John Turturro, who do dramatic readings of important selections from Beat writings.

In contrast to the documentaries are the Hollywood productions; these offer some flavor from the Beat era, but most are virtually unwatchable because of wretched acting and dumb scripts. Nevertheless, in *The Wild One* (1954) and *Rebel without a Cause* (1955), one does see Marlon Brando and James Dean suggest the hero disconnected from society. In *The Connection*, director Shirley Clarke presents Jack Gelber's play as performed by the Living Theater. Drug-dependent jazz musicians await the arrival of their connection, and a filmmaker compiles a documentary of their existence in the Beat apartment. The musicians address the camera tauntingly, and Shirley Clarke allows the camera to swerve and creates abrupt transitions between scenes.

Other films engage in mere exploitation of the news coverage afforded to the Beats in the late 1950s. *A Bucket of Blood* (1959) and *The Beat Generation* (1959) absurdly reflect the stereotypes of Beat culture and now serve only as laughable selections. *The Subterraneans* (1960) supposedly is based on Kerouac's novel of the same title, but the interracial love theme is dropped and the movie plods on miserably.

*Heart Beat* (1979), based on the memoir by Carolyn Cassady, promises to be an excellent Hollywood interpretation of the Beats, especially because of the cast, which includes John Hurt, Nick Nolte, and Sissy Spacek, but the movie is a bomb. Subsequent Hollywood films, such as *Peggy Sue Got Married* (1986), *Barfly* (1987), *Hairspray* (1988), and *Drugstore Cowboy* (1990) recreate to some degree the Beat scene, the social context, or a Beat character. In *Hairspray,* the heroine mistakenly enters a Beat pad and encounters a mad Beat painter and a "stoned chick" who reads from "Howl." In *Drugstore Cowboy,* William Burroughs plays Tom Murphy, a drug addict–priest who describes the rise of the international police because of hysteria about drugs.

*Naked Lunch* (1991) succeeds in rendering the bizarre mood and environment of Burroughs's novel; the film ultimately is not based on the novel itself, however, but on the life of the author during the time of the composition of the novel. Burroughs and Joan Vollmer are the focus of attention in *Beat* (2000), but weak acting by Kiefer Sutherland and Courtney Love make the film tedious. *The Last Time I Committed Suicide* (1997) is based on a letter by Neal Cassady, but as a biography of Cassady, the movie has little interest.

The biggest of all the Hollywood issues for the Beats and their followers is the question of the production of *On the Road.* Francis Ford Coppola has the rights to produce the film. Over the years various stories have emerged about selections for the cast. However, the film has never gone into production, and the difficulties of transforming Kerouac's novel into a viable film script are significant. With so many film treatments of the Beats already in existence, perhaps a stubborn insistence on quality for *On the Road* will make the wait for the film worthwhile.

—*Andrea Powell*
*William Lawlor*

**Bibliographical References**

Ray Carney, *The Films of John Cassavetes: Pragmatism, Modernism, and the Movies* (1994) thoroughly discusses Cassavetes's work; in *Beat Culture and the New America,* ed. Lisa Phillips, 1995, Carney is the author of "Escape Velocity: Notes on Beat Film," and a thorough listing of films associated with the Beat movement follows the article. In *Beat Culture* one also finds John G. Hanhardt, "A Movement Toward the Real: *Pull My Daisy* and the American Independent Film 1950–1965." David E. James, ed., *To Free the Cinema: Jonas Mekas and the New York Underground,* 1992, gives background on independent filmmakers. David Sterritt's *Mad to Be Saved,* 1998, analyzes the Beats' position in history and connects the Beats to film productions. Jack Sargeant, *Naked Lens, Vol. 1,* 2002, is an updated edition of a previous work by the same title; this updated edition discusses *Pull My Daisy* and includes interviews with Allen Ginsberg and Jonas Mekas. The liner notes for the audio recordings *The Beat Generation,* 1992, include a review and listing of Hollywood interpretations of the Beats.

*See also* Kerouac, Jack; Ginsberg, Allen; Burroughs, William Seward; Corso, Gregory; Ferlinghetti, Lawrence; Mekas, Jonas; Theater

## First Poetry-Jazz Concert

A collaborative jazz-poetry performance by Howard Hart, Philip Lamantia, Jack Kerouac, and David Amram at the Brata Gallery on East 10th Street in Manhattan in early October 1957.

Amram, a musician, and Kerouac, a poet and prose writer, enjoyed and frequently took part in spontaneous combinations of their art. Hart and Lamantia added their poetry to the work of Amram and Kerouac.

Originally the performance was intended for the Museum of Modern Art. Frank O'Hara tried to establish a connection with the events coordinator at the museum, but when the coordinator balked, O'Hara helped schedule the performance at the Brata Gallery. Promotion was limited to flyers distributed at the Cedar Tavern, the Five Spot, the Kettle of Fish, the White Horse Tavern, and the San Remo; nevertheless, a full house greeted the performers, whose communal prayer before the show was answered when the show successfully combined jazz and three styles of poetry.

—*William Lawlor*

**Bibliographical Reference**

See David Amram, *Offbeat: Collaborating with Kerouac,* 2002: 8–15.

*See also* Amram, David; Lamantia, Philip; 6 Gallery Reading; Kerouac, Jack

## Florida House of Kerouac

A home in the College Park area northwest of downtown Orlando, Florida, where Jack Kerouac and his mother lived together in 1957 around the time of the publication of *On the Road* (1957); now a location for the Jack Kerouac Writers in Residence Project, which sponsors stays at the house for writers.

Shaded by a large oak tree, the home is located at 1418 Clouser Avenue, where Kerouac and his mother shared the back-porch apartment. In the late summer of 1957, Kerouac left the residence for New York to be in the city at the time of the publication of *On the Road.*

With the success of *On the Road,* Kerouac soon had the opportunity to sell another book. In the Clouser Avenue apartment, he wrote *The Dharma Bums* (1958), working mostly late at night when the Florida heat abated.

Cofounded by Bob Kealing, the Jack Kerouac Writers in Residence Project is dedicated to the development of Kerouac's literary legacy in Orlando. The full house, not just the back apartment, is now offered, rent-free and with utilities paid, to successful applicants for residencies in writing.

—*William Lawlor*

### Bibliographical References

Thomas Swick, "Beat City," *South Florida Sunsentinel*, 22 February 2004: 1G, gives details about the house, its connection to Kerouac, and the opportunity for residencies for writers. Bob Kealing, *Kerouac in Florida: Where the Road Ends*, 2004, is an informative book by the cofounder of the Jack Kerouac Writers in Residence Project.

*See also* Kerouac, Jack; *On the Road, New York Times* Review of

## Frank, Robert

Swiss photographer and filmmaker who came to the United States in 1947 and worked for the *New York Times* and *Harper's Bazaar.* After gathering materials for the 1953 Museum of Modern Art exhibition *Post-War European Photographers*, he received a fellowship from the Guggenheim Foundation in 1955.

Frank traveled across the United States with Jack Kerouac and compiled *The Americans* (1959), a collection of black-and-white photographs insightfully revealing citizens in their daily lives. Kerouac wrote the introduction.

In 1958, Frank and Alfred Leslie produced *Pull My Daisy*, the experimental film that became a Beat classic because of Kerouac's narration and the acting of Allen Ginsberg, Peter Orlovsky, Gregory Corso, Larry Rivers, and David Amram.

—*William Lawlor*

Artist Robert Frank in his studio, New York City, 1986. (Christopher Felver/Corbis)

### Principal Works

*Pull My Daisy*, 1959, is available on video; *Story Lines*, 2004, is Frank's most recent volume of collected photos; *The Americans*, 1959, includes the introduction by Jack Kerouac; other volumes include *Frank Films: The Film and Video Work of Robert Frank*, 2004; *Robert Frank: London/Wales*, 2003; a broad survey is *Robert Frank: Moving Out*, 1994.

### Bibliographical References

See John G. Hanhardt, "A Movement toward the Real: *Pull My Daisy* and the American Independent Film, 1950–65" in *Beat Culture and the New America: 1950–1965*, ed. Lisa Phillips, 1995: 215–233; Terence Diggory, "What Abstract Art Means in *Pull My Daisy*" in *Reconstructing the Beats*, ed. Jennie Skerl, 2004: 135–149.

*See also* Film; Photography

## Furthur/Further

"Furthur" was the inscription written on the destination placard of the 1939 International Harvester school bus that novelist Ken Kesey (*One Flew Over the Cuckoo's Nest, Sometimes a Great Notion*) and the Merry Pranksters drove across the country in 1964 to attend the New York World's Fair and the release party for Kesey's second novel. By association, "Furthur" was also the name given to the multicolored bus.

In many ways, the "Furthur" destination on the bus—piloted by Neal Cassady, inspiration for the character Dean Moriarty in Jack Kerouac's *On the Road*—represented the mind-set of the transition from Beat culture to the more heavily drug-infused hippie culture and the LSD-laced psychedelic culture, with Ken Kesey, Neal Cassady, the Merry Pranksters, and the Grateful Dead—all alumni of the Acid Tests—as ambassadors and guides on that cognitive and conceptual journey.

The bus, which at one time was sought after by the Smithsonian Institution, rests in a grove of trees on property owned by Kesey, where it has faded and rusted. A reincarnation of the bus has emerged in recent years, and the surviving members of the Merry Pranksters display the latest edition of the bus at their public appearances. Although the original destination read "Furthur," the spelling was later changed to "Further," and the latest version of the bus bears the destination "Further."

The cultural iconography of "Furthur" led to the "Furthur Festival," a series of post–Jerry Garcia tours of the remaining members of the Grateful Dead, and the establishment of the Furthur Foundation, a San Francisco–based charitable foundation composed of many members of the Grateful Dead's extended family.

—*Timothy D. Ray*

### Bibliographical References

Ken Kesey, *The Further Inquiry*, 1990; Paul Perry and Ken Babbs, *On the Bus: The Complete Guide to the Legendary Trip of Ken Kesey and the Merry Pranksters and the Birth of the Counterculture*, 1990; Tom Wolfe, *The Electric Kool-Aid Acid Test*, 1968.

*See also* Kesey, Ken Elton; Cassady, Neal; Merry Pranksters

# G

## Gaddis, William (1922–1998)

Before William Gaddis published his first novel, *The Recognitions* (1955), he was acquainted with Jack Kerouac, Allen Ginsberg, Chandler Brossard, Alan Ansen, and William Burroughs. The middle third of *The Recognitions* dramatizes scenes from Greenwich Village parties where they mixed, and he seems to have provided the template for characters in several Beat works, notably Harold Sand in Kerouac's *The Subterraneans*, and Harry Lees in Brossard's *Who Walk in Darkness*, and he is also the focus of part of Ansen's "Epistle to Chester Kallman."

Gaddis was born in Manhattan on 29 December 1922. He published four innovative novels in forty years. He died before two final works were published.

—*Stephen J. Burn*

### Principal Works

*The Recognitions*, 1955; *JR*, 1975; *Carpenter's Gothic*, 1985; *A Frolic of His Own*, 1994; *Agapē Agape*, 2002; *The Rush for Second Place: Essays and Occasional Writings*, 2002.

### Bibliographical References

There are brief references to Gaddis's connection with Kerouac in biographies like Gerald Nicosia's *Memory Babe: A Critical Biography of Jack Kerouac*, 1983; but more useful are the accounts included in the introduction to John Kuehl and Steven Moore's *In Recognition of William Gaddis*, 1984; and in Moore's *William Gaddis*, 1989. Moore (and other contributors) expanded this account on a "Gaddis in Fiction" website, http://www.williamgaddis.org/infiction/index.shtml (cited October 23, 2003)

## Gaillard, Slim (1916–1991)

Jive-talking, tap-dancing, guitar-playing showman known for 1930s hits such as "Flat Foot Floogie" and "Cement Mixer," which he recorded anew with Charlie Parker and Dizzy Gillespie in the 1940s. Born Bulee Gaillard in Detroit, Michigan (or Santa Clara, Cuba, Slim sometimes said), Slim Gaillard invented Vout, a variety of jive talking with many words ending in "orooni, "oreeni," or "vout." Gaillard spoke and sang this language with masterful fluency and combined his verbal dynamics with clever jazz.

In *On the Road*, Jack Kerouac describes the performance of Slim Gaillard in a San Francisco night club (176–177). Slim hypnotizes the audience with his jive talk and especially impresses Dean Moriarty, who views Slim as a divinity.

—*William Lawlor*

### Principal Works

Available on the set of CDs (*Laughing in Rhythm*, 2003) are 103 selections from the career of Slim Gaillard; "Yip Roc Heresy" is included on a set of CDs or tapes called *The Beat Generation*, 1992.

## Genet, Jean (1910–1986)

Originally a thief and pimp, Genet became an important figure in French letters as a novelist and playwright, beatified by Sartre as an existentialist saint. Genet was rescued from a life sentence in prison through the advocacy of Jean Cocteau and Sartre. His early novels, especially *Our Lady of the Flowers* (1942), with its lyrical treatment of the marginalized, entered the Beat circle through William Burroughs and Jack Kerouac, becoming an important statement. His early plays, *Death Watch* (1949) and *The Maids* (1947), show the themes and neoclassical economy of Sartre. His later plays *The Balcony* (1956), *The Blacks* (1958), and *The Screens* (1961) are significant contributions to the Theater of the Absurd.

—*Thomas L. Cooksey*

### Principal Works

Major Prose: *Le Condamné à mort,* 1942 (in English *The Man Sentenced to Death,* 1981); *Notre-Dame des Fleurs,* 1942 (in English *Our Lady of the Flowers,* 1949); *Chants secrets,* 1945; *Miracle de la rose,* 1946 (*Miracle of the Rose,* 1949); *Pompes funèbres,* 1947, revised 1948 (in English *Funeral Rites*); *Querelle de Brest,* 1947, revised 1953 (in English *Querelle of Brest,* 1966); *La Galère,* 1947; *Journal du voleur,* 1949 (in English *The Thief's Journal,* 1954); *Un Captif amoureux,* 1986.

Drama: *Haute Surveillance,* 1949, revised 1965 (in English *The Death Watch,* 1954); *Les Bonnes,* 1954 (in English, *The Maids,* 1954); *Le Balcon,* 1956, revised 1962 (in English *The Balcony,* 1957, 1960); *Les Nègres, clownerie,* 1958 (in English *The Blacks,* 1960); *Les Paravents,* 1961 (in English, *The Screens,* 1962).

### Bibliographic References

Joseph McMahon, *The Imagination of Jean Genet,* 1963, is an important study; Jean-Paul Sartre, *Saint Genet, Actor and Martyr,* trans. Bernard Frechtman, 1963, is an existentialist classic that helped to gain Genet's pardon and to define him as an existential hero; Philip Thody, *Jean Genet: A Study of His Novels and Plays,* 1968, is a standard general study of Genet's work; see also Richard C. Webb and Suzanne A. Webb, *Jean Genet and His Critics: An Annotated Bibliography,* 1982; Edmund White, *Genet: A Biography,* 1993, is a thorough recent biography by novelist White and is strong on Genet from a gay perspective.

*See also* Influences

## Gillespie, John Brinks (Dizzy) (1917–1993)

Virtuoso trumpet player whose beard, beret, and horn-rimmed shades gave him a distinctive cool appearance. The bell of his horn was turned upward at a right angle, and his cheeks puffed out as he played.

Dizzy Gillespie's father was a bandleader and amateur musician and made a variety of instruments available to his son, who eventually attended Laurinburg Institute in North Carolina on a music scholarship. Throughout the latter half of the thirties, Dizzy Gillespie worked with band leaders such as Mercer "Duke" Ellington and Cab Calloway and began developing his own style, which later came to be known as bebop. A fistfight on-

In both his musical style and cool attire, Dizzy Gillespie appealed to the Beats. (Library of Congress)

stage led to his departure from Calloway's band, and throughout the forties he played in New York clubs with musicians such as Thelonious Monk, Charlie Parker, and Earl Hines. Gillespie's improvisational style and innovative harmonies had a profound influence on Beat writers such as Jack Kerouac, who, according to Allen Ginsberg in an interview originally published in *Composed on the Tongue* (1980), but reprinted in *Spontaneous Mind* (2001), "learned his line" listening to early bebop.

—*David Arnold*

**Bibliographical References**

Alyn Shipton, *Groovin' High: The Life of Dizzy Gillespie*, 1999; Allen Ginsberg, *Spontaneous Mind: Selected Interviews 1958–1996*, ed. David Carter, 2001.

*See also* Music

## Ginsberg, Allen (1926–1997)

Poet, founding member of the Beat Generation, controversial social and political activist—Allen Ginsberg was one of the best known and most influential literary figures of the twentieth century. "Howl," his lengthy breakthrough poem, which appears in *Howl and Other Poems* (1956), influenced a generation of poets and musicians, and triumphed in a notorious obscenity trial that set a standard still held today; its opening line—"I saw the best minds of my generation destroyed by madness"—(9) remains one of the most often quoted lines in the history of American poetry. Ginsberg's alignment with antiwar, free-speech, and gay liberation causes, among others, brought him additional fame, placing him at the forefront of the tumultuous 1960s and making him as famous for his politics as he was for being a poet. He remained active in his later years, although he devoted much of his time to teaching, photography, and affirming the legacy of the Beat Generation.

Born on 3 June 1926, Irwin Allen Ginsberg was the product of parents who were enormously influential throughout his life. Louis Ginsberg, Allen's father, enjoyed a modest reputation as a lyric poet,

publishing his work in newspapers and small poetry journals. Allen and his older brother Eugene always remembered the way Louis walked about the house, doing chores and reciting poetry the way some people sang the songs of the day while they worked. Naomi Ginsberg, Allen's mother, was a strong-willed woman who, like her husband, taught school until mental illness forced her into retirement in her early twenties. A Russian immigrant, Naomi Ginsberg identified strongly with communism, and her love of the working class and oppressed masses was passed on, often not so subtly, to Allen.

By all appearances, Allen Ginsberg's youth was typical. He enjoyed swimming and running, made friends easily, and excelled in school. As he later confessed, however, he also experienced great psychological stress. His parents quarreled often, usually over politics or money, and his mother was often away, confined to sanitariums for long periods of time when her paranoid schizophrenia became too disruptive at home. As he entered his adolescence, Allen Ginsberg became painfully aware of his homosexuality, which, as the times dictated, he went to great lengths to keep hidden.

Many of the crucial events of Ginsberg's youth are contained in "Kaddish," his lengthy masterwork dedicated to his mother. Brutally frank yet equally tender, "Kaddish," with its accounts of Naomi Ginsberg's descent into mental disability, is shocking in its depiction of Naomi's paranoid ravings (she insisted, throughout her life, that Hitler, Roosevelt, and even Louis Ginsberg's mother, were plotting against her) and disruptive behavior, including her nudism around her two young sons. The poem includes an account of an attempted suicide and, in perhaps the most striking episode, the detailing of the time when Allen, who had been kept out of school to watch over his mother, grew alarmed at her public behavior and, after a series of harrowing misadventures, admitted her to a rest home, only to be admonished by his father when he returned home later that evening.

Ginsberg's ambivalent feelings toward his mother, along with the sense of guilt that he felt later, as an adult, when he authorized Naomi's lobotomy, haunted him throughout his life, provoking countless nightmares and inspiring some of his finest work. The conflicting emotions also evolved into an enormous empathy for the disenfranchised, the suffering, and the downtrodden of the world—an empathy that fueled his poetry and political proclamations.

After graduating from high school, Ginsberg enrolled at Columbia University, where he intended to study to become a labor lawyer. These ambitions were quickly cast aside. Shortly after beginning his studies at Columbia, Ginsberg met Lucien Carr, an aspiring writer two years his senior. Ginsberg was immediately attracted to the strikingly handsome, fiercely intellectual St. Louis native, and the two spent many hours discussing what they called a "New Vision" for American literature. Through Carr, Ginsberg met Jack Kerouac and William Burroughs, two men who, in the decades to come, became Ginsberg's two primary confidants and influences.

Burroughs and Kerouac could not have been more unalike. Burroughs came from a wealthy St. Louis background, Kerouac from a blue-collar family in Lowell, Massachusetts. Burroughs, who had studied anthropology at Harvard, exuded a world-weary cynicism, while Kerouac, who had briefly attended Columbia on a football scholarship, was an American romantic in the Thomas Wolfe tradition. The two older men had an immediate impact on Ginsberg, Burroughs as an elder and mentor, Kerouac as a literary influence. Kerouac had written a prodigious amount of work by the time he met Ginsberg in 1944, and he encouraged Allen to follow his interests in writing poetry. Burroughs, a student of abnormal, rebellious, and even criminal behavior, introduced Ginsberg to a menagerie of unusual acquaintances, including petty thieves and drug addicts, Times Square hustlers and small-time mobsters. Burroughs and Kerouac wound up being as important to Ginsberg's intellectual development as any of Allen's teachers at Columbia.

The conflict between Ginsberg's formal and informal education mirrored the conflicts between his parents, with Louis Ginsberg replaced by the likes of Lionel Trilling, Mark Van Doren, and Ray-

Allen Ginsberg, shown in this photo from 1958, was the author of "Howl," a central work of the Beat Generation. (Bettmann/Corbis)

mond Weaver, and with Naomi Ginsberg replaced by Allen's new circle of friends. Ginsberg was as dependent on his educators and new friends as he had been on his parents, and his behavior at Columbia reflected that dependency. He wrote imitations of his father's (and teachers') favorite poets, excelled in his studies, and openly sought his teachers' approval; conversely, he also earned a reputation for nonconformist behavior, from his classroom discussions to his physical appearance, which was more bohemian than Ivy League

Few questioned his talent. Throughout his time at Columbia, Ginsberg contributed highly polished, rhymed poems to the university's literary journal. He showed his works-in-progress to his father, who critiqued the work and offered encouragement.

Ginsberg and his friends met regularly, often at Burroughs's apartment or at the West End Bar on Manhattan's Upper West Side. The group members, including Kerouac's girlfriend, Edie Parker, and Burroughs's friend, Joan Vollmer, discussed literature and the social issues of the day, their ideas decisively unorthodox. Burroughs, in particular, urged his friends to think outside the margins. Ginsberg was impressed, and he continually sought Burroughs's advice on the books he should be reading.

The circle was broken in August 1944, as a result of a bizarre event that became part of Beat Generation legend. Back in St. Louis, Lucien Carr had met an older man, David Kammerer, who had been so taken with Carr's physical beauty that he stalked Carr across the country, first to the University of Chicago and, eventually, to Columbia. Kammerer had also known Burroughs in St. Louis, and while Kammerer was never part of the inner circle of friends, he was tolerated.

On August 14, 1944, Kammerer's infatuation with Carr reached a tragic ending. After an evening of excessive drinking at the West End, Carr and Kammerer walked to a nearby park. They argued vehemently over Kammerer's feelings toward Carr, and Kammerer threatened to murder Carr and commit suicide if Carr failed to submit to his advances. A physical struggle ensued, and Carr pulled out a pocket knife and stabbed Kammerer in the heart. Carr weighed down Kammerer's body with rocks and dropped him in the Hudson River. He then visited Burroughs, who encouraged him to turn himself in to the police, and Kerouac, who helped him dispose of Kammerer's glasses and the pocket knife. When Carr eventually surrendered to the authorities, Kerouac and Burroughs were arrested as material witnesses. Burroughs's family helped him avoid a jail sentence, and Kerouac escaped by marrying Edie Parker and moving to Michigan. The media portrayed the event as an honor slaying, and Carr eventually received a light sentence for second-degree manslaughter.

The scandal set university officials on edge and did little to dispel Ginsberg's reputation as an eccentric. When Ginsberg attempted to write an account of the tragedy for a class assignment, he was informed that the subject matter was unacceptable. Later, when Kerouac, already persona non grata on the Columbia campus, stayed overnight in Ginsberg's dormitory room, Ginsberg was suspended from the university for harboring an unauthorized guest and for scribbling obscene slogans and drawings in the grime on his dorm windows. If not for the support from his influential professors, Ginsberg might have been permanently banished from the school.

Not that Ginsberg would have protested too vehemently: he had long abandoned his labor-lawyer aspirations, and with encouragement from Kerouac, he was devoting extensive time to his poetry. Ginsberg and Kerouac had grown very close, and Ginsberg had revealed his homosexuality to Kerouac during one particularly intense conversation. Kerouac, who had bisexual tendencies of his own, was sympathetic.

Through a mutual friend, Ginsberg and Kerouac met Neal Cassady, a young Denver hustler who influenced their lives. Cassady was a smooth, good-looking, fast-talking young man of incredible energy, and his boasts about his sexual escapades intrigued Kerouac, who viewed him as a kind of Western American hero. Ginsberg was physically attracted to Cassady, and although he was essentially heterosexual, Cassady reciprocated. After a tender sexual encounter detailed in Ginsberg's poem, "Many Loves," Ginsberg offered to help Cassady with his writing in exchange for his sexual favors. Cassady agreed.

The relationship was doomed from the beginning. Because Cassady preferred women to men, Ginsberg had to settle for his very limited availability. Then there was the issue of geography: Cassady lived two thousand miles away, and when he was gone, he and Ginsberg exchanged letters that found Ginsberg alternately happy, anxious, frustrated, jealous, warm, bitchy, and romantic. The relationship was typical of the love affairs Ginsberg had throughout his life. He had a tendency to fall the hardest for heterosexual men, and this problematic attraction inevitably led to great anxiety and depression. Later poetic works such as "Please Master" and "C'mon Jack" reveal a sadomasochistic inclination, undoubtedly cultivated in these difficult relationships.

By 1947, Ginsberg reached a crossroads in his long-distance relationship with Cassady. He was weary of competing for Cassady's affections—Cassady was married to a teenaged girl and had a number of simultaneous flirtations with other women; and in an effort to force the issue to some kind of conclusion, Ginsberg traveled to Denver to meet with Cassady.

The trip to Denver was a nightmare. Cassady had turned back to his womanizing ways, and Ginsberg, mired in self-pity, brooded alone in his small apartment. His journal entries from the period bounced back and forth between lengthy diatribes saturated in self-pity and beautifully descriptive passages, including an entry describing a young laborer at work. The passage eventually became "The Bricklayer's Lunch Hour," which Ginsberg later called his first truly successful poem. Seeing little hope for improvement in the future, Ginsberg decided to drop out of school, take a job on a ship bound for Africa, and straighten out his life when he returned. During his voyage to Africa, Ginsberg wrote "Dakar Doldrums," a lengthy poem more noteworthy for its expression of the poet's state of mind than for its literary accomplishment.

Ginsberg continued to work on his rhymed poems, including a couple of epic-length works that never met his approval. The poetry, although accomplished in its imitation of classical forms, was bogged down by dense, excessive symbolism and Ginsberg's devotion to form over content. In addition, Ginsberg was studying a variety of prophetic and mystical writers, including William Blake, St. John of the Cross, and Christopher Smart, and Ginsberg was far too young and inexperienced to apply what he had absorbed from those writers to his own work.

These studies, along with Ginsberg's fragile emotional state, led to an extraordinary event that preoccupied him for the next decade and a half. During the summer of 1948, Ginsberg experienced a series of what he called "visions," in which he heard what he perceived to be the voice of William Blake speaking to him through the ages. The first

vision occurred one early evening when Ginsberg was alone in his Harlem apartment, lying in bed and staring out his window at the nearby rooftops. He suddenly heard a deep voice reciting Blake's "Ah Sunflower," a poem that seemed to address Ginsberg's innermost feelings. Both shaken and exuberant, Ginsberg was utterly convinced that he had arrived at a personal epiphany, that Blake, by speaking to him through eternity, had shown him that poetry had a mystical power that transcended time. Other visions, all involving Blake's poetry, followed. Ginsberg vowed that he would never deny or forget the experience.

The Allen Ginsberg of this period was eventually recorded—to Ginsberg's displeasure—in *Go*, novelist John Clellon Holmes's roman à clef about Kerouac, Ginsberg, Cassady, and others in the group. David Stofsky, the name Holmes gave to his fictitious Ginsberg character, was alternately brooding and hyperactive, strongly intellectual yet emotionally shattered, focused on his poetry and visions yet prone to grossly exaggerated behavior. In his later years, Ginsberg cringed at this portrayal, as well as at the journals and diaries from his youth and young adulthood, to the extent that he refused to write an introduction to a new edition of *Go*, issued decades after its initial publication. Significantly, he also refused to publish any of his early journals during his lifetime.

His troubles, it turned out, were racing toward a climax. After Ginsberg told Kerouac of Allen's visions, Jack Kerouac feared for his friend's sanity, as did Louis Ginsberg, who urged his son to "exorcise Neal," finish his schooling, and lead a normal life. In early 1949, Ginsberg invited an acquaintance, a Times Square hustler named Herbert Huncke, to stay in his apartment. Huncke had recently been released from jail and had nowhere to stay, and after living on the street he was sickly and depressed. A sympathetic Ginsberg offered his apartment for as long as it took Huncke to recover.

In no time, Ginsberg's apartment was converted into a warehouse for stolen goods. Huncke hooked up with a couple of small-time burglars, and Ginsberg watched helplessly as they went on their nightly runs and returned with everything from men's clothing to a cigarette machine. Finally, not long after Huncke and his friends burglarized a detective's home, Ginsberg insisted that the goods be removed from the apartment. Unfortunately, while they were in the process of doing so, with Ginsberg riding in what turned out to be a stolen car, the driver made a wrong turn on a one-way street and came face-to-face with a police officer. The driver of the stolen car panicked, and a wild chase ensued. The driver crashed the car, and although Ginsberg escaped before the police reached the scene, it was only a matter of hours before the police arrived at his apartment. He was charged with being an accomplice in the burglary ring.

If not for the efforts of Columbia University's faculty and attorneys, Ginsberg might have received a jail sentence. Instead, an agreement was reached and Ginsberg was sent to a psychiatric hospital for treatment. While in the hospital, Ginsberg met Carl Solomon, an eccentric intellectual seemingly hell-bent on self-destruction. Solomon had been arrested and institutionalized for stealing a peanut-butter sandwich and showing it to the police, and at the time of his meeting with Ginsberg, he had been undergoing shock treatments. To Ginsberg, who spent hours discussing life and literature with the troubled patient, Solomon was proof of a great mind being destroyed by madness, not unlike the sorrow Allen felt when he considered his mother's mental decline.

Once released from the psychiatric institute, Ginsberg tried to conform to what the rest of the world considered to be normal. He found a job, lived at home with his father and new stepmother, and even struck up a romantic relationship with a woman. His poetry took a dramatic turn for the better when he met and was befriended by William Carlos Williams, New Jersey's unofficial poet laureate. Williams had little use for Ginsberg's rhymed poetry, and he encouraged Ginsberg to use concrete images and everyday speech in his work. Ginsberg complied by rewriting some of his journal entries into poetry. Happy with the results, Williams promised to help Ginsberg find a publisher, and although years passed before that connection occurred, the poems written by Ginsberg during this period, eventually published as *Empty Mirror,* represented an important new direction for Ginsberg's poetry.

While Ginsberg tried to conform to the suggestions made by his psychiatrists, his friends were seeing major changes taking place in their lives. Neal Cassady was now married and living in California. Jack Kerouac published his first book, *The Town and the City,* a novel written in the style of Thomas Wolfe and telling the stories of characters modeled after Kerouac, Ginsberg, Burroughs, Huncke, and others. Burroughs had run afoul of the law again, this time in Mexico, when, according to some reports, he accidentally shot and killed Joan Vollmer during a drunken game of William Tell, during which Vollmer had placed a glass on her head and dared Burroughs to shoot it off. Horrified by the news, Ginsberg worried about the future of his friend and mentor.

In 1951, Ginsberg met Gregory Corso, a young, aspiring poet who became a lifelong friend. In many ways, Corso was the personification of a "Beat" poet. He had had a difficult childhood, with much time spent fending for himself on the street, and by the time he met Ginsberg, Corso had spent time in reformatories and jails, educated himself on the classic writers and poets, and written some excellent early work. Like Neal Cassady or Herbert Huncke, Corso was a natural storyteller, yet he possessed a poet's instincts and sensibilities. For the next four-plus decades, Ginsberg acted as Corso's biggest apologist, defending him when he acted out, promoting his work to anyone who listened, and taking him in when he had no place to live.

Ginsberg's efforts to conform might have kept him out of harm's way, but they also left him unhappy. By all indications, he was adrift in an ocean of uncertainty. He was writing as much as ever, yet very little was being published; he had engaged in several heterosexual relationships, yet he knew they were a sham, that he was and always would be homosexual at the core. His jobs earned him money but took him nowhere. Even a brief fling with William Burroughs—back in New York after years of rambling around the United States and Mexico—ended poorly, with Ginsberg rejecting

Burroughs and Burroughs leaving the country for Tangier.

Desperate for any kind of movement in his life, Ginsberg left New York for an extended stay in Mexico. He explored the Mayan ruins in the Yucatán, pondering the fate of the great yet long-gone civilization and wondering if the same was in store for modern Western civilization. It was a happy period, even if Ginsberg had little money and had to rely on the generosity of a female archeologist who befriended him. "Siesta in Xbalba," one of Ginsberg's stronger early works, details his adventures and inner discoveries during his trip to Mexico.

Ginsberg eventually became known for his extensive travels, and his trip to Mexico, taken when he was nearly twenty-eight, was his first extended time away from home. This time away proved to be critical to Ginsberg's personal development. Away from friends and family, he was forced to think and act independently, and by all indications, Ginsberg had grown dramatically by the time he left Mexico in May 1954. His journal entries, published in *Journals Early Fifties Early Sixties*, display a maturation in his thinking and poetry.

From Mexico, Ginsberg moved up the California coastline to San Jose, where he hoped to rendezvous with Neal Cassady and possibly rekindle their affair. He was only partially successful. Cassady was preoccupied with his job and a domestic life that included a wife and children, and after a brief stay with the family, Ginsberg was banished from the household when Carolyn Cassady caught him in bed with her husband. She drove Ginsberg to San Francisco and ordered him to stay away from Neal.

Although these events at first seemed troublesome, Ginsberg could not have written a better script for his life. San Francisco had a teeming arts community, and the city was tolerant of bohemian and alternative lifestyles. Ginsberg wasted no time in getting involved in San Francisco's thriving poetry community, which was essentially guided by poets Kenneth Rexroth and Robert Duncan. Jack Kerouac was in and out of town, as was Neal Cassady, so for Ginsberg, San Francisco represented a reunion of the central figures in his East Coast life

nearly a decade earlier. During his first year on the West Coast, Ginsberg also met poets Gary Snyder, Philip Whalen, and Michael McClure, who all became lifelong friends and, in the cases of Snyder and Whalen, influences in Ginsberg's study of Buddhism and Eastern thought.

Shortly after arriving in San Francisco, Ginsberg met Peter Orlovsky, who became Allen's lifelong lover. Orlovsky, seven years younger than Ginsberg, was emotionally fragile, and, in the wake of his recent affairs with Cassady and Burroughs, Ginsberg moved slowly in developing their relationship. The fact that Orlovsky was mainly heterosexual also posed a potential problem, but it was an issue Ginsberg was prepared to address. In February 1955, the two exchanged informal marriage vows and moved into an apartment together.

The relationship was never easy. Ginsberg could be possessive and demanding, and Orlovsky could be quite moody. In time, as Ginsberg gained international fame, Orlovsky all but disappeared into the background, and, at times, he was subjected to brutal disapproval and criticism from Ginsberg's friends. Orlovsky struggled with alcohol and drug dependency for much of his life, and he and Ginsberg separated for great stretches of time, but the relationship endured for more than four decades. Orlovsky was at Ginsberg's bedside during the final hours of his life.

Ginsberg's poetry reflected the dramatic changes in his life. He filled the pages of his journals (eventually published as *Journals Mid Fifties*) with notes and new poems, dream entries, drawings, and accounts of his day-to-day life. Some of the poems from his early days in California—"America," "In the Baggage Room at Greyhound," "A Supermarket in California," and "Sunflower Sutra," a stunning piece of spontaneous composition, hurriedly written while Kerouac waited for Ginsberg to join him for a party—rank among the best works Ginsberg produced.

During this productive period Ginsberg wrote his signature work, a poem that not only gained him international fame but actually changed the face of modern poetry. Ironically, "Howl" began as an artistic exercise and, by Ginsberg's account, was never intended for publication. Jack Kerouac had been experimenting in spontaneous composition with his fiction, and he had been urging Ginsberg to try spontaneity with his poetry. One evening in August 1955, Ginsberg sat down at his typewriter and, remembering Kerouac's advice and thinking about the long sax lines played by jazz musicians, attempted a work that summoned forth a rush of thoughts and sympathies for all his friends and acquaintances whose unorthodox thinking and behavior had been trampled by an unsparing society. There were lines devoted to Carl Solomon, Herbert Huncke, Bill Cannastra (a friend who died in a tragic subway accident), and others, and although Naomi Ginsberg was never specifically mentioned in the poem, she and her plight were a strong influence in the writing. The long lines looked to be straight out of Whitman, but there was no question that "Howl" was the work of a powerful contemporary voice.

At first, Ginsberg felt ambivalent about the massive work. As spontaneous writing, as well as emotional expression, the poem had undeniable value. Still, as Ginsberg saw it, the subject matter of "Howl" was far too private to be published.

Ginsberg read the first part of "Howl" during a historic reading at San Francisco's 6 Gallery on 7 October 1955. Hosted by Kenneth Rexroth, the reading featured new work by such younger, relatively unknown poets as Philip Lamantia, Michael McClure, Philip Whalen, Gary Snyder, and Ginsberg, but no one in the room was prepared for the impact of Ginsberg's contribution. Jack Kerouac had declined an invitation to read, but he was very much a presence, passing around wine jugs and punctuating the end of each long line of "Howl" with shouts of "Go!" and "Yes!" The audience joined in, and Ginsberg, a little drunk when he took the stage and emboldened by the encouragement, responded by delivering his poem in a manner nothing short of astonishing. Poet Lawrence Ferlinghetti, owner of the City Lights Bookstore and publisher of small volumes and pamphlets under his City Lights Books imprint, witnessed Ginsberg's performance and sent him a telegram: "I greet you at the beginning of a great career," Ferlinghetti

wrote, imitating a letter Ralph Waldo Emerson had sent Walt Whitman after the publication of *Leaves of Grass.* "When do I get the manuscript?"

Despite the poem's length, Ginsberg felt that it was incomplete, and over the next several months he wrote two new sections for it, as well as what he labeled a "Footnote to Howl." Although spontaneously composed, each section was subsequently worked and reworked until Ginsberg was satisfied. To complete his first collection of poems, Ginsberg gathered a sampling of his best new poems, along with four short works he had completed while staying with the Cassadys in San Jose. William Carlos Williams provided an introduction. The booklet, *Howl and Other Poems*, became the fourth installment in Lawrence Ferlinghetti's "Pocket Poets" series.

Suddenly, with Ginsberg and "Howl" largely to thank, San Francisco was enjoying a poetry "renaissance." Major publications ran articles and photos of the poets; readings enjoyed increases in attendance. Ginsberg, quite comfortable with all the attention, used his new celebrity status as a means of promoting the works by his friends, and although he wasn't always successful in convincing editors to publish their books, he was able to keep their names circulating in literary circles. Throughout his life, Ginsberg championed the work of unknown and unpublished poets and writers, eventually establishing a nonprofit organization, Committee on Poetry, to help fund their works. San Francisco was just a starting point.

The reaction to "Howl" was fiercely mixed, with some critics praising it as a breakout poem signaling the beginning of a new type of poetry, while others condemned it for its profane language, graphic references to homosexuality, and confrontational, antiestablishment stance. The poem (and Ginsberg) enjoyed a huge boost in publicity in 1957 when Ferlinghetti and Shig Murao, a City Lights Bookstore clerk, were arrested and charged with selling an obscene book. The trial garnered national attention, and by the time a "not guilty" verdict was rendered, *Howl and Other Poems* had sold more than 10,000 copies. The trial set precedents used in future First Amendment court cases, including the San Francisco obscenity trial of social satirist Lenny Bruce.

Ginsberg was away from the United States during the trial. He and Peter Orlovsky had left the country in early 1957, first for Tangier, where they visited William Burroughs, and Ginsberg assisted him in the editing of a novel he was calling *Naked Lunch*. Then Allen and Peter were off to Europe, where Ginsberg divided his time writing poetry, hanging out with artists and writers, and exploring the sites and museums of Spain, Italy, France, and England. Much of his time was spent in Paris. Ginsberg, Orlovsky, and Gregory Corso resided in a run-down, inexpensive hotel (known in Beat Generation lore as "The Beat Hotel").

For Ginsberg, Europe was another eye-opening experience, much like his earlier excursion to Mexico. Every time he visited an art museum or cultural landmark, Ginsberg was reminded of Europe's rich history—a history now threatened by modern world events. The Cold War had heightened tensions between the United States and the Soviet Union, and Ginsberg feared that a power struggle, culminating with nuclear warfare, could bring an end to the world. His poetry, a portion of which was eventually published in *Kaddish and Other Poems,* underscored his concerns.

Meanwhile, back in the United States, the term "Beat Generation" was becoming a household phrase. Jack Kerouac's *On the Road* was published shortly after the "Howl" obscenity trial ended, and the novel made a huge impression on critics and readers alike. A year later, Kerouac published *The Dharma Bums,* his account of his friendship with Gary Snyder, their interest in Buddhism, and the San Francisco Poetry Renaissance. Scholarly essays and articles in general interest magazines spawned a lively debate over the merits of the works by Kerouac, Ginsberg, and others, and the freewheeling lifestyles in *On the Road* and *The Dharma Bums* were analyzed. The naturally shy Kerouac basked briefly in the spotlight, but ultimately found it too hot for his liking.

Ginsberg eventually returned to the States, settled into an apartment in New York, and resumed his leadership role in promoting the works of Beat Generation writers. He acted as a guest editor for magazines clamoring for new work by these controversial writers, and he made a point of attending high-visibility publishing parties and functions. Ferlinghetti requested a new manuscript of poems, but Ginsberg felt the volume lacked a big poem to anchor it, as "Howl" had anchored his first book.

He had a strong inclination about what that poem would be. For more than two years, he had been attempting to write a long eulogy to his mother, who had died shortly before the publication of *Howl and Other Poems.* Ginsberg had been haunted by the fact that there had been so few people at her gravesite that a kaddish had not been read for her; Naomi Ginsberg's life, difficult and tormented by mental disorder, seemed to have been swallowed up and forgotten. Allen himself had missed her funeral and burial. Over the ensuing years, Ginsberg had written several false starts to his own version of a kaddish, and while in Paris, he had actually succeeded in writing a fragment that met his approval.

"Kaddish," the most striking and moving work Ginsberg ever wrote, came about as unexpectedly as "Howl." In mid-November 1958, it all came together. Ginsberg had been up all night one Friday evening, sitting in a friend's apartment and listening to music, and when he returned home, he sat down at his desk, pulled out a sheaf of blank typing paper, and began writing, in longhand, an account of his mother's life, the details striking and unsparing, complete with moments of breathtaking beauty followed by lines of agonizingly painful memory. The mental breakdowns, graphic descriptions of Naomi Ginsberg's nudism, the political rantings and ravings, the paranoid fantasies, the horrors of two boys watching their mother's mental disintegration, Naomi's lonely years in sanitariums—nothing was left out. Ginsberg wept as he wrote, his teardrops staining the pages and becoming part of the manuscript. He wrote for forty continuous hours, taking breaks only to go to the bathroom or eat, his flagging energy refueled by coffee and Dexedrine. When he finished, he had filled fifty-eight pages with some of the most affecting writing ever produced by an American poet. As with "Howl," Ginsberg wrote additional sections to accompany the main body of his new poem, and numerous revisions of the poem preceded submission for publication.

Not surprisingly, Louis Ginsberg was both deeply moved and shocked when he read "Kaddish" for the first time. The more personal and embarrassing descriptions and events, he surmised, needed to be trimmed from the poem. Allen disagreed. In his view, art reflected everyday life, warts and all. It was an idea that he, Lucien Carr, and Jack Kerouac had discussed with all their talk of a "New Vision" in the mid-forties, and it was a practice employed by a number of American poets, from Whitman to Williams. The more conservative or traditionally minded critics were harsh in their judgments of what they considered to be the excesses of the Beat Generation's literature, but Ginsberg, Kerouac, and the others held their ground. "My poetry is a graph of my mind—who I am and what I'm seeing and thinking," Ginsberg explained in defense of his writing during a personal interview with Michael Schumacher.

This graph of Ginsberg's mind included the subconscious as well as the conscious. From his earliest journals on, Ginsberg kept a record of many of his dreams, and some of his most arresting poems, including "White Shroud," were transcriptions of dreams. Different levels of consciousness attained under the influence of drugs applied as well. Ginsberg had experimented with different drugs since his college days, hoping to probe the depths of his mind, and a number of poems had been colored by the drugs Ginsberg had taken during their composition. "The message," Ginsberg explained in an interview with Michael Schumacher, was "to widen the area of consciousness."

In 1960, at the urging of William Burroughs, Ginsberg traveled to South America in search of the powerful, mind-expanding *ayahuasca,* or *yagé.* Ginsberg had sampled LSD in a controlled environment at Stanford University a year earlier, and he had been exhilarated by its effect on his mind. Experiments with other drugs, including nitrous oxide, followed, with Ginsberg attempting to write under the influence of drugs, or at least capture

their effects afterward. In the Amazon, a *curandero* introduced Ginsberg to *ayahuasca,* and the experience shook Ginsberg to his roots. Ever since his Blake visions in 1948, he had been hoping for another visionary experience; *ayahuasca* thrilled him with hallucinations of death, eternity, and all points between heaven and hell.

After returning to New York, Ginsberg contacted Timothy Leary, a Harvard psychology lecturer conducting experiments with psilocybin, a synthetic of the sacred hallucinogenic mushrooms used in religious ceremonies in Mexico and Central America. Leary supervised Ginsberg's initial experience with psilocybin, and the trip, recalled in Leary's autobiography *Flashbacks,* was a memorable one. To Ginsberg and Leary, psilocybin offered the possibilities for a revolution in human consciousness with the help of this mind-expanding drug: behavior could be altered for the better; violence and aggression could be controlled. Although he openly endorsed the drug and encouraged his friends to try it, Ginsberg correctly predicted that a day would come when authorities, from the government to Harvard officials, would find a way to thwart Leary's work.

Ginsberg was at a critical juncture in his study of consciousness. He yearned for the ultimate spiritual or metaphysical experience, and he seemed to have hit a roadblock with Western philosophy and religion. In 1961, he turned to the East, traveling throughout India and consulting with the subcontinent's gurus, holymen, poets, and even the Dalai Lama. Ginsberg was surprised to hear essentially the same message wherever he went: rather than take flight from the body, one should return to it; one should not seek an escape, but, rather, acceptance from within. "If you see something horrible, don't cling to it," Ginsberg was advised. "If you see something beautiful, don't cling to it" (quoted in *Dharma Lion,* 379). Ginsberg was profoundly affected by the advice, which seemed to free him from the trap of pursuing visionary experiences—an obsession since his Blake visions.

Ginsberg spent two years in India and the Far East, and when he returned to the United States, he brought back a wisdom he had attained from his travels. The Civil Rights movement was gaining momentum, the war in Vietnam was showing signs of being a conflict requiring more than cursory U.S. effort, and the country's baby boomers were hitting their stride. Unlike Kerouac and Burroughs, who had little use for politics, Ginsberg immersed himself in social and political causes. He shed his Beat Generation skin and moved ahead. He busied himself with First Amendment cases, continued his campaign for a greater exploration of mind-expanding drugs, and, in general, moved into the front ranks of what would become a countercultural movement.

Ginsberg had been interested in visiting Cuba since the Fidel Castro–led revolution, and in January 1965 he was asked to judge a poetry contest in the country. The trip, however, was disastrous from the start. Ginsberg intended to use the occasion to speak out in favor of free speech, and to criticize the Cuban government's oppression of homosexuals and use of capital punishment. His statements on these issues, offered to students and the Cuban press, were dealt with sternly by the Cuban government, which ultimately expelled him from the country.

Ironically, due to the travel restrictions between the United States and Cuba during the time, Ginsberg was expelled to Czechoslovakia, another Iron Curtain country, and although he was much more cautious in his public statements while visiting the European country, his trip to Czechoslovakia was also destined for trouble. Ginsberg met with students well versed in Beat Generation literature, and he read his poetry at universities and coffee houses. He took meaningful sidetrips, as well. He fulfilled a lifelong dream of visiting the Soviet Union and, later, Poland. But he ran afoul of government authorities when he returned to Czechoslovakia and was elected *Kral Majales* (King of May) by university students. The authorities considered his election an insult and embarrassment, and Ginsberg was immediately stripped of the honor. In the days following the election, Ginsberg had one of his journals stolen, and he was followed by shadowy figures on the street; one evening, he was attacked and beaten, and subsequently taken into custody. Shortly thereafter, he was thrown out of the country, the officials claiming that he was a bad influence on Czechoslovakian youth.

Ginsberg's next stop—England—was much more pleasant. "Swinging London" was in full bloom, and during his stay in the city, Ginsberg spent time with Bob Dylan, who was touring the country and making his film *Don't Look Back*. Through Dylan, Ginsberg met the four members of the Beatles, and though their initial encounter was edgy and less than memorable, it was still an important introduction: both John Lennon and Paul McCartney later influenced Ginsberg. On the plane from Czechoslovakia to England, Ginsberg had written "Kral Majales," his account of his problems in Czechoslovakia, but in England, Ginsberg was in a more conciliatory mood. He read his newly written "Who Be Kind To" at the International Poetry Reading at London's Royal Albert Hall on 11 June 1965.

Back in the United States, Ginsberg turned his attention to the growing dissatisfaction with the Vietnam War. At that point, a majority of Americans still supported the war effort, but the numbers were shrinking and a protest movement was mounting, especially on college campuses. Ginsberg flew to California, where a huge demonstration was planned by students and activists in Berkeley. The demonstration, the largest of its kind to date, promised to be violent, especially when the Hell's Angels motorcycle club threatened to disrupt the scheduled peace march and beat any demonstrators in their way. Ginsberg, author Ken Kesey (*One Flew over the Cuckoo's Nest*), Neal Cassady, and others met with a faction of the Hell's Angels, and rather than bicker over politics, the group took LSD, listened to music, and talked, the Angels eventually concluding that Ginsberg and his friends were not the enemy. The demonstration and peace march commenced without a hitch. Ginsberg's essay, "How to Make a March/Spectacle," served as a blueprint for planning demonstrations and peacefully resolving potentially violent confrontations between two opposing sides. "Flower Power" was born.

Ginsberg increased his political activism throughout the sixties. In addition to his public opposition to the Vietnam War, Ginsberg campaigned tirelessly for free speech, defending controversial social satirist Lenny Bruce, battling New York City officials trying to restrict cabaret licenses (and thus control the content of material presented at these clubs), acting as an advocate for The Living Theatre. He continued to openly support the use of marijuana and LSD, and, in 1966, he testified on the use of mind-expanding drugs before a Senate subcommittee. His poetry, particularly the epic antiwar poem, "Wichita Vortex Sutra," reflected his political concerns, as well as his strong interests in spontaneous composition.

By 1966, Ginsberg had the physical appearance for which he is now best remembered. Although he was balding, he had long, shoulder-length hair and a black beard; he wore black horn-rimmed glasses. With his jeans, T-shirts, and tennis shoes, he dressed more like college students a generation his junior. He was now probably as well known as a public figure as he was as a poet. He lectured and read his poetry all across America, maintaining the kind of touring schedule associated with rock stars, crisscrossing the country, recording his observations onto a tape recorder, and transcribing the lines later. These spontaneously composed works, many appearing in *The Fall of America,* captured the mood of a country caught up in a political storm.

Ginsberg's popularity among America's youth was easy to understand. His physical appearance largely reflected the look of the "hippie" culture sprouting on either coast, and his "Flower Power" gentility fell in step with the antiwar sentiments growing on college campuses. His appearance at the "Human Be-In" in San Francisco's Golden Gate Park on January 17, 1967, placed him at the white-hot center of countercultural activity. Ironically, he spent 1967's "Summer of Love" outside the United States. He traveled to Europe, taking part in the "Dialectics of Liberation" conference in England and visiting the different countries in the United Kingdom. In Wales, while under the influence of LSD, he wrote the beautifully pastoral "Wales Visitation," universally accepted as one of his greatest works. Later that summer, he visited Italy and had a memorable encounter with Ezra Pound, the expatriate American poet disgraced by his anti-Semitic statements

Allen Ginsberg in 1973 at the age of 47. (Hulton-Deutsch Collection/Corbis)

during World War II. Pound, who had maintained a strict silence for years, stunned Ginsberg by admitting that he had made a terrible mistake in his pronouncements—a confession he'd avoided making to anyone in the past.

The following year, 1968, proved to be one of the most turbulent years in American history. The Vietnam War had become an issue tearing the country apart; civil rights leader Martin Luther King, Jr., and presidential candidate Robert Kennedy were assassinated. Ginsberg watched in horror and anger as the United States stood at the threshold of what appeared to be another civil war. It was a presidential election year, and Ginsberg traveled to Chicago to attend the Democratic National Convention, which political radicals and dissidents were threatening to disrupt. The Chicago police, under orders from Mayor Richard Daley, were prepared to drive back forcefully the demonstrators and protest marchers, and although Allen Ginsberg, poet Ed Sanders, peace activist David Dellinger, and others attempted to instill a spirit of passive resistance to the convention week, a series of violent confrontations between law enforcement officers and the youths visiting the city—later labeled "a police riot"—left Ginsberg badly shaken.

This dark period also found Ginsberg considering his mortality, with the deaths of two of his closest friends, Neal Cassady in 1968 and Jack Kerouac in 1969. Both seemed to exemplify the awful price one could pay for celebrity. Kerouac had never been comfortable with his celebrity status, and, in his later years, he became almost reclusive, devoting more time to drinking than writing, his alcoholism finally claiming his life. Cassady, on the other hand, loved the spotlight, and his association with Ken Kesey (recalled in Tom Wolfe's *Electric Kool-Aid Acid Test*) kept his lifestyle on the fast track. He died of exposure in Mexico after an afternoon of drinking and ingesting drugs, his body found near the railroads tracks he had been counting in one final aimless journey.

Ginsberg addressed the personal and political crises as he always did: with strong, energetic bursts of creative activity. He filled his journals and notebooks with new poetry and political observations, his musings grounded in two major influences of his youth: Walt Whitman, who had once warned that America would fall victim to its own heartlessness, and William Blake, whose prophetic poetry had affected Ginsberg's early work. With the assistance of Barry Miles, the British writer and bookstore owner who had introduced him to the Beatles, Ginsberg set selections of Blake's *Songs of Innocence and Songs of Experience* to music, writing music to accompany Blake's poetry. Ginsberg had been singing and chanting mantras at poetry readings since his return from India, and while his voice was far from polished, the sincerity that he brought to the Blake songs impressed critics reviewing the eventually released recordings.

Ginsberg's interest in writing and recording music typified a subtle change in life and career at the end of the sixties and the early seventies. His nonstop activity during the sixties, coupled with the turmoil around him, had exacted emotional and psychological tolls: the aftermath of the Chicago Convention, including Ginsberg's testimony at the Chicago conspiracy trial of seven activists arrested during convention week, had left Ginsberg despairing about the future of America. The Vietnam War showed little sign of letting up, despite the huge number of people now opposing it, and President Richard Nixon's priorities for the United States seemed, to Ginsberg, to be leading the country away from democracy and closer to a police state. Needing to find a place to retreat, Ginsberg purchased a farm in upstate New York, where he could often be found when he wasn't on the lecture and reading circuit.

The period found Ginsberg renewing his studies of Buddhism and meditation. He had always been interested in Buddhism—at Kerouac's urging, he had begun an informal yet intense study of Buddhism in the early fifties, and he had continued to look into Buddhism in the sixties, especially after his visits to India and the Far East—and a chance meeting with Chögyam Trungpa Rinpoche, a Tibetan Buddhist teacher and spiritual leader, led to a new, invigorating period of study that ultimately led to Ginsberg's taking formal Buddhist vows. The controversial Trungpa Rinpoche, criticized by purists for his unorthodox preaching and Western lifestyle, was an ideal teacher for Ginsberg: Trungpa's "wild wisdom" teachings reminded Ginsberg of his mother, Carl Solomon, William Burroughs, and any number of other unconventional figures in his life; Trungpa's interest in improvisation reminded him of Jack Kerouac's preachings about spontaneous writing. In an arrangement reminiscent of his earlier vows with Neal Cassady and Peter Orlovsky, Ginsberg agreed to assist Trungpa Rinpoche in his pursuits of poetry in exchange for the Buddhist's acting as his spiritual teacher.

The Ginsberg-Trungpa association profoundly affected the direction Ginsberg took for the remainder of his life. Trungpa had founded the Naropa Institute in Boulder, Colorado, the university dedicated to aligning Eastern and Western thought and scholarship, and Ginsberg, along with poet Anne Waldman, cofounded Naropa's poetics school, playfully called the "Jack Kerouac School of Disembodied Poetics." By following Trungpa's meditation practice, which involved focusing on one's breath, Ginsberg not only stepped up his daily meditation practice, but he also applied many of the principles to the way he wrote poetry.

The 1973 publication of *The Fall of America,* and the volume's subsequent winning of the National Book Award a year later, brought Ginsberg a measure of critical and academic acceptance that he'd found elusive in the past. Whitmanic in its tone and scope, *The Fall of America,* by far the largest of Ginsberg's poetry collections, was an expansive gathering of works written between 1968 and 1972, largely composed on the road, when Ginsberg was racing back and forth across the United States and witnessing the tremendous social and political upheaval of the times.

The founding of the Naropa poetics school nudged Ginsberg into another new direction in life. He enjoyed teaching, and he had taught sporadically, usually at seminars or when he was reading at college campuses, for nearly two decades. His Naropa duties were more substantial and formal. Every summer, from the founding of the poetics school to the end of his life, Ginsberg lectured and appeared in seminars at Naropa, his fame bringing in students from all over the country and attracting such guest lecturers as Norman Mailer, William Burroughs, Gregory Corso, and other writers, musicians, poets, and artists associated with the Beat Generation. Over the years, at Naropa and, later, Brooklyn College in New York, Ginsberg taught courses on William Carlos Williams, William Blake, and others, as well as a general course he called "The Literary History of the Beat Generation."

In 1975, Bob Dylan invited Ginsberg to join in a touring troupe of musicians he was calling the Rolling Thunder Revue. Ginsberg, along with Jack Kerouac, Lawrence Ferlinghetti, and other Beat poets, had been huge influences on Dylan, and he was acknowledging as much by asking Ginsberg to read his poetry onstage in an eclectic ensemble that including Dylan, folksinger Joan Baez, former Byrds leader Roger McGuinn, and a host of others. Unfortunately, Ginsberg's participation was cut short by teaching obligations and by the news that his father was dying of cancer. He was at Naropa when Louis Ginsberg passed away on 8 July 1976. On his flight back to New Jersey, Allen wrote the lyrics to "Father Death Blues," a song that became the centerpiece of a series of poems he wrote about his father's final days, and by far his finest song.

Louis Ginsberg's death signaled the beginning of an especially difficult period in Allen Ginsberg's life. A few months after Louis's death, Allen had to contend with a controversy that split the poetry community and threatened the future of Naropa's poetics school. At a Halloween party in Snowmass, Colorado, a drunken Chögyam Trungpa Rinpoche, along with a number of his followers, had publicly humiliated poets W. S. Merwin and Dana Naone by ridiculing them and stripping them naked in front of the partygoers, the incident outraging Trungpa's critics and receiving plenty of attention in the local press. Although he had been out of town at the time, Allen became involved, first, when he tried to act as an intermediary in the dispute between Trungpa supporters and enemies, and, later, when he defended Trungpa in a magazine interview. Ginsberg's comments infuriated a number of poets and critics, and for the next several years, a bitter feud divided the poetry community, with a depressed Allen Ginsberg trying to soothe both sides. Funds to Naropa dried up, and Ginsberg wound up paying most of the poetics school's bills out of his own bank account.

To make matters worse, he was going through a prolonged period of writer's block. *Mind Breaths,* published in 1978, contained some noteworthy work, especially the poems addressing Ginsberg's Buddhism and meditation practices, but in comparison to *The Fall of America,* the book fell short of the standard Ginsberg had set for himself. His foray into songwriting and recording apparently distracted him, and some grumbling critics felt that Ginsberg was more dedicated to becoming a rock star than in writing good poetry.

His struggles with "Plutonian Ode" was a case in point. The poem, written a day after Ginsberg, Peter Orlovsky, and a small group of protesters were arrested for civil disobedience at the Rocky Flats nuclear facility in Colorado, was another exercise in spontaneous writing, a diatribe against nuclear energy and the threat that it posed to the environment and future generations. Ginsberg badly wanted to write another masterwork, and "Plutonian Ode" had all the potential of becoming a work in the "Wichita Vortex Sutra" tradition, but Ginsberg was unable to pull it off. He toiled through draft after draft of the poem, and while he would use it to anchor his 1982 collection, *Plutonian Ode: Poems 1977–1980*, he was never totally satisfied with the way it turned out.

In all likelihood, Ginsberg was falling victim to a combination of his tireless pursuit of his various interests and his advancing age. He still possessed an incredible energy that was the envy of his friends and associates, but he had reached an age that demanded certain concessions he was reluctant to make. His teaching duties at Naropa took up his summer months, and he still used the spring and fall months for reading and lecturing tours, although the number of cities visited was decreasing. He also had to contend with his past: with members of the Beat Generation growing older or dying, there was an increasing demand for historical perspective. For Ginsberg, the workload was staggering. *As Ever,* his selected correspondence with Neal Cassady, had been published in 1977, and in 1980, he published *Straight Hearts Delight,* his love poems to Peter Orlovsky and selected correspondence with him. That same year, *Composed on the Tongue,* a collection of interviews and literary essays, was also released. A Naropa conference honoring Jack Kerouac on the occasion of the twenty-fifth anniversary of the publication of *On the Road,* and featuring nearly every Beat Generation writing figure still around, along with such counterculture luminaries as Abbie Hoffman and Timothy Leary, was a high-visibility event demanding much of Ginsberg's time. Ginsberg, always a willing proponent of Beat Generation writers and writings, now found himself addressing his past almost as much as he was living his present.

One project of particular interest was the gathering of Ginsberg's poems into one volume. City Lights had published all of Ginsberg's major poetry collections since 1956, and although that work alone would have formed a large volume, Ginsberg had also published a sizable number of other small collections, pamphlets, booklets, and broadsides for other small presses. His ambitious plans for a book of collected poems included a complete compilation, arranged in chronological order, of all his published poetry; comprehensive notes on the individual poems, complete with photographs and brief biographies of the important figures in the poems; and indices of proper names, poem titles, and first lines. The project spelled an end to Ginsberg's long association with City Lights. He hired an agent, who landed him a six-book, six-figure contract with a large New York publisher, and, in 1984, *Collected Poems 1947–1980* appeared to great critical acclaim. City Lights continued to publish its earlier collections of Ginsberg's poetry, but HarperCollins issued the rest of his new work.

Ginsberg traveled extensively throughout the eighties and nineties, combining his long-established reading tours with journeys charged with political implications. A trip to Nicaragua, coming at a time when the United States was engaged in testy relations with the country's government, and a trip to China—both under the sponsorship of poetry conferences—found Ginsberg pondering human rights issues and writing arresting new work. In Nicaragua, Ginsberg teamed up with Russian poet Yevgeny Yevtushenko and Nicaraguan poet Ernesto Cardenal in a manifesto inviting writers from all over the world to visit the Central American country and draw their own conclusions about the people and their revolutionary government. In China, Ginsberg wrote some of his best poetry in years, from beautifully descriptive street scenes to a pair of powerful poems originating from dreams Ginsberg had about his mother: "Black Shroud," based on a nightmare, focused on Ginsberg's lifelong sense of guilt over how he addressed his mother's mental illness; "White Shroud," conversely, offered a peaceful resolution, in which Ginsberg, finding Naomi still alive and living as a homeless woman in the Bronx, takes his mother under his care.

*White Shroud* (1986) and *Cosmopolitan Greetings* (1994), the final two volumes of new poetry published during Ginsberg's lifetime, proved that Ginsberg still had plenty of excellent poetry in him, with a range that seemed to cover nearly every form, from haiku to rock 'n' roll lyrics, list poems to rhymed works similar to those written by his father. More time was passing between the publication of collections than in Ginsberg's youthful years, but that seemed to be due more to Ginsberg's pursuits of other interests than any loss of creativity.

His recording career thrived. His two-record *First Blues*, released in 1982 and produced by John Hammond, the renowned producer who had discovered Bob Dylan and Bruce Springsteen, among others, received generally good reviews and seemed to prompt a string of new works, including a collaboration with Philip Glass. *The Lion for Real* set classic Ginsberg poems to musical arrangements, with Ginsberg reading his work to the accompaniment of some of the music industry's most respected avant-garde artists. In 1994, Rhino Records issued *Holy Soul Jelly Roll*, an ambitious 4-CD boxed set covering Ginsberg's entire career, all but guaranteeing that Ginsberg's voice would be heard long after he was gone, the recording acting as an impressive companion piece to *Collected Poems*.

Perhaps most surprising—and rewarding, personally and financially—of Ginsberg's alternate careers was his work as a photographer. From the time he had met Jack Kerouac, William Burroughs, Neal Cassady, and the other figures of the Beat Generation, Ginsberg had felt a need to document their lives and times. As a photographer, he had been a natural, with a good eye for framing the dramatic and ironic, as well as the historically important. His photographs had been published in newspapers, magazines, and books for more than two decades, but never with the intention of showing them as artistic works. In the eighties and nineties, under the guidance of such esteemed photographers as Robert Frank and Bernice Abbot, and with considerable assistance from Raymond Foye, Ginsberg gathered the best of nearly a half-century's worth of photographs, which were catalogued and, in many cases, printed on museum-quality archival paper. The results, published in *Allen Ginsberg Photographs,* were stunning. Ginsberg began selling the prints to collectors, and gallery showings of his photographs popped up around the world.

By the mid-nineties, Ginsberg began to experience serious health problems. He had heart problems and diabetes, which he managed to keep under control with careful monitoring of his diet; he had also been exposed at one time or another to all three types of hepatitis. Walking up a couple of flights of stairs to his apartment or office became a chore. A new office building with an elevator was located, and, after selling his archives to Stanford University for a million dollars, Ginsberg bought a huge loft in the East Village. The loft not only afforded him plenty of space in which to live and work, but it also had an extra room that he could provide to his aging stepmother, Edith, whenever she visited.

In March 1997, Ginsberg became ill and was hospitalized in New York. Doctors, discovering an advanced state of liver cancer, told him that, at best, he had a matter of months to live. Although badly weakened, Ginsberg returned home, set his affairs in order, visited with family and friends, wrote a handful of final poems and journal entries, and prepared for the death that had been a preoccupation for much of his life. In the early morning hours of 5 April 1997, Allen Ginsberg died peacefully in his sleep, surrounded by a handful of close friends. After a Buddhist funeral service, his remains were cremated and his ashes distributed to three locations: a gravesite with his father in New Jersey; the Sacred Heart Buddhist monastery in Michigan; and the Rocky Mountain Shambhala Center in Colorado.

Ginsberg's works have continued to appear after his death. *Last Poems*, a collection of poetry written between the publication of *Cosmopolitan Greetings* and Ginsberg's death, was published in 1998; *Deliberate Prose,* a volume of selected essays, reviews,

Allen Ginsberg studies his contact sheet. (Photo by Gordon Ball)

speeches, dust jacket blurbs, and other nonfiction, appeared in 1999; *Spontaneous Mind,* a large selection of Ginsberg's interviews given over four decades, was issued in 2000, and *Family Business,* the selected correspondence between Allen and Louis Ginsberg, appeared in 2001. Other volumes of journals, lectures, and correspondence are also being prepared, assuring a continuation of the Ginsberg literary canon for years to come.

—*Michael Schumacher*

## Principal Works

Poetry: *Howl and Other Poems,* 1956; *Kaddish and Other Poems,* 1961; *Empty Mirror,* 1961; *Reality Sandwiches,* 1963; *Planet News,* 1968; *The Fall of America,* 1972; *Iron Horse,* 1972; *The Gates of Wrath,* 1973; *First Blues,* 1975; *Mind Breaths,* 1978; *Poems All Over the Place, Mostly Seventies,* 1978; *Plutonian Ode,* 1982; *Collected Poems 1947–1980,* 1984; *White Shroud,* 1986; *Howl, Original Draft Facsimile, Fully Annotated,* ed. Barry Miles, 1986; *Cosmopolitan Greetings,* 1994; *Selected Poems 1947–1995,* 1996; *Illuminated Poems* (with Eric Drooker), 1996; *Death and Fame,* 1999.

Prose: *Indian Journals,* 1970; *The Yage Letters* (with William Burroughs), 1963; Gay Sunshine Interview (with Allen Young), 1974; *Allen Verbatim: Lectures on Poetry, Politics, Consciousness,* ed. Gordon Ball, 1974; *Visions of the Great Rememberer,* 1974; *Chicago Trial Testimony,* 1975; *To Eberhart from Ginsberg,* 1976; *As Ever: Collected Correspondence Allen Ginsberg & Neal Cassady* (with Neal Cassady), ed. Barry Gifford, 1977; *Journals Early Fifties Early Sixties,* ed. Gordon Ball, 1977; *Composed on the Tongue,* 1980; *Straight Hearts Delight* (with Peter Orlovsky), ed. Winston Leyland, 1980; *Howl: Original Draft Facsimile, Fully Annotated,* ed. Barry Miles, 1986; *Journals Mid-Fifties,* ed. Gordon Ball, 1994; *Luminous Dreams,* 1997; *Deliberate Prose: Selected Essays,* ed. Bill Morgan, 2000; *Spontaneous Mind: Selected Interviews 1958–1996,* ed. David Carter, 2001; Family *Business: Selected Letters Between a Father and a Son* (with Louis Ginsberg), ed. Michael Schumacher, 2001.

Recordings: *Howl and Other Poems,* 1959; *Kaddish,* 1966; *Wm. Blake's Songs of Innocence & Experience,* 1970; *First Blues: Rags, Ballads, and Harmonium Songs,* 1981; *First Blues,* 1982; *The Lion for Real,* 1989; *Howls, Raps, & Roars,* 1993;

*Hydrogen Jukebox* (with Philip Glass), 1993; *Holy Soul Jelly Roll: Poems & Songs 1949–1993,* 1994; *Howl U.S.A.* (with Kronos Quartet), 1996.
Photographs: *Scenes along the Road* (with Ann Charters), 1970; *Allen Ginsberg Photographs,* 1990; *Snapshot Poetics,* 1993.

## Bibliographical References

A useful collection of articles is Louis Hyde, ed., *On the Poetry of Allen Ginsberg,* 1984; one should compare Paul Carroll, *The Poem in Its Skin,* 1968, with Jonah Raskin, *Allen Ginsberg's "Howl" and the Making of the Beat Generation,* 2004; John Lardas, *The Bop Apocalypse,* 2001, interprets the religious dimensions of Ginsberg's work; James Campbell, *This Is the Beat Generation,* 2001, offers a general view of Ginsberg and the Beats. For biographical background, one may turn to Carolyn Cassady, *Off the Road,* 1990; Michael Schumacher, *Dharma Lion,* 1992; Barry Miles, *Ginsberg: A Biography,* 1989; Graham Caveney, *Screaming with Joy,* 1999. Ginsberg in Paris receives attention in Barry Miles, *Beat Hotel,* 2000.

## Life of Allen Ginsberg

3 June 1926: Allen Ginsberg is born in Newark, New Jersey.

1932: Because of problems with mental health, Naomi Ginsberg hospitalized.

1935: Naomi Ginsberg enters New Jersey's Greystone State Mental Hospital.

1937: After an apparent suicide attempt, Naomi is returned to Greystone State Mental Hospital.

27 June 1939: Allen graduates from elementary school and enters Paterson's Central High. Mother Naomi returns from Greystone State Mental Hospital.

December 1941: Allen takes his mother to New Jersey in search of a rest home. The event is later recounted in "Kaddish."

23 June 1943: Allen completes his studies at Paterson's East Side High School.

September 1943: Allen enters Columbia University in New York City. He intends to become a labor lawyer.

December 1943: Allen meets Lucien Carr, David Kammerer, and William S. Burroughs.

June 1944: Through Lucien Carr, Allen Ginsberg discovers the group of people who often congregate at the apartment of Edie Parker and Joan Vollmer. Allen meets Edie's boyfriend, Jack Kerouac.

14 August 1944: Lucien Carr kills David Kammerer. Kerouac and Burroughs are arrested as material witnesses. Carr is sent to Elmira Reformatory but is released in 1946.

January 1945: William Burroughs meets Herbert Huncke, a Times Square hustler and thief. Burroughs is introduced to narcotics.

16 March 1945: For writing vulgar and discriminatory remarks in the accumulated dust in his dormitory room, Allen Ginsberg is suspended from Columbia. He moves into the apartment on West 115th Street, where Joan Vollmer and Edie Parker have created a center for artistic activity.

1945: Allen serves in the Merchant Marines.

September 1946: Allen Ginsberg resumes studies at Columbia University.

December 1946: Hal Chase, a friend of Ginsberg and Kerouac, presents Neal Cassady and his wife, LuAnne Henderson, who are newly arrived from Denver, Colorado, to members of the group at the 115th Street apartment.

January 1947: Intending to grow marijuana, William Burroughs and wife Joan (*née* Vollmer) move to a farm near New Waverly, Texas, and are later joined by Herbert Huncke.

March 1947: Neal Cassady returns to Denver.

July 1947: Allen visits Neal Cassady, the object of his unrequited affection, in Denver, only to find Neal preoccupied with his girlfriend, Carolyn Robinson. In Ginsberg's ongoing attempt to hold on to Cassady, Ginsberg invites Cassady to accompany him on a journey to Texas to visit William and Joan Burroughs.

September 1947: Allen departs the United States on the SS *John Blair* destined for Dakar from a port in Galveston, Texas. The trip terminates in New York in October of the same year.

November 1947: Allen receives a letter from doctors at Pilgrim State Hospital, where Naomi was residing, recommending his mother receive a frontal lobotomy. Since Louis divorced her, the legal responsibility falls to her sons; Allen signs the papers.

July 1948: Allen experiences a vision of Blake in his Manhattan apartment.

February 1949: Herbert Huncke moves in with Ginsberg. Huncke is soon joined by Vicki Russell and Little Jack Melody. These individuals use the apartment as a repository for stolen goods.

21 April 1949: Allen decides to transfer his personal papers to his brother's home. Unwittingly, he travels in a stolen car laden with items stolen by Herbert Huncke, Vicki Russell, and Little Jack Melody. After the police chase the car overturns, and Allen is taken into custody. To avoid imprisonment, Allen agrees to enter Columbia Psychiatric Institute, where he meets Carl Solomon the first day of his stay.

1949: Louis Ginsberg, Allen's father, takes Edith Cohen as his wife.

September 1949: Joan Vollmer and William Burroughs move to Mexico City.

September 1949: Jack Kerouac uses the term "Beat generation" in a conversation with John Clellon Holmes.

27 February 1950: Ginsberg is discharged from Columbia Psychiatric Institute.

March 1950: Kerouac's first novel *The Town and the City* is released.

March 1950: William Burroughs begins an autobiographical narrative that is later published as *Junky*.

March 1950: Allen meets Gregory Corso.

30 March 1950: After hearing William Carlos Williams speak at New York's Guggenheim Museum, Ginsberg writes to Williams and introduces himself.

August 1951: Allen and Lucien Carr visit Joan Burroughs in Mexico City, just missing William, who is in Ecuador seeking *yagé*, a hallucinogen used by natives.

6 September 1951: William Burroughs shoots his wife, Joan, in Mexico City.

September 1953: William Burroughs moves to New York from Mexico and works with Ginsberg on *The Yage Letters*. Although a homosexual relationship forms, Allen chooses to end it.

December 1953: William Burroughs moves to Tangier, Morocco.

December 1953: Allen travels to Mexico.

June 1954: Returning from Mexico, Allen lives with Neal and Carolyn Cassady in San Jose, California. Carolyn discovers Allen and Neal in bed together. Allen moves to San Francisco in August.

December 1954: Allen Ginsberg views a painting of Peter Orlovsky at the residence of painter, Robert LaVigne, in San Francisco. Peter enters the room and Allen falls in love with Peter at once.

August 1955: Allen begins to write "Howl."

September 1955: Ginsberg, Kenneth Rexroth, Gary Snyder, Philip Whalen, and Michael McClure collaborate in planning a reading at the 6 Gallery.

September 1955: Allen lives in a tiny home in Berkeley, California. He writes "Strange New Cottage in Berkeley," "A Supermarket in California," and "Sunflower Sutra." He teaches part time at San Francisco State University and works as a baggage handler at a Greyhound bus station.

7 October 1955: At the 6 Gallery Allen reads the first part of "Howl" for the first time. Rexroth is the moderator, and Philip Lamantia, Michael McClure, Gary Snyder, and Philip Whalen also read. Imitating Emerson's letter to Whitman, Lawrence Ferlinghetti telegrams Allen: "I greet you at the beginning of a great career. When do I get the manuscript?"

18 March 1956: Allen reads "Howl" in its entirety at a poetry reading in Berkeley.

9 June 1956: Naomi Ginsberg dies.

October 1956: City Lights Books publishes *Howl and Other Poems* as the fourth book in the Pocket Poets Series.

November 1956: Ginsberg, Corso, and Peter and Lafcadio Orlovsky visit Jack Kerouac in Mexico.

March 1957: Allen and Peter Orlovsky head for Morocco to meet William Burroughs and help edit *Naked Lunch*. They travel on to Europe later that year.

21 May 1957: Police arrest Shig Murao and Lawrence Ferlinghetti for selling *Howl and Other Poems.*

10 June 1957: Allen and Peter depart Tangier and go to Europe. They journey from Spain to Paris in September and reside at the "Beat Hotel." Corso joins them. Allen stays almost a year.

3 October 1957: "Howl" is deemed "not obscene" by Judge Clayton Horn.

November 1957: Allen begins "Kaddish."

January 1958: William Burroughs joins Allen and the others at the "Beat Hotel" in Paris.

17 July 1958: Allen returns to New York.

5 February 1959: At Columbia University, Allen reads an early version of "Kaddish" for the first time.

May 1959: Allen agrees to take LSD-25 at Stanford University's Mental Research Institute in Palo Alto, California, as part of a scientific study.

1959: Olympia Press publishes William Burroughs's *Naked Lunch.*

April 1960: With Lawrence Ferlinghetti, Allen travels to Chile to attend a literary conference. He travels on to Bolivia and Peru and experiments with *yagé.*

15 September 1960: Allen completes "Kaddish" and submits the work to City Lights.

26 November 1960: Dr. Timothy Leary introduces Ginsberg to psilocybin.

23 March 1961: In Paris, Ginsberg and Peter Orlovsky seek out William Burroughs.

29 April 1961: *Kaddish and Other Poems* is published by City Lights.

15 July 1961: After failing to find Burroughs in Paris, Ginsberg and Orlovsky continue to Tangier, where they find him.

24 August 1961: Allen arrives in Greece and stays there several months.

21 January 1962: Allen meets Peter Orlovsky in Israel.

21 January 21, 1962: Ginsbeg and Peter Orlovsky attend a rally in Nairobi, Kenya.

15 February 1962: Allen and Peter Orlovsky visit Bombay, India. They meet Gary Snyder and Joanne Kyger in Delhi.

15 May 1963: Peter remains in India, but Allen travels through Southeast Asia, including Bangkok, Saigon, and Cambodia. With Kyger and Snyder, Ginsberg visits Japan.

July 1963: Allen participates in a poetry conference in Vancouver, British Columbia, on July 17. He proceeds to San Francisco, where he stays until November, and then goes on to New York.

October 1964: Ken Kesey and Neal Cassady arrive in New York on Further, the psychedelic bus. Ginsberg arranges a reunion of Cassady and Kerouac.

15 January 1965: Allen visits Cuba, but makes remarks about homosexuality that are not well received. Allen is deported to Prague.

18 March 1965: In Moscow Ginsberg confers with Russian poets Yevgeny Yevtuchenko and Andrei Voznesenski.

1 May 1965: Allen returns to Prague and is crowned "King of May"; infuriated, police seize Ginsberg's notebook and deport him.

9 May 1965: Bob Dylan and Allen perform at London's Albert Hall.

11 June 1965: At the Albert Hall Ginsberg convenes an international gathering of poets, including Ferlinghetti, Voznesenski, Burroughs, Harry Fainlight, and Ernst Jandl.

July 1965: Allen attends the Berkeley Poetry Conference with Amiri Baraka, Robert Duncan, and John Wieners. With Gary Snyder, Ginsberg ventures to Oregon and Washington to camp and reflect.

14 June 1966: Allen speaks to the U.S. Senate Judiciary Subcommittee on juvenile delinquency and urges that LSD not be prohibited.

14 January 1967: Ginsberg, Leary, Jerry Rubin, Ferlinghetti, Snyder, the Grateful Dead, and Jefferson Airplane participate in the "Human Be-In."

5 July 1967: Allen reads poetry at the Spoleto Festival in Italy.

28 October 1967: Allen meets with Ezra Pound in Italy.

5 December 1967: Allen is arrested along with pediatrician Dr. Benjamin Spock and 264 others at an antidraft demonstration in New York City.

3 February 1968: Neal Cassady is found dead near the railroad tracks close to San Miguel de Allende, Mexico.

July 1968: Allen purchases a farm near Cherry Valley, New York.

August 24–30, 1968: Allen is in Chicago during the Democratic National Convention.

October 21, 1969: Jack Kerouac dies in St. Petersburg, Florida. Ginsberg attends the funeral in Lowell, Massachusetts.

December 1969: Allen testifies in the trial of the Chicago Seven.

August 1970: Allen meets Chögyam Trungpa Rinpoche.

September 1971: Allen visits India and West Bengal. As a result of floods and famine in West Bengal, around seven million people are homeless.

December 1972: *Fall of America* receives the National Book Award for Poetry.

February 1973: Allen becomes a member of the National Institute of Arts and Letters.

1974: Ginsberg cofounds with Anne Waldman the Jack Kerouac School of Disembodied Poetics at Naropa in Boulder, Colorado.

27 October 1975: Allen joins Bob Dylan's Rolling Thunder Review tour late in 1975 and through parts of 1976.

7 July 1976: Louis Ginsberg dies at age eighty.

July 1978: At the Rocky Flats nuclear facility in Colorado, Ginsberg, Orlovsky, Daniel Ellsberg, and others protest nuclear proliferation.

October 1981: Allen takes up residence in Boulder, Colorado, and is active at Naropa Institute.

1982: Allen travels to Nicaragua to read at the Poetry Festival in Managua.

July 1982: Ginsberg, William Burroughs, Gregory Corso, Peter Orlovsky, Robert Creeley, Lawrence Ferlinghetti, Michael McClure, Diane di Prima, Ken Kesey, Ted Berrigan, Carl Solomon, Ray Bremser, Jack Micheline, Robert Frank, Herbert Huncke, David Amram, Anne Waldman, Abbie Hoffman, Timothy Leary, Jan Kerouac, and others attend the Twenty-fifth Anniversary National Celebration of *On the Road* at Naropa.

October 1984: With Gary Snyder, Toni Morrison, William Gass, and Harrison Salisbury, Ginsberg travels to Beijing, China, as part of an American Academy of Arts and Letters delegation. Ginsberg travels through China for two months.

1984: Harper and Row publishes *Collected Poems 1947–1980*.

1986: Allen accepts a position as distinguished professor of English at Brooklyn College.

4 April 1987: Chögyam Trungpa Rinpoche dies.

1990: Allen's photographs are printed in an oversize format by Twelvetrees Press.

1994: A boxed set of four CDs titled *Holy Soul Jelly Roll* presents highlights of various readings by Ginsberg. Stanford University in California pays $1 million for Allen Ginsberg's archive. HarperCollins publishes *Cosmopolitan Greetings: Poems 1986–1992*.

5 April 1997: Ginsberg dies of liver cancer at age seventy in New York.

*See also* Photography; Be-In; Drugs; Cowen, Elise; Influences; Eastern Culture; New York City; Huncke, Herbert; Carr, Lucien; Kerouac, Jack; Burroughs, William Seward; Denver, Colorado; Mexico City; Brooks, Eugene; Holmes, John Clellon; Corso, Gregory; Ginsberg Archive, Sale of the

## Ginsberg Archive, Sale of the

A collection of about 300,000 items from the life and career of Allen Ginsberg, including personal diaries, correspondence, tape recordings, drafts of poems, personal effects, and domestic records, sold to Stanford University for about $1 million in September 1994.

Ginsberg had hoped that the materials could find a home at Columbia University or at the New York Public Library, but no bid emerged from either collection. Stanford University, usually conservative in its outlook, had acquired materials by Denise Levertov and Robert Creeley and in buying the Ginsberg archive sought to enhance Stanford's avant-garde collection.

For Ginsberg, the transaction seemed lucrative, but taxes for the federal, state, and city governments sapped 56 percent of the money. Tony Angiletta, the agent who arranged the sale, drew 5 percent, and Bill Morgan, the archivist for Ginsberg, collected 10 percent after ten years of work. With the remaining funds, Ginsberg bought a loft on the Lower East Side in Manhattan, accommodating his need for a home and office in a building with an elevator.

The archive is noteworthy for its completeness and eccentricity. In addition to letters, notebooks, journals, manuscripts, and personal records, the archive includes photos, audio and video recordings, teaching materials, artwork, and musical scores. Of special interest are clippings from Ginsberg's beard, the sneakers he reportedly wore in 1965 when he was expelled from Czechoslovakia, and dried-out hallucinogenic plants.

—*William Lawlor*

### Bibliographic References

David Margolick, "An Unlikely Home for Ginsberg's Archive," *The New York Times,* 20 September 1994: C5, offers most of the details of the sale of the archive; at Allenginsberg.org, the entry for 1994 on Ginsberg's lifeline offers additional details.

*See also* Ginsberg, Allen

## Glass, Philip (1937–)

Innovative American composer, and with Steve Reich, La Monte Young, and Terry Riley, a leading figure in musical Minimalism. Influenced by Indian sitarist Ravi Shankar, Glass developed a musical idiom that rejected the atonality of Modernist music for a style based on syncopated rhythm, developed in a diatonic structure. Prolific, his compo-

Philip Glass is a prolific composer of orchestral arrangements, film scores, and "character operas." (Christopher Felver/Corbis)

sitions range over vocal, instrumental and orchestral work, film scores, including *Koyaanisqatsi* (1983), *Powaqqatsi* (1988), and *Naqoyqatsi* (2002), and his groundbreaking "character operas," *Einstein on the Beach* (1975), *Satyagraha* (1980), and *Akhnaten* (1984). Glass's interest in jazz, non-Western music, rock, and small ensemble performance, as well as his aesthetic rejection of Modernism, has many parallels with the Beats. He collaborated with Allen Ginsberg on the oratorio *Hydrogen Jukebox* (1990).

—*Thomas L. Cooksey*

### Selected Discography

Instrumental and Orchestral: *North Star,* 1977, with CD in 1988; *Glassworks,* 1982, with CD in 1990; *Organ Works,* 1993; *Itaipu: The Canyon,* 1993; *Music in 12 Parts: Parts 1 & 2,* 1974, with CD in 1996; *Symphony No. 2/Concerto for Saxophone Quartet and Orchestra,* 1998; *Violin Concerto,* 2000; *Symphony No. 3,* 2000; *Symphony No. 5 (Choral): Requiem, Bardo, Nirmaakaya,* 2000; *Music in the Shape of a Square,* 2002.

Dramatic and Multimedia: *The Photographer,* 1983, with CD in 1990; *Einstein on the Beach,* in collaboration with Robert Wilson, 1993; *Satyagraha,*1985, with CD in 1990; *Songs from Liquid Days,* 1986, with CD in 1990; *Akhnaten,*1987, with CD in 1990; *1000 Airplanes on the Roof,* 1989, with CD in 1992; *In the Upper Rooms/Glasspieces,* 1990; *Hydrogen Jukebox,* with libretto by Allen Ginsberg, 1993; *La belle et la bete,* 1995; *the CIVIL warS, a tree is best measured when it is down: Act V; the Rome section,* in collaboration with Robert Wilson, 1999; *A Descent into the Maelstrom,* 2002.

Film Scores: *Koyaanisqatsi,* 1983, with CD in 1998; *Mishima,* 1985, with CD in 1990; *Powaqqatsi,* 1988, with CD in 1990; *Kundun,* 1997; *Dracula,* 1999; *The Music of Candyman,* 2001; *Naqoyqatsi,* 2002.

## Bibliographical References

See William Duckworth, *Talking Music: Conversations with John Cage, Philip Glass, Laurie Anderson, and Five Generations of American Composers,* 1999; Philip Glass, *Opera on the Beach: Philip Glass on His New World of Music Theatre,* 1988, presents Glass's views on his innovations to the opera and musical theater; see also Richard Kostelanetz and Robert Flemming, eds., *Writings on Glass: Essays, Interviews, Criticism,* 1999; Robert Maycock, *Glass: A Biography of Philip Glass,* 2002, is the first major biography on Glass; Wim Mertens, *American Minimal Music: La Monte Young, Terry Riley, Steve Reich, Philip Glass,* trans. J. Hautekeit, 1995, is a seminal study on musical Minimalism; Keith Potter, *Four Musical Minimalists: La Monte Young, Terry Riley, Steve Reich, Philip Glass,* 2002, is an important study on American Minimalism, although highly technical in places.

*See also* Music; Ginsberg, Allen

## Goddard, Dwight (1861–1939)

Writer, promoter of interreligious dialogue. Goddard is best known as the editor of *A Buddhist Bible* (1938), the "best book" that heavily informed Jack Kerouac's study and interpretation of Buddhism. Born in Worcester, Massachusetts, Goddard, an engineer, was led by a series of personal crises to missionary work, first as a Congregationalist and, in 1928, as a Zen "monk-novice." From his Thetford, Vermont, estate Goddard corresponded and collaborated with scholars such as D. T. Suzuki (1870–1966) and even attempted to found an itinerant *sangha* (monastery). His prolific writings and translations, arranged for popular consumption by an American audience and culminating in the *Bible,* stressed the individual's experience of the "adventure" of Buddhism.

—Matt Stefon

## Bibliographic References

See Rick Fields, *How the Swans Came to the Lake: A Narrative History of Buddhism in America,* 1986; see also Dwight Goddard, ed., *A Buddhist Bible,* 2nd Beacon ed., 1994; Dwight Goddard, in *The Buddha's Golden Path: The Classic Introduction to Zen Buddhism,* 1st Square One ed., 2002, patterned his book as three "adventures" into Buddhism; Jack Kerouac, letter to Allen Ginsberg, 1954, in *Jack Kerouac: Selected Letters: 1940–1956,* ed. Ann Charters, 1996, discusses Ginsberg's study of Buddhism.

*See also* Kerouac, Jack; Eastern Culture

## Goodrow, Garry (?–)

Actor and writer. Played Ernie in *The Connection* (1962), the film directed by Shirley Clarke based on the play by Jack Gelber and performed by The Living Theatre. In this pseudodocumentary, a group of Beat heroin addicts awaits a delivery from the group's drug connection.

Goodrow also performed with the comedy troupe The Committee, which arose in San Francisco in the 1960s and did edgy, political humor. Fellow performers in the Committee included Richard Dreyfus, Rob Reiner, and Avery Schreiber.

Goodrow has worked as a character actor or writer in connection with many films and television shows, including *Lemmings* (1973), *Eating Raoul* (1982), and *Dirty Dancing* (1987).

—William Lawlor

## Film References

Skits from The Committee can be seen in *The Committee,* 1969, which is directed by Del Jack; *The Connection,* 1962, is also available on video.

*See also* Film; Theater

## Gordon, Dexter (1923-1990)

A native of Los Angeles, Gordon began studying music theory and playing the clarinet at 13, later switching to alto sax and finally to tenor when, in 1940, he joined a local band called the "Harlem Collegians." Later that year he began a three-year stint with Lionel Hampton's band, following which he worked on both coasts with musicians such as Louis Armstrong and Billy Eckstein. In 1945, he returned to New York with Charlie Parker, where he formed a part of the growing bebop movement, working to merge the qualities of the tenor saxophone with the idiosyncrasies of bebop. Along with musicians such as Parker and Thelonious Monk, Gordon had a profound influence on the writers of the Beat Generation, whose prose and poetry came to reflect the improvisational lyricism of bebop. In *On the Road* by Jack Kerouac, Sal Paradise and Dean Moriarty listen to "The Hunt" by Dexter Gordon and Wardell Gray at a New Year's party as Sal and Dean play catch, tossing Marylou back and forth over a couch.

—*David Arnold*

### Bibliographic References

Stan Britt, *Dexter Gordon: A Musical Biography*, 1989; Allen Ginsberg, *Spontaneous Mind: Selected Interviews 1958–1996*, ed. David Carter, 2001.

*See also* Music

## Gorky, Arshile (1904-1948)

Abstract Expressionist painter born Vasdonik Manoog Adoian in Van, Armenia. He took Gorky as his last name from the Russian writer Maxim Gorky.

He left Armenia around 1915 to avoid the Turkish campaign of genocide against the Armenians and arrived in the United States around 1920. Gorky was initially influenced by Joan Miró, Cezanne, and Pablo Picasso but later drew ideas from the European artists who arrived in New York as the outbreak of World War II raised threats against artists in Europe. In particular, André Breton inspired Gorky's interest in Surrealism.

From 1926–1931, Gorky taught at the Grand Central School in New York City. He shared a studio with Willem de Kooning in the 1930s. Many of his works were lost in a studio fire, and he suffered physically after surgery and an auto accident.

He took his own life on 21 July 1948.

—*William Lawlor*

### Bibliographical References

A biographical study is Hayden Herrera, *Arshile Gorky: His Life and Work*, 2003; a collection of essays is Dore Ashton, *Arshile Gorky: The Breakthrough Years*, 1995; a review of the paintings is Jim Jordan, *The Paintings of Arshile Gorky: A Critical Catalogue*, 1982.

*See also* Painting; de Kooning, Willem; Pollock, Jackson; Breton, André

## Grauerholz, James (1952-)

Longtime secretary, editor, and personal assistant for William S. Burroughs. Editor, biographer, and scholar specializing in topics related to Burroughs.

—*William Lawlor*

### Bibliographical References

Grauerholz is the editor for two works by William S. Burroughs: *Interzone*, 1989, and *Last Words*, 2000. With Ira Silverberg, Grauerholz is coeditor of William S. Burroughs, *Word Virus*, 1998; with Barry Miles, Grauerholz is coeditor of *Naked Lunch, The Restored Text*, 2001.

*See also* Burroughs, William Seward

## Gray, Wardell (1921-1955)

Jazz tenor saxophonist gifted with great improvisational ability. Gray played with the Earl Hines band from 1943–1945, was briefly with the Billy Eckstein Band, and then joined Benny Carter's band in 1946. In the late 1940s, Gray played in Los Angeles jazz clubs on Central Avenue and was especially successful in making live recordings with Dexter Gordon.

In *On the Road,* Jack Kerouac refers to the frantic pleasure of Dean Moriarty and Sal Paradise as they listen to a live recording of "The Hunt" by Dexter Gordon and Wardell Gray while Sal and Dean are in the home of Sal's brother (112). The reserved southerners in the brother's house cannot comprehend Dean's ecstasy. In "About the Beat Generation," which appears in *The Portable Jack Kerouac,* ed. Ann Charters (1995), Kerouac refers to the music of Wardell Gray and others as Kerouac tries to explain the mood and activity as the Beat Generation was taking shape (559).

Gray was found dead of a broken neck in the desert near Las Vegas in 1955, and although the death was ruled an accident, some remain unconvinced that the death was accidental.

—*William Lawlor*

## Bibliographic References

See Ira Gitler, *The Masters of Bebop,* 2001; compare Scott DeVeaux, *The Birth of Bebop,* 1997; Lewis MacAdams, *The Birth of the Cool,* 2001, discusses bebop in the context of other artistic movements. *Central Avenue Sounds,* 1999, is a sound recording that includes "The Chase" by Wardell Gray and Dexter Gordon.

*See also* Music; Gordon, Dexter

## Guthrie, Woody (1912–1967)

In the 1930s and 1940s, Woody Guthrie redefined the folk ballad into a medium for observation and social protest, writing hundreds of original songs and a biography based on his travels as he hitchhiked across America during the Depression. He influenced the Beats, who also wrote about America as they hitchhiked across it. Guthrie's music influenced songwriters such as Bob Dylan.

Woody Guthrie grew up in Okemah, Oklahoma, where he learned to play guitar, mandolin, fiddle, and harmonica. In 1940, he moved to New York, joining its left-wing community. He died in 1967

from Huntington's chorea. In 1988, Guthrie was inducted into the Music Hall of Fame.

—*Lisa A. Wellinghoff*

## Principal Works

Recordings: Smithsonian Folkways has released *Ballads of Sacco & Vanzetti,* 1996; *Bound for Glory: Songs and Stories of Woody Guthrie,* 1956; *Buffalo Skinners, The Asch Recordings,* Vol. 4, 1999; *Cowboy Songs on Folkways,* 1991; *Folkways: The Original Vision,* 1988; *Hard Travelin', The Asch Recordings,* Vol. 3, 1989; *Long Ways to Travel: The Unreleased Folkways Masters, 1944–1949,* 1994; *Muleskinner Blues, The Asch Recordings,* Vol. 2, 1997; *Nursery Days,* 1992; *Sing Folk Songs,* Vol. 1, 1989; *Songs to Grow On for Mother and Child,* 1991; *Struggle,* 1990; *That's Why We're Marching: World War II and The American Folk Song Movement,* 1996; *This Land Is Your Land, The Asch Recordings,* Vol. 1, 1997; and *Woody Guthrie Sings Folk Songs,* 1989; the Elektra Entertainment Group has released *Mermaid Avenue,* 1998; and *Mermaid Avenue,* Vol. II, 2000; Rounder Records has released *Columbia River Collection,* 1987; *Library of Congress Recordings,* 1988; Columbia Records has released *Folkways: A Vision Shared: Tribute to Woody Guthrie & Leadbelly,* 1988; Vanguard has released *Greatest Songs of Woody Guthrie,* 1972; Budda Records has released *Dust Bowl Ballads,* 2000; and Warner Bros. has released *Tribute to Woody Guthrie,* 1989.

Books: *Born to Win,* 1965; *Bound for Glory,* 1983; *Pastures of Plenty: A Self-Portrait,* 1990; *Seeds of Man: An Experience Lived and Dreamed,* 1995; *Woody Sez,* 1975; with Alan Lomax and Pete Seeger, *Hard Hitting Songs for Hard-Hit People,* 1999.

## Bibliographical References

Serge R. Denisoff, *Great Day Coming: Folk Music and the American Left,* 1971; Joe Klein, *Woody Guthrie: A Life,* 1999; Harold Leventhal and Marjorie Guthrie, eds., *The Woody Guthrie Songbook,* 1976; Robert Santelli and Emily Davidson, eds., *Hard Travelin': The Life and Legacy of Woody Guthrie,* 1999; Jim Longhi, *Woody, Cisco, and Me: Seamen Three in the Merchant Marine,* 1997; Richard A. Reuss and JoAnne C. Reuss, *American Folk Music and Left-Wing Politics, 1927–1957,* 2000; Janelle Yates, *Woody Guthrie: American Balladeer,* 1995.

*See also* Music; Dylan, Bob

Woody Guthrie inspired the Beats with his love for America and his readiness to make music a form of social protest. (Library of Congress)

## Gysin, Brion (1916–1986)

Painter, poet, novelist, and conceptual artist, Brion Gysin was a major influence on the Beats, including William Burroughs and Allen Ginsberg, as well as later subterranean figures from David Bowie to Genesis P-Orridge. Gysin's life and work crossed national borders and disciplinary boundaries and brought the sensibilities of the international avant-garde to the Beat movement in Paris in the late fifties and early sixties.

Living with Burroughs, Corso, and Ginsberg at the "Beat Hotel" in 1959, Gysin invented the cut-up technique, slicing sections of ready-made texts and rearranging them to form new, critical, or absurd works. Gregory Corso, Sinclair Beiles, and Burroughs all created cut-ups, published as *Minutes to Go* in 1960. Burroughs was captivated by the technique and used it as the technical basis of his groundbreaking *Nova* trilogy. Corso and Ginsberg were more critical, fearing the cut-ups usurped the role of the author. Burroughs had no such reserva-tion, and together with Gysin wrote *The Third Mind,* devoted to the theory and practice of collage in literature and visual arts.

Gysin continued to develop multimedia techniques. He used calligraphic writing to create a unique style of painting emphasizing the material nature of language. This interest in the material nature of language led Gysin to create permutation poetry with early computers and sound poetry using tape recorders. Gysin also coinvented the *Dreama-chine* with Ian Sommerville, an optical flicker device used to induce hallucinatory states.

—*David Banash*

### Bibliographic References

Jason Weiss, ed., *Back in No Time: The Brion Gysin Reader,* 2001; José Férez Kuri, ed., *Brion Gysin: Tuning in to the Multimedia Age,* 2003; *The Third Mind* (with William S. Burroughs), 1978.

***See also*** Burroughs, William Seward; Sommerville, Ian

# H

## Happening

A work of performance art that relies on the circumstances of a given moment. Artists may collaborate, but their activity, or lack thereof, may be spontaneous or apparently disconnected from the work as a whole. The happening is sometimes a community event that draws the audience into the performance.

John Cage's "Theater Piece #1," performed in 1952 at Black Mountain College with M. C. Richards, David Tudor, Robert Rauschenberg, and Merce Cunningham, may have been the first happening, but the form soon had a life of its own. Any gathering of people who viewed their interaction or co-presence as art might claim to be part of a happening.

The happening was appropriated for Hollywood in *The Happening* (1967), starring Anthony Quinn, Faye Dunaway, and George Maharis. In this weak movie, a few hippies abduct an organized crime leader, but the intended comic effects are barely realized.

—*William Lawlor*

*See also* Cage, John; Theater

## Hawkins, Coleman (1904–1969)

Coleman Hawkins was one of the premier tenor saxophonists of his generation. He had a booming, robust sound and influenced a great many musical and literary contemporaries. More at home in the traditional jazz of the 1920s, with a playing style suited to swing or big band, Hawkins nonetheless comfortably made the transition into the bebop style that influenced the writing techniques of the Beats. According to Arthur Knight in *The Beat Vision* (79), Ginsberg often listened—with Jack Kerouac and John Clellon Holmes—to Hawkins playing alongside bebop greats such as Charlie Parker, Dizzie Gillespie, Thelonious Monk, Miles Davis, and Max Roach on the all-night radio program "Symphony Sid," which originated from the famous Birdland club in New York City.

—*David N. Wright*

**Bibliographical References**

See Ira Gitler, *Swing to Bop*, 1985; Arthur Winfield Knight, *The Beat Vision*, 1987; Thomas Owens, *Bebop: The Music and its Players*, 1995; and Lewis Porter and Michael Ullman, *Jazz: From Its Origins to the Present*, 1993.

*See also* Music

## Herms, George (1935–)

Visual artist who helped to establish in San Francisco the Assemblage movement, a group of artists dedicated to gathering scrap and waste material and unifying it for presentation as art. Herms's fellow artists included Wallace Berman and Ed Kienholz. Herms interacted with poets and writers of the Beat period, such as David Meltzer, William Burroughs, Jack Kerouac, Lawrence Ferlinghetti, and Allen

Coleman Hawkins performing with the Coleman Hawkins Quartet, 1965. (Library of Congress)

Ginsberg. Herms's "The Librarian" (1960), "Poet" (1960), "The Meat Market" (1960–1961), and "Burpee Seed Collages" (1962) were included in the Whitney Museum exhibition on Beat culture in 1995.

—*William Lawlor*

### Bibliographic References

George Herms, *Then and Now: Fifty Years of the Assemblage Movement*, 2003, includes an introduction by Charles Simic. A large color image of "The Librarian" is included in *Beat Culture and the New America: 1950–1965*, ed. Lisa Phillips, 1995.

***See also*** Sculpture; Berman, Wallace

## Holiday, Billie (1915–1959; born Eleanor Gough McKay; aka Lady Day)

Although many liken Billie Holiday's voice to the voice of blues giant Bessie Smith, Holiday is nonetheless regarded as the essence of jazz. Gravelly but warm and emotive, her voice lacked range but was filled with expression, revealing a unique timbre that blended pain and playfulness. She made her debut recording in 1933 with Benny Goodman, and throughout the thirties she gained international fame recording under her own name and with bandleaders such as Count Basie and Artie Shaw. Allen Ginsberg later called the jazz and blues tradition that Holiday embodied one of the

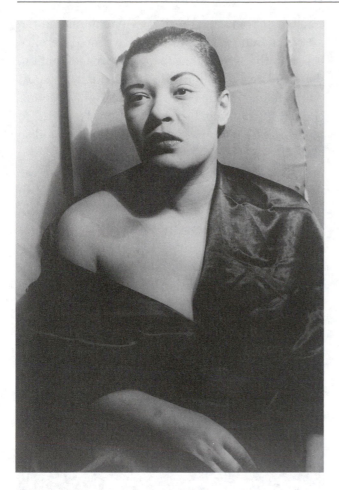

Portrait of Billie Holiday, 1949. (Library of Congress)

most "powerful contemporary lyric forms." In *How I Became Hettie Jones*, Jones mentions that Billie Holiday showed up outside a reading by Jack Kerouac at the Seven Arts Gallery in New York City. She battled narcotics addiction most of her adult life and was arrested on her deathbed a few days after her last performance.

—David Arnold

**Bibliographical References**

Donald Clarke, *Billie Holiday: Wishing on the Moon*, 2002; Michael Schumacher, *Dharma Lion: A Critical Biography of Allen Ginsberg*, 1992; Hettie Jones, *How I Became Hettie Jones*, 1990.

## Holmes, John Clellon (1926–1988)

Although John Clellon Holmes mainly operated on the fringe of the Beat movement and never became widely known, a large part of his work offers a personal and perceptive view of the Beat Generation. It was in a conversation with Holmes, whom Jack Kerouac had befriended in 1948, that Kerouac coined the term "Beat generation." Holmes's friendship with Kerouac is also at the root of his first novel, *Go*, which was the first full-fledged published account of the kind of life led by Holmes, Kerouac, Allen Ginsberg, Herbert Huncke, Neal Cassady, and other figures associated with the Beat movement at the end of the 1940s. In a much-discussed essay that Holmes wrote after the publication of *Go* in 1952, "This Is the Beat Generation," he attempted to describe the changes in American society that had led to the emergence of the Beat Generation. Although and perhaps even because Holmes distanced himself from the Beat movement in the course of the 1950s, he was able to present both personal and objective insights into the Beat Generation and some of its key figures in essays that are still highly readable. Although Holmes was not a major novelist, his fiction, essays, and poems make him a notable presence among the Beats and a distinguished figure in his own right.

John Clellan Holmes was born in Holyoke, Massachusetts, on 12 March 1926. He started to write in his early teens, first poetry, but soon fiction as well. From June 1944 to June 1945, he was in the U.S. Navy Hospital Corps. His experiences there shocked him, but his time in the navy also allowed him to catch up on his reading. After his discharge, Holmes and his first wife settled in New York City. Although he did not have a high school diploma, he spent most of 1945 and 1946 at Columbia University on the G.I. Bill. From 1948 onward, Holmes's poems began to appear in magazines such as *Poetry* and *Partisan Review*, at first under the name Clellon Holmes to avoid confusion with the poet John Holmes. Holmes's early poems owe a great deal to W. H. Auden and W. B. Yeats; showing the influence of the New Critics, the poems are highly formal and allusive, strongly affected by Elizabethan and metaphysical poets. It was especially the ironic tone of these early poems, however, with which Holmes grew increasingly disenchanted, and in 1952 he decided not to write another poem until, as he himself put it in an interview published in *Interior Geographies* (1981), "emotion overcame craft" (5).

Four years earlier, in July 1948, Holmes had met both Jack Kerouac and Allen Ginsberg, who, according to an unpublished thesis by Dana Burns Westberg (1976), in Holmes's view were "really talking about freedom of being, feelings rushing out, candor and honesty" (57). Kerouac in particular later played a major role in Holmes's career as a writer and is a prominent character in *Go* (1952). Holmes's first novel is a minimally fictionalized and convincing account of Holmes's experiences with some of the writers and personalities related to the Beat Generation. Holmes's own persona in the book is Paul Hobbes, a struggling young writer in New York City who has recently befriended the young novelist Gene Pasternak (based on Kerouac) and the budding poet David Stofsky (based on Ginsberg). Other figures are also easily recognizable: Hart Kennedy was modeled on Neal Cassady; the original of Albert Ancke was Herbert Huncke; and Bill Agatson was based on Bill Cannastra, a self-destructive young lawyer and friend of W. H. Auden. Yet *Go* is not an autobiography. Some of its material is based on the imagination, and Holmes also frequently changed the order of the real-life events to accentuate the book's major theme: the conflict between an old morality, illustrated by Agatson's cold intellectuality and nihilism, and new values, based on spontaneity and intuition, which are represented by Pasternak and Stofsky. In *Go*, Hobbes has to choose between the old morality and the new values, but in the end he is unable to do so. This indecision is reflected in Holmes's writing, which in *Go* sometimes has a cerebral and rather stilted quality, and which lacks the spontaneity that is inherent in much Beat literature. The same detachment from Beat values that is to be noted in *Go* is also characteristic of "This Is the Beat Generation," an article that Holmes contributed to the *New York Times Magazine* in November 1952 at the request of Gilbert Millstein, a journalist who had been struck by Holmes's use of the term "Beat generation" in *Go*. In the article Holmes recognizes "Beat" aspects in the behavior of many young Americans, and he makes a striking

comparison between the Beat Generation and the Lost Generation. In Holmes's view, one difference between the two is that for the Beat Generation, the problem of modern life is essentially "a spiritual problem." In fact, in his article Holmes comes close to attributing the connotation "beatific" to the word "Beat" some time before Kerouac did so himself.

Critical reactions to *Go* were mixed and the book sold only 2,500 copies. The novel became a financial boon for Holmes, however, when, still in 1952, Bantam bought the paperback rights for $20,000. The Bantam paperback never materialized, but overnight Holmes became fairly affluent. This financial success allowed Holmes to leave New York and buy a house in Old Saybrook, Connecticut, where he and his second wife spent the

Novelist, poet, and essayist John Clellon Holmes wrote "This Is the Beat Generation," an influential article in the *New York Times Magazine* dated November 16, 1952. (Christopher Felver/Corbis)

major part of the rest of their lives. Holmes's temporary financial success nettled Kerouac, which led to Kerouac's portrayal of Holmes in *The Subterraneans* (1958, but written in 1953) as his "arch literary enemy Balliol MacJones," a successful writer who has been able to cash in on what his friend Leo Percepied (Kerouac) told him about the Beat Generation, but who is not really in the know. The problem between Kerouac and Holmes increased when Holmes began to write a novel about jazz. Kerouac felt that Holmes encroached on material that he had been planning to use, but he endorsed the first chapter of Holmes's book, which was published as a short story called "The Horn" in *Discovery* in 1953. Holmes completed his jazz novel in 1957, after the death of Charlie Parker had given him an idea for the ending of the book. It was published as *The Horn* in 1958, during the height of the Beat craze of the late 1950s.

Set in 1954, *The Horn* deals with the last twenty-four hours in the life of tenor saxophonist Edgar Pool, a legendary forerunner of bop music who has fallen on evil days. The book describes Pool's peregrination through New York, while he is trying to raise the money for the bus back to his hometown, Kansas City. Pool turns to several fellow musicians for support, but they cannot give him the help he needs. The jazz musicians Holmes used as models in *The Horn* are easily recognizable. Thus, Edgar Pool's prototype is clearly Lester Young. The similarities between Pool and Young are closest in the first two chapters, however; in the rest of the book Holmes used details from the life of Charlie Parker to characterize Pool. Among the other musicians in *The Horn* with recognizable traits are Curny Finley, based on Dizzy Gillespie, and Geordie Dickson, based on Billie Holiday. Holmes wanted his book also to be about American literature, however, so the musicians in *The Horn* are also meant to represent some of the great writers of the American Renaissance. Although the resemblances between characters and writers are not as obvious as those between characters and jazz musicians, the epigraphs that open each chapter make it easy to identify the fictional characters with writers such as Edgar Allan Poe, Mark Twain, and Emily Dickinson. Arguably,

some of Holmes's literary comparisons may be forced, but they resemble the methods of jazz musicians: the way jazzmen incorporate strains from other tunes in their improvisations, Holmes took elements from the realm of literature to make his tale of the bop era more meaningful. And while Holmes's writing about jazz may lack some of the fire and spontaneity of Kerouac's jazz scenes, one of the virtues of *The Horn* is the lively sense that Holmes is able to create of the jazz world.

Holmes's third and final completed novel, *Get Home Free,* was published in 1964. Although its two protagonists tell their story from the point of view of the sixties, the events they describe take place in the early fifties. *Get Home Free* covers six months in the lives of Daniel Verger and May Delano, a young couple sharing a loft in Greenwich Village. Their relationship is not a happy one: disappointed with each other, both have taken to drink and are thinking of a way to end their affair. Dan decides to return to his hometown, Grafton, Connecticut, for a while, after which he makes a trip to Europe. In the meantime, May returns to her former home in Louisiana. The end of the book, when Dan and May meet again, seems to suggest that their relationship will have a second chance. *Get Home Free* is Holmes's most personal novel. He himself was never happy with the structure of the book; originally he intended it to be two novellas, and these do not wholly merge with the connecting episodes that were added later. Holmes had come into his own as a stylist, however, and *Get Home Free*'s pared-down language is clearly in line with the book's frequently stern subject matter.

The same distinctive style marks the essays that Holmes began to write in the early sixties, most of which were collected in *Nothing More to Declare* (1967). Although this collection deals with a variety of subjects, nearly everything in it is in some way connected with Holmes's view of the Beat Generation. The oldest essays in the book are, in fact, "This Is the Beat Generation" (1952) and "The Philosophy of the Beat Generation" (1958). Particularly successful is the section "Representative Men," which consists of four character sketches of friends, all of whom Holmes met on the July 4th weekend of

1948. Two of these friends, folklorist Gershon Legman and editor and entrepreneur Jay Landesman, were not writers of fiction or poetry, and their influence on Holmes was mainly spiritual. Allen Ginsberg and Jack Kerouac, however, were later strong literary influences and friends. Holmes's essay on Ginsberg, "The Consciousness Widener," contains a valuable and perceptive survey of Ginsberg's work. "The Great Rememberer" (reprinted in *Gone in October: Last Reflections on Jack Kerouac*, 1985) is a moving account of Holmes's friendship with Kerouac, but at the same time a penetrating essay on Kerouac's life and art. Other outstanding essays in *Nothing More to Declare* are "The Silence of Oswald," an attempt to understand Lee Harvey Oswald's motives for killing President John F. Kennedy, and a long autobiographical section, "The Raw Materials," in which Holmes looks back at his own development. *Nothing More to Declare* proves that Holmes is a distinguished essayist, with a good eye for societal changes.

Holmes did not write much in the 1970s. Lack of money forced him to try his luck at teaching; after having been visiting professor at various universities in the 1960s and 1970s, he became full professor at the University of Arkansas between 1980 and 1987. Holmes's university career was not conducive to the writing of fiction, and for the last twenty years of his life, he expressed himself mainly in a number of essays and in poetry, which he had begun to write again in 1959. Holmes's later poems use open forms and while most of them have a private character, Holmes is always able to objectify and universalize his experiences, and to write strong lines in which feeling is balanced by a sharp mind. Some of Holmes's later poems were published in small press publications like *The Bowling Green Poems* (1977), *Death Drag: Selected Poems 1948–1979* (1979), and *Dire Coasts* (1988). In fact, it was the smaller presses that kept an interest in Holmes alive until the late 1980s, when Holmes's three novels were reissued by a New York publishing house and when the University of Arkansas Press brought out a three-volume edition of Holmes's essays, which also contained unpublished material. Unfortunately, Holmes was unable to benefit from the upsurge of interest in the Beats in the 1990s. He had developed cancer in the early 1980s and died in Middletown, Connecticut, on 30 March 1988.

—*Jaap van der Bent*

## Principal Works

Fiction: *Go*, 1952; *The Horn*, 1958; *Get Home Free*, 1964.

Essays: *Nothing More to Declare*, 1967; *Gone in October: Last Reflections on Jack Kerouac*, 1985; *Displaced Person: The Travel Essays*, 1987; *Representative Men: The Biographical Essays*, 1988; *Passionate Opinions: The Cultural Essays*, 1988.

Poetry: *The Bowling Green Poems*, 1977; *Death Drag: Selected Poems 1948–1979*, 1979; *Dire Coasts*, 1988; *Night Music: Selected Poems*, 1989.

## Bibliographical References

A full-scale study of Holmes's work is not yet available; a thorough but slightly dated overview of Holmes's work is Richard Kirk Ardinger, "John Clellon Holmes," in *The Beats: Literary Bohemians in Postwar America*, 1983; an essay on *The Horn* is Theo D'haen, "John Clellon Holmes' Intertextual Beat," in *Beat Indeed!*, 1985; in Gregory Stephenson, *The Daybreak Boys: Essays on the Literature of the Beat Generation*, 1990, a chapter "Homeward from Nowhere: Notes on the Novels of John Clellon Holmes" discusses Holmes's novels; a discussion limited to Holmes's poetry is Jaap van der Bent, "The Maples Will Enleaf Again, and Consciousness Relent: The Poetry of John Clellon Holmes," *American Poetry Review* 23.6 (1994); Cynthia Hamilton, "The Prisoner of Self: The Work of John Clellon Holmes," in *The Beat Generation Writers*, 1996, is a valuable study of Holmes's work; a recent appraisal of Holmes's life and work is Jim Burns, "John Clellon Holmes: The Quiet Man," in *Beat Scene* 40 (2002); an extended interview with Holmes is Arthur Winfield Knight and Kit Knight, eds., *Interior Geographies: An Interview with John Clellon Holmes* (1981); bibliographical data may be found in Richard K. Ardinger, *An Annotated Bibliography of Works by John Clellon Holmes*, 1979; *The Kerouac Connection* 15 (1988), the "John Clellon Holmes Issue," was entirely devoted to Holmes.

***See also*** Kerouac, Jack; Ginsberg, Allen; Cassady, Neal; Young, Lester; Parker, Charles Christopher;

Gillespie, John Brinks; Holiday, Billie; Legman, Gershon; Landesman, Jay, and Fran Landesman

## Huncke, Herbert (1915–1996)

Storyteller, drug addict, and thief whose use of the slang term "Beat" gave Jack Kerouac the name for a generation. His name coincidentally rhyming with "junky," Huncke first met William S. Burroughs in New York in 1944 when the latter wanted to unload a stolen shotgun and a stash of morphine syringes. Although Huncke was a troublemaker and self-described parasite, he was also intelligent and well read, and he mesmerized friends with stories of his youth in Chicago, his travels around the country, and his Beat life in New York. If Burroughs and Ginsberg were upset when he stole their possessions—it seems not even Huncke could get past Kerouac's watchdog mother—they also recognized that it was a small price to pay for the intrigue and literary stimulation that Huncke offered them.

Herbert Edwin Huncke was born on 9 January 1915 to Herbert Spenser Huncke and Marguerite Bell Huncke in Greenfield, Massachusetts. A teenaged bride, his mother was the pampered daughter of a wealthy Wyoming cattle rancher. His German American father was an auto mechanic who had delivered a car to the Bell ranch. After working as an apprentice in a Greenfield machine-parts factory, the elder Huncke moved his family first to Detroit and then to Chicago, his hometown, where he started his own machine-parts company. The Hunckes' marriage fell apart, and young Herbert felt the brunt of the family's dissolution. His mother confessed her marital woes to him, while his father, seeming to sense that his son was homosexual, regarded him with disgust. As an old man, Huncke found that recollections of his childhood caused him to weep uncontrollably.

At twelve, he ran away from home. From the North Side apartment where he lived with his mother and younger brother (his parents were separated and later divorced), he rode the trolley to the end of the line and began hitchhiking east. He was bound for New York, with a vague desire to see

his Massachusetts birthplace as well. A hundred miles outside of Chicago, he was sexually molested. His nervous assailant gave him a ten-dollar bill and sped away. Huncke later wrote of the assault with equanimity. He was happy about that ten-dollar bill.

In the years following this aborted escapade, which ended when police caught up with him in Geneva, New York, Huncke found solace among Chicago's lost souls. Prominent among them was a heroin-addicted hermaphrodite whom Huncke described movingly in "Elsie John." A bright student who won accolades for a school speech about Abraham Lincoln, he got most of his education on the streets. His best friend, Johnny, shared his delinquent ways. By the time Johnny got shot in the middle of a drug deal, Huncke had a genuine habit. With his startled mother's assistance, he gradually weaned himself of drugs. But from then on, he was never clean for long.

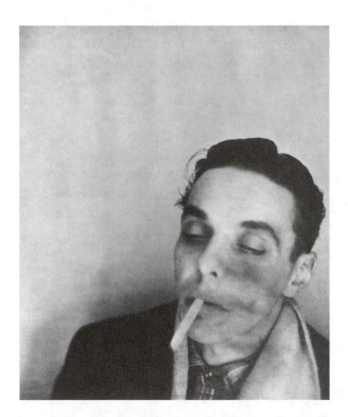

Herbert Huncke connected the world of drugs and hustling with the Beat passion for conversation and writing. (Allen Ginsberg/Corbis)

Alienated from his family and uninterested in traditional paths to success, he dropped out of high school and began crisscrossing the country, working odd jobs when he had to. His travels took him to the Deep South and west to California. He learned how to ride freight trains and developed a sixth sense for finding drugs in any town, large or small. He met criminals and drifters and later scrawled their stories in little notebooks, which provided the basis for future publications. Presaging Kerouac's notion of spontaneous prose, many of his stories were apparently written in a single draft, with only a few revisions penciled in. He was fond of the dash (as Kerouac was to be later on), a punctuation mark well suited to his discursive, lyrical descriptions of his friends and his own anguished emotions.

Huncke landed in New York City in 1939. Working as a gay hustler, he quickly became a familiar sight on 42nd Street, but he still needed to steal to support his drug habit. He found partners-in-crime in seedy bars and cafeterias. With one of them, he shipped out with the Merchant Marines. Along the way, Huncke acquired Jocko, a shipboard pet. Huncke was the rare addict who literally had a monkey on his back. Sometimes Jocko was just as high as Huncke was, since he exposed Jocko to marijuana fumes. Ostensibly seeking to kick his habit on his voyage, Huncke came back from the sea (sans monkey) more addicted than ever. This pattern recurred in his life.

His criminal misadventures, along with his candor and his elegant manners, made him an interesting person to know. Small of stature, in a silk shirt and ascot, with his large hazel eyes staring out the window at Bickford's cafeteria, he got to know hundreds, possibly thousands of people in New York. His engaging ways charmed friends and neutralized enemies for the fifty years he lived there. It was Huncke whom Dr. Alfred Kinsey, the famed sex researcher, turned to when he needed a reliable informant on Times Square. Kinsey interviewed Huncke about his sexual activities and then paid him a couple of dollars for everyone (including Burroughs, Ginsberg, and Kerouac) Huncke could procure for an interview. It was Huncke, furthermore,

whom Burroughs wanted as a long-term houseguest when he and his common-law wife, Joan Vollmer Adams Burroughs, had a farm outside New Waverly, Texas. For most of 1947, Huncke lived on the farm and helped with chores, including drug runs to Houston.

His life was not often so bucolic. In 1949, just released from Rikers Island, a sick and destitute Huncke wandered the city before dragging himself to Ginsberg's York Avenue apartment. With biblical imagery no doubt flashing through his mind, Ginsberg washed his friend's bloody feet and put him to bed. In time, Huncke recovered. He rearranged the furniture, commandeered Ginsberg's bed, and wrote up shopping lists for his intimidated host. Worst of all, he brought the thief Little Jack Melody and Little Jack's girlfriend, Vickie Russell—a redheaded, six-foot-tall prostitute—into the household. Ginsberg watched in stupefaction as his home filled up with stolen loot.

Then, one April day in 1949, with Allen and Vickie along for the ride, Little Jack wrecked a stolen car full of stolen goods and Ginsberg's personal papers. The police had been in hot pursuit of the car for a traffic violation, but the resulting bust was worthy of coverage in *The New York Times*. Although Huncke wasn't involved in this particular debacle, he was arrested along with Little Jack, Vickie, and Allen. Wanted for numerous break-ins, he was the only one of the four who served time. Over the course of his life, Huncke spent eleven years in the New York prison system.

When Huncke used the word "Beat," he always maintained that he meant down and out, exhausted—and he knew what that felt like—but his trademark word could be used in so many ways that it is no wonder Kerouac appropriated it. Always attuned to people who could teach him something, Kerouac admired Huncke's talent as a storyteller and recognized his psychological complexity. Huncke was a true hipster, as Beat as people come, but his genuine compassion for his friends and his pained awareness of life's fleeting nature were equally important to his makeup. These characteristics found their way into Kerouac's expanded notion of "Beat" as sympathetic and spiritual as well as tired and broken down.

With his haunted gaze and velvet voice, Huncke appeared, virtually unretouched, in many of his friends' novels and poems. Kerouac called him Junkey in *The Town and the City* (1950) and Elmer Hassel in *On the Road* (1957), and Burroughs renamed him Herman in *Junky* (1953). Ginsberg immortalized Huncke and his blood-soaked shoes in "Howl" (1956). Huncke also surfaces in John Clellon Holmes's novel *Go* (1952) and Irving Rosenthal's novel *Sheeper* (1967) and in poems by John Wieners, Janine Pommy Vega, and Marty Matz.

Huncke himself finally published a book at age fifty. Diane di Prima published *Huncke's Journal* (1965) through her Poet's Press. The collection contains stories and vignettes that Huncke scooped up and handed to her when she asked him for a manuscript. Less affected than Jean Genet, an obvious influence, Huncke is a storytelling shaman who evokes his own and other people's feelings with great skill and delicacy. His next publication was a limited-edition chapbook, *Elsie John & Joey Martinez* (1979), which his friend Rlene Dahlberg published through her Pequod Press. The following year, Cherry Valley Editions published a collection of stories, *The Evening Sun Turned Crimson* (1980). Raymond Foye's Hanuman Press published a short version of Huncke's autobiography, *Guilty of Everything* (1987), as a miniature book. Paragon House released an expanded edition of the autobiography in 1990. The most comprehensive collection of his work to date is *The Herbert Huncke Reader* (1997).

In the 1980s and 1990s, Huncke was buoyed by the Beat renaissance. At the Rare Book Room, a small bookstore on Greenwich Avenue owned by Roger and Irvyne Richards, he and Gregory Corso held forth for young men in love with all things Beat. In 1982, Huncke attended the Naropa Institute's conference marking the twenty-fifth anniversary of *On the Road*'s publication. Jerome Poynton, a new acquaintance who later became one of Huncke's close friends, recalled his conference interview with the wizened cult figure: Asked about the writing workshop he was supposed to lead, Huncke quipped: "I don't know what a writing workshop is, but I don't like the sound of that word 'work.'"

Huncke stayed addicted to an assortment of illegal drugs until the end of his life. His methadone treatment was a supplement rather than a substitute. Typically he ran through his monthly Social Security check in a few days, buying cocaine and fresh flowers and throwing a party for his young admirers. His aged body withstood physical and emotional traumas that would have destroyed almost anyone else. When his beloved friend Louis Cartwright was stabbed to death on the New York streets in 1994—theories vary as to why and by whom—Huncke was devastated. Nevertheless, he went on a reading tour in Europe the following year. He was down but still not completely out.

His friends helped prop him up. With assistance from the Grateful Dead's Rex Foundation, art curator and publisher Raymond Foye secured a room for Huncke at the Chelsea Hotel, the 23rd Street home to many bohemian artists. Old friends and new ones tended to him there and later at Beth Israel Hospital. Sometimes their ministrations involved urging doctors to increase his dose of pain-easing morphine; other times, they sneaked in the cocaine that he craved. An addict to the end, he also retained his winning way with words. When Timothy Moran asked Huncke the night before he died of congestive heart failure on 8 August 1996 if he wanted anything, Huncke replied, "The moon with a fence around it."

—Hilary Holladay

## Principal Works

*Huncke's Journal*, 1965; *Elsie John and Joey Martinez*, 1979; *The Evening Sun Turned Crimson*, 1980; *Guilty of Everything*, 1987; *Guilty of Everything: The Autobiography of Herbert Huncke*, 1990; *The Herbert Huncke Reader*, 1997.

## Bibliographical References

The only biography, written in German, is Alfred Hackensberg's *"I am beat": das Leben des Hipsters Herbert Huncke—und seine Frunde Burroughs, Ginsberg, Kerouac*, 1998; excerpts from an interview with Huncke appear in *Jack's Book: An Oral Biography of Jack Kerouac*, 1978; John Tytell's interview is in *the unspeakable visions of the individual* 3.1–2 (1973): 3–15; Ted Morgan's biography of Burroughs, *Literary Outlaw*, 1988, contains a portrait of Huncke; in the essay "'Why Do We always Say Angel?': Herbert Huncke and Neal Cassady," in *The Beat Generation Writers*, ed. A. Robert Lee, 1990, Clive Bush analyzes Huncke's relation to the other Beats; in *The Herbert Huncke Reader*, 1997, Jerome Poynton's "Biographical Sketch" and Raymond Foye's "Introduction" provide useful background and context.

**See also** Drugs; Burroughs, William Seward; New York City; Kerouac, Jack; Kinsey Report; New Waverly, Texas; Ginsberg, Allen; Pommy Vega, Janine; Juvenile Delinquency

## Hunt, Tim (1949–)

Distinguished scholar on Robinson Jeffers and Jack Kerouac. Hunt's *Kerouac's Crooked Road: The Development of a Fiction* (1981) helped to establish the sequence of Kerouac's preparation of manuscripts, especially in connection with *Visions of Cody* and *On the Road*.

—*William Lawlor*

### Bibliographical References

*Kerouac's Crooked Road: The Development of a Fiction* was reprinted as a paperback by the University of California Press in 1996. Hunt is the editor of *The Selected Poetry of Robinson Jeffers*, 2001, and the five-volume *Collected Poems of Robinson Jeffers*, 1988–2001.

# I

## Influences

Influences on the Beat Generation are diverse and innumerable, and because the Beats themselves are diverse, numerous, and exceptionally erudite, a catalog of influences on them inevitably falls short of completeness. The Beats draw from the ancient Greeks and Romans, from the Bible, and from Shakespeare. The metaphysical poets, the neoclassical writers, the Romantics, and the moderns all contribute to the shaping of the Beats. Dada, surrealism, existentialism, imagism, abstract expressionism, and spontaneous jazz influence the creative processes of the Beats. Finally, inasmuch as the Beats are innovators and rebels, even the ideas and writings that they reject have influence over them because the Beats use such works as a springboard to new approaches and new ways of thinking.

In the case of Jack Kerouac, the influence that is most often cited is Thomas Wolfe, especially his novel *Look Homeward, Angel* (1929). Kerouac's *The Town and the City* (1950), which was written slowly and extensively revised, has the autobiographical design and the stylistic luxuriance of Wolfe's writing. However, beyond Wolfe, Kerouac's writing clearly arises from multifarious sources. In "Author's Introduction," which is included in *Lonesome Traveler* (1960), Kerouac refers proudly to the class he took with Mark Van Doren on Shakespeare at Columbia—a course in which Kerouac got an A (iv). In "Author's Introduction" Kerouac goes on to mention Jack London, William Saroyan, and Ernest Hemingway as early influences and

mentions Thomas Wolfe as a subsequent influence (v), but Kerouac suggests that his literary outlook is a product of lifelong private study, as revealed in the remark that he failed to attend many classes at Columbia so that he could read authors such as Louis Ferdinand Celine rather than the authors typically assigned in college courses (vi).

In a letter to Donald Allen dated 1 October 1959, which is included in *Jack Kerouac: Selected Letters: 1957–1969,* ed. Ann Charters (1999), Kerouac outlines the history of his development as a writer. Referring again to London, Saroyan, Hemingway, and Wolfe, Kerouac notes the transformation of his own writing from the terse prose of Hemingway to the flowing rhythms of Wolfe (248). But Kerouac went beyond Wolfe to explore James Joyce, whom Kerouac says he imitated in *Vanity of Duluoz* (1968). Joyce's influence is also evident in Kerouac's sound poem appended to *Big Sur* (1962); in "Sea," Kerouac attempts to recreate the sounds of the ocean near Big Sur. After Joyce, according to Kerouac's letter to Donald Allen, Fyodor Dostoyevsky contributed to Kerouac's formation, and then William Blake and Arthur Rimbaud exerted a Romantic influence (248). Finally, Kerouac refers to Johann Wolfgang Goethe's six-volume autobiographical work *Aus Meinem Leben: Dichtung und Warheit* (1811–1822) and says that this work gave him a Western sense of academic pursuits (248).

The letter to Donald Allen reveals that in considering such literary influences, one must not overlook

Ezra Pound made imagism and translations of Eastern writers inspiring to Beat writers. (National Archives)

influences. Kerouac cites William Carlos Williams as the source of his sense of pause, sound, and timing based on ordinary speech (484). Wilhelm Reich, the controversial psychologist, inspired Kerouac's sense of writing based on orgasm—a writing that is free from conscious restriction and instead springs from a subconscious source. And if one considers the Legend of Duluoz, one must acknowledge the influence of Marcel Proust. Like Proust, Kerouac makes his powerful memory the source for much of his writing, and again like Proust, Kerouac envisions his life's literary output as one great book.

The broadest influences on Kerouac come from music and religion. Based on a great repertoire of musical resources and an ability to combine them spontaneously and seamlessly with any performance in progress, the jazz style of Charlie Parker is an object of emulation for Kerouac. Buddhism, Catholicism, and God are always at work in Kerouac's creative process because he feels holy in his commitment to writing and seeks heaven as his reward.

Whitman, too, should be mentioned in the list of influences on Kerouac because Whitman embodies a broad love of America and its ceaseless parade of extraordinary individuals. Kerouac expresses such love profoundly; however, in turning to Whitman, one sees that his most sweeping influence is on Allen Ginsberg. The frankness and personal intensity of Whitman are found in Ginsberg's "Howl" and "Kaddish." Whitman's long lines and extensive catalogs of specific details influence Ginsberg's composition of lines and help him to create a line based not on meter but on the breath of the poet speaking. Whitman's exuberance in the accumulative effect of his long lines and extensive catalogs corresponds to the emotional intensity of Ginsberg's writing. Expressed with sincerity and passion, the homosexuality of Whitman is a touchstone for the homosexual expression of Ginsberg. Whitman's status as a hero for Ginsberg is clear because "Howl" begins with an epigraph taken from Whitman, and Ginsberg's "Supermarket in California" features Whitman as a wandering homosexual.

But just as Kerouac is not solely influenced by Wolfe, Ginsberg is not solely influenced by Whit-

the influence of people much closer to Kerouac, especially Gerard Kerouac, the brother who taught Kerouac how to draw, who inspired Kerouac with saintly behavior, and who died of rheumatic fever at age nine, piercing Kerouac's soul (248). In addition, in "Author's Introduction," Kerouac refers to Sebastian Sampas as the friend who made him decide to be a writer and later died at Anzio (v). In the letter to Donald Allen, Kerouac does not overlook the influence of the letters of Neal Cassady, whose free and frank style helped him discover the spontaneous energy he needed for his own original style, as well as the friendships he had with Allen Ginsberg and William Burroughs (248).

If one looks to Kerouac's "Essentials of Spontaneous Prose" and "Belief & Technique for Modern Prose," which are included in *The Portable Jack Kerouac,* ed. Ann Charters (1995), one sees additional

man. During his early years in writing, Ginsberg pursued conventional styles of writing and imitated Thomas Wyatt, Andrew Marvell, John Donne, John Milton, William Shakespeare, Lord Brooke, Philip Sydney, and Thomas Campion. In "Appendix IV: Model Texts Inspirations Precursor to HOWL," which is included in *Howl: Original Draft Facsimile,* ed. Barry Miles (1986), Ginsberg, making an assessment of influences on his major works, presents a selection of poems (175–188). He begins with an acknowledgment of Whitman, but accounts further for his long line by citing Christopher Smart, the eighteenth-century British author of "Jubilate Agno," whose capacity to vary the measure of lines—according to Ginsberg—is superior to that of any other poet. For intensity of poetic spirit, Ginsberg salutes Percy Bysshe Shelley, who rises to ecstasy in "Adonais" and "Ode to the West Wind" and sets the standard for the height of consciousness that Ginsberg wishes to attain. In this respect, Hart Crane in "Atlantis" also inspires Ginsberg with the spiritual ascent of the poet. Ginsberg credits Guillaume Apollinaire for adding the details of the modern world to Smart's variable line and for creating abrupt shifts in imagery and compressed linkings of references not usually brought together. In Kurt Schwitters, Ginsberg finds a source for the sound of poetry—sound that in "Priimiitittiii" is separate from any intention to convey meaning. Moreover, Schwitters's recurrent initial sound in each line is consistent with the fixed-base opening Ginsberg uses in both "Howl" and "Kaddish." In Vladimir Mayakovsky's "At the Top of My Voice," Ginsberg finds the poet asserting his immortality through his poetry, and Ginsberg seeks to make himself immortal through his poetry. In Antonin Artaud, Ginsberg finds the besieged spirit. In "Van Gogh—The Man Suicided by Society" Ginsberg hears Artaud crying out in the midst of his own destruction and Ginsberg takes that desperation as energy for his writing. In contrast, Federico Garcia Lorca, as shown in "Ode to Walt Whitman," expresses the spirit rising above its destruction through powerful surreal images. Finally, in "To Elsie" by William Carlos Williams, Ginsberg finds a calming, sensible balance between what is heavenly and what is devilish.

Walt Whitman's uninhibited expressiveness and stylistic freedom formed the base for Beat creativity. (Library of Congress)

While Ginsberg's analysis of the authors who influenced him is thorough, it is not complete. Certainly William Blake must be recognized as a key influence, because in July 1948 Ginsberg experienced a powerful vision of Blake—a vision that affected him for many years to come. Blake's mysterious imagery is inspiration for Ginsberg's poetic images, and Ginsberg was so moved by Blake's *Songs of Innocence and Experience* that he set the words to music, performed the songs in countless appearances, and recorded them. In addition, Carl

Solomon, to whom "Howl" is dedicated, is certainly a strong influence. When he and Ginsberg were receiving treatment at the Psychiatric Institute in New York City, they stimulated each other with references to Dostoyevsky. After receiving shock treatments, Solomon spoke expressively, and Ginsberg took down some of the phrases and set them down in "Howl." In addition to Solomon, Jack Kerouac influenced Ginsberg, particularly in connection with spontaneous writing. Ginsberg learned from Kerouac that writing must go unrevised if it is to have its full power.

Beyond literary influences, Ginsberg's family was highly significant in shaping Ginsberg's career. Louis Ginsberg, Allen's father, was also a poet. Though Louis Ginsberg was more conventional than his son, Louis joined his son for readings on numerous occasions. On the occasion of the death of Louis, Allen Ginsberg wrote "Father Death Blues," one of his most enduring songs. Naomi Ginsberg, Allen's mother, had a profound influence over him throughout his life. In childhood, Allen learned to appreciate the kindness in the hearts of many people in the Communist Party. When Naomi was afflicted with mental illness, Allen was seriously affected, and his troubling experiences with his mother became the substance of "Kaddish," the poem many readers consider Ginsberg's masterpiece. Naomi reappears in "White Shroud," the dream poem Ginsberg wrote near the end of his career.

In the case of William Burroughs, one faces a writer who was influenced by many, but who also exerted a great deal of influence. In an interview with Kathy Acker, Burroughs acknowledges Brion Gysin, who remarks that writing is always a half century behind painting; with this lag in mind, Burroughs finds that he as a writer is working with techniques, such as the montage, that painters took advantage of well before he did. Burroughs also recognizes his debt to Jean Genet, Joseph Conrad, Graham Greene, William Shakespeare, Arthur Rimbaud, and Charles Baudelaire.

A peculiar combination of life experiences also contributes to the texture of Burroughs's writing. On one hand, he is a Harvard man and has the refinement that goes with such an education. He ma-

jored in English and later studied anthropology. While in Europe, he attended medical school in Vienna. This combination of studies informs Burroughs's prose and gives his work a scientific flavor. However, Burroughs also came under the influence of Herbert Huncke, who made the underworld of narcotics, hustling, and thievery accessible to Burroughs. Thus, Burroughs's writing includes street language and an awareness of the culture of the underworld.

Because Burroughs was older than either Kerouac or Ginsberg and because he had a superior education, he became an influence over his friends. By introducing Kerouac and Ginsberg to works such as Oswald Spengler's *Decline of the West* and Wilhelm Reich's *The Function of the Orgasm* Burroughs forced the younger writers to revise their thinking.

The autobiographical prose of Thomas Wolfe shaped Jack Kerouac's early prose style. (Bettmann/Corbis)

Other artists of the Beat Generation came under significant influences as well. Lawrence Ferlinghetti, like William Burroughs, responded to visual art, and in many cases, Ferlinghetti's writings are reactions to famous drawings or paintings by Goya, Klimt, Monet, Picasso, Motherwell, or other artists. Ferlinghetti, like Ginsberg, takes Whitman as a special hero, showing Whitman's empirical approach to life in "Dog," a poem included in *A Coney Island of the Mind* (1958) and Whitman's free distribution of lines on the page in almost all poems. Like Ginsberg, Gregory Corso takes Shelley as a model, and in "I Held a Shelley Manuscript," which is included in *The Happy Birthday of Death* (1960), Corso shows his reverence for Shelley. In "Marriage," which is in the same collection, Corso refers to Rimbaud, Tacitus, Bach, Della Francesca, and H. Ryder Haggard, and his writing style blends street idiom and archaic diction. Gary Snyder is strongly indebted to Robinson Jeffers, but his imagistic style derives largely from William Carlos Williams, Ezra Pound, and Chinese and Japanese writers. In his independence and his intimacy with the environment, Snyder hearkens back to Henry David Thoreau and Ralph Waldo Emerson. John Clellon Holmes, who is the author of "The Philosophy of the Beat Generation," which appears in *Passionate Opinions* (1988), finds that the Beats as a whole are influenced by existentialism, but more in the manner of Kierkegaard than that of Jean Paul Sartre.

—*William Lawlor*

## Bibliographical References

See Jack Kerouac, "Author's Introduction," in *Lonesome Traveler,* 1960; the letter to Donald Allen dated 1 October 1959 is in *Jack Kerouac: Selected Letters: 1957–1969,* ed. Ann Charters, 1999; "Essentials of Spontaneous Prose" and "Belief & Technique for Modern Prose" appear in numerous places, but can be easily found in *The Portable Jack Kerouac,* ed. Ann Charters, 1995; Ginsberg's "Appendix IV: Model Texts Inspirations Precursor to HOWL" is included in *Howl: Original Draft Facsimile,* ed. Barry Miles, 1986; the connection between Carl Solomon and Allen Ginsberg is briefly treated in *The Portable Beat Reader,* ed. Ann Charters, 1992; Burroughs's comments about influences on his career can be found in an interview conducted by Kathy Acker for the video *William Burroughs: With Kathy Acker,* 1995; details of Burroughs's life at Harvard and in Europe are in Ted Morgan, *Literary Outlaw,* 1988; Ferlinghetti's writings in response to paintings and other works of visual art are in *When I Look at Pictures,* 1990; Corso's debt to various authors can be seen in *The Happy Birthday of Death,* 1960; Snyder's furthering of the work of the imagists is clear in *Turtle Island,* 1974; John Clellon Holmes's essay "The Philosophy of the Beat Generation" is included in *Passionate Opinions,* 1988.

*See also* Kerouac, Jack; Ginsberg, Allen; Burroughs, William Seward; Allen, Donald; Charters, Ann; Anderson, Joan, letter about; Rimbaud, Arthur; Williams, William Carlos; Reich, Wilhelm; Parker, Charles Christopher; Eastern Culture; Solomon, Carl; Gysin, Brion; Huncke, Herbert; Ferlinghetti, Lawrence; Corso, Gregory; Holmes, John Clellon

# J

## Joans, Ted (1928–2003)

As much as that of any other Beat writer, Ted Joans's peripatetic lifestyle exemplified the quintessential image of the "on the road Beat poet" captured in the popular imagination. André Breton, the founder of surrealism and Joans's mentor and friend, famously called Joans the "only Afro-American surrealist" (qtd. by James Miller in *Dictionary of Literary Biography* 16: 268). An exceptional poet, Joans was also an accomplished musician and painter. His painting "Bird Lives" hangs in the de Young Museum in San Francisco. Yet most importantly, Joans used himself as an example of the possibility to live an alternative, bohemian lifestyle even into old age. For anyone who would say that it was too hard to live "on the road" after the 60s or after one turns sixty, all Joans would have to do was give a brief history of his own life.

Theodore Jones (he later changed the spelling of his surname to distinguish himself) was auspiciously born on a riverboat on 4 July 1928 in Cairo, Illinois. His father was a riverboat entertainer who was killed in 1943 during a race riot in Detroit, Michigan. After attending Indiana University, where he studied painting, Joans found himself immersed in the bohemian scene of Greenwich Village. Initially, his interests were focused on painting. With the encouragement of Allen Ginsberg, Joans became one of the most popular performing poets of the time. He became friends with most of the major Beat poets: Ginsberg, Peter Orlovsky, Jack Kerouac, Gregory Corso, LeRoi Jones (now Amiri Baraka),

Ray Bremser, Diane di Prima, Tuli Kupferberg, and Bob Kaufman. He also became close with the New York school poet Frank O'Hara. Unlike these poets, Joans rarely submitted work to magazines, journals, anthologies, or publishing houses. He was later included in Ann Charters' *The Portable Beat Reader* (1992) in hardcover and had one of his phrases used as the title for one of the book's sections, but he was removed over a financial dispute in the paperback version. Joans believed that a poet's life was more important than being widely published, anyway. Skip Gates, in an interview in *Transition* 48 (April-June 1975), indicated that Joans once said, "I'm a living poem. It's a poem I'm living and I live it automatically" (5).

Kerouac introduced Joans to the jazz scene in Harlem. According to Richard Meltzer, the author of "Another Superficial Piece about 158 Beatnik Books," which appears in Holly George Warren, ed., *The Rolling Stone Book of the Beats* (1999), one night at the Five Spot, Joans wrote a poem for Kerouac that includes the lines, "I know a man who's neither white nor black / And his name is Jack Kerouac" (86). Joans later eulogized Kerouac in the poem "The Wild Spirit of Kicks." According to Joans, the *Village Voice* could not find anyone willing to write an obituary poem when Kerouac died, so Joans decided to honor his old friend. For a time, Charlie Parker, Kerouac's favorite musician, was Joans's roommate, and the social scene Joans remembers included Steve McQueen, James Dean, Harry Belafonte, and Sidney Portier. When Parker died in 1955, Joans and his friends scrawled "Bird Lives" throughout New York City. Joans also met the famous abstract expressionist painters Jackson Pollock, Willem de Kooning, Mark Rothko, and Franz Kline during his Village years. Joans gave parties to raise money for his rent, and everyone chipped in a few dollars, drank, danced, sang, and recited poetry. He also made a name for himself as one of the major players in the "rent-a-beatnik" scheme started by Fred McDarrah as a joke in the *Village Voice*. Joans rented himself out to unsuspecting "square" New Yorkers and suburbanites who thought they would spice up their parties with "beatniks." Joans delivered witty diatribes against their lifestyles, as in his famous poem "The Sermon." Joans was known for reading his poetry with the beautiful and wild intonations of jazz. Langston Hughes was impressed with the jazz quality of Joans's readings and became one of Joans's important supporters and mentors. Joans later said that he had two artistic fathers: André Breton and Langston Hughes. One might say that from America Joans took jazz, from Europe he took surrealism, and from Africa he took his vitality. Most of his life was spent traveling around America, Europe, and Africa. Yet this lifestyle contributed greatly to the scholarly neglect of Joans's work.

He began his worldly travels after saving money from his Beat readings. In 1961, disillusioned with America, Joans became part of the expatriate scene associated with Paul Bowles and William S. Burroughs in Tangier, Morocco. He traveled the cities of Europe in the summer and explored Africa in the winter, supporting himself by selling African artwork. Apparently he became involved in some African societies, but in *Black World* (August 1970), he declined to comment on his initiation to Poro society—a traditional assembly of males associated with the Mende people of Sierra Leone in West Africa (72). In the late 1960s and 1970s, Joans's aesthetic aligned him with the black power and black arts movements. Yet he was disappointed with many of the African American promoters of Africa who had not bothered to actually visit the continent. Until the end of his life, Joans continued to travel around the world, give poetry readings, and write

poems, often accompanied with drawings by his love, Laura Corsiglia.

The American Book Awards recognized Joans for lifetime achievement in 2001. Joans was found dead in his Vancouver, British Columbia, apartment on 7 May 2003. He apparently had died from complications with diabetes on 25 April.

—Kurt Hemmer

**Principal Works**

Poetry: *Jazz Poems*, 1959; *All of Ted Joans and No More*, 1961; *The Hipsters*, 1961; *Black Pow-Wow: Jazz Poems*, 1969; *Afrodisia: New Poems*, 1970; *A Black Manifesto in Jazz Poetry and Prose*, 1971; *Spetrophilia: Poems, Collages*, 1973; *The Aardvark-Watcher: Der Erdferkelforscher*, 1980; *Sure, Really I Is*, 1982; *Merveilleux Coup de Foudre Poetry of Jayne Cortez & Ted Joans*, 1982; *Teducation: Selected Poems 1949–1999*, 1999; *Our Thang: Selected Poems, Selected Drawings* (by Laura Corsiglia), 2001.

**Bibliographical References**

There is distressingly little written about Joans. James A. Miller's piece in the *Dictionary of Literary Biography, Volume 16: The Beats: Literary Bohemians in Postwar America*, edited by Ann Charters, 1983; and Jon Woodson's essay in the *Dictionary of Literary Biography, Volume 41: Afro-American Poets since 1955*, 1985, provide some background material, but there is a need for much more scholarly attention on this intriguing artist. The Skip Gates interview is "Ted Joans: Tri-Continental Poet" *Transition* 48 (April-June 1975): 4–12. A short introduction and a selection of poems appears in the hardcover edition of Ann Charters, ed., *The Portable Beat Reader*, 1992.

*See also* New York City; Paris, The Beats in; Tangier; Painting

## Johnson, Joyce (1935–)

Writer and editor Joyce Johnson is the author of the award-winning *Minor Characters: A Beat Memoir* (1983), an elegant, clear-eyed account of her involvement with the Beats that elucidates women's activities in the movement. Her writing addresses issues of independence, choice, and feminism by examining the link between women's personal and professional lives. Johnson's career as an editor spanned more than twenty years. She also served as an adjunct professor of creative writing in Columbia University's graduate writing program in the 1980s.

Johnson was born in New York City on 27 September 1935 to Rosalind (née Ross) and Daniel Glassman. Her mother wanted her to become a composer of musical comedies, but Johnson's creative interests flowed in another direction. At Hunter High School, she was a classmate of Audre Lorde and Diane di Prima, budding poets who edited the school magazine, *Argus,* which published Johnson's first story.

Soon Johnson was sneaking off to Greenwich Village to experience real life and gather information for her writing. As a student at Barnard College, she met Elise Cowen, who introduced her to Donald Cook, a psychology instructor and friend of the poet Allen Ginsberg. Over the next couple of years, Johnson met Ginsberg and others associated with the Beat movement. She also fell in love with Cook, with whom she had a short but intense affair that fizzled in 1955. By then, Johnson had left home, determined to support herself while she wrote a novel.

In 1957, when Jack Kerouac came to town, Allen Ginsberg set Kerouac up on a date with Johnson. After she bought dinner for him, Kerouac came home with her, and the two of them had an on-and-off affair for approximately two years. This relationship drew her deeper into the artistic culture of New York, as she began frequenting the Cedar Tavern and the Five Spot, listening to John Coltrane and Billie Holliday and conversing with Willem de Kooning and John Chamberlain. The relationship with Kerouac ended in the fall of 1958, after Johnson decided she could no longer put up with Kerouac's drinking and carousing. Nevertheless, when Random House published her first novel *Come and Join the Dance* (1962), under her maiden name of Glassman, Kerouac provided the blurb: "The best woman writer in America." Johnson married her first husband that year, James Johnson, an expressionist painter who died in a motorcycle accident in 1963.

Despite Kerouac's endorsement, Johnson's novel went unnoticed, and in 1965 she embarked on a career as an editor and married her second husband, Peter Pinchbeck. Though the couple divorced in 1971, they had one son, Daniel. Johnson began as an associate editor at William Morrow, then moved to Dial Press as a senior editor, later working for McGraw-Hill and the Atlantic Monthly Press. In 1987 she became a contributing editor for *Vanity Fair* magazine.

Johnson never gave up on her writing, using it to explore themes of women's independence, showing how complex their choices had become within the context of the feminist movement. *Bad Connections* (1978) is the tale of a divorced woman named Molly raising a young son while pursuing the perfect romantic relationship. *In the Night Café* (1989) tells of Joanna, an aspiring actress in the early 1960s, who marries an artist named Tom, an alcoholic who meets a tragic death. The last chapter of that book, "The Children's Wing," had been published as a short story and won the 1987 O. Henry Award.

*Minor Characters* (1983) catapulted Johnson into prominence as a chronicler of the Beat movement, earning her the National Book Critics Circle Award. Few people had ever considered the role of women in the movement until the appearance of *Minor Characters,* and it has been instrumental in providing a fuller picture of the Beats and of the changing lives of American women in the postwar period. Johnson shows in her memoir that just prior to the emergence of the counterculture and the women's liberation movement of the 1960s, Beat women blazed their own trail of independence.

Her next nonfiction writing project concerned the 1987 murder of six-year-old Lisa Steinberg. *What Lisa Knew: The Truths and Lies of the Steinberg Case* (1990) explores the complicity of Hedda Nussbaum, Joel Steinberg's live-in lover, who did nothing to stop his abuse of the little girl.

Johnson published a fuller account of her relationship with Jack Kerouac in *Door Wide Open: A Beat Love Affair in Letters, 1957–1958* (2000). More intimate and precise than the passages in *Minor Characters,* this collection shows that Johnson was a fine writer even before the publication of her first novel. Taken together, these two books show Johnson as a keen participant in and observer of the Beat movement.

—*Theresa Kaminski*

## Principal Works

Fiction: *Come and Join the Dance*, 1962; *Bad Connections*, 1978; *In the Night Café*, 1989.

Nonfiction/Memoir: *Minor Characters: A Beat Memoir*, 1983; *What Lisa Knew: The Truth and Lies of the Steinberg Case*, 1990; *Door Wide Open: A Beat Love Affair in Letters, 1957–1958*, 2000.

## Bibliographical References

An extended critical review of Johnson's work can be found in Nancy Pear's entry on Johnson in *Contemporary Authors*, 1990. Brenda Knight includes a chapter called "Joyce Johnson: A True Good Heart" in *Women of the Beat Generation: The Writers, Artists and Muses at the Heart of a Revolution*, 1996, which presents some biographical information along with excerpts from *Minor Characters*. Johnson contributed an article, "Beat Queens: Women in Flux," to *The Rolling Stone Book of the Beats*, 1999, assessing her role in the movement and analyzing its feminist implications. The book also contains "Talkin' 'Bout Our Generations," a dialogue between Johnson and her son Daniel Pinchbeck concerning the New York literary scene in the 1950s. Johnson appears in Susan Cahill's collection *Writing Women's Lives: An Anthology of Autobiographical Narratives by Twentieth-Century American Women Writers*, 1994. Penguin Putnam released a new edition of *Minor Characters* with a different subtitle and an introduction by literary scholar Ann Douglas, *Minor Characters: A Young Woman's Coming-of-Age in the Beat Orbit of Jack Kerouac*, 1999.

*See also* Cowen, Elise; Kerouac, Jack

## Jones, Hettie (1934–)

Memoirist of the Beat era and editor of the early Beat magazine *Yugen*, Hettie Jones influenced the Beat Generation by promoting and distributing Beat writing and later provided in her memoir, *How I Became Hettie Jones*, an intimate view into the lives of many Beat figures, most notably that of her husband LeRoi Jones, later Amiri Baraka. Hettie Jones also remains significant as one of the few women immediately involved in the Beat lifestyle, literature, and performances as she chose to remove herself from her suburban Jewish upbringing and live independently in New York before marrying a black writer and creating a biracial family.

Hettie Jones was born Hettie Cohen in Brooklyn, New York, on 16 July 1934. Her family soon moved from Brooklyn to Laurelton, New York, where Jones grew up in a largely Jewish neighborhood. As a girl, she studied piano and dance, but theater came to be her primary interest. At seventeen, she turned down acceptance at Vassar College to attend Mary Washington, the women's college of the University of Virginia. There Jones pursued a degree in drama and began writing poetry, which was published in the college's literary magazine, *The Epaulet*. She also combined her love of theater and poetry in a thesis on "The Poet in the Theater."

Following graduation, Jones moved to Manhattan in October 1955 to attend graduate school at Columbia. For a weekly salary of forty-five dollars and three tuition units at Columbia, Jones worked in the Center for Mass Communication (CMC), a small film library, where she researched films and wrote promotional literature. After the defunding of the CMC, Jones became subscription manager at the *Record Changer*, a magazine published for collectors of records. During this time she met and fell in love with the new shipping manager, LeRoi Jones. Through LeRoi, Jones found herself more educated about current music, philosophy, and social politics as well as being introduced to two of the Beat Generation's most recognized writers, Allen Ginsberg and Jack Kerouac.

By 1957, Jones had moved from the *Record Changer* to *Partisan Review*, where she continued her education in revolutionary thought and writing and developed her skills as an editor. At the same time, LeRoi struck up a correspondence with Allen Ginsberg that led the Manhattan couple into contact with Beats such as Gregory Corso, Diane di Prima, and Frank O'Hara. Further, Jones's job at *Partisan Review* provided her not only with the editorial skills that allowed her to take a primary role in the production of *Yugen,* but also provided the Beats with a connection to an established publication; LeRoi and others were published in its pages, and a few Beats, such as di Prima, found in *Partisan Review* a periodic means of employment.

In 1958, Jones and LeRoi initiated the literary magazine *Yugen: a new consciousness in arts and letters.* Though the inspiration behind the magazine was LeRoi's, Jones had the skills and enthusiasm to physically put the magazine together using a borrowed T-square on her kitchen table. Using her connections with the distributors for *Partisan Review,* Jones also increased the distribution of *Yugen* beyond local coffeehouses and newsstands. By this time, the Jones's apartment had become not only a center for printing but also a Beat salon where figures from Allen Ginsberg and Peter Orlovsky to Jack Kerouac, Diane di Prima, and Joyce Johnson appeared for impromptu dinners and late-night editing and pasting sessions for the next *Yugen.*

Jones continued to live with LeRoi for the next five years—despite his affairs with other women, one being fellow writer Diane di Prima—and Hettie and LeRoi had two children together and founded Totem Press. She kept house, raised the children, and worked to provide an income whenever necessary, allowing LeRoi time to write and publish his poetry. At the same time, she wrote poems, though she deemed her poetry inferior to LeRoi's and seldom showed the work to anyone, contenting herself with being an editor and aide to others.

Often a lesser issue in Beat writing, racial inequality and unrest also marked this period in American history, and as an interracial couple, Hettie and LeRoi could not remain apart from it. In her memoir, Jones writes of her own naiveté with respect to interracial relationships, but the white/black and Jew/black combination that she and LeRoi represented ended that naiveté in increasingly invasive ways ranging from jeering comments hurled at them to the eventual breakdown of the marriage. During the early 1960s, LeRoi turned to writing drama, and with the production of *Dutchman* in 1964, fame invaded the Jones's household, a fame that focused on LeRoi as a black writer with a white wife. With the success of *Dutchman* and later *The Slave* came marital breakdown as LeRoi found it necessary to live out the black activist image his plays extolled and one impossible to hold onto while married to a white wife.

With LeRoi's departure, Jones found more time and space for her own writing, from writing curricula for a Head Start program to poetry, short stories, and children's books. She continues to live in New York and teach writing workshops for the homeless and at the New York Correctional Facility for Women as well as at New York University, Hunter College, and the University of Wyoming.

—*Jennifer Love*

## Principal Works

Poetry: *Drive,* 1998.
Prose: *Having Been Her,* 1981; *How I Became Hettie Jones,* 1990;
Children's Stories: *The Trees Stand Shining, Poetry of the North American Indians,* 1971; *Big Star Fallin' Mama, Five Women in Black Music,* 1974
Edited Works: *Yugen,* 1958–1962; *Poems Now,* 1968.

## Bibliographical References

Jones's memoir, *How I Became Hettie Jones,* 1990, provides the most intimate biography; Joyce Johnson also discusses Jones in *Minor Characters,* 1983; a brief biography appears with selected works in Brenda Knight's anthology *Women of the Beat Generation,* 1996; in her anthology *Beat Down to Your Soul,* 2001, Ann Charters includes Jones's comments during the panel discussion with women writers of the Beat Generation, 1994.

*See also* Baraka, Amiri; Little Magazines

## Jones, LeRoi

*See* Baraka, Amiri

## Juvenile Delinquency

Although teenagers and young adults during President Dwight Eisenhower's 1950s did have legal problems as a result of their improper behavior, juvenile delinquency was also an object of sensationalism for the media. Beat writers William S. Burroughs, Allen Ginsberg, and Herbert Huncke did run afoul of the law, but the characterization of the Beats as hoodlums and criminals was an unfair generalization.

The troubling phenomenon of juvenile delinquency—popularized in films such as *The Wild One* (1953), in which a motorcycle gang led by Johnny (Marlon Brando) terrorizes a California town—had its roots in the disruption of societal norms on the home front during World War II, according to Bernard Williams, the author of the 1949 exploitation classic, *Jailbait: The Story of Juvenile Delinquency*. Written under the pseudonym William Bernard, the book offers up offenses as exotic as teen prostitution rings, forced lesbian school encounters, school and street-gang wars, extortion schemes, car thefts, drinking sprees, thrill and rage killings, seductions by ministers and teachers, and preteen rapes. *Jailbait* is stuffed with salacious tales of teenage lust, with enough vandalism, rowdyism, and voyeurism thrown in to make the character Jim Stark in *Rebel without a Cause* (portrayed in 1955 by James Dean) seem mild. This wild stream of anecdotal evidence is offset with more stoic chronicles such as *Juvenile Offenders,* a 1963 textbook by Illinois sociologist Clyde Vedder. As late as 1960, according to Vedder, juveniles were responsible for almost one-half of America's reported robberies and nearly three-fourths of the country's reported car thefts (17–18). "A wayward child's misbehavior can usually be traced to lack of proper guidance and supervision during the formative years," suggests John E. Winters in *Crime and Kids: A Police Approach to Prevention and Control of Juvenile Delinquency* (1959). "The family is the first great training school in behavior or misbehavior" (60). According to Harvard scholars Sheldon and Eleanor Glueck—authors of *Delinquents in the Making: Paths to Prevention* (1959), who tackled the problem at least partly by poring over photographs of some 500 antisocial boys—young, male juvenile delinquents were four times more likely to have a physique with "a strong masculine component" (100). "Delinquency itself encompasses a wide variety of behavior patterns and deviations of behavior that are to a certain extent community-determined," Herbert Bloch suggests in his 1956 text, *Delinquency: The Juvenile Offender in America Today.* "Not only is the range of misbehavior a wide one, but to a large extent the youngsters involved have normal intelligence and their conduct cannot be attributed to gross physical or heredity defects" (532).

Some of the Beat writers described delinquency in their works. William Burroughs, raised in privileged St. Louis society and educated at Harvard, celebrated the dark underbelly of the drug world in *Junkie,* published under a pseudonym as a cheap, mass-market paperback in 1953. Herbert Huncke, a heroin addict and hustler in New York's Times Square, provided the real-life background for the fiction. In an autobiographical sketch in *Junkie,* the narrator fondly recalls his aimless childhood career as a wandering vandal and would-be burglar and his youthful admiration for a small-time crook. The narrator writes that he and his accomplices entered an empty factory, smashed windows, and stole a tool. The delinquents were apprehended, and each boy's parent was held responsible for the destruction. William Lee, the novel's narrator, admits that his actions were senseless. If he broke into a home, he merely walked around and took nothing (xii-xiii).

Burroughs's own connection to delinquency reached tragic proportions in September 1951, when he pulled the trigger on a pistol and sent a bullet flying into the brain of his wife, Joan Vollmer Adams. This accident led to profound legal complications, yet Burroughs later claimed that the event set his life's course as a writer.

Huncke, who inspired Jack Kerouac to coin the phrase "Beat Generation," lived in prison during the 1950s. His obituary in *The New York Times* (9 August 1996) describes Huncke as a "charismatic street hustler, petty thief and perennial drug addict" (B7). A high school dropout junky who sold his body to men on the streets of New York at a time when other boys were playing sandlot baseball, Huncke appears as a character in Ginsberg's seminal poem, "Howl" (1956) and Kerouac's prototype Beat novel, *On the Road* (1957). Neal Cassady, the inspiration for Kerouac's Dean Moriarty, was the son of an alcoholic father. Neal spent all of 1944 in a Colorado reformatory for stealing cars. Convicted of marijuana possession in California in 1958, Cassady served two years in San Quentin. Married three times (once bigamously) and addicted to gambling, alcohol, and drugs, Cassady developed an obsession with risks that defined his life. Ginsberg was unfairly implicated in 1949 in one of Huncke's many burglary schemes and spent eight months in a New York mental hospital. Huncke writes about Ginsberg at the jailhouse in *The Herbert Huncke Reader* (1997) and recalls Ginsberg's sadness in the cell. Ginsberg had never experienced imprisonment (266).

In addition to Burroughs's shooting of his wife, the Beat Generation's most notorious crime connection is Lucien Carr, a nineteen-year-old friend of Burroughs and Kerouac. In 1944, Carr used his Boy Scout knife to kill David Kammerer, a friend who pursued homosexual contact with Carr. Kerouac and Burroughs were held as material witnesses.

Many years later, Jack Kerouac regretted that the Beats were associated with delinquency and crime because that reputation detracted from the appreciation of the literature the Beats created.

—*Mark W. Scarborough*

## Bibliographical References

The most accessible edition of Herbert Huncke's work is *The Herbert Huncke Reader,* 1997; Burroughs's autobiographical sketch is included as a prologue in the "unexpurgated" Penguin Books edition of *Junky,* 1977; Cassady's life is chronicled by Matt Theado in *The Beats: A Literary Reference,* 2001; Theado includes a *New York Daily News* account (8 September 1951) of Burroughs's shooting of his wife, as well as reports of Lucien Carr's arrest; "scientific" studies of juvenile delinquency include Sheldon and Eleanor Glueck, *Delinquents in the Making: Paths to Prevention,* 1952; Herbert Bloch, *Delinquency: The Juvenile Offender in America Today,* 1956; and Clyde Vedder, *Juvenile Offenders,* 1963; anecdotal studies of juvenile delinquency include William Bernard (Bernard Williams), *Jailbait: The Story of Juvenile Delinquency,* 1949; and John Winters, *Crime and Kids: A Police Approach to the Prevention and Control of Juvenile Delinquency,* 1959.

***See also*** Burroughs, William Seward; Ginsberg, Allen; Huncke, Herbert; Film; Cassady, Neal; Kammerer, David Eames; Carr, Lucien; Vollmer Adams Burroughs, Joan; Drugs

# K

## Kammerer, David Eames (1911–1944)

William S. Burroughs's childhood friend, whose death in August 1944 at the hands of young Lucien Carr shocked the original New York Beat circle. Born in St. Louis in late 1911, Kammerer was two years older than Burroughs; they met in the early 1920s as children when both were at the Community School. After 1925 they were classmates at John Burroughs School in the St. Louis suburb of Clayton/Ladue, Missouri, along with David's younger brother Richard Kammerer (1912–2001) and Burroughs's boyhood friend and Clayton neighbor, Kells Elvins (1913–1961).

Kammerer studied at Washington University in St. Louis 1930–1934, and later taught there as an English instructor. In summer 1933, after Burroughs's first year at Harvard, he and Kammerer traveled to England and France. In Paris's 11th arrondissement they visited the rue de Lappe, famous for its bohemian nightclubs frequented by wild young "Apaches," as the thugs, pimps, and prostitutes of the quarter were known. In an interview with Ted Morgan taped in the mid 1980s, Burroughs remembered Kammerer as "tall and thin and not handsome at all. He had red hair, rangy features, big nose." Burroughs added that Kammerer "was always very funny, the veritable life of the party, and completely without any middle-class morality."

While working as a youth group counselor at the Community School, Kammerer met fourteen-year-old Lucien Carr and became progressively more infatuated with the handsome blond boy's looks and personality during 1939–1944. Kammerer lost his teaching job because of his involvement with some student pranks. With Carr's mother's approval, he took Carr on a long trip to Mexico in summer 1940. Then, when Carr was at prep school in Andover in Massachusetts and later at Bowdoin in Maine, Kammerer showed up in his automobile to lead the youth and his friends on wild adventures, in both cases contributing to Carr's withdrawal from those schools.

When Carr transferred to the University of Chicago in fall 1942, Kammerer also moved to Chicago, as did his childhood friend William Burroughs, then aged twenty-eight and recently discharged from the army on psychological grounds after a very brief enlistment. Kammerer and Carr continued drinking heavily together and trying to outdo each other with wild, spontaneous pranks; Burroughs clucked disapprovingly, but on some level he enjoyed the high jinks. These antics got Burroughs thrown out of his rooming house, and reached a crescendo in spring 1943 when Carr was found unconscious near a gas stove, apparently suicidal. Carr spent two weeks in Cook County Hospital's psychiatric ward, then went to New York, where his mother then lived; in fall 1943 he enrolled at Columbia University.

Again Kammerer followed Carr. He moved to 48 Morton Street in Greenwich Village and found work variously on the New York docks, teaching at a high school, and washing windows. He had now grown a red beard, adding to his strange appearance. Burroughs also moved to the Village in fall 1943, renting a flat at 69 Bedford Street, one block away from Kammerer. The writer Chandler Brossard (1922–1993) also lived in the Morton Street building and observed Kammerer's and Burroughs's social circle, which included Donna Leonard and Louise McMahon—and, of course, Lucien Carr, who in December met fellow Columbia student Allen Ginsberg (1926–1997) and introduced Ginsberg to Kammerer's Morton Street coterie. Carr had also encountered Jack Kerouac (1922–1969), a former Columbia student, around the West End Bar, and thus did Kerouac, Ginsberg, and Burroughs first meet.

During spring and summer 1944, Kammerer pursued Carr, who avoided him at times but accepted his attentions at others. Carr's friends mostly saw Kammerer as pathetic and oppressive, and tended to avoid him as well. Burroughs always believed that, despite the intensity of Kammerer's desires, he never succeeded in having sex with Carr.

In the early hours of 13 August 1944, on a hillside at the foot of 115th Street near Riverside Drive, Kammerer and Carr were alone. Carr had spent the night drinking and avoiding Kammerer, who had been looking for him all over town and who seems to have presented Carr with a do-or-die romantic ultimatum. A struggle ensued, and Carr stabbed the older man twice with a small folding knife. In a panic, Carr weighted the unconscious body with stones and rolled it into the Hudson River. He went to Burroughs's apartment and confessed to him, then found Kerouac and told him the story. Carr's mother found a lawyer and the young man turned himself in to the police that afternoon. Kammerer's body was not recovered until two days later.

Soon Burroughs and Kerouac were arrested as material witnesses, but Burroughs's father came from St. Louis and got his son released; Kerouac married his girlfriend Edie Parker (1922–1993) in jail, and her family provided funds to bail out their new son-in-law. Carr pled guilty to a reduced charge of first-degree manslaughter and was sen-

tenced in October to Elmira Reformatory for one to twenty years; he was released after two years for good behavior. Kammerer was buried in his family's plot in St. Louis's Bellefontaine Cemetery.

The killing received considerable newspaper coverage, and because Carr was able to ward off any implications of homosexuality on his part, there was much sympathy for his act of "self-defense" against his homosexual pursuer. In November 1944, Ginsberg attempted to write a novel based on the story, which he melodramatically called "The Bloodsong," but the chairman of the English Department forbade him to continue it, seeking both to protect Carr and to avoid bad publicity for the university. Kerouac also worked on a version of the affair, writing an unfinished novella, "I Wish I Were You," by himself and then a longer work called "And the Hippos Were Boiled in Their Tanks" in collaboration with Burroughs, alternating chapter authorship.

Not only these members of what Ginsberg in his journals called "the libertine circle" were affected by the story: James Baldwin began a related work titled "Ignorant Armies," which he later abandoned, using elements of the story in his gay-themed 1956 *Giovanni's Room;* Chandler Brossard's 1952 first novel, *Who Walk in Darkness*, includes the story, as does Alan Harrington's 1955 first novel, *The Revelations of Dr. Modesto*. But it was Kerouac who—in his first novel, *The Town and the City* (1950), and in his last book, *Vanity of Duluoz* (1968)—published the most detailed fictional versions of the characters and events around the tragic death of David Kammerer.

—*James Grauerholz*

## Bibliographical References

Ted Morgan, *Literary Outlaw: The Life and Times of William S. Burroughs,* 1988; Barry Gifford and Lawrence Lee, *Jack's Book: An Oral Biography of Jack Kerouac,* 1978; James Grauerholz, Unpublished interview with Lucien Carr, 11 October 1999; Jack Kerouac, *The Town and the City,* 1950; Jack Kerouac, *The Vanity of Duluoz: An Adventurous Education, 1935–1946,* 1968.

***See also*** Carr, Lucien; Ginsberg, Allen; Elvins, Kells; Burroughs, William Seward; Brossard, Chandler; Juvenile Delinquency

## Kandel, Lenore (1932–)

Lenore Kandel has been both inspiration and innovator, character and creator. From her relationship with Lew Welch to her poetry collections, *The Love Book* (1965) and *Word Alchemy* (1967), she has established herself as a leading female figure among the Beats. As an activist for free speech, sexual freedom and empowerment, gender-role diversification, and Buddhism, Kandel combines the spiritual and the sensual/sexual. However, with *Word Alchemy* out of print, with *The Love Book* available only in a limited reprint edition, and with her withdrawal from public life, her position and reputation among the Beats is tenuous.

Kandel was born in 1932 in New York City. Kandel's family relocated to Los Angeles in her infancy, so that her father, novelist Aben Kandel, could work on a film adaptation of one of his novels. Kandel's childhood marked her first interest in Buddhism and poetry around the age of twelve. She became fascinated by books in general and the study of religions in particular and spent her formative years analyzing anything she could get her hands on. She decided early on that she wanted to be a professional writer.

In 1959 she had her first works published, but they did not gain her widespread notice. She came to visit San Francisco one weekend, and ended up staying long-term. In San Francisco, she met Lew Welch, Gary Snyder, and others at the East-West House co-op of Zen-minded students and was soon introduced into all the circles of leading Beat/San Francisco Renaissance writers. She traveled to Big Sur with Kerouac, Welch (with whom she was romantically involved from 1960–1961), and others on the trip that inspired Kerouac's novel, *Big Sur*. She was immortalized by Kerouac in that text as the "monster beauty," Romana Schwartz.

She spent the next few years living at the East-West House and studying with Shunryu Suzuki Roshi (after first sitting *zazen* in 1959). She was fascinated by Kerouac's works and found him a strong inspiration for her own creative efforts, but her primary interest remained Buddhism and a search for a link between spiritualism and physical actions. This search involved experiments with psychotropic substances, including peyote and acid (LSD). She became an active participant in the Summer of Love, working with the Diggers, Richard Brautigan, and others to spread the message.

On 17 November 1966 newly-elected California governor Ronald Reagan (who had campaigned on promises to crack down on the emerging hippie movement) ordered a largely symbolic raid of the infamous Psychedelic Shop in Haight-Ashbury (as well as a raid on Ferlinghetti's City Lights). One of the targets was Kandel's new book of poetry, *The Love Book*, which was confiscated.

During a five-week hearing, Kandel defended *The Love Book* as the culmination of her lifelong quest for expressing the sacredness of love, dubbing her text "holy erotica." She stated that *The Love Book* is "a twenty-three year search for an appropriate way to worship" and is meant to "express her belief that sexual acts between loving persons are religious acts" (quoted by Knight, 281). While the poems celebrate the pleasures of sex and love they do not promote a "wild" sexual lifestyle, and although she liberally utilizes the word *fuck*, the book is considered tame by comparison to other literature available at the time, which tended to be far more vulgar and explicit.

The situation peaked when the jury declared the book obscene and lacking in any redeeming social value on 28 May 1967. Sales soared, and Kandel gleefully thanked the police by offering 1 percent of all profits to the Police Retirement Association for their part in raising public consciousness through her book. On appeal, the decision was overturned, and the book continued to sell well.

As with Ginsberg's *Howl*, the book's trial made the book well known among bohemians as a cause célèbre. The timing of the raid and the fact that many of the poems had been previously published without incident in an anthology the year before only added fuel to the general consensus that this prosecution was an attempt of the establishment to assert control over the forces of the underground and not an actual attempt to control an indecent text. Incidentally, *The Love Book*'s trial marked the last time a book was dragged into court in San Francisco on obscenity charges.

Kandel's second collection, *Word Alchemy*, appeared in 1967 and, although it is far less notorious than its predecessor, it is generally regarded as the more stylistically and thematically developed text. While still focusing on sex and love, Kandel also treats drugs and mental illness in the poems. Her work is praised (both by writers within the Beat movement and those outside it) for its originality and the boldness of her linguistic expressions, as well as her fresh melding of the spiritual and the bodily. Much of her poetry is explicitly Buddhist or tantric in nature.

In 1970, Kandel was incapacitated from a motorcycle accident with her then-husband, Hell's Angel William Fritsch (aka Sweet William). Her life since then has been marked by a great deal of physical pain.

She enumerated her poetic principles in "Poetry Is Never Compromise," a commentary made available in 1973. Since the late 1970s, after participating in a number of gatherings with prominent Beat and hippie figures, she has largely disappeared from public life. Although it is claimed that she is still active as a writer, her current whereabouts are not entirely known (though she is believed to be in or around San Francisco).

Kandel's disappearance from the public sphere is tragic. She was considered one of the best and brightest upcoming writers, but fell into a potentially destructive situation through her relationship with the volatile Hell's Angels. Today she is largely unknown, though with increased scholarly and public interest in the Beats, her name has become more visible again.

With the republication of *The Love Book* in 2003, she remains an important figure in the Beat movement whose work rewards the enterprising reader willing to seek it out and explore its originalities and nuances.

—*John M. Carey*

## Principal Works

*The Love Book*, 1965 (rpt. 2003); *Word Alchemy*, 1967 (currently out of print).
Poems are available in *The Women of the Beat Generation*, ed. Brenda Knight, 1996; *Beat Voices*, ed. David Kherdian, 1995; *Big Sky Mind*,

ed. Carole Tonkinson, 1995. "Poetry Is Never Compromise" is available in Donald Allen and Warren Tallman, eds., *The Poetics of the New American Poetry*, 1973.

## Bibliographical References

Information on Kandel is most recently available in Brenda Knight, *The Women of the Beat Generation*, 1996; David Kherdian, *Beat Voices*, 1995; Carole Tonkinson, *Big Sky Mind*, 1995; and Bruce Cook, *The Beat Generation*, 1994. See also Ann Charters, *The Beats: Literary Bohemians in Postwar America*, 1983, and Barry Gifford and Lawrence Lee, *Jack's Book*, 1978.

*See also* Kerouac, Jack; Censorship; Be-In

## Kaufman, Bob (1925–1986)

Though not the best known of the Beat poets, Bob Kaufman led a life that closely resembled the lifestyle of the Beats. Before Kaufman had ever published a major collection of verse, he was a legendary figure in the North Beach section of San Francisco. He was known for performing poetry and discussing a multitude of subjects at the Co-existence Bagel Shop. Arrested repeatedly for screaming his poetry to people on street corners and to cars on the street, he lived the life of a vagabond. He was also called the "bebop man" for his frequent pronouncements about music and the way in which his lifestyle paralleled the lives of musicians such as Charlie Parker and Miles Davis.

The facts of Bob Kaufman's life are difficult to ascertain, for as he told Raymond Foye, who wrote the "Editor's Note" for Kaufman's collection *The Ancient Rain*, "I want to be anonymous" (ix). He was born on 18 April 1925, one of fourteen children. Both of his parents were African American, though at times he spread the legend that he was of mixed parentage, part African American and part German and Jewish. Whatever the actual facts of his heritage, he consciously cast himself in the role of outsider. In a letter to the *San Francisco Chronicle* that is now reprinted in *Cranial Guitar*, ed. Gerald Nicosia (1996), Kaufman stated, "One thing is for certain. I'm not white. Thank God for that" (96–97).

Kaufman spent a good portion of his early life in the merchant marines, during which time he traversed the globe many times and read extensively. Later, while working at various jobs in California, he became acquainted with Allen Ginsberg, Jack Kerouac, and William Burroughs. With them, he became one of the seminal figures in the early days of the Beat movement. He published three broadsides through Ferlinghetti's City Lights Bookstore in the late 1950s: *The Abomunist Manifesto* (1959), *Second April* (1959), and *Does the Secret Mind Whisper?* (1960). In 1965, New Directions published his first major collection of poems, *Solitudes Crowded with Loneliness*. City Lights published the legendary *Golden Sardine* in 1967. Kaufman took a Buddhist vow of silence after the assassination of John Kennedy in 1963 and supposedly did not speak or write until 1973 when the Vietnam War ended. On that day at a public gathering, he spontaneously recited Thomas à Becket's speech from T. S. Eliot's *Murder in the Cathedral*. In 1980, through the tireless work of Raymond Foye, New Directions published Kaufman's last collection of poems, *The Ancient Rain, Poems 1956–1978*. Addicted to drugs and in trouble with the law for much of his life, Kaufman succumbed to emphysema on 12 January 1986.

Kaufman showed relatively little interest in publishing his poetry. Much of it was found written on napkins, envelopes, and toilet paper. Some of it was entirely oral, never recorded at all. All of his poetry might have remained oral had not his wife, Eileen, whom he met in 1957, urged him to publish his poems, recording many of them herself. To read Kaufman's published poetry is to enter a world where words seem to exist on the cusp of the moment. His language has an immediacy and a sense of improvisation that makes it like the jazz he emulated—bebop. Though all of the Beat poets claimed an affinity to jazz, Kaufman understood jazz more than any of them. He knew many of the famous musicians of the bebop years, such as Charlie Parker, Charles Mingus, and Miles Davis. He named his son "Parker" for Charlie Parker. But more importantly, he understood and felt their rhythms, as well as the meaning of what they did.

Poems such as "War Memoir" and "Walking Parker Home" (*Solitudes Crowded with Loneliness*) are among the best poems ever written reflecting the world of jazz. They precisely use the fresh, unpredictable, and often frenetic rhythm of bebop, but they also probe into the subversive meaning of jazz, suggesting that music is more than sound and that words can sometimes work as sound and rhythm without having meaning. Kaufman is the heir to the blues/jazz tradition that began in American poetry in the Harlem Renaissance, but more than that, he is its master.

Critics have attempted to fit Kaufman's work into niches such as surrealism, automatic writing, jazz poetry, or Beat poetry. Anyone who reads Kaufman carefully will find these categories to be inadequate. Poems such as "Song of the Broken Giraffe" (*Solitudes Crowded with Loneliness*) are surrealistic, just as poems such as "Novels from a Fragment in Progress" (*The Ancient Rain*) are automatic writing. But many of Kaufman's poems are in Duke Ellington's phrase, "beyond category." They create a world for themselves. Poems like "San Francisco Beat" from *Solitudes Crowded with Loneliness* or "Waiting" from *Golden Sardine* invite readers to live on the edge of language where meaning is made new with every word, where language is constantly morphing into mere sound.

—*H. William Rice*

## Principal Works

Most of Kaufman's collected poetry is contained in three volumes. *Solitudes Crowded with Loneliness*, 1965, published by New Directions, contains his first two City Lights broadsides, *The Abomunist Manifesto*, 1959, and *Second April*, 1959, as well as other poems. A third broadside, *Does the Secret Mind Whisper?* appeared in 1960 from City Lights and was not a part of any other later collections. *The Ancient Rain, Poems 1956–1978*, 1980, published by New Directions and edited by Raymond Foye, contains uncollected poems from the fifties as well as poems that Kaufman wrote in the sixties and seventies. *Cranial Guitar*, published in 1996 by Coffee House Press, contains all of *Golden Sardine* (published by City Lights in 1965), as well as selections from *Solitudes* and many uncollected poems. It is by far the most complete collection of Kaufman's work.

## Bibliographical References

Though scant at this time, criticism on Kaufman is growing. The single best article is T. J. Anderson's "Body and Soul," in *African American Review* 34.2 (2000): 329–347. Anderson is at work in 2005 on a book-length study of the work of Kaufman and other jazz-influenced poets. Another article of merit is Kathryne Lindberg's "Bob Kaufman, Sir Real, and His Revisionary Surreal Self-Presentation." It appears in Aldon Lynn Nielsen's *Reading Race in American Poetry: "An Area of Act,"* 2000. Two older articles also deserve attention: Lorenzo Thomas's "'Communicating by Horns': Jazz and Redemption in the Poetry of the Beats and the Black Arts Movement," in *African American Review* 26.2 (1992): 291–299, and Barbara Christian's "Whatever Happened to Bob Kaufman" from Lee Bartlett's *The Beats: Essays in Criticism*, 1981. By far the best introduction to Kaufman's life and work is David Henderson's introduction in *Cranial Guitar*, 1996, ed. Gerald Nicosia. *Cranial Guitar* also contains an excellent bibliography.

*See also* San Francisco; Little Magazines

## Kenton, Stan (1911–1979)

Bandleader, pianist, arranger, and educator, Stan Kenton led the Progressive Jazz Orchestra and played at Carnegie Hall in 1949, inspiring the movement in jazz that took its name from Kenton's group. During the period 1950–1951, Kenton led a forty-three-piece band on tours, but the size of the band proved impractical, and Kenton subsequently reduced the size of the groups he led. Many soloists came into prominence after their work with Kenton—among them Lee Konitz and Zoot Sims.

—*William Lawlor*

## Bibliographical References

Compare Lillian Arganian, *Stan Kenton: The Man and His Music*, 1989, with Carol Easton, *The Story of Stan Kenton*, 1973.

## Kerouac Archive, Sale of the

In August 2001 the literary archive of Jack Kerouac, including unpublished works and materials previously unseen by scholars, was sold for an undisclosed amount to the New York Public Library. Formerly held in a bank vault in Kerouac's hometown of Lowell, Massachusetts, the archive now rests in the library's Henry W. and Albert A. Berg Collection of English and American Literature.

Though it includes neither the famous scroll containing the first draft of *On the Road*, which had been on deposit within the library until its sale at auction earlier in the year, nor several letters and personal effects resting either in other archives or in private collections, the library's archive is by far the largest collection of Kerouac manuscripts. Included are over 1,000 prose and poetic manuscripts, notebooks for almost all of his works, journals and diaries spanning from 1934 to his death in 1969, and 1,800 pieces of correspondence. Personal effects include the crutches Kerouac used when he suffered a football injury as a student at Columbia University and notebooks and materials relating to the fantasy baseball game he invented in his youth.

Historian Douglas Brinkley of the University of New Orleans, given exclusive first access to the papers, has edited *Windblown World* (2004), a selection from Kerouac's journals, and Brinkley is writing a Kerouac biography. Though some items were briefly put on display in the library in 2002, the archive is currently being catalogued, and public access to the collection is restricted until 2005 or until Brinkley's biography is published.

—*Matt Stefon*

## Bibliographical References

Douglas Brinkley, "Inside the Kerouac Archive," *Atlantic Monthly*, November 1998; Henry W. and Albert A. Berg Collection of English and American Literature. Archive website: http://www.nypl.org/research/chss/spe/brg/berg.html; Hillel Italie, "Archives Reveal Diamond: Kerouac's Baseball League," *Boston Globe*, 22 August 2001; "New York Public Library Buys Kerouac Archive," *New York Times*, 22 August

2001; Christopher Scott, "Beating It to the Big Apple," *Lowell Sun,* 22 August 2001.

## Kerouac, Jack (1922–1969)

Known as "the chronicler of the Beat Generation," or "the martyred King of the Beats," Jack Kerouac was from Lowell, Massachusetts, a New England milltown with a strong French Canadian community. Famous primarily for having written the quintessential Beat Generation novel, *On the Road,* Kerouac was also the author of many other novels including *The Subterraneans, The Dharma Bums, Desolation Angels,* and *Tristessa,* as well as books of poetry, *Mexico City Blues* and *Book of Haikus.* As a prose fiction stylist, he exerts considerable influence on American letters, particularly on the New Journalism of writers such as Hunter S. Thompson and Tom Wolfe, and on poets. In addition to being an author, he was also a cult figure, his image melding with the more generalized images of rebellious youth in the culture at large. In the movies, Marlon Brando's leather-clad appearance on a motorcycle in *The Wild One* and James Dean's image in *Rebel without a Cause* are surely prototypes—along with *On the Road*'s principal characters Sal Paradise and Dean Moriarty—of this disaffection with American life and culture in the mid-twentieth century.

Kerouac's early years were marked by the deaths of his brother Gerard, his boyhood friend Sebastian Sampas, and his father. Kerouac made a deathbed promise to his father Leo to take care of his mother Gabrielle, affectionately known as Mémère. This trust adversely affected his relationships with women throughout his life. Nevertheless, he married three times (to Edie Parker; to Joan Haverty, with whom he had a daughter, Jan Michelle; and to Stella Sampas, the sister of his friend Sebastian, who had died at Anzio during World War II). In Lowell, he attended a French Canadian school in the mornings and continued his studies in English in the afternoons. He went on to the Horace Mann School in New York on a football scholarship. There he met Henri Cru, who introduced Kerouac to his first wife, Edie, and helped

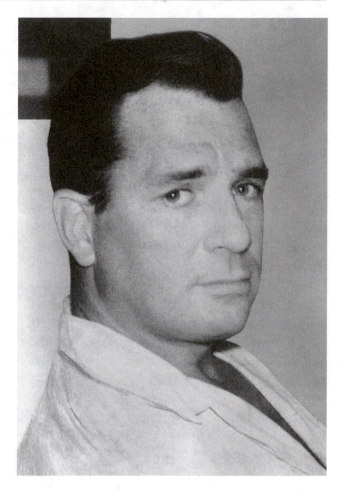

The youthful Jack Kerouac was strikingly handsome yet slightly shy. (Bettmann/Corbis)

Kerouac find jobs as a merchant seaman. He also met Seymour Wyse, who introduced Kerouac to jazz. Later on, at Columbia University, Kerouac met Allen Ginsberg and William S. Burroughs, lifelong friends who together with Kerouac are the seminal figures of the literary movement known as Beat.

William Burroughs in "Remembering Jack Kerouac," which is included in *Beat Down to Your Soul,* ed. Ann Charters (2001), said of Kerouac, first and foremost, "Kerouac was a writer. That is, he wrote" (63). By the time Kerouac and Burroughs met in 1944, Kerouac had already written a million words and was completely dedicated to his chosen trade. His boyhood ambition was to write the "great

American novel." Kerouac's first novel, *The Town and the City* (1950), was favorably reviewed but deemed derivative of the novels of Thomas Wolfe, whose *You Can't Go Home Again* and *Time and the River* were all the rage. Even as he was writing in the late 1940s under Wolfe's influence, Kerouac was dissatisfied with the pace of his prose. Inspired by the bebop musicians of the times, Charlie Parker and Thelonious Monk, and the manic verbal drive of a young hustler named Neal Cassady, the son of a Denver wino, Kerouac developed what Allen Ginsberg in his dedication to "Howl" called Kerouac's "spontaneous bop prosody," which he perfected through novel after novel. *The Dharma Bums* (1958), *Subterraneans* (1958), *Visions of Cody* (published posthumously in 1972), and *Desolation Angels* (1965) remain classics of his stylistic progression, his "road" books. A more nostalgic rhapsodic style was developed in his "Lowell" books, concerning his hometown, his memories of childhood and a nightmare Catholicism, his first love, and the death of his saintly brother Gerard at age nine when Jack was four: *Dr. Sax* (1959), *Maggie Cassidy* (1959), and *Visions of Gerard* (1963). *Vanity of Duluoz* (1968) remains a masterpiece of his mature style. He considered these works his "true life" novels and wished they could all be seen as a Divine Comedy of the Buddha, as one vast book, his Legend of Duluoz.

After the respectable but ultimately disappointing debut of his first novel, Kerouac attempted to develop a voice and vision more in keeping with the world as he was beginning to see it. Jack Kerouac found himself a national sensation when his second novel, *On the Road*, received rave recognition from a second-string *New York Times* critic, Gilbert Millstein, in 1957. While Millstein extolled the literary merits of this book, to the American public the novel represented a departure from traditions, particularly in its characterization of the American hipster and a lifestyle of movement back and forth across the American landscape. Disappointed with having achieved fame for the wrong reason, Kerouac never quite recovered from his "success." He was dismayed that little attention went to the excellence of his writing, but most attention went instead to the novel's radically different characters and their

nonconformist celebration of the joys of sex, jazz, and endless movement. In fact, many critics regarded the long sweeping sentences of *On the Road* as grammatically derelict, with the punctuation and other formalities of the English language abandoned. The critic Norman Podhoretz famously wrote his essay "The Know-Nothing Bohemians," accusing the Beat writers of ignorance. Kerouac became despondent and retreated into drink. Jack Kerouac thought of himself as an American writer in the tradition of Walt Whitman, Herman Melville, Jack London, and Thomas Wolfe. This place in the canon continues to elude him now, nearly thirty-five years after his death. The critical assessment continues to lag behind popular fascination. In typical irony, the original manuscript of *On the Road* sold at auction in 2001 for the highest price ever paid for a literary work.

*On the Road*'s composition is legendary. Not only was *On the Road* a stylistic departure, written on a roll of paper as one huge sentence, grammatically *exclamatio* (in the manner of Melville's *Moby Dick*), as if every moment were a simultaneous highest high and lowest low describing the antics of two travelers across the vast body and expanse of America in a fast car, but the novel was also a thematic departure with its refrain of "Everything is collapsing" (56 and 99). Following *The Town and the City*, which anticipated this breakdown of the very foundation of American life (the family, government, institutions), in their articulation of "The New Vision," the characters in *On the Road* were considered revolutionary hipsters, satiric in their defiance of American hypocrisies. American picaros, they were Huck Finn and Jim, the raft on the Mississippi supplanted by the automobile.

## The New Vision

Inspired by the Beat writers' reading of Oswald Spengler's *Decline of the West*, for Kerouac "The New Vision" was first articulated in *The Town and the City* and defined the characters of *On the Road*. Early Beat history had its center near Columbia University in the mid-1940s, where Kerouac met Allen Ginsberg and William S. Burroughs, seminal Beat figures. Early scandals—perhaps an adolescent response to the Gidean "acte graduit"—cemented friendships: Lucien Carr killed his gay stalker, Dave Kammerer, and Kerouac became an accessory to the crime. Scandals made art imperative: William Burroughs accidentally shot his common-law wife, Joan Vollmer, in a William Tell routine, and thereafter, Burroughs resolved to redeem himself, to exorcise the "Ugly Spirit" through writing. The radical nature of this concept is defined in Norman Mailer's 1957 essay, "The White Negro." Published originally in *Dissent* and now reprinted in *The Portable Beat Reader*, ed. Ann Charters (1992), the essay contextualized these characters' nature, positing a connection between the Beat outsiders and the anomie of the post–World War II period, when individuals could be quantified by the number of teeth that could be extracted from their mouths, the number of lampshades made from their skin. Mailer took the imagery of the concentration camps and post-Hiroshima period to describe the correlative emotional state of the hipster. If the individual could be so threatened as to be collectively murdered, mounded in mass graves, or atomically annihilated, then the teleology of organized religions, with their concerns with God's organization in matters of life, death, and afterlife, had no bearing on contemporary civilization. The American existentialist lived in a perpetual NOW, disconnected from the past and future, as if each moment were his last. To be Beat, one decides to "encourage the psychopath in oneself, to explore the domain of experience where security is boredom and therefore sickness, and one exists in the present, in that enormous present which is without past or future, memory or planned intention, the life where a man must go until he is beat" (in Charters, 584).

The character of Dean Moriarty depicts this American archetype, just as *On the Road* celebrates a new kind of hero, one who embodies IT. Kerouac wrote in the voice of his onlooker, Sal Paradise, explaining his fascination with Dean Moriarty, Rollo Greb, and jazz players: "the mad ones, the ones who are mad to live, mad to talk, mad to be saved" (5). In other words, Paradise admired a character like the jazzman in the moment of creation, wrested from the rules, strictures, and confines of straight society, for whom the perpetual NOW is all.

Readers in Kerouac's time confused Kerouac with the amoral hipster he so poetically portrayed, but his truth was far from it. Seeking all along the "hearthside" ideal, the solidity of family and home, and the girl next door, Kerouac found through writing the romantic quest for the promise of America, for the comforts of Catholicism, the peace and serenity of his adopted Buddhism. Considering himself marginalized by the "Beat" label foisted on him by Allen Ginsberg, repulsed by the cultish aspects of the Beat movement and their myths, and thereafter the hippies who claimed his paternity, Kerouac wished only to be considered in the mainstream American tradition, a man of letters like Herman Melville, Walt Whitman, Ernest Hemingway, and Jack London.

## Linguistic Experimentation

Controversial, too, was his dictum, "First Thought, Best Thought." Kerouac refused to revise. This outrageous stance was on appearance a rebellion itself, revision being the artist's chief control. As an artist, his quest was for language—pure, natural, unadulterated language, or the open heart unobstructed by what Kerouac saw as the lying of revision. And yet as book followed upon book roughly recounting the same material, the writer's life, he was in fact revising with each new novel. The original scroll of *On the Road* makes it quite clear that, in the words of Malcolm Cowley, his editor at Viking Press, he revised, and did so quite well (Gifford and Lee 206). Both large and small changes in his pencil scrawl appear on the tattered original. In addition, Kerouac considered repetition as a form of revision. The recasting of his words in variations such as *Visions of Cody* explains Kerouac's unconventional literary strategy.

He also outlined his methods himself in essays that were published in the *Evergreen Review:* "Essentials of Spontaneous Prose" (Summer 1958) and "Belief and Technique for Modern Prose" (Spring 1959). On the grammatically irreverent sentences, Kerouac extolled a "method" eschewing conventional punctuation in favor of dashes. In "The Essentials of Spontaneous Prose," which is reproduced in *The Portable Jack Kerouac*, ed. Ann Charters

Near the end of his life, Kerouac was troubled by fame and alcoholism. (Allen Ginsberg/Corbis)

(1995), Kerouac favored the "vigorous space dash separating rhetorical breathing (as jazz musician drawing breath between outblown phrases)" because the dash allowed Kerouac to deal differently with time, making time less prosaic and linear, more poetic. Moreover, Kerouac's descriptions usually begin with the privileged image of the "jewel center," from which he writes in a "semi-trance," "without consciousness" as his language is governed by sound, by poetic affect of alliteration and assonance, until he reaches a plateau. From there he begins a new "jewel center," stronger than the first and spiraling out as he continues his "riffing" on the analogy with a jazz musician. And so in the smaller interior structures of writing he duplicated the repetitive process operating in his legend at large, book to book. This process accounts for the unusual organization of his writing, not haphazard or ragged, but systematic in the most individualized sense. This concept of spontaneity explains Kerouac's distinct voice.

## Kerouac as Poet

Though he was best known as a prose fiction stylist, Jack Kerouac wrote books of poetry as well. Among the Beats, Jack Kerouac was known as a poet supreme, who worked in several poetry traditions including sonnets and odes, and blues (which he based on blues and jazz idioms). His *Mexico City Blues* was published in 1959. After meeting the poet Gary Snyder in 1955, he also mastered the haiku, the three-line, seventeen-syllable Japanese form going back to Basho. Ezra Pound had modeled his short poem "In a Station of the Metro" after the Japanese haiku. Kerouac went further to define the American haiku tradition, departing from the seventeen-syllable, three-line form.

Like Ezra Pound, Kerouac consciously felt he was creating a new version of this highly compact poetic genre, at least in English, as he remained convinced of the supremacy of the Japanese masters, Buson, Shiki, Issa, as well as Basho. In his essay, "Origins of Joy in Poetry," which serves as a preface for *Scattered Poems* (1971), he extolled the haiku form as "pointing out things directly, purely, concretely, no abstractions or explanations, wham wham the true blue song of man." He defined his practice further in *Scattered Poems:*

I propose that the "Western Haiku" simply say a lot in three short lines in any Western language.

Above all, a Haiku must be very simple and free of all poetic trickery and make a little picture and yet be as airy and graceful as a Vivaldi Pastorella. Here is a great Japanese Haiku that is simpler and prettier than any Haiku I could ever write in any language:

A day of quiet gladness,—
Mount Fuji is veiled
In misty rain.
(Basho) (1644–1694) (*Scattered Poems*, 69)

Thus in this tradition, Kerouac wrote:

Birds singing
in the dark
-Rainy dawn.

Elephants munching
on grass—loving
Heads side by side.

Missing a kick
at the icebox door
It closed anyway.

Perfect moonlit night
marred
By family squabbles.
(*Scattered Poems*, 71)

In terms of Kerouac's oeuvre, the short, compact poetic form is a contrast to the long, looping, panoramic, spontaneous sentences or riffs of his highly poetic novels. His creative range includes the crafting of both a long, sweeping pan and an instantaneous snapshot that deepens as it is contemplated.

Jack Kerouac was not the first American poet to experiment in haiku aesthetics. Before him, Ezra Pound, William Carlos Williams, Amy Lowell, and Wallace Stevens all created haiku-inspired verse. It was not until after the Second World War that attention to the genre arose, with the first volume of R. H. Blyth's four-volume *Haiku* appearing in 1949, bringing the classical traditions of haiku and Zen to the West.

Kerouac turned to Buddhist study and practice after his "road" period, from 1953 until 1956, in the lull between the writing of the seminal *On the Road* in 1951 and its publication in 1957—that is, before fame changed everything. When he finished *The Subterraneans* in the fall of 1953, fed up with the world after the failed love affair on which the book was based, he picked up Thoreau and fantasized a life separate from civilization. Then he happened upon Asvaghosha's *The Life of Buddha*, and immersed himself in Zen study.

Kerouac began his genre-defying book *Some of the Dharma* in 1953 as a collection of reader's notes on Dwight Goddard's *The Buddhist Bible* (1938);

the endeavor grew into a massive compilation of spiritual material, meditations, prayers, and haiku, a study of his musings on the teaching of Buddha. By 1955, while living in North Carolina with his sister, he worked on two other Buddhist-related texts: *Wake Up*, his own biography of the Buddha, and *Buddha Tells Us*, translations of "works done by great Rimbauvian Frenchmen at the Abbeys of Tibet," what he refers to in his letters as "a full-length Buddhist Handbook."

Haiku came to the West Coast poets through Gary Snyder. Inspired by D. T. Suzuki's *Essays in Zen Buddhism* (1927) in the fall of 1951, Snyder spent the early 50s traveling in Japan, studying and practicing Zen Buddhism. Philip Whalen and Lew Welch became avid haiku practitioners through his influence. Kerouac, Ginsberg, Snyder, and Whalen spent time together in Berkeley in 1955, talking, drinking, and trading their own versions of Blyth's haiku translations, which they were reading in all four volumes. Through Blyth's translations and his extraordinary commentary on the Japanese works, Kerouac found emotive and aesthetic sympathies. Even though he attempted to meditate; wrote a sutra, *The Scripture of the Golden Eternity* (1956), at Gary Snyder's behest; and thought of his entire oeuvre, the Legend of Duluoz, as a "Divine Comedy" based on Buddha, Buddhism stayed a literary concern for him, not a meditative or spiritual practice as it was for Snyder and Whalen. Later, when he told Ted Berrigan in his 1968 *Paris Review* interview that he was a serious Buddhist, but not a Zen Buddhist, the distinction was to separate his interest from the prevalent scholarly study of dogma in favor of Buddhist essence. The practice of haiku, however, persisted throughout his life, becoming an important medium for rendering the Beat ideal of "shapely mind," and for crafting an American mysticism in the manner of Thoreau. For a new generation of poets, Kerouac ended up breaking ground at a pioneering stage of an American haiku movement.

Allen Ginsberg in his *Paris Review* interview, which is reprinted in *Spontaneous Mind*, ed. David Carter (2001), speaks perhaps hyperbolically of Kerouac as the "only *master* of the haiku" (51). Ginsberg adds that Kerouac "talks that way and thinks that way" and "is the only one in the United States who knows how to write haikus" (51). What Kerouac "got" perhaps more than any other Beat poet working in this genre was the rendering of a subject's essence, and the shimmering, ephemeral nature of its fleeting existence. This sensitivity to impermanence appears again and again in his work, from *The Town and the City*, constructed around the death of the father, through *The Book of Dreams*, which evokes the frail individual beset with a harsh, indifferent society, at times succumbing, defeated.

One of Kerouac's classic haiku images is of a sole animate entity in a wide, cavernous expanse. From a 1959 cross-country trip Kerouac took with Albert Saijo and Lew Welch during which they passed the time tossing off haiku after haiku and which became the basis of the volume *Trip Trap: Scenes along the Road*, published in 1973:

The windmills of
Oklahoma look
In every direction

And, from a 1960 unpublished notebook:

One flower
on the cliffside
Nodding at the canyon.

That isolated being—here "looking" or "nodding"—is the quintessential Kerouacean persona seen again and again in his Legend of Duluoz.

Seeking visual possibilities in language, Kerouac combined his spontaneous prose with sketching, a technique suggested to him by Ed White, a friend during his Columbia University days in the late 40s. According to Dennis McNally, author of *Desolate Angel* (1979), White recommended that Kerouac "try sketching like a painter, but with words" (139).

"'Keep the eye STEADILY on the object,' for haiku," Kerouac exhorted himself in his notebooks, which are kept at the New York Public Library. "WRITE HAIKUS THEN PAINT THE SCENE DESCRIBING THEM!" He also likened good

haiku to good painting. The best haiku gave him "the sensation" that he got when he was "looking at a great painting by Van Gogh, it's there & nothing you can say or do about it, except *look* in dismay at the power of looking." The extraordinary juxtapositions often noted in Kerouac's sketched prose—in *Visions of Cody* (written in 1951 and 1952, a portion published in 1959 as *Visions of Neal*), *Doctor Sax* (written in July 1952, published in 1959), and "October in the Railroad Earth" (written in 1952; portions published in *Black Mountain Review* and *Evergreen Review* in 1957; a full version included in *Lonesome Traveler* in 1960)—especially evoke haiku spirit, even before he was fully immersed in composing haiku.

The discovery of haiku through Dr. Suzuki's work and Blyth's translations is the starting point of one of Kerouac's most popular books, *The Dharma Bums*. The struggle to perfect haiku becomes part of the narrative motif in this novel, published in 1958, and dedicated to Han Shan, the Chinese poet whose work Snyder was translating. Calling his mentor Gary Snyder "Japhy Ryder" in slant rhyme, Kerouac has this nature-boy, Zen mystic, and poet supplant the speedy Dean Moriarty of *On the Road* as catalyst for the Kerouac persona, this time named Ray Smith, in learning the ways of "dharma bums."

In the course of the novel, the two decide to go mountain climbing, Japhy as Virgil to Ray's Dante. They engage in a sharing of poetry, observation of nature, and speculation on haiku practice. Says Smith, perusing a fresh pure lake, "by God it's a haiku in itself" (55). The ensuing conversation reveals Kerouac's vision of the haiku:

"Look over there," sang Japhy, "yellow aspens. Just put me in the mind of a haiku . . . 'Talking about the literary life—the yellow aspens.'" Walking in this country you could understand the perfect gems of haikus the Oriental poets had written, never getting drunk in the mountains or anything but just going along as fresh as children writing down what they saw without literary devices or fanciness of expression. We made up haikus as we climbed, winding up and up now on the slopes of brush.

"Rocks on the side of the cliff," I said, "why don't they tumble down?"

"Maybe that's a haiku, maybe not, it might be a little too complicated," said Japhy. "A real haiku's gotta be as simple as porridge and yet make you see the real thing, like the greatest haiku of them all probably is the one that goes 'The sparrow hops along the veranda, with wet feet.' By Shiki. You see the wet footprints like a vision in your mind and yet in those few words you also see the rain that's been falling that day and almost smell the wet pine needles." (59)

## Haiku Prose

Kerouac's use of haiku was not limited to poetry, and as is typical for this artist for whom language was paramount, he was interested in incorporating his haiku aesthetic into his prose. Reviewing *The Dharma Bums* in *The Village Voice* on 12 November 1958, Ginsberg noted that: "The sentences are shorter (shorter than the great flowing, inventive *Doctor Sax*), almost as if he were writing a book of a thousand haikus. . . . *Dharma Bums* winds up with a great series of perfectly connected associations in visionary haikus (little jumps of the 'freedom of eternity'). Two images set side by side that make a flash in the mind" (3–5). Kerouac, in the interview in *Paris Review* (1968), which is reprinted in *Beat Writers at Work*, ed. George Plimpton (1999), also saw that leap:

A sentence that's short and sweet with a sudden jump of thought is a kind of haiku, and there's a lot of freedom and fun in surprising yourself with that, let the mind willy-nilly jump from the branch to the bird. (117)

Haiku seeps into his prose style in other ways. In *The Dharma Bums*, Kerouac writes, "The storm went away as swiftly as it came and the late afternoon lake-sparkle blinded me. Late afternoon, my mop drying on the rock. Late afternoon, my bare back cold as I stood above the world in a snowfield digging shovelsful into a pail. Late afternoon, it was I not the void that changed" (241–242). The repet-

itive "late afternoon" sequence—Kerouac's "visionary haikus" here written out as prose phrases—echoes the manner in which he wrote haiku in his journals, often repeating a line with a variation.

These "late afternoon" haiku also appear in the notebooks marked "Desolation Peak 1956" when, in an attempt to replicate the experience of isolation favored by the reclusive Chinese poet Han Shan, Kerouac spent sixty-three days atop Desolation Peak, which is in the state of Washington. Handwritten, these poems follow the three-line haiku form and are also included in a 1956 typed haiku manuscript consisting of seventy-two numbered poems, which he dubbed "Desolation Pops." As he explained in *Some of the Dharma*, completed in 1956, when he decided to call haiku by the name of "pops," a "pop" is an American haiku, that is, a short three-line poem aimed toward enlightenment. Kerouac recounted this experience at Desolation Peak in *Desolation Angels* (1965) using haiku as bridges between sections of spontaneous prose, as a bridge is a connective in jazz.

## Connection with and Disconnection from the Beats

Kerouac was curiously absent or nonparticipatory in some of the Beat literati's peak moments. At the pivotal 6 Gallery poetry reading in San Francisco in 1955, an event said to have triggered the San Francisco Renaissance, Kerouac passed jugs of wine while Ginsberg wowed the crowd with a premier reading of "Howl." Ginsberg organized the 7 October reading, inviting Michael McClure, Philip Lamantia, Kenneth Rexroth, Gary Snyder, and Philip Whalen. Kerouac had, of course, been invited to read but claimed shyness. "Poet ain't court jester, I say. He, tho, gets up on stage and howls his poems," said Jack declining to read (Kerouac, *Selected Letters 1940–1956*, 519). However he was instrumental on one historical occasion: Passing through Europe in 1957, Kerouac made a stop in Tangier and helped organize and type up—along with Allen Ginsberg, Alan Ansen, and Brion Gysin—the disparate pages of the manuscript of William S. Burroughs's *Naked Lunch*, also supplying its title.

In San Francisco, Adler Alley was renamed Jack Kerouac Street in 1988. (Mark L. Stephenson/Corbis)

By the sixties Kerouac had finished most of his significant writing, accomplished in the long period between the writing of *On the Road* in 1951 and its actual publication in 1957. However one significant book remains to be reevaluated, *Vanity of Duluoz*. Typically autobiographical, Kerouac recounts his early years as a school athlete and as a young writer in New York. The book retells the stories of his childhood, his schooling, and the dramatic scandals that defined the early Beat experience. An alcoholic, he eventually drank himself to death in 1969, broke and with many books out of print. Living in St. Petersburg, Florida, with his third wife, Stella Sampas, as well as his mother, and given to inciting brawls outside bars, he died a week after he had been beaten up, of internal hemorrhaging, while watching *The Galloping Gourmet* on television. Having contributed profoundly to the Beat move-ment, creating an aesthetic that defined Beat, Kerouac showed that his death made him the ultimate martyred King of the Beats.

## A Chronology of the Life of Jack Kerouac

1922: Born at 5:00 P.M. on 12 March in Lowell, Massachusetts—the third child and second son of Leo and Gabrielle Kerouac.

1926: Gerard, Kerouac's saintly brother, dies of rheumatic fever after a long illness.

1934: On the Moody Street Bridge in Lowell, Kerouac is deeply disturbed after witnessing, in the company of his mother, the sudden death of a man bearing a watermelon across the bridge.

1936: The rising flood waters of the Merrimack River ruin Leo Kerouac's printing business.

1937: Kerouac scores the winning touchdown in Lowell High School's victory over Lawrence High School.

1938: Kerouac meets Mary Carney, whom he later recreates in *Maggie Cassidy.*

1939: Kerouac graduates from Lowell High School, wins a football scholarship to attend Columbia University, and begins preparatory studies at Horace Mann School in New York City.

1940: Kerouac begins studies at Columbia College and during a football game breaks his leg.

1942: Kerouac joins the merchant marines; on the SS *Dorchester* he sails to Greenland.

1943: Kerouac enlists in the navy but is discharged in less than a year. He becomes a merchant marine and on the SS *George Weems* travels to Liverpool, England.

1944: Friendship develops with William Burroughs, Lucien Carr, and Allen Ginsberg. When Carr kills David Kammerer, Kerouac is implicated in the crime, but by marrying Edie Parker, Kerouac secures money for bail. The newlyweds travel to Michigan to be with Edie's parents, and the marriage begins to disintegrate.

1945: With Burroughs, Kerouac writes *And the Hippos Were Boiled in Their Tanks.*

1946: Leo Kerouac succumbs to stomach cancer. Kerouac meets Neal Cassady. Kerouac and Edie Parker annul their marriage.

1947: Kerouac journeys to Denver and San Francisco and returns to New York in October.

1948: Kerouac completes *The Town and the City* and composes an early draft of *On the Road.* Friendship with John Clellon Holmes begins.

1949: With Cassady, Kerouac visits Burroughs near New Orleans. They proceed to San Francisco, but Kerouac ends his second trip across the country when he completes a bus ride to his sister's home in North Carolina. He receives an advance of $1,000 for *The Town and the City* from Harcourt Brace.

1950: *The Town and the City* is published. With Neal Cassady, Kerouac drives from Denver to Mexico City, where they reconnect with Burroughs. Back in New York in November, Kerouac marries Joan Haverty. Neal Cassady's "Joan Anderson Letter" amazes the newlyweds.

1951: In a three-week typing marathon, Kerouac prepares the legendary scroll of *On the Road* on a paper scroll. Kerouac and Joan Haverty separate. Kerouac composes *Visions of Cody.*

1952: Jan Kerouac, daughter of Jack Kerouac and Joan Haverty Kerouac, is born on February 16. Kerouac lives with Neal and Carolyn Cassady in San Francisco. In Mexico, during another reconnection with Burroughs, Kerouac writes *Dr. Sax.*

1953: Kerouac writes *Maggie Cassidy, The Subterraneans,* and "Essentials of Spontaneous Prose."

1954: Buddha enters Kerouac's life: after he reads Dwight Goddard's *A Buddhist Bible,* he begins writing *Some of the Dharma.* Sterling Lord becomes Kerouac's literary agent. The paternity suit involving Jan Kerouac, Jack's daughter, leads to Kerouac's arrest for his failure to provide for his daughter's care.

1955: Kerouac's "Jazz of the Beat Generation" is published in *New World Writing.* Kerouac's "The Mexican Girl," which is part of the manuscript for *On the Road,* appears as the lead story in *Paris Review.* In Mexico City, Kerouac begins composition of *Tristessa* and writes *Mexico City Blues.* In San Francisco, Kerouac attends the legendary reading at the 6 Gallery. Accompanied by Gary Snyder and John Montgomery, Kerouac climbs the Matterhorn, which is located in the area east of Yosemite National Park in California.

1956: Kerouac finishes *Visions of Gerard.* Kerouac takes a post as a fire lookout on Desolation Peak in the state of Washington. In

September, he returns to Mexico City, completes *Tristessa,* and begins *Desolation Angels.*

1957: Kerouac and Joyce Glassman meet. In Tangier, Kerouac visits Burroughs and types a manuscript for Burroughs's *Naked Lunch.* Kerouac proceeds to France and England and then returns to New York. *On the Road* is published and receives a stunning review in the *New York Times.* The issue of *Evergreen Review* that focuses on the San Francisco scene includes Kerouac and other Beats. In Florida, Kerouac finishes writing *Dharma Bums.* Kerouac does the first jazz/poetry reading session with David Amram in New York. Kerouac writes a play entitled *The Beat Generation.*

1958: *The Subterraneans* and *The Dharma Bums* are published. Kerouac and Steve Allen combine to produce an album. Kerouac travels with photographer Robert Frank.

1959: Robert Frank and Al Leslie produce *Pull My Daisy,* a film based on the third act of *The Beat Generation,* a play by Kerouac. Kerouac's *Doctor Sax, Mexico City Blues,* and *Maggie Cassidy* are published. On 16 November, Kerouac appears on the *Steve Allen Show.* Kerouac drives to New York with Lew Welch and Al Saijo and contributes to a book of haiku.

1960: *Tristessa* and *Lonesome Traveler* are published. *The Subterraneans* is produced as a film. New Directions publishes *Visions of Cody,* but the work is an abbreviated edition. Kerouac suffers a breakdown near Big Sur, California.

1961: Timothy Leary introduces Kerouac to psychedelic experimentation. *Book of Dreams* is published. In Florida Kerouac writes *Big Sur* in ten days.

1962: Kerouac settles the paternity suit involving Jan Kerouac by agreeing to make support payments. *Big Sur* is published.

1963: *Visions of Gerard* is published.

1964: Neal Cassady presents Kerouac to the Merry Pranksters. On 19 September, Kerouac's sister, Nin, dies.

1965: *Desolation Angels* is published. To investigate his ancestry, Kerouac flies to Paris.

1966: *Satori in Paris* is published 9 September. Kerouac's mother, Gabrielle, has a stroke. Kerouac marries Stella Sampas in Hyannis, Massachusetts.

1967: Kerouac takes up residence in Lowell with his mother and wife. He is interviewed for *Paris Review* by Ted Berrigan, Aram Saroyan, and Duncan McNaughton. November: Kerouac's daughter Jan visits her father in Lowell.

1968: Neal Cassady dies of exposure. *Vanity of Duluoz* is published. Kerouac appears on William F. Buckley's television show *Firing Line.*

1969: "After Me, the Deluge" appears in the *Chicago Tribune.* On 21 October, Kerouac dies. His body is taken to Lowell for the funeral and burial.

1971: *Pic* is published.

1972: *Visions of Cody* is published in its entirety.

1973: Ann Charters's *Kerouac: A Biography* is published. Gabrielle Kerouac dies.

1974: The Jack Kerouac School of Disembodied Poetics opens at the Naropa Institute in Boulder, Colorado.

1978: *Jack's Book,* an oral history of Kerouac's life and career, is edited by Barry Gifford and Lawrence Lee.

1979: Dennis McNally's *Desolate Angel: Jack Kerouac, the Beat Generation, and America,* a detailed biography of Kerouac, is published.

1982: At the University of Colorado, dozens of friends and associates of Kerouac celebrate the twenty-fifth anniversary of the publication of *On the Road* by participating in a special conference.

1983: Gerald Nicosia publishes *Memory Babe,* the longest biography of Kerouac; in *Minor Characters,* Joyce Johnson recounts her love relationship with Kerouac.

1984: Tom Clark publishes *Jack Kerouac*, another biography.

1985: A complete version of *Old Angel Midnight* is published in England.

1988: Jack Kerouac Street is dedicated in San Francisco. Jack Kerouac Park, including monuments featuring selections from the writings of Kerouac, is dedicated in Lowell, Massachusetts.

1990: *Off the Road*, a memoir by Carolyn Cassady, is published. Joan Haverty, Kerouac's second wife, dies, Stella Sampas, Kerouac's third wife, dies.

1992: *Pomes All Sizes* published.

1993: *Old Angel Midnight*, which originally appeared in a shortened version in the magazine *Big Table* in 1959, is published in its entirety for the first time in the United States. *Good Blonde and Others*, a collection of essays, is published. Edie Parker, Kerouac's first wife, dies.

1995: Writings of Jack Kerouac Conference held at New York University. *The Portable Jack Kerouac*, ed. Ann Charters, and *Jack Kerouac: Selected Letters 1940–1956*, ed. Ann Charters, are published.

1996: Jan Kerouac dies.

1999: *Some of the Dharma* is published. *Jack Kerouac: Selected Letters: 1957–1969*, ed. Ann Charters, is also published. *Atop an Underwood*, ed. Paul Marion, is also published.

2000: *Door Wide Open*, a collection of letters by Joyce Johnson and Jack Kerouac, is published.

2001: The scroll of *On the Road* is sold at auction for more than 2 million dollars.

2002: *Orpheus Emerged* is published.

2003: Regina Weinreich edits *Book of Haikus*. University of Massachusetts, Lowell, hosts Jack Kerouac Conference on Beat Literature.

2004: The scroll of *On the Road* goes on the road as a traveling exhibit at various libraries and historical centers. Ed Adler edits *Departed Angels: The Lost Paintings of Jack Kerouac*. Douglas Brinkley edits *Windblown World*, a selection of materials from the journals of Jack Kerouac.

2007: Readers celebrate the fiftieth anniversary of the publication of *On the Road*.

—*Regina Weinreich*

## Principal Works

*The Town and the City*, 1950; *On the Road*, 1957; "Essentials of Spontaneous Prose," *Evergreen Review* (Summer 1958): 72–73; *The Dharma Bums*, 1958; *The Subterraneans*, 1958; "Belief & Technique for Modern Prose," *Evergreen Review* (Spring 1959): 9; *Doctor Sax*, 1959; *Visions of Neal*, 1959; *Maggie Cassidy*, 1959; *Mexico City Blues*, 1959; *Lonesome Traveler*, 1960; *The Scripture of the Golden Eternity*, 1960; *Tristessa*, 1960; *The Book of Dreams*, 1961; *Big Sur*, 1962; *Vision of Gerard*, 1963; *Desolation Angels*, 1965; *Satori in Paris*, 1966; *Vanity of Duluoz: An Adventurous Education, 1935–1946*, 1968; *Pic*, 1971; *Scattered Poems*, compiled by Ann Charters, 1971; *Visions of Cody*, 1972; with Lew Welch and Albert Saijo, *Trip Trap: Haiku along the Road from San Francisco to New York*, 1959 (rpt. 1973); *Heaven and other Poems*, 1977; *Pomes All Sizes*, 1992; *Good Blonde & Others*, 1993; *Book of Blues*, 1995; *Selected Letters, 1940–1956*, ed. Ann Charters, 1995; *Some of the Dharma*, 1997; "Paris Review Interview," *Beat Writers at Work*, ed. George Plimpton, 1999: 97–133. *Selected Letters, 1957–1969*, ed. Ann Charters, 1999; with Joyce Johnson, *Door Wide Open: A Beat Love Affair in Letters, 1957–1958*, 2000; *Book of Haikus*, ed. Regina Weinreich, 2003.

## Bibliographical References

Ann Charters, *Kerouac: A Biography*, 1973; Ann Charters, ed., *The Portable Beat Reader*, 1992; Ann Charters, ed., *Beat Down to Your Soul*, 2001; Rick Fields, *How the Swans Came to the Lake: A Narrative History of Buddhism in America*, 1992; Barry Gifford and Lawrence Lee, *Jack's Book: An Oral Biography of Jack Kerouac*, 1978; Allen Ginsberg, *Allen Verbatim: Lectures on Poetry, Politics, Consciousness*, ed. Gordon Ball, 1974; Allen Ginsberg, "Review of *The Dharma Bums*," *Village Voice*, 12 November 1958: 3–5; Allen Ginsberg, "*Paris Review* Interview" in *Beat Writers at Work*, ed. George Plimpton, 1999; Dwight Goddard, ed., *A Buddhist Bible*, 1938; John

Clellon Holmes, *Nothing More to Declare: Of the Men and Ideas That Made This Literary Generation*, 1967; Joyce Johnson, *Minor Characters: A Beat Memoir*, 1983; Joyce Johnson, *Door Wide Open: A Beat Love Affair in Letters 1957–1958*, 2000; Jack Kerouac, "Paris Review Interview" in *Beat Writers at Work*, ed. George Plimpton, 1999; Seymour Krim, *Shake It for the World, Smartass*, 1970; John Lardas, *The Bop Apocalypse: The Religious Visions of Kerouac, Ginsberg and Burroughs*, 2001; Dennis McNally, *Desolate Angel: Jack Kerouac, the Beat Generation, and America*, 1979; Barry Miles, *Jack Kerouac: King of the Beats*, 1998; Norman Podhoretz, "The Know-Nothing Bohemians" *Partisan Review* 25 (Spring 1958): 305–311, 313–316, 318; Gary Snyder, *The Gary Snyder Reader: Prose, Poetry, and Translations, 1952–1998*, 1999; David Sterritt, *Mad to Be Saved: The Beats, the '50s, and Film*, 1998; Carole Tonkinson, ed. *Big Sky Mind: Buddhism and the Beat* Generation, 1995; John Tytell, *Naked Angels: The Lives and Literature of the Beat Generation*, 1976; John Tytell, *Literary Outlaws: Remembering the Beats*, 1999; Barbara Ungar, *Haiku in English*, Stanford Honors Essay in Humanities Number XXI, 1978; Steven Watson, *The Birth of the Beat Generation: Visionaries, Rebels, and Hipsters, 1944–1960*, 1995; Regina Weinreich, *The Spontaneous Poetics of Jack Kerouac: A Study of the Fiction*, 1987; Regina Weinreich, Interview with Allen Ginsberg, in *Five Points: A Journal of Literature and Art* (Fall 1997).

**See also** *On the Road, New York Times* Review of; *On the Road*, Sale of the Scroll of; Burroughs, William Seward; Ginsberg, Allen; Mexico City; New York City; Kammerer, David Eames; Carr, Lucien; Mailer, Norman; 6 Gallery Reading; Holmes, John Clellon; Cassady, Neal; Cassady, Carolyn; Anderson, Joan, Letter about; Vollmer Adams Burroughs, Joan; Krim, Seymour; Sampas Kerouac, Stella; Kerouac, Jan; Kerouac, Joan Haverty; Parker, Edie; Thompson, Hunter Stockton; Wolfe, Tom; Influences; Eastern Culture; Mountains, Beats in the; Juvenile Delinquency; Beatitude; Music; Film; Photography; Painting; Johnson, Joyce; Native American Cultures; Sea, The Beats at; Memory; Mental Illness; Fellaheen.

## Kerouac, Jan (1952–1996)

Daughter of Jack Kerouac and Joan Haverty, born 16 February 1952, in Albany, New York. Jack Ker-

ouac denied paternity, but blood tests taken when Jan was nine served as legal confirmation that Jan was Jack Kerouac's daughter. Jan Kerouac is noteworthy for three autobiographical novels whose content reveals the zeal for travel that her father displayed, but whose style is original rather than an imitation of Jack Kerouac's jazz-inspired prose.

Jan met her father only twice during her life, the first time at age nine when he underwent a paternity test, and the second time at age fifteen when she visited him at his home. During adolescence, Jan Kerouac had problems with delinquency and drug abuse and spent some time in detention centers. Like her father, she experienced life on the road and worked at various jobs to support herself. She was twice married and twice divorced. She was childless.

Eventually, she connected with the writers who had been friends of her father, including Lawrence Ferlinghetti, Allen Ginsberg, and William Burroughs. She wrote *Baby Driver* (1981) and *Train-*

Jan Kerouac, the only child of Jack Kerouac, speaks at a 1994 conference on the Beat Generation at New York University. (AP Photo/Ed Bailey)

song (1988), but was not able to complete *Parrot Fever* during her lifetime.

She spoke at the 1994 New York University conference on the Beat Generation and performed with David Amram.

She later was involved in a legal dispute with the estate of Jack Kerouac, which was under the control of the heirs of Stella Sampas, Jack Kerouac's third wife. Jan Kerouac contested the validity of the will of Gabrielle Kerouac, who inherited everything from Jack Kerouac and who upon her death passed everything on to Stella Sampas. Jan died of kidney failure before her suit could yield results, and Gerald Nicosia, who pursued the case as Jan Kerouac's representative, could not make legal action against the estate go forward.

—*William Lawlor*

**Principal Works**
In 1998, Thunder's Mouth Press published new and expanded editions of *Baby Driver* and *Trainsong;* in 2005, the same publisher released *Parrot Fever,* the book Jan could not complete before her death.

**Bibliographical References**
Brenda Knight, "Jan Kerouac: Next Generation," in *The Women of the Beat Generation,* 1996, summarizes Jan Kerouac's life and includes a short memoir by Gerald Nicosia and a selection from *Trainsong.* James Jones, *Use My Name,* 1999, analyzes Jan's connection to her father.

*See also* Kerouac, Joan Haverty; New York University Conferences on Beat Culture; Kerouac, Jack

# Kerouac, Joan Haverty (1931–1990)

Friend of Bill Cannastra, a Harvard Law School graduate whose recklessness led to a fatal accident in a New York Subway station; second wife to Jack Kerouac and mother of his daughter, Jan Kerouac; author of the autobiography *Nobody's Wife* (2000), which offered insights about Kerouac's personality and family.

As told in Part V of *On the Road,* Sal Paradise was lost in Manhattan and was trying to find his way to a party. From the street, he called up to an apartment, and Laura answered. She invited Sal to come upstairs for hot chocolate, and Sal and Laura fell instantly in love. They planned to move to San Francisco in an old truck with Dean Moriarty at the wheel, but Dean showed up before money could be raised and the move was deferred.

In real life, Sal was Jack Kerouac, and Laura was Joan Haverty, whose friendship with Bill Cannastra ended suddenly on 12 October 1950, when Cannastra impulsively tried to exit a subway car through a window as the train left the Bleecker Street Station. Cannastra died, and Kerouac, Cannastra's friend, subsequently discovered his attraction to Joan Haverty. Two weeks after meeting, Kerouac and Haverty were married, but within eight months they were divorced. From the union, one child—Jan Kerouac—was born, but for nearly a decade Kerouac denied paternity.

During the marriage, the couple lived in a brownstone apartment on West 20th Street, where Kerouac received legendary letters from Neal Cassady, including the "Joan Anderson Letter." Inspired by Cassady's free-flowing style, in April 1951 Kerouac sat at his typewriter and produced the scroll version of *On the Road* that ultimately sold for 2.4 million dollars.

Despite an affliction with breast cancer, to which she succumbed in 1990, Joan Haverty relentlessly revised her autobiography, *Nobody's Wife,* which was finally published in 2000.

—*William Lawlor*

**Bibliographical References**
*Nobody's Wife,* 2000, is the product of posthumous editing by John Bowers and includes an introduction by Jan Kerouac; Brenda Knight, "Joan Haverty Kerouac: Nobody's Wife," in *Women of the Beat Generation,* 1996, summarizes Joan Haverty's life and presents a selection from the autobiography. James Jones, *Use My Name,* 1999, offers valuable analysis of the relationship between Haverty and Kerouac; Dennis McNally, *Desolate Angel,* 1979, provides additional commentary.

*See also* New York City; *On the Road,* Sale of the Scroll of; Kerouac, Jan; Kerouac, Jack; Cannastra, Bill; Anderson, Joan, Letter about

## Kesey, Ken Elton (1935–2001)

Ken Kesey was a transitional figure between the 1950s Beats and the 1960s hippies, helping to transform the nature of antiestablishment society through his fiction, experimentation with drugs, and leadership of the Merry Pranksters. Kesey published his first and most important novel, *One Flew Over the Cuckoo's Nest*, in 1962, a book that immediately established him as a major force in American fiction. However, a 1964 trip across much of the United States in a bus painted in psychedelic colors secured his position in the country's counterculture. The trip featured Kesey and some of his Merry Prankster friends, veterans of Kesey's so-called acid tests, including Neal Cassady, the model for Dean Moriarty in Jack Kerouac's novel *On the Road* (1957). Kesey's trip was chronicled in Tom Wolfe's *Electric Kool-Aid Acid Test* (1968), which solidified Kesey's position as a cultural icon.

Ken Kesey was born on 17 September 1935 in La Junta, Colorado, to Fred and Geneva Kesey. In 1946, after Fred's World War II service in the U.S. Navy, the family—by that time including a second son (Joe, known as Chuck)—moved to Springfield, Oregon. Fred became a prominent figure in the dairy industry in Oregon, running a successful creamery and founding the Eugene Farmers Co-operative.

Kesey's high school and college years gave little indication of the type of cultural outlaw that he later would become. At Springfield High School, he was named "most likely to succeed" among the 1953 graduates. A well-rounded student, he did well academically, while also participating in football and wrestling, designing sets for plays, and winning an award for his acting. At the University of Oregon, Kesey majored in speech and communications, starred in wrestling (almost making the 1960 Olympic team), acted in university productions, began to write fiction, married childhood sweetheart Faye Haxby, and earned a Woodrow Wilson Fellowship to graduate school.

With his Wilson fellowship, Kesey entered the creative writing program at Stanford University in the fall of 1958. There he studied under such writing luminaries as Wallace Stegner, Malcolm Cow-

Ken Kesey established a strong bridge between the Beats and the psychedelic revolution. (Christopher Felver/Corbis)

ley, and Frank O'Connor (the latter two visiting professors) and encountered several other students who later became successful authors, including Larry McMurtry, Robert Stone, and Wendell Berry. He also met Ken Babbs, who became a lifelong friend and had a major impact on Kesey's life.

Kesey and his wife lived in a one-block area of Menlo Park near Stanford called Perry Lane. In this bohemian neighborhood, Kesey and friends modeled their lifestyle on the Beat culture of San Francisco's North Beach. Their parties featured heavy wine drinking, marijuana and LSD, body painting, strobe lights, and unusual costumes. Vic Lovell, one of Kesey's Perry Lane friends and the person to whom Kesey dedicated *One Flew Over the Cuckoo's Nest*, encouraged Kesey to volunteer for drug experiments at the Veterans' Hospital in Menlo Park. Kesey did so during 1961, taking LSD and other hallucinatory drugs and then writing accounts of their effects on him. Kesey later worked at the hospital as a psychiatric aide.

Kesey's Veterans' Hospital experiences provided much of the material for *Cuckoo's Nest* and further cemented the connection to drugs that shaped Kesey's public persona for the rest of his life. The novel is narrated from the hallucinatory point of view of Chief Bromden, an inmate in a psychiatric ward. The novel received both popular and critical acclaim, quickly becoming a standard in college classrooms. It was usually interpreted as an exposition of an unfeeling, authoritarian society (represented by Nurse Ratched) attempting to destroy individual freedom and spontaneity (as Randle Patrick McMurphy, a former work-farm prisoner, tries to encourage individual, nonconformist expression by his fellow inmates, only to be subjected to a lobotomy).

The Keseys were forced to leave Perry Lane in 1963 when a developer purchased the area and bulldozed the houses. The Keseys then bought a home at La Honda, California, where their new friends included Neal Cassady. In the following spring, Kesey completed the novel *Sometimes a Great Notion* (1964). At his new home, he hosted parties that continued the extravagant recreational practices of Perry Lane. Kesey referred to these events as acid tests, due to the participants' generous use of LSD surrounded by blaring music and Day-Glo colors. Surviving the party meant passing the "test." Eventually, Kesey made his parties more public by holding them in the Longshoreman's Hall, at Muir Beach, or in other public venues.

When publication of *Sometimes a Great Notion* required a trip to New York, Kesey purchased a 1939 International Harvester school bus; named it Furthur; gave it a psychedelic painting; outfitted it with movie, stereo, and recording equipment; and stocked it with marijuana and LSD. Accompanied by a group of friends called the Merry Pranksters, Kesey took a circuitous route to New York across the South. The trip began in June 1964, with Neal Cassady doing much of the driving. Kesey and his Pranksters punctuated their trip with performances on top of the bus, a journey chronicled by Tom

Wolfe in his book *The Electric Kool-Aid Acid Test* (1968). In New York City, Kesey was introduced by Cassady to the prominent Beats Allen Ginsberg and Jack Kerouac. Kesey and the Pranksters, with Ginsberg along, then visited LSD guru Timothy Leary in Millbrook, New York. During the trip from La Honda to New York and back, Kesey and the Pranksters shot a great deal of film, which they called "The Movie." Kesey's combination of drug use, psychedelic colors, and a communal lifestyle, made all the more notable by his personal fame and flamboyance, helped to establish hallmarks of the hippie culture throughout the decade and into the 1970s.

After the first two novels and the bus trip with the Merry Pranksters, Kesey's writing career and personal life both slid off track. He was arrested in April 1965 for marijuana possession, but continued his acid-test parties in his house, adding to his guest list members of the Hell's Angels motorcycle gang, to whom he had been introduced by journalist Hunter S. Thompson. His extensive use of drugs began seriously to affect him physically and mentally. He imagined himself a kind of omnipotent god and at times was unable to speak coherently. He put on increasingly public acid tests, distributing LSD to anyone who came, behavior that alienated him from mainstream society.

Kesey was found guilty of drug possession on 17 January 1966 and two days later was arrested again for possession of drugs while with nineteen-year-old Carolyn Adams, known as Mountain Girl, with whom he had a daughter, Sunshine. Kesey fled to Mexico, where he remained for most of 1966; he finally returned in September and was apprehended by the authorities in October. Two trials ended in hung juries, after which Kesey pleaded *nolo contendere* to knowingly being in the presence of marijuana. He entered San Mateo Country Jail in June 1967 to serve his time for both this marijuana charge as well as the previous conviction. Kesey later was transferred to the San Mateo County Sheriff's Honor Camp and released in November.

After his release, Kesey moved with Faye and their children, daughter Shannon and sons Zane and Jed, to Pleasant Hill, Oregon. Sunshine, whose mother had married Merry Prankster George Walker during Kesey's stay in Mexico, also lived with the Keseys.

In Oregon, Kesey embarked on a much calmer life, returning to his rural roots on a farm where he raised cattle. He also regained his writing focus, although no subsequent publication equaled *One Flew Over the Cuckoo's Nest* in popularity.

Kesey coedited with Paul Krassner *The Last Supplement to the Whole Earth Catalogue* in 1971. In the same year the film version of *Sometimes a Great Notion* was released, starring Paul Newman and Henry Fonda, with Newman also directing; and the stage version of *Cuckoo's Nest* opened in New York, where it had enjoyed an earlier run in 1963 with Kirk Douglas in the lead.

Kesey's *Garage Sale* was published in 1973, a collection including letters, interviews, and unpublished writings, among them the screenplay "Over the Border," based on Kesey's adventures as a fugitive in Mexico. Also during the 1970s, Kesey visited Egypt to write a five-part series called "The Search for the Secret Pyramid" for *Rolling Stone*, published the partly autobiographical "Abdul and Ebenezer" in *Esquire* about life on a dairy farm, and began a magazine called *Spit in the Ocean*, which ran for seven issues from 1974 to 2003, with the last issue serving as a tribute to Kesey edited by Ed McClanahan. In *Spit in the Ocean*, Kesey serialized a novel entitled *Seven Prayers by Grandma Whittier*. In addition, he worked on the screenplay for *One Flew over the Cuckoo's Nest* but left the project after a dispute over the film's changed perspective from Chief Bromden to Randle Patrick McMurphy, played by Jack Nicholson. Although Kesey did not approve of the final product, the 1975 film was named best picture of the year by the Academy of Motion Picture Arts and Sciences and also won Oscars for best director (Milos Foreman), best actor (Nicholson), and best actress (Louise Fletcher as Nurse Ratched).

During the final decades of his life, Kesey continued to raise cattle on his Oregon farm and write, while also teaching and performing. Later books included *The Day after Superman Died* (1980), a tribute to Neal Cassady that originally appeared in *Esquire*; *Demon Box* (1986), a collection of essays and articles; the novel *The Further Inquiry* (1990), which includes an imagined trial of Neal Cassady's ghost with a courtroom re-creation of the 1964 bus trip; another novel, *Sailor Song* (1992), featuring hippies in an Alaskan fishing village overrun by a movie company; *Last Go Round* (1994), a fictional account of the last Oregon roundup, which occurred in 1911; and the children's books *Little Tricker the Squirrel Meets Big Double the Bear* (1990) and *The Sea Lion* (1991). Ironically, the counterculture hero made the Library of Congress's list of recommended children's books in 1991 with *Little Tricker*.

During the late 1980s, Kesey returned to the classroom setting, where he had excelled as a student, to teach at the University of Oregon. He also took to the stage, sometimes with longtime friend Ken Babbs, to offer audiences a look at Ken Kesey the Prankster. Attired in black-and-white-striped pants, striped shoes, and top hat, and traveling in a Mark II version of his original psychedelic bus, he offered humor, readings, and film footage from the 1960s. Unfortunately, these later years were not without personal tragedy, as Kesey lost one of his sons, Jed, in a van accident in 1984. An athlete like his father, Jed was traveling with his University of Oregon wrestling team when the accident occurred.

Ken Kesey died on 10 November 2001 of liver cancer in an Oregon hospital. A man of many accomplishments, he nonetheless will be remembered primarily for his novel *One Flew Over the Cuckoo's Nest*, the 1964 Merry Pranksters bus trip, his prominent position in the 1960s drug culture, and his role as a major transitional figure from the Beats to the hippies.

—*Edward J. Rielly*

## Principal Works

*One Flew over the Cuckoo's Nest*, 1962; *Sometimes a Great Notion*, 1964; *Ken Kesey's Garage Sale*, 1973; "The Search for the Secret Pyramid," *Rolling Stone* 21 November 1974; "Abdul and Ebeneezer," *Esquire* March 1976; *The Day after Superman Died*, 1980; *Demon Box*, 1987; *The Further Inquiry*, 1990; *Little Tricker the Squirrel Meets Big Double the Bear*, 1988; *Sailor Song*, 1992; with Ken Babbs, *Last Go Round*, 1994; *Kesey's Jail Journal*, 2003.

## Bibliographical References

Ken Babbs and Paul Perry, *On the Bus: The Complete Guide to the Legendary Trip of Ken Kesey and the Merry Pranksters,* 1990; Lawrence Kappel, *Readings on "One Flew Over the Cuckoo's Nest,"* 1999; Barry H. Leeds, *Ken Kesey,* 1981; M. Gilbert Porter, *The Art of Grit: Ken Kesey's Fiction,* 1982; Elaine B. Safer, *The Contemporary American Comic Epic: The Novels of Barth, Pynchon, Gaddis, and Kesey,* 1988; George J. Searles, ed., *A Casebook on Ken Kesey's "One Flew Over the Cuckoo's Nest,"* 1992; Stephen L. Tanner, *Ken Kesey,* 1983; Peter O. Whitmer and Bruce Vanwyngarden, *Aquarius Revisited: Seven Who Created the Sixties Counterculture That Changed America,* 1987.

**See also** Merry Pranksters; Furthur/Further; Perry Lane; Cassady, Neal; Drugs; Kerouac, Jack; Wolfe, Tom; Native American Cultures; Mental Illness

## Kinsey Report

In 1948, Dr. Alfred Kinsey of Indiana University published his groundbreaking study *Sexual Behavior in the Human Male*—better known as the first "Kinsey Report." In this volume, to widespread controversy, Kinsey published the results of face-to-face interviews with thousands of American men who revealed sexual habits that were both shocking and enormously liberating at the same time. Most men confessed that they masturbated on a regular basis, many described having sex outside of marriage, many had had homosexual experiences, and a small number even confessed to intercourse with animals.

In his analysis of these surprising results, Kinsey made a point of insisting that sexual activity should be separated from traditional moral judgments. He was one of the first people to take this position in an official capacity, and his report had an enormous influence on the Beat culture of the 1950s, when bohemian lifestyles became increasingly acceptable—at least in places like Greenwich Village—for the very first time.

Although happily married, Kinsey was basically homosexual by inclination, with a strong sadomasochistic bent. Many conservative critics of the Kinsey Report came to believe that Kinsey's work

Alfred Kinsey's studies helped Americans to understand their own sexual behavior. (Library of Congress)

grew out of his compulsion to "prove" that homosexuality is "normal." These allegations have recently been repeated in a pair of controversial biographies of Kinsey, *Alfred C. Kinsey: A Public/Private Life,* by James H. Jones, published in 1997; and *Kinsey: Crimes and Consequences,* by Judith Riesman, published in 1999.

Alfred Kinsey's untimely death in 1956 was believed by many to be the result of his tendency toward overwork, exacerbated by the pressure and outcry over the publication of the second "Kinsey Report," *Sexual Behavior in the Human Female,* which was published in 1953.

—*Mikita Brottman*

## Bibliographical References

Jonathan Gathorne-Hardy, *Sex: The Measure of All Things,* 2000; James H. Jones, *Alfred C. Kinsey: A Public/Private Life,* 1997; Paul A. Robinson, *The*

*Modernization of Sex: Havelock Ellis, Alfred Kinsey, William Masters, and Virginia Johnson*, 1976; Judith Riesman, *Kinsey: Crimes and Consequences*, 1999.

## Kline, Franz (1910–1962)

Painter; central figure in abstract expressionist movement. Born in Wilkes Barre, Pennsylvania, Kline studied at the Boston Art Students' League and at London's Heatherley's Art School during the 1930s. He established residence in New York City in 1939 and began to produce cityscapes, landscapes, murals, and portraits. In 1943 he began his association with Willem de Kooning, and soon he was also friends with Jackson Pollock. In the late 1940s Kline came into the mature period of his abstract expressionism, completing works in black and white marked by bold, slashing strokes. His solo exhibit at the Egan Gallery in New York in 1950 established him as a major figure in the abstract expressionist movement. After his death, the Gallery of Modern Art in Washington, D.C., opened a memorial exhibition.

In "New York Scenes," which is included in *Lonesome Traveler* (1960), Jack Kerouac refers to Franz Kline as a mysterious, wondrous American painter known for his black spiderwebs (116). In *The Gay Sunshine Interview* (1974), which is reprinted in *Spontaneous Mind*, ed. David Carter (2001), Allen Ginsberg refers to his excitement about Franz Kline and other artists who were Ginsberg's friends and part of a fresh artistic movement in New York (322).

—*William Lawlor*

### Bibliographical References

Compare Fielding Dawson, *An Emotional Memoir of Franz Kline*, 1967, with Harry F. Gaugh, *The Vital Gesture: Franz Kline*, 1985; Daniel A Siedell, "Art Criticism as Narrative Strategy: Clement Greenberg's Encounter with Franz Kline," *Journal of Modern Literature* 26.3/4 (Summer 2003): 47–62, considers Kline's critical reception.

*See also* Painting

## Konitz, Lee (1927–)

Saxophonist; plays alto, soprano, and tenor saxophone, but is best known for a smooth sound and a style that is free from unnecessary complications. Konitz worked with Miles Davis on the *Birth of the Cool* sessions in the late 1940s.

In "New York Scenes," which is included in *Lonesome Traveler* (1960), Jack Kerouac refers to the performances of Lee Konitz in clubs in Greenwich Village such as the Village Vanguard and the Village Gate, but Kerouac laments that the high prices at such clubs stifle the enjoyment of jazz (114).

—*William Lawlor*

### Bibliographical References

On the set of audio recordings called *The Beat Generation*, 1992, one can hear "Bernie's Tune," which features Lee Konitz with the Gerry Mulligan Quartet. On the CD *Birth of the Cool*, 1989, one can hear Konitz play alto sax with Miles Davis and other musicians. Ira Gitler, *Jazz Masters of the Forties*, 1966, gives background on Konitz's life and career.

*See also* Music

## Krebs, Maynard G.

Bob Denver's caricature of the beatnik presented on *The Many Loves of Dobie Gillis*, a television comedy popular in the United States (1959–1963).

Based on Max Shulman's book *The Many Loves of Dobie Gillis*, the program featured Dobie, played by Duane Hickman, who often sat in front of Rodin's *The Thinker* (1880), assuming the pose of the thinker and pondering personal problems. Maynard, who was not part of Shulman's original text, was Dobie's "good buddy." Although Maynard failed to live up to the values that parents endorsed, he appealed to young viewers because of his mild and lovable rebellion.

Maynard wore a goatee and sweatshirt. His walk was expressively personalized, his language peppered with phrases such as "like," "like wow," and the responsive question "You rang?" He was fascinated by the film *The Monster that Devoured Cleve-*

*land,* which perpetually was screened at the Bijou, and he loved to watch the wrecking ball smashing against the old Endicott Building. Denver says he visited bohemian coffee houses in order to develop the language, style, attitude, and appearance he needed for the role.

Maynard remained a caricature of the Beats, and despite references to bop musicians and expressions of bohemian taste, he never revealed the understanding of literature, religion, and history that was connected with the real Beats. Nevertheless, Maynard popularized an alternative lifestyle and opened hearts in young America to his peculiar yet charming personality.

—*William Lawlor*

## Bibliographical References

See Max Shulman, *The Many Loves of Dobie Gillis,* 1951; see also Bob Denver, *Gilligan, Maynard, and Me,* 1993. See also Nina C. Liebman, *Living Room Lectures: The Fifties Family in Film and Television,* 1995; John J. O'Connor, "The Many Loves of Dobie Gillis," *New York Times,* 3 February 1974: 2.19.

***See also*** Beat and Beatnik; Styles of Dress, The Beats and.

## Krim, Seymour (1922–1989)

Seymour Krim's stature as a Beat writer stems primarily from three sources: the no-holds-barred confessional journalism of his first collection, *Views of a Nearsighted Cannoneer* (1961), his editing of *The Beats* (1960), and "The Kerouac Legacy," originally printed as the introduction to Jack Kerouac's *Desolation Angels* (1965). Though none of Krim's four collections is currently in print, his critical voice offers a prescient perspective on American literary culture of the 1950s and 1960s.

Born in 1922 and raised in Manhattan, Krim briefly attended the University of North Carolina before returning to New York. His primary visibility until the mid-1950s was as a critic in conventional literary venues such as *The New York Times Book Review, Commentary, Commonweal,* and the *Partisan Review.* After a mental breakdown in 1955, Krim reemerged in the late 1950s as a writer clearly

working closer to the bone, producing a highly personal, engaged journalism that presaged Tom Wolfe's and Hunter Thompson's work in the 1960s. *The Beats,* in which Krim's own "The Insanity Bit" appears, gathered for the first time in a single volume representative work of Ginsberg, Kerouac, Snyder, Corso, Holmes, di Prima, Burroughs, Selby, Ferlinghetti, Mailer, and others. Krim's "The Kerouac Legacy," written at a time when Kerouac's critical and personal star was at ebb, is perhaps the first serious revision of Kerouac's oeuvre following a decade of critical disparagement of his work. Aside from the aforementioned texts, Krim's work is collected in *Shake It for the World, Smartass* (1970), *You & Me* (1974), and a posthumous collection. He died an apparent suicide in 1989.

—*Tracy Santa*

## Principal Works

The posthumous collection is *What's This Cat's Story? The Best of Seymour Krim,* ed. Peggy Brooks, 1991; *Views of a Nearsighted Cannoneer,* a set of autobiographical essays, appeared first as an incomplete edition in 1961, but the complete edition, including a foreword by Norman Mailer, appeared in 1968. Krim's other works include *Shake It for the World, Smartass,* 1970, and *You and Me,* 1974. Krim is the editor of two books: *The Beats,* 1960, and *Manhattan: Stories of a Great City,* 1954.

## Bibliographical References

In Ann Charters, ed., *The Beats: Literary Bohemians in Postwar America,* 1983, Joseph Wenke's "Seymour Krim" provides background on Krim. In Theodore Solotaroff, *The Red Hot Vacuum and Other Pieces on the Writing of the Sixties,* 1970, one finds a review of Krim.

## Krupa, Gene (1909–1973)

Jazz drummer; major figure of the swing era; educator. In the early 1930s Krupa recorded with Benny Goodman and played with Goodman's big band. In 1938, Krupa left Goodman to form his own band, which featured, among many others, Roy Eldridge. In 1943, Krupa faced charges that he had contributed to the delinquency of a minor, and these charges stalled his career. However, overcoming the charges on appeal, Krupa reestablished himself in the late forties as a top band leader, especially because of his showmanship in performing drum solos. Later in his career Krupa dedicated himself to teaching percussion to young musicians.

—William Lawlor

## Bibliographical References

Compare Bruce H. Klauber, *World of Gene Krupa: That Legendary Drumming Man*, 1990, with Bruce Crowther, *Gene Krupa: His Life and Times*, 1987.

*See also* Music

## Kupferberg, Tuli (1923–)

Poet, self-proclaimed anarchist, and vocalist for the the Fugs, Tuli Kupferberg is a foundation figure in the Beat Generation. A native New Yorker and graduate of Brooklyn College, Kupferberg wrote poetry that was a staple of the Beats in the 1950s. His voice remained prominent among the hippies of the 1960s, when his raucous vocals and lyrics for the Fugs exposed the angry nerve pulsating just beneath the veneer of the Summer of Love.

Generally perverse in tone and obscene in content, Kupferberg's poetry satirizes almost every facet of human life. Sexual repression and politics are among the most prominent of Kupferberg's subjects. Often illustrated with his own cartoons, Kupferberg's publications include books such as *In Media's Feces* (1986). Many of his approximately twenty books have titles that refer to a thousand and new ways to do things, as in *1001 Ways to Beat the Draft* (1967).

A nonmusician who could neither read music nor play an instrument, Kupferberg nevertheless became a founding member of the 1960s band "The Fugs." For Kupferberg, however, poetry and music are the same thing, so a nonmusician becoming famous as a member of an avant-garde New York rock band is not incongruous to him. Known for encouraging audience participation in the Fugs' performances, Kupferberg has developed a style that often includes taking well-known melodies, such as "My Country Tis of Thee," and setting new lyrics to them. The new lyrics are almost always obscene and scatological and usually promote Kupferberg's anarchist ideas. After the band's dissolution in the late 1960s, Kupferberg continued producing performance art with The Revolving Theater and films.

—Larry Adams

## Principal Works

After founding the magazine *Birth* in 1958, Kupferberg created Birth Press, which enabled him to produce three of his own books: *Beating*, 1959; *Selected Fruits and Nuts, from One Crazy Month in Spring Not So Long Ago*, 1959; and *Snow Job Poems 1946–1959*, 1959.

## Bibliographical References

Fred W. McDarrah and Gloria S. McDarrah, *Beat Generation*, 1996; Fred W. McDarrah, *Kerouac and Friends*, 1985; Barry Miles, *The Beat Hotel*, 2000; Jon Pareles and Patricia Romanowski, eds., *Rolling Stone Encyclopedia of Rock & Roll*, 1983.

*See also* Sanders, Ed; Little Magazines

## Kyger, Joanne (1934–)

Writer and one of the few women intimately involved with both the Beat movement and the San Francisco Renaissance of the late 1950s and early 1960s, Joanne Kyger combined the Beat wanderlust and struggle for uncensored self-expression with Zen Buddhism, producing written works rooted in daily life. Kyger turned to poetry after the "Howl" obscenity trial was in full swing and from the opposite coast of the New York–based Beats, and she brought a singular female presence to the San Francisco Renaissance surrounding Jack Spicer and Robert Duncan. Later, as the Beats journeyed west, she met and traveled with Gary Snyder and Allen Ginsberg. Her *Japan and India Journals* (1981) detail this experience, including her increasing interest in Zen Buddhism and writing poetry. As both a memoirist of the Beat Generation and a poet, Kyger created an inviting and instantaneous voice. Because of her integration of the New York Beats and the San Francisco Renaissance, Kyger remains an important figure, both as a balance to the male dominance of these movements and as a writer who explored the quotidian through the cosmic.

Kyger was born on 19 November 1934 in Vallejo, California. The daughter of a career naval officer, Kyger spent her early years with the American naval force in China. Her family returned to Long Beach, California, where Kyger attended elementary school and published her first poem, a work dictated to her teacher, who submitted it to the school's literary magazine. Subsequently, Kyger's family moved to Santa Barbara, where Kyger became a features editor for the high school newspaper. Afterwards, she attended the University of California at Santa Barbara, studying philosophy and experimenting with poetry at a workshop hosted by the Santa Barbara Public Library.

Leaving the university one unit shy of a degree, Kyger made her way to San Francisco in 1957, where she took an apartment in North Beach, discovered City Lights Bookstore, and read "Howl" as it was on trial for obscenity. Tremendously excited by "Howl," Kyger worked her way into the North Beach poetry scene. Through Joe Dunn, she met the enclave surrounding Jack Spicer and Robert Duncan, wherein she became known as "Miss Kids," for calling others "kid" and for being the youngest poet there. The Beat writers had traveled west by this time, and Kyger also worked with them, and over the next three years her writing and pursuit of Zen Buddhism flourished as she moved into the East-West House, a communal living project based in Buddhism and Japanese culture.

By 1960, Kyger was in love with Beat poet Gary Snyder, and she agreed to accompany him to Japan. Under the dictates of Snyder's sponsor, the director of Kyoto's Zen Institute, Kyger and Snyder married in order to live together at the Institute, where Snyder was to teach part-time. During her four years in Japan, Kyger continued to write, taking refuge in a journal later published as *The Japan and India Journals*. She chronicled her experiences studying flower arranging, practicing Zen Buddhism, and writing poetry, as well as confronting the difficulties of daily life in another culture—from drawing seventy-five buckets of well water for a bath to taking English-speaking parts in low-budget Japanese films. These years provided the foundation for her first book of poems, *The Tapestry and the Web*, and after returning to San Francisco in 1964 and divorcing Snyder, she saw this book published in 1965. These poems exemplify Kyger's primary poetic concerns: the movement and placement of the line on the page, the Buddhist notion of fully inhabiting a moment, and the connection of the individual to the archetypal. Structuring the work around Homer's *Odyssey*, Kyger allowed herself the Penelope role, but centralized that role to explore her place as a woman surrounded by the mythic male poets of the Beats and San Francisco Renaissance.

Following this publication, Kyger traveled to Europe and New York before settling in Bolinas, California, in 1969. Although she met poets Anne Waldman and Lewis Warsh in New York and their Angel Hair Press published her book *Joanne: A Novel from the Inside Out* (1970), Kyger disliked New York and returned to San Francisco, where she has remained except when teaching at the Naropa Institute in Boulder, Colorado.

*The Japan and India Journals* remains Kyger's most widely read work, yet her poetry contains some of the wisest Beat expressions of Buddhism as the poems focus on a single, often domestic moment wherein the verse experiences a fully present being. Further, in recognizing the value of these domestic moments, Kyger opened the Beat movement's urgency for enlightenment on the road to transcendence within the home.

—*Jennifer Love*

## Principal Works

Poetry: *The Tapestry and the Web*, 1965; *Joanne: A Novel from the Inside Out*, 1970; *Places to Go*, 1970; *Trip Out and Fall Back*, 1975; *All This Every Day*, 1975; *Up My Coast*, 1977; *The Wonderful Focus of You*, 1980; *Mexico Blonde*, 1981; *Going On: Selected Poems 1958–1980*, 1983; *Phenomenological*, 1989; *Just Space: Poems*

1979–1989, 1991; *Some Life*, 2000; *Selected Works*, 2001.

Prose: *The Japan and India Journals, 1960–1964*, 1981.

## Bibliographical References

No biography of Joanne Kyger exists; however, biographical material can be found in several sources: Brenda Knight provides a brief biography in *Women of the Beat Generation*, 1996; in *San Francisco Beat: Talking with the Poets*, 2001, David Meltzer interviews Kyger regarding her life as a poet; Alice Notley provides a feminist analysis in "Joanne Kyger's Poetry" in *Arshile, A Magazine of the Arts* 5 (1996); in *Big Sky Mind: Buddhism and the Beat Generation*, 1995, Carole Tonkinson comments on Kyger's Buddhist works; Kyger's correspondence from 1957–1975 is housed at the University of California, San Diego.

***See also*** Snyder, Gary; Eastern Culture

## La Vigne, Robert (1928–)

Painter, especially of portraits of members of the Beat Generation. In 1954, La Vigne met Allen Ginsberg by chance in San Francisco at Foster's Cafeteria, and they had a lively conversation about art and painters. La Vigne invited Ginsberg to view La Vigne's work at the painter's nearby apartment. Several nudes of a young man intrigued Ginsberg, and when asked who the model was, La Vigne informed Ginsberg that the model was Peter, who also lived in the apartment. At that moment Peter Orlovsky walked into the room, and Allen immediately fell in love. At that time, La Vigne and Orlovsky were homosexually involved, but soon Ginsberg and Orlovsky established their lifelong connection.

The exhibition "Beat Culture and the New America 1950–1965" at the Whitney Museum in 1995 included La Vigne's painting and sketches of Orlovsky, portraits of Gregory Corso and Jack Kerouac, and cover art for John Wiener's *The Hotel Wentley Poems*. La Vigne also won an Obie Award (1967–1968) for his set designs for *A Midsummer Night's Dream* and *Endecott and the Red Cross*.

—*William Lawlor*

### Bibliographical References

Ginsberg relates the story of meeting Orlovsky in *Spontaneous Mind*, ed. David Carter, 2001: 322–324. *Beat Culture and the New America*, ed. Lisa Phillips, 1995, reproduces some of La Vigne's sketches and drawings; in the same book is a photo of La Vigne at the Hotel Wentley—in the background is the famous nude of Peter Orlovsky.

*See also* Ginsberg, Allen; Orlovsky, Peter; Wieners, John; Whitney Museum Exhibition: Beat Culture and the New America 1950–1965; Painting

## Lamantia, Philip (1927–2005)

Philip Lamantia is perhaps most aptly called a surrealist poet, rather than a Beat. His poetry is predominantly visionary in scope and style. However, he has deep ties to members of the Beat Generation, not least of which was his participation at the famous 6 Gallery reading, where "Howl" was unleashed to the world. Further ties to the Beat Generation come from his work being published by Lawrence Ferlinghetti's City Lights Press, and his position as the initial bond between Allen Ginsberg and the Beats and Kenneth Rexroth's circle of writers. More generally, Lamantia shares a sense of mystic spiritual desire with Ginsberg, Kerouac, and the other major Beat voices.

Philip Lamantia was born on 23 October 1927 in San Francisco. His parents were Italian immigrants, connecting him with many of his Beat peers as a first-generation American. Lamantia discovered poetry early on in school, but wrote in a more daring and precocious style than is typical for children. By junior high school he had discovered writers of the macabre like H. P. Lovecraft and Edgar Allan Poe. Choosing to imitate his new heroes, he found himself expelled for a period for "intellectual delinquency."

By his high school years, Lamantia had moved on to more academic surrealists. After a visit to the San Francisco Museum of Art featuring an exhibit of Dali and Miro, Lamantia began to write surrealist poetry. He first rose to the attention of Kenneth Rexroth, who recognized in Lamantia an emerging poetic talent. Through Rexroth's guidance, Lamantia realized that for his growth as a surrealist to continue he would have to relocate to New York, then the heart of the surrealist movement. He found himself welcomed with open arms by the ruling surrealists, with André Breton taking him firmly under his wing as a protégé.

Breton lavished praise on Lamantia and helped guide his poetic development, introducing him to a wide range of writers and artists. Breton aided Lamantia in publishing his poetry as part of Breton's project, *VVV*, in 1943 (with Lamantia still just fifteen). Through Breton's guidance, Lamantia placed many poems with various avant-garde poetry journals, including Charles Henri Ford's *View*. Three years later, Lamantia published his first full collection of poetry, *Erotic Poems* (1946).

Lamantia also met many of the leading modernists, including Tennessee Williams. While these writers were interesting to Lamantia, none held the powerful position for him that Rexroth or Breton did. Following World War II, Lamantia decided to relocate back to San Francisco, where he rejoined Rexroth's greatly expanded circle—a group that now included Robert Duncan and William Everson. The four poets found themselves linked through a common desire for mystical and visionary advancement. Each possessed an individual perspective on the subject, but there was a common thread that bound them to one another.

Yet Lamantia never felt comfortable lumped in with any one group of writers, and this continued sense of restless dissatisfaction caused him to travel back to New York in the late 1940s. Now, Lamantia encountered the rising figures of the Beat Generation—people like Allen Ginsberg and Carl Solomon. Lamantia found a shared sense of vision with these writers and they became fast friends. It was Lamantia who helped encourage Ginsberg and his cohorts to come out to San Francisco and meet up with Rexroth and his circle of poets.

In 1956, with Rexroth serving as master of ceremonies, the historic 6 Gallery reading was arranged. Lamantia was slated to participate, along with the diverse poetic voices of Michael McClure, Allen Ginsberg, Philip Whalen, and Gary Snyder. Lamantia was the first poet to read that night, but instead of using his own surrealist poetry, he presented the work of his friend, John Hoffman, who had recently died of an apparent peyote overdose. This activity is emblematic of the relationship that exists between Lamantia and the Beats—he is a sympathetic fellow traveler, but not one walking exactly the same path. In fact, Kerouac, in his send-up of the reading found in *Dharma Bums*, mocks Lamantia's reading as prissy, although Kerouac claimed he later came to appreciate Lamantia's work. Lamantia's path often crossed that of the Beats—in San Francisco he was frequently seen hanging out in Beat favorites, such as Foster's Cafeteria (a subject he immortalized in one of his poems). Lamantia was often in the company of Allen Ginsberg and later Peter Orlovsky.

Lamantia's second book of poetry, *Ekstasis* (1959), appeared following the 6 Gallery reading and solidified his growing reputation as the leading American-born surrealist of his generation. This text is often viewed in light of his latter-day Catholicism to mark the beginning of his serious interest in more traditional Western spiritual forms. The text was inspired by a visionary experience Lamantia had while traveling in northern Mexico—the experience itself is ambiguously related, but its spiritual impact on Lamantia is unquestionable. Lamantia's poetry suggests that it was a powerful vision of a Christian God figure, rather than the more varied and personal beings that populate most Beat literature.

Lamantia's poetry can be said to fully embrace the surrealist vision of tension in life between reality and a realization of the ubiquitous presence of suffering in that life. Lamantia's poetry, however, follows its own unique path. His work is clearly mystical—inspired by a questing desire for faith and understanding. This quest is mixed with his surrealist visions, producing startling and profound imagery. He is fascinated by the darkness underneath the veneer that makes up normal life and seeks ways to broach it. Lamantia has also served as a contributing editor of *Arsenal: Surrealist Subversion* and for decades has remained active in avant-garde poetry circles.

In more recent years, Lamantia has increasingly turned toward traditional Catholicism. His lifelong vision quest—after trips through drugs, mysticism, and Eastern philosophies—appears to have brought him toward Franciscan and Dominican modes of belief. Lamantia is often quoted stressing the importance of St. Francis in the future (and past) of his beloved San Francisco.

—*John M. Carey*

## Principal Works
*Erotic Poems,* 1946; *Ekstasis,* 1959; *Touch of the Marvelous,* 1966; *Becoming Visible,* 1981; and *Meadowlark,* 1986. *Selected Poems (1943–1966)* was published in 1967 by City Lights. *Bed of Sphinxes: New & Selected Poems (1943–1993)* followed from City Lights in 1997.

## Bibliographical References
Nancy J. Peters offers background on Lamantia in "Philip Lamantia" in Ann Charters, ed., *The Beats: Literary Bohemians in Postwar America,* 1983: 329–336; Steven Watson includes commentary on Lamantia in *The Birth of the Beat Generation,* 1995: 215–217; Neeli Cherkovski includes the chapter "Mostly Visible" in *Whitman's Wild Children,* 1988: 81–99.

*See also* 6 Gallery Reading; Breton, André

## Landesman, Jay (1919–), and Fran Landesman (1927–)

Born Irving Ned Landesman in St. Louis in 1919, Landesman changed his name to Jay after reading *The Great Gatsby* as a child. While never himself a headline maker, Jay Landesman and his wife Fran were both responsible for bringing to public attention some of the most talented but still at the time unrecognized writers, artists, performers, and

thinkers of the 1950s and 1960s. In notes on the back cover of *Rebel without Applause* (1987), Landesman is credited by critic Kenneth Rexroth as being "the founder of the Beat generation," and by Norman Mailer as "the man who can be accused of starting it all." Landesman's most significant contribution to Beat culture was perhaps his originally conceived and executed lifestyle that, set against the conformity of the Eisenhower years, placed him at the center of a group of influential writers and thinkers who permanently changed American cultural values.

In the spring of 1948, Landesman published the first issue of his new journal *Neurotica,* a quarterly that became popular in the early fifties. Featuring work by Marshall McLuhan, Lawrence Durrell, Allen Ginsberg, and others, *Neurotica* was a smart mixture of literature and psychoanalysis, and now remembered mainly as the journal of the Beat writers. Vaguely dedicated to the proposition that a great deal could be said about "a culture clearly going insane," it was often daring and always interesting. In the first issue, Landesman set out the magazine's aims:

> *Neurotica* is a literary exposition, defense, and correlation of the problems and personalities that in our culture are defined as "neurotic." It is said that if you tie a piece of red cloth to a gull's leg its fellow-gulls will peck it to pieces: and *Neurotica* wishes to draw an analog to this observation and the plight of today's creative "anxious" man. We are interested in exploring the creativeness of this man who has been forced to live underground.

The early issues contained articles that mixed a serious intellectual tone with outlandish and controversial subjects, such as a piece on prostitution as a force for social good, and another on homosexuals who marry women. Another article covered fetishists like "Jack the Snipper"—a local fiend who secretly cut off locks of women's hair in the cinema—and another analyzed the attractions and drawbacks of the bar as a pick-up place. After eight issues of *Neurotica,* Landesman turned the magazine over to the joint editorship of Gershon Legman and John Clellon Holmes. However, Legman's "Castration" issue (Winter 1952) fell afoul of government censorship, and the magazine folded shortly afterwards. But in its prime, *Neurotica* had a national audience of a few thousand readers, some of whom still remember it very fondly.

Landesman and his wife Fran soon became well known in the Greenwich Village of the 1950s for their open-house parties, where friends and strangers mingled to the sounds of bop and jazz. Guests included Philip Rahv, the editor of *Partisan Review*, poet Delmore Schwartz, jazz singer Stella Brooks, and psychoanalyst Gregory Zilboorg. However, financial constraints eventually forced Landesman to return with Fran to his hometown of St. Louis, where in 1951 he took over his family's antique business. The stability of regular employment eventually gave the Landesmans the freedom to open their innovative cabaret theater, the Crystal Palace.

In this renovated building, like a cross between a church and a movie palace, the Landesmans introduced an unsuspecting audience to a wide range of radical performers, including Mike Nichols and Elaine May, Judith Malina, Leonard Bernstein, and the Smothers Brothers. Because many of these acts were not initially successful, Jay Landesman began staging productions of his own, and on 4 March 1959 the first production of *The Nervous Set*, a play about the Beat generation, featuring music by Tommy Wolf, took place. Lyrics to Wolf's tunes were penned by Fran Landesman, whose song "Spring Can Really Hang You Up the Most" was hailed as the Beat answer to T. S. Eliot.

*The Nervous Set* was an instant success in St. Louis. *Variety* particularly praised the musical numbers, noting that they "punctuate a tragi-comic scene that shifts back and forth from square Connecticut to beat Greenwich Village and Manhattan's tony Sutton Place," and are "tailored to the assorted beatniks, squares and snobs who punctuate the three acts" (qtd. in *Rebel without Applause* 216–217). The show was quickly sold to Broadway where, with a different cast, it failed to find an audience, becoming tagged as "that Beatnik show" at a time when beatniks were rapidly going out of fashion. The Landesmans' next theatrical venture, a musical version of Nelson Algren's novel *A Walk on the Wild Side* (1956), fared even worse, and was dismissed as an out-and-out flop.

The Landesmans had more success in the early 1960s with their lineup at the Crystal Palace, which hosted early performances by Woody Allen, Barbra Streisand, Lenny Bruce, and Phyllis Diller. Experimental theatrical productions—critically acclaimed, though often financially disastrous—included Mailer's *The Deer Park* (1955), Ionesco's *The Chairs* (published in French in 1954; translated into English in 1958), Beckett's *Krapp's Last Tape* (1958), and quirky one-act plays by Chandler Brossard. Fran Landesman soon became a well-known songwriting talent, responsible for such numbers as "I'm Bidin' My Time," and "The Ballad of the Sad Young Men."

By the midsixties Gaslight Square in St. Louis—home of the Crystal Palace—was becoming increasingly crime ridden, and the beatnik scene was long forgotten. Earlier visits to London had convinced the Landesmans that the scene in Chelsea was similar to that of Greenwich Village in the early 1950s, and that—unlike many Americans—the "angry young men" of the London scene fully appreciated the cultural significance of writers like Kerouac and Ginsberg. In 1964 the Landesmans made the move to London, where they settled with their two children, Cosmo and Miles.

In London, Fran Landesman continued her successful career as a songwriter, penning lyrics for songs by Jason McAuliffe, Alex Wilder, Steve Allen, George Shearing, and Dudley Moore. Jay first opened a talent agency, then promoted natural macrobiotic foods, then finally founded Polytantric Press, devoted to the publication of previously neglected or suppressed works of literature. The press was noted for such titles as *By Grand Central Station I Sat Down and Wept*, *The Punk*, and *The Private Case*. The entire run of *Neurotica* was reprinted in 1963 as *The Compleat Neurotica;* Jay Landesman's memoirs of the Beat years, *Rebel without Applause*, were published in 1987 by The Permanent Press. The Landesmans' eldest son, Cosmo

Landesman, is now well known as a British journalist, and his brother Miles is a music producer.

—*Mikita Brottman*

### Bibliographical References

See Jay Landesman, *Rebel without Applause,* 1987; Jay Landesman, ed., *Neurotica, 1948–1951,* 1981, is a reprint of *The Compleat Neurotica,* 1963; A CD of Jay Landesman, Fran Landesman, and Tommy Wolfe, *The Nervous Set,* 2000, has been released.

*See also* Theater

## Language and Idiom of the Beats

Chief amongst the concerns of Beat writers was the creation and codification of a new language or idiom that would capture and perpetuate their way of life. As a result, many of the words and sayings that were current with the Beats have become part of our everyday lexicon. Apart from old words reenergized with new meanings, as well as neologisms, which appear in Beat texts such as Allen Ginsberg's *Howl and Other Poems* or Jack Kerouac's *On the Road,* some early Beat writers took it upon themselves to collect and arrange catalogues of words or glossaries to explain the new lingo to the uninitiated and to give a more general view of how a living language was coming into being.

Dan Burley, in his *Original Handbook of Harlem Jive,* offers "The Jiver's Bible" in closing, in which he gives a list of some 1,000 words in alphabetical order. Earl Conrad, who wrote the introduction to the book, writes: "Dan's job represents a chemical change on language. Not a change that he has worked up himself, but rather one that he has seen in embryo on all sides of himself, and has picked it up, reported it, added to it and polished it" (5). For example, take these two better-known terms:

*Dig*—To understand, consider, appeal to, to comprehend, to remember, to sample, take, conceive, perceive, think, hand over (137).
*Groovy*—In keeping with a situation, the best thereof, highly enjoyable and/or entertaining, superb, great, tops, excellent. (139)

The Beats used a single, often one-syllable word to invoke a wide variety of related and unrelated meanings. However, an equally important aspect of Burley's collection is the somewhat rarer, but all the more interesting, longer sayings, which may sound strange to our ears today:

*Broom to the slammer that fronts the drape crib*—
Walk to the door of the closet where your clothes are kept (135).
*Playing the dozens with one's uncle's cousins*—
Doing everything wrong. (145)

These two idioms show how rhythm and rhyme can be used to create a memorable saying and reveal that a metaphor can intensify even the most banal events of daily life. With Beat idiom, the strict line that existed in America between the ways blacks and whites talked was forever blurred.

Another writer who took it upon himself to explain the new idiom was William S. Burroughs. At the end of *Junky,* which relates the narrator's agonizing addiction to heroin, Burroughs includes a "glossary" of about a hundred words, for which he provides an introduction. The narrator distinguishes between the language of pot smokers (jive talk) and the idiom of heroin addicts (junk talk); however, as the use of addictive drugs crosses over to groups that formerly only used marijuana, the two kinds of talk blend (153). If Burley's collection is concerned with jive talk, then that of Burroughs is concerned with junk talk. Thus, idiom within the Beat movement is marked by differences between one generation and the next.

Two expressions suffice to exemplify Burroughs's somewhat pessimistic rendition of Beat idiom. A "hot shot" is toxic and most often includes strychnine. Sold disguised as heroin or another addictive drug, the hot shot is provided by the drug seller as punishment to an addict who is serving as an informer to the authorities.

According to Burroughs's narrator, "kick" signifies multiple ideas. An intoxicating effect may be a kick. If a location spurs a reaction in a person, the place may be said to provide good or bad kicks. When combined with the word "on," the word

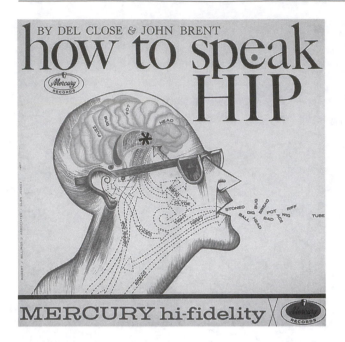

BY DEL CLOSE & JOHN BRENT
how to speak HIP
MERCURY hi-fidelity

All people who wanted to be cool needed to learn how to speak in hip language.

"kicks" creates the idea of special perception. The person "on kicks" perceives reality uniquely (156).

Burroughs's list provides examples of the words being used, while Burley's does not. Even with this minimal selection, one sees how equivocal some of these Beat terms actually were, and continue to be. Burroughs himself notes in closing that the language of drug users and hipsters evolves quickly, making the significance of phrases different with each passing year. Burroughs advises that hip language constantly renews itself (158).

A final, key player in Beat idiom is Lord Buckley. Buckley provided yet another link between black English vernacular and mainstream culture: first to the Beat youths in the 1950s, then to the AM disc jockeys of the 1960s, who brought the new language to the masses. Today, Lord Buckley's collection of words and sentences can be found online at his official website (www.lordbuckley.com). Called the "HIPesaurus," the list includes hundreds of entries such as these rare sentences and words: In the section "Nero," the phrase is "ALL HIGH FLIP OUT IN ORBIT MOTHER TO END ALL MOTHERS," which is meant to suggest the ultimate example of something. The narrator in "Nero" says, "Yeah, Nero was an All High Flip Out in Orbit Mother to end All Mothers!" In "The Gasser," the special language is "wanged," which conveys the idea of having a hard time. The speaker says, "Your Majesty, I've been billed, willed and twilled, I've been flung, wanged and looned, but I never dug no jazz like this last riff you put me on."

Taken as a whole, Beat idiom should thus be considered one of the lasting achievements of this important generation of American writers. Like a time capsule, these glossaries and indexes carry with them traces of their time that we can look back to both in wonder and surprise.

—Antony Adolf

**Bibliographical References**

If Lord Buckley, *Hiparama of the Classics* (1960) is difficult to acquire, one may visit www.lordbuckley.com. A fiftieth anniversary edition of William S. Burroughs, *Junky*, ed. Oliver Harris (2003) includes the glossary. See *Dan Burley's Original Handbook of Harlem Jive* (1944). See also Gregory Stephenson, *The Daybreak Boys: Essays on the Literature of the Beat Generation* (1990): 14–15; and David Herd, "'After All, What Else Is There to Say?': Ed Sanders and the Beat Aesthetic," *The Review of Contemporary Fiction* 19.1 (1999): 122–38.

## Leary, Timothy (1920–1996)

Timothy Leary, for all of his work as a behavioral psychologist, college professor, author, and lecturer, will be best remembered as a pioneer in the 1960s "Psychedelic Revolution," during which millions of people worldwide experimented with such mind-expanding drugs as psychedelic mushrooms, peyote, psilocybin, and, above all, LSD. Although not a member of the Beat Generation in the strictest sense, Leary served as an important bridge between the Beat Generation of the 1950s and the hippies a decade later.

Rebellious and precocious as a youth growing up in Massachusetts, Leary was the product of a hard-drinking, womanizing, often-absent father, who had difficulty holding a job, and a strict, conservative, deeply religious mother who prayed that her son would study for the Catholic priesthood. Leary, who idolized Mark Twain for his brilliance and wit, straddled the line between the straight-and-narrow and the mischievous, his youthful years marked by impressive academic achievement undermined by acts of rebellion that prohibited him from reaching a social and academic stature he otherwise might have easily attained.

He edited his high school's newspaper, only to fall into disfavor with the principal when he wrote an editorial rejecting the school's motto. In 1940, while a cadet at West Point, Leary received a formal "silencing" (an extended period during which he was forbidden to speak and others were forbidden to talk to him) after he confessed to providing liquor to underclassmen at the Army-Navy football game. After transferring to the University of Alabama, Leary was expelled for spending a night in the girls' dormitory. He eventually enlisted in the army for a stint that found him completing his undergraduate education, attending officers' training school, and meeting his first wife, Marianne. After military service, he received his master's degree in psychology from Washington State University and his Ph.D. from the University of California at Berkeley.

The early years of Leary's career were filled with great promise. His work as a clinical researcher was highly regarded, and his first book, *The Interpersonal Diagnosis of Personality* (1957), was voted book of the year by the American Psychological Association. He and his wife had two children, Susan and Jack, and by all indications they lived perfect, middle-class lives. However, the Leary marriage was a troubled one, and Marianne suffered from depression. When she committed suicide on Leary's birthday in 1959, Leary found himself at a professional crossroads, wondering if the study and practice of psychology were as useful as he once believed. He and his children moved to Europe, where Leary hoped to finish a new book. While in Italy, Leary met a vacationing Harvard dean and was eventually offered a lecturing position at the Ivy League school.

Leary ingested psychedelic mushrooms for the first time during the summer of 1960 while vacationing in Mexico, after completing his first year at Harvard. His introduction to the mushrooms was far from accidental. He had heard much about their effects on consciousness, and he was curious about how they might affect human personality and behavior. He was not disappointed. His initial encounter with mushrooms was a powerfully religious experience.

From that point on, Leary, convinced that these drugs could alter behavior for the better, approached mind-expanding drugs with the passion of a religious zealot. He plunged into an expansive study of their history and usage, and, through the Sandoz Laboratories in Switzerland, he obtained a large supply of psilocybin (a synthetic of the mushrooms) and, later, LSD. To the dismay of his Harvard peers, he and colleague Richard Alpert conducted numerous experiments with Harvard graduate students, inmates at a nearby prison, and students at a divinity school—all with encouraging results. Leary also offered the drugs to artists, musicians, and writers, including Allen Ginsberg, Jack Kerouac, and William S. Burroughs. Kerouac and Burroughs were unimpressed with psilocybin, but Ginsberg shared Leary's enthusiasm for the drug's potential to change behavior, and he and Leary, along with other Leary colleagues, began planning what they believed would be nothing less than a revolution in human consciousness.

Leary and Alpert were dismissed from Harvard in 1963, but not before their lectures, writings, and experiments attracted worldwide attention. Over the next few years, Leary published a series of controversial books, including *The Psychedelic Reader* (1965, an anthology of scholarly articles about mind-expanding drugs, which Leary edited); *The Politics of Ecstasy* (1968, a collection of his own articles and interviews); *The Psychedelic Experience* (1964, a guide for the psychedelic drug user, modeled on the *Tibetan Book of the Dead*); and *High Priest* (1968, the first of several Leary autobiographies). He

Dr. Timothy Leary was famous for his advice during the psychedelic revolution: "Turn on, tune in, drop out." (Library of Congress)

moved into a mansion in upstate New York, where he met his second wife, Rosemary Woodruff, and lived a communal life with Alpert and their followers. They stepped up their studies of psychedelic drugs, especially LSD.

Before long, Leary's name had become a household word. His slogan "turn on, tune in, drop out," became a catchphrase for a generation of youths as much at odds with the status quo as the Beat Generation youths had been a decade earlier. John Lennon mentioned Leary by name in his anthem, "Give Peace a Chance," and the Moody Blues immortalized him in their song, "Legend of a Mind."

The attention stroked Leary's substantial ego, but it also led to hardship. For more than a decade, Leary was harassed and arrested by the police and

vilified by government and scientific leaders. He was eventually arrested and convicted for a minor marijuana violation, and given a lengthy prison sentence. He escaped prison, fled to Africa and Europe (detailed in his 1973 book, *Confessions of a Hope Fiend*), and was captured in Kabul and returned to the United States. By the time he was released from prison, his influence and notoriety had greatly diminished, and while he was still popular on the college lecture circuit, he was never again viewed as more than an oddity or nostalgia item.

Leary used his explorations into the mind and consciousness in future studies, first when he delved into the artificial intelligence of computers and the evolution of the Internet, and, finally, when he learned that he had terminal cancer and was facing the ultimate transition in consciousness. He spent the last year of his life preparing for death, but rather than view it as a sad ending, he celebrated it as another adventure in life. His final book, *Design for Dying* (1997), addressed the important ways in which an individual could prepare for dying. After his death, some of his cremated remains were shot into space, as he had requested.

—*Michael Schumacher*

## Principal Works

*Interpersonal Diagnosis of Personality,* 1957; with Ralph Metzner and Richard Alpert, *The Psychedelic Experience,* 1964; *Psychedelic Prayers,* 1966; *Start Your Own Religion,* 1967; *High Priest,* 1968; *The Politics of Ecstasy,* 1968; *The Eagle Brief,* 1970; *Jail Notes,* 1970; *Neurologic,* 1973; *Confessions of a Hope Fiend,* 1973; *Starseed,* 1973; *Terra II,* 1974; *The Curse of the Oval Room,* 1974; *What Does a Woman Want?,* 1976; *Exo-Psychology,* 1977; *Neuropolitics,* 1977; *The Intelligent Agents,* 1979; *The Game of Life,* 1980; *Changing My Mind, among Others,* 1982; *Flashbacks,* 1983; ed., with Michael Horowitz and Vickie Marshall, *Chaos and Cyber Culture,* 1994; *Design for Dying,* 1997.

## Bibliographical References

Barry Miles, *Hippie,* 2004, includes discussion of Leary. Peter O. Whitmer, *Aquarius Revisited,* 1987, also covers Leary.

*See also* Drugs; Ginsberg, Allen; Be-In

## Legacy

If the Beat Generation begins in the 1940s and comes to public attention in the 1950s, then one must also see that the Beats have an enduring legacy. A second and third generation follows the Beats, and these succeeding generations carry forth the individuality and expressiveness that are the hallmarks of Beat culture.

*The Source* (1999), a film by Chuck Workman, suggests that the Beat Generation was the inspiration for the hippies and the counterculture of the sixties and early seventies. In Workman's view, the Beats established an alternative culture that the hippies recognized, appreciated, and applied. Michael McClure, who appears in the film, is satisfied that when he speaks to young people, he can see the Beat outlook in them. Johnny Depp, John Turturro, and Dennis Hopper visibly bring the literature of Beats forward to the next generation with their dramatic interpretations of famous passages from Kerouac, Ginsberg, and Burroughs.

Ed Sanders in "The Legacy of the Beats," which appears in *Beat Culture and the New America,* ed. Lisa Phillips (1995), describes various things that the Beats left as lessons for those who came after them (244–247). For example, Sanders suggests that Beats taught that people ought to overcome their tendency to be withdrawn; instead, people should be expressive and outgoing; moreover, people must appreciate the difficulty one has in overcoming inhibitions. Sanders says the Beats showed that people could stop saying no and could instead simply go, and when they went, they could find beauty in art and in their sensory experiences. The Beats insisted that to be gay is OK. And the Beats helped people know the pleasure of spontaneity, the beauty of the American environment, and the possibility of social change without violence.

Allen Ginsberg's prologue for *Beat Culture and the New America,* ed. Lisa Phillips (1995), provides an itemized list of effects the Beat Generation produced in society (17–19). Ginsberg refers to spiritual freedom, sexual freedom, and freedom from censorship. He credits the Beats with a revelation of the foolishness of laws prohibiting the use of marijuana. According to Ginsberg, the Beats contributed with their influential poetry and prose to developments in music that led to the acceptance of rhythm and blues, rock and roll, and other emerging musical forms as substantive art forms. And the Beats resisted militarization, industrialization, and regimentation in order to promote individuality, spirituality, and respect for native people, wildlife, and the environment.

Finally, one cannot overlook the legacy of the Beats in language and style. The Beat Generation is "cool" and their speech is "hip." Because of the choices the Beats made about their clothing, many restrictive and uncomfortable conventions in dress have faded away.

—*William Lawlor*

**Bibliographical References**

Ed Sanders's poem "The Legacy of the Beats" appears in *Beat Culture and the New America,* ed. Lisa Phillips, 1995: 244–247; *The Source,* 1999, is available in video; Allen Ginsberg's list of the effects of the Beat Generation is in *Beat Culture and the New America,* ed. Lisa Phillips, 1995: 17–19.

*See also* Sanders, Ed; Film; Ginsberg, Allen; Language and Idiom of the Beats; Styles of Dress, The Beats and

# Legman, Gershon (1917–1999)

Once described as "the Diderot of the dirty joke," Gershon Legman, who died in 1999, influenced Beat culture, and his erudition in the field of sexual humor remains unsurpassed. Alfred Kinsey's first official bibliographer, Legman's work was first given national attention by Jay Landesman in the Beat magazine *Neurotica*. Legman's most important works include *Love and Death* (1949), a study of sex and violence in comics; *The Fake Revolt* (1967), a condemnation of hippie culture; and his two enormous collections of sexual humor, *Rationale of the Dirty Joke* (1968), and *No Laughing Matter* (1978).

—*Mikita Brottman*

**Bibliographical Reference**

John Clellon Holmes offers a chapter on Gershon Legman in *Representative Men*, 1988.

# Lexington, Kentucky

The connection of Lexington, Kentucky, to the Beat Generation primarily is the construction in 1935 of a "narcotics farm," a place where, in accordance with a federal law passed in 1929, addicts received treatment to break their dependence on drugs.

In the fiftieth anniversary issue of *Junky*, ed. Oliver Harris (2003), the narrator refers to his experience at the Lexington Narcotics Farm (50–57,) which later was known as the U.S. Public Health Service Hospital. Sick with withdrawal symptoms, the narrator checks into the facility. He gets relief through an initial round of injections, and he gives an account of the population—a group of irredeemable thieves and hustlers who tell each other stories and share information. One patient refers to the Do-Rights, whose prospects for successful reform lead to extra shots and better accommodations, but the narrator does not get placed in such a group. Without completing the cure, the narrator leaves. These events in *Junky* apparently correspond to Burroughs's stay at the Lexington facility in January 1948.

—*William Lawlor*

**Bibliographical References**

William S. Burroughs, *Junky*, ed. Oliver Harris, 2003; Ted Morgan, *Literary Outlaw*, 1988.

*See also* Vollmer Adams Burroughs, Joan; Burroughs, William Seward

# Library Holdings

The work of Beat writers and related paraphernalia have been collected, preserved, and housed in American libraries. Research institutions such as Stanford; the University of California, Berkeley; the New York Public Library; the University of North Carolina, Chapel Hill; and the State University of New York, Buffalo, have amassed significant collections of both original and secondary source material on the Beats.

Stanford University houses the Allen Ginsberg papers; the New York Public Library owns Jack Kerouac's archives; and the University of California, Berkeley, has the Lawrence Ferlinghetti papers. Moreover, SUNY Buffalo possesses a notable collection of poetry publications, including small magazines, rare and handmade volumes, and poet trading cards. William Burroughs's works are distributed throughout the aforementioned sources.

The journey of some works to their current homes has only been in the 1990s or early 2000s. For example, Jack Kerouac's widow kept his archival materials after his death in 1969 until she died in 1990. Upon Mrs. Kerouac's death, the archives were willed to her siblings, who donated the materials to the New York Public Library in 2001. They are now part of the Henry W. and Albert

...ction of English and American Liter-... ...erouac's archive includes notebooks, manu-...pts, journals, and childhood memorabilia. One of the more unusual items in the archives is a set of crutches Kerouac used while recovering from a football injury. All of these items can be searched directly through the New York Public Library catalog at http://catnyp.nypl.org/. The archive items are noncirculating, however.

For the Berg Collection at the New York Public Library, a press release notes, "There are also small but significant collections of manuscripts and correspondence of Allen Ginsberg, William Burroughs, Gary Snyder, and several other Beat writers" (http://www.nypl.org/press/kerouac.html). While this information is made available to the public through the library's website at www.nypl.org, not all of the research institutions publicly detail how and when their Beat collections were acquired. Nevertheless, examining the contents of each collection gives one insight into how the pertinent author collected them and indicates what was of interest to the author. For example, Allen Ginsberg's collection includes 88,000 photographs, 78,000 taken by Ginsberg and the remainder taken by others. This collection of photos reflects Ginsberg's great interest in photography as both hobby and creative tool. One can also see Ginsberg's friendly and open personality in that he allowed Jerry Aronson to film extensive interviews with Ginsberg's family, friends, and colleagues for Aronson's documentary film *The Life and Times of Allen Ginsberg* (1993). All of this information can be found in the Allen Ginsberg Papers collection at Stanford University's Department of Special Collections in the Cecil H. Green Library.

Of all the Beat authors, Ginsberg appears to have documented his own life most thoroughly in the form of written and audio-visual records. His papers even include teaching files from his time as a professor at institutions like Columbia University, the Naropa Institute, and Brooklyn College, where he taught until his death. The entire Allen Ginsberg Papers take up about 1,200 linear feet at Stanford's library. One may search the contents using the online finding guide at http://dynaweb.oac.cdlib.org/ dynaweb/ead/stanford/mss/m0733/ or the printed version available on-site.

Somewhat smaller is the Lawrence Ferlinghetti Archive at the Bancroft Library on the University of California, Berkeley, campus. The entire archive fills about twenty-eight linear feet. Manuscripts are primarily available as holographs, with holographic versions also available of revisions made by the author. All printed materials have a provenance. Ferlinghetti's archive also contains various audio-visual materials, such as audiocassettes and films. The materials are noncirculating and the contents may be searched using the finding guide in person, or the online version at http://www.oac.cdlib.org/cgi-bin/ oac/berkeley/bancroft/ferling.

William S. Burroughs's manuscripts and other archive materials are spread throughout U.S. research institutions and private collections. A good overview can be found in the Library of Congress National Union Catalog of Manuscript Collections at http://www.loc.gov/coll/nucmc/nucmc.html. The University of Virginia, Ohio State University, and Arizona State University seem to have the most extensive collections that are open to the public. The Library of Congress does, however, catalog private collections as well. It is unclear as of this writing whether a central repository of Burroughs's papers will ever be instituted.

SUNY Buffalo's Poetry/Rare Books Library (PL) houses poetry magazines by Beat writers and assorted other items of interest, such as journals, poet trading cards, handmade volumes, and rare books. This material is of most interest to the scholar who is looking for original source material that is not available elsewhere. For example, if one's local research institution does not possess a handmade book that an author contributed to, SUNY Buffalo's Poetry/Rare Books Library is a good place to look. All of the items in the library are specially stored and can be viewed only on-site. Of the authors examined in this article, Allen Ginsberg leads the PL listings, with 352 records attributed to him, while Jack Kerouac has 225 listings, Lawrence Ferlinghetti 224, and William Burroughs 86. Materials in the library collection can be searched by guest users online via the SUNY Buffalo library catalog at

http://ublib.buffalo.edu/libraries/e-resources/
bison/off.html.

The institutions have fairly open accessibility policies in that most of them allow access to the general public, but the materials in each archive collection are generally noncirculating. This policy is encouraging because rare or original materials can be preserved more easily within the confines of a library with archival specialists on staff. Contents of each collection include both published and personal papers and ephemera. The attention given to obtaining and preserving each collection indicates how far the Beats have come in literary and scholarly circles.

—Lisa Loderhose

## Bibliographical References

Go to Arizona State University Libraries at http://catalog.lib.asu.edu/. The Department of Special Collections and University Archives, Stanford University Libraries, offers a "Guide to the Allen Ginsberg Papers, 1937–1994," which has been processed and encoded by Steven Mandeville—visit http://dynaweb.oac.cdlib.org/dynaweb/ead/stanford/mss/m0733/. One can also visit "Ferlinghetti (Lawrence) Papers" at the Online Archive of California (OAC): http://www.oac.cdlib.org/cgi-bin/oac/berkeley/bancroft/ferling. The Library of Congress National Union Catalog of Manuscript Collections (NUCMC) is at http://www.loc.gov/coll/nucmc/nucmc.html. William McPheron's "American Literary Studies: Allen Ginsberg Papers" at the Stanford Library can be reached at http://library.stanford.edu/depts/hasrg/ablit/amerlit/ginsberg.html. One can study the holdings of the New York Public Library at http://catnyp.nypl.org/. Information on the Jack Kerouac Archive is included in "The New York Public Library Acquires Archives of Jack Kerouac: Literary Manuscripts, Correspondence, Journals, and Fantasy Sporting Records Provide Insight to Distinctive Literary Figure," and this information can be seen at http://www.nypl.org/press/kerouac.html. Additional facts are available in "New York Public Library Opens Its Cabinet of Curiosities for Exhibition of Unusual and Unexpected Items," which may be reached at http://www.nypl.org/press/curiosities2.html. Resources at the Ohio State University Libraries can be searched at http://www.lib.ohio-state.edu/. Berkeley's library is searchable via http://sunsite2.berkeley.edu:8000/.

The online catalog at Stanford is at http:// stanford.edu/uhtbin/cgisirsi/GyWWKFgUSe/6800 56/60/668/X. The "Virgo Online Catalog" at the University of Virginia Libraries is at http://virgo.lib.virginia.edu/. The University at Buffalo Libraries Catalog is at http://ublib.buffalo.edu/libraries/e-resources/bison/off.html.

*See also* Naropa Institute

## Lipton, Lawrence (1898–1975)

Writer, jazz-poetry enthusiast, and chronicler of Beat culture, Lawrence Lipton wrote creative works that encompassed multiple genres and thrived on change. Born in Lódz, Poland, on 10 October 1898, he came to the United States in 1903 and as a young man worked as a graphic artist, journalist, and cinema publicist. He belonged to the circle of 1920s Chicago writers that included Sherwood Anderson, Edgar Lee Masters, Carl Sandburg, and others. After his first marriage to Dorothy Omansky, Lipton married Betty Weinberg and had his only child, James. In the 1930s, he married prolific mystery novelist Georgiana "Craig" Rice (1908–1959). During World War II, Lipton published two protest novels, and in 1948 he married Nettie Esther Brooks, who moved with him to Southern California in the 1950s. Lipton wrote articles for *The Nation* in 1956 on poetry and the vocal tradition. His experiments with poetry and improvisational jazz led to his involvement in The West Coast Poetry and Jazz Festival, recorded and later released as the LP *Jazz Canto: An Anthology of Poetry and Jazz* (World Pacific Records, 1958). Lipton's *The Holy Barbarians* (1959) offered a sociological-biographical sketch of Beat writers such as Gregory Corso, Lawrence Ferlinghetti, Allen Ginsberg, Kenneth Rexroth, Kenneth Patchen, and Dylan Thomas. Using taped interviews and partially fictionalized case studies, he presented *The Holy Barbarians* as "the first complete inside story" of the Beats. In *Life* (September 1959), Lipton is shown performing his poetry with accompaniment by jazz musicians, and the lifestyle of Lipton and his fellow performers is contrasted with the activities in a "square" Kansas town. Lipton appeared as "King of the Beatniks" in George Blair's film *The Hypnotic Eye* (1960) and later focused his energies on sexual liberation, made manifest in *The Erotic Revolution* (1965). He died 9 July 1975 in Southern California.

—*Brad E. Lucas*

## Principal Works

*Brother, the Laugh is Bitter*, 1942; *In Secret Battle*, 1944; *Rainbow at Midnight*, 1955; *The Holy Barbarians*, 1959; *The Erotic Revolution: an Affirmative View of the New Morality*, 1965; *Bruno in Venice West, and Other Poems*, 1976.

## Bibliographical References

John Arthur Maynard, in *Venice West: The Beat Generation in Southern California*, 1991, refers to Lipton various times. A photo of Lipton reading poetry with jazz accompaniment appears in *Life* 21 September 1959: 31.

*See also* Venice West

## Literary Forms

Beat writers sought to express their new vision in new forms; their published works confronted, changed, and expanded traditional literary forms. As a result, some early reviewers questioned the literary merit of Beat works when those publications fell outside the expected ranges of traditional forms. Awareness of the benefits and limitations of various genres and the ways they overlap can help readers understand the wide-ranging exploratory nature of Beat Generation literature.

Traditionally, the term *genre* refers to the grouping of literary works according to form or technique. Classical genres include tragedy, comedy, epic, lyric, and pastoral; until recent centuries these types were composed in verse. Today distinctions of genre also include the novel, short story, essay, and television and movie scripts. Works can be classified further by subject matter; literary works can be considered westerns, romances, detective stories, and so on. Identifying a literary work by genre helps readers approach the material and aids critical scrutiny. However, characteristics of one genre may overlap with those of another, making clear identification problematic. A literary work may exhibit the qualities of prose and of poetry—the result is sometimes called a prose-poem—or it may contain elements of both tragedy and comedy—a tragi-comic work.

Jack Kerouac, the most prodigious writer of the Beat Generation, published works in a variety of the generally recognized genres. Poems, essays, short stories, collected letters, and even a record of his actual dreams have all been published under his name, yet he is best known for his novels. The term *novel* applies to an extended work of prose fiction. Though there may be as many ways to write a novel as there are writers to do the job, novels typically adhere to certain characteristics. For one thing, they usually represent characters who undergo development as the result of a series of events. They also generally follow a plausible plot and make use of recognizable details. Kerouac's first published book, *The Town and the City*, is a traditionally structured novel with a *bildungsroman* theme—the development toward maturity of a young central character. Another Kerouac novel that depicts a coming-of-age story, *Doctor Sax*, features characteristics of the Gothic horror story. Kerouac's best-known novel, *On the Road*, is a picaresque adventure novel, while *Maggie Cassidy* and *Tristessa* are romance novels. The Beat writers drew much of their material from their own lives and examined their experiences in their work. Kerouac's close friend, John Clellon Holmes, published the first Beat Generation novel, *Go*, which, like most of Kerouac's novels, is a *roman à clef*, a novel that recounts experiences based on actual occurrences with little narrative creativeness other than name changes. Some critics hesitate to classify Kerouac's books as novels at all because they so closely trace biographical events. Yet these works are neither biography nor autobiography in the strictest sense, as Kerouac intensified the biographical elements for artistic purposes. William Burroughs's early work *Junky* is also a *roman à clef*. However, one should not label *Naked Lunch*, also by Burroughs, as such, for though Burroughs based the work on his own life, careful reading does not render the re-creation of biographical events. Although many Beat works are autobiographical in nature, Beat writers produced few true autobiographies. Neal Cassady's *The First Third* is an autobiography in the traditional sense as the writing is an attempt to render and examine his own life from birth to the moment of composition.

Kerouac's popular reputation rests largely with his thematic content of quest and adventure, jazz and drugs, but he is also known as an experimenter with style. After the publication of *The Town and the City*, Kerouac declared that he would write no more novels in the traditional format for literary fiction that he had studied in school and would instead create new prose forms. The deviation of Kerouac's prose from the expected styles generally allowable for novels led to criticism. Kerouac's most important development began with a writing technique that he called "sketching," which involved writing quickly and on the spot, without revision. He compared the method to that of painters, particularly the French impressionists, who brought their easels out of the studios so that they might paint directly from the scene in the available light. One further might consider the impressionists' predicament in the art of painting; when they eschewed traditionally accepted notions of line and light their works fell outside the accepted realms of the genre of landscape painting. Kerouac developed his ideas of sketching into a new method of composition that he called "spontaneous prose." Most of the books Kerouac wrote after *On the Road* were composed according to this method. Kerouac stated that he had developed a new prose and a new form, so traditional genres of book classification are not applicable.

Although Kerouac's experimental novels were his main form of expression, he published several short stories as well. None of the Beat writers produced short stories abundantly, yet Kerouac did have several well-placed pieces: "Jazz of the Beat Generation" in *New World Writing*, "The Mexican Girl" in *The Paris Review*, and "A Billowy Trip in the World" in *New Directions* were all excerpts from *On the Road* published as short stories. Other Kerouac short stories include "Good Blonde" and "The Rumbling, Rambling Blues."

Poetry was the bastion of the Beat Generation. One of the Beats' chief contributions to contemporary culture is their reintroduction of poetry to everyday society. Literary poetry had been for several generations the purview of scholars and the literary elite; in the 1950s, the Beats brought verse down to the streets and into the clubs by writing of personal and often confessional topics in a jazz vernacular. All Beat writers were in some sense poets, and they seemed to insist that every human being could be a poet, too. Allen Ginsberg is best known for "Howl" and his lifelong commitment to poetry, but Kerouac himself, primarily a novelist, published a half dozen books of verse. Other notable Beat poets include Gregory Corso, Michael McClure, Gary Snyder, Philip Whalen, Lawrence Ferlinghetti, Bob Kaufman, Amiri Baraka, Diane di Prima, John Wieners, and Ted Joans. Although many of the poets worked with traditional forms in their early years, Beat poetry is almost invariably *vers libre*, or free verse, and intended to be read aloud. Ginsberg worked with various spiritual forms, including the Hindu *sutra* and the Hebrew *kaddish*.

Another genre of literary expression is the memoir, written recollections of one who has been a witness to significant events. Memoirs differ from autobiographies in that they do not deal with the author's life in an extended narrative focused on introspection. Memoirs tend to be accounts of selected incidents that often focus on people other than the writer. The most notable memoir writer of the Beat Generation is Herbert Huncke. Huncke's published literary output is sparse, and his friends recall him primarily as a storyteller. His straightforward storytelling suits the memoir form. Ed Sanders and Carl Solomon have also written of their interactions with the Beat Generation in *Tales of Beatnik Glory* and *Mishaps, Perhaps*, respectively. Some notable contributions by women of the Beat Generation have come in the form of memoirs; Joyce Johnson is a primary example. Other women memoir writers include Hettie Jones, Carolyn Cassady, Diane di Prima, and Brenda Bremser Frazer.

The Beat Generation's primary playwrights include Amiri Baraka and Michael McClure. Baraka has published more than twenty plays, beginning with *A Good Girl Is Hard to Find* in 1958. His most anthologized play might be *Dutchman* (1964), which takes place entirely in a subway car. McClure has also published more than twenty plays, his most well known being *The Beard*, which features a meeting between Billy the Kid and Jean Harlow and faced charges of obscenity after its first month of performances in 1965. Other writers associated with the Beat Generation have produced plays, including Diane di Prima, who had several plays produced by the Living Theater in New York City. After the success of *On the Road*, Kerouac worked on a play he tentatively titled *The Beat Generation*. The play was not produced, but he salvaged much of the script for use in the film *Pull My Daisy*.

Many writers' journals have been published for the light they shed on the writers' lives. Ginsberg and Kerouac wrote extensive journals with the awareness that these journals would one day be published. Most Beat writers kept journals, but for the most part, only excerpts have appeared. Letters are another window to writers' personal lives, and through the years writers have composed letters with one eye toward publication. Thousands of letters written from one Beat writer to another now have been published. Beats also wrote essays; the first and perhaps most well known is John Clellon Holmes's "This Is the Beat Generation" published in the *New York Times Magazine* (16 November 1952). McClure also produced essays, most notably his collection *Scratching the Beat Surface* (1982). While many of the Beats, including Kerouac and Ginsberg, have published essays, some of the best essays are by contemporary essayists seeking to explain the Beat esthetic. Among these essayists is Seymour Krim, who wrote for such journals as *Commentary*, *Partisan Review*, and *Hudson Review*. His essays have been collected in *Views of a Nearsighted Cannoneer* (1961) and *Shake It for the World, Smartass* (1965).

—*Matt Theado*

## Bibliographical References

The novels of Jack Kerouac include *The Town and the City*, 1950; *On the Road*, 1957; *Doctor Sax*, 1959; *Maggie Cassidy*, 1959; and *Tristessa*, 1960. The novels of Burroughs include *Junky*, 1953;

and *Naked Lunch*, 1959 (in Paris) and 1962 (in the United States). Neal Cassady's autobiography is *The First Third*, 1971—revised and expanded in 1981; Kerouac's short prose includes "Jazz of the Beat Genration," *New World Writing* 7 (1955): 7–16; "The Mexican Girl," *Paris Review* 11 (Winter 1955): 9–32; "A Billowy Trip in the World," *New Directions* 16 (1957): 93–105; "The Rumbling, Rambling Blues," *Playboy*, January 1958; and "Good Blonde," which appears in *Good Blonde & Others*, ed. Donald Allen, 1993. Of the many poems published by Beat writers, "Howl" is the most famous, and it is included in *Howl and Other Poems*, 1956. The numerous memoirs by Beat writers include two by Herbert Huncke: *Guilty of Everything*, 1990; and *The Evening Sun Turned Crimson*, 1980. Other noteworthy memoirs are Ed Sanders, *Tales of Beatnik Glory*, 1973; Carl Solomon, *Mishaps, Perhaps*, 1966; Joyce Johnson, *Minor Characters*, 1983; Hettie Jones, *How I Became Hettie Jones*, 1990; and Carolyn Cassady, *Off the Road*, 1990. Plays by Beat writers include Amiri Baraka, *A Good Girl Is Hard to Find*, 1958; and *Dutchman*, 1964. Michael McClure is the author of the play *The Beard*, 1967; and Kerouac's script for *Pull My Daisy*, 1960, is derived from his attempt to write a play entitled *The Beat Generation*. Essays by Beat writers include John Clellon Holmes, "This Is the Beat Generation," which appeared in the *New York Times Magazine* 16 November 1952: 10–22; McClure's *Scratching the Beat Surface*, 1982, is a book-length essay. The essays of Seymour Krim may be found in *Views of a Nearsighted Cannoneer*, 1961, and *Shake It for the World, Smartass*, 1965.

*See also* Corso, Gregory; McClure, Michael; Whalen, Philip; Ferlinghetti, Lawrence; Kaufman, Bob; Baraka, Amiri; di Prima, Diane; Wieners, John; Joans, Ted; Holmes, John Clellon; Krim, Seymour; Kerouac, Jack; Ginsberg, Allen; Burroughs, William Seward; Huncke, Herbert; Sanders, Ed; Solomon, Carl; Bremser, Bonnie; Johnson, Joyce; Jones, Hettie; Cassady, Carolyn; Censorship; Scholarship and Critical Appreciation, A Survey of; Theater

## Little Magazines

Numerous little magazines and small presses provided forums for Beat expression prior to major publications, during periods of editorial rejection, and in counterbalance to caricatures, censorship, and sensationalism.

Some of the magazines were produced on mimeograph machines and assembled at collating parties. Others were produced on small letter presses. Some were individually produced works of art that combined printing with drawing, collage, and assemblage.

In the *Dictionary of Literary Biography,* George F. Butterick lists 245 little magazines that reflect the Beat spirit. The magazines originated in the late 1940s, became numerous in the 1950s, connected with the broadening counterculture in the 1960s and 1970s, and continued through the 1980s and 1990s. Many of these magazines were based in New York, Chicago, and San Francisco, but the geographical range of publications extended throughout the United States, into Mexico and Canada, and in various instances into Europe.

Funding for the magazines was a difficulty because virtually no advertising was included, except for announcements of similar publications. To establish a base of paying subscribers was a challenge, and many magazines were produced in a limited series because editors could not absorb the continuing costs. Nevertheless, various magazines were sustainable because the mimeograph machine made production inexpensive, and generous individuals contributed paper or postage stamps. Using a mailing list principally made up of fellow artists, editors produced their magazines and sent them across the nation promptly, keeping people in different locations aware of day-to-day changes in creative activity.

These magazines presented the Beats in an accommodating environment free from condescension. For example, in *Big Table,* a magazine first created in 1959 when university authorities imposed content restrictions on the *Chicago Review,* the editors published episodes from *Naked Lunch* prior to the book's vindication in censorship trials. *Big Table* printed Ginsberg's "Kaddish" prior to its City Lights release in 1961. The lead item in the first issue of *Big Table* was Jack Kerouac's experimental prose piece "Old Angel Midnight."

Two of the key magazines of the era were *Black Mountain Review* and *Evergreen Review.* The seventh issue of *Black Mountain Review* (1957) was edited by Robert Creeley with contributing editors Allen Ginsberg, Irving Layton, Charles Olson, and Jonathan Williams. This issue, which established an interconnection among West Coast, Black Mountain, and Beat writers, included works by Allen Ginsberg, Jack Kerouac, Philip Whalen, Michael McClure, William Burroughs, Gary Snyder, and William Carlos Williams. The second issue of *Evergreen Review* (1957), also known as the San Francisco Scene issue, was edited by Donald Allen and Barney Rosset, who took advantage of support from Grove Press and produced their magazine in runs that exceeded 100,000 copies. The famous second issue included Ginsberg, Kerouac, Ferlinghetti, Kenneth Rexroth, Henry Miller, and Robert Duncan.

In New York, LeRoi Jones and Hettie Cohen published *Yugen,* and shortly thereafter, Jones and Diane di Prima produced *Floating Bear.* These magazines defied censors and academics, affording a forum to Ginsberg, McClure, Whalen, Corso, Snyder, Burroughs, and many others. With *Floating Bear,* the mimeo production and direct-mail delivery created an immediacy rivaling today's e-mail.

On the West Coast in 1959, *Beatitude* took up the mimeo style, established rotating editorial leadership, and gave space to diverse and inventive Beat writers. In addition to Kerouac, Ginsberg, and Ferlinghetti, the reader finds Bob Kaufman, Lenore Kandel, Richard Brautigan, and many others. According to prefatory remarks in the first issue, the magazine aimed "to extol beauty and promote the beatific life among the various mendicants, neoexistentialists, christs, poets, painters, musicians, and other inhabitants and observers of North Beach, San Francisco, California, United States of America." In the preface, the editors described themselves as "a few hardy types who sneak out of alleys on Grant Avenue."

In contrast to the mimeographed magazines was *Semina,* the magazine produced by Wallace Berman in very limited editions and distributed to his friends. *Semina* was not bound, but was enclosed in envelopes. Berman included poetry by Beat writers such as David Meltzer and Michael McClure, but also included drawings and pictures.

Berman combined aspects of the little magazine with aspects of sculpture and visual art.

In the end, the little magazines and small presses provided the best Beat fidelity. When the censor loomed, the small press prevailed. When major editors doubted and rejected, small press editors comprehended and published. Today, when the Beats enjoy growing acceptance, the sustaining force of the little magazines is sometimes overlooked but nevertheless crucial. Those who would go beyond the distortion of media and popular culture to see the naked truth about the Beats cannot avoid the little magazines. Hundreds of periodicals feature the Beats on pages that prove to be their most comfortable home.

—*William Lawlor*

### Bibliographical References

Steven Clay and Rodney Phillips, *A Secret Location on the Lower East Side*, 1998, offers background information and photos of magazine covers for many little magazines associated with the Beat Generation. See also "The Little Magazine in America: A Modern Documentary History," *TriQuarterly* 43 (Fall 1978), an issue devoted to the analysis of the little magazine.

*See also* Censorship; Carroll, Paul; Baraka, Amiri; di Prima, Diane; Jones, Hettie

## London

A center for Beat activity, including personal travel, interaction of important personalities, and professional performance.

In "Big Trip to Europe," which is included in *Lonesome Traveler* (1960), Jack Kerouac describes his visit to London after his travels to Tangier and France (167–171). Unshaven and bearing a pack on his back, Kerouac at first has problems with British immigration, but he manages to establish his identity and enters London. He walks through the city, noting Victoria Station, Buckingham Palace, St James's Park, the Strand, Trafalgar Square, Fleet Street, and St. Paul's Cathedral. On Good Friday he hears an impressive performance of the St. Paul's choir. At the British Museum he looks up his family name and discovers that the family motto is plain, simple, and apt: "Love, work, suffer" (171).

Allen Ginsberg visited London after being expelled from Cuba and Czechoslovakia in 1965. He met with Bob Dylan and the Beatles. He enjoyed the spring weather in London, and when several friends arrived, he helped to organize an international poetry reading at the Royal Albert Hall on 11 June 1965. Nineteen poets, including Lawrence Ferlinghetti, William Burroughs, Harry Fainlight, Gregory Corso, and Andrei Voznesensky, contributed to the performance before an audience of 7,000.

At the center of underground activity in London was Barry Miles, who shared ownership of the Indica Book Shop in London's Southampton Row and collaborated on the *International Times*, an underground newspaper. The Indica featured many books by Beat writers and attracted a clientele that included the Beatles.

William Burroughs resided in London for many years (1966–1973), but his life was not happy there, perhaps because problems with the health of his mother and his son in the United States were disquieting. Burroughs did write four books while in London, but when he had the opportunity to sell his archive for an amount of cash that permitted his exit from London, he left.

—*William Lawlor*

### Bibliographical References

See Barry Miles, *The Sixties*, 2002; Michael Schumacher discusses the international poetry reading at the Albert Hall in *Dharma Lion*, 1992; Jack Kerouac's "Big Trip to Europe" is included in *Lonesome Traveler*, 1960; Ted Morgan covers Burroughs's years in London in *Literary Outlaw*, 1988.

*See also* Ginsberg, Allen; Burroughs, William Seward; Kerouac, Jack

## Lowell, Massachusetts

The City of Lowell was planned and founded as an industrial center on the banks of the Merrimack River in northeastern Massachusetts in the early nineteenth century. Its primary, perhaps sole, significance for Beat culture is as the birthplace of Jack Kerouac (Jean Louis Lebris de Kerouac, 12 March 1922) and as the setting for several of Kerouac's novels. The city's history informs the cultural milieu into which Kerouac was born and in which he spent his boyhood and adolescence.

Lowell was established according to plans for the expansion of integrated textile manufacturing already developed at Waltham, Massachusetts, exploiting the drop of water at the Pawtucket Falls (approximately thirty feet) to power machinery in the mills. Lowell's early history offers a remarkable example of industrial and social engineering. The first mill began production in 1823, nearly 100 years before Kerouac's birth; but the development of Lowell from town (1826) to city (1836) and its differentiation from a highly organized and homogenized socioindustrial experiment into a sprawling metropolis of ethnic enclaves provides a background both predictably provincial and curiously cosmopolitan for Kerouac's own development and writing.

Those who conceived and executed the designs of the presiding Boston Company—an "enterprising elite" including Francis Cabot Lowell (for whom the city was named, although he died before it was established) and Nathan Appleton, among numerous others—worked from tried engineering principles copied from British factories (these Francis Lowell memorized on a trip to the north of England) and conservative economic and moral principles. Its original factory workforce was composed of young girls from New England farms generally intending to work for a few years in the mills and accumulate savings to establish themselves economically for a nonfarming life. This workforce was paternalistically protected by the corporation, boarded in company-owned housing, and supervised by "moral police." The city was notable enough by the mid-nineteenth century for Charles Dickens to comment extensively upon it in *American Notes* (1842) (based on a visit in 1842); and out of the industrial milieu was produced a journal of the writings of the women working in the mills, *The Lowell Offering* (1840), and the later memoir, *A New England Girlhood* (1889) by Lucy Larcom. For a time it seemed an enormously successful social experiment. Prints and etchings from the pre–Civil War period represent the relation of factory and dormitory to surrounding countryside as bucolic, like that of a college to its environs.

Textile manufacture is, however, enormously susceptible to markets, both to procure raw goods and to sell manufactured ones, and the onset of the Civil War was disastrous to the enormous productive power of the mills as a consequence of the disruption of the supply of cotton. Huge mills were shut down and raw goods precipitously sold off for fear that a long-enduring conflict and disruption of trade would erode invested capital. The workforce of "mill girls" was dispersed and never attracted to the mills again. When manufacture began to arise again after the war, the workforce came principally from displaced immigrants.

First among these groups were the Irish, who had been employed in constructing canals and building factories, and who had inhabited a more or less unsupervised and unincorporated part of the city called "the Acre." Successive immigrant groups included French Canadians (who by the end of the nineteenth century achieved their own Roman Catholic parish, French-language schools, and a residential enclave), Greeks, Poles, Central European Jews, Portuguese, Armenians, Syrians, and Lebanese—in all, including about forty different ethnic, linguistic, and national groups, lacking only a significant number of African Americans, Italians, and Spanish speakers. Compelling motivations for the immigration of these groups were, first, to escape from poverty, pogroms, and displacement; and, second, to succeed in a new environment. Among them, the Irish gained political and economic ascendancy, for a variety of reasons: the hierarchy of the Roman Catholic diocese of Boston was predominantly Irish, as were other urban political and administrative units (e.g., police organizations); the immigrant Irish spoke English as a home language; and the Irish had apprenticed and established themselves in trades earlier than those in other groups. Cohesion among ethnic groups was encouraged by the fact that, until after World War II, surrounding farmland was not suburbanized. Each group could maintain many of its dietary traditions because some members took to farming in the area. As communicated in Kerouac's writing set in Lowell, the local ethos that developed despite ethnic, intraethnic, and religious differences included a sense of identity as Americans—being from and of Lowell, and therefore from and of a defining American experience. But, equally, that sense of identity included a sense of estrangement from the mainstream and ambivalence and *ressentiment* toward the wider and more established social order.

The most Lowell-centered of Kerouac's works include his first book, *The Town and the City* (1950), which pays lyrical homage to the Merrimack River in its romantic opening; *Dr. Sax* (1958); *Maggie Cassidy* (1958); and *Visions of Gerard* (1959), which pays homage to Kerouac's older brother, who died when Kerouac was four and about whom Kerouac wove legend and fantasy. Kerouac left Lowell after high school, with his parents, and moved to New York, where he attended the Horace Mann School for a year and Columbia for less than a year, and then began an itinerant life. He maintained some of his local connections through letter writing and returned to Lowell in 1966, after he married Stella Sampas, from the same family as his fictionalized Greek American hero Sammy Sampaticus. Kerouac, wife Stella, and his mother Gabrielle (Mémère) moved away again in 1968, and he died a year later in Florida. He was buried in the Edson Cemetery in Lowell—an event memorialized in Allen Ginsberg's poem "Memory Gardens."

Lowell figures in Kerouac's work as a romanticized background to and explanation for inchoate aspirations. The most Lowell-centered of biographical treatments of Kerouac is *Visions of Kerouac: The Life of Jack Kerouac* (1973, 1974) by Charles E. Jarvis (Constantine Xiavros). The book benefits from Jarvis's talents as a minor novelist, as he adds dialogue freely from memory (though research may show that he kept contemporaneous notes) and provides a convincing portrait of Lowell from the Depression up through the time of his writing. Kerouac is the only literary writer of the twentieth century of comparable talent and significance to emerge from and remember Lowell as a subject in his fiction. At the beginning of the twenty-first century, Lowell memorializes Kerouac in publications and events that attempt an understanding of the writer and of its own history.

—Stephen Hahn

**Bibliographical References**
Robert F. Dalzell Jr., *Enterprising Elite: The Boston Associates and the World They Made*, 1987; Charles Dickens, *American Notes*, 1842; Benita Eisler, *The Lowell Offering: Writings by New England Mill Women (1840–1845)*, 1977; Arthur L. Eno Jr., ed., *Cotton Was King: A History of Lowell, Massachusetts*, 1976; Allen Ginsberg, "Memory Gardens" in *Collected Poems: 1947–1980*, 1984; Raymond P. Holden, *The Merrimack*, 1958; Charles E. Jarvis, *Visions of Kerouac: The Life of Jack Kerouac*, 1973; Lucy Larcom, *A New England Girlhood*, 1889.

***See also*** Kerouac, Jack

# M

## Mailer, Norman (1923–)

Norman Mailer has been widely praised for his novels and for his fusion of fiction and nonfiction in works that defy easy categorization, while also being both lauded and attacked for his controversial public persona. Mailer achieved his first great writing success with the novel *The Naked and the Dead* (1948), based on the author's World War II experiences in the United States Army. A long line of other novels followed, including the Pulitzer Prize–winning *The Executioner's Song* (1979), but many critics located Mailer's greatest creative accomplishments in his fusion of fiction and nonfiction, especially in *Miami and the Siege of Chicago* and *Armies of the Night*, both published in 1968. Mailer's many marriages, heavy drinking, excursions into politics, and appearances on such television talk programs as *The Dick Cavett Show* made him one of America's most recognized writers.

Norman Mailer was born in Long Branch, New Jersey, on 31 January 1923. He graduated from Harvard University in 1943; served in the army (1944–1946) as a field artillery observer and infantry rifleman in the Philippines and Japan; studied at the Sorbonne in Paris, France (1947–1948); and established himself as a major literary force at the age of twenty-five with his first novel. *The Naked and the Dead* occupied the number one position on the *New York Times* best-seller list for eleven weeks. Later novels included *The Deer Park* (1955), the only novel that Mailer completed in a projected eight-novel cycle about a mythical hero named Sergius O'Shaugnessy; *An American Dream* (1965), about a psychology professor who murders his wife; the prize-winning *The Executioner's Song* (1979), a somewhat fictionalized account of convicted murderer Gary Gilmore, who was executed in 1977; and *The Gospel According to the Son* (1997), a supposed autobiography of Jesus in the first person.

Among Mailer's nonfiction works, the most praised are the two 1968 books *The Armies of the Night: History as a Novel, the Novel as History* and *Miami and the Siege of Chicago*. The former, based on an antiwar demonstration at the Pentagon in 1967, received both the Pulitzer Prize and the National Book Award in 1969 for nonfiction. Its subtitle reflects the creative merging of fiction, history, and autobiography that characterizes some of Mailer's best writing. *Miami and the Siege of Chicago*, about the 1968 national political conventions, won the National Book Award for nonfiction in 1968. Among his other notable nonfiction works are an account of the first moon landing, *Of a Fire on the Moon* (1970); *Pablo and Fernande: Portrait of Picasso as a Young Man: An Interpretive Biography* (1994); and an attempt to unlock the mystery of President Kennedy's assassin, *Oswald's Tale: An American Mystery* (1995). Mailer also wrote plays and screenplays, receiving an Emmy nomination for the screenplay of *The Executioner's Song* (1982).

Mailer's essay "The White Negro," which is included in *The Portable Beat Reader*, ed. Ann Charters (1992), has special relevance to the study of the Beat Generation because Mailer explores the outlook of the hipster. Mailer recognizes contextual factors, including the horrors of World War II, the anxiety of the Cold War, and the boredom of conformity. Hipsters need to cultivate the freedom that lurks within them and speak their own idiom.

Norman Mailer reached his highest level of controversy during the 1960s as a result of his outspoken opposition to the Vietnam War, two unsuccessful campaigns for mayor of New York City, and an argument with second wife Adele Morales that led to Mailer stabbing her twice at a party. This controversy lessened the public's esteem for Mailer but did not impede his continuing literary successes nor seriously reduce his status as one of the most imaginative prose writers of the twentieth century.

—Edward J. Rielly

## Principal Works

*The Naked and the Dead*, 1948; *Barbary Shore*, 1951; *The Deer Park*, 1955; "The White Negro," 1957; *Advertisements for Myself*, 1959; *An American Dream*, 1964; *Cannibals and Christians*, 1966; *Why Are We in Vietnam?* 1967; *Miami and the Siege of Chicago*, 1968; *The Idol and the Octopus*, 1968; *The Armies of the Night*, 1968; *Of a Fire on the Moon*, 1970; *The Prisoner of Sex*, 1971; *Deaths for the Ladies*, 1971; *St. George and the Godfather*, 1972; *Existential Errands*, 1972; *Marilyn, a Biography*, 1973; *Genius and Lust*, 1976; *Some Honorable Men*, 1976; *A Transit to Narcissus*, 1978; *The Executioner's Song*, 1979; *Of Women and Their Elegance*, 1980; *Pieces and Pontifications*, 1982; *Ancient Evenings*, 1983; *Tough Guys Don't Dance*, 1984; *Harlot's Ghost*, 1991; *The Spooky Art: Thoughts on Writing*, 2003.

## Bibliographical References
Mary V. Dearborn, *Mailer: A Biography*, 1999; Adele Mailer, *The Last Party: Scenes from My Life with Norman Mailer*, 1997; Robert Merrill, *Norman Mailer Revisited*, 1992; Carl Rollyson, *The Lives of Norman Mailer*, 1991.

## Marriage

For some members of the Beat Generation, marriage was as open and spontaneous as prose and poetry. For others, the sacred ritual served as a constant reminder of conformities and conventional restrictions placed upon sexual orientation and behavior. Marriage, with its bohemian flavor, feminine influence, and revolutionary looseness, became part of an iconoclastic lifestyle plagued with infidelities and divorce.

An eclectic mix of religions, ethnicities, and sexual orientations, Beat marriages varied in length and purpose. William S. Burroughs's marriage to Ilse Klapper was a matter of convenience. Burroughs married Klapper so she could escape persecution and emigrate to the United States. Burroughs's marriage to Joan Vollmer was a common-law relationship, and it ended in tragic violence. Kerouac married, divorced, and remarried. Kerouac denied paternity in connection with his daughter, Jan Kerouac. Many of the women associated with the Beats, including Joanne Kyger, Joanna McClure, and Joan Haverty, were divorced before they even became involved with Beat men. Some, including the Cassadys and the Kaufmans, experienced on-and-off relationships. In the Beat culture, interracial marriage, such as the marriage between Hettie Cohen and LeRoi Jones, was easily accepted, even though society in general was not ready to accept such unions. Joyce Johnson questioned the limitations that marriage enforced upon her parents, but she married twice herself.

Gregory Corso focuses on marriage in his poetry. "Marriage," published in 1960, is a 111-line ambling debate satirizing American middle-class values. One of Corso's most famous poems, "Marriage" chronologically examines the institution itself, offering serious criticism about societal expectations with a comic voice. Corso contrasts the advantages of marriage (companionship, children, and responsibility) with the disadvantages of marriage (henpecking, conformity to community standards, loss of freedom), while providing much of the sentiment felt by other writers, colleagues, friends, and lovers. "Marriage" reveals the anxiety that men feel about women. "Marriage" mocks the conformity that tradition embodies.

Feminist writer Barbara Ehrenreich, in her chapter "The Beat Rebellion: Beyond Work and Marriage" in *The Hearts of Men: American Dreams and the Flight from Commitment* (1983), argues that because roles such as worker, husband, and father, were undesirable for the Beats, they became part of a strong American male movement in which men were actually the first to flee their commitments. Because of the infamous "boy gang" associated with the Beats, women often became second-class entities and, consequently, took on traditional female roles. Brenda Knight's comments in her forward to *Women of the Beat Generation* (1996) reveal hard realities of time and place: "Women of the fifties in particular were supposed to conform like Jell-o to a mold. There was only one option: to be a housewife and mother" (3). She adds that "being Beat was far more attractive than staying chained to a brand new kitchen appliance. For the most part, the liberal arts educations these young women were given created a natural predilection for art and poetry, for living a life of creativity instead of confining it to the occasional hour at the symphony. Nothing could be more romantic than joining this chorus of individuality and freedom, leaving behind boredom, safety, and conformity" (3).

—*Patricia Hillen*

**Bibliographical References**
Joan Haverty Kerouac, *Nobody's Wife,* 1990; Brenda Knight, ed., *Women of the Beat Generation,* 1996; Barbara Ehrenreich, *The Hearts of Men: American Dreams and the Flight from Commitment,* 1983; Steven Watson, *The Birth of the Beat Generation,* 1995.

*See also* Kerouac, Jack; Corso, Gregory; Burroughs, William Seward; Burroughs, Ilse Herzfeld Klapper; Vollmer Adams Burroughs, Joan; Kerouac, Jan; Kyger, Joanne; McClure, Joanna; Kerouac, Joan Haverty; Parker, Edie; Cassady, Carolyn; Jones, Hettie; Johnson, Joyce; Bremser, Bonnie

## Marshall, Edward (1932–)

Author of "Leave the Word Alone," which was published in *Black Mountain Review* 7 (1957) and *The New American Poetry,* ed. Donald Allen (1960). In 1979, Pequod Press published the poem as a pamphlet with an introduction by Allen Ginsberg, who cites Marshall's poem as inspiration for "Kaddish." Ginsberg says that he imitated Marshall's un-

restricted form, uncontrolled line, and exquisite confession about his mother's mental illness.

—*William Lawlor*

**Bibliographical Reference**
Ginsberg's introduction to the pamphlet is reproduced in *Beat Down to Your Soul,* ed. Ann Charters, 2001: 333–334, and Marshall's complete poem follows.

*See also* Ginsberg, Allen

## Martinelli, Sheri (1918–1996)

Sheri Martinelli's career as an artist and writer has flown beneath the radar of most chronicles of Beat culture. This lack of attention belies her contribution to art and literary culture of the 1940s, 1950s, and 1960s. Martinelli's presence inhabits the work of William Gaddis, Anais Nin, Anatole Broyard, H. D. (Hilda Doolittle), Allen Ginsberg, and Ezra Pound. Her essays of the 1950s exhibit a protofeminism little evident among other writers of the era. Her paintings have enjoyed international acclaim, though little exposure. The recent publication of her correspondence with Charles Bukowski would argue for closer scrutiny of Martinelli's career and influence.

Born Shirley Burns Brennan in 1918, Martinelli was raised in and around Philadelphia and attended the Philadelphia School of Industrial Arts, where she studied ceramics and met painter Ezio Martinelli. By the early 1940s, Sheri Martinelli was living in Manhattan and separated from her husband. According to Steven Moore, Martinelli appears as a figure in Anais Nin's diaries of 1945; she impressed Nin as a younger version of herself (30). William Gaddis acknowledges that Martinelli served as a model for Esme in *The Recognitions;* the central figure in Anatole Broyard's posthumously published memoir *Kafka Was the Rage* is a thinly disguised facsimile of Martinelli.

In 1952, Martinelli moved to Washington, D.C., at the urging of Ezra Pound, then a patient at St. Elizabeth's Hospital. Martinelli devoted six years of her life to serving as Pound's confidante and companion. Pound wrote the foreword and facilitated the publication of Martinelli's single collection of paintings (*La Martinelli,* 1956). Martinelli's role in Pound's life is manifest in *The Cantos* composed in this period (1956). Pound left for Europe without Martinelli in 1958. H. D. chronicled similar abandonment decades prior in *End of Torment: A Memoir of Ezra Pound* (1979). Martinelli appears as Undine in H. D.'s work.

Martinelli settled in 1959 in San Francisco and began publishing the *Anagogic & Paideumic Review,* in which appeared some of Charles Bukowski's earliest work as well as her own "Duties of a Lady Female." A tart, protean account of the war between the sexes, "Duties" was reprinted in Diane di Prima's journal *Floating Bear* (1966) and Richard Peabody's collection *A Different Beat* (1997). For two decades Martinelli lived south of San Francisco with husband Gilbert Lee. Aside from a one-woman show in Cleveland in 1964 and occasional commentary on Pound or Nin, there is little available evidence of Martinelli's work over the final thirty years of her life. She returned to Washington, D.C., in 1983 and died in Falls Church, Virginia, in 1996.

—*Tracy Santa*

## Bibliographical References

Charles Bukowski and Sheri Martinelli, *Beerspit Night and Cursing: The Correspondence of Charles Bukowski and Sheri Martinelli, 1960–1967,* ed. Steven Moore, 2001; Steven Moore, "Sheri Martinelli: A Modernist Muse," in *Gargoyle* 41 (1998).

## Materialism

Materialism has two quite distinct yet complementary meanings in Beat culture. The first is derived from the Marxist philosophy of dialectical materialism. This kind of materialism was of interest to the Beats not so much because of the writings and actions of Marx, Engels, Lenin, Stalin, or Trotsky, but rather because of the success of Mao Zedong as the leader of the Chinese revolution of 1949. The other meaning of materialism prevalent among the Beats defined the word in negative terms as consumer society based on the glorification of the acquisition of houses, cars, fashionable clothes, and appliances. This materialism led to U.S. capitalist exploitation of the rest of the world, particularly oppressed peoples in colonial and neocolonial countries, which China had been. The Beats could entertain both of these views in the 1950s as part of a general opposition to the dominant cultural values of affluence, political conservatism, and the suburban lifestyle.

Their interest in Marxist materialism was fed by the vehement anticommunism of J. Edgar Hoover of the F.B.I. and United States Senator Joseph McCarthy, who set up hearings across the country designed to ferret out communists and communist sympathizers, particularly in the Hollywood entertainment industry and on college campuses. Targets of these hearings included faculty members who taught the Beats at Reed College, for instance, where Gary Snyder, Philip Whalen, and Lew Welch attended school in the late 1940s and early 1950s. Looking at the Chinese revolution, the Beats could identify with the overturning of tradition and the glorification of the common person, the worker, and the peasant. The interest in China was also fed by a strong West Coast taste for anything "Oriental" as represented by Kenneth Rexroth's translations of Chinese and Japanese poems, the study and promotion of Chinese, Japanese, Indian and Tibetan Buddhism, as well as Hindusim, by such figures as Joseph Campbell and Alan Watts, and the popularization of Zen by D. T. Suzuki.

Although philosophically closer to the egalitarian, antiorganizational spirit of anarchism than to Marxism, with its rigidly hierarchical party structure, democratic centralism, and dictatorship of the proletariat, the Beats could celebrate the spirit of revolution and upheaval, the ideal of rapid social change, and the utopian spirit of cultural transformation the Chinese communists were believed to embody. The kind of materialism represented, then, by Marxism and the Chinese revolution could be embraced by many of the Beats as a positive belief in the capacity of human beings to transform their lives and their societies based on being grounded in real people and the real, material world rather than institutions, dogmas, and traditions.

Curiously enough, then, materialism could be defined as positive when associated with socialism and the liberation of people and nature on the one hand, and defined as negative when associated with consumerism, conformity, capitalism, the enslavement of people, and the destruction of nature on the other hand. Many Beats, for instance, opposed the Korean War on this basis in the early 1950s and then the Vietnam War in the 1960s. For the most part, the Beat generation had grown up during the Great Depression of the 1930s and the strict rationing and relative scarcity of consumer goods during World War II and its immediate aftermath. The majority of their parents' generation embraced the relative stability and prosperity of the Eisenhower years from 1952 through 1960, finally being able to afford the housing, automobiles, household amenities, and general explosion of consumer goods, especially electrical gadgets. They bought into the promise of the good life represented by suburbia, even if it meant living in a house identical to a hundred others in the same development, with the same white picket fence, and a homogeneous style of clothing and public behavior. But the Beats resolutely rejected this image of the "American Dream."

Despite their often romantic sentiments about socialism and the naiveté of supporting anyone attacked by the United States as necessarily progressive, many Beats found themselves at odds with Marxist materialism because of its stridently antispiritual, atheistic orientation, particularly by the time of the Chinese invasion of Tibet and the suppression of religious freedom in that country, as well as in China. The strong spiritual orientation of the Beats toward Buddhism, Tantrism, and esoteric religious traditions, then, turned them against both Marxist materialism and American consumerism. As a result, the second negative meaning of "materialism" as consumerism came to dominate Beat writing. The spiritual tradition and anarchist spirit of the Beats promoted the image of "the dharma bums" that Kerouac celebrated and made famous as the 1950s counterculture set out upon a rucksack, road-trip revolution promoting voluntary poverty as freedom from possessions and the responsibilities that came with ownership. Work was something to be done as needed, and, despite their frequent Ivy League educations, they often took blue-collar, temporary employment to pay the rent on an apartment or house shared by as many as would fit, with frequent transient visitors.

One sees this anticonsumerism with both a strong spiritual imagery and a clear Marxist influence in Ginsberg's "Howl," which drew heavily from Blake's romantic anticapitalist imagery in *Songs of Innocence and Experience* on the one hand and from Fritz Lang's dystopian, anticapitalist film *Metropolis* (1927), with its explicit biblical allusions to Moloch. One also sees it early in Snyder's poetry in "A Berry Feast," which he read at the same 6 Gallery reading where Ginsberg performed "Howl," as well as in his 1960s prose volume *Earth House Hold: Technical Notes and Queries for Fellow Dharma Revolutionaries,* and such poems as "Revolution in the Revolution in the Revolution." The phrase, "Dharma Revolutionaries," of course, acknowledges Kerouac's novel, *The Dharma Bums,* in which the main character, Japhy Ryder, is modeled on Snyder and links following a spiritual path in life with transforming society, including its economic base. Clearly, these aspects of the Beats as a cultural movement, and not just a literary one, helped spawn the hippie movement in the later sixties and linked the older Beat leaders and celebrities with the younger politicized countercultural youth coming of age in the 1960s, particularly on the West Coast, who were not only opposed to the Vietnam War itself, but saw it as proof that American society was corrupt, gluttonous, and destructive at its core. The Human Be-In at Golden Gate Park in 1968 probably marked the culminating event where these two generations most clearly converged.

—*Patrick D. Murphy*

## Bibliographical References

William Blake, *Songs of Innocence and Experience,* 1977; Allen Ginsberg, *Howl and Other Poems,* 1956; Jack Kerouac, *The Dharma Bums,* 1958; Gary Snyder, "A Berry Feast" in *The Back Country,* 1968; Gary Snyder, *Earth House Hold: Notes and Queries for Fellow Dharma Revolutionaries,* 1969.

*See also* Communism and the Workers' Movement; Conformity; Ginsberg, Allen; Kerouac, Jack; Snyder, Gary; Anarchy, Christian

## McClure, Joanna (1930–)

Joanna McClure developed friendships with Beat artists, including Michael McClure, Robert Duncan, Jess Collins, Kenneth Rexroth, Allen Ginsberg, Gary Snyder, Philip Lamantia, Philip Whalen, Jack Kerouac, and Diane di Prima. McClure wrote poetry that integrated naturalism and autobiography—two elements of Beat writings her male contemporaries also infused into their own works. Though she wrote simultaneously with her male contemporaries and as prolifically as they did, her work remained largely private and unpublished despite its refreshing spirituality and naturalism.

Joanna Kinnison, born in 1930 on an Arizona ranch near Tucson, grew up in the Southwest, Mexico, and Latin America. Her early experiences materialize in her work's references to desert plants and animals and its sensitivity to nature. At the University of Arizona, she met Michael McClure, whom she later married. Her move to San Francisco in 1954 placed her in an exciting intellectual community in which she discussed poetry and art with Robert Duncan and Jess Collins and their circle of intellectuals.

Joanna and Michael moved to a Fillmore flat in 1956 that quickly became a center for other artists and poets. She wrote her first poem, "Dear Lover," while exploring the California coast to Big Sur. She continued to write privately in her notebook describing the beauty of the coastline and renewing her own earlier relationship with nature. Another brief move to New York in 1960 brought her into contact with the New York Beats. Now divorced from Michael McClure, she lives in San Francisco, where she continues to write poetry.

—Lisa A. Wellinghoff

### Principal Works

*Wolf Eyes*, 1974; *Extended Love Poems*, 1978; "Dear Lover," in Arthur and Kit Knight, eds., *unspeakable visions of the individual* 8 (1978): 112–114.

### Bibliographical References

An entry on Joanna McClure appears in *Dictionary of Literary Biography, Vol. 16, The Beats: Literary Bohemians in Postwar America*, 1983; see also Barbara Gravelle, "Six North Beach Women" and "California Living," *San Francisco Examiner*, 21 October 1979; in Jack Kerouac, *Big Sur*, 1962, Joanna and Michael McClure are the McLears; see also Robert Peters, "Joanna and Josephin," *Margins* (1975): 46–47; additional information is included in *Women of the Beat Generation*, ed. Brenda Knight, 1996.

*See also* McClure, Michael; Marriage

## McClure, Michael (1932–)

Though most famous as a poet, Michael McClure is also an author of plays and essays. His central themes are intimacy, the environment, and art. In San Francisco he participated in literary groups led by Kenneth Rexroth and Robert Duncan, and with Rexroth serving as moderator, McClure was a featured reader at the 6 Gallery on 7 October 1955. Selected for publication in Donald Allen's *The New American Poetry* and the second issue of *Evergreen Review*, which paid tribute to the San Francisco Scene, McClure's writing became prominent in the San Francisco Poetry Renaissance. As an editor, McClure combined writers from the Black Mountain school with San Francisco writers in *Ark II/Moby I*, and McClure's *The Beard* (1965), which faced problems with censorship, nevertheless won two Obie awards. *Scratching the Beat Surface* (1982), an interpretation of the Beat Generation by one of its major players, is a commentary of enduring value.

Born in 1932 to Thomas and Marian Dixie Johnston McClure, Michael McClure grew up in Marysville, Kansas. His parents subsequently divorced, and McClure lived with his maternal grandfather in Seattle, Washington, where forests and beaches were inspiring. The grandfather had interests in medicine, birds, and plants and encouraged Michael to appreciate these topics. When McClure was twelve, his mother remarried, and McClure returned to Kansas, where he lived with his mother and stepfather.

Abstract expressionist painters, including Clyfford Still, Mark Rothko, and Jackson Pollock, captured the imagination of McClure and his high school friend Bruce Conner. Nevertheless, McClure wrote conventionally, submitting a sequence of villanelles at Wichita University. At the University of Arizona, while taking classes in anthropology and painting, McClure met Joanna Kinnison. After marrying, the couple went to San Francisco. McClure hoped to meet Mark Rothko and Clyfford Still, but neither was teaching any longer in San Francisco. Despite this disappointment, McClure was inspired by the impressive natural environment, and meeting Robert Duncan, McClure found new reason to concentrate on poetry. Duncan advised McClure to experiment, and McClure began to reevaluate his traditional style. The McClures also met Kenneth Rexroth, whose literary soirees further broadened McClure's concepts for writing.

In 1956, McClure published two villanelles dedicated to Theodore Roethke in *Poetry*. McClure executes the villanelle competently, but in "Premonition," he aspires to transcend the fulfillment of formal requirements. A thrush and a water spirit represent McClure's longings, but they are not converted to realities. McClure takes Roethke as a model for theme and artistry, but signals his intent to go beyond such boundaries in his future work.

In the same year, McClure coedited *Ark II/Moby I*, a little magazine. San Francisco writers were featured on the same pages as Black Mountain writers, such as Charles Olson and Robert Creeley. As a result of an extended correspondence with Olson, McClure continued to develop his artistic ideas. In 1956, *Passage*, McClure's first book of poetry, appeared.

In 1957 six poems by McClure, among them poems from *Passage* and *Hymns to St. Geryon*, were published in the issue of *Evergreen Review* subtitled the "San Francisco Scene." In "Night Words: The Ravishing" McClure is at peace. He appreciates the beauty of a room, and distinguishes between art and real life. Passionate, he speaks of touching his lover with the ecstasy of jazz. Even so, the poem is not the act itself. However, despite the shortcomings of words, a poem can be exhilarating. In "The Robe,"

McClure tells his lover that they are transcendent, that they know jazz, and that they have the forms of flowers. This issue of *Evergreen Review* presents McClure as a member of the "San Francisco Scene," marking him as a major contributor to the San Francisco Poetry Renaissance.

In 1960, *The New American Poetry* edited by Donald Allen presented together the Black Mountain writers, the San Francisco Renaissance writers, the Beats, the New York poets, and a geographically undefined group of young poets. McClure's work appears in this landmark publication. In particular, "Hymn to St. Geryon, I" lays out a design for poetry. McClure cites abstract expressionist Clyfford Still, who commits himself to unreserved productivity in art. To communicate is no longer the intention. Rather than express an idea, the poem must be the record of the artist in the act of creation.

Poet and playwright Michael McClure reads his work. (Time Life Pictures/Getty Images)

In "Peyote Poem, Part I," McClure describes his experience with drugs. While McClure's mind soars with the effect of peyote, his discomfort in his stomach cannot be ignored. Even so, he smiles and enjoys knowledge and feeling. Peyote takes McClure to a new height of experience. Like "Peyote Poem," "For Artaud" discusses drugs, in this case heroin and peyote. Since McClure is free, he can accept pain and suffering. Like Antonin Artaud, McClure deranges his senses to make them provide a new form of information.

McClure is a transformed poet in *The New American Poetry*. Instead of observing the rigors of forms such as the villanelle, McClure experiments. Lines do not have to be aligned, but can be freely distributed on the page. Rhyme and metrics are set aside as McClure seeks to record action.

*Meat Science Essays* (1961) provides scientific and ecological background for McClure's other writings.

A production of McClure's play *The Beard* was offered at the Actor's Workshop in San Francisco in 1965, but police objected to sexual frankness and harassed and arrested actors and producers of several performances. With support from the American Civil Liberties Union, *The Beard* survived efforts to stifle its production.

McClure's autobiographical novel, *The Mad Cub* (1970), establishes many of the central themes, moods, and goals for McClure's writing.

In 1986, McClure published *Selected Poems*, which gathered material from nine of his previous books. From *The New Book/A Book of Torture* (1961) McClure selects "Ode to Jackson Pollock," a tribute to the abstract expressionist who showed that disorder can be beautiful, disclosed the mysteries of color, and pressed experience through himself "onto the canvas." From *Little Odes* (1969) appears "Hummingbird Ode," in which McClure addresses a dead hummingbird. McClure speaks to the bird, which met its end by smashing into a plate glass window, asking it what it can see now that it has crossed into death. From *The Star* (1970), McClure selects "The Surge," an exclamatory poem that he, in a prefatory note, admits is not the exquisite poem he tried to write. McClure insists that there is more to apprehend. He asserts that men and women must be joined if life is to be whole. From *September Blackberries* (1974), McClure includes "Gray Fox at Solstice," a poem in honor of the fox, who savors starlight and ocean sounds. In his habitat, the fox in the brush scurries like a dancer. A similar appreciation of wildlife occurs in "To a Golden Lion Marmoset," which is selected from *Jaguar Skies* (1975). The animal is an endangered species, and McClure declares that the marmoset's continuing existence gives continuing value to human life. From *Antechamber & Other Poems* (1978) McClure includes a long selection from the title poem, which resounds with his affirmation of human possibilities. He calls for powerful creativity and declares that he is both a mammal and a patriot. Participants in the universe are members of an angelic family. From *Fragments of Perseus* (1983), McClure chooses "Listen Lawrence," a poem addressed to Lawrence Ferlinghetti that laments the wasting of the environment and calls for an abandonment of politics. McClure admits that humans naturally procreate excessively and prey on other species. However, human potential is without limits and humans can make wise choices. A selection from the long poem "Rare Angel" (1974) concludes *Selected Poems*. This poem asserts its vertical arrangement and engages the possibilities of chance. McClure tests the limits of perception, consciousness, and reality. McClure notes that he does not include any sampling of *Ghost Tantras* (1964) in *Selected Poems* because "beast language" does not coordinate with his other verse. *Ghost Tantras* is poetry based exclusively on sound rather than meaning.

The most recent poetry of McClure looks both to the past and present. *Huge Dreams* (1999) regathers the work of the early Beat period, and *Three Poems* (1995) presents anew "Rare Angel" and "Dark Brown" (1961), McClure's long and boldly erotic poem. New in *Three Poems* is "Dolphin Skull," a long poem revealing subconscious and conscious artistic production. McClure calls for the suspension of time so that the moment can be isolated and scientifically examined. Both *Rain Mirror* (1999) and *Touching the Edge* (1999) are intended as vertical poems that scroll down. In *Rain Mirror,* the first series of poems is titled "Haiku Edge," and McClure pits trickery against awareness and violence against nature's serenity. The haikus often focus on such dualities. The second series of poems is "Crisis Blossoms," a sequence in which the poet explores memories and contemplates death. He says goodbye to a sweet past and sees a smiling pleasure in supernatural existence. *Touching the Edge* is a set of dharma devotions divided into three sequences: "RICE ROARING," "OVAL MUDRA," and "WET PLANK." McClure asks to be happy and reserved as he reflects on the diversity around him, noticing not only fruit, flowers, and wildlife, but also chain saws, airplanes, and asphalt. He is calmly aware of both destruction and creation, and ultimately concludes that these forces are one and the same.

With these varied accomplishments behind him, McClure now pursues a diverse and prolific artistic career. Addressing a larger audience, he publishes collections of his work with New Directions, Penguin, Delacorte, and the University of New Mexico Press. Nevertheless, his interest in broadsides and specially crafted editions has kept him connected to Auerhahn Press, Black Sparrow Press, Grey Fox Press, and other small presses. McClure is an avant-garde figure whose participation in and commentaries about spontaneity, music, art, and the environment are central to understanding his artistic generation. McClure remains committed to full and open exploration of consciousness, perception, sexual fulfillment, and artistic action. To this end, he pursues an interdisciplinary approach. An experimental man, he has taken hallucinogens in a quest for special awareness. McClure argues against environmental destruction and seeks to protect and enhance the planet. In all, McClure stands as a positive and unifying force in art, science, literature, and ecology. Often produced through small presses dedicated to artistry in the making of books, his work reflects a combination of spontaneous creativity and enduring, specialized publication. His awards include a Guggenheim Fellowship and a Rockefeller grant. The National Poetry Association has honored McClure for distinguished lifetime achievement in poetry.

—*William Lawlor*

## Principal Works

Poetry: *Passage*, 1956; *Peyote Poem*, 1958; *For Artaud*, 1959; *Hymns to St. Geryon and Other Poems*, 1959; *The New Book/A Book of Torture*, 1961; *Dark Brown*, 1961, 1967; *Ghost Tantras*, 1964, 1969; *13 Mad Sonnets*, 1965; *Poisoned Wheat*, 1965; *Dream Table*, 1965; *Unto Caesar*, 1965; *Mandalas*, 1965; *Love Lion Book*, 1966; *Hail Thee Who Play*, 1968, 1974; *The Sermons of Jean Harlow and the Curses of Billy the Kid*, 1968; *The Surge*, 1969; *Hymns to St. Geryon/Dark Brown*, 1969, 1980; *Little Odes & The Raptors*, 1969; *Star*, 1970; *The Book of Joanna*, 1973; *Solstice Blossom*, 1973; *Fleas 189–195*, 1974; *An Organism*, 1974; *Rare Angel (writ with raven's blood)*, 1974; *September Blackberries*, 1974; *A Fist Full (1956–1957)*, 1974; *Jaguar Skies*, 1975; *Man of Moderation*, 1975; *Antechamber & Other Poems*, 1978; *Fragments of Perseus*, 1983; *Selected Poems*, 1986; *Rebel Lions*, 1991; *Simple Eyes and Other Poems*, 1994; *Three Poems: Dolphin Skull, Rare Angel, and Dark Brown*, 1995; *Lie, Sit, Stand, Be Still: A Poem*, 1995; *Soul Cinders*, 1996; *Huge Dreams*, 1999; *Rain Mirror: New Poems*, 1999; *Touching the Edge: Dharma Devotions from the Hummingbird Sangha*, 1999; *The Masked Choir: A Masque in the Shape of an Enquiry into the Treena and Sheena Myth*, 2000.

Plays: McClure is the author of more than twenty plays. A production in New York of *The Beard* (1965) won Obie awards for best play and best director. In 1977, McClure's *Josephine, The Mouse Singer* was produced at the WPA Theatre in New York and won the Obie award for best play of the year in 1978.

Prose: *Scratching the Beat Surface* (1982) and *Lighting the Corners* (1993) offer theories of art, memoirs of the Beat Generation, and interviews. See also *Meat Science Essays*, 1961. *The Mad Cub*, 1970, is autobiographical fiction.

Editing: McClure's work as an editor is revealed in *Ark II/Moby I* (1956–1957) and *Journal for the Protection of All Beings* (1961–1978).

## Bibliographical References

John Jacob, ed., *Margins 18* (1975) is a special issue entirely devoted to analysis and discussion of McClure; Rod Phillips, "Let Us Throw Out the Word *Man*: Michael McClure's Mammalian Poetics" is a chapter in *"Forest Beatniks" and "Urban Thoreaus": Gary Snyder, Jack Kerouac, Lew Welch, and Michael McClure*, 2000, in which Philips emphasizes McClure's fascination with nature and his combination of poetry with biology and ecology; Gregory Stephenson, "From the Substrate: Notes on the Work of Michael McClure," is a chapter in *The Daybreak Boys: Essays on the Literature of the Beat Generation,* 1990, in which Stephenson provides a clear and thorough survey of McClure's writings, appreciating McClure's effort to heal humankind, to reconcile body and spirit, and to develop harmonious coexistence with the environment; Geoffrey Thurley, "The Development of the New Language: Michael McClure, Philip Whalen, and Gregory Corso," in *The Beats: Essays in Criticism,* 1981, is an examination of McClure as a poet experimenting with hallucinogens, especially in "Peyote Poem," but Thurley expresses reservations about the validity of McClure's triumphs in perception while under the influence of narcotic substances; Steven Watson, "Michael McClure," *The Birth of the Beat Generation,* 1995, provides a sketch of McClure's youth, education, and career, with recognition for McClure's interdisciplinary role among the Beats and his dedication to science and the environment.

***See also*** Censorship; San Francisco; Theater; Painting; Conner, Bruce; Pollock, Jackson; Duncan, Robert; Rexroth, Kenneth; Ferlinghetti, Lawrence; Black Mountain, North Carolina, and Black Mountain College; San Francisco Renaissance; Drugs; Environmentalism; Legacy

## Mead, Taylor (1924–)

Quintessential Beat actor, perhaps the best and most famous independent actor in the sixties. A filmmaker and poet in his own right, Mead was the star of many key films of the independent film movement known as the New American Cinema. Focused around spontaneity and improvisation, this movement found that Taylor Mead was the perfect star to express Beat alienation and nonconformist attitudes.

Mead first gained attention after starring in Ron Rice's *The Flower Thief* (1960), in which he plays a carefree loner who frolics through the streets of San Francisco, steals a flower, and subsequently deals with a series of misadventures. P. Adams Sitney in *The American Avant-Garde* has referred to the film as "the purest expression of the Beat sensibility in cinema" (351). Mead, reminiscent of the

court jester whose foolishness equals his perceptiveness, celebrates in his performance irrational states that are the polar opposites of so-called acceptable social behavior. His performance style calls attention to itself and is freed from traditional acting conventions. Mead does not conceal the fact that he is acting, which is further reminiscent of the role of the harlequin.

Mead is the modern incarnation of the fool who, through his play-acting style, blurs the line between fiction and reality. Faced with Mead's performances, the audience has difficulty in determining whether he is performing or simply playing himself. In the end, the audience is enlightened by such a liberated and free-form performance style, for according to Enid Welford in *The Fool: His Social and Literary History* (1966), Mead "draws out the latent folly in his audience" (28).

Mead, much like William Burroughs, turned his back on a well-to-do upbringing. His father arranged a job at Merrill Lynch for him as a stockbroker, but Mead quit soon after to hitchhike across the country, in the tradition of Kerouac, and settled in San Francisco, where he met many innovative artists and filmmakers, including Ron Rice. Other important New American Cinema films Mead starred in were Vernon Zimmerman's *Lemon Hearts* (1960) and Adolfus Mekas's *Hallelujah the Hills* (1963).

Mead starred alongside Winifred Bryan in Rice's last, unfinished film before his untimely death, *The Queen of Sheba Meets the Atom Man* (1963–1982). Perhaps one of the New American Cinema's most carnivalesque of films, here again Mead showcases his improvisational style of performance as the Atom Man, a pseudomadman who takes on various personae, such as a drug-crazed fool, a businessman, a doctor, a proper gentleman, a mad scientist, and a servant. Mead possesses the ability to symbolically change "masks" depending on his situation and environment.

Mead is also well known for his performances in some of Andy Warhol's films between 1963 and 1968, including the title role of Tarzan in *Tarzan and Jane Regained . . . Sort Of* (1964).

—*Ari Grief*

## Bibliographical References

Ari Grief, *Breaking Frozen Cinematic Ground: Carnival and the New American Cinema,* 2001; P. Adams Sitney, *The American Avant-Garde,* 1974; Enid Welsford, *The Fool: His Social and Literary History,* 1966.

*See also* Film

## Mekas, Jonas (1922–)

Seminal figure in underground cinema, which he later referred to as the New American Cinema; producer of various films, among them *Guns of the Trees* (1962), *The Brig* (1963), *Walden* (1969), *Lost, Lost, Lost* (1975), *Reminiscences of a Voyage to Lithuania* (1972), and *Zefiro Torna* (1992); publisher of the magazine *Film Culture;* founder and director of Anthology Film Archives in New York City; cofounder of the Filmmakers' Cooperative; author of a column on filmmaking for the *Village Voice.*

Born in Lithuania, Mekas studied at the University of Mainz in Germany, but the outbreak of World War II did not allow for the beginning of an artistic career. In 1949 he arrived in the United States and distinguished himself as an avant-garde filmmaker. He is also the author of six volumes of poetry in Lithuanian. His principal themes are family, friendship, and memories of childhood. *Guns of the Trees* may be the film that most clearly connects Mekas to the Beats. Allen Ginsberg narrates, and the film explores the oppressive mood created by the nuclear threat, racial contrasts, and the world of work. Ginsberg and Mekas introduced a screening of *Guns of the Trees* at the conference on the Beat Generation at New York University in 1994.

—William Lawlor

## Bibliographical References

David James, *To Free the Cinema,* 1990; John G. Hanhardt, "A Movement Toward the Real," in *Beat Culture and the New America,* ed. Lisa Phillips, 1995, offers some comment on Mekas; Jonas Mekas, *There Is No Ithaca,* 1996, is a selection of Mekas's early poetry translated by Vyt Bakaitis, with a preface by Czeslaw Milosz.

*See also* Film

## Meltzer, David (1937–)

David Meltzer, who worked at the Cellar and began writing poetry as early as age eleven, associated with Beat writers such as Michael McClure, Lew Welch, Jack Spicer, Robert Duncan, and Philip Whalen. Meltzer considers himself to be a late-generation Beat, having arrived in San Francisco later than other Beats. His poetry resonates with the musical qualities of jazz and folk songs, the same forms of music that inspired the Beats themselves. Meltzer has become a preserver of manuscripts written by Beats and other California poets. He is also a teacher of poetics, ensuring that students study, write, and read poetry in the future.

David Meltzer, born 17 February 1937, grew up in Rochester, New York, where his parents, Rosemunde Lovelace and Louis, worked as a musician and a writer, respectively. His father moved the family to Manhattan to enrich his career as a comic writer and Meltzer enjoyed the culturally rich neighborhood of his childhood. His early years in New York united poetry with music and performance, a foundation Meltzer's own poetry and life reflect. While his father wrote comic scripts for radio and television, young Meltzer sang on the *Horn and Hardhart Children's Hour* program in New York City. In 1946 he was introduced to bebop when he saw Charlie Parker perform at the Royal Roost. Meltzer has even described his experiences reading as a young child: he felt as if he were hearing a voice in a performance.

The link between music, poetry, and performance he felt as a child continued when he moved to Los Angeles in 1951. He continued to listen to bebop and jazz and he read Joyce and Faulkner. He sang on the *Al Jarvis Show* and *Stairway to the Stars.* From 1955–1956, he attended L.A. City College, where he discovered haiku poetry, and he attended U.C.L.A. from 1956–1957. Although his formal education ended, his informal education continued. He traveled in a circle of young artist friends who were all participating in the Los Angeles Renaissance. At one of his various jobs, he cast fake Ming dynasty horses for Rare Junk on Santa Monica Boulevard. He also contributed to Wallace Berman's publication, *Semina,* handmade collections of poetry meant to be given away instead of sold for money.

He and Berman moved to San Francisco in 1957. Meltzer often went to City Lights to hear and read poetry. He met Christina Meyer in his group of friends in San Francisco. Meltzer read his own poetry at the Cellar in North Beach, where he worked and organized readings for other local poets. He heard the Beats read their poetry at Joe Dunn's flat where open readings and discussions were encouraged. At the flat, he met and befriended Lew Welch, John Wieners, and Michael McClure while participating in discussions and readings.

He married Christina Meyer, an artist, teacher, and singer in 1959, and he was manager of Discovery Book Shop near City Lights from 1959–1967. He also founded Minotaur Books, which sold mail-order contemporary literature. His interest in music evolved when he and his wife participated in the Bay Area folk revival with Janis Joplin, David Crosby, Dino Valentino, and Jerry Garcia. They performed and recorded together as folk singers. Meltzer had a psychedelic band, Serpent Power, and in the late sixties, he worked as a musician in Snopes Country Camp Followers.

His interest in music, which blended with his interest in writing, continued to prevail at the end of the sixties, but in an interesting new form. Science fiction novels and erotica became forums for Meltzer in the late sixties and early seventies. He wrote extensively to pay the bills. While living in Mill Valley, Meltzer wrote erotic novels; he believed they were the only genre in which a writer could still rant without the pressures and burdens of canonicity. Erotica and science fiction were fresh genres, alive with new possibilities. His erotic novels, from 1968–1970, granted him a space for a voice against the Vietnam War, because he considered pornography a perfect metaphor for war.

In Bolinas, Meltzer and his wife lived among literary neighbors, who included Joanne Kyger, Robert Creeley, and Lawrence Ferlinghetti. Often Anne Waldman, Philip Whalen, Robert Duncan, and Robert Kelly visited the area. Meltzer has described the atmosphere as a "literary hot spot." He became involved with preserving the memory of such hot spots by persuading California institutions that the archival material of his Beat peers was valuable and worth procuring. He supports and encourages efforts to archive materials of Californians who participated in the Los Angeles and San Francisco Renaissances. He received awards and grants from the Coordinating Council for Literary Magazines in 1973–1974 and 1981, the National Endowment for the Arts in 1974, and the California Arts Council in 1979. The latter award granted him money to teach and sponsor writing workshops for prisoners.

Meltzer began a teaching career at Urban School, a private high school in San Francisco; he taught jazz history and was head of a dream workshop from 1975–1976. From 1979–1981, he taught a writing workshop at Vacaville State Prison in California. His poetry in the 1981 edition of *Art/Veil* records his experience teaching at the prison. He currently teaches in the poetics program at New College in San Francisco. He teaches graduate and undergraduate poetics and has worked there with Robert Duncan and Duncan McNaughton.

His most recent book is *Beat Thing* (2004), a long poem that reviews Beat legend and Beat personalities. Other recent books have been anthologies on jazz. Some of his own poetry can be found anthologized in *The New American Poetry 1945–1960* (1960), *Beatitude Anthology*, ed. Lawrence Ferlinghetti (1960), and *The Real Bohemia* (1961). David Meltzer has not only participated in the Beat movement by writing his own music and performance-inspired poetry, learning from the Beats themselves, but he has also continued to be a teacher and promoter of poetry and music. By teaching poetics, ensuring the preservation of Beat materials, and writing and/or creating his own poetry, Meltzer continues the spirit of the Beat movement.

—*Lisa Wellinghoff*

## Primary Works

Poems (with Donald Schenker), 1957; *Ragas: Poems*, 1959; *The Clown: A Poem*, 1960; *We All Have Something to Say to Each Other*, 1962; *Bazascope Mother*, 1964; *Blackest Rose*, 1964; *The Process*, 1965; *In Hope I Offer a Fire Wheel: A Poem*, 1965; *The Dark Continent*, 1967; *Nature Poem*, 1967;

*Journal of Birth*, 1967; *How Many Blocks in a Pile*, 1968; *The Agency*, 1968; *The Agent*, 1968; *Orf*, 1968; *The Martyr*, 1969; *Yesod*, 1969; *Luna*, 1970; *The Brain Planet Tetralogy: Lovely, Healer, Out and Glue Factory*, 1970 (reprinted together in 1970, separately in 1969); *Round the Poem Box Rustic & Domestic Home Movies for Stan & Jane Brakhage*, 1969; *Star*, 1970; *Hero/Lil*, 1973; *Tens: Selected Poems 1961–1971*, 1973; *Bark: A Polemic*, 1973; *Six*, 1976; *Two Way Mirror: A Poetry Note-Book*, 1977; *The Art/Veil*, 1981; *The Name: Selected Poetry 1973–1983*, 1984; *The Agency Trilogy*, 1994; *Arrows Selected Poetry 1957–1992*, 1994; *No Eyes: Lester Young*, 2000; *Beat Thing*, 2004.

Works Edited: *Journal For the Protection of All Beings #1: A Visionary and Revolutionary Review* (with Lawrence Ferlinghetti and Michael McClure), 1960; *Journal for the Protection of All Beings* (with Lawrence Ferlinghetti, Gary Snyder, and Michael McClure), 1968; *The San Francisco Poets*, 1971; *Golden Gate: Interviews with Five San Francisco Poets*, 1976; *The Secret Garden: An Anthology in the Kabbalah*, 1976; *Birth: Hymns, Prayers, Documents, Myths, and Amulets*, 1981; *Death: An Anthology of Ancient Texts, Songs, Prayers, and Stories*, 1985; *Reading Jazz*, 1993; *Writing Jazz*, 1999; *San Francisco Beat: Talking with the Poets*, 2001.

Audio Recordings: From Vanguard: *Poet Song*, 1969; and *Serpent Power*, 1986. From S-Tapes: *Re-Runs*, 1980; and *Nurse*, 1982. From Membrane Tapes: *David Meltzer Reading*, 1981. From Folkways Records: *Faces: New Songs for Kids*, 1985; and from Living Room Tapes: *Just Folks*, 1985; *Just Standards*, 1986; *For*, 1987; and *Stars*, 1988.

## Bibliographical Sources

*Dictionary of Literary Biography, Part 2: M-Z, The Beats: Literary Bohemians in Postwar America*, Vol 16., 1983; Barbara R. Gitenstein, *Apocalyptic Messianism and Contemporary Jewish-American Poetry*, 1986; David Kherdian, *Six Poets of the San Francisco Renaissance*, 1965; David Kherdian, *Meltzer: A Skeleton from Memory and Descriptive Checklist*, 1965; and Michael Perkins, *The Secret Record: Modern Erotic Literature*, 1976.

**See also** San Francisco; Ferlinghetti, Lawrence

## Memory

A central source for Beat inspiration and composition. Because the Beats frequently write in the au-tobiographical or confessional mode, memory pro-vides the substance of their work.

According to Dennis McNally in *Desolate Angel* (1979), Jack Kerouac's nickname was Memory Babe (250). In 1958, Kerouac even started a novel that took the nickname for its title. Gerald Nicosia, one of Kerouac's biographers, titled his life of Ker-ouac *Memory Babe: A Critical Biography of Jack Kerouac* (1994). Allen Ginsberg, when asked to compose an introduction for Kerouac's *Visions of Cody*, read the book slowly and carefully, compiling extensive notes. This response to Kerouac's novel was eventually published as *Visions of the Great Rememberer* (1974). Current paperback printings of *Visions of Cody* now include Ginsberg's lengthy introduction.

Kerouac's literary method is founded on mem-ory. In "Belief & Technique for Modern Prose," which is included in *The Portable Jack Kerouac*, ed. Ann Charters (1995), the seventeenth article in his "List of Essentials" specifies that writing is an act of recollection that the writer does for personal satis-faction (483). "Essentials of Spontaneous Prose," which is also in *The Portable Jack Kerouac*, allows for the artist to respond to immediate reality, but the writer has the alternative to sketch from mem-ory (484).

Kerouac sought to record his life as the Legend of Duluoz—Kerouac's individual works were meant to be joined ultimately as one huge book similar to Marcel Proust's *Remembrance of Things Past* (1913–1927).

As a visionary writer, Kerouac makes his reliance on memory very clear. *Visions of Gerard* (1963) is based on Kerouac's power to recall himself as a toddler witnessing the saintliness and suffering of his elder brother. *Visions of Cody* recalls Cody Pomeray, the fictional character who corresponds to Neal Cassady, Kerouac's inspiring friend.

Ironically, Jack Kerouac's tragic death made Ker-ouac himself a memory. Allen Ginsberg's "Memory Gardens," an elegy for Kerouac written in the days following Kerouac's funeral in Lowell, Massachu-setts, in 1969, rues the loss of Ginsberg's friend and fellow writer, but recalls the images of his life. Like Kerouac's work, Ginsberg's "Howl" and "Kaddish" are autobiographical and confessional, drawing on memory for their power.

—William Lawlor

## Bibliographical References

Dennis McNally, *Desolate Angel*, 1979; Gerald Nicosia, *Memory Babe: A Critical Biography of Jack Kerouac*, 1994; "Belief & Technique for Modern Prose" and "Essentials of Spontaneous Prose" appear in *The Portable Jack Kerouac*, ed. Ann Charters, 1995; Ginsberg's "Memory Gardens" is included in *Collected Poems 1947–1980*, 1984; Ginsberg's *Visions of the Great Rememberer*, 1974, is available as a separate volume, but *Visions of Cody*, 1993, includes this introductory essay.

*See also* Kerouac, Jack; Ginsberg, Allen; Confession

## Mental Illness

A recurrent topic in the lives and literature of the Beat Generation, with an ultimate challenge being made about society's definition of insanity; society's role in causing depression, mental instability, and mental illness; and the medical profession's inappropriate treatment of psychological problems.

In *One Flew Over the Cuckoo's Nest,* Ken Kesey explores the issue of mental illness within the confines of a mental hospital. Randle P. McMurphy thinks that he can avoid the inconveniences of his jail sentence by getting himself transferred to a mental ward. Ironically, he ends up facing consequences far worse than any his jail sentence would have entailed, because Nurse Ratched asserts her power to control the men on the ward, especially McMurphy, and she arranges electroshock treatments and lobotomies. In the end, one sees that Nurse Ratched is the one with mental problems, not McMurphy.

Kesey's discussion of mental illness is especially poignant because Bromden, the narrator, is delusional at the start of the novel. He does not speak, and he has extraordinary visions of the Combine's control over everything in the ward and the world. The treatment afforded to the patients, including daily medication and group therapy discussions, provides little relief for the patients, but does enhance Nurse Ratched's control. McMurphy's antics and enthusiasm are more therapeutic, especially for Bromden, who emerges from his delusions in the course of the novel and becomes mentally sound. Saddened by the effects of the lobotomy on McMurphy, Bromden kills McMurphy, thereby placing him beyond the nurse's control, and Bromden escapes. The other patients, who are in the ward on a voluntary basis, also leave. Therefore, the inmates prove themselves to be saner and shrewder than the people who are supposed to cure the sick.

While the use of electricity to treat mental problems dates back to the ancient Romans, the modern beginning of electroshock therapy is usually credited to Ugo Cerletti, who in 1938 achieved positive results with a psychotic patient. He led other health professionals to take up the practice and soon the procedure, which was reasonably simple and not unduly expensive, was widely applied. Beat Generation figure Seymour Krim underwent electroshock treatment. However, electroshock treatment was sometimes used inappropriately and too often. In some cases, treatments were used to punish patients in mental wards rather than relieve their problems. Despite such problems, electroshock treatment, now called electroconvulsive therapy, is still used today, and, according to some doctors, the treatment produces positive results when properly applied. In 2001 the American Psychiatric Association published *The Practice of Electroconvulsive Therapy: Recommendations for Treatment, Training, and Privileging*, second edition, and this book indicates when this treatment is appropriate, how it should be administered, how outcomes can be assessed, and what side effects may occur.

Lobotomy as a treatment for mental illness gained favor in the years following World War II. State hospitals were crowded, conditions deteriorated, and numerous veterans who suffered from mental disturbances could not find effective treatment. In 1938, Portuguese physician Egas Moniz and his associate Almeida Lima applied to twenty patients a surgical treatment that tests on monkeys and chimps suggested was effective. Moniz recorded positive findings in a monograph, and in the United States, Dr. Walter Freeman and Dr. James Watts responded to Moniz in 1942 with their book *Psychosurgery*. Magazines such as *Time* and *Life* reported favorably on lobotomies, and by 1950 Freeman and Watts had performed lobotomies on over 1,000 patients. In 1949, Egas Moniz won the Nobel Prize in physiology and medicine, and the door swung fully open. Many other practitioners performed the procedure, and in the postwar years approximately 40,000 lobotomies were done. By the late 1950s, some of the undesirable side effects were evident, and medications seemed to be a preferable alternative to surgery. Nevertheless, with the rise of a vigorous counterculture and the occurrence of race riots in the 1960s, lobotomies again seemed purposeful, and concerned citizens expressed their apprehensions.

The sorrows, horrors, and dangers of mental illness are key factors in the life and writings of Allen Ginsberg. "Kaddish" tells the harrowing story of the mental problems of Naomi Ginsberg, Allen Ginsberg's mother. Though tender and loving, Naomi had repeated problems with delusions and unfounded suspicions of others. In "Kaddish" Ginsberg unfolds the struggles of Naomi, her erotic fantasies, and the agony of surgeries, including the lobotomy for which Allen himself, in accordance with the advice of Naomi's doctors, formally gave approval. The poem is a prayer following Naomi's death and a confession of Allen Ginsberg's own mental anguish.

Ginsberg's "Howl" has similar emphasis on mental illness. The poem opens with the declaration that Ginsberg has witnessed the most brilliant people of his time being driven insane. The poem is dedicated to Carl Solomon, and an extended portion of the poem makes reference to the author's stay at a mental hospital in which Solomon was a fellow patient. In the end, however, Ginsberg seems to say that the crazed behavior of the many people he refers to is justifiable in view of the madness that surrounds them. The evil spirit of Moloch prevails, and an atomic doom is possible at any second. Ginsberg's fellows are angels on a visionary quest for holiness, but an insane world surrounds them.

Society's view of mental health had special implications for women of the Beat Generation. In a report about the celebration of Allen Ginsberg's life at the Naropa Institute in the summer of 1994, Stephen Scobie quotes Gregory Corso, who responded to a question about the absence of women in the Naropa program in particular and in the Beat Generation in general by insisting that women were represented among the Beats; however, Corso explained that society rarely permitted women to experiment with nonconformity, and the consequence for women who did rebel was institutionalization and electroshock treatment.

Elise Cowen is perhaps an example of the situation to which Corso refers. Her successful parents expected Elise to graduate from Bard and pursue a respectable life. When she associated with unconventional people and experimented with sex and drugs, her parents sought professional help. Elise also became involved with Allen Ginsberg, and for a time a relationship seemed to form, but when Ginsberg pursued his homosexual identity, Elise became obsessed. She descended into the drug world, lost her grip on reality, and wound up at Bellevue Hospital. Released to the care of her parents, she could not tolerate life and leapt to her death from the window of her parents' apartment in Manhattan.

Natalie Jackson further illustrates the struggle of Beat women with mental instability. Jackson was Neal Cassady's lover in San Francisco in 1955, and when she was with Neal, she brimmed with energy and enthusiasm. However, by degrees she became nervously anxious and filled with worries. As her tensions grew worse, she made repeated attempts to slash her wrists, and when she did so on a rooftop and police tried to restrain her, she slipped away and plunged from the roof to her death. In *The Dharma Bums*, Jack Kerouac describes Natalie Jackson as Rosie Buchanan, who has irrational fears about the police and an international conspiracy to jail people and endlessly interrogate them. Ray Smith, the narrator, does not take Rosie seriously, but by morning she slips away to the roof, tries to slash her wrists, and falls from the roof when the police try to control her.

Problems with mental health afflicted various other people associated with the Beats. Jack Kerouac had difficulty in adjusting to his service in the navy and was eventually discharged. In *Big Sur*, Kerouac tells the story of his alcohol-induced crackup at Bixby Canyon. Charlie Parker had a nervous breakdown in 1946 and spent months at Camarillo State Hospital. Lew Welch, after starting a master's degree program at the University of Chicago, suffered a nervous breakdown and could not continue. Welch's problems subsided for a while, but eventually the pressures of life forced him into an apparent suicide. Richard Brautigan went through a period of instability and entered Oregon State Hospital for treatment. Like Welch, Brautigan eventually surrendered to suicide.

—*William Lawlor*

## Bibliographical References

Ken Kesey, *One Flew Over the Cuckoo's Nest,* 1962; Allen Ginsberg, "Howl," in *Howl and Other Poems,* 1956; Allen Ginsberg, "Kaddish," in *Kaddish and Other Poems,* 1960; Elliot S. Valenstein, *Great and Desperate Cures,* 1986, gives a detailed history of the rise of the lobotomy; the National Commission for the Protection of Human Subjects of Biomedical and Behavioral Research, *Report and Recommendations: Psychosurgery,* 1977, is specific but less detailed than Valenstein's work; Timothy Kneeland, *Pushbutton Psychiatry,* 2002, gives the history of electroshock treatment in the United States; Josephine Marcotty, "Electroshock Therapy Revised," *Minneapolis Star and Tribune,* 17 November 1999, provides a quick review. See the relevant section of Stephen Scobie's report on Naropa in Brenda Knight, ed., *Women of the Beat Generation,* 1996. Knight also has information on Elise Cowen and Natalie Jackson. Jackson's fictional identity as Rosie Buchanan is in Jack Kerouac, *The Dharma Bums,* 1958.

*See also* Kesey, Ken Elton; Ginsberg, Allen; Cowen, Elise; Kerouac, Jack; Krim, Seymour; Solomon, Carl; Welch, Lew; Brautigan, Richard

## Merry Pranksters

The name given to a group of friends and followers of novelist Ken Kesey (*One Flew Over the Cuckoo's Nest; Sometimes a Great Notion*), who are immortalized in Tom Wolfe's 1968 book *The Electric Kool-Aid Acid Test.* That book described their 1964 cross-country trip in a multicolored 1939 International Harvester school bus to attend the 1964 New York World's Fair and the release party for Kesey's second novel. It further described the ongoing experimentations by Kesey and the Pranksters with LSD to try to achieve a "group mind"—experimentations that led to the famous LSD-laced and multimedia-infused "acid tests" of 1965–1966, featuring the Grateful Dead. Kesey and the Pranksters filmed their adventures and planned to release a film, *Intrepid Traveler and His Merry Band of Pranksters Look for a Cool Place,* but only portions of the voluminous footage were ever released. A traveling commune, the Pranksters lived up to their name through their reputation for constantly pulling pranks on friends and strangers—a practice that typically recalled their own self-styled motto: "Never trust a Prankster."

A product of the Beat culture, the Pranksters, through their frequent use of marijuana and LSD, were at the forefront of the transition from the less drug-laden Beat culture to the more drug-infused hippie culture and were vanguards of psychedelic culture. Indeed, while the Pranksters were led by Kesey, their bus driver the vast majority of the time was Neal Cassady, the inspiration for Dean Moriarty in Jack Kerouac's *On the Road.* Straddling both Beat culture and hippie culture, Cassady was further immortalized in song by the Grateful Dead as "Cowboy Neal at the wheel of a bus to never-ever land" ("That's It for the Other One"). Further, through Wolfe's documentation of the Pranksters' exploits, the American lexicon was enriched by references to whether someone was either "on the bus" or "off the bus"—phrases that were interpreted most often metaphorically in reference to whether someone was "cool" or "hip" or "with it."

The acid tests, conducted during a time when LSD was still legal in California, began in November 1965 in San Jose, California, and approximately a dozen were held between then and February 1966 in and around San Francisco, in Los Angeles, in Oregon, and even in Mexico, where Kesey fled

Neal Cassady, also known as Speed Limit, safely drove a colorful bus across the nation, carrying Ken Kesey and the Merry Pranksters to numerous locations. (Ted Streshinsky/Corbis)

in 1966 to avoid prosecution on a marijuana possession charge and where he was subsequently followed by the Pranksters. The acid tests, oftentimes held in dance halls, typically featured the Grateful Dead, then just starting out as a band, as musical entertainment, along with the Merry Pranksters playing their own interpretation of music in another area of the dance hall, while sound and light shows enhanced the sensory experience and contributed to the audience being as much a part of the show as the performers. A trash can or two filled with LSD-laced "electric Kool-Aid" provided the chemical stimulus for the evening. The acid tests derived their name from a card that was used to promote the first production and that featured a

traditional armed forces recruiting picture of Uncle Sam with the words "CAN YOU PASS THE ACID TEST?"

—*Timothy D. Ray*

## Bibliographical References

Ken Kesey, *The Further Inquiry,* 1990; Dennis McNally, "The Bus Came By (11/13/65–2/5/66)," in *A Long Strange Trip: The Inside History of the Grateful Dead,* 2002; Timothy Miller, "The New Communes Emerge, 1960–1965" in *The 60s Communes: Hippies and Beyond,* 1999; Paul Perry and Ken Babbs, *On the Bus: The Complete Guide to the Legendary Trip of Ken Kesey and the Merry Pranksters and the Birth of the Counterculture,* 1990; William Plummer, *The Holy Goof: A Biography of Neal Cassady,* 1981;

Tom Wolfe, *The Electric Kool-Aid Acid Test*, 1968.

*See also* Cassady, Neal; Drugs; Furthur/Further; Kesey, Ken Elton

## Merton, Thomas (1915–1968)

Poet and writer, Merton, a Trappist monk subsequently known as Father Louis, is widely regarded as one of the most influential writers in twentieth-century American Catholicism. While not a member of the Beats, his spiritual restlessness, his love of jazz, and his later interest in Asian mysticism and social criticism attracted them. Jack Kerouac dedicated several poems to Merton.

The first twenty-six years of his life are described in his most famous work, the spiritual autobiography *The Seven Storey Mountain* (1948). This work traces his growth from a state of atheism and little personal discipline through his education at Columbia University, and culminates in his conversion to Catholicism in 1938. In 1941, Merton entered the Abbey of Gethsemane, Kentucky, receiving ordination into the Cistercian Order of the Strict Observance (the Trappists). The next twenty-seven years of his life were devoted to teaching and writing. In his last years, Merton received special dispensation to become a hermit. Despite his separation from the world, he played an active role as social critic, opposing the war in Vietnam and the nuclear arms race, supporting the civil rights movement, and exploring the dehumanizing effects of technology.

A prolific writer, Merton produced some sixty books, many published by New Directions. These included twelve books of poetry, volumes of autobiographical writings, many devotional works and essays, including the influential collections *Mystics and Zen Masters* (1967) and *Zen and the Birds of Appetite* (1968), both of which influenced an interest in Eastern mysticism, states of consciousness, and Zen Buddhism. Merton also produced translations and edited several books on peace and on Gandhi and nonviolence.

—*Thomas L. Cooksey*

### Principal Works

*Figures for an Apocalypse*, 1948; *The Seven Storey Mountain*, 1948; *The Waters of Siloe*, 1949; *Seeds of Contemplation*, 1949; *The Sign of Jonas*, 1952; *No Man is an Island*, 1955; *The Living Bread*, 1956; *Mystics and Zen Masters*, 1967; *Zen and the Birds of Appetite*, 1968; *Contemplation in a World of Action*, 1971.

### Bibliographical References

James Baker, *Thomas Merton—Social Critic*, 1971, is a study of Merton's later commitment to social justice and peace; Lawrence Cunningham, *Thomas Merton and the Monastic Vision* is an examination of Merton's religious convictions from the perspective of monasticism; Victor A. Kramer, *Thomas Merton*, 1984, is a standard introduction to Merton's work; John Laughlin, *Reading Thomas Merton: A Guide to his Life and Works*, 2000, is an important handbook, briefly discussing Merton's entire body of work; Sister Therese Lentfoehr, *Words and Silence: On the Poetry of Thomas Merton*, 1979, is the best study of Merton's poetry; Anthony Padovano, *The Human Journey: Thomas Merton, Symbol of a Century*, 1982, is a solid intellectual biography that looks at Merton's religious and social concerns in the context of modern spiritual desires; see also William H. Shannon, and others, *The Thomas Merton Encyclopedia*, 2002; George Woodcock, *Thomas Merton: Monk and Poet*, 1978, is an important early biography.

## Mexico City

The capital megalopolis of the nation of Mexico, known as México, D.F. (*Distrito Federal*), or, to North Americans, as Mexico City. The city's population doubled in the decade before 1950, to about 3 million; in 2005 there are more than 16 million persons living in the Valle de México, in one of the planet's largest and most polluted megacities.

Along with New York City, Paris, San Francisco, and London, Mexico City is one of the key cities on the Beat map. William S. Burroughs and Jack Kerouac both lived there for extended periods and wrote major works set in the city. A host of other Beat characters either visited or lived there during 1949–1968 as well, including David Kammerer

(1911–1944), Lucien Carr (b. 1925), Kells Elvins (1913–1961), Joan Vollmer (1924–1951), Neal Cassady (1926–1968), Bill Garver (1913?–1954), Hal Chase (b. 1923), Allen Ginsberg (1926–1997), Gregory Corso (1930–2001), Peter Orlovsky (b. 1933), Howard Hart (1927–2002), Philip Lamantia (1927–2005), and Ray Bremser (1934–1998) and his wife, Bonnie (Brenda Frazer, b. 1939), among others.

The Pan American Highway's 775-mile section linking Laredo, Texas, to Mexico City was finally completed in July 1937. Automobile tourism from North America grew by leaps and bounds every year in the following decade, from less than 20,000 annually in 1936 to more than 200,000 by 1941; for centuries Mexico's leading industry had been silver, but now it changed almost overnight to tourism. The lifting of gasoline rations after the war and a 35 percent devaluation of the peso in 1949 boosted the annual number of *turistos gringos* past 300,000. The Mexican government subsidized the promotion of tourism, and many U.S. magazine and newspaper stories extolled our southern neighbor as an exotic, affordable destination.

Four influential novels helped to shape the "Mexican imaginary" for literate North Americans in this period: *The Plumed Serpent*, by D. H. Lawrence (1926); "Hacienda," by Katherine Anne Porter (1934); *The Power and the Glory*, by Graham Greene (1940); and *Under the Volcano*, by Malcolm Lowry (1947).

Lawrence and Porter each lived in Mexico in the early 1920s, only a decade after the Mexican Revolution of 1910. Lawrence depicts a newly independent Mexico struggling to throw off her centuries-old Spanish-Catholic yoke, but caught between contesting European ideologies of communism and fascism, and the irresistible "Oriental" imperatives of her ancient Aztec religion. Porter portrays, with a certain cynicism, the social microcosm of Mexican cultural revolutionaries and visiting international avant-garde artists.

Greene and Lowry were each in Mexico in the late 1930s; the postrevolutionary governments of Presidents Calles and Obregón had put down the *Cristero* revolt of the 1920s, but they continued to persecute the Catholic Church. Greene (a 1926 convert to Catholicism) captures the complexity and pathos of the worldly wise "Whiskey Priest," an existentialist antihero who acquiesces to a martyr's fate. Lowry was by 1936 a desperately ill alcoholic, although he intermittently recovered sufficiently to rewrite the book for ten more years before finishing it. His vision of Mexico is both gloomy and bitterly humorous; his protagonist, "the Consul," is another bleak, doomed antihero.

Condescension, naïve mythification, projection, and the "imperial gaze" of late colonialism mark the reactions of all the Beat writers who lived in and wrote about Mexico during 1949 to 1957—but the same can also be said of Lawrence, Porter, Greene, Lowry, and others. Much of what they saw in Mexico was what they brought to it: interwar sexual liberationism, post-Stalin era political chagrin (or idealism), Catholic existentialism, mystical fatalism, etc.

To these viewpoints, the Beats—or rather, Burroughs, who was specifically influenced by the four cited works, and who in turn influenced his younger friends—brought also the ideas of Oswald Spengler (1880–1936), whose 1918/1922 masterwork, *The Decline of the West*, provided the *fellaheen* concept: the nameless native masses, caught between great historical moments whose meanings are beyond their understanding, and living in an eternal, historyless present. Kerouac in particular felt a kinship between himself and his Beat friends and these ahistoric denizens of an idealized urban-peasant Eden; in Mexico, and later in Morocco, Kerouac saw *fellaheen* everywhere. The sentimental myopia of this simplistic view has been much noted in recent critical studies of the Beats' culture-centric, late-colonial outlook on the non-American world.

Apparently the earliest Beat-related visitor to Mexico was William Burroughs's friend from his St. Louis days, David Kammerer, who in 1939 (aged twenty-eight) was able to get permission from the mother of his protégé, Lucien Carr (aged fourteen), to take the precocious boy from St. Louis to Mexico City for a summer vacation trip. But Burroughs was the first of the Beats to live in Mexico City, and it was his presence that drew the other Beat writers there.

Burroughs himself was initially drawn to Mexico by his boyhood friend Kells Elvins, who had inherited farmland and citrus groves in the Texas border town of Pharr. In the summer of 1946, Elvins enticed Burroughs to join him in his farming venture with tales of how the money was just waiting to be picked off the trees in South Texas. Burroughs, who was living back at home in St. Louis following a drug arrest in New York City, thought the plan sounded good. They were in business together in the valley for three years. By late 1949, a second drug bust (in New Orleans), and his failing fortunes as a farmer, led Burroughs to "jump" across the border, escaping his pending drug charges to live in a land he believed was "free" in a way America no longer was.

Burroughs, his wife Joan, and their two children all moved to Mexico City in September 1949. They first lived at 37 Cerrada de Medellín (today Calle José Alvarado), but later moved to an apartment at 210 Orizaba Street—still within the Colonia Roma neighborhood around Mexico City College, where Burroughs was taking classes in anthropology.

In his "Introduction" to Queer (written in 1985), Burroughs described Mexico City at that time as a city of 1 million inhabitants overarched by a piercing blue sky. (He undercounted the population by two-thirds.) Food was cheap, rent was cheap, and the whorehouses were "fabulous." He initially saw Mexico City as a place of nearly total freedom, where the cops had as much authority as a streetcar conductor and both boys and drugs were plentiful. He used such enticing descriptions of Mexico City to lure Jack Kerouac and Neal Cassady down there in April 1950, a trip recorded in the famous "Mexico" section of On the Road. Lucien Carr was also drawn to return to Mexico; he visited Burroughs and Vollmer there in August 1950.

Lucien Carr visited Mexico City again, this time with Allen Ginsberg, in August 1951, just two weeks before the tragic moment that would define Burroughs's life thereafter—his accidental shooting of Joan in a "William Tell" scene they performed at a party above the Bounty Bar and Grill at 122 Calle Monterrey in Mexico City on 6 September 1951. Burroughs's flamboyant lawyer, Bernabé Jurado,

got him out of jail in record time (thirteen days) on a $2,300 bond, but Mexico City was never the same for Burroughs thereafter. When Jurado himself was forced to leave the country in November 1952, Burroughs finally followed suit. He had lived there three years, he said, and didn't even have anyone to say goodbye to. From a place of promise and freedom, Mexico had become (for him) a sinister "Oriental" land filled with chaos.

Still, it was that very chaos that inspired him in his writings about Mexico City. Mexico City was the kind of place where anything could happen, a dreamlike place. Although the city shows up as a setting in almost all of his works, it is most important as a setting at the end of Junky and in Burroughs's major book set there, Queer.

Written in 1952 but not published until 1985, Queer tells the story of Burroughs's seduction of a straight young man named Eugene Allerton (Lewis Marker in real life). Both are Mexico City College students. The action takes place in the bars and restaurants of Colonia Roma, near the college. Toward the end of the book, Lee and Allerton leave the city on an expedition to South America in search of the hallucinogenic vine called yagé. Finally Lee (Burroughs) returns to the city alone, abandoned by Allerton. Although the 1952 text makes almost no mention of Joan Vollmer, Burroughs later confessed that the book, in veiled ways, is all about what is not written: Joan's death. Eerie, premonitory scenes in the book—such as one in a Mexico City bar where Lee shoots a rat being dangled by its tail—reveal this story within a story.

The other great Beat writer whose work was indelibly influenced by Mexico City is Jack Kerouac. In 1947, Kerouac went "on the road" for the first time, from New York to Denver and on to San Francisco; on his way back that autumn, he spent two weeks in a romantic border idyll with an anonymous "Mexican girl," before returning to New York. In 1947–1949 he was following Neal Cassady around the country, or traveling across it with him, and when Cassady caught up with Kerouac in Denver in spring 1950, at the wheel of a late-model "drive-away" Cadillac, he easily convinced his impressionable friend to head south with him.

As Kerouac describes it in *On the Road*, Dean Moriarty exhorts Sal Paradise, referring to the Pan American Highway: "Think if you and I had a car like this what we could do. Do you know there's a road that goes down Mexico and all the way to Panama?—and maybe all the way to the bottom of South America where the Indians are seven feet tall and eat cocaine on the mountainside? Yes! You and I, Sal, we'd dig the whole world with a car like this because, man, the road must eventually lead to the whole world" (231).

In April 1950, Kerouac, Neal Cassady, and his fellow Denverite, Frank Jeffries, crossed the border at Laredo, Texas, on a road trip chronicled in Part Four, Chapters 4–6, of *On the Road*. Kerouac's description of Mexico on this trip closely reflects Burroughs's description of Mexico in his letters to Kerouac: it is a virtual paradise of freedom and easy living. After smoking huge marijuana cigarettes rolled in newspaper and enjoying a wild night in a whorehouse in Gregoria, they continued their trip on down to Mexico City, where Burroughs, Joan, and the kids were their hosts.

For a few days, the American visitors sampled the food and the prostitutes, wandering the streets of the city, but Kerouac fell ill with dysentery, and Cassady returned to the United States without him. (Jeffries would stay on as a Mexico City College student.) When Kerouac recovered, he further explored the city, finding it to be similar, in many ways, to his hometown of Lowell, Massachusetts. In *On the Road* he would claim that because of his French Canadian and Indian heritage, he actually was, in some way, a Mexican. This first visit to Mexico City would thus prove to be an inspiration both for *On the Road* and *Doctor Sax*, his novel about growing up in Lowell.

Two years later, in April 1952, Kerouac again visited Mexico City, crossing the border south of Tucson, Arizona, on the newly opened western route from Nogales to Guadalajara and Mexico City (see "Mexican Fellaheen" in *Lonesome Traveler*)—twice as long as the eastern route through Nuevo Laredo. He quickly hooked up with a young Mexican hipster named Enrique, who accompanied Kerouac to Culiacán, where they smoked opium with a local medicine man. Kerouac abandoned Enrique in Mexico City, however, and moved in with Burroughs.

Burroughs was not the same man after the traumatic experience of shooting his wife, and he was closely watched by the Mexican authorities. Often, Kerouac hid out in Burroughs's toilet to smoke and write. Kerouac's marathon pot-smoking sessions and bad roommate manners annoyed the police-shy Burroughs, and the visit strained their friendship.

From May to June 1952, while living with Burroughs, Kerouac produced one of his finest books: *Doctor Sax*. Although the book is about Kerouac's childhood in Lowell, Massachusetts, the history of Mexico City accounts for the wild ending of the often-allegorical novel, in which a serpent is carried aloft by a bird of paradise. According to legend, the Aztecs chose the site of Mexico City as their capital when they observed an eagle catching a serpent and flying off with it clutched in its beak.

Kerouac next visited Mexico City in August 1955, and he wrote about the events of this two-month stay in Part Two of *Desolation Angels* and in *Tristessa*. In "Passing through Mexico" (*Desolation Angels*), he presents a much different view of the city than he had in *On the Road:* it is a sad, dreary place, and he no longer romanticizes the Mexican people as representing Oswald Spengler's noble *fellaheen*. Burroughs had never returned (he was now in Tangier), but their mutual friend Bill Garver, a junky from the New York City scene, had arrived not long before Burroughs's departure in late 1952, and he still remained, in his final decline.

Garver had an apartment he shared with a prostitute and drug dealer named Esperanza, and Kerouac took up residence on the roof of the building. He performed menial tasks for Garver in exchange for lodging, but spent most of his time writing—his main reason for coming to Mexico City. This peace was broken by the arrival of Allen Ginsberg, Peter Orlovsky, and Gregory Corso. Kerouac took them on a tour of Mexico City's slums, and they climbed nearby pyramids and discussed the violent history of the Aztecs and Mayans. Corso hated Mexico because of (as he saw it) her people's obsession with death.

In spite of the interruptions caused by visitors, this two-month period was among Kerouac's most productive as a writer. He wrote the first parts of both *Tristessa* and *Desolation Angels* and composed his poetic masterpiece, *Mexico City Blues*. *Tristessa* tells the story of his romance with Bill Garver's companion and drug supplier, Esperanza (Kerouac changed her name from "hope" to "sadness"). In addition to being one of Kerouac's best meditations on love, the book is also an insightful portrait of Mexico City's underworld, like Kerouac's portrait of New York City's underworld (translated to San Francisco) in *The Subterraneans*. But perhaps his greatest achievement from this period is his collection of poems entitled *Mexico City Blues*. Each morning, buoyed by coffee and a joint, Kerouac sat on the rooftop of the Orizaba Street apartment and spontaneously composed what turned out to be the 244 "choruses" of the book. Inspired by jazz and Buddhism, the poems were meant to be a poetic primer for Kerouac's friend Allen Ginsberg.

Kerouac's final trip to Mexico City, in August 1957, involved yet another doomed romantic relationship, this one with the aspiring novelist Joyce Glassman. Kerouac invited Glassman to join him in Mexico City, where he had retreated after a fight with his brother-in-law. He hoped that the city would once again bring some peace to his life and some much-needed literary inspiration. This time, however, Mexico was decidedly gloomy: Garver was dead, Esperanza was missing, and his hotel room was rattled by a severe earthquake. Kerouac had convinced the twenty-one-year-old Glassman that Mexico City was the perfect place for her to finish her novel (*Come Join the Dance,* 1962) because she could live there so cheaply and because the city itself had a special atmosphere conducive to creativity; now he wrote to Glassman telling her not to come, and spent two depressed weeks alone in the city.

Kerouac fictionalized these events at the end of *Desolation Angels;* Glassman, writing under her married name of Joyce Johnson, tells her side of this story in her memoir *Minor Characters* (1983). Glassman's most recent book, *Door Wide Open: A Beat Love Affair in Letters 1957–1958* (2001), con-

tains their letters about this obstructed romance and about Kerouac's influence on her as a writer. After this last, abortive visit, Kerouac never returned to the Land of the Eagle and Serpent.

Not every Beat associate went to Mexico just for drugs, sex, and easy living. When Kells Elvins moved to Mexico City in early 1951 with his second wife, Marianne, he was continuing his studies in criminal psychology; he had completed a master's degree in Texas, and he enrolled at the National University of Mexico to study with Erich Fromm there. Haldon "Hal" Chase, a member of the 1945–1946 Beat household of Joan Vollmer and Edie Parker, finished his anthropology studies at Columbia and enrolled in 1951 at Mexico City College to study the Zapotecan language. Even Burroughs was not merely fleeing American drug laws in fall 1949; he was also drawn to the illustrious anthropology faculty of Mexico City College, where he studied the ancient Mayans and their written glyph language.

After the publication of Burroughs's *Junkie* (by "William Lee," with its final scenes set in Mexico City) in 1953, and Kerouac's *On the Road* in 1957 and *Mexico City Blues* in 1959, Mexico's place as a Beat mecca was established. *Junkie,* and Burroughs's letters from Mexico City in 1952, show that a U.S. bohemian hipster scene was already growing up around Mexico City College in the postwar years.

With the famous 6 Gallery reading in October 1955, Ginsberg and company effectively colonized the San Francisco Renaissance poetry movement; thus, poets like Philip Lamantia (who had a transformative Christian vision while traveling in northern Mexico in the 1950s), and Howard Hart (Lamantia's friend, a jazz drummer, who joined him in Mexico City for a while) also fell under this broad mantle.

By the time that Ray Bremser (a friend of Ginsberg and Corso by 1958) fled to Mexico in the early 1960s with his young wife, Brenda Frazer, and their infant daughter Rachel, to avoid a narcotics charge, the glory days of "Beat Mexico" were nearing their end. After five years in Mexico, while Ray wrote poetry and pimped for his wife's prostitution, which supported their family, she left him in Mexico and put their daughter up for adoption at the border, arriving in New York with a new name, Bonnie Bremser. Her autobiography, *Troia: Mexican Memoirs,* was published in 1969.

Mexico still had one Beat card left to play: in the 1960s (his post-"*Road*" years), Neal Cassady was the driver for Ken Kesey's psychedelic bus and an elder guru to Kesey's "Merry Pranksters." On a visit to San Miguel de Allende in early February 1968, Cassady left a party, drunk, to walk fifteen miles to town; he was found beside the railroad tracks after dawn, in a coma, and died later that day, 4 February. The news of Cassady's death was a final blow to Kerouac, whose slide into late-stage alcoholism was mercifully ended by his own death on 21 October 1969.

—*Rob Johnson*
*James Grauerholz*

## Bibliographical References

Stefan Baciu, "Beatitude South of the Border: Latin America's Beat Generation," in *Hispania* 49: 4 (Dec. 1966); William S. Burroughs, *Junky: The Restored Text,* ed. Oliver Harris, 2003 (first published 1953), and *Queer,* 1985; Howard Campbell, "Beat Mexico: Bohemia, Anthropology, and 'the Other,'" *Critique of Anthropology* 23: 2 (June 2003); Brenda Frazer, *Troia: Mexican Memoirs,* 1969; Norman S. Hayner, "Mexico City: Its Growth and Configuration" in *American Journal of Sociology* 50: 4 (Jan. 1945); Joyce Glassman Johnson, *Minor Characters: A Memoir of a Young Woman of the 1950s in the Beat Orbit of Jack Kerouac,* 1983; Joyce Johnson and Jack Kerouac, *Door Wide Open: A Beat Love Affair in Letters 1957–1958,* 2001; Rob Johnson, "Tiger in the Valley: William S. Burroughs on the Texas-Mexico Border, 1946–1950" (unpublished manuscript); Jack Kerouac, *On the Road,* 1957, *Doctor Sax,* 1959, *Mexico City Blues,* 1959, *Lonesome Traveler,* 1960, *Tristessa,* 1960, and *Desolation Angels,* 1965; John Lardas, *Bop Apocalypse: The Religious Visions of Kerouac, Ginsberg, & Burroughs,* 2000; Jon Panish, "Kerouac's *The Subterraneans:* A Study of 'Romantic Primitivism,'" in MELUS, 19: 3 (Autumn 1994); Cecil Robinson, "The Extended Presence: Mexico and Its Culture in North American Writing," in MELUS 5: 3 (Autumn 1978); Mel van Elteren, "The Subculture of the Beats: A Sociological Revisit," in *Journal of American Culture* 22: 3 (Fall 1999).

*See also* Kerouac, Jack; Burroughs, William Seward; Ginsberg, Allen; Carr, Lucien; Kammerer, David; Vollmer Adams Burroughs, Jane; Drugs; Fellaheen; Johnson, Joyce; Bremser, Bonnie; Bremser, Ray; Cassady, Neal; Kesey, Ken Elton

## Micheline, Jack (1929–1998)

A minor poet typically associated with the Beat movement, Jack Micheline has exerted a literary influence out of proportion with his stature. Micheline was in many ways a very paradoxical personality. His early work came to prominence in large part because it was endorsed by some of the major figures among the Beats, but he was soon very publicly dismissing the concept of a "Beat movement" as an oxymoron, as the creation of a literary establishment that wished to transform the Beats' imaginative and spiritual energy into an intellectual commodity. Likewise, Micheline's great vitality and his commitment both to his own work and to the broader Beat vision of the artist as the itinerant troubadour of social revolution won him a number of lasting literary associations and personal friendships; yet he seemed perversely predisposed to alienate anyone in the publishing industry who exhibited an interest in his work. Although there is not a single entry about his work in the *MLA Bibliography,* throughout his lengthy career Micheline won awards for his readings, and a number of younger poets working in the Beat tradition have acknowledged that his readings convinced them to commit themselves to a kind of poetry that might energize imaginations and thereby liberate both the flesh and the spirit from impoverishment.

On 6 November 1929, the poet was born Harold Martin Silver in Brooklyn, New York, to Herman and Helen (Micheline) Silver. Shortly after his birth, his parents changed his first name to Harvey; he later claimed that because he was a small and delicate infant, they wished to fool the angel of death by the name change. His parents were of Russian and Romanian ethnicity. His father worked at a number of ordinary jobs, most lengthily as a

next two decades, he produced eleven more books of poetry. Most notably, in *North of Manhattan* (1975), the poems from all but his last book were collected.

Micheline's poetry was composed to be read aloud, and it suffers from some of the reliance on catch-phrase, refrain, and expression of overt sentiment that defines successful song writing. Despite these limitations, Micheline often achieves moments of compelling lyricism (as in "I Kiss the Face of a Russian Girl") and creates vivid portraits of "street" characters and scenes (as in "Librizzi's Childhood").

—*Martin Kich*

### Principal Works

Poetry: *River of Red Wine*, 1958; *I Kiss Angels*, 1962; *The World Is Getting Better*, 1963; *In the Bronx and Other Stories*, 1965; *Tell Your Mama You Want to Be Free, and Other Poemsongs*, 1969; *Yellow Horn, and Other Poemsongs*, 1969; *Poems of Dr. Innisfree*, 1975; *Purple Submarine*, 1976; *Last House in America*, 1976; *North of Manhattan: Collected Poems, Ballads, and Songs, 1954–1975*, 1977.

Stories: *Skinny Dynamite, and Other Short Stories*, 1980.

Play: *East Bleeker*, 1967.

### Bibliographical References

Scott Harrison, "Jack Micheline and His Painted Room," *Poets on the Line* 9–10 (2000): Item 46; "The Jack Micheline Foundation." http://www.jackmicheline.com/

Itinerant poet Jack Micheline was best known for his expressive readings. (Christopher Felver/Corbis)

mechanic and as postman, and Micheline grew up in a working-class, politically progressive environment. In 1947–1948, he served with the U.S. Army Medical Corps. After his discharge, he decided to commit himself to the underground literary "scenes" that he found first in Greenwich Village and then in San Francisco. He began using the pseudonym Jack Micheline, acknowledging the influence of Jack London and taking his mother's maiden name; he changed his name legally to Jack Micheline in 1963 after he and his father had a bitter falling out.

In 1958, Micheline's first book of poems, *River of Red Wine*, included an introduction by Jack Kerouac, and it was reviewed prominently by Dorothy Parker in *Esquire*. Ironically, Micheline's subsequent work never received anything approaching this level of formal critical endorsement. Over the

## Miles, Barry (1943–)

Biographer; co-owner of Indica Book Store in London, England; prolific writer on the history of the counterculture.

—*William Lawlor*

### Bibliographical References

The biographical works include *Beat Hotel*, 2000; *Ginsberg*, 1989; *Jack Kerouac*, 1998; *Paul McCartney*, 1997; *William Burroughs*, 2002; the studies of cultural history include *Hippie*, 2004; and *In the Sixties*, 2002; Miles edited Allen Ginsberg, *Howl: Original Draft Facsimile*, 1986;

he compiled *John Lennon: In His Own Words,* 1981.

*See also* London

## Mingus, Charles (1922–1979)

Charles Mingus was one of the most influential jazz bassists of all time. One of the most recognizable composers of twentieth-century jazz, he was known for a stormy temper and innovative improvisational composition technique, which influenced the Beats' writing practices, particularly what Ginsberg in his dedication to "Howl" called Kerouac's "spontaneous bop prosody." Mingus was formally trained in classical music, and his compositions are both artfully constructed and open to interpretive play, equally at home within both traditional and avant-garde styles. In *Venice West,* Arthur Maynard suggests that the syncopated playing style of bebop artists like Mingus influenced the loose rhythms of Beat poetry and prose (48).

—*David N. Wright*

**Bibliographical References**

See Timothy Hunt, *Kerouac's Crooked Road: Development of a Fiction,* 1981; John Arthur Maynard, *Venice West,* 1991; Alan M. Perlman and Daniel Greenblatt, "Miles Davis Meets Noam Chomsky: Some Observations on Jazz Improvisation and Language Structure," in *The Sign in Music and Literature,* ed. Wendy Steiner, 1981; Regina Weinreich, *The Spontaneous Poetics of Jack Kerouac,* 1987.

## Moloch (also Molech)

A false god; the fire god of the Canaanites to whose flames children were sacrificed in ritual worship. Biblical references to Moloch include 1 Kings 11:7, 2 Kings 23:10, Leviticus 18:21, Leviticus 20:2–5, and Jeremiah 32:35.

In Part II of "Howl," Allen Ginsberg refers repeatedly to Moloch, using the name to establish the fixed-base form for his lines. The biblical reference to Moloch, according to Ginsberg in his journal (quoted by Schumacher 206), suggests the society that strips humans of their individuality and makes people believe they are crazy unless they deny what is truly in their hearts.

Ginsberg's vision of Moloch stems from his viewing of the Sir Francis Drake Hotel in San Francisco. In particular, on a walk with Peter Orlovsky in 1955, Allen was high on peyote and was impressed by the illuminated monstrous hotel in the night sky.

—*William Lawlor*

**Bibliographical References**

One can see various drawings of Moloch in *Howl: Original Draft Facsimile,* ed. Barry Miles, 1986: 139–140; in the same book on page 141 is a large photo of Ginsberg and Orlovsky at night with the Sir Francis Drake Hotel in the background. In *Beat Culture and the New America,* ed. Lisa Phillips, 1995, one can see on page 16 a large photo of Ginsberg pointing to the monstrous hotel. Michael Schumacher, in *Dharma Lion,* 1992, recounts on pages 205–206 the story of Ginsberg's visionary encounter with Moloch during his walk with Peter in 1955 in San Francisco.

## Monk, Thelonious Sphere (1917–1982)

Thelonious Monk is known, along with Charlie Parker and Dizzy Gillespie, as one of the inventors of the jazz idiom known as bebop. An innovative pianist and composer, he worked irregularly throughout the forties, usually alone or in small combos. He began receiving widespread critical acclaim only during the fifties, and in 1959 he fronted his own orchestra in a performance at New York's Town Hall. But it was through the many performances in smaller New York clubs, alongside artists like Kenny Clark and Bud Powell, as well as Parker and Gillespie, that Monk undoubtedly had his most profound influence on Beat writers such as Jack Kerouac, who emulated the rhythmic and harmonic intricacies of bebop in his spontaneous prosody.

—*David Arnold*

**Bibliographical References**

Thomas Fitterling, *Thelonious Monk: His Life and Music,* 2d ed., trans. Robert Dobbins, 1997; Allen

Ginsberg, *Spontaneous Mind: Selected Interviews 1958–1996*, ed. David Carter, 2001.

*See also* Music

## Montgomery, John McVey (1919–1992)

Poet, publisher, postman, and mountain-climbing librarian, Montgomery is celebrated as Henry Morley and Alex Fairbrother in Jack Kerouac's *The Dharma Bums* (1958) and *Desolation Angels* (1965). Born in Spokane, Washington, on 2 May 1919, the only child of John McVey and Belle Murray Montgomery, John was raised on the West Coast, where he developed a love for the outdoors. After completing a bachelor's degree in economics at Berkeley, he served briefly in the army before going on to earn a master's degree in library science at George Peabody College for Teachers in Tennessee (1958) and a master's in creative writing at San Francisco State College (1964). Montgomery married twice: first to Frances Cooney (1948), then to Dora Dale Rogers (1974). He and Cooney had a daughter, Laura.

Part of Kenneth Rexroth's San Francisco literary circle, Montgomery attended the 6 Gallery reading on 7 October 1955, where Allen Ginsberg's reading of "Howl" launched the Beat movement. Montgomery supported himself working at various jobs, finding his niche finally in the post office. Although he gave occasional readings and contributed to poetry journals, he published only one book of poetry in his lifetime: *Hip, Beat, Cool & Antic* (1988).

Montgomery's main contribution to Beat literature was not as a poet but as a small press publisher and an indefatigable promoter of Kerouac's work. When Kerouac's reputation was at its lowest, Montgomery's Fels & Fern Press publications and his voluminous correspondence with Beat scholars worldwide helped keep the flame alive. Montgomery generously shared his expertise (as well as the latest gossip) in densely packed letters and postcards, usually typed in a small italic font that added to the eccentricity of his writing style. Putting scholars and collectors in touch with one another, he played an important role in reshaping Kerouac's reputation at the end of the twentieth century. Montgomery died of a heart attack on 5 June 1992 in San Rafael, California.

—*William M. Gargan*

### Principal Works

Poetry: *Hip, Beat, Cool & Antic*, 1988.
Prose: *Jack Kerouac: A Memoir*, 1970; *Kerouac West Coast*, 1976; *The Kerouac We Knew*, 1982; *Kerouac at the "Wild Boar,"* 1986.

### Bibliographical References

*A Man of Letters: Montgomery Remembered*, 1993, compiled by his daughter, Laura Petersen, offers seventy-three memoirs and tributes. Jim Christy's entry for the *Dictionary of Literary Biography, Volume 16: The Beats*, 1983, is the most extensive biography.

*See also* Kerouac, Jack

## Motherwell, Robert (1915–1991)

Painter, writer, philosopher, and theoretician; key figure in the abstract expressionist movement.

Born in Aberdeen, Washington, Motherwell attended the California School of Fine Arts, Stanford University, Harvard University, Grenoble University, and Columbia University. He arrived in New York in 1940, traveled to Mexico with Robert Matta, and then returned to New York, where his association with Willem de Kooning and Jackson Pollock began. In 1946 he had a solo exhibition at the Guggenheim Museum and became friends with Mark Rothko. Solo exhibitions at the Arts Club of Chicago and at the San Francisco Museum of Art followed. He was included in the exhibit "Fourteen Americans" at the Museum of Modern Art in New York, and thereafter he steadily was featured in exhibitions throughout the world.

He is noteworthy for his series of more than one hundred paintings titled *Elegy for the Spanish Republic* (1948–1990). Influenced by Freudian dream theories and psychological interpretations of the unconscious mind, Motherwell painted abstractly and symbolically, sometimes in black and white, sometimes in color, sometimes with elements of the collage. He was the editor of the fifteen-volume *Documents of Modern Art* (1944–1961), *Modern Artists in America* (1952), and *The Dada Painters and Poets* (1951). Motherwell's extensive writings are gathered in *Collected Writings of Robert Motherwell* (1993).

—*William Lawlor*

## Bibliographical References

Mary Ann Caws, *Robert Motherwell: What Art Holds*, 1996; Jack Flam, *Motherwell*, 1991; Robert Saltonstall Mattison, *Robert Motherwell: The Formative Years*, 1987.

*See also* Painting; Pollock, Jackson; Gorky, Arshile; de Kooning, Willem

## Mountains, Beats in the

Mountain ranges are central to the lives and literature of the Beat Generation. The Beats climbed many mountains, and in solitude on mountaintops, the Beats studied literature, increased their artistic output, and developed a spiritual connection to the mountains themselves. Mountains figure prominently in such Beat works as *The Dharma Bums, Desolation Angels, Myths and Texts, Mountains and Rivers without End,* and *On the Road.*

Gary Snyder was the Beat with the greatest competence in mountaineering. He made his first snow-peak climb in 1945, ascending Mt. St. Helens. In 1946 he climbed Mt. Hood. By 1952, Snyder had climbed Mt. Hood fourteen times and had eight years of climbing under his belt. In the summer of 1952, Snyder worked as a fire lookout on Crater Mountain for the United States Forestry Service.

Snyder joined the Mazamas Mountain Club in Portland, Oregon, and later was a member of "Youngsteigers," a group of youthful climbers. The Youngsteigers took the Himalayas as the standard to evaluate all other mountains, and these young climbers often combined an interest in skiing with their climbing. Gary Snyder accepted these ideas, but also developed an outlook based on animism. He viewed the mountains as beings and sought not to conquer them, but to achieve self-knowledge.

When opportunities arose to serve as fire lookouts in the North Cascades, Beat writers took advantage. Sitting on top of a mountain and watching out for fires did not require a full day of persistent attention; with seventeen hours of sunlight in summer months, one could take advantage of complete solitude and read many books, write journals, and complete extensive literary projects.

In 1953, Gary Snyder and Philip Whalen became fire lookouts, with Snyder taking a post at Sourdough Mountain and Whalen accepting an assignment at Sauk Lookout. Whalen and Snyder had been friends at Reed College and continued their close connection in San Francisco. Their mutual interest in poetry, Asian cultures, and Asian religions solidified their alliance when they worked in the North Cascades as lookouts. From Sourdough Mountain, Snyder enjoyed a panoramic view of peaks, headwaters, and streams generated from thawing glaciers. Though not as remote as Sourdough, Whalen's post also afforded inspiring views.

In 1955 blacklisting affected Snyder's application for another season at Sourdough, and when Snyder could not work, Whalen took his place. Whalen's experience inspired "Sourdough Mountain Lookout," one of Whalen's most enduring poems. The poem combines references to daily life as a lookout, including musings on rocks, insects, animals, and weather, with quotations from Empedocles and Heraclitus; Whalen merges the words of his father and grandmother with a reconsideration of his own place in time and space.

In October 1955, Gary Snyder and Jack Kerouac climbed the Matterhorn in the area east of Yosemite. They spent two nights at an elevation of 10,000 feet. This experience is memorably recorded in fictional form in *The Dharma Bums* (1958).

In June 1956, after Snyder departed for Buddhist studies in Japan, Kerouac accepted a post as lookout on Desolation Peak. For Kerouac, the solitude he faced was beyond any measure of privacy he had previously experienced. His view included Hozomeen, which some refer to as the Hozomeen Range because of the multiple peaks. Though Jack Mountain stood a thousand feet higher than Hozomeen, and though Crater Peak could be seen to the south, Kerouac found Hozomeen the most captivating view. Kerouac passed sixty-three days on Desolation Peak, and this experience is included in *The Dharma Bums* and *Desolation Angels.*

In *On the Road,* mountain experiences are significant in several places. In Part One, Sal Paradise and his friends ascend a mountain to Central City, a Colorado mining town two miles above sea level, where in formal dress Sal attends an opera in the company of Babe Rawlins and is part of a subsequent party. *Fidelio* is an enjoyable opera, and the party starts out well, but soon fights begin, and the experience degenerates. After spending a night on a dusty mattress, Sal wakes up sneezing and coughing, and a breakfast of stale beer does not set things right. The ride down the mountain is miserable.

In the climactic Part Four of *On the Road,* Sal, Dean, and Stan journey to Mexico and ascend the snow-capped mountains in an old Ford. The road winds through the clouds to reach a plateau. The companions meet sad Indians, and among the natives life seems mystical; the natives have a somber perspective that links them to antiquity. Arriving in Gregoria, the travelers meet Victor, whose guidance makes activities spin into a frenzy, including marijuana, Mexican dance music, a variety of prostitutes, and a refreshing bath. Though the intensity of the experience is reinforced by the setting in the mountains, Kerouac ends Part Four sadly. The travelers go downhill from Gregoria, and in Mexico City, Dean abandons Sal, who falls victim to dysentery.

The connection of the Beats to mountain experiences is also shown in *Tracking the Serpent,* a memoir by Janine Pommy Vega, who describes her journeys in Peru and Nepal. Like most Beat writers, Vega takes the ascent of the mountain as a spiritual event. Her respect for the mountain and the people who live atop it help her to grow emotionally and intellectually.

In "Cordillera Blanca," Pommy Vega describes her experience in the Andes. Her intended destination is Huaraz, a town in the Callejon de Huaylas, which is about 250 miles to the north of Lima. Pommy Vega explains that Callejon means "alley,"

and she is fascinated by the valley of Huaylas, which extends for more than a hundred miles between the Cordillera Blanca and the Cordillera Negra, which are mountain ranges named for the color of their peaks.

A specific threat that Pommy Vega faces in the Andes is the Shining Path, a guerilla group, but climbing itself is also complicated by her own health problems, including atrial fibrillation. Despite these dangers, Pommy Vega takes pride in her Spartan approach to mountain climbing, especially when she sees German hikers, who travel on a familiar road with a team of burros and a crew of assistants.

In "The Old Way," Pommy Vega describes her trip into the Himalayas, where she seeks out "the heart of worship, not the brain" (135). She seeks out "altars tended by women" who keep "devotion alive" (135). Her quest is never fulfilled, but her mountain experience is satisfying. She reaches the Tibetan Plateau and begins the slow climb to the Thorung Phedi.

In the end, Pommy Vega's mountaineering is more ambitious than the climbs of Snyder, Whalen, or Kerouac, but her focus is on the trek itself rather than extended solitude on the peaks of the earth.

—*Valentina Peguero*

## Bibliographical References

John Suiter's *Poets on the Peaks* (2002) discusses Snyder, Whalen, and Kerouac in the Northern Cascades and presents photos from the past and present. In *The Dharma Bums* (1958), *Desolation Angels* (1965), and *On the Road* (1957), Jack Kerouac refers extensively to experiences in the mountains; Gary Snyder refers to the mountains in almost all his poems, essays, and interviews, but *Myths and Texts* (1978) and *Mountains and Rivers without End* (1997) are excellent examples. Philip Whalen's "Sourdough Mountain Lookout" and other works referring to mountains are in *Overtime: Selected Poems* (1999). Janine Pommy Vega's *Tracking the Serpent* (1997) recounts her experiences in the Himalayas and the Andes.

***See also*** Kerouac, Jack; Snyder, Gary; Whalen, Philip; Pommy Vega, Janine; Mexico City

## Museum of Modern Art Exhibition: "Fantastic Art, Dada, and Surrealism" (1936)

As the Museum of Modern Art's second major retrospective since its founding, the 1936 exhibition "Fantastic Art, Dada, and Surrealism" (1936) formally introduced American audiences to two European movements that had, ironically, made museums and tradition the objects of scorn and satire. The show included work by Dada and surrealist precursors such as Marcel Duchamp and Giorgio De Chirico, as well as later practitioners such as Raul Hausmann, Hans (Jean) Arp, Max Ernst, Salvador Dalí, and Réné Magritte. Illustrating the art of children and "the insane," as well as tracing precursors of "irrational" art from the Renaissance to its most recent incarnations, the MoMA exhibit showcased alternative approaches to writing and art making—practices that were already familiar to a growing number of American painters and poets.

Formed in the international, pacifist circles of Zurich during World War I, and spreading to Berlin, Hanover, and Paris, the Dada movement experimented with automatism (as in Tristan Tzara's poem games) and collage, and emphasized collective, communal participation. These activities in turn influenced the Parisian surrealists, who sought to shatter social codes and shock bourgeois sensibilities with an art of uncensored eroticism. Gravitating primarily around the writer André Breton, surrealists believed that their "fantastic" and hallucinatory images could help to reshape cultural and social modes. As Alfred H. Barr, the MoMA's exhibition organizer, put it in his catalogue, art (and "anti-art") was for these individuals "a philosophy, a way of life" (18).

Dada and surrealist activities proved to be lightning rods for those across the Atlantic exploring unconventional methods of artistic and literary expression in 1950s America. Though abstract expressionism became the predominant style of painting in the years following World War II, aspects of Dada and surrealist practice lived on in American Beat culture, particularly through the exploration of the most marginal aspects of social life, and in the desire to create anew the systematic arrangement of society. Ginsberg's momentous 1956 poem "Howl," dedicated to Carl Solomon, celebrated expulsion from formal schools because of eccentric behavior and the printing of erotic poetry. "Howl" announced Ginsberg's own scandalous iconoclasm and echoed Ginsberg's debts to Dada and surrealism. The Beats' desire to fashion a utopian collectivity out of "down-and-out-ness," their battles with consumerist and conformist ways of life, and their focus upon alternative states of mind found eminent precedents in a recent Dada and surrealist past.

—Ara H. Merjian

### Bibliographical References

Of primary importance is the show's original catalogue *Fantastic Art, Dada, and Surrealism,* 1936, with introductions by Alfred H. Barr and essays by George Hugnet. A more recent account of Dada and surrealism, which considers the overlappings, divergences, and legacies of these movements in Europe and abroad, is Matthew Gale's comprehensive and accessible *Dada & Surrealism,* 1997. Fundamental for any understanding of Beat countercultural activities is the catalogue of the Whitney Museum's 1995 exhibition, *Beat Culture and the New America, 1950–1965,* 1995. Thomas Crow's *The Rise of the Sixties: American and European Art in the Era of Dissent,* 1996, offers an excellent background to the artistic, historical, and political climates out of which strains of Beat culture arose, particularly in California. For an overview of Dada's and surrealism's influences upon California-based painting and photography, both prior to and following the MoMA's 1936 exhibit, see Susan Ehrlich, ed., *Pacific Dreams,* "Currents of Surrealism and Fantasy in California Art," *Performing Arts Journal* 52, 18.1 (1996): 72–80.

*See also* Ginsberg, Allen; Painting

## Music

An artistic form that influenced the Beats and in which the Beats themselves participated and influenced; in particular, Beat writings arose from the forms and methods of music, and through live and recorded performances, the Beats became part of the musical landscape.

For the members of the Beat Generation, music manifests itself in numerous forms and styles and has a profound influence on daily life and creativity. Beat writers appreciate the tradition, evolution, style, and phrasing of jazz, blues, and bebop. For Beat writers such as Jack Kerouac, Bob Kaufman, and Allen Ginsberg, performers such as Charlie Parker, Dizzy Gillespie, Louis Armstrong, Thelonious Monk, and Miles Davis are heroes whose innovation, virtuosity, and improvisation give birth not only to "the cool," but also what Allen Ginsberg on the dedication page in "Howl" calls "spontaneous bop prosody"—the heart of Beat poetics.

The taste of the Beats in music goes well beyond jazz, blues, and bop; the connection of the Beats to folk and folk-rock, whose lyrics not only celebrate American individuality and the vast beauty of the American environment, but also protest the mistreatment of workers and the problems of racism and war, is clearly evident. In addition, the Beats' connection to music extends to rock, as Beat writers such as Burroughs, Ginsberg, and Ken Kesey interact with performers such as the Beatles and the Grateful Dead, whose ceaseless and influential innovations steered countless listeners through an era of psychedelic experimentation, political upheaval, and the elevation of human consciousness. Even movements such as new wave, punk rock, and grunge show a connection to the Beats, as William Burroughs and Allen Ginsberg win admiration from young musicians. The Beats are also involved in the experimental music of artists such as John Cage and Philip Glass, sometimes writing in response to the music and sometimes collaborating with the musicians. Finally, the Beats themselves are often musical performers, as they combine poetry with jazz, as they sing with various forms of musical accompaniment, and as they design musical scores for films.

The connection of the Beats to jazz is perhaps the plainest connection to see. In "Jazz of the Beat Generation," which is included in *The Portable Jack Kerouac,* ed. Ann Charters (222–232), Jack Kerouac provides his thumbnail history of the "children of the modern jazz night" (230). Kerouac acknowledges the basic contributions of New Orleans musicians—"the tuba and trombone kings who paraded on official days" (229) and transformed the marches of Sousa with ragtime innovations. Kerouac recognizes the magical horn and voice of Louis Armstrong, who established a jazz tradition, and Roy Eldridge, who made swing music exert a broad influence on the evolution of jazz (229). With the arrival of Charlie Parker, Kerouac sees a youth of Kansas City beginnings and tireless practice shaped by idols such as Count Basie, Bennie Moten, and Hot Lips Page. In Kerouac's vision, Parker joins Monk and Dizzy in New York and plays out his youthful heart (230). In the course of this evolution of jazz, central and abiding figures are Lester Young and Billie Holiday (230) and a culminating factor is "architectural Miles Davis logics" (229).

Another indication of the connection of the Beats to jazz and jazz history is evident in the work of LeRoi Jones (Amiri Baraka). Because Jones worked extensively as a reviewer of jazz records for various magazines, he developed a broad knowledge of artists and their recordings. *Blues People: Negro Music in White America* (1963) joins musical history with Jones's interpretation of cultural history. According to Jones, the music of the blues draws from West African music, which involves a unique musical scale, call-and-response structures, and spontaneous invention of lyrics. Another African characteristic is the coordination of music with daily life, and this coordination is part of the blues because the music, like African music, accompanies work, family traditions, and courtship. In contrast, Jones argues, white music is disconnected from the quotidian life. In *Blues People* Jones explains the process of making African music into American music by noting the history of black people and artists. Louis Armstrong, Duke Ellington, and many others are named as key players. In Jones's view, African music becomes American when white people open their ears to African music and adopt what they understand.

The Beats had a great taste for blues, jazz, and bop, and their pleasure in this music was evident in homage paid to great musical artists. *Mexico City Blues,* a collection of poetry by Jack Kerouac, repeatedly turns to Charlie Parker. In the 239th chorus, Parker is the "Perfect Musician," whose look, like the Buddha's, was "calm, beautiful, and profound" (241). In the 240th chorus, Parker is given equal standing with Beethoven, with Parker's sax complementing "string orchestras" with "perfect tune & shining harmony" (242). In the 241st chorus, Kerouac pleads for the prayers of Parker, who in Kerouac's mind holds the power to redeem (243). Bob Kaufman also pays tribute to Parker in "On," which is included in *Cranial Guitar.* Kaufman refers to "yardbird corners" and "parker flights" (92). In "Walking Parker Home" (102) Kaufman refers to "excursions to tribal Jazz wombs and transfusions" (102) and "birdland nights on bop mountains" (102). "Bagel Shop Jazz" captures the shadowy spirit of people in a coffee shop who hope "the beat is really truth" and speak "of Bird and Diz and Miles" (108).

In "Kaddish," Allen Ginsberg establishes a tragic mood in his opening lines by declaring that he has gone without sleep "listening to Ray Charles blues shout blind on the phonograph" (7). In *Junky,* William Burroughs also refers to the power of blues and jazz heard on the phonograph. According to William Lee, the narrator, one can get through drug withdrawal by smoking marijuana, consuming paregoric, and listening to recordings of Louis Armstrong (28).

The admiration of the Beats for jazz artists transcends appreciation of the power of the music to reach a holistic view of artists and their music. Even though dress styles, including beard, shades, and beret, became stereotypical, the clothing of jazz artists, as well as their posture and walk, expressed an understated rebellion and individuality. Kerouac's sympathetic imagination penetrated the mind and cultural history of the jazz performers he admired, enabling him to get inside the complexities and simplicities of the jazz artist to recognize that they were *cool;* indeed, they were the fundamental source of coolness. An important part of this coolness was the expressive speech of jazz musicians, and their idiom became part of Beat expression. Slim Gaillard, a jazz musician, is appreciated in *On the Road* (176–177) for his musicianship and bongo playing, but also for "orooni" and "ovauti,"

suffixes that he attaches to many words to stylize his speech. Similarly, Dizzy Gillespie makes scat sounds the basis for "Oop-Pop-A-Da" (on Rhino's *The Beat Generation* recordings). These expressive freedoms demonstrated by musicians perhaps influence Kerouac's experimentations with the music of language, as in the concluding sound poem for *Big Sur* (219–241).

As shown in Beat literature, jazz performances are magical and exalted. In *On the Road,* when Dean and Sal hear George Shearing at Birdland in 1949 (128), chords emerge from the piano in "great rich showers" (128). When Shearing completes his performance and leaves the stage, covered in sweat, Dean looks at the empty seat and declares, "God's empty chair" (128). In San Francisco, after Dean and Sal hear a tenorman magically perform "Close Your Eyes," the tenorman repudiates Dean's unrelenting pursuit of gratification, declaring that "life's too sad to be ballin all the time" (200). His wisdom stands in contrast to Dean's frenzy. The experience of hearing music in an intimate jazz club and witnessing the artist in the coolness of performance can lift the Beat listener to "it"—to ecstatic satisfaction.

The direct expressions of admiration for jazz artists, particularly Charlie Parker, gain resonance as one realizes that Beat writing and performance take their form and measure from jazz, blues, and bop musicians. In *On the Road,* and in many other writings, Kerouac intentionally develops a jazz effect in his prose, with rhythm, pauses, syncopations, pops, and onomatopoeia. Sal Paradise's description of Dean Moriarty working as a frantic parking attendant (6) and Ti Jean's childlike narration in *Visions of Gerard* waft and wail like a melodious sax.

In "Howl," by Allen Ginsberg, Michael Schumacher notes three musical movements determined by three jazz styles: in the opening section Ginsberg composes "hot saxophonic expressions" in the manner of Charlie Parker and Lester Young; in the second part, Schumacher hears "squawks" similar to the style of Miles Davis; in the third part, Schumacher senses "a cool bluesy and lyrical feeling" in the manner of John Coltrane (*Dharma Lion* 207).

Bob Kaufman also learns from the jazz masters, but instead of transferring melody, rhythm, and stylings to prose or poetry, Kaufman adopts methods of improvisational performance. Charlie Parker knew a vast assortment of melodies and in the midst of performance could produce a particular melody in response to any suggestion, smoothly integrating the improvisation in the established musical framework. In similar fashion, Bob Kaufman retained a huge selection of phrases, quips, and routines, and on the spur of the moment could fit these into a performance of poetry, making a presentation uniquely suited to the moment.

The Beats combined literary performances with jazz accompaniment. In 1958, Kenneth Patchen recorded "The Murder of Two Men by a Young Kid Wearing Lemon Colored Gloves" with the Chamber Jazz Sextet. Kenneth Rexroth recorded "Thou Shalt Not Kill" in 1957 with jazz accompaniment at the Cellar in San Francisco. Rexroth's performance, combined with readings by Lawrence Ferlinghetti, who performed "Autobiography" and "Statue of St. Francis," was released as a Fantasy LP. Ferlinghetti went on to do another LP that included "Moscow in the Wilderness Segovia in the Snow" done with guitar accompaniment.

David Amram plays an especially conspicuous role in Beat musical performances. He composed the music and developed the musical soundtrack for *Pull My Daisy*, the experimental film by Robert Frank and Alfred Leslie. Amram took part in the first-ever jazz-poetry reading with Jack Kerouac, Philip Lamantia, and Howard Hart at the Brata Gallery in New York in 1957.

Kerouac combined various times with Steve Allen to enhance Beat literature with music. In 1959 a Hanover LP of Allen and Kerouac's recordings appeared, including Kerouac's readings of "October in the Railroad Earth" and selections from *Mexico City Blues*. Unforgettable is Kerouac's appearance on *The Steve Allen Show* on 16 November 1959, when Steve Allen accompanied Jack Kerouac's readings from *On the Road* and *Visions of Cody*.

Kerouac's *Blues and Haikus* LP featured jazz artists Zoot Sims and Al Cohn. The artists engaged in call and response, with Kerouac's readings of haikus prompting saxophone riffs from Sims and Cohn. The blues recordings from this LP diverged from the short impressions of Kerouac's haikus in order to give life to blues selections from Kerouac. Al Cohn plays piano, and Kerouac sings in a homely but expressive style. Kerouac also reads selections from *Book of Blues*.

Perhaps Allen Ginsberg is the Beat artist most diversely connected to music. In his career, he interacted or performed with Bob Dylan, the Jefferson Airplane, Quicksilver Messenger Service, the Grateful Dead, John Lennon, Phil Ochs, the Fugs, Philip Glass, Marianne Faithfull, the Clash, John Hammond, Paul McCartney, and many others. Always fascinated with Blake, Ginsberg set poems by Blake to music, and with the help of Barry Miles and other musicians, Ginsberg produced a musical adaptation of Blake's *Songs of Innocence and Experience*. With the help of John Hammond, Ginsberg recorded *First Blues*, his collection of poems written in the blues format.

Though Ginsberg's musical performances are sustained more by enthusiasm and personality than by musicianship, he made musical performances a regular part of his speaking engagements. In the last fifteen years of his career, he typically included in his public presentations musical selections based on Blake, "CIA Dope Calypso," "Do the Meditation Rock," "Capitol Air," and "Airplane Blues." His performance of "Father Death Blues" was especially moving, and on the occasion of Ginsberg's death, this poem in memory of Louis Ginsberg often was played in memory of Allen himself. Ginsberg's harmonium, an instrument comparable to Blake's pump organ, was at the center of innumerable performances and became a symbol of Ginsberg's life. Sotheby's, when the harmonium was offered at auction in 1999, asked for $3,000–5,000.

In 1993, Ginsberg worked with classical composer Philip Glass to produce *Hydrogen Jukebox*, with Ginsberg writing the libretto. In 1996, working with Paul McCartney, Philip Glass, and others, Ginsberg recorded *Ballad of the Skeletons*. In 1997, *The Lion for Real* drew together both musical and nonmusical pieces from all parts of Ginsberg's career.

The experimental musician John Cage had an extraordinary effect on Lawrence Ferlinghetti. In

"Monet's Lilies Shuddering," which is included in *When I Look at Pictures* (1990), Ferlinghetti complicates his response to an installation of Monet's paintings at the Chicago Art Institute by referring to the museum's "Debussy piano soundtrack" (20) and a woman's film showing lilies near the "'Bridge at Giverny'" (20). Ferlinghetti marvels at Monet's inability to anticipate the future manifestations and effects of his work, including an occurrence during Ferlinghetti's attendance at a John Cage performance of "Cello with Melody-driven Electronics" at the University of Chicago on the evening after Ferlinghetti's visit to the Art Institute. Hearing Cage's music, Ferlinghetti recalls Monet's lilies and in Ferlinghetti's mind "those lilies shudder and shed/ black light" (20).

The link between folk artists and the Beats is not as immediate as the connection to jazz, but cannot be overlooked. The folk songs of Woody Guthrie, such as "This Land Is My Land," convey the love for America's geographic grandeur that one finds in Snyder and Kerouac; furthermore, the support of Guthrie and other folk artists for union workers clearly parallels Ginsberg's early desire to be a labor lawyer and his interest in socialist causes his mother favored, as revealed in "America." Guthrie's interest in disenfranchised and marginal individuals regularly arose in his music, and this sympathetic spirit arose in the thinking of the Beats, too.

The compositions and performances of Mimi and Richard Fariña draw an even closer connection between the Beats and folk music. Though best known for the novel *Been Down So Long It Looks Like Up to Me*, whose title is a reference to a famous blues lyric, Richard Fariña and his wife, Mimi, combined to produce *Reflections in a Crystal Wind*, a haunting collection of original folk music. The couple's music is available on various Vanguard collections of folk music.

Like Ginsberg and Kerouac, William Burroughs collaborated with musicians in order to enhance readings of his writings. *Spare Ass Annie*, recorded in combination with the Disposable Heroes of the Hiphoprisy, provided background music for readings of familiar routines such as "Did I Ever Tell You about the Man Who Taught His Asshole How to Talk?" and "Dr. Benway Operates." *Dead City Radio* featured musical support by Sonic Youth, John Cale, and the NBC Symphony. *Priest, They Called Him* is Burroughs's narration of a "Christmas story" about drug addiction, and after the narration was recorded, a wailing guitar interpretation of "Silent Night" by Kurt Cobain was added.

In addition, Burroughs collaborated with Laurie Anderson, U2, and Tom Waits. Living at the "Bunker," a residence in the Bowery in Manhattan, Burroughs gained insight about the punk rock scene at a club called CBGB's. Burroughs's writings inspired new groups to choose their names from his pages; thus the Soft Machine, the Mugwumps, and Steely Dan all are names of contemporary bands but also are allusions to Burroughs's work. Burroughs is sometimes cited as the coiner of the phrase "heavy metal."

The Beatles recognized the significance of Burroughs by including his image in the collection of people on the cover of *Sgt. Pepper's Lonely Hearts Club Band*. Ginsberg interprets the form and implications of this monumental album in a PBS television program *It Was Twenty Years Ago Today* created on the twentieth anniversary of the release of *Sgt. Pepper's Lonely Hearts Club Band*.

—*James E. Lawlor*

## Bibliographical References

One can see Kerouac's taste and passion for music, especially jazz, blues, and bop, in *On the Road*, 1957; "Jazz of the Beat Generation," in *The Portable Jack Kerouac*, ed. Ann Charters, 1995; *Mexico City Blues*, 1959; *Visions of Gerard*, 1963; *Visions of Cody*, 1972; *Big Sur*, 1963; and *Book of Blues*, 1995. To hear the performances of Kerouac with Steve Allen, Zoot Sims, and Al Cohn, one can acquire *The Kerouac Collection*, 1990. Ginsberg's dedication page in "Howl" in *Howl and Other Poems*, 1956, refers to the "spontaneous bop prosody" of Kerouac; in the opening lines of "Kaddish" in *Kaddish and Other Poems*, 1961, Ginsberg refers to Ray Charles; and in "America," a poem in *Howl and Other Poems*, one sees Ginsberg's reference to the Wobblies. Recordings of Ginsberg's music are numerous: *Holy Soul Jelly Roll*, 1994, is the most complete collection and features adaptations of Blake, "Capitol Air," "CIA Dope Calypso," "Airplane Blues," "Father Death

Blues," and others. Ginsberg also recorded *First Blues*, 1983, with John Hammond; with Philip Glass, Ginsberg helped to produce *Hydrogen Jukebox*, 1993; with Paul McCartney, Ginsberg recorded "Ballad of the Skeletons," 1996. Michael Schumacher provides an interpretation of musical movements in "Howl" in *Dharma Lion*, 1992. A shortened version of *Blues People*, 1963, is available in the *Amiri Baraka/LeRoi Jones Reader*, ed. William J. Harris, 1991. Bob Kaufman's poems are collected in *Cranial Guitar*, ed. Gerald Nicosia, 1996; to listen to the poetry-and-jazz recordings of Patchen, Rexroth, and Ferlinghetti, one may turn to *Howls, Raps, and Roars*, 1993, and the Rhino recordings *The Beat Generation*, 1992, which include helpful liner notes. David Amram's "Pull My Daisy" is on this collection, too, and details of the first-ever jazz-poetry reading are in Amram's memoir *Offbeat*, 2002. Ferlinghetti's "Monet's Lilies Shuddering," which reveals admiration for John Cage, appears in *When I Look at Pictures*, 1990. In *Junky*, 1953, Burroughs refers to Louis Armstrong, and various combinations of Burroughs with musicians are available in *Spare Ass Annie*, 1993, which features the Disposable Heroes of Hiphoprisy, and *Priest, They Called Him*, 1993, which includes Kurt Cobain's guitar. Richard Fariña's *Been Down So Long It Looks Like Up to Me*, 1966, complements the beautiful folk album *Reflections in a Crystal Wind*, 1965.

**See also** Blakey, Art; Coltrane, John; Gillespie, John Brinks; Gordon, Dexter; Mingus, Charles; Monk, Thelonious Sphere; Gaillard, Slim; Gray, Wardell; Hawkins, Coleman; Holiday, Billie; Kenton, Stan; Konitz, Lee; Krupa, Gene; Cage, John; Glass, Philip; Guthrie, Woody; Dylan, Bob; Fariña, Richard; Kupferberg, Tuli; Sanders, Ed; Ginsberg, Allen; Kerouac, Jack; Burroughs, William Seward; Amram, David; Kaufman, Bob; Ferlinghetti, Lawrence; Rexroth, Kenneth; Patchen, Kenneth; First Poetry-Jazz Concert.

# N

## Nakedness

Central to the Beat outlook is the need to be naked, in both the literal sense of wearing no clothing and the figurative sense of baring the soul. A Beat poet may actually disrobe during a reading; a Beat actor may play a theatrical part in the nude. Unashamed of their bodies, Beats may be nude subjects in photographs and paintings. In *The Dharma Bums* by Jack Kerouac, Alvah and George walk around naked at a party, but they do not try to enforce nakedness upon anyone else; in fact, they stand around the fire and talk about international occurrences with Rheinhold Cacoethes and Arthur Whane, who are in formal attire. More important than such nakedness, however, are the metaphorical implications of nakedness. Thriving on candor, the Beat strips away dishonesty and secrecy. Allen Ginsberg declares that frankness eliminates the need for unwarranted suspicions. In *Pull My Daisy*, Jack Kerouac insists that people need to divulge the dirty thoughts they hide within themselves. To be truly Beat, a person must be frank and willing to explore and confess the things upon which society has imposed unnatural restrictions.

—*William Lawlor*

### Bibliographical References

John Tytell, *Naked Angels*, 1976; Allen Ginsberg, *Allen Ginsberg Photographs*, 1990.

*See also* Kerouac, Jack; Ginsberg, Allen

## Naropa Institute

Situated in the foothills of the Rockies in Boulder, Colorado, on 5.5 acres of land, Naropa University, a private, nonprofit, small liberal arts college, formerly known as the Naropa Institute, was founded in 1974, in the Buddhist tradition, by Tibetan meditation master and scholar, Chögyam Trungpa Rinpoche. Naropa's unique origins of Buddhist traditions and educational philosophies were patterned after Nalanda University, a sixth-century Indian university, presided over in the eleventh century by the Buddhist scholar, Naropa. Housing both the Allen Ginsberg Library and the Jack Kerouac School of Disembodied Poetics, Naropa offers undergraduate and graduate degrees in psychology, education, environmental studies, gerontology, religious studies, creation spirituality, and the arts.

Dedicated in 1993, the Allen Ginsberg Library has a specialized 26,000-volume collection with strong holdings in contemporary American poetry, psychology, and Buddhist studies. The Special Collections multimedia section includes over 6,000 audio cassettes of recorded educational and cultural events of Naropa's history.

Naropa University's Department of Writing and Poetics, inaugurated as the Jack Kerouac School of Disembodied Poetics, cofounded by Allen Ginsberg and Anne Waldman in 1974, offers a bachelor of arts degree in writing and literature and a master of fine arts degree in writing and poetics. Waldman continues as distinguished professor of poetics and artistic director of the summer writing program, a four-week-long intensive convocation of students, poets, scholars, and Buddhist teachers. Creative writing workshops host such visiting Beats as Amiri Baraka, Robert Creeley, Diane di Prima, Joanne Kyger, and Gary Snyder.

In 1975, Naropa was associated with what has come to be known as the "Merwin Incident." Poet William S. Merwin and a female companion, Dana Naone, refused to participate in a party that required nudity, and a violent altercation with Trungpa ensued, prompting controversy in the American poetry community and a two-year investigation (1978–1980), chronicled in Tom Clark's *The Great Naropa Poetry Wars* (1980) and Ed Sanders's *The Party* (1977).

In 1976, Trungpa appointed Osel Tendzin as his successor, and another scandal ensued, further tainting Naropa's reputation, as Tendzin contracted the AIDS virus and knowingly infected others.

Despite various controversies, Naropa's development continues. The school aims to join intellect and intuition and seeks to embody an appreciation and respect for various contemplative traditions. Moreover, Naropa continues to be a forum for countercultural humanities where religion and poetry, Buddhism and Beat literary sensibilities, permeate the landscape.

—*Patricia Hillen*

### Bibliographical References

One can get basic information about Naropa University at http://www.naropa.edu/index.html. Information on Naropa's history, including various controversies is in Michael Schumacher, *Dharma Lion*, 1992; and Ted Morgan, *Literary Outlaw*, 1988.

**See also** *On the Road*, 1982 Conference on Twenty-fifth Anniversary of the Publication of; Trungpa, Chögyam; Waldman, Anne; Ginsberg, Allen; Sanders, Ed

## Native American Cultures

In "Prologue," a revised version of "Definition of the Beat Generation" that is published in *Beat Culture and the New America: 1945–1960* (1995), Allen Ginsberg claims for the members of the Beat Generation a special distinction for understanding and appreciation of Native American culture (19). Though the Beat Generation's affinity for Native American cultures is debatable, the Beats do show a recurrent interest in Native American families, myths, traditions, languages, and problems.

In "Author's Introduction," which appears in *Lonesome Traveler* (1960), Jack Kerouac describes himself as partly Native American; though he is mostly French, intermarriage among his ancestors makes him partly Mohawk and Caughnawaga (v). In "Among the Iroquois," which appears in *City Lights Journal* (1963), Kerouac refers to an Iroquois who theorized that Kerouac had Iroquois ancestry.

In Part Four of Kerouac's *On the Road*, Sal Paradise esteems the Indians he sees as he crosses the Sierra Madre Mountains on the way to Mexico City. Sal theorizes that the poor people of the equatorial regions of the world, whom he calls the fellaheen, know the basic truths of life and hold these truths silently and soberly. For Sal, the Indians in the Mexican mountains have this mystic quality. He declares that the earth and the Indians are fundamentally interconnected. Those who would know the earth can do so by knowing the Indians (280).

However, Sal's vision of the Native Americans also includes innocence. Extending their hands, Indian women from remote mountain regions approach Sal and Dean, but Sal remembers that these Indians are unaware of the white man's nuclear warfare (298). If the bomb falls, Sal thinks, then the white men will be as poor as the Indians and will have nothing to offer.

The writings of Gary Snyder also reveal awareness and appreciation of native cultures. At Reed College in 1951, Snyder wrote "He Who Hunted Birds in His Father's Village," an anthropological study of a native myth. A selection of this study is now published in *The Gary Snyder Reader* (1999). In studying the myth, Snyder explores connections to culture, the worldwide catalog of myths, and human nature in general.

"A Berry Feast," which Snyder read at the 6 Gallery reading on 7 October 1955, includes various references to native myths, including stories involving coyote, the bear, and the magpie. The poem was subsequently reprinted in *The Back Country* (1968) and *The Gary Snyder Reader*.

Snyder explores Native American culture further in *Myths and Texts* (1960), which pits the experience of speakers, either contemporary or historical, against established myths and myths still undergoing formation in the poems themselves. Myth and culture, Snyder demonstrates, function reciprocally, with myth reflecting culture, and with culture borrowing from myth. For example, in "6," which is written for bears, Snyder recounts the native myth of a woman whom a bear takes for his wife. She gives birth multiple times, but ultimately is freed by her brothers, who trap the bear. The recounting of the mythic story is broken by Snyder's reference to himself: he declares that he wants to hunt bears, but the poem answers mockingly that such an idea is foolish because Snyder does not know the first thing about bears.

Snyder's *Turtle Island* (1974) takes its title from a Native American myth that envisions the continent as a turtle. In *Turtle Island*, Snyder compares contemporary American life, which is wasteful, destructive, and unsustainable, with Native American life, which is efficient, compatible with wildlife and environment, and sustainable. When whites drive their cars and build their houses, whites squander resources and generate pollution. In contrast, Indians waste no part of an animal they kill and do not threaten the earth with garbage.

In an interview published in *Paris Review*, which is reprinted in *The Gary Snyder Reader* (1999), Snyder responds to questions and comments about the problem of appropriation of native myths. Snyder acknowledges that he is not an Indian, but affirms that he is a Native American in the sense that he inhabits the territory. For Snyder, being a true inhabitant is difficult and is only achieved through sustained endeavor, but once such habitation is real, the myths belong to the inhabitant (336–337). According to Patrick Murphy in *A Place for Wayfaring: The Poetry and Prose of Gary Snyder* (2000), Snyder eventually concluded that white people cannot experience full involvement in Na-

tive American spirituality (6); for that reason, Snyder turned to Eastern religion and culture, which appeared more open.

In *One Flew Over the Cuckoo's Nest* (1962), Ken Kesey makes native identity central to his story because an Indian, Chief Bromden, is the narrator. The triumph of the story is the chief's matching of his physical size with a discovery of his gigantic spirit. In the background, Kesey reveals the abuse and suffering of Bromden's tribe. The martyrdom of Randle McMurphy has Promethean proportions, but Chief Bromden, by killing the lobotomized McMurphy, foils Nurse Ratched's quest for control and achieves clarity for his own mind.

William Burroughs does not make an Indian the narrator of his writings, but he showed a special interest in Native American culture when he arrived in Mexico City in 1949. Taking advantage of the GI Bill, Burroughs enrolled in archeology courses at Mexico City College. However, the purpose of Burroughs's studies apparently was to enable him to gain access to hallucinogens associated with natives. In 1951, seeking out the native drug *yagé*, Burroughs traveled to Panama and Ecuador; in 1953, Burroughs went on a second quest for *yagé*, visiting Panama and Colombia, experimenting with a sample of the drug provided for him by a native medicine man; he extended this expedition for *yagé* into Peru. In all, Burroughs's journeys in search of *yagé* demonstrate his intense desire for total derangement of his senses through drug experiences, and the frustrations he had in seeking *yagé* led him to express contempt for the natives, who took advantage of him and robbed him when the opportunities arose.

Allen Ginsberg also ventured to Mexico and while in the southern region took time to appreciate the evidence of Mayan culture. In 1954, Ginsberg visited Chiapas, meeting Karena Shields, an archeologist who had learned of Mayan history and culture from the Karivis Indians. Shields's cocoa farm was in a region the natives called Xbalba, which in native myth refers to purgatory or limbo. Inspired, Ginsberg later wrote "Siesta in Xbalba."

Ginsberg's subsequent travels in Mexico led him to Zapata and Acavalna, where volcanic activity was causing tremors. Ginsberg did not find an active volcano or secret mountain lake, but when he returned to Zapata, forty Indians asked him to travel with them to the east to verify the existence of a huge cave. After a journey over rugged terrain, Ginsberg arrived at the opening of a large cave. *Acavalna,* Ginsberg learned, is a native word for "house of night," and the large cave he viewed explained the naming of the volcanic mountain.

A gloomy view of Native Americans appears in the poetry of Gregory Corso, who is the author of "Death of the American Indian's God," which is included in *Long Live Man* (1962). Corso indicates that the wildlife that sustains Indians is exhausted, and the Indians themselves are defeated. Corso's lament for the extinction of the American Indian is reiterated in "Spontaneous Requiem for the American Indian," which appears in *Elegiac Feelings American* (1970). Assuming that the American Indian is dead, Corso laments the death and pays homage.

Diane di Prima also expresses sadness in connection with Native American cultures, but in "American Indian Art: Form and Tradition," which appears in *Pieces of a Song* (1990), di Prima demonstrates that displays in museums fail to capture the vitality of Indians. The poem suggests that a museum such as the Walker Art Center in Minneapolis is a cold place. When artifacts are fixed in display cases, the energy of the people who wore the clothing or used the baskets is absent (101).

—*James E. Lawlor*

## Bibliographical References

Allen Ginsberg's "Prologue" appears in *Beat Culture and the New America: 1945–1960,* ed. Lisa Phillips, 1995; Ginsberg's short writing was originally published as "A Definition of the Beat Generation" in *Friction* 1 (Winter 1982): 50–52. "Author's Introduction" is the opening portion of Jack Kerouac, *Lonesome Traveler,* 1960; "Among the Iroquois" appears in *City Lights Journal* 1 (1963): 44. Sal Paradise's references to Indians are in Part 4 of *On the Road,* with an introduction by Ann Charters, 1991. Grey Fox Press has published the complete text of Gary Snyder's *He Who Hunted Birds in His Father's Village: Dimensions of a Haida Myth,* 1979, but one can also refer to a selection in *The Gary Snyder Reader,* 1999. "A Berry Feast" is included in *The Back Country,* 1962, but is reprinted in full in *The Gary Snyder Reader.* Kesey's story of Chief Bromden is told in *One Flew Over the Cuckoo's Nest,* 1962, which was made into a famous film with the same title. Details of Burroughs's searches for *yagé* are in Ted Morgan, *Literary Outlaw,* 1988; Ginsberg's Mexican journeys are described in Michael Schumacher, *Dharma Lion,* 1992. Corso's elegies for Indians are in *Long Live Man,* 1962, and *Elegiac Feelings American,* 1970. Di Prima's "American Indian Art: Form and Tradition" is included in *Pieces of a Song,* 1990.

**See also** Kerouac, Jack; Snyder, Gary; Burroughs, William Seward; Kesey, Ken Elton; Ginsberg, Allen; Corso, Gregory; di Prima, Diane

## New Orleans

Major Louisiana city famous for its nightlife, music, and cultural history. Known as the Big Easy, New Orleans hosts the Mardi Gras, an occasion for inhibitions to be set aside so that parades, parties, and revelry can be fully enjoyed. Despite this well-deserved reputation for good times, in the literature and experience of the Beats, New Orleans is mostly a disappointment.

In Jack Kerouac's *On the Road,* Sal and Dean have high expectations for excitement and pleasure in New Orleans, but their expectations are not fulfilled. As the travelers approach the city, the tropical environment seems luscious with rich smells and beautiful women. The Mississippi River suggests the richness of America to Sal. Nevertheless, Sal and Dean visit Old Bull Lee in Algiers, across the river from New Orleans, and Bull's house is dilapidated. When they visit the French Quarter in New Orleans, Bull takes Sal and Dean to the dullest bars.

Bull Lee is Kerouac's character based on William S. Burroughs, whose real-life experience in New Orleans was far from pleasing. In Texas, Burroughs was arrested for committing indecent acts and being drunk in public; to avoid severe penalties for any further offenses, he came to New Orleans. However, in 1949 he was arrested in New Orleans on a firearms charge, and a letter from Allen Ginsberg in Burroughs's possession made incriminating references to drugs. Police tried to prosecute Burroughs, but with the help of an attorney, Burroughs was admitted to a sanitarium for drug rehabilitation, and with this case pending, Burroughs retreated from New Orleans to Pharr, Texas. He ultimately decided to move on to Mexico rather than return to New Orleans to face the charges.

William Lee, the narrator of *Junky* by William Burroughs (1953), remarks that some citizens in New Orleans have never left the city. Their accent is remarkably similar to the accent of Brooklynites. People in the French Quarter are supposed to have fun, but noise interferes with pleasure. Bars are crowded with homosexuals, and hustlers are ready to exploit fools in search of sex or drugs. In *Junky*, Burroughs's arrest in New Orleans is re-created in the experience of William Lee (66–77).

Charles Bukowski in "Young in New Orleans" speaks favorably of New Orleans, but he seems pleased by negativity. New Orleans is a refuge, a place where one need not feel shame if others must do without. In New Orleans, according to Bukowski, a young person can sink into depravity and the city will leave him alone.

In *Desolation Angels* (1965), Jack Kerouac and his mother visit New Orleans briefly. The prices in a restaurant are too high, and Jack and his mother leave the place to politicians and executives, preferring a simple oyster bar. Jack's mother enjoys wine and conversation with the oyster man and has fun buying tourist items as gifts for Jack's sister (380–381).

—*Valentina Peguero*

### Bibliographical References

On pages 140–157, Jack Kerouac's character Sal Paradise narrates his experience in New Orleans in *On the Road*, 1957; in the fiftieth anniversary issue of *Junky* published in 2003, William Burroughs's William Lee delivers a narration about the underworld in New Orleans (57–87). Bukowski's "Young in New Orleans" appears in *The Last Night on Earth Poems*, 1982. Ted Morgan, *Literary Outlaw*, 1988, covers the details of Burroughs's experience in New Orleans.

*See also* Bukowski, Charles; Burroughs, William Seward; Kerouac, Jack; Algiers, Louisiana

## New Waverly, Texas

William S. Burroughs's postal address from November 1946 to May 1948, when he lived with his common-law wife Joan Vollmer (1923–1951), her daughter Julie, and their infant son Bill Jr. in a primitive farmhouse on Winters Bayou in San Jacinto County, thirteen miles east of New Waverly.

After a narcotics arrest (his first) in April 1946 in New York, Burroughs left behind his friends in Manhattan, including Joan Vollmer, as a condition of his suspended sentence. He spent the summer with his parents in St. Louis, where he was reunited with his childhood friend Kells Elvins (1913–1961). Elvins had done graduate work in criminal psychology at Harvard and the University of Texas, and he worked at the Texas State Prison in Huntsville during 1939–1940; Burroughs first saw the piney woods of east Texas when he visited Elvins there in the summer of 1939. When Elvins's father, Politte Elvins, died suddenly in January 1943, Kells inherited his father's citrus and vegetable farms near Pharr, Texas, in Hidalgo County on the Rio Grande River.

By early October 1946, Burroughs was farming in partnership with Elvins in Pharr, but he returned to New York later that month to retrieve Joan Vollmer after her release from Bellevue Hospital following her treatment for benzedrine psychosis. Burroughs brought Joan and her infant daughter Julie (b. 1944) to Texas, where he planned to set himself up as a farmer, like Kells. In addition to vegetables, Burroughs intended to grow illegal marijuana for the New York market, and to that end he found a remote ninety-nine-acre tract near the tiny hamlet of Pumpkin, Texas, and purchased it on 23 November 1946.

Burroughs's neighbors were mostly longtime residents of San Jacinto County, families such as the Ellisors, the Hoots, and the Browders; the ones he met were Arch Ellisor and a tenant farmer, Mr. Gilley. Cold Spring was the county seat, and the courthouse regulars there made a strong impression on Burroughs when he encountered them while buying his land. The heyday of the Ku Klux Klan in Texas was the early 1920s, but even after World War II and the Klan's fragmentation, many citizens of east Texas continued to cling to its violently racist beliefs. A decade later, in drafts for his 1959 novel, *Naked Lunch*, Burroughs satirized the "County Clerk" and his associates as grotesquely ignorant, bigoted, backwoods characters.

By January 1947, Joan was two months pregnant with Burroughs's child, and Burroughs sent money to their Times Square hustler friend, Herbert Huncke (1915–1996), in New York, so he could join them on Winters Bayou as their "farmhand" while Joan came to term. Burroughs "commuted" to his south Texas farm several times that spring and summer, while Huncke made occasional trips to Houston to buy benzedrine strips for Joan's habit. Far from being inconspicuous in his deep-woods hideaway, Burroughs and his odd *ménage* stood out as eccentric, well-off Yankees—and possibly even gangsters, with Burroughs's constant pistol practice audible to his neighbors.

On 21 July 1947, at the hospital in nearby Conroe, Texas, Joan gave birth to William Seward Burroughs III. Within two weeks Burroughs's mother and father visited east Texas from St. Louis to see their new grandson and to shower gifts on the young family. A few weeks later Allen Ginsberg and Neal Cassady arrived at the east Texas farm, after hitchhiking from Denver; this was meant to be the romantic climax of Ginsberg's long infatuation with the bisexual Cassady, but the affair went sour after only a few days at the farm. In early September, Ginsberg shipped out from Houston on a coal ship bound for Dakar, in Africa; Cassady remained for another month.

Harvest time for the marijuana came in October, and Burroughs broke up the household, sending Joan and the children to New York by train while Cassady drove Burroughs and Huncke in Burroughs's Jeep, carrying the crop packed in Mason jars inside duffel bags. The three men arrived a few hours late at the Grand Central Station meeting point, only to find that Joan and her children had been taken to Bellevue by police suspicious of her apparent disorientation. After Burroughs obtained her release, they stayed in the New York area—first in Yonkers, then in Atlantic Beach—for several weeks, and Burroughs became readdicted that winter. Trying to kick the habit, he and Joan drove to St. Louis where, over his parents' objections, Joan insisted on Burroughs's wish to go to the federally run "narcotics farm" at Lexington, Kentucky. By late February he was back at the Winters Bayou house.

In May 1948, Burroughs and Vollmer were returning from south Texas, after buying forty acres of farmland on 6 May 1948, when they were arrested in Beeville, Texas, and charged with public indecency for drunkenly having sex in the car by the roadside. Burroughs lost his Texas driver's license and decided to sell out in east Texas and move to New Orleans, which he did by early June. At a notary's office in New Orleans he signed papers selling his east Texas farm on 28 June 1948.

—James Grauerholz

### Bibliographical References

Ted Morgan, *Literary Outlaw: The Life and Times of William S. Burroughs,* 1988, offers basic information; see also William S. Burroughs, *Junky,* 1953 (rpt. 2003); and William S. Burroughs, *The Letters of William S. Burroughs, 1945–1959,* ed. Oliver Harris, 1993; in the so-called "tape" section, Jack Kerouac, *Visions of Cody,* 1972, one finds references to New Waverly.

*See also* Burroughs, William Seward; Elvins, Kells; Drugs; Huncke, Herbert; Vollmer Adams Burroughs, Joan; Burroughs, William S., Jr.

## New York City

New York City gave birth to the Beat Generation at Columbia University on Broadway and 116th Street in the heady years surrounding World War II. The Ivy League campus on Morningside Heights, crowded with soldiers enrolled in officer-training courses, continued to attract some of the nation's best students, including Jack Kerouac, a scholar-athlete from Lowell, Massachusetts, and Allen Ginsberg, an idealistic poet from Paterson, New Jersey, who dreamed of becoming a labor lawyer. Early in 1943, Ginsberg met Lucien Carr, a transfer student from the University of Chicago, in his dormitory at Union Theological Seminary. Carr's family had sent him to Columbia in order to remove him from the unwholesome influence of

David Kammerer, a former teacher and Boy Scout leader, who had been pursuing Carr since prep school. Their effort proved unsuccessful. Carr soon introduced Ginsberg to Kammerer, who had moved to 48 Morton Street in Greenwich Village, and to his friend William S. Burroughs, who lived nearby at 69 Bedford Street. Carr took an art class with Edie Parker, Kerouac's girlfriend, who was living with Joan Vollmer Adams in apartment #62 at 421 W. 118th Street. Soon afterwards Kerouac met Ginsberg and Burroughs there and the first Beat pad soon became their private hedge school. Here and at the West End Bar on Broadway and 113th Street, the rebellious undergraduates sat at the feet of an older, more worldly William Burroughs, ruminating on the poetry of Arthur Rimbaud, the esoteric system of William Butler Yeats's *A Vision*, the linguistic theories of Alfred Korzybski, and the philosophical insights behind Oswald Spengler's *The Decline of the West*. The group sought to create a "new vision" in art and literature, one that emphasized above all else the importance of self-expression and expanded consciousness. In August 1944, however, an act of violence overshadowed their artistic endeavors.

Carr and Kammerer left the West End late one night and walked over to Riverside Park at 116th Street, where Carr fatally stabbed Kammerer. Carr turned himself in to the police, claiming that he had killed Kammerer while fending off a homosexual advance. The New York tabloids reported the lurid details, describing the crime as an "honor slaying." Found guilty of manslaughter, Carr spent the next two years in an Elmira reformatory. Burroughs and Kerouac, who had been arrested as material witnesses, were badly burned by their brush with the law. After being released, Burroughs returned home to St. Louis, while Kerouac married Edie Parker and went to live with her family in Grosse Point, Michigan.

Back in New York City a year later, the circle reformed in apartment #51 of the "Cragsmoor" at 419 W. 115th Street. The occupants included Joan Vollmer, Edie Parker, Kerouac, Burroughs, and newcomer Hal Chase, a Columbia anthropology student from Denver, who later introduced the group to Neal Cassady. Kicked out of his dorm room in Hamilton Hall for writing obscenities on his windows and having Kerouac as an unauthorized overnight guest, Ginsberg joined his friends at the "Cragsmoor" in March 1944. When Burroughs brought over Herbert Huncke, a merchant seaman he befriended over the course of a sale of some guns and morphine Syrettes, the circle was complete. Huncke, whose use of the word *beat* was to provide a name for the new literary movement, became a fixture at the "Cragsmoor," regaling his new friends with stories of the seedier side of life in the Big Apple. A hustler, drug addict, and petty thief, Huncke became their guide to the fringes of New York's underworld.

The Times Square area was Huncke's base of operation. A beehive of activity throughout the war years, the neon lights of its movies, restaurants, and penny arcades burned twenty-four hours a day, attracting people from all walks of life. When not stealing suitcases at the bus terminals or hustling in Bryant Park, Huncke could usually be found in the all-night cafeterias and bars around Times Square. He introduced his new friends to his favorite hangouts, including Grants (220 W. 42nd Street), Bickford's (225 W. 42nd Street), Chase's Cafeteria (210 W. 42nd Street) and the Horn & Hardart Automat (250 W. 42nd Street). The food, ranging from a crock of baked beans to a Salisbury steak dinner, was plain and inexpensive, and customers were welcome to sit and talk all night over a cup of coffee. Kerouac immortalizes these eateries, particularly Grants, in the "New York Scenes" chapter of *Lonesome Traveler* (1960). The group also frequented the Angler Bar, an L-shaped gin mill popular with gangsters and rough trade, at 674 Eighth Avenue. Huncke met here with Alfred Kinsey, who sought his assistance in enlisting subjects for his research on the sexual behavior of the American male. Receiving two dollars for each referral, Huncke quickly recruited Kerouac, Ginsberg, and Burroughs. In *Junkie* (1953), Burroughs changed the name of the bar from Angler to Angle, creating some confusion for later Beat scholars.

A little farther uptown, the Beats went to hear the latest jazz bands on and around 52nd Street. In places like Bop City (1619 Broadway), the Three Deuces (72 W. 52nd), and the Clique (1678 Broadway), which became Birdland in 1949, they listened to jazz greats such as Charlie Parker, Lester Young, Ben Webster, and Billie Holliday. They frequently followed the performers uptown to nightclubs in Harlem, particularly Minton's Playhouse at 210 W. 118th Street, where the musicians played in after-hours jam sessions that gave birth to bebop, the music that came to define the era. It was at Minton's that Jack and his Columbia friend Jerry Newman recorded Dizzy Gillespie's "Kerouac."

The Beats were attracted to the jazz musicians and the underworld figures of Huncke's world because their lifestyles seemed exciting and more authentic than their own. They learned all too soon, however, that there was a price to be paid for their experiments with drugs and criminality. After Huncke and Burroughs were arrested on drug-related charges, and Joan was hospitalized in Bellevue with an amphetamine-induced psychosis, the 115th Street apartment broke up. Ginsberg moved into a rooming house at 200 W. 92nd Street and focused on his studies at Columbia. Kerouac returned to his parents' home at 133–01 Crossbay Boulevard in Ozone Park, Queens. A commemorative plaque now marks the spot where the tyro author finished *The Town and the City* (1950) and began the earliest version of *On the Road* (1957).

In the summer of 1948 Ginsberg lived briefly at 321 E. 121st Street. Here, while reading William Blake, he heard the poet's voice aloud. The hallucinatory experience haunted and obsessed him for many years to come. Shortly afterwards he moved to 1401 York Avenue between 74th and 75th Street. Huncke found Ginsberg here and soon moved in with him. Before long, he and two associates, Jack Melody and Priscilla Arminger (also known as Vicki Russell), were using the place as a thieves' den. On 21 April 1949, Melody, with Ginsberg and Arminger as passengers, turned over his stolen car at sixty miles an hour on 205th Street in Bayside, Queens, while trying to outrun the police. Allen and Arminger escaped without serious injury but evidence at the crash site led the police to the stolen goods at the York Avenue apartment. Huncke, who

had a criminal record, got five years in prison; Ginsberg, a first offender with a history of mental problems, was sent for treatment to the New York State Psychiatric Institute of Columbia Presbyterian Hospital at 722 W. 168th Street, where he met Carl Solomon.

John Clellon Holmes learned of the arrests in the newspaper reports that followed. He had last seen his friends at his apartment at 681 Lexington Avenue on 20 April at a party he threw to celebrate the acceptance of Kerouac's *The Town and the City* by Harcourt-Brace and Company. Although Holmes took classes at Columbia before and after the war, he did not meet Kerouac or Ginsberg until July 1948. Kerouac and Holmes became close friends and, after Kerouac and his mother moved to 94–21 134th Street in Richmond Hill, Queens, Kerouac frequently visited Holmes at the above address and at a later apartment Holmes had at 123 Lexington Avenue. Holmes was with Kerouac when Jack first coined the phrase "Beat Generation" in November 1948 and Holmes was the first to use the term in print in his novel *Go* (1952). *Go* ends with the death of Agatson, a character modeled on Bill Cannastra, a Harvard law school graduate who died in a bizarre subway accident at Bleecker Street station. After the accident, Kerouac married Cannastra's girlfriend, Joan Haverty. They lived together briefly at 454 W. 20th Street, where Kerouac typed out the scroll version of *On the Road*. With the money he made on *Go*, Holmes bought a Victorian house in Old Saybrook, Connecticut, where he could write away from Manhattan's distractions. Kerouac, Ginsberg, and Burroughs spent much of the next few years on the road. When the Beat scene returned to New York City, it shifted downtown.

In the 1950s, lured by low rents and a budding literary and artistic renaissance, more and more writers moved to Greenwich Village and the more remote East Village. The preferred hangout for the Beats in the early 1950s was the San Remo bar at 93 MacDougal on the corner of Bleecker. The regulars included a wide range of writers such as Jack Kerouac, William Burroughs, Gregory Corso, John Clellon Holmes, Chandler Brossard, James Baldwin, Anatole Broyard, and Allen Ginsberg. Coincidentally, Gregory Corso's birthplace is just across the street from the San Remo at 190 Bleecker. The Beats also drank around the corner at Fugazzi's (305 6th Avenue), a bar Ginsberg made famous in "Howl."

While the writers frequented the San Remo, the artists of the same period chose the Cedar Tavern at 24 University Place as their favorite watering hole. Every night artists like Jackson Pollock, Willem de Kooning, Larry Rivers, and Franz Kline could be found drinking here. The poet Frank O'Hara, who knew all of the painters through his work at the Museum of Modern Art, was a confidant of both groups and through him Kerouac, Ginsberg, Corso, and other writers found their way to the Cedar.

From 1952 until December 1953 Ginsberg lived in the first of his several East Village apartments at 206 E. 7th Street. Quickly, it became a central meeting place for friends such as Kerouac, Burroughs, Holmes, Carr, and Gregory Corso who, shortly after his release from Clinton prison, met Ginsberg at the Pony Stable, a lesbian bar at 150 W. 4th Street. When Burroughs, in the wake of his accidental shooting of Joan Vollmer during a game of William Tell, returned to New York, he stayed there with Ginsberg. Ginsberg left his apartment at the end of 1953 and did not return to live in New York City until 1958. By that time he had written "Howl" and was quickly becoming the most famous poet of his generation.

Upon his return, Ginsberg settled into an apartment at 170 E. 2nd Street, where he lived for three years and wrote his greatest poem "Kaddish." A plaque on the building commemorates his stay there. Herbert Huncke also lived there after his release from prison in 1959. Ginsberg encouraged Huncke's writing and supported him in his first public reading at the Seven Arts Coffee Gallery at 496 Ninth Avenue, close to his old stomping grounds in Times Square. The gallery featured readings by some of the best poets of the day, including Ginsberg, Corso, Ray Bremser, LeRoi Jones (now Amiri Baraka), and Diane di Prima.

During the years the Beats were becoming famous worldwide, coffeehouses featuring poetry readings, similar to the Seven Arts, were springing up all over the Village. The center of the scene in the late 1950s was MacDougal Street between Bleecker and W. 3rd Street. The Gaslight at 116 MacDougal was among the first to have readings. The trend spread quickly to other places, such as the Cafe Bizarre at 106 W. 3rd and the Kettle of Fish at 114 MacDougal. The Kettle also attracted younger folksingers, such as Bob Dylan, Phil Ochs, and Eric Andersen, who were influenced by the elder Beats. The Kettle's "BAR" sign became the backdrop for the well-known photo of Kerouac that appears in the GAP advertisement, as well as on the dust jacket of Joyce Johnson's *Minor Characters* (1983). The bar, along with the neon sign, has moved to 59 Christopher Street, the former home of another famous literary pub, the Lion's Head.

Just across Sheridan Square, in the basement of 178 Seventh Avenue South, the Village Vanguard offered jazz nightly with a sprinkling of poetry. In December 1957, Jack Kerouac performed there and met talk show host Steve Allen, with whom he later recorded *Poetry for the Beat Generation* (1959). Shy and ill at ease in public, Kerouac drank heavily throughout his performances and the critics were less than enthusiastic. On the whole, the experience was less satisfying for Kerouac than his October performance with David Amram and Philip Lamantia at the Brata Gallery at 89 E. 10th Street.

In the 1960s, the poetry readings moved east to places like Les Deux Megots at 64 E. 7th Street and the Cafe Le Metro at 149 Second Avenue. St. Mark's Place and Tompkins Square Park supplanted MacDougal Street and Washington Square Park as gathering places for up-and-coming poets and artists. Finally, in the mid-1960s, the poetry readings found a more permanent home with the St. Mark's Poetry Project at St. Mark's in the Bowery Church on Second Avenue at 10th Street. Nearly every Beat poet from Ferlinghetti, Snyder, Ginsberg, and Corso to the next generation of poets such as Diane di Prima, Janine Pommy Vega, and Anne Waldman have read at St. Mark's. The Five Spot, located at 5 Cooper Square and later at 2 St. Marks Place, became the hot spot for jazz, featuring performances by Charlie Mingus, Thelonious

Monk, and Cecil Taylor, among others. Beat listeners at the Five Spot included Kerouac, Ginsberg, David Amram, and Leroi and Hettie Jones, who lived at nearby 27 Cooper Square.

Several bookstores played an important role in promoting the Beat movement in New York City. The Eighth Street Bookshop (32 W. 8th Street, later 17 W. 8th Street), founded by brothers Ted and Eli Wilentz, was one of the most prominent. Poets met there, read their work, and sometimes used the place as a mail drop. The Wilentzes joined their Corinth imprint with LeRoi Jones's Totem Press in the 1960s and published several important Beat works, including Jack Kerouac's *Scripture of the Golden Eternity* (1960) and Allen Ginsberg's *Empty Mirror* (1961). In the mid-1960s, Ed Sanders, poet and founder of the rock group "The Fugs," opened the Peace Eye Bookstore (383 E. 10th Street) and sold and published irreverent new works by many of the Beats. His mimeographed publication, *Fuck You: A Magazine of the Arts,* was required reading for anyone who would be hip. The Phoenix Bookshop at 18 Cornelia Street (later 22 Jones) also specialized in Beat literature, though its focus was more on rare books. While living at 309 E. Houston, Diane di Prima worked at the Phoenix and published early issues of *The Floating Bear* on the bookstore's mimeograph machine. These bookstores followed in the tradition of Frances Steloff's Gotham Book Mart at 41 W. 47th Street, supporting and promoting the best in avant-garde literature.

From the 1970s on, the East Village remained the heart of Beat activities in New York City, primarily because Allen Ginsberg spent the rest of his life there. After leaving his E. 2nd Street apartment in 1961, he lived at 704 E. 5th Street and then 408 E. 10th Street until 1975. Around that time the neighborhood was at its most dangerous, and after being mugged on the street, Ginsberg moved to 437 E. 12th Street, where he lived for the next twenty years. By this time Ginsberg was perhaps the most recognizable poet in the world, and his presence in the East Village enhanced the neighborhood's reputation for literary and artistic innovation.

Burroughs returned to New York City in 1973, accepting a teaching position in the MFA program at City College, CUNY, at 138th Street and Convent Avenue, just a few subway stops from Columbia. From 1975 to 1981, he lived at 222 Bowery, near the punk rock club CBGB, in a windowless apartment he dubbed "The Bunker." Ginsberg and Burroughs saw a good deal of each other once again, until Burroughs moved to Lawrence, Kansas, where he remained for the rest of his life.

Brooklyn beckoned to the Beats in the 1980s. After substituting for John Ashbery, Ginsberg was appointed a distinguished professor in the English department at Brooklyn College, CUNY, where he remained until his death. He brought numerous Beat writers to the Flatbush Avenue campus, including Burroughs, Corso, Huncke, Carl Solomon, Ray Bremser, Robert Creeley, Philip Whalen, Michael McClure, and Gary Snyder. Huncke was also living in Brooklyn at the time at 276 Henry Street, just a few blocks from the brownstone at 293 State Street that Kerouac shared with relatives when he first arrived in New York to attend Horace Mann.

New York said goodbye to most of the Beats who remained in the city in the 1990s. Herbert Huncke, who returned to Manhattan, lived briefly at 269 E. 7th Street and at the Chelsea Hotel (222 W. 23rd Street). He died at Beth Israel hospital on 8 August 1996. A memorial service was held for him at the Friends Meeting House at 221 E. 15th Street. Ginsberg, who had used the proceeds from the sale of his archive to Stanford University to buy a loft in an elevator building at 404 E. 14th Street, died there on 5 April 1997, surrounded by friends and old loves, including Peter Orlovsky. There was a Buddhist funeral service at the Shambhala Meditation Center at 118 W. 22nd Street and later memorial services at the St. Mark's Poetry Project, Central Park, and the Cathedral of St. John the Divine. Gregory Corso, who had lived in the city off and on over the years, had finally settled with friends at 26 Horatio Street, where he spent the last ten years of his life. He died peacefully on 18 January 2001. A funeral mass was held at Our Lady of Pompeii on Carmine Street, a stone's throw from his birthplace.

Like Ginsberg's Denver, New York is lonesome for its Beat heroes, but the city remains a mecca for writers and artists with a new vision.

—*William M. Gargan*
*Bill Morgan*

## Bibliographical References

The most comprehensive guide to the Beats in New York City is Bill Morgan's *The Beat Generation in New York: A Walking Tour of Jack Kerouac's City,* 1997. Steven Watson's *The Birth of the Beat Generation,* 1995, provides good coverage of the movement's early days. Ronald Sukenick's *Down and In: Life in the Underground,* 1987, captures the ambience of the Beat scene in Greenwich Village and the East Village in the 1950s and 1960s, particularly the pubs and coffeehouses. Other books focusing on Greenwich Village include Fred and Gloria McDarrah's *Beat Generation: Glory Days in Greenwich Village,* 1996; Fred and Patrick McDarrah's *The Greenwich Village Guide,* 1992; and Terry Miller's *Greenwich Village and How It Got That Way,* 1990. *Greenwich Village: Culture and Counterculture,* 1993, edited by Rick Beard and Leslie Cohen Berlowitz, contains an informative essay by Beat historian Barry Miles. John Gruen's *The New Bohemia,* 1966, and *A Secret Location on the Lower East Side: Adventures in Writing 1960–1980,* 1998, edited by Steven Clay and Rodney Phillips, target the East Village. Magazine articles include Patrick Fenton's "Kerouac in Queens," *The Newsday Magazine,* 1 April 1990, 9–12, 17; "The Cedar Bar," by Larry Rivers with Carol Brightman in *New York,* 5 September 1979, 39–44; Aaron Latham's "The Columbia Murder That Gave Birth to the Beats," *New York,* 19 April 1976, 41–58; and Ann Charters's "Allen Ginsberg and Jack Kerouac, Columbia Undergraduates," *Columbia Library Columns* 20.1 (1970): 10–17.

*See also* Music; Parker, Charles Christopher; Young, Lester; Holiday, Billie; Gillespie, John Brinks; Holmes, John Clellon; Cannastra, Bill; Corso, Gregory; Pollock, Jackson; de Kooning, Willem; Kline, Franz; Bremser, Ray; di Prima, Diane; Baraka, Amiri; Kerouac, Jack; Ginsberg, Allen; Carr, Lucien; Kammerer, David Eames; Burroughs, William Seward; Vollmer Adams Burroughs, Joan; Parker, Edie; Pad, The Beat; Chase, Haldon "Hal"; Huncke, Herbert; Kinsey Report; Ferlinghetti, Lawrence; Pommy Vega, Janine; Mingus, Charles; Monk, Thelonious Sphere; Amram, David; Jones, Hettie; Sanders, Ed; Creeley, Robert; Whalen, Philip; McClure, Michael; Snyder, Gary; Orlovsky, Peter

## New York University Conferences on Beat Culture (1994 and 1995)

"The Beat Generation: Legacy and Celebration" (17–22 May 1994), organized by New York University's School of Education, marked a watershed in terms of academic acceptance for the Beat Generation. Fifty years after the birth of the Beat movement on the Columbia University campus (116th Street and Broadway), the movement's founders, denounced by Columbia alumnus Norman Podhoretz as "know-nothing bohemians," were being honored for their profound influence on American culture, only five miles from where the Beat Generation all began.

With Allen Ginsberg and Ann Charters serving as honorary cochairs, the conference at the Loeb Student Center attracted a veritable who's who of Beat artists, including David Amram, Carolyn Cassady, Gregory Corso, Lawrence Ferlinghetti, Joyce Johnson, Hettie Jones, Jan Kerouac, Ken Kesey, Joanne Kyger, Michael McClure, Jack Micheline, Harold Norse, Ed Sanders, Cecil Taylor, Hunter S. Thompson, and Anne Waldman. Serving on panels with distinguished scholars such as Gordon Ball, Douglas Brinkley, Gerald Nicosia, Michael Schumacher, John Tytell, and Regina Weinreich, the movement's founders discussed the history and influence of the Beat Generation, including its contributions to literature, music, the visual arts, philosophy, and education. Among the more specific topics explored were "The Beat Generation and Censorship," and "Women and the Beat Generation." At less formal "current research" sessions, paper topics ranged from Beat spirituality to Kerouac and food.

A wide variety of cultural and social activities offered conference participants a chance to rub elbows with Beat legends. These included a twenty-four-hour poetry and music insomniacathon (18 May), an evening of jazz and poetry at "The Beat

Cabaret" (20 May), a marathon reading of *On the Road* in Washington Square Park (22 May), and a production of James Mirrione's play *The Last Stop, Will and Testament, Saint Jack Kerouac*, which ran for eight performances (20–28 May) at the Black Box Theatre.

One of the conference's high points, a gala event at Town Hall (19 May), featured musical performances by David Amram and Doors band member Ray Manzarek accompanying Michael McClure; a telephone greeting from William Burroughs in Kansas; and poetry readings by Allen Ginsberg, Lawrence Ferlinghetti, Gregory Corso, and others. The audience was particularly appreciative of Corso who, succumbing to its requests, read his popular poem "Marriage."

An art exhibit and film festival documented Beat contributions in the visual arts. The art show at 80 Washington Square East Galleries ran through 10 June 1994 and featured work by and about Beat artists, including Kerouac, Ginsberg, Burroughs, Ferlinghetti, and Corso. While works such as Ginsberg's and Fred McDarrah's photographs had been exhibited or published previously, others, such as Kerouac's paintings, seen here publicly for the first time, generated fresh excitement. The film festival (17–21 May), showcased over two dozen films, including experimental works such as Anthony Balch's *Towers Open Fire* (1963), documentaries such as *What Happened to Kerouac* (1985), and Hollywood productions such as *The Subterraneans* (1960).

The conference was not without controversy. There were arguments over the role of women in the Beat Generation and calls for more recognition of African American contributions to the movement. A lawsuit filed by Jan Kerouac against the executors of Kerouac's estate over the validity of Gabrielle Kerouac's will and the disposition of Kerouac's archive occasioned heated exchanges by supporters of both sides at several meetings. The legal battle had greater repercussions on the Kerouac conference held at NYU the following year.

"The Writings of Jack Kerouac" (4–6 June 1995) was smaller in scope but similar in format to the 1994 conference. A Beat walking tour of Greenwich Village and an open reading of *Mexico City Blues* in Washington Square Park on Sunday afternoon preceded the scholarly programs scheduled for Monday and Tuesday. From the opening session on, however, controversy seemed to upstage scholarship. Conference participants voted to reject a bid by Jan Kerouac and biographer Gerald Nicosia to air their grievances and, after several disruptions, moderator Allen Ginsberg had to ask security to escort them from the auditorium. Adding to the irony, "The Unbearables," a group of poets who equated academic recognition with selling out, protested the conference's $120 registration fee. The conference closed on Tuesday with an evening of readings and musical performances at Town Hall.

—*William M. Gargan*

**Bibliographical References**

Reviews on the 1994 conference include John Pareles, "Some Original Beatniks on a Trip to the Past," *New York Times*, 21 May 1994, Section 1: 13; Adrian Dannatt's "On the Road Again," *Times* (London), 24 May 1994, Arts section: 39; and Todd Bauer's reports in *Beat Scene*, issue 21: 4–6 and issue 22: 4–5. The *Kerouac Connection* 27 (1995 Winter) is a special issue devoted to the conference. A review of the 1995 conference by Edward Lewine is in the *New York Times*, 11 June 1995, Section 13: 8. Gerald Nicosia presents his view in "Buddha-gate at NYU," *Beat Scene* 24: 23–33.

***See also*** Burroughs, William Seward; Amram, David; Cassady, Carolyn; Charters, Ann; Corso, Gregory; Ferlinghetti, Lawrence; Ginsberg, Allen; Johnson, Joyce; Jones, Hettie; Kerouac, Jan; Kesey, Ken; Kyger, Joanne; McClure, Michael; Micheline, Jack; Norse, Harold; Sanders, Ed; Thompson, Hunter Stockton; Waldman, Anne; Nicosia, Gerald; Tytell, John; Music; Painting; Photography; Curriculum, Beats in the; Censorship; Sexism and Misogyny; Film

# News Media and Publicity, The Beats and

Whether supportive or antagonistic, always a force to keep the Beats in public attention. Major newspapers, widely circulated magazines, Hollywood movies, and television programs all gave significant attention to the Beats, making their spirit an inextinguishable flame.

The *New York Times* is at the center of the media attention to the Beats. In the *New York Times Magazine,* in 1952, John Clellon Holmes's "This Is the Beat Generation" appeared, providing an insider's view of a cultural phenomenon still in formation. In 1956, Richard Eberhart's "West Coast Rhythms" in the *New York Times Book Review* called attention to innovative artistry in California and paid particular attention to Allen Ginsberg, as well as Lawrence Ferlinghetti, Philip Whalen, and Gary Snyder. Gilbert Millstein's review of Jack Kerouac's *On the Road* in the *New York Times* on 5 September 1957 gave an incalculable boost to the rising Beats.

The *New York Times,* however, was not always favorable. Almost as soon as Millstein's review appeared, David Dempsey reviewed *On the Road* a second time (this time in the *New York Times Book Review*), recognizing the book's quality but finding glaring weakness in Kerouac's development of characters. Reviews in the *New York Times* of subsequent Beat publications often showed limited enthusiasm. Nevertheless, the *Times* always paid attention to the Beats, and in 2004, Walter Kirn in the *New York Times Book Review* hailed the publication of Kerouac's journals, comparing Kerouac's stature as a writer to that of Whitman, Twain, and Faulkner.

Like the *New York Times, Life* magazine gave significant support to the rise of the Beats, even when it sought to demean them. The 1957 article "Big Day for Bards at Bay" brought national attention to the censorship trial involving Allen Ginsberg's *Howl and Other Poems* (1956). The 1959 article "Squaresville U.S.A. vs. Beatsville," with its photo spread comparing small-town Kansas with hip Venice Beach, California, connected the Beats with coolness in the minds of countless Americans. Nevertheless, Paul O'Neil's "The Only Rebellion Around," published only two months after the "Squaresville" piece, clearly took a negative view of the Beats, mocking the Beat "pad," and dismissing the Beats as foolish, inartistic rebels.

*Time* magazine paid consistent attention to the Beats with short articles, principally derogatory. With items such as "Bam; Roll on with Bam," "Bang Bong Bing," and "Endsville: Zen-Hur," *Time* mocked the Beats as weirdos on the fringe of normal society; even so, *Time* proved that even negative publicity serves promotional purposes.

Numerous other magazines and newspapers contributed to the notoriety of the Beats. *Saturday Review,* the *Nation, Esquire, Playboy,* the *New York Post,* the *San Francisco Chronicle,* the *New Yorker,* the *Village Voice, Mademoiselle,* the *Chicago Tribune,* the *New Republic, Partisan Review,* and many other magazines covered the Beats. But even when reviewers went on the attack, they wound up helping the Beats because the attacks were sometimes unduly venomous, thereby making numerous readers perceive the commentators as nasty serpents.

Hollywood films carried the Beat message forward, sometimes suggestively, sometimes foolishly and pathetically. Certainly Marlon Brando in *The Wild One* (1954) and James Dean in *Rebel without a Cause* (1955) established the mysterious, troublesome, and yet engaging character that audiences could associate with the Beat outlook. Films such as *The Beat Generation* (1959), *The Subterraneans* (1960), and *Heart Beat* (1979) exploited the Beat experience in distorted, stereotypical presentations with horrible acting.

Television intensified media's support of the Beats. *The Many Loves of Dobie Gillis* (1959–1963), with its lovable Maynard G. Krebs, made the beatnik immensely popular with young people. *Route 66* (1960–1964), a program featuring Martin Milner and George Maharis as two young men driving in a Corvette across the country in search of an accommodating community, might well have been a take-off on Kerouac's *On the Road.*

Other programs, such as *Alfred Hitchcock Presents* (1955–1962) and *The Twilight Zone* (1959–1965), reinforced general interest in the Beats. Segments of these programs often included scenes in bars and coffeehouses with characters who suggested the Beats through their dress, speech, and posture.

—*William Lawlor*

## Bibliographical References

Among many items on the Beats in the *New York Times* are John Clellon Holmes, "This Is the Beat

Generation," *New York Times Magazine* 16 November 1952: 10–22; Gilbert Millstein, "Books of the Times," *New York Times*, 5 September 1957: 27; Richard Eberhart, "West Coast Rhythms," *New York Times Book Review*, 2 September 1956: 7; David Dempsey, "In Pursuit of 'Kicks,'" *New York Times Book Review*, 8 September 1957: 4; Walter Kirn, "The Rush of What Is Said," *New York Times Book Review* 10 October 2004: 6–7. The key articles on the Beats in *Life* are "Big Day for Bards at Bay," *Life*, 9 September 1957: 105–108; "Squaresville U.S.A. vs. Beatsville," *Life* 21 September 1959: 31–37; and Paul O'Neil, "The Only Rebellion Around," *Life*, 30 November 1959: 119–130. To see a full listing of articles on the Beats in numerous magazines and newspapers, see William Lawlor, *The Beat Generation: A Bibliographical Teaching Guide*, 1998: 59–80. Barbara Ehrenreich, "The Beat Rebellion: Beyond Work and Marriage" in *The Hearts of Men: American Dreams and the Flight from Commitment*, 1983, reviews the place of Beats in the media on pages 52–67.

***See also*** Film; Holmes, John Clellon; *On the Road, New York Times* Review of; Ginsberg, Allen; Styles of Dress, The Beats and; Language and Idiom of the Beats; Venice West

## Nicosia, Gerald (1949–)

Scholar, biographer, journalist, film consultant, poet; author of *Memory Babe* (1983), the lengthy critical biography of Jack Kerouac; literary executor for the estate of Jan Kerouac. Nicosia battled with the estate of Jack Kerouac to win a share of Kerouac's estate for Jan Kerouac, the daughter of Jack Kerouac. Nicosia also sought to prevent the piece-by-piece sale of Jack Kerouac's estate, but was thwarted in his legal efforts.

—*William Lawlor*

### Bibliographical References

*Memory Babe*, 1983, was reprinted by the University of California Press in 1994; *Home to War*, 2001, was reprinted in 2004.

## Norse, Harold (1916–)

Acknowledged as one of the most technically accomplished of the Beat poets, Harold Norse has never achieved the stature as a poet that he has unabashedly sought. His work has, however, received some fresh attention with the increased interest in "queer" studies. A secretary to W. H. Auden and a protégé of William Carlos Williams, Norse recounted his Parisian experiences with prominent Beats in the memoir *Beat Hotel* (1975) and later achieved some notoriety with his broader autobiography, *Memoirs of a Bastard Angel* (1989). Ironically, because of its opinionated portraits of a wide range of literary figures and its explicit chronicling of Norse's sexual exploits, *Memoirs of a Bastard Angel* has brought more attention to Norse than any of his collections of poetry—even though he presents a running argument throughout the book that his poetic achievement has been unaccountably slighted. The title of the autobiography comes from Norse's stint as editor and publisher of a literary magazine, *Bastard Angel*, which appeared from 1972 to 1974 and included the work of Beat poets.

Harold Norse was born on 16 July 1916, in New York City. He received a baccalaureate degree from Brooklyn College in 1938 and a master's degree from New York University in 1951. From 1949 to 1952, he taught at Cooper Union. In 1953, he became an expatriate and lived for the next decade and a half in French North Africa and several European countries. During that time, he taught English at several secondary and postsecondary institutions. Fluent in several languages, Norse also translated poetry into English. When he returned to the United States, he settled in San Francisco. From 1973 to 1975, he taught creative writing at the University of California at San Jose.

—*Martin Kich*

### Principal Works

Poetry: *The Undersea Mountain*, 1953; *The Dancing Beasts*, 1962; *Karma Circuit*, 1966; *Charles Bukowski, Philip Lamantia, Harold Norse*, 1969; *Hotel Nirvana: Selected Poems 1953–1973*, 1974; *I See America Daily*, 1974; *Carnivorous Saint: Gay Poems 1941–1976*, 1977; *Harold Norse, The Love Poems, 1940–1985*, 1986; *In the Hub of the Fiery Force: Collected Poems of Harold Norse*, 2003.

Translations: *The Roman Sonnets of G. G. Belli*, 1960.

Memoirs: *Beat Hotel,* 1975; *Memoirs of a Bastard Angel,* 1989.

Correspondence: *The American Idiom: A Correspondence,* with William Carlos Williams, 1990; *Fly Like a Bat out of Hell: The Letters of Harold Norse and Charles Bukowski,* 2002.

## Bibliographical References

*Ole* 5 (1966) is an issue devoted to Norse; in "An American Catullus," in *Advocate* 19 (Oct. 1977), Tony Sarver and W. I. Scobie focus on the gay themes in *Carnivorous Saint;* in "Harold Norse," in *Advocate* 26 (May 1987): 31–34, Ron Bluestein provides a profile, identifying the major themes in Norse's poetry; in "Poet Harold Norse: Searing Notes from Inroads of the Heart," in *Advocate* 25 (Nov. 1986): 57–59, Rudy Kikel focuses on the major themes of *Love Poems, 1940–1985;* in "The Return of the Bastard Angel," in *San Francisco Weekly,* 8 November 2000, Mark Athitakis provides a detailed commentary on Norse's life and work while deriding his association with a controversial figure in the regional gay community; in "Harold Norse's Poetic Imagination," in *Gay and Lesbian Review Worldwide* 10 (Jan./Feb. 2003): 24, Jim Nawrocki presents a brief profile, focusing as much on Norse's autobiography as on his poetry. Neeli Cherkovski, on pages 197–222 of *Whitman's Wild Children,* 1988, presents "Becoming a Man," a memoir and analysis of Norse's poetry.

***See also*** Williams, William Carlos

# O

## O'Hara, Frank (1926–1966)

Frank O'Hara was a major figure in the New York school of poetry and helped to reestablish poetry and painting as "sister arts." O'Hara moved to New York City in 1951 and immersed himself in both poetry and art, with the city remaining the center of his personal and professional activities until his death in 1966. O'Hara published several collections of poetry, received credit for establishing the New York school of poetry (with John Ashbery, Kenneth Koch, and James Schuyler), collaborated with painters on multimedia projects, befriended Allen Ginsberg and other members of the Beat Culture, and worked for the Museum of Modern Art (MoMA).

Frank O'Hara was born Francis Russell O'Hara to Irish-Catholic parents in Baltimore, Maryland, on 27 March 1926. He enlisted in the navy in 1944 and served throughout the remainder of World War II, primarily as a sonarman on the destroyer *Nicholas*. After being discharged in 1946, he attended Harvard University, where he pursued his love of literature and art. Winning the Avery Hopwood Award in poetry at the University of Michigan, where he earned a master's degree in contemporary literature, propelled him into a career as a poet.

O'Hara moved to New York City in 1951 in order to live a lifestyle devoted to the arts and open to the expression of his homosexual orientation. He was employed by MoMA in 1951 to sell tickets, publications, and souvenirs. He left for an editorial position with *Art News* in 1953, a publication to which he had been contributing articles. His reviews of art shows established his credentials in the art world, leading to a return to MoMA in 1955, initially to help organize traveling exhibitions, and later as an assistant curator preparing painting and sculpture exhibitions.

O'Hara developed friendships with many artists, including the major abstract expressionists Jackson Pollock and Willem de Kooning. He engaged in a number of joint creative efforts with painters, typically combining his poetry with their paintings, such as *A City Winter and Other Poems* (1952) with Larry Rivers, an exhibition of twelve poems entitled "Oranges" with paintings by Grace Hartigan at the Tibor de Nagy Gallery (1953), and two special comic-strip issues of the underground magazine *C* with Joe Brainard (1963).

O'Hara wrote exhibition catalogs and plays, but his primary accomplishment was in poetry. *Meditations in an Emergency* (1957) established his reputation, *Second Avenue* (1960) and *Odes* (1960) contributed to it, and inclusion of fifteen of his poems in Donald Allen's *The New American Poetry: 1945–1969* (1960) assured national recognition. The same anthology placed O'Hara prominently within the "New York school," further establishing his importance.

O'Hara's poems are noted for their descriptions of the people and places of New York City and for their detailed and relatively unadorned reciting of the poet's daily experiences. His poems have been compared to diary entries, and O'Hara himself likened many of his poems to personal phone calls.

Frank O'Hara died on 25 July 1966 of injuries suffered when he was struck by a dune buggy on a beach on Fire Island, New York. His posthumous *The Collected Poems of Frank O'Hara* (1971), edited by Donald M. Allen, received the National Book Award in 1972. Since then, his poetic reputation has remained secure.

—*Edward J. Rielly*

## Principal Works

*A City Winter, and Other Poems*, 1952; *Meditations in an Emergency*, 1956; *Odes*, 1960; *Second Avenue*, 1960; *Lunch Poems*, 1964; *Love Poems (Tentative Title)*, 1965; *In Memory of My Feelings*, 1967; *The Collected Poems of Frank O'Hara*, ed. Donald Allen, 1971; *Selected Poems*, 1974; *Collected Plays*, 1978.

## Bibliographical References

Alan Feldman, *Frank O'Hara*, 1979; Brad Gooch, *City Poet: The Life and Times of Frank O'Hara*, 1993; Marjorie Perloff, *Frank O'Hara: Poets among Painters*, 1977; Geoff Ward, *Statutes of Liberty: The New York School of Poets*, 2d ed., 2001.

*See also* Painting; Pollock, Jackson; de Kooning, Willem

## Olson, Charles (1910–1970)

The poet and essayist Charles Olson, born in 1910 in Worcester, Massachusetts, is known primarily for his long poem *The Maximus Poems* and a manifesto on poetics entitled "Projective Verse." His manifesto is often cited as central to Beat experiments with spontaneous composition and using the syllable rather than grammar as a unit of poetic measure. While rector of the influential Black Mountain College, he coedited, with Robert Creeley, *The Black Mountain Review*, publishing numerous contributions from major Beat figures, including Ginsberg's "America" and Kerouac's "Essentials of Spontaneous Prose."

With the demise of Black Mountain College in the midfifties, Olson became connected with the San Francisco Beat scene through his friendship with Robert Duncan and his leadership of the Black Mountain school of poetry. While clearly an influence on the younger Beats, Olson's poetics proved academic and pedantic compared to their more street-savvy compositional modes and poetic subjects. Nonetheless, the Beats and Olson shared a common aesthetic in their assertion that literature be the spontaneous record of the mind recording or recounting experiences.

Olson's achievements in terms of poetic form are notable. He used the typewriter exclusively for composition, feeling that it best captured the spontaneous energy of the mind constructing words into ideas. Approaching the page as a "field" in which to place recorded language, Olson abandoned traditional ideas about form and instigated a more spatial organization. By placing words and phrases all over the page unhindered by the constraints of margins and spacing, Olson felt that he more accurately captured the compositional process of the creative mind.

In his early poems, such as "The Kingfisher," Olson offered a fractured, highly allusive, and symbolic narrative culled from multifarious sources; a poetic effort that came to be recognized as the beginnings of the postmodern movement in poetry. Along with experiments in poetic form and content, Olson presented many interesting commentaries on history, perception, and language in his numerous essays, which were in themselves vast, highly esoteric assemblages, taking their compositional cues from his experiments in poetry. His complex rhetorical style is most evident in transcripts and recordings of lectures at Berkeley and Vancouver as part of writing conferences often featuring prominent members of the Beat movement.

Like his poetic mentor Ezra Pound, Olson chose to devote most of his later poetic career to the construction of a long poem, which built on the modes of poetic expression that he had been working with since he began writing poetry. Olson's *Maximus Poems* uses an epistolary style to recount the cultural history of a small fishing town, Gloucester, Massachusetts, through the eyes of the poem's protagonist, Maximus. It continues the organizational, compositional, and formal experiments of his earlier poetry in an attempt to render a modern American poetic epic.

Olson took up poetry seriously only in his midthirties after pursuing graduate studies on Herman Melville at Harvard University and working for the Office of War Information as assistant chief of the Foreign Language Division during the Second World War.

—David N. Wright

## Principal Works

Poetry: *Y & X*, 1948; *In Cold Hell, in Thicket*, 1953; *The Distances*, 1960; *The Maximus Poems*, 1960; *The Maximus Poems, IV, V, VI*, 1968; *Archeologist of Morning*, 1970; *The Maximus Poems, Volume Three*, eds. Charles Boer and George F. Butterick, 1975; *The Maximus Poems*, 1983; *The Collected Poems of Charles Olson: Excluding the Maximus Poems*, 1987.

Prose: *Call Me Ishmael*, 1947; *Projective Verse*, 1950; *The Mayan Letters*, 1953; *A Bibliography on America for Ed Dorn*, 1964; *Human Universe and Other Essays*, ed. Donald Allen, 1965; *Proprioception*, 1965. *Selected Writings*, ed. Robert Creeley, 1966; *Casual Mythology*, 1969; *The Special View of History*, ed. Ann Charters, 1970; *Additional Prose*, ed. George F. Butterick, 1974; *The Post Office: A Memoir of His Father*, 1974; *Collected Prose*, 1997.

Drama: *The Fiery Hunt and Other Plays*, 1977.

Selected correspondence and lectures: Ralph Maud's edition of *Charles Olson: Selected Letters*, 2001; George F. Butterick's *Charles Olson and Robert Creeley: The Complete Correspondence*, 1980; *Muthologos: The Collected Lectures and Interviews Volumes I and II*, 1978; Catherine Seeyle, *Charles Olson & Ezra Pound: An Encounter at St. Elizabeths*, 1975; and Albert Glover, *Letters for Origin, 1950–56*, 1970 offer a comprehensive view of Olson's prolific letter writing.

## Bibliographical References

The most recent biography is Tom Clark, *Charles Olson: The Allegory of a Poet's Life*, 1991, while Charles Boer's *Charles Olson in Connecticut* covers the last days of the poet's life. A general view of Olson's writing and significance can be found in Judith Halden-Sullivan's *The Topology of Being: The Poetics of Charles Olson*, 1991; Paul Christensen, *Charles Olson: Call Him Ishmael*, 1979; and in Robert von Hallberg, *Charles Olson: The Scholar's Art*, 1978. Studies by Ralph Maud in *Charles Olson's Reading: A Biography*, 1996, and Ann Charters in *Olson/Melville: A Study in Affinity*, 1986, detail some of Olson's early influences. Comprehensive studies such as those offered by Daniel Belgrad in *The Culture of Spontaneity: Improvisation and the Arts in Postwar America*, 1998, and Paul Sherman in *Olson's Push: Origin, Black Mountain, and Recent American Poetry*, 1978, serve as valuable resources for understanding Olson's influence. Finally, George F. Butterick's *A Guide to the Maximus Poems of Charles Olson*, 1978, is an invaluable source for the student of the *Maximus Poems*.

**See also** Black Mountain, North Carolina, and Black Mountain College; Creeley, Robert

# On the Road, New York Times Review of

On 5 September 1957, in the portion of the *New York Times* called "Books of the Times," Gilbert Millstein's review of Jack Kerouac's *On the Road* appeared. Millstein said that Kerouac was the incarnation of the Beat spirit and his book was a beautifully artistic interpretation of the Beat Generation, comparable to Ernest Hemingway's interpretation of the Lost Generation.

Joyce Johnson, who was with Kerouac on the evening that Millstein's review reached the newsstands, reports that she and Jack read the review under a streetlamp. They knew the review was very favorable, but could not anticipate the review's full effect.

That night, Jack went to bed an unknown man, but arose to a bright new world of notoriety, with reporters pursuing him and his book rising onto the best-seller list.

—William Lawlor

## Bibliographical References

See Gilbert Millstein, "Books of the Times," *New York Times*, 5 September 1957: 27. See Joyce Johnson, *Minor Characters*, 1983; Johnson's description of the night Kerouac read the review is reprinted in *The Portable Beat Reader*, ed. Ann Charters, 1992.

## On the Road, 1982 Conference on the Twenty-fifth Anniversary of the Publication of

In July 1982, Naropa Institute held the "Jack Kerouac *On the Road* Conference," the twenty-fifth anniversary celebration of the book's publication. The ten-day event reunited many Beat luminaries, including William S. Burroughs, Gregory Corso, Lawrence Ferlinghetti, and Herbert Huncke, with Allen Ginsberg as host. The conference, documented both on videotape (housed in the Special Collections section in the Ginsberg Library) and in John Montgomery's book, *The Kerouac We Knew*, drew over 350 participants and cost each participant $260. Attracting not only academics, but also LSD guru Timothy Leary, political activist Abbie Hoffman, the media, and Kerouac groupies from afar, the conference reveled in the bohemian lifestyle, while keeping the legacy of Kerouac alive.

The day after the event, Henry Allen wrote in the *Washington Post* (2 August 1982) that the conference was intended "to celebrate and commemorate Kerouac, who died at 47 in 1969, author of 19 published books that changed the American psyche with their celebration of spontaneity, drugs, aimlessness, esoteric religion, jazz, blacks, and a sort of sidewalk dadaism they called 'goofing'" (C1). Kerouac wrote almost exclusively about himself and his friends, many of whom were in attendance. Because Beat literature helped to pave the way for political change, a cultural revolution was celebrated as well, including the merchandising and sale of Beat memorabilia, such as Jack Kerouac posters and T-shirts.

Workshops included studies of disembodied poetics, analysis of the bop prosody style, and discussions of the artistry of Kerouac, but according to a somewhat disenchanted John Clellon Homes, some participants were perplexed: "What disturbs me is thinking that by following somebody else's way, they can write. I think the audience was puzzled by the panel on Kerouac as an artist. They don't think of him as an artist. They think of him as a personality" (qtd. by Allen, C1). The conference was also criticized for its lack of literary discussion and its surge of political commentary, not to mention a drunken opening speech given by Chögyam Trungpa Rinpoche.

—*Patricia Hillen*

### Bibliographical References

See Henry Allen, "'On the Road Again and Mad to Remember," *Washington Post*, 2 August 1982: C1; in the postscript to *Dharma Lion*, 1992, Michael Schumacher offers valuable information on the Kerouac conference; Ann Charters, *Beats and Company*, 1986, offers a brief summary of the conference and a series of photos.

## On the Road, Sale of the Scroll of

On 22 May 2001, the fiftieth anniversary of its completion, the scroll upon which Jack Kerouac typed *On the Road* sold for $2.43 million at Christie's in Manhattan. The buyer, James Irsay, owner of the Indianapolis Colts and collector of pop culture artifacts, including a guitar once played by Elvis Presley, was admittedly willing to pay more. Irsay's $2.2 million bid, not including a premium of $226,000, was almost $1 million more than the highest preauction estimate and broke the world record for the auction price of a literary manuscript.

The decision by the Kerouac estate to auction the 120-foot scroll to a private owner rather than to place it with a public archive met harsh criticism from scholars, writers, and others associated with the Beat movement, including Carolyn Cassady, former wife of Neal Cassady, and Gerald Nicosia, a Kerouac biographer who once contested control of the Kerouac estate in court. But the heirs to the estate, who inherited it upon the death of Kerouac's third wife, Stella Sampas, stated that the scroll was sold separately from the rest of the archive in order to pay the nearly $1 million estate tax. And, to assuage fears that the public would be denied access to Kerouac's most famous and most democratic work, Irsay made and has kept a promise to exhibit the scroll in archives across the country. In honor of the novel's fiftieth anniversary in 2007, the scroll itself will go "on the road" and be displayed at various universities and libraries around the United States.

—*Matt Stefon*

The original manuscript of the first draft of Jack Kerouac's *On the Road* is displayed in Indianapolis, Tuesday, January 6, 2004. Jim Irsay, owner of the Indianapolis Colts, bought Kerouac's epic, a 50-year-old, 120-foot scroll containing the single-spaced typewritten account of his trip wandering across America, for $2.43 million. Beginning in 2004 at the Orange County History Center in Orlando, Florida, and ending with a three-month stay at the New York Public Library in 2007, Kerouac's *On the Road* scroll made a thirteen-stop, four-year national tour of museums and libraries. (AP Photo/Darron Cummings)

## Bibliographical References

John Ezard, "Auction of Kerouac Manuscript 'Blasphemy,'" *Guardian*, 5 April 2001; Jack Minch, "Sale Brings 'Mixed Feelings' for One of Three Local Estate Heirs," *Lowell Sun*, 23 May 2001; "*On The Road* Sets Record on the Block," *New York Times*, 23 May 2001; Richard Pyle, "Toll to Get 'On The Road' at Auction: $2.46M," *Lowell Sun*, 23 May 2001; Kathryn Shattuck, "First, Elvis's Guitar; Now *On The Road*," *New York Times*, 3 June 2001.

***See also*** Kerouac, Jack; Spontaneity, The Beat Generation and the Culture of; New York City

## Orlovsky, Peter (1933–)

Peter Orlovsky is not only Allen Ginsberg's longtime companion and lover, but a poet as well. Known for political activism, he protested nuclear sites and drug laws. With Ginsberg, he frankly displayed and discussed their homosexual union to spread consciousness and acceptance for alternative lifestyles.

Orlovsky was born on 8 July 1933 on the Lower East Side of New York. Orlovsky's parents separated when he was a teenager and he soon dropped out of school to work a number of odd jobs until he could later complete a diploma. Although drafted in 1953

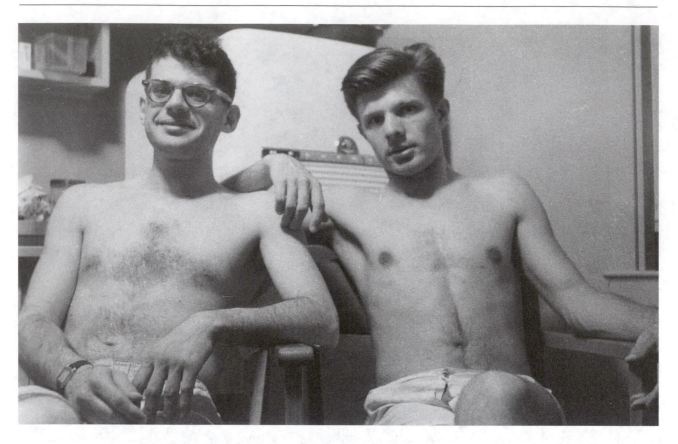

Allen Ginsberg (left) and Peter Orlovsky (right) were lifetime lovers. (Allen Ginsberg/Corbis)

for service in Korea, he was deemed unfit by military psychologists and served instead as a medic in San Francisco.

Upon discharge he stayed in San Francisco, moving in with painter Robert La Vigne as a model and companion. In 1954, Ginsberg visited La Vigne and became interested in Orlovsky after seeing a painting he had modeled for. They soon became lovers and moved in together. The relationship lasted until Ginsberg's death in April 1997, although Orlovsky's propensity for heterosexual affairs (and Ginsberg's for homosexual ones) sometimes complicated things. However, the couple was nearly inseparable for thirty years and Ginsberg and Orlovsky provided each other steady artistic inspiration and personal gratification.

It was not until his relationship with Ginsberg that Orlovsky began to assert himself as a poet. He began writing in Paris in 1957, trying spontaneous compositional forms. He soon began (like Ginsberg) to carry notebooks for jotting down observations and poetry. His work, though similar in style to Ginsberg's, remains distinct. His output has dropped off since the 1970s.

—*John M. Carey*

## Principal Works

*Clean Asshole Poems & Smiling Vegetable Songs: Poems 1957–1977*, 1978; with Allen Ginsberg, *Straight Hearts' Delight: Love Poems and Selected Letters*, 1980; *Lepers Cry*, 1972. Poems are also available in Ann Charters, ed., *Portable Beat Reader*, 1992; David Kherdian, *Beat Voices*, 1995; and Anne Waldman, ed., *The Beat Book*, 1996.

## Bibliographical References

Biographies of Allen Ginsberg contain ample information on Orlovsky: Michael Schumacher, *Dharma Lion*, 1992; Barry Miles, *Ginsberg: A Biography*, 1989; Jane Kramer, *Allen Ginsberg in America*, 1969.

***See also*** Ginsberg, Allen; New York City; Moloch

# P

## Pad, The Beat

*Pad*, in Beat idiom, refers to a living space, whether that is a house, apartment, cottage, or shack. The term *Beat pad* came to mean a place in which Beats lived and worked. Though the term refers simply to living space, the Beat pad took on a legendary status in American culture as a site of squalor, drug use, and sexual promiscuity. As a result of film and print media, including a full-page illustration in *Life Magazine* (November 1959), the Beat pad came to include stock elements: bare mattresses, abandoned beer cans and wine bottles, espresso coffee pots, marijuana, hypodermic needles, a guitar and/ or bongos available for late-night revelry, battered furniture, and abstract paintings that were hung, or better yet, painted directly onto the walls alongside posters for poetry readings.

The actual Beat pads came into existence as Beat writers and artists moved into cities, most notably the area surrounding Columbia University, the Lower East Side in Manhattan, the Greenwich Village area of New York, the Venice Beach area near Los Angeles, and the North Beach area of San Francisco. The Beats forsook the conventional 1950s emphasis on family and career, instead choosing to write, paint, act, and politically revolt against the conformity, consumerism, and repressive McCarthyism of the age. However, the Beats usually had little money, so the Beat pad arose as low-rent housing that could provide shelter along with the means for personal expression. Beat pads often offered no heat, no hot water, and a bathroom shared among several private rented rooms on a floor of an apartment building. Because of their location in poor urban areas, sanitation problems led to rodent and insect life sharing the space with the Beats. In addition, the pads were furnished with whatever furniture came to hand, from used sofas and mattresses to orange crates for bookcases.

In "Howl," which appears in *Howl and Other Poems* (1956), Allen Ginsberg writes about "the supernatural darkness of cold-water flats" (9), and in "Marriage," which appears in *The Happy Birthday of Death* (1960), Gregory Corso refers to "hot smelly tight New York City/ seven flights up, roaches and rats in the walls" (31). In *On the Road* (1957), Kerouac describes the Denver pad of Carlo Marx, who lived in a basement with "one bed, a candle burning, stone walls that oozed moisture, and a crazy makeshift ikon that he had made" (47). In *Memoirs of a Beatnik,* Diane di Prima describes the Manhattan apartment where she entertained guests and served large quantities of lentil soup.

For three years, Ginsberg lived in an apartment at 170 E. 2nd Street, where he wrote "Kaddish." After leaving his E. 2nd Street apartment in 1961, he lived at 704 E. 5th Street and then 408 E. 10th Street until 1975.

The Beat pad provided space for writers and artists to gather, discuss writing, share meals, and prepare literary magazines, sculptures, paintings, and various crafts. The pads often hosted a revolving occupancy, as people came and went depending on need and inclination, bringing whatever payment

A group of young people in beatnik attire (berets and sunglasses) watch a boy reclining on his back and playing the bongos, 1960. (Jack Moebes/Corbis)

they could afford from wood to fuel the fire to canned goods or produce to supplement dinner for that evening's group. Joan Vollmer Adams, who lived in apartment #62 at 421 W. 118th Street, established a famous communal residence for the Beats.

*Life* magazine brought the Beat pad to nation-wide attention in September 1959 in an article titled "Squaresville U.S.A. vs. Beatsville" comparing the midwestern town of Hutchinson, Kansas, to beatnik life in Venice, California. Meant to be shocking, the pictures contrasted wholesome interior design and lovingly displayed family albums to dirty mattresses and discarded beer cans in a

Venice Beat pad. Film and other media developed the legendary version of the Beat pad by regimenting the essentials along the lines of stereotype and caricature rather than exploring individual differences based upon the pad's occupants.

—*Jennifer Love*

## Bibliographical References

*Life* magazine provides a photographic journey through a Beat pad in "Squaresville U.S.A. vs. Beatsville" (September 1959); *Life* also provides an annotated illustration of the "well-equipped" Beat pad in "The Only Rebellion Around" (November 1959); the CD-ROM *The Beat*

*Experience* offers an interactive representation of a Beat pad, 1996; Diane di Prima's *Memoirs of a Beatnik,* 1969, also offers titillating descriptions of Beat pads and what happened there.

*See also* New York City; San Francisco; Vollmer Adams Burroughs, Joan; Venice West

# Painting

The cultural, historical, political, and aesthetic forces of the 1940s to the 1960s that shaped the Beat poets found parallel expression in the visual arts, especially painting. The restlessness, anxiety, nonconformity, love of jazz, spiritual search, and quest for an authentic American art that informed Burroughs, Kerouac, Corso, Ferlinghetti, and the other Beat writers also contributed to the work of abstract expressionism and the New York school and the work of painters such as Jackson Pollock, Mark Rothko, Robert Motherwell, and Willem de Kooning. These factors also contributed to later developments such as pop art, and junk and funk art, with their playfulness, their critique of consumer commercialism, and their appeal to spontaneity and to assemblages, installations, and happenings. In turn, many of the Beats themselves explored various visual idioms that indicated their affinity with the artistic currents around them.

Abstract expressionism represents one of the most important American contributions to modern art. While the term was first applied in the 1920s to the work of Vasily Kandinsky, it was used in 1946 by the critic Robert Coates to describe the work being done in America by Arshile Gorky (1905–1948), Willem de Kooning (1904–1997), and Jackson Pollock (1912–1956). The term *New York school* was coined to describe the first generation of these painters living and working in New York at the time. In addition to Gorky, de Kooning, and Pollock, they include most notably William Baziotes (1912–1963), Adolph Gottlieb (1903–1974)—the only member of the New York school actually born in New York—Philip Guston (1913–1980), Hans Hofmann (1880–1966), Franz Kline (1910–1962), Robert Motherwell (1915–1991), Lee Krasner (1911–1984), Barnett Newman (1905–1970), Ad Reinhardt (1913–1967), Mark Rothko (1903–1970), Clyfford Still (1904–1980), and Mark Tobey (1890–1976).

Abstract expressionism is less a coherent style than an attempt to capture a direct response to visual experience. Flourishing in the 1940s and 1950s, abstract expressionism represents a response and reply to various currents of European modernism, especially Dada, fauvism, cubism, and surrealism, as well as to more indigenous styles such as social realism and American scene painting. Most of the painters of the movement grew up during the Depression in midwestern and western rural or industrial settings, their early work manifesting a tension between the individual and his or her environment. Disenchanted with realist orthodoxy, they sought an aesthetic that went beneath the level of experience. Thus, they were attracted to the ideas and work of surrealist Max Ernst and other émigrés who came to New York after the fall of Paris to the Nazis in 1940. They were especially drawn to the surrealist concept of automatism, which seemed to link the image with the unconscious, turning the work into a direct expression, rather than a representation of consciousness. For similar reasons they were also drawn to primitive art and Jung's theory of archetypes and the collective unconscious.

Their work responds to the aesthetics of European modernism. All were attracted to the bright colors of the fauves and the use of a unified picture plane by the cubists. They differed, however, in that while Picasso and Matisse still grounded their fragmented images in the representation of objects, the expressionists focused on the expressive potential of form and color independent of representation. Picasso's *Les Demoiselles d'Avignon* (1907) is a cubist representation of five bathers. Pollock's drip painting *Lavender Mist* (1950) or Rothko's *Houston Chapel* (1964–1967) is about how color and form evoke emotion.

Loosely speaking, abstract expressionism falls into two stylistic groups, gestural painting, also known as action painting, and color field painting. The categories are not absolute, but the first group conventionally includes most prominently Kline, Pollock, and De Kooning, and the second, Rothko,

Jackson Pollock's "Silver over Black, White, Yellow, and Red" (1948) is a clear example of abstract expressionism. (CNAC/MNAM/Dist Réunion des Musées Nationaux/Art Resource, NY)

Newman, and Still. Others, such as Motherwell, seem to fall into both camps. The term *action painting* was coined by critic Harold Rosenberg to describe the practice of Pollock and others, and probably inspired by the photographs of Pollock at work that earned him the epithet "Jack the Dripper." Such descriptions, however, belie the meticulous care that the abstract expressionists took in both composition and execution, contributing to the caricature of the Beat painter simply throwing paint at a canvas. The technique of dripping paint looks back to Hans Hofmann. Playing on spontaneity and chance, the action or gestural artists treat the canvas as an event rather than a picture, throwing and dripping paint, then manipulating the results with

sticks or towels to create carefully composed rhythms of color and form. Many of De Kooning's paintings, such as his series of female nudes, have a subject, but are painted with violent brushstrokes to suggest sexual energy. Kline's images are also marked by their strong black brushwork on a white painted surface. In paintings such as *Dahlia* (1959) or *Painting Number 2* (1954) the abstracted forms suggest the iconic qualities of Chinese calligraphy. Color field paintings, such as Rothko's *Black on Maroon* (1958) or the various numbered canvases with their glowing, floating rectangles, present monumental fields of color that create visual tensions between void and presence. The effect, Rothko insisted, was not abstraction, but the expression of human emotion. The same may be said of Gottlieb's *Blast* series, which relates a red disc and a black mass on a large field.

Art patron Peggy Guggenheim, the wife of surrealist Max Ernst, promoted the New York school. In 1951 the Museum of Modern Art presented the exhibition "Abstract Painting and Sculpture in America." In 1958–1959 it mounted "The New American Painting," the first major recognition of abstract expressionism. Although the painters celebrated at this show influenced subsequent painters such as Joan Michell and Helen Frankenthaler, the show also marked the decline of abstract expressionism. While aesthetically liberating, abstract expressionism is also inherently constrained in what it can say because of the limited nature of its visual language and because it tends to focus on a single act. To create variety and open the range of expression, many painters produced series of pictures, which allowed them to introduce a succession of variations. Too often, however, much in abstract expressionism loses its power to be expressive, becoming merely decorative. In response to these limitations as well as the solemnity of much of the work, many painters in the 1960s, initially inspired by the possibilities of abstract expressionism, turned to new directions, most notably pop, neo-Dada, and funk art.

In the late 1950s, pop art enjoyed parallel, but independent developments in Britain and America. The critic Lawrence Alloway first applied the term to the work of the Independent Group in London, and especially the collages and paintings of Richard Hamilton, Eduardo Paolozzi, and Peter Blake. American pop includes most notably Jasper Johns (1930–), Roy Lichtenstein (1923–1997), Claes Oldenburg (1929–), Robert Rauschenberg (1925–), James Rosenquist (1933–), Andy Warhol (1928–1987), and Tom Wesselmann (1931–). Both British and American pop share a fascination with the images and icons of advertising, consumerism, and mass media, especially pertaining to themes of glamour, gimmickry, and the transient. American pop, however, tends to be less ironic, or at least more ambivalent in its tone than its British counterpart. Warhol, for instance, explored the relationship between machine production and fame in his many silk-screened treatments of celebrity figures, such as the *Marilyn Diptych.* In an inversion of Dadaist "readymades," such as Duchamp's *Fountain* (1917), which presented ordinary objects (in this case a urinal) as works of art, pop artists produced works in the form of ordinary objects, as in the case of Warhol's iconic Campbell's Soup cans, Lichtenstein's formalized enlargements of comic strip pages, or Oldenburg's vinyl sculptures of toilets, cheeseburgers, and monumental lipstick holders. Each either posits the aesthetic value found in ordinary objects, or suggests that consumer goods represent modern art.

In reducing ordinary objects to their formal properties, pop reveals an underlying affinity to abstract expressionism, drawing the viewer to the expressive possibilities found in the form of everyday things. Jasper Johns, for instance, painted rows of numbers, bull's-eye targets, and American flags on large canvases and different bright colors to make the viewer conscious of what the "mind already knows." Similarly Rauschenberg created assorted "combines," three-dimensional collages that combined painting with newspaper clippings, photographs, and "found" objects. In this method he took inspiration from both the Dadaists and the expressionists. Pop artists also applied the techniques of expression and spontaneity to stage art events or happenings. Rauschenberg, who had studied at Black Mountain College (1948–1949), worked with composer John Cage and choreographer Merce Cunningham. Similarly, Oldenburg was involved in the happenings produced in the late 1950s by Allan Kaprow and Jim Dine.

While pop largely centered in New York, junk and funk art thrived around Berkeley and the San Francisco Bay area. Frequently linked with neo-Dadaists and the Beats, funk artists sought to break down the barriers between life and art. They include Bruce Connor (1933–), George Herms (1935–), and Ed Kienholz (1927–1994). Also of relevance are Wallace Berman (1926–1976), Jay DeFeo (1929–1989), Jess [Collins] (1923–), Robert Frank (1924–), and Larry Rivers (1923–). Junk took its name from the practice of creating sculpture assembled out of found castoffs, picking up the surrealist spirit of spontaneity. The term *funk,* as in "funky," derived from the bad smell of some of the junk, what Kienholz termed, "the leftovers of human experience." Unlike pop, funk has an explicit social dimension, exhibiting rage against injustice, victimization of the marginalized, and war. Aspiring to shock, its expressions and images were often complex, bizarre, tattered, sexual, and frequently characterized as sick. Bruce Connor's *Couch* (1963) seems to be the remains of a crumbling corpse on a crumbling Victorian couch. His mixed media, *Black Dahlia* (1959), that combines the photograph of the victim of a sensationalized Hollywood murder case with various fetishistic objects in a nylon bag, is equally disturbing. Similarly Kienholz's installation *Roxy's* (1961) uses animal bones and the simulated parts of women to reconstruct a famous Las Vegas brothel. George Herms's *The Meat Market* (1960–1961) arranges various assemblages of objects, including mannequin torsos embracing, a cow skull in a basket, and a table with an x-ray photo, dolls, a pickle jar, and a butcher's sign.

Wallace Berman and Jay DeFeo, both deeply admired by the Beat poets, are variously classified among the abstract expressionists and funk artists, though there tends to be a dimension of spirituality and a play with esoteric imagery in their work that is absent from funk. A pair of gelatin silver prints done by Berman and DeFeo in collaboration shows a nude DeFeo (front and back) posed before a sunburst in an attitude reminiscent of Leonardo DaVinci's *Vitruvian Man* and the Kabalistic Adam Kadmon (the primordial man). Berman's most famous and innovative works are his Verifax collages mounted on canvas made with the aid of an early copying machine. This technique allowed him to deploy a series of images with variations, somewhat like Jasper Johns's sequences of numbers. In other cases, Berman incorporated text and letters, especially Hebrew, into and around his images, creating a tension between the visual and the verbal, between modes of perception and consciousness. Also of importance is Berman's publication *Semina* (seeds); each issue consisted of a multimedia folio of loose-leaf pages that combined poetry, prose,

photographs, and drawings by Berman and others. DeFeo's work ranges over a variety of styles. *Dr. Jazz* (1958) is expressionistic in its brushwork. Her collages *Blossom* (1956) and *Applaud the Black Fact* (1958) are almost surrealistic. Her most admired piece, however, is *The Rose* (1959–1966), a monumental painting done in muted tones. It is 7.5 by 11 feet in dimension. DeFeo applied the paint impasto, sometimes 8 inches thick, creating a paradoxical relationship between sheer physicality and lightness, a mystical expressiveness not unlike that found in Rothko's glowing rectangles. In addition, both Berman and DeFeo participated in various happenings around the Bay area, several with Claes Oldenburg.

Of the Beat writers who experimented with visual media, William Burroughs was the most radical and prolific, innovating the techniques of collage, photomontage, and text-image to challenge the boundaries of the visual and the verbal. Burroughs's early entrance into the visual arts came through the "cut-up" and "fold-in" techniques clearly recognizable in *Minutes to Go* (1960). Friend and frequent collaborator, artist Brion Gysin, discovered the technique when he lay together strips of newspaper text that he had accidentally cut while trimming a matte. While the "cut-up" has prototypes in the work of the Dadaists and surrealists, Burroughs and Gysin extended its potential to generate complex nonlinear narratives, not merely individual images. From this they produced a series of scrapbook experiments in which they arranged texts and pictures. *Green Scrapbook* (1971–1973) constructed an elaborate narrative out of the association of ideas produced by placing various images together. In turn, photographs of these collages became complex elements in yet other collages. Filling about twenty notebooks, the most ambitious of the scrapbook experiments was *The Third Mind* (1963–1972), which includes typescript, clippings of articles and headlines, comic book strips, book jacket illustrations, and advertisements. These experiments inspired numerous collages and photomontages arranged on grids. Most notable are *The Dreamachine* (1965) and *The Death of Mrs. D.* (1965). In the 1980s, in a series of experiments that look back to action painting as well as funk and neo-Dada, Burroughs explored the visual effects produced by shooting at sheets of plywood with a shotgun or revolver. Sometimes he included containers of paint on the panels to produce various splatter patterns. From the end of the 1980s until his death, Burroughs turned to more conventional means of painting, and in the spirit of Jackson Pollock, moved paint on smooth paper with various objects, including brushes, markers, spray paint, and (he claimed) mushrooms. Some of these works resemble the calligraphic forms of Franz Kline. Others, such as an untitled 1982 series of red streaks on a yellow background or the black and white *Rub out the Word* (1989) resemble Pollock's work. In *Research Animal* (1989) and *Call* (1991), he laid various cutouts and objects on a prepared surface, then spray painted over them to produce a negative or silhouette effect. In addition to his collaboration with Gysin, Burroughs worked with a number of other painters, including Robert Rauschenberg for a series of lithographs called *American Pewter with Burroughs* (1981), and graffiti artist Keith Haring for the series *Apocalypse* (1988), an association that Timothy Leary characterized as Dante working with Titian.

Although Jack Kerouac joked that he could paint better than Franz Kline, the paintings and drawings of Kerouac and Gregory Corso are primitive, though enthusiastic. Kerouac's famous typing of *On the Road* at one sitting, on a 120-foot roll of paper echoes both the expressionist gesture of action painting and machine production of pop, turning text into a visual object or product. His actual paintings are technically less sophisticated, but reveal the underlying spiritual dimension of his aesthetic. Most interesting is his canvas *Buddha* (1956–1960), resembling the color and iconography of Tibetan painting, but reduced to the abstraction of an oil sketch. Painted on a red background, the Buddha hovers in a flat picture plane. In one corner sits a Buddhist monk with halo, and in the other a demonic face or skull, suggesting the imagery of the Mexican Day of the Dead.

The paintings and drawings of Corso tend to be lighter in tone and brighter in color. Many of his drawings illustrate or accompany his poems.

*There's a Chineseman in my Dreams* is a pen-and-ink sketch of five naked men posed on a bed with a Chinese figure in the background. *Capt. Poetry & His Magical Lyre & Pegasus* combines the imagery of comic book superheroes with Greek mythology. His paintings are witty, if primitive, treatments of his friends and favorite poets of the past. *Rarely, Rarely Comst Thou Spirit of Delight, Keats and Shelley* (1980s) portrays the two Romantic poets. Another colorful canvas features Kerouac, Corso, and Allen Ginsberg seated in the foreground, in Buddhist posture. Looming in the sky behind them as divine presences are Emily Dickinson, Walt Whitman, Burroughs, and Edgar Allan Poe.

Lawrence Ferlinghetti has long been interested in the visual arts, both as an art critic and practitioner. As a poet, he was inspired by the typographical layouts innovated by French poet Guillaume Apollinaire's 1914 *Calligrammes*, breaking and deploying the verse lines to create a visual effect. At Columbia University, he wrote a master's thesis on the Victorian critic John Ruskin and Ruskin's treatment of the painter J. M. W. Turner. Ferlinghetti took up painting in Paris, while working on his doctorate at the Sorbonne, in the late 1940s. His visual work ranges over drawing, graphics, and painting in various media. In Paris, he was drawn to the surrealists, and early paintings such as *Deux* (1950) strongly resemble the spare classical/symbolist images of Jean Cocteau. In the 1950s abstract expressionists de Kooning and Kline introduced Ferlinghetti to the possibilities of visual expression and color. The oil on canvas *Vajra Lotus* (1957–1960) shows the influence of Kline, with an abstract figure painted with strong, broad strokes on a plain surface, suggesting Chinese or Sanskrit. More recent work, such as *Two Poets at Berlin Wall* (1992), done in collaboration with Duane Foster, and *Lady Whose Shrine* (2002), returns to a treatment of image as text and text as image. The first shows silk-screened portraits of Ferlinghetti and Russian poet Andre Voznesensky in front of an abstract, graffiti-marked wall. The second, the *Nike of Samothrace (Winged Victory)* is suspended before an abstract background of blue strokes, superimposed with lines by T. S. Eliot.

Black Beat poet Ted Joans has long been an active painter. Of special interest are his collages, such *as The Manhattan Mau Mau Return from Mexico* (1959), and *First Lady Diane Di Prima* (1961). Both are in his 1961 *Hipster Series* and feature bizarre constructions of images borrowed from Victorian periodical engravings. They resemble the style and images by Max Ernst and Georg Grosz, and also the illustrated novels of the proto-surrealist writers Alfred Jarry (1873–1907) and Raymond Rousel (1877–1933).

—*Thomas L. Cooksey*

## Bibliographical References

Edward Adler and Bernard Mindich, *Beat Art: Visual Works by and about the Beat Generation,* 1994, is a brief but important essay and catalog on Beat art; David Anfam, *Abstract Expressionism,* 1990, is a well-illustrated standard introduction; Anna C. Chave, *Mark Rothko: Subjects in Abstraction,* 1989, is an important treatise on Rothko and the aesthetics of abstract expressionism; Thomas E. Crow, *The Rise of the Sixties: American and European Art in the Era of Dissent,* 1996, is a short but sharp examination of the variety and complexity of radical art movements in the 1960s beyond New York; Robert Hughes, *The Shock of the New,* 1981, is a witty, cranky, and articulate examination of the currents of modern painting; Edward Lucie-Smith, *Movements in Art since 1945: Issues and Concepts,* 1995, is a frequently updated handbook on the currents in modern art; Tilman Osterwold, *Pop Art,* 1991, is a well-illustrated catalog; Lisa Phillips, ed., *Beat Culture and the New America: 1950–1965,* 1995, is a series of essays by different authors on various aspects of Beat culture, prepared for the 1995–1996 exhibition at the Whitney Museum of American Art, New York. The volume is richly illustrated with photographs and reproductions and is an important source, but lacks an index; Stephen Polcari, *Abstract Expressionism and the Modern Experience,* 1993, is a revisionist treatment, with close attention to the historical and intellectual roots of abstract expressionism in the 1930s and 1940s. Polcari includes chapters on each of the major painters; Carter Ratcliff, *The Fate of a Gesture: Jackson Pollock and Postwar American Art,* 1996, analyzes Pollock and his art in its cultural context; Robert A. Sobieszek, *Ports of Entry: William S.*

*Burroughs and the Arts,* 1996, is a series of essays and an exhibition catalog on the paintings and drawings of Burroughs and on his relations with other artists. This work serves as the starting point for any consideration of Burroughs as a visual artist.

***See also*** Conner, Bruce; Herms, George; Berman, Wallace; DeFeo, Jay; Frank, Robert; Joans, Ted; New York City; San Francisco; Black Mountain, North Carolina, and Black Mountain College; Cage, John; Cunningham, Merce; Burroughs, William Seward; Kerouac, Jack; Corso, Gregory; Ferlinghetti, Lawrence; Pollock, Jackson; Motherwell, Robert; de Kooning, Willem; Kline, Franz; Rauschenberg, Robert; Gysin, Brion

## Paris, The Beats in

A hotel still stands at 9 rue Git-le-Coeur in Paris, France. The Relais Hotel du Vieux Paris is not, however, the magnet for avant-garde artists that its predecessor was. It boasts four stars and all the amenities favored by modern tourists, the very things shunned by the bohemians of the Beat Generation who flocked to Paris in the 1950s and 1960s. Artists such as Allen Ginsberg, Gregory Corso, William Burroughs, Brion Gysin, Guy Harloff, Sinclair Beiles, and Ian Somerville were all involved in the bohemian life in Paris's Latin Quarter and most were residents of Madame Rachou's hotel.

The defining characteristic of Rachou's hotel was that it was inexpensive. Allen Ginsberg and Peter Orlovsky were unable to get a room in the hotel when they first arrived in Paris and had to rent one elsewhere for about $1.75 per night, more than the $30 per month they expected to pay at 9 rue Git-le-Coeur. By 1958, William Burroughs rented a room there for $25 per month. Rachou's hotel boasted no rugs, no private baths, no toilet paper (they used newsprint instead), no room service, no maid service, and no guarantees. Gregory Corso's attic room was so small he was able to stand fully erect only in the center, and the roof leaked in heavy rain. Bathing for the Beats was a weekly affair, if that often; there was a surcharge for this "service." Linens were changed even less frequently. Beats often shared rooms at the hotel with sometimes as many as three or four people sleeping in one or two beds. In addition to the cheap rent, Monsieur and Madame Rachou were extremely tolerant of their guests' eccentricities, even encouraging them most of the time. Madame Rachou also tolerated late rents and even took paintings and other art in lieu of payment, although she gave most of them away, thinking they would never have any great value. Consequently, the hotel became a focal point for the creative bohemians.

Even with the low rent, however, the Beats who stayed there were chronically cash poor and needed to find other means to pay their bills. Some of the beatniks/bohemians in Paris had independent sources of income. Orlovsky, for example, had a military pension. Ginsberg was receiving small royalty checks from his book sales in the United States. Those who did not have independent means, however, lived on the largesse of wealthier benefactors, or, as was true for many, wrote pornography for a local press dedicated to the genre.

Perhaps the primary factor drawing the American Beats to Paris in the 1950s and 1960s was the freedom life there offered. The cultural atmosphere of the restaurants, bars, and public attractions of the 9 rue Git-le-Coeur area was one of tolerance and openness. Almost all of them stayed open until the early morning hours. By way of contrast, London bars were required by law to close at 10 P.M. Drugs were easily obtainable, and the nightlife offered numerous opportunities for the Beats to hone their skills in poetry, music, and the visual arts. Most nights were spent in smoky cafes drinking, talking, and creating art. Jazz was the music of choice, and many times impromptu sessions sprang up in which poetry was read to the driving jazz beat. A *Toronto Star* article once described the atmosphere in these cafes as akin to being in the birdhouse at the zoo, both aurally and in olfaction. Experimentation was the driving force and format behind the creativity these artists displayed. Brion Gysin was trying out new recording techniques, and painters, sculptors, writers, and musicians were also experimenting with the forms of their respective arts.

Experimentation was also the norm for interpersonal relationships. Sexual relations were indiscriminate, often as not including same-sex partners. People came and went from the various rooms in Madame Rachou's hotel, often dropping in unannounced. Ginsberg and Orlovsky were also fascinated by the young bohemians who had dropped out of society and were trekking all over Europe with nothing more than rucksacks and the will to see the continent. For the Beats, it was an unparalleled time of productivity and excitement. Allen Ginsberg wrote a portion of "Kaddish" here. Likewise, Gregory Corso wrote "Bomb" at 9 rue Git-le-Coeur.

By the 1980s, the beatniks/bohemians had virtually left Madame Rachou's hotel and Paris's Latin Quarter. The movement was over, but the individuals within it had scattered throughout the world, taking their ideas and experiences with them.

—*Larry Adams*

### Bibliographical References
Fred McDarrah and Gloria S. McDarrah, *Beat Generation*, 1996; Fred W. McDarrah, *Kerouac and Friends*, 1985; Barry Miles, *The Beat Hotel*, 2000; Jon Pareles and Patricia Romanowski, eds., *Rolling Stone Encyclopedia of Rock & Roll*, 1983.

**See also** Pad, The Beat; Ginsberg, Allen; Burroughs, William Seward; Corso, Gregory

## Parker, Charles Christopher (Charlie) (1920–1955)

Encouraged to play alto saxophone by his mother, Charlie Parker left school at fifteen to pursue a career as a musician. At this time he also developed the narcotics habit that followed him throughout his life. He worked irregularly during the thirties and forties but forged a loose association with Dizzy Gillespie that had a profound influence on the history of jazz, as well as on the Beat writers then frequenting New York jazz clubs. Along with artists such as Gillespie and Thelonious Monk, Parker, who soon acquired the nicknames Bird or Yardbird, became known as one of the founders of bebop, a rhythmically complex, improvisational idiom that influenced Jack Kerouac's spontaneous approach to prose writing. Jack Kerouac honors

Saxophonist Charlie Parker inspired the Beats with his spontaneity and cool style. (Bettmann/Corbis)

Charlie Parker in the final three choruses of *Mexico City Blues*, praising Parker's musical genius, recognizing his human position, and appealing to Parker for prayer on behalf of Kerouac.

—*David Arnold*

### Bibliographical References

Carl Woidek, *Charlie Parker*, 1998; Allen Ginsberg, *Spontaneous Mind: Selected Interviews 1958–1996*, ed. David Carter, 2001.

*See also* Music; Kaufman, Bob; Ginsberg, Allen; Kerouac, Jack

## Parker, Edie (1923–1992)

A native of Grosse Point, Michigan, who came to Columbia University in 1941; with Joan Vollmer Adams Burroughs, the renter of apartment #62 at 421 West 118th Street, where many key figures from the early years of the Beat Generation gathered; the first wife of Jack Kerouac.

After an on-and-off relationship, Edie Parker and Jack Kerouac wed on 22 August 1944, when Kerouac, desperate to get out of jail, promised to marry Edie in exchange for making arrangements to raise bail. Held as a material witness in connection with Lucien Carr's stabbing of David Kammerer, Kerouac could not get assistance from his father, and Kerouac married Parker while in custody. After his release, he traveled with Edie to Grosse Point, where he worked only long enough to repay his debt to her family. The couple subsequently reunited in New York City, but the reunion failed and soon Edie returned to Michigan, where she arranged for an annulment. When Edie Parker learned of Kerouac's success with *On the Road* in 1957, she proposed a renewal of the relationship, but nothing came of this proposal.

In interviews, Edie referred to the day she ate six sauerkraut hotdogs and impressed Kerouac so thoroughly that he knew he was completely in love with her. She and Kerouac attended after-hours jazz performances at Minton's in New York City and enjoyed the unrestrained music. Debunking the myth of the Beat pad, Edie insisted that the people who gathered at her apartment were more interested in talking about books than in having orgies.

Married four times, Edie Parker apparently did not find sustained happiness in her life. Disappointed that her autobiography, *You'll Be Okay*, drew no good offers for publication, she died in 1992.

—*William Lawlor*

### Bibliographical References

Brenda Knight, "Edie Parker Kerouac," in *Women of the Beat Generation*, 1996, summarizes Edie Parker Kerouac's life and presents a selection from the unpublished autobiography; James Jones in *Use My Name*, 1999, insightfully reviews Parker's connection to Kerouac; Dennis McNally, *Desolate Angel*, 1979, reviews the circumstances of Parker's relationship with Kerouac.

*See also* New York City; Kammerer, David Eames; Vollmer Adams Burroughs, Joan

# Party, The Beat

One of the fundamental aspects of Beat literature is the incorporation and retelling of real-life events based on the writer's experiences. Central to this focus on real-life events are Beat parties—celebrations that gathered together the diverse and dynamic personalities who immortalized the Beat Generation within popular culture. Beat parties were verifiable occurrences, but in some instances the parties took on legendary status.

Parties helped the Beats transcend the restrictions of conformist Eisenhower America and provided a platform for experimentation and carnivalesque exaggeration. Ginsberg immortalized his first meeting with Ken Kesey in the poem "First Party at Ken Kesey's with Hell's Angels." Diane di Prima wrote about her experiences in *Memoirs of a Beatnik,* where one notable scene describes an "orgy" involving di Prima, several dancers, Kerouac, and Ginsberg. Faced with the co-opting of the Beats within popular culture, Ted Joans, the self-styled "Afro-American Surrealist performance poet," went to parties as a "rent-a-beatnik," further solidifying the popular-culture beatnik stereotypes of the dark poet figure sporting a black beret and sunglasses.

In a sense, the Beat Generation came into being at a party. The 1955 San Francisco 6 Gallery reading of Allen Ginsberg's poem "Howl," among others, can be seen as the first official Beat party. Kerouac described the event in *The Dharma Bums.* Ray Smith, the narrator, noticed that all the important members of the artistic community were present and that the atmosphere was celebratory. After gathering contributions from the people on hand, Smith bought large bottles of local wine and passed the bottles around, heightening the mood of the audience so that when Alvah Goldbook read his long poem, "Wail," the listeners responded with enthusiasm. The reading went so well that Rheinhold Cacoethes, the moderator, was brought to tears. In this particular case, most of those present remember the night in much the way Kerouac described. Perhaps a universal consciousness was created, and an artistic movement was born.

Kerouac's *On the Road* contains various party scenes. After the opera in Colorado, the cast and other various types come back to the miner's shack where Sal is staying. Kerouac's prose energetically describes the scene of women, dancing, booze, and singing. Sal mentions that he longs for the presence of Carlo Marx and Dean Moriarty, but checks his own thinking. Sal recognizes that Carlo and Dean have a subterranean outlook and represent the emergence of the Beat consciousness. Sal feels that he is taking on that outlook, but Sal knows the mood of the party in the miner's shack would sadden and disorient Carlo and Dean. Sal and his friends eventually leave the party to hit the bars. As Kerouac subtly implies, this party was not his scene.

Later in the book, Kerouac describes the series of parties in New York City for New Year's weekend 1948, which lasted three days and nights. Back in his element—the New York Beat element—the chapter and parties end on a more positive note. After sketching the various happenings, conversations, and people throughout the weekend, Kerouac suggests that Sal is being enlightened by the entire experience and sensing that he is changing, even if the change is drug-induced. Sal momentarily feels that he cannot comprehend his surroundings, but then attributes this confusion to the marijuana supplied to him by Dean. The marijuana gives Sal a feeling that a revelation is at hand and soon everything will be clearly known.

Spiritual enlightenment can occur at a party, much like a communion, and such enlightenment was something Kerouac explored in more depth in *The Dharma Bums,* in which he describes a three-day farewell party for Gary Snyder who was about to leave for two years of study in Japan. Kerouac's exuberance for the party has him foreshadow the event in preceding chapters. Talk of Buddhism, enlightenment, and heaven are interspersed with naked dancing girls, bongo playing, and people sitting around a fire in the yard. Indeed, the Beat stereotypes that were soon claimed by popular culture emerged from Kerouac's vivid descriptions.

Another example of Beat art imitating Beat life in the form of a party is the film *Pull My Daisy*

(1959) by Robert Frank and Alfred Leslie. Narrated by Kerouac, the film is based on the third act of his unstaged play *The Beat Generation*, depicting an actual occasion at Neal and Carolyn Cassady's home when a priest and his mother came for a visit. The film presents a party atmosphere from the onset when Ginsberg and Gregory Corso barge into the apartment of Milo (Larry Rivers) and his wife (Delphine Seyrig) early in the morning. They sit, discuss poetry, smoke a joint, and drink wine. Later when everyone else arrives, the party moves into full swing when the bishop is peppered by Milo's Beat friends with all sorts of theological and philosophical questions. They want to know if baseball, alligators, and countless other things are imbued with holiness. Eventually, a short jam session occurs, and the mentally exasperated bishop leaves with his mother and sister. Milo's son Pablo awakes from his sleep to join in on a jam session led by Mez (Amram) on the French horn. Then, in typical Beat fashion, Milo has an argument with his wife about his friends' behavior around the bishop and leaves with the friends to continue the festivities late into the New York night.

Interestingly enough, the production of the film can in itself be described as carnivalesque, as a drunken Kerouac regularly arrived on set with drinking buddies or hangers-on from the Bowery. The filmmakers found this behavior so distracting that they eventually banned Kerouac from the set. According to David Amram, the production of the film was far from orderly, and Robert Frank deserves credit for recording wondrous scenes under such conditions. Indeed, *Pull My Daisy* captures a unique time and place, structured around a party scene that is uniquely Beat.

The "Merwin Incident" might have been the ultimate carnivalesque Beat party. In 1976, during a seminary meeting led by Chögyam Trungpa Rinpoche near Snowmass, Colorado, the prize-winning poet W. S. Merwin and his companion Dana Naone retired from a party at which nudity was required. Trungpa subsequently directed several people to break into a barricaded room to drag the reluctant pair to the gathering, where they were forcibly stripped of their clothing. The fiasco haunted the Naropa Institute for several years, setting off the "poetry wars," severing numerous friendships and drawing public criticism.

Parties allowed the Beats to create their own special world—an alternate life free from conventional rules and public restrictions. Parties further helped liberate the participants from the constraints of the physical, but also from the restrictions of the spiritual, as imposed upon the public by ecclesiastical hierarchies. Beat parties were playgrounds for sexual and drug experimentation and meeting places for mad discussions about literature and spirituality.

—*Ari Grief*

## Bibliographical References

Carolyn Cassady, *Off the Road. My Years with Cassady, Kerouac, and Ginsberg*, 1990; Diane di Prima, *Memoirs of a Beatnik*, 1998; Allen Ginsberg, *Howl and Other Poems*, 1956; Allen Ginsberg, "First Party at Ken Kesey's with Hell's Angels" in *The Compact Bedford Introduction to Literature: Reading, Thinking, Writing*, 6th ed., 2003; Ari Grief, *Breaking Frozen Cinematic Ground: Carnival and The New American Cinema*, 2001; Jack Kerouac, *The Dharma Bums*, 1958; Jack Kerouac, *On the Road*, 1957; Lisa Phillips, *Beat Culture and the New America: 1950–1965*, 1995.

***See also*** 6 Gallery Reading; Naropa Institute; Film; Kerouac, Jack; Ginsberg, Allen; Amram, David

## Patchen, Kenneth (1911-1972)

Kenneth Patchen was a product of the Great Depression, a proletarian poet who found his stride in poems that took a strong stand against the horrors committed during the second World War, both in the name of fascism and in the cause of defeating fascism. Over the last three decades of a consistently productive career, Patchen's primary subject remained the ways in which history victimizes the ordinary person—the disjunction between the great ideals that are ostensibly preserved by great sacrifices and the terrible ways in which such sacrifices are exacted and then impact individual lives. In the late 1940s and the 1950s, the Beat writers were influenced by Patchen's blending of a moving expression of radical political conviction and a lyrical, mystical quest for personal, spiritual awareness. In the late 1950s, Patchen experimented with writing and recording poems to jazz accompaniment, and in the 1960s, he experimented with illustrating his poems with his own primitive, avantgarde drawings. Eventually, he even combined the literary and graphic modes, imbedding the words of some poems in the drawings. Despite the continuing inventiveness evident in these experiments, his poetry remained consistently accessible. In combination with his political convictions and his spiritual sensibility, his accessibility and his interest in formal experimentation ensured his continuing popularity among the post-Beat writers and readers of the 1960s and 1970s.

Patchen was born in Niles, Ohio, on 13 December 1911. His father worked in a steel mill, and Patchen himself at times worked in mills and at other manual labor until a back injury in 1937 left him permanently disabled. In 1929 and 1930, he attended Alexander Meikeljohn's Experimental College in Wisconsin and Commonwealth College in Arkansas. Despite these experiences, Patchen described himself and was typically described by others as a largely self-taught poet. In the first years of the Great Depression, Patchen, like many young men of that generation, took to the road in search of opportunity and adventure. Eventually he ended up in Boston, where he met and married Miriam Oikemus in 1934. In their first half-decade of marriage, he and his wife moved from Boston to New York City, then to Los Angeles, to Connecticut, and then back to New York. Still, he found time to write his first three books of poetry while also writing for several publications, including the *New Republic*. In 1947, the Patchens moved again to Connecticut, and then in 1951, they moved to the San Francisco area, where they lived for the rest of their lives.

In 1950, Patchen underwent the first in a series of operations on his back. Instead of improving his condition, these surgeries actually had the cumulative effect of making it worse. A spinal fusion in 1956 was followed by another major back surgery in 1959 that left Patchen crippled. Still, he remained a prolific poet, and his books were now being published by New Directions and reaching a broader audience. In 1967, Patchen received an award from the National Foundation on the Arts and Humanities for "life-long contribution to American letters." Despite this level of recognition and his sustained popularity, especially among younger writers and readers, Patchen has not received equivalent attention from academic critics.

—*Martin Kich*

## Principal Works

Poetry: *Before the Brave*, 1936; *First Will and Testament*, 1939; *Teeth of the Lion*, 1942; *The Dark Kingdom*, 1942; *Cloth of the Tempest*, 1943; *An Astonished Eye Looks Out of the Air*, 1945; *Outlaw of the Lowest Planet*, 1946; *Selected Poems*, 1946; *Pictures of Life and Death*, 1947; *They Keep Riding Down All the Time*, 1947; *Panels for the Walls of Heaven*, 1947; *CCCLXXIV Poems*, 1948; *Red Wine and Yellow Hair*, 1949; *Orchards, Thrones and Caravans*, 1952; *Fables and Other Little Tales*, 1953; *The Famous Boating Party and Other Poems in Prose*, 1954; *When We Were Here Together*, 1957; *Hurrah for Anything: Poems and Drawings*, 1957; *Poemscapes*, 1958; *To Say If You Love Someone*, 1959; *Because It Is*, 1960; *Love Poems*, 1960; *Poems of Humor and Protest*, 1960; *Selected Love Poems*, 1965; *Like Fun I'll Tell You*, 1966; *Hallelujah Anyway*, 1966; *But Even So*, 1968; *Love and War Poems*, 1968; *The Collected Poems of Kenneth Patchen*, 1969; *Aflame and Afun of Walking Faces*, 1970; *Wonderings*, 1971; *In Quest of Candlelighters*, 1972; *The Argument of Innocence*, 1977; *Still Another Pelican in the Breadbox*, 1980; *What Shall We Do without Us? The Voice and Vision of Kenneth Patchen*, 1984.

Fiction: *The Journal of Albion Moonlight*, 1941; *The Memoirs of a Shy Pornographer: An Amusement*, 1945; *Sleepers Awake*, 1946; *See You in the Morning*, 1948.

Plays: *Now You See It (Don't Look Now)*, 1966; *Patchen's Lost Plays*, 1977.

## Bibliographical References

Alan Clodd compiled *Tribute to Kenneth Patchen*, 1977, a collection of brief reminiscences and appreciative comment. Book-length biocritical studies include Larry Smith's TUSAS volume

*Kenneth Patchen,* 1978; Raymond Nelson's *Kenneth Patchen and American Mysticism,* 1984; and Smith's appreciative reappraisal in *Kenneth Patchen: Rebel Poet in America,* 2000. Richard G. Morgan's *Kenneth Patchen: A Collection of Essays,* 1977, remains the only collection of critical essays; Gene Detro's *Patchen: The Last Interview,* 1976, is a pamphlet that includes a foreword by Miriam Patchen and an afterword by Henry Miller; Gail Eaton compiled an early bibliography, *Kenneth Patchen: A First Bibliography,* 1948; and Richard Morgan a more definitive, later bibliography, *Kenneth Patchen: An Annotated, Descriptive Bibliography,* 1978; Frances Steloff's "Kenneth Patchen" in *Journal of Modern Literature* 4 (Apr. 1975): 805–808, is a reminiscence; critical essays include David Pichaske's "Kenneth Patchen, Norbert Blei: The Literary Text as Graphic Form," in *Crossing Borders: American Literature and Other Artistic Media,* ed. Jadwiga Maszewska, 1992; Stephen J. Robitaille's "Vulcan Revisited: Kenneth Patchen's *Journal of Albion Moonlight*" in *Forms of the Fantastic,* eds. Jan Hokenson and Howard D. Pearce, 1986; Carroll F. Terrell's "Kenneth Patchen" in *Contemporary Literature* 27 (Spring 1986); Amos N. Wilder's "A Poet in the Depression: Letters of Kenneth Patchen, 1934–1941" in *Sagetrieb: A Journal Devoted to Poets in the Pound-H. D.-Williams Tradition* 5 (Winter 1986): 111–126; Tomaz Lazar's "The Little Journal of Kenneth Patchen" in *Acta Neophilologica* 11 (1978); and James Schevill's "Kenneth Patchen: The Search for Wonder and Joy" in *The American Poetry Review* 5 (Jan.-Feb. 1976).

*See also* Music

# Paterson, New Jersey

An industrial town in northeastern New Jersey near the waterfalls of the Passaic River; hometown of Allen Ginsberg; title reference of multivolume masterwork by William Carlos Williams.

Though some sources indicate that Allen Ginsberg was born in Paterson, he actually was born in Newark, New Jersey, and did not arrive in Paterson until he was a toddler. Allen's father, Louis Ginsberg, taught at Paterson Central High School and Allen was a graduate of Eastside High School in Paterson.

Naomi Ginsberg took her sons, Gene and Allen, to parks in Paterson. On 23 October 1966, Allen and Louis Ginsberg did a joint reading in Paterson, and the audience responded enthusiastically to the contrast in poetic styles between the father and the son and to Allen's reading of his poem "Paterson."

During the reading in Paterson, Allen mentioned that he and his father had visited Passaic Falls on the previous day, and Allen revealed that he had smoked marijuana while looking at the falls. Ginsberg returned to New York City immediately after the reading, but Paterson Police responded to complaints about Ginsberg's public admission of pot smoking and mistakenly arrested a bearded man on the street.

Ginsberg also refers to Paterson in the opening section of "Kaddish."

William Carlos Williams is the author of a five-volume work *Paterson,* a poem that is impressionistic in its style and philosophical in its message. In the poem Williams addresses the responsibilities of the literary artist. In *Desolation Angels* (1965), Jack Kerouac refers to the love William Carlos Williams has for Irwin Garden (Allen Ginsberg), who hails from Paterson, which is very close to Williams's home in Rutherford, New Jersey (323). In Kerouac's *On the Road* (1957), Sal Paradise lives in Paterson with his aunt.

—*William Lawlor*

## Bibliographical References

Michael Schumacher gives the details of Ginsberg's youth in Paterson in *Dharma Lion,* 1992; he also recounts the details of Allen's joint reading with his father; in Allen Ginsberg, *Collected Poems* (1984), one can find "Paterson" (40–41) and "Kaddish" (209–227).

*See also* Ginsberg, Allen; Williams, William Carlos

## Performance Humor

Exemplified in its purest expressions by the routines of Lord Buckley and Lenny Bruce, what might be called Beat performance humor played on the rhythms and language of the hip to confront the dominant values of the 1950s and early 1960s.

Like the Beats, these humorists targeted those aspects of American culture that alienated, marginalized, and isolated certain groups. The performer played the role of a knowing, sophisticated insider of the marginalized group. By this means, the would-be hipster from the dominant group entered the marginalized group. The effect was to make the marginal the center, and to exorcise the dominant values by putting them outside the hip circle of what was cool. At its height in the 1950s, this humor focused on the confrontation between the cultures of black and white, Jew and Gentile, and to a lesser extent, gay and straight.

Thus, Lord Buckley picked up the idiom of the black urban hipster with his jive renditions of Shakespeare, the Gettysburg Address, and his hip sermons on "the Naz" (Jesus), and "the Hip Gahn" (Gandhi). In the world of the black jazzmen, this code of the hipster had been a way of protecting themselves from racial persecution. Buckley, a white man, used the code of the black hipster to confront the white world, making it acceptable to take black on its own terms, rather than conforming to a white stereotype. His act differed from an Amos 'n' Andy routine in that Buckley did not draw on the white stereotype imposed on blacks, but an authentic manner borrowed from black hipster culture. He laid the groundwork for black comedians like Dick Gregory to be a "colored funnyman," and not a "funny colored man." In a similar manner, Lenny Bruce played on the biases common within the Jewish community to confront stereotypes held by the Gentile world—the private inside joke brought to the larger public. His routine "Christ and Moses" played on Jewish paranoia about the Catholic Church. "How to Relax Your Colored Friends at Parties" confronted white racial hypocrisy, while "Lima, Ohio" looked at Jewish racial hypocrisy. In a similar manner, though to a lesser degree, Louis Nye's character, Gordon Hathaway from the old *Steve Allen Show* (1956–1961), with his signature, "Hi Ho, Steverino!" played on gay stereotypes, as did Bruce with his more explicit "Thank You Masked Man."

In its purest expression, the venue for this kind of performance humor reflected its origins in jazz.

Thus, while Buckley, Bruce, and others performed on television, they developed their routines and took them to their logical extreme in the uninhibited atmosphere of small, smoky jazz and nightclubs such as Jazz Gallery, the Village Gate, and the Hungry I in New York, Jazz City in Los Angeles, or similar establishments in Chicago and San Francisco. These environments emphasized a hip, urban identity that licensed the unconventional and the off-color. The routines typically took on the form of a free-floating monologue, punctuated with the rhythms and vocabulary of jazz, and in the case of Buckley, came close to scat. Albert Goldman quipped that Bruce's goal was to make the boys in the band laugh. This remark could summarize the essence of Beat performance humor in general.

A more generic form of Beat performance humor found occasional mainstream expression in radio and television. Such performances can be found in the animated character Go Man Van Gogh and Wildman of Wildville (both with the voice of Buckley) in Bob Clampett's *Beany and Cecil* cartoon series (1959–1962). Bob Denver (in his pre-Gilligan days) created the character Maynard G. Krebs, the bearded beatnik in the television series, *The Many Loves of Dobie Gillis* (1959–1963), and Stan Freberg created a spider-hating beatnik bongo player in his "Banana Boat Song," a send up of Harry Belafonte's calypso music. Most significant is the character Sergeant Bilko created by Phil Silvers for his television show (1955–1959), what one commentator described as the hippest comedy show ever to reach television. Silvers's Ernie Bilko is a street-smart hustler, playing off the square Colonel Hall (played by Paul Ford). The shows subsequently informed the Hanna-Barbara cartoon series *Top Cat* (1961–1962), further spreading and domesticating the "cool cat."

It is valuable to look at comic forms developed within the black bebop world of the 1940s and the "sick Jew black humor" of the 1950s in order to understand the origins and contexts of Beat performance humor. In the 1930s and 1940s, black jazzmen developed a jive slang to communicate among themselves. It also offered possibilities for performance and comedy. Cab Calloway (1907–1994), who authored a *Hipster's Dictionary* (1938), stands as perhaps the first black performer who could create his own hip persona not based on the Uncle Tom image that dominated the media of the day. Several other names are worth mentioning. Slim (Bulee) Gaillard (1916–1991), often teamed with Slam Steward in the novelty duo "Slim and Slam," invented a jive language called "voutoreenie," and created such riff tunes as "the Flat Foot Floogie," and the "Groove Juice Symphony." Leo Watson (1898–1950) developed scat dialect into a sort of "stream of consciousness." Babs Gonzales (Lee Brown) (1916 or 1919–1980) was famous for his slapstick routines, including his own jive version of the Gettysburg Address. Also of note is the white performer, Harry "the Hipster" Gibson (1916–1991), who created comic songs such as "Who Put the Benzedrine in Mrs. Murphey's Ovaltine." He was linked with Gaillard in the 1950s by *Time* magazine as exemplifying why bebop was supposedly a corrupting influence.

"Sick Jew black humor" developed out of the "Borscht Belt" circuit, which had been directed at a Jewish audience. Whereas earlier Jewish comedians such as Jack Benny, the Marx Brothers, and Milton Berle tended to play down their Jewishness in order to conform to the Gentile world, comics such as Bruce, Mort Sahl, Shelley Berman, Nichols and May, Mel Brooks, Soupy Sales, Sandy Baron, and later Woody Allen played on their identities as Jews and accompanying tensions as the source for their material. The comic routines developed out of the strains between the third-generation American Jews and their parents and immigrant grandparents, focusing on the problems of assimilation in relation to what it means to be a Jew, expressed variously in contemptuousness and nostalgia, sophistication and hysteria. Such a complex of tensions fits naturally with Beat performance humor.

—*Thomas L. Cooksey*

## Bibliographical References

Roy Carr, Brian Cox, and Fred Deller, *The Hip: Hipsters, Jazz and the Beat Generation*, 1986, is a valuable, if colloquial, study of the various manifestations of the hip from its origins in black culture through the Beats and beyond. This work is good on hipster performance humor. Ross Firestone, ed., *Breaking It Up: The Best Routines of the Stand-Up Comics*, 1975, is a handy collection of classic stand-up routines from Mort Sahl and Lenny Bruce through Jay Leno and Franklyn Ajaye; Albert Goldman, *Freakshow: The Rocksoulbluesjazzsickjewblackhumoursexpoppsych Gig and Other Scenes from the Counter-Culture*, 1971, is a collection of insightful reviews and articles on popular culture, especially on Lenny Bruce and on Jewish "sick humor"; Norman Mailer, *Advertisements for Myself*, 1992, is an important collection of Mailer's writings, including "The White Negro," and other reflections on the hipster; Gerald Nachman, *Seriously Funny: The Rebel Comedians of the 1950s and 1960s*, 2003, is a current and valuable source; Ronald Lande Smith, *The Stars of Stand-up Comedy: A Biographical Encyclopedia*, offers biographical articles on 100 major American comedians from Weber and Fields to Steve Martin.

***See also*** Buckley, Lord; Bruce, Lenny; Language and Idiom of the Beats; Allen, Steve; Gaillard, Slim

## Perkoff, Stuart Z. (1930–1974)

Stuart Z. Perkoff was a poet and collage artist widely regarded as the central figure of the Venice West community. He was born in St. Louis on 29 July 1930, and moved to New York in the late 1940s, where he engaged in draft resistance. His first poems appeared in *Resistance* and Cid Corman's *Origin*, and attracted the attention of Charles Olson and Robert Creeley. Perkoff moved to the West Coast in the early 1950s, married, and eventually settled in Venice, California, where he encountered, befriended, and encouraged other poets such as Bruce Boyd, Frankie Rios, Tony Scibella, Maurice Lacy, and John Thomas. Perkoff's first book, *The Suicide Room*, was published by Jargon Books in 1956, and many poems appeared in magazines such as Wallace Berman's *Semina*, *Ark II/Moby I*, *Yugen*, *Hearse*, *Floating Bear*, *Trace*, *Stooge*, *Tree*, and *Invisible City*, as well as Donald Allen's anthology *New American Poetry* and Paul Vangelisti's *Specimen '73*. Perkoff participated in the West Coast Poetry and Jazz Festival in 1957 and in the following year cofounded Venice West Café. Although he quickly sold it at a loss, the café managed to survive as a community gathering place until 1966. Reputedly a charismatic reader of his own poetry, Perkoff's heroin addiction forestalled any substantial attempt to get another manuscript published until after he served four years of a prison sentence for dealing drugs. After his parole in Southern California in 1970, he lived in the Bay Area as well as briefly in Colorado. Two collections of his poetry, *Alphabet* and *Love Is the Silence*, were published by Red Hill Press. In 1973, Perkoff returned to Venice and died in Los Angeles of cancer on 25 June 1974. Perkoff's *Voices of the Lady: Collected Poems* was published by the National Poetry Foundation in 1998.

—*Bill Mohr*

## Principal Works

Poetry: *The Suicide Room*, 1956; *Eat the Earth*, 1971; *Kowboy Poems, 1973; Alphabet*, 1973; *Love Is the Silence: Poems 1948–1972*, 1975; *Voices of the Lady: Collected Poems*, 1998.

Prose: Perkoff's journals constitute a sporadic glimpse into the development and dissolution of Venice West. They constitute the primary contents of his archive at the University of California, Los Angeles.

## Bibliographical References

Perkoff's relationship to the Beat movement is briefly discussed in *Utopia and Dissent: Art, Poetry and Politics in California* by Richard Candida Smith, 1995.

*See also* Venice West

## Perry Lane

Place of residence in Menlo Park, California, just off the Stanford University golf course, where novelist Ken Kesey and other notable figures of the time lived an intellectual, bohemian existence. Writer Tom Wolfe describes Perry Lane in *The Electric Kool-Aid Acid Test:*

Perry Lane was Stanford's bohemian quarter. As bohemias go, Perry Lane was Arcadia, Arcadia just off the Stanford golf course. It was a cluster of two-room cottages with weathery wood shingles in an oak forest, only not just amid trees and greenery, but amid vines, honeysuckle tendrils, all buds and shoots and swooping tendrils and twitterings like the best of Arthur Rackham and *Honey Bear*. Not only that, it had true cultural cachet. Thorstein Veblen had lived there. So had two Nobel Prize winners everybody knew about though the names escaped them. The cottages rented for just $60 a month. Getting into Perry Lane was like getting into a club. Everybody who lived there had known somebody else who lived there, or they would never have gotten in, and naturally they got to know each other very closely too, and there was always something of an atmosphere of communal living. Nobody's door was ever shut on Perry Lane, except when they were pissed off. (34)

A graduate student in the writing program at Stanford University at the time, Kesey resided on Perry Lane when he first volunteered as a subject in experiments that the U.S. government was conducting on LSD at the local VA hospital. These experiences led in part to the creation of his greatest work, *One Flew Over the Cuckoo's Nest*. They also led to his later role as the West Coast counterpart to Timothy Leary in the development of psychedelic culture, a role that started with parties he threw at his place, during which he served his famous LSD-laced venison chili. The gatherings attracted the likes of Jerry Garcia, Larry McMurtry, Neal Cassady, and others. Kesey's band of Merry Pranksters first began to coalesce on Perry Lane and then later followed him to a new place in La Honda, California, where he moved after a developer bought up the cheap bungalows on Perry Lane and razed them to build more expensive housing.

—*Timothy D. Ray*

## Bibliographical References

Malcolm Cowley, "Ken Kesey at Stanford," in *Kesey*, ed. Michael Strelow, 1977; see the Merry Prankster History Project, Perry Lane Page, at http://www.pranksterweb.org/perry.htm; Timothy

Miller, *The '60s Communes: Hippies and Beyond*, 1999; Tom Wolfe, *The Electric Kool-Aid Acid Test*, 1968.

***See also*** Kesey, Ken Elton; Merry Pranksters; Drugs

## Photography

Photography, in Beat culture, begins as a series of perspectives on "typical" 1950s American life and becomes the medium that most fully cements and later confronts media-generated "beatnik" stereotypes. In the 1960s, photographs of the Beats become more humanizing and document them as serious writers at work and at home; the Beats are revealed as active, public figures of the counterculture. In later decades, photos capture these "angry young men" as they enter old age. Photography also speaks to the spirit of collaboration in this community—as some Beat figures worked closely with photographers or took pictures themselves.

The first photography book associated with Beat sensibilities and culture is Robert Frank's *The Americans* (1959). This collection, arguably the most influential book-length collection of photos since World War II, documents Frank's observations of American life in 1955 and 1956 as he traveled coast to coast across the United States. In this collection, Frank captures social mores of the 1950s, from the heartland to the Deep South to the life on the coasts and in the American West. Frank captures racial stratification, class divides, and perhaps most importantly America's love affair with the automobile—young lovers make out on a blanket spread in front of a car; young men sit in the backseat of a car at the drive-in; a homeless man in Venice, California, sleeps on a car seat underneath an American flag. These photographs serve as a visual analogue to the America of Kerouac's *On the Road*. Kerouac's admiration for and affinity with Frank is clear in his own introduction to *The Americans* and later in his essay "On the Road to Florida"—an account of a trip from New York to Florida he took with Frank in 1959 (reprinted in *Good Blonde and Others*, Grey Fox Press, 1993).

Fred McDarrah, former adman for the *Village Voice* and resident of Greenwich Village in the 1950s and 1960s, offers an astute, observant, and unobtrusive look at Beat life of the period. His photographs, collected in *Kerouac and Friends* and more recently in *Beat Generation: Glory Days in Greenwich Village*, provide the perspective of an invited observer. Through McDarrah's eyes the viewer gets a sense of the "scene" from loft parties to poetry readings at the Gaslight Cafe, Five Spot Cafe, and in various bars on MacDougal Street and throughout the Village. More intimate moments in these photographs are interior shots of Allen Ginsberg's East Side apartment and a number of pictures of Jack Kerouac at readings, surrounded by groupies and admirers, and at McDarrah's own apartment, collaborating with Lew Welch and Albert Saijo on what would become their poem "Trip Trap." McDarrah also chronicles the "Rent-a-Beatnik" scene and the staged "Beatnik" parties—popular among the effete and upper middle class of the period.

Gordon Ball's photography is most closely associated with Allen Ginsberg. Editor of Ginsberg's *Mid-Fifties Journals (1954–1958)* and later collaborator on *Allen Verbatim*, a book of Ginsberg's essays, Ball subsequently became a professor at the Virginia Military Institute. Ball, in a thirty-year sequence called "Ginsberg and Beat Fellows," chronicles Ginsberg and a number of his contemporaries (Burroughs, Corso, Ferlinghetti, Orlovsky). Ball's photographs include a number of now famous shots of the Naropa Institute poetry community as it was beginning in the 1970s, as well as portraits of gatherings at Ginsberg's Cherry Valley, New York, farm in the late 1960s and early 1970s. More recent photographs include a notorious 1991 shot of VMI cadets reading "Howl" in the classroom as well as stills from Ginsberg's funeral in 1997.

Christopher Felver's work includes inspired photographic histories of Beat poets in maturity. Drawing from the observation that Allen Ginsberg was seldom by himself, Felver, in *The Late Great Allen Ginsberg: A Photo Biography* (2003), illuminates Ginsberg's incredible social and literary network. Showing Ginsberg leading workshops, giving readings, dealing with admirers, and working as a writer, these photos from 1980–1987 reveal Ginsberg's tireless humanitarianism, sensitivity, and intellect. Felver's interest in friendships within the Beat community and its periphery is also evident in his *Ferlinghetti: Portrait* (1998) and in his earlier collection *The Poet Exposed* (1986).

Allen Ginsberg himself is a central figure in the Beat photography canon. From the late 1940s on Ginsberg captured a number of friends and contemporaries from New York to San Francisco to India to Tangier and back again. A number of these photographs appeared in collage form on the jackets of Penguin's Kerouac editions beginning in the early 1990s. Some of the finest of these are the early photographs of the first New York Beat triumvirate: Ginsberg, Kerouac, and Burroughs. The three are photographed around Columbia and in Ginsberg's East Side apartment. Many of these photos are available in *Snapshot Poetics* (including shots from the 1970s and 1980s as the generation grew older) and in his collaboration with Kerouac biographer/bibliographer/editor Ann Charters, *Scenes along the Road.* Charters herself, during her early collaboration with her husband Sam on *Blues People,* took some seminal photographs. In *Beats and Company* (1986), she documented Kerouac in Hyannis, Massachusetts, near the end of his life as they collaborated on his complete bibliography.

John Suiter's *Poets on the Peaks* (2002) is a photo-history of the Beat presence in Washington's Northern Cascades where Gary Snyder, Philip Whalen, and Jack Kerouac all served as fire lookouts in the 1950s. This book is a rich biographical study of these three writers during this period, chronicling their experiences atop Crater Mountain, Sourdough Lookout, and Desolation Peak—places that inspired some of the richest, most evocative Beat nature writing from all three writers. Suiter includes his own recent photographs of the lookout stations and mountain ranges and juxtaposes these with historical photographs. Suiter's text makes use of newly accessible Kerouac journals and letters as well as recent interviews from Gary Snyder and Philip Whalen. This book is also a penetrating history of the Forest Service's presence in the North Cascades as well as an evocation of San Francisco literary life.

—*Matt Kelley*

## Bibliographical References
Ann Charters and Allen Ginsberg, *Scenes along the Road: Photographs of the Desolation Angels 1944–1960,* 1970; Ann Charters, *Beats and Company,* 1986; Christopher Felver, *The Poet Exposed,* 1986; Christopher Felver, *The Late Great Allen Ginsberg,* 2003; Christopher Felver, *Ferlinghetti: Portrait,* 1998; Robert Frank, *The Americans,* 1959; Allen Ginsberg, *Snapshot Poetics: Allen Ginsberg's Photographic Memoir of the Beat Era,* 1993; Fred McDarrah and Gloria S. McDarrah, *Beat Generation: Glory Days in Greenwich Village,* 1996; Fred McDarrah, *Kerouac and Friends: A Beat Generation Album,* 1985; John Suiter, *Poets on the Peaks: Gary Snyder, Philip Whalen and Jack Kerouac in the North Cascades,* 2002.

*See also* Mountains, Beats in the; Kerouac, Jack; Ginsberg, Allen; Film

## Pleasure in Life
According to Jack Kerouac, what the Beat Generation was all about.

In an interview with William F. Buckley on the television program *Firing Line* (1968), Kerouac tried to distinguish the real desires of the Beats from the false information reported by journalists. Kerouac insisted that the Beats were not hoodlums, delinquents, or angry rebels; instead, the Beats were pure in their hearts; they were in pursuit of pleasure in life and beatitude—a blessed state of happiness.

—*William Lawlor*

## Bibliographical References
Segments of the interview are included in John Antonelli's film *Kerouac* (1984), which has been reproduced under various titles, including the video *On the Road with Jack Kerouac* (1990) and the DVD *Jack Kerouac: King of the Beats* (2003). One can also see, in either DVD (2003) or video (1985), segments of the *Firing Line* interview in *What Happened to Kerouac?* Kerouac is drunk during the interview, but his remarks are nevertheless witty and insightful.

*See also* Beatitude; Juvenile Delinquency

# Plymell, Charles (1935–)

Younger than most of the principal Beat writers, Plymell holds an unsteady relationship to them. Although belonging to what he calls the pot-and-amphetamine "hobohemian" generation, Plymell grew increasingly critical of the Beats' commercial motivations and artistic ideologies. He was born 26 April 1935, in Holcomb, Kansas. While attending Wichita State University (1955–1961), Plymell worked as a printer, also publishing campus literary magazines. He moved to San Francisco in 1963, living with Allen Ginsberg and Neal Cassady during the summer. Throughout the 1960s, Plymell served as an editor and publisher, and in 1967 he published the first issue of *Zap Comix*, an independent comic illustrated by Robert Crumb. Plymell married Pamela Beach on 3 September 1966. He soon published his first book, *Apocalypse Rose* (1967), followed by *Neon Poems* (1970). Upon receiving a fellowship at Johns Hopkins University, Plymell moved to Maryland in 1970 and completed *The Last of the Moccasins* (1971), which documents his Bay Area experiences in the 1960s. Plymell and Beach moved to New York and founded Cherry Valley Editions, publishing works by Ginsberg, William S. Burroughs, Herbert Huncke, and others. In many ways a proletarian writer, Plymell has worked in construction, farming, and mining. A major collection of his poetry appeared as *The Trashing of America* (1975), and *Hand on the Doorknob: A Charles Plymell Reader* (2000) anthologizes his ever-evolving work. Considered by some critics as a second-generation, latter-day, post-Beat writer, Plymell is connected to the Beats more by association than style, tracing his work to writers such as Hart Crane and Loren Eiseley more than to the Beats.

—*Brad E. Lucas*

## Principal Works

*Apocalypse Rose*, 1966; *Neon Poems*, 1970; *The Last of the Moccasins*, 1971; *Over the Stage of Kansas*, 1973; *The Trashing of America*, 1975; *Blue Orchid Numero Uno*, 1975; *In Memory of My Father*, 1977; *Are You a Kid?*, 1977; *Forever Wider: Poems New and Selected, 1954–1984*, 1985; *The Harder They Come*, 1985; *Hand on the Door: A Charles Plymell Reader*, 2000.

## Bibliographical References

Brown Miller, "Charles Plymell," on pages 448–452 in Ann Charters, ed., *The Beats: Literary Bohemians in Postwar America*, 1983, gives a summary of Plymell's life and work. An interview with Plymell appears in *The Harder They Come*, 1985.

*See also* Cherry Valley, New York

# Pollock, Jackson (1912–1956)

Painter, leading figure of the abstract expressionist movement. Pollock's unorthodox technique of "poured paintings" on large canvases in the 1950s made him the most important American painter of this century. Paul Jackson Pollock was born 28 January 1912. He began studying painting in 1929 at the Art Students' League and moved to New York in 1930 and studied under Thomas Hart Benton. He worked for the Federal Art Project of the WPA from 1938 to 1942. In the late 1940s, Pollock began his best-known stylistic innovation, the so-called drip or splash paintings, also called action painting. In these works Pollock took artistic risks by laying large canvases on the floor, giving primacy to the act of painting and emphasizing all parts of the canvas. Though often ridiculed as "Jack the Dripper," Pollock used unconventional methods that paved the way for many younger American artists. Pollock's frequent bouts with alcohol led to treatment through Jungian psychoanalysis, and his works became increasingly abstract and surrealistic. Pollock's legendary status as an artist was sealed by his untimely death at age forty-four in a car crash on 1 August 1956.

—*Gary Kerley*

## Bibliographical References

Justin Spring, *The Essential Jackson Pollock*, 1998; B. H. Friedman, *Jackson Pollock: Energy Made Visible*, 1995; Steven W. Naifeh, *Jackson Pollock: An American Saga*, 1989; Bryan Robertson, *Jackson Pollock*, 1960; Frank O'Hara, *Jackson Pollock*, 1959.

*See also* de Kooning, Willem; Painting; New York City

Instead of painting with brushes, Jackson Pollock dripped paint onto his canvases. (Burckhardt Rudolph/Corbis Sygma)

## Pommy Vega, Janine (1942–)

A mystical wayfarer continually in search of transcendence, Janine Pommy Vega writes poetry that is a chronicle of the many spiritual and temporal journeys she has embarked upon during the latter half of the twentieth century. According to Ronna C. Johnson and Nancy M. Grace, editors of *Girls Who Wore Black: Women Writing the Beat Gener-* *ation*, Pommy Vega emerged during the third wave of the women Beat writers (14). Unlike many of her female predecessors, Pommy Vega's aesthetic was influenced by both the emerging feminist and countercultural, political schema of the 1960s. While Pommy Vega does not attempt to rewrite the mythos of the male Beat writers, her poetry does call into question some assumptions of the male

Beat poets, in particular those aspects that ignore expressions of female wanderlust and creativity. As is the case with many of the female Beat writers, an assessment of Pommy Vega's contribution to the Beat movement is long overdue (Damon 219).

Born on 5 February 1942 to working-class New Jersey parents, Janine Pommy was valedictorian of her high school class. Bored with the confines of her suburban upbringing, she made frequent treks at age sixteen to New York City, often stopping by coffee shops frequented by Beat writers. After striking up friendships with Herbert Huncke, Peter Orlovsky, and Elise Cowen, Pommy began writing creatively. For a short while, she lived with Elise Cowen before Cowen's suicide. In 1962 at age twenty Pommy met the Peruvian painter Fernando Vega and traveled with him extensively. The pair married in Israel and pursued their respective interests of poetry and painting in Europe and Israel. Both also sought creative inspiration in frequent drug use. An extended stay in the Spanish island of Ibiza resulted in Vega's hospitalization for mescaline use. In the aftermath of her husband's death from a heroin overdose, Pommy Vega dedicated her first book of poems to Fernando's memory. Entitled *Poems to Fernando,* the work describes the couple's turbulent life together as they endured numerous separations from one another and Vega's mental illness. Over the course of the epic, Pommy Vega's distinctive style and thematic approach emerge. As R'lene H. Dahlberg notes, *Poems to Fernando* acts as an "exquisite chronicling of the birth of a poet through pain" (523). A Whitmanesque strain runs through the works. The last stanza from "poem to your lean face, leaning down eyes," sums up the tenor of the collection: "O love pure love in the universe/ pierce me and pour in/ that I live outside the wall/ the flourish of wilderness grasses/ High—& see not that/ familiar circle of leaves/ to step back to" (in *A Different Beat* 201).

After her husband's death, Pommy Vega relocated to San Francisco. During a brief stay at Woodstock, Pommy Vega chose the destination for her next adventure via the flip of a coin. Of the three possibilities, Peru, Ireland, or Australia, Peru emerged as her destination (Dahlberg 525). She began her second book, *Journal of a Hermit,* during her sojourn in Peru, occasionally teaching English to support herself. In 1980, Pommy Vega was temporarily laid up from injuries sustained from a serious automobile accident. During her recuperation, she became interested in studying prepatriarchal, goddess-centered cultures. Not one to succumb to stagnation, she embarked on various excursions to the Himalayas, the Peruvian Andes, the Amazon, and the south of England, all of which are recounted in her travel narrative, *Tracking the Serpent: Journeys to Four Continents* (1997), published by City Lights Books. The implications of her spiritual odyssey can be summed up in these lines from *Tracking the Serpent:* "At the end of the road/ there is no fair haven/ no hero's welcome no pot of tea/ at the end of the road/ is the road/ stretching in both directions/ in your heart" (186).

In New York State, Pommy Vega has been teaching inmates in state correctional facilities for twenty-five years. At universities and writing conferences Pommy Vega lectures and reads. She also tours frequently throughout North and South America with her band Tiamalu. In addition, she is director of Incisions/Arts, a group of writers who lead poetry workshops for prison inmates. In recent works such as "Which Side Are You On?" and "To You on the Other Side of This," Pommy Vega reveals a deep sympathy for the downtrodden and the neglected casualties of modern life, interspersed with omnipresent elements of the natural world. In "To You on the Other Side of This," which appears in *Mad Dogs of Trieste* (2000), she writes, "Months Passed. You have taken away/ his forward momentum, but not himself/ his spirit still alive in the midst of my grieving./ You crossed over into the mystery of someone else's life/ stopped by your hands/ And no one will join you in the ring as you wrestle with that" (239).

—*Patricia Gott*

## Principal Works

Pommy Vega's poetry includes *Morning Passage,* 1976; *The Bard Owl,* 1980; *Drunk on a Glacier, Talking to Flies,* 1988; *Threading the Maze,* 1992;

*The Road to Your House Is a Mountain Road,* 1995; *Mad Dogs of Trieste: New and Selected Poems,* 2000; *The Green Piano,* 2005; and various chapbooks. She has also edited numerous anthologies, including an anthology entitled *Voices under the Harvest Moon: An Anthology of Writing from Eastern Correctional Facility,* 1999. *Tracking the Serpent: Journeys to Four Continents,* 1997, is a collection of essays on travel.

### Bibliographical References

R'lene H. Dahlberg, "Janine Pommy Vega," in *Dictionary of Literary Biography: The Beats: Literary Bohemians in Postwar America,* ed. Ann Charters, 1983; Maria Damon, "Revelations of Companionate Love; or, The Hurts of Women: Janine Pommy Vega's 'Poems to Fernando,'" in *Girls Who Wore Black: Women Writing the Beat Generation,* eds. Ronna C. Johnson and Nancy M. Grace, 2002; Ronna C. Johnson and Nancy M. Grace, eds., *Girls Who Wore Black: Women Writing the Beat Generation,* 2002; Richard Peabody, ed., *A Different Beat: Writings by Women of the Beat Generation,* 1997.

*See also* Mountains, Beats in the

## Publishers

In most cases small and independent enterprises whose editorial policies were open minded and whose convictions included opposition to censorship and a world view of literature; in some cases private artistic presses that produced fine, limited editions; in other cases, full-scale publication companies with capacity for broad distribution and active promotion.

City Lights Books is one of the most noteworthy of the small presses giving opportunities to the Beats. City Lights Bookstore served as a base for operations for City Lights Books and its Pocket Poets Series. Peter Martin and Lawrence Ferlinghetti opened the Pocket Bookshop in San Francisco in 1953, but in 1955, as the publication of the Pocket Poets Series began, the store became the City Lights Bookstore. City Lights Books has always made room for dissent, innovation, and international perspectives. The publications of City Lights include Garcia Lorca, Arthur Rimbaud, Pablo Picasso, Pablo Neruda, Yevgeny Yevtushenko, and many others. The Pocket Poets Series—the small, slender volumes with simple cover designs—has provided opportunities for numerous Beat writers, including Allen Ginsberg, Lawrence Ferlinghetti, Gregory Corso, Diane di Prima, Robert Duncan, Philip Lamantia, Jack Kerouac, Michael McClure, and many others. Allen Ginsberg's *Howl and Other Poems* (1956), despite the public efforts to halt the book's sale and distribution, has been a perennial best-seller for City Lights, enabling the press to take on other projects by writers not favored at traditional publication houses.

Similar to the Pocket Poets Series was the production of poetry pamphlets by Totem Press under the direction of LeRoi Jones. With a small offset press, Jones produced works by Diane di Prima, Michael McClure, Charles Olson, Jack Kerouac, Frank O'Hara, and Philip Whalen. Combining interests with Eli Wilentz of Corinth Books, Jones tried to enhance the distribution of the small volumes of poetry.

Presses like City Lights and Totem Press simplified production and cut costs so that publication could be diverse and continuous. David Haselwood of Auerhahn Press (later David Haselwood Books) strove to make the books as excellent as the poetry published in them. Artwork often adorned the books, which sometimes featured luxurious paper, binding, and covers. A signed copy of Michael McClure's *Dark Brown,* published in 1961 by Auerhahn Press with leather binding, gilt stamping, and fine Japanese paper, sells for more than a thousand dollars in 2005. A copy of Charles Olson's *Human Universe and Other Essays* (1965) featuring full-color artwork by Robert La Vigne and a photo of the author sells in 2005 for more than two hundred dollars.

If not simple and basic and if not elegant and artistic, Beat publications were sometimes large-scale productions for wide distribution. New Directions Press, founded by James Laughlin in 1936, established itself by publishing authors such as Ezra Pound, William Carlos Williams, and Tennessee Williams. Always open to the publication of innovative new authors, foreign authors in translation, and worthy authors whose works have fallen out of print, New Directions has been especially helpful to Beat writers. Lawrence Ferlinghetti's *A Coney Island of the Mind* (1958), which reportedly has outsold all other paperback volumes of poetry, is a New Directions book. Numerous titles by Gary Snyder, Gregory Corso, Robert Creeley, Robert Duncan, Bob Kaufman, Michael McClure, Kenneth Patchen, and Kenneth Rexroth stay in print because of New Directions.

Barney Rosset, whose publication style was consistent with the practices of New Directions, transformed Grove Press in 1951 when he became a partner. Rosset began to publish diverse examples of world literature, including books by Samuel Beckett, Jean Genet, and Eugene Ionesco. Unafraid of the courts, Rosset fought against censorship and won important decisions involving D. H. Lawrence's *Lady Chatterly's Lover* (1928) and Henry Miller's *Tropic of Cancer* (1934). Among many Grove publications that were helpful to Beat authors, *The New American Poetry,* ed. Donald Allen (1960), was a key text, as Allen's edition brought various schools of poetry together in a single volume, giving space to Jack Kerouac, Michael McClure, LeRoi Jones, and many other Beat writers. Grove Press in 1962 published the first United States edition of William Burroughs's *Naked Lunch* (1962) and has published various other works by Burroughs since that time. In addition, works such as Lenore Kandel's *Word Alchemy* (1967), Jack Kerouac's *Mexico City Blues* (1959), and Hugh Selby's *Last Exit to Brooklyn* (1964) have appeared in Grove editions.

Because the Beats have been successful as well as innovative, large publishing houses have brought Beat writers to market, too. A notable publisher is Viking Press, which published *On the Road* (1957) and *The Dharma Bums* (1958). Penguin Group, which now owns Viking, produces a broad variety of books connected to the Beat Generation, including Kerouac's *Desolation Angels* (1965), Joyce Johnson's *Minor Characters* (1983), and *The Portable Beat Reader,* ed. Ann Charters (1992). Before his death, Allen Ginsberg negotiated a contract for multiple books with Harper Perennial, and this contract led to *Collected Poems* (1984), *Cosmopolitan Greetings* (1995), *Death and Fame* (2000), and other works.

—*William Lawlor*

## Bibliographical References

For information on small presses, see Steven Clay and Rodney Phillips, *A Secret Location on the Lower East Side,* 1998; on-line catalogs are available for City Lights, New Directions, Grove Press, Viking, Penguin, and Harper Perennial.

## Rauschenberg, Robert (1925–)

Artist, painter, printmaker, sculptor, and performance artist; influential figure in the avant-garde movement away from abstract expressionism since the 1950s.

Milton E. Rauschenberg—he changed his name to Robert while a student at the Kansas City Art Institute (1947–1948)—was born 22 October 1925, in Port Arthur, Texas. He also studied at Black Mountain College (1948–1949), where he was influenced by such visionaries as Buckminster Fuller, Merce Cunningham, and John Cage, and did further work at the Art Students' League in New York, where he moved in 1949. By the 1950s Rauschenberg's enthusiasm for popular culture led to what he termed "combines," in which cast-off bits of disparate materials blurred the lines between painting and sculpture and influenced the American pop art scene.

As silk-screen painter, performance artist, and printmaker, Rauschenberg continues to experiment with theater, choreography, and happenings. In 1998 the Guggenheim Museum exhibited a retrospective of 400 of his works.

—*Gary Kerley*

### Bibliographical References

Robert Mattison, *Robert Rauschenberg: Breaking Boundaries*, 2003; Sam Hunter, *Robert Rauschenberg*, 1999; Mary Lynn Kotz, *Rauschenberg: Art and Life*, 1990; Calvin Tomkins, *Off the Wall: Robert Rauschenberg and the Art World of Our Time*, 1980.

*See also* Pollock, Jackson; Black Mountain, North Carolina, and Black Mountain College; Painting

## Red Scares (First and Second)

Two "red scares" plagued politically progressive Americans during the twentieth century, isolating these citizens by casting them as part of a communist threat to American society. Many writers of the Beat Generation—including Allen Ginsberg, William S. Burroughs, and Lawrence Ferlinghetti—shared a passion for radical politics that, among their other challenges to established norms, placed them outside the power structure of their time. For many, the Beats became beatniks, with the suffix connoting a connection between the Beats and the Reds.

U.S. Attorney General A. Mitchell Palmer orchestrated the first crackdown on homegrown American communists, a process that started with the passage of federal espionage and sedition acts in 1917 and 1918. Advocating a forced change in the U.S. government became a crime, as did criticism of America's involvement in World War I. As a consequence, radical politician Eugene V. Debs served a three-year prison sentence, while African American activist Marcus Garvey, feminist Emma Goldman, and thousands of other Americans were jailed or deported in retaliation for their political beliefs. Postal officials also simultaneously attacked efforts of pioneer birth control advocate Margaret Sanger, prosecuting her for obscenity. The first scare reached a fever pitch with the 1927 execution of anarchists Bartolomeo Vanzetti and Nicola Sacco, but ran out of steam by 1933, when President Franklin D. Roosevelt recognized the legitimacy of Joseph Stalin's government in the Soviet Union. Prominent during the first scare was a young lawyer, John Edgar Hoover, who was appointed the first director of the agency that eventually became the Federal Bureau of Investigation.

The second scare started about 1938, when the Un-American Activities Committee of the U.S. House of Representatives began an investigation of communists in American unions, federally funded theatrical troupes, and other alleged Red "front" organizations. Later, the search for communists was extended to Hollywood and the U.S. military. The Smith Act of 1940, akin to the earlier espionage and sedition acts, again criminalized radical dissent. By 1948, first-term U.S. Representative Richard M. Nixon (R-CA) had exposed a communist connection to the U.S. State Department by helping to convict former presidential advisor Alger Hiss of perjury. Julius and Ethel Rosenberg were executed two years later for an unsuccessful attempt to pass atomic bomb secrets to Russia. A 1950 West Virginia speech by rampaging U.S. Senator Joseph R. McCarthy (R-WI) made communists in government a bread-and-butter issue for all America. Despite four years of investigation, however, McCarthy never found a communist. Before his 1954 Senate censure removed him from power, McCarthy's smear tactics and innuendo created a national mood that encouraged employers to blacklist writers, entertainers, and academics accused of communist sympathies. Prominent progressives targeted included mystery writer Dashiell Hammett, actor John Garfield, presidential advisor Philleo Nash, scientist Albert Einstein, and singer Pete Seeger. The second scare evaporated about 1960, when blacklisted screenwriter Dalton Trumbo was hired under his own name to write a movie script. McCarthy died in 1957, his liver destroyed by alcoholism. Nixon, elected president in 1968, traveled to communist China in 1972. Facing impeachment in the wake of the Watergate scandal, Nixon was forced to resign the presidency in 1974.

Although the Beat writers faced charges that they were Reds, the truth is that the Beats expressed varying degrees of dissent and no particular advocacy of communism. Ginsberg, Ferlinghetti, and Burroughs were the most radical, while Jack Kerouac moved from a nearly nonpolitical stance to a neoconservative approach by the time of his 1968 appearance on William F. Buckley Jr.'s television show, *Firing Line*. Ferlinghetti collided with the U.S. government in 1957, after he was charged with obscenity for publishing Ginsberg's best-known work, *Howl and Other Poems*. Burroughs's contempt for the American presidency was best shown in his short performance pieces, especially "When Did I Stop Wanting to Be President?" (1975) and "Keynote Commentary, Roosevelt after the Inauguration" (1978).

By the 1980s, the pages of Ginsberg's redacted FBI file were stacked three feet high. J. Edgar Hoover himself considered Ginsberg an unbalanced radical who was potentially suicidal and likely to help destroy America's government. Ginsberg's radicalism—honestly acquired from his schoolteacher mother, who took him to Communist Party meetings when he was still in grade school—prompted the U.S. Information Agency to ban his participation in poetry readings sponsored by the government. Ginsberg's poems "America" (1956) and "Kaddish" (1961) touch. on the radical politics of his family. Ginsberg writes in "America" about his childhood experiences with 1930s-era American communism and speaks of the tenderness of the people in the Communist Party (*Collected Poems: 1947–1980*, 147). Yet, as the poet acknowledged during a mid-1960s interview published in *The Paris Review*, hard-line Leninism-Marxism was never the answer to America's problems. "The general idea of revolution against American idiocy is good," Ginsberg said. "But what's gonna follow—the dogmatism that follows is a big drag." (*Beat Writers at Work: The Paris Review Interviews*, ed. George Plimpton, 48).

—*Mark Scarborough*

## Bibliographical References

For Kerouac's friendship with Buckley, see Gerald Nicosia, *Memory Babe: A Critical Biography of*

*Jack Kerouac*, 1983; Ginsberg's FBI file is detailed in Herbert Mitgang, *Dangerous Dossiers: Exposing the Secret War against America's Greatest Authors*, 1988; Ginsberg's *Collected Poems: 1947–1980* was published in 1984; editor George Plimpton's *The Beat Writers at Work: The Paris Review*, 1999, offers interviews with Burroughs, Kerouac, Ginsberg, Ferlinghetti, and others; Burroughs speaks for himself on the compact discs of *The Best of William Burroughs*, 1998; America's Red Scares are described in Robert K. Murray, *Red Scare: A Study in National Hysteria, 1919–1920*, 1955, and M. J. Heale, *McCarthy's Americans: Red Scare Politics in State and Nation, 1935–1965*, 1998.

*See also* Cold War

## Reich, Wilhelm (1897–1957)

Medical doctor; psychiatrist; theorist who drew a connection between the blocked sexuality of the individual and the sickness of society as a whole; researcher who determined that physical and mental well-being depends on the accumulation of life energy through the collection of orgones from the atmosphere and the release of life energy through sex. Wilhelm Reich's extensive writings and investigations influenced Beat writers, who were interested in liberation of sexual attitudes and full sexual satisfaction.

Reich was born in 1897 in Galicia, which then was part of the Austro-Hungarian Empire, but which now is in Ukraine. He was a German-speaking Austrian citizen, and as World War I began, Russian troops advanced into his homeland and he served in the Austrian army as a lieutenant. In 1918, as the war ended, he entered the University of Vienna. By 1922 he completed his studies and became a medical doctor. He worked in the Neurological and Psychiatric University Clinic and became a student of Freud. Learning of psychoanalysis from Freud, he also worked in Freud's Psychoanalytic Polyclinic in Vienna.

Freud developed the theory that society can sometimes inhibit natural sexual behavior and thereby produce neurosis; furthermore, Freud developed the concept of the libido—the sexual energy in the mind and the body. Though Freud eventually viewed the libido as a speculative concept, Reich seized upon the idea and theorized that the failure to release energy through sex leads to neurosis and an alteration of character, which Reich described as the development of character "armor." In contrast, the fully healthy person achieves "orgastic potency," which involves the full discharge of sexual energy in the sex act.

Reich believed that the problem of sexual dysfunction should be solved through reform of society. Because people must adjust themselves to achieve the successful release of life energy through sex, society must adjust itself so that people are not inhibited in the pursuit of fulfillment. Reich was in favor of sex education, birth control, access to divorce, and improvements in housing, because each of these factors contributes to the potential of a person to achieve orgastic potency. Freud, in contrast to Reich, believed that people need to adjust to their cultural surroundings. This point of contention led to a split between Reich and Freud. Reich pursued his research in Oslo, Norway, but when Reich published his findings about orgone energy (Reich's term for life energy), a public outcry against him followed. Finally, in 1939, Reich accepted a position at the New School for Social Research in New York and traveled to the United States, where he continued his investigations.

In the United States, Reich sought a means to gather orgone energy and developed the orgone energy accumulator around 1940. The accumulator was at first only a small box with sides made of alternate layers of metallic and nonmetallic materials. Cotton, wool, or plastic absorbed the orgone energy, and steel and iron attracted and transferred the energy, accumulating the energy within the box. Reich went on to construct enclosures with a similar design but of a size that could accommodate a person who would enter the chamber and thereby gain an enriching exposure to orgone energy. A person might enter the accumulator, charge himself or herself with life energy, and subsequently externalize that energy through sex, achieving pleasure, satisfaction, and health.

Controversy developed when Reich faced accusations that he was fraudulently promising health benefits through the use of the orgone accumulator. Mildred Edie Brady wrote "The Strange Case of Wilhelm Reich" in the *New Republic* (26 May 1947), raising questions about Reich, his research, and his practices. The Food and Drug Administration investigated and charged Reich with making false claims about curing diseases through the use of the orgone accumulator. On 7 May 1956, Reich was found guilty and tons of materials at his research center in Maine were destroyed. When his appeal failed, Reich was imprisoned in 1957. He died in prison of heart failure on 3 November 1957.

In "Essentials of Spontaneous Prose," which is included in *The Portable Jack Kerouac*, ed. Ann Charters (1995), Jack Kerouac refers to Reich. Kerouac suggests that Reich's theory that orgasmic energy starts within and is brought to the surface and discharged is analogous to writing, which is based on an energy that must come from within and be made external on the page (485).

In *On the Road*, Sal and Dean visit Old Bull Lee in Algiers, Louisiana, and Bull has an orgone accumulator constructed near his home (152). Bull apparently subscribes to the theories of Reich and seeks to enhance his life by properly gathering orgones for the benefit of his body. Sal apparently knows about Reich and orgone energy because he refers to Reich and the theory that people are afflicted with cancer because they have insufficient orgone energy (152).

Old Bull Lee is based on William Burroughs, and in *Literary Outlaw* (1988), Ted Morgan describes Burroughs's connection to Reich (140–143). Though Burroughs thought Reich was foolish for creating the circumstances that allowed the authorities to incarcerate him, Burroughs was interested in Reich's analysis of the orgasm and the connection of disease to sexual dissatisfaction. The orgone accumulator really worked, Burroughs believed, and he constructed several of them.

In *The Job*, ed. Dan Oldier (1974), Burroughs comments further on Reich (16–17). Burroughs refers to the electrode that Reich attached to the penis in order to measure the quality of an orgasm. He speaks of various designs for orgone accumulators and praises the effects of one accumulator he used, claiming that he achieved a spontaneous orgasm (without manual stimulation). The action taken against Reich by the Food and Drug Administration, Burroughs insists, is proof that Reich's work is important (122). The government usually suppresses things that are important.

—*James E. Lawlor*

### Principal Works

*The Function of the Orgasm*, 1942 (trans. Nancy Bod Higgins, 1973); *Character Analysis*, 1945 (trans. Vincent R. Carfagno, 1972); *Discovery of the Orgone*, trans. Theodore P. Wolfe, 1948; *Early Writings*, trans. Philip Schmitz, 1975.

### Bibliographical References

Jerome Greenfield, *Wilhelm Reich vs. the USA*, 1974; Eustace Chesser, *Reich and Sexual Freedom*, 1973; Myron R. Sharaf, *Fury on Earth: A Biography of Wilhelm Reich*, 1983.

***See also*** Burroughs, William Seward

## Reinhardt, Ad (1913–1967)

Painter; educator; writer. Avant-garde artist whose series of black paintings and numerous writings marked a departure from abstract expressionism and influenced the development of minimalism.

Reinhardt attended Columbia University (1931–1935) and the American Arts School (1936–1937). Around this time he was involved in the WPA Federal Art Project. In the 1940s, Reinhardt was known for simple, full-colored, and neat abstractions, but by the 1950s, he dedicated himself to paintings in a single color. His series of black paintings appear to be canvases that are simply painted with uniform black paint, but closer inspection reveals subtle gradations in tone. Reinhardt taught at Brooklyn College and also lectured at Yale, the California School of Fine Arts, and Hunter College.

In 1980, Reinhardt's work was on display at the Guggenheim Museum. The Museum of Modern Art exhibited Reinhardt's work in 1991.

—*William Lawlor*

**Bibliographical References**

Ad Reinhardt, *Art as Art: The Selected Writings of Ad Reinhardt*, ed. Barbara Rose, 1975; *Ad Reinhardt: Early Works*, 1999, is a catalog from an exhibit at the Marlborough Gallery.

## Religion, The Beats and

Throughout their careers Beat writers maintained an ambivalent relationship with organized religion. For example, William S. Burroughs, Jack Kerouac, and Allen Ginsberg—Protestant, Catholic, Jew—simultaneously drew upon their childhood faiths even as they found them lacking in certain areas. Rather than privilege or dismiss the Judeo-Christian heritage of Beat writers, one must be aware of how the religious language of their youth was translated into the aesthetic language of their adulthood. The Beats also reinterpreted traditional religious themes and searched for religious meaning in the least obvious of places—in popular culture, in sexual ecstasy, on the open road, in drugs, and among marginalized members of society. More often than not the Beats looked for religious insight not in the seminary libraries or the church pews but in the works of Wilhelm Reich, Oswald Spengler, and linguist Alfred Korzybski; the saxophone wails of Charlie Parker and Lester Young; and the elegance of William Carlos Williams, William Blake, and Arthur Rimbaud. In an era when church attendance reached unprecedented heights and theological debate raged, the Beats collectively pursued religious strategies for personal empowerment and sought leverage for their cultural criticism.

In many ways, the Beat writers reveal a strong connection to traditional religious beliefs. Jack Kerouac attended Catholic schools and always kept in mind the wisdom and suffering of Jesus Christ. The Stations of the Cross and the crucifix were enduring and powerful symbols in his community, family, and home. Kerouac's solitude atop Desolation Peak is comparable to Christ's solitude, and *Visions of Gerard*, written in memory of Kerouac's older brother, who succumbed to rheumatic fever at age nine, is a work of hagiography, cutting out a place for Gerard among the saints. In Allen Ginsberg's family, Judaism did not always manifest itself in formal ritual, but Ginsberg's "Kaddish," the work that many consider his masterpiece, draws its form from the sequence of the Jewish prayers for the dead. William Everson, also known as Brother Antoninus, for many years was a Dominican friar.

While the Beats had many connections to traditional faith, one must also recognize that every era needs an avant-garde in order to challenge, and eventually revise, definitions of nature, authenticity, and the really real. This struggle over the "real" lies at the heart of religion, a struggle that involves not only how the world is conceived in essence but how one should act in accordance with this conception. Since the mid-nineteenth century, the struggle among Americans to align metaphysics with ethics has taken place within an industrialized, technological, and market-driven culture and outside the precincts of institutionalized religion. As theological discourse became untethered from the traditions of theology in the mid-nineteenth century, artists, writers, and ordinary folk have more often assumed the authority to make pronouncements about what constitutes ultimate reality and why. During a time of unprecedented industrial expansion and spread of capitalist markets, America witnessed a proliferation of new religious movements that privileged the capacity of the individual mind over the authority of doctrine or creed. Transcendental provocations such as Ralph Waldo Emerson's *Nature* (1836) and Henry David Thoreau's *Walden* (1855) set a standard of religious dissent from which another group of writers later drew inspiration.

In the mid-1940s, Burroughs, Kerouac, and Ginsberg came together at a subcultural crossroads: not the brooks and streams of New England but the intersection of Times Square addicts and petty criminals, Greenwich Village bohemia, and Columbia University intellectual circles. Together they initiated a project of literary and spiritual development, what they termed the "new vision." Because of their close association during the 1940s and 1950s, these writers garnered the group label "Beat," a self-descriptive and Catholic-tinged adjective that Kerouac first applied to the entire generation of postwar American youth—beaten down by society but capable of overcoming oppression through religious transcendence. Religion, in this sense, becomes positively destabilizing—a way to carve out an alternative space that challenges the legitimacy of the majority culture by the very process of existing alongside it.

The term *Beat* has come to embody a distinct literary sensibility shared by a wide range of artists: New York writers such as John Clellon Holmes, Gregory Corso, LeRoi Jones (Amiri Baraka), and Diane Di Prima, as well as West Coast poets Gary Snyder, Joanne Kyger, Michael McClure, Philip Whalen, Lawrence Ferlinghetti, and Lew Welch among others. In his essay, "The Beat Surface," which is included in *Scratching the Beat Surface,* McClure broaches the wider significance of the Beat writer's reorientation to "nature." Not simply nature as in the seas and the trees, but a heretofore underutilized category of human experience— "Much of what the Beat Generation is about is nature—the landscape of nature in the case of Gary Snyder, the mind as nature in the case of Allen Ginsberg. Consciousness is a natural organic phenomenon. The Beats shared an interest in Nature, Mind, and Biology—areas that they expanded and held together with their radical political or antipolitical stance" (11).

As McClure suggests, what bound Beat works together in common cause was an interest in the category of nature, or more precisely, their deepfelt suspicions about and radical critique of the "American way of life" as unnatural. Often claiming the mantle of America, they offered both ecological and epistemological jeremiads, calling home those who had wandered in the wilderness of corporate and mechanized America. The Beats were of the homegrown lineage of American romanticism and its recourse to "natural" forms and "natural" objects of worship. Within American religious history this diffuse movement has often been the site of spiritual resistance to dominant codes of morality and accepted understandings of the really real.

Although the Beats are known primarily as an urban phenomenon, "angel headed hipsters" in Ginsberg's telling phrase, barreling down the New York or San Francisco streets, nature, as both a category of religious experience and as a material phenomenon, played a crucial role in their respective works. Just as Emerson had sought an "original orientation" to the universe, so, too, did the Beats. Indeed, their work not only helped revive literary experimentation within America, but filtered the Romantic worship of nature through idioms as varied as bebop jazz, drug use, sexual ecstasy, the orgone psychology of Wilhelm Reich, and the prophecies of Oswald Spengler's *The Decline of the West.* Works such as Ginsberg's *Howl and Other Poems* (1956), Kerouac's *On the Road* (1957), and Burroughs's *Naked Lunch* (1959) were direct extensions of what the Beats termed the "new vision" and their attempts to challenge accepted definitions of nature, authenticity, and the really real. In language that expresses the spirituality of Emerson or Thoreau in a new, decidedly urban American key, Kerouac wrote in *Visions of Cody* that through the "brownlit windows of Sixth Avenue semi-flophouses" he could see "a piece of litter in the gutter" and "a beat gray coupe." He declares, "I know the city, and the universe" (17–18).

Given their desire to participate in an alternative social reality, many Beat writers sought to realize a new means of natural expression, or rather, a new means of expression as perception. To the extent that the boundaries dissolved between subject and object, conscious and unconscious, description and explanation, the Beats' poetics sought to achieve an uninterrupted and complete account of reality. In their attempt to unearth the unspeakable visions of the individual, Beat writers strove for more natural modes than those espoused by either the New Critical literary establishment or middle-class decorum. Kerouac's spontaneous compositions, Ginsberg's attention to individual breath as a measure of his poetry, and McClure's physically based poetics were variations upon automatic writing with the common goal of achieving a confessional honesty.

Burroughs, for example, began with the assumption that language was a system of unnatural control that "locked" consciousness into certain patterns of thought and expression. Beginning in the late 1950s, Burroughs began his "cut-up" experiments—a strategy of conversion that resembled the missionary zeal of evangelical Protestantism. (It should be noted that Burroughs's maternal grandfather was a Methodist circuit rider from Georgia.) This method of writing was designed to do a number of things: (1) reduce language to a state of naked materiality, (2) confront the censorship of consciousness, and (3) serve to expose the authoritarian agendas of contemporary political, economic, and moral orders. The cut-up method involved the process of cutting out passages from various texts—literary works, newspapers, advertisements—and reassembling them at random. Its goal was to create a text that would defy traditional classifications and logic, one that could potentially propel the reader into unexplored areas of consciousness and action.

The Beats' religious energies must not be understood solely in terms of Asian systems and outlooks. Ginsberg became familiar with haiku and Zen koans in the early 1950s, but even then he read them in terms of bebop, Cézanne, Blake, and the prophets of the Hebrew scriptures. Kerouac's spontaneous method had already matured by the time he began serious study of Buddhism in the early 1950s, reading such works as Dwight Goddard's *The Buddhist Bible* and Paul Carus's *The Gospel of Buddha*. Burroughs, who had actually sparked Kerouac's interest in the tradition of automatic writing, spent most of the 1950s attempting to "disabuse" Kerouac of his Buddhist leanings. Although Eastern spirituality cannot be discounted when looking at the Beats and religion, their creative borrowing from a variety of established religious and philosophical traditions defies simple categorization.

Even the most self-consciously Buddhist individual from among the Beats, Gary Snyder, mixed Native American myths and an ecological sensitivity with traditional Asian outlooks. Given his lifelong commitment to Buddhism, the work of Gary Snyder offers the most sensitive portrayal of nature as both state of mind and material condition. Along with Ginsberg, McClure, Whalen, and Philip Lamantia, he participated in the 6 Gallery reading in October 1955 that was the first public show of

force of a burgeoning literary phenomenon. At this event Snyder read "A Berry Feast" (later published in *The Back Country* in 1968) in which a Coyote trickster figure notes the ironies of human industry and impositions upon the land:

The chainsaw falls for boards of pine,
Suburban bedrooms, block on block
Will waver with this grain and knot,
The maddening shapes will start and fade
Each morning when commuters wake—
Joined boards hung on frames,
A box to catch a biped in. (4)

Influenced by his study of Native American and Buddhist sources as well as his own wilderness experiences, Snyder has consistently explored the metaphorical capacities of nature. His corpus of works—from *Myths & Texts* (1960), *Earth House Hold* (1969), and the Pulitzer Prize–winning *Turtle Island* (1974)—have inspired environmentalists and cultural critics since the 1950s. Never comfortable with the label "Beat," Snyder has produced work that nonetheless exemplifies the religious attentiveness to nature on the part of Beat writers. Snyder writes in the preface to *No Nature: New and Selected Poems* (1993), "There is no single or set 'nature' either as 'the natural world' or 'the nature of things.' The greatest respect we can pay to nature is not to trap it, but to acknowledge that it eludes us and that our own nature is also fluid, open and conditional" (v). The religious legacy of the Beats, particularly the ongoing literary activism of Snyder, has often been cited as an important influence by the proponents of Deep Ecology.

The legacy of the Beat poets is not only complicated but also somewhat contradictory. On one hand, their physical poetics celebrated ecstatic experience wherever it could be had, atop a tenement apartment or a lookout on Big Sur. On the other hand, their religious appreciation for those places and individuals whom they understood to be outside the matrix of Western civilization helped recast the aesthetics and politics of ecological concern. In other words, their radical deconstruction of "nature" and "authenticity" could also renew appreciation for traditional understandings. Direct heirs to the Beats' "natural" piety include Richard Brautigan and Ed Sanders, not to mention the Americanization of Buddhism as celebrated in the life and works of Ginsberg, Snyder, Lamantia, Whalen, and the Buddhist popularizer Alan Watts. The Beat sensibility is also evident in the ethnopoetics movement of the 1960s and the publication of *Technicians of the Sacred: A Range of Poetries from Africa, America, Asia, Europe & Oceania* (1967), edited by Jerome Rothenberg, as well as the journal *Alcheringa* (1970–1980). In *Juniper Fuse: Upper Paleolithic Imagination & the Construction of the Underworld* (2003), Clayton Eshleman has offered a series of poetic meditations on the Paleolithic art in which he carries on the Beat interest in the plurality of human consciousness. Although influence is, at base, uncategorizable, one senses in the works of Edward Abbey and Annie Dillard a Beat-inflected transcendentalism.

In the name of a more natural society, Beat poetics interrogated a Cold War patriotism celebrated in the proliferation of consumer goods, the will to geopolitical dominance, and the intense focus on technological innovation. Much of Beat writing, in both form and content, calls into question the "naturalness" of such a world and, instead, searches for alternative ways of living and expression. Although differing in their understanding of nature and sometimes plagued by their era's conservative views of gender, Beat writers' openness to alternative systems of knowledge—from improvisatory jazz to Buddhism to Native American beliefs—continues to challenge normative conceptions of reality, a challenge that is part and parcel to the religious imagination.

—*John Lardas*

## Bibliographical References

Michael Davidson, *The San Francisco Renaissance: Poetics and Community at Mid-century,* 1989; Jack Kerouac, *Visions of Cody,* 1993; John Lardas, *The Bop Apocalypse: The Religious Visions of Kerouac, Ginsberg, and Burroughs,* 2001; Michael McClure, *Scratching the Beat Surface,* 1982; Rod Phillips, *"Forest Beatniks"* and *Urban Thoreaus": Gary Snyder, Jack Kerouac, Lew Welch, and Michael McClure,* 2000; Stephen Prothero, "On the Holy Road: The Beat Movement as Spiritual Protest," *Harvard Theological Review* 84: 2 (1991); Gary Snyder, *The Back Country,* 1968.

*See also* Eastern Culture; Reich, Wilhelm; Kerouac, Jack; Ginsberg, Allen; Snyder, Gary; Burroughs, William Seward; Parker, Charles Christopher; Young, Lester; Williams, William Carlos; Influences; New York City; Mountains, Beats in the; Environmentalism

## Rexroth, Kenneth (1905-1982)

Poet, critic, translator, journalist, activist, and visionary for the San Francisco Renaissance, Rexroth was a Renaissance man who inaugurated the Beat generation of writers in the mid-1950s. Rexroth's sixty-year career reached its height in the 1930s through 1950s as he set forth his left-leaning, social reform program. His elitism, however, eventually made him unattractive to younger audiences. Ginsberg, Kerouac, and other writers appealed to Americans coming of age in the late 1950s and 1960s, whose increasing disenchantment with "establishment" values found expression in the Beats' freewheeling style and search for enlightenment. Rexroth, a more disciplined, classically minded poet, wasn't looking for *satori*, the Buddhist secret of life, argues critic Morgan Gibson. Rexroth cherished "being for being's sake," transforming careful observations of the mundane into some of the most beautiful, deceptively simple poetry of the last century (qtd. in Meltzer, *Kenneth Rexroth,* 22). At the time of his death, Rexroth had published nearly sixty books, married four times, fathered two daughters, and become an expert on subjects ranging from Chinese and Japanese poetry, philosophy, medieval theology, and avant-garde art to classical languages, Buddhism, and jazz. *Living* was Rexroth's *satori*.

Son of Charles Rexroth, a pharmaceutical salesman, and Delia Reed, a fragile woman who inculcated in her son an abiding love of knowledge, Kenneth Charles Marion Rexroth was born in South Bend, Indiana, in 1905. A little over a decade later, his sickly mother died, and in 1919, his father, an alcoholic, followed. Already a precocious artist, poet, and translator, Rexroth went to live with his Aunt Minnie, Uncle Paul, and their five children, and immediately enrolled in the Chicago Institute of Art. But school wasn't for him, and he began educating himself by reading practically anything he could get his hands on and keeping company with a colorful array of artists, writers, jazz musicians, gangsters, and bums. When he wasn't discussing philosophy, art, and politics, he worked as a wrestler, soda jerk, horse wrangler, diet-book salesman, and reporter for a Wobbly newspaper; he also co-owned a brothel, for which he was briefly imprisoned. Rexroth lived in New York briefly but soon took to the open road and fell in love with the West Coast. In 1927, he settled in San Francisco, and for the next forty years made that city his home and a hotbed of literary activity.

California's mountains, forests, and ocean sparked Rexroth's interest in regional literature, and he helped to launch the San Francisco literary magazines *Circle* and *Ark* and to revive the *Illiterati*. His dreams for San Francisco did not end there, however. He wanted to import European culture—especially Paris's avant-garde intellectualism—to San Francisco. By the late 1940s, his home on Potero Hill became a mecca for sophisticated, Continental thought, serving disaffected academics and "disaffiliated" members of society as both a literary salon and an educational resource several nights a week.

In his early poetry, Rexroth experimented with surrealism and cubism, but largely abandoned these aesthetics later for more direct, passionate verse about nature, love, and revolution. Poetry is spoken word, he argues in *Assays*, and must therefore be read before a live audience (189). His best known poem, "Thou Shalt Not Kill" (1953), memorializes Dylan Thomas by holding cultural conformists responsible for his death. The poem became part of Rexroth's standard repertoire, and at Beat gatherings he read it to musical accompaniment.

In 1955, Rexroth presided over the 6 Gallery reading of new Beat poets, where Allen Ginsberg read "Howl" for the first time, while Jack Kerouac beat time on a wine jug. Rexroth unflaggingly supported many Beat writers yet severed personal ties with some of them after Kerouac caricatured him in *The Dharma Bums* (1958) as Rheinhold Cacoethes ("a bowtied wildhaired old anarchist"), and, along with Ginsberg, Snyder, and Whalen, caused a drunken brawl at one of Rexroth's literary soirees. When *Time* magazine dubbed Rexroth the leader of the Beats, he replied with characteristic wit and indignance that "an entomologist is not a bug" (qtd. in the introduction to Bradford Morrow's *Rexroth: Complete Poems*, xxvi).

By the late 1960s, Rexroth had won many prestigious literary awards and was finally enjoying widespread popularity; generally speaking, the end of his life was the happiest part. Most memorable of his later work is his erotic verse, especially his inventive 1978 collection *The Love Poems of Marichiko*, which is narrated in the voice of a Japanese poetess.

Rexroth died in 1982 of a massive heart attack after suffering two strokes that left him barely able to speak. His modest grave in Santa Barbara, on a hilltop overlooking his beloved ocean, bears an epitaph from *The Silver Swan* poems, part of his last series of works, and an exquisite example of meditative thought "crystallized" into a single, evocative image: "As the full moon rises/ The swan sings/ In sleep/ On the lake of the mind."

—*Sarah Pogell*

## Principal Works

Poetry: *The Dragon and the Unicorn*, 1952; *In Defense of the Earth*, 1956; *Natural Numbers: New and Selected Poems* and *The Homestead Called Damascus*, 1963; *The Collected Shorter Poems*, 1966; *The Heart's Garden/The Garden's Heart*, 1967; *The Collected Longer Poems*, 1968; *Sky, Sea, Birds, Trees, Earth, House, Beasts, Flowers*, 1973; *New Poems*, 1974; *Selected Poems*, 1984.

Translations: *One Hundred Poems from the Japanese*, 1955; *One Hundred Poems from the Chinese*, 1956; *Poems from the Greek Anthology*, 1962; *The Orchid Boat: Women Poets of China*, 1972; *Thirty Spanish Poems of Love and Exile*, 1973; *The Burning Heart: Women Poets of Japan*, 1977.

Prose: *Assays*, 1961; *An Autobiographical Novel*, 1966; *Classics Revisited*, 1968; *With Eye and Ear*,

*Bird in the Bush: Obvious Essays,* and *The Alternative Society: Essays from the Other World,* 1970; *American Poetry in the Twentieth Century,* 1971; *Communalism: From Its Origins to the Twentieth Century,* 1974.

## Bibliographical References

The major biography is Linda Hamalian's *A Life of Kenneth Rexroth,* 1991. Critical works include Morgan Gibson's *Kenneth Rexroth,* 1972, and *Revolutionary Rexroth, Poet of East-West Wisdom,* 1986; and Ken Knabb's *The Relevance of Rexroth,* 1990. David Meltzer's *San Francisco Beat: Talking with the Poets,* 2001 (Rexroth entry rpt. www.bopsecrets.org), includes wonderful interviews and conversations with Beat poets and critics. *The Modern American Poetry* website (www.english.uiuc.edu/maps/poets) includes the most up-to-date (and updated) scholarship on Rexroth by Bradford Morrow, Donald Guitierrez, Sam Hamill, and others. See also the introduction to Bradford Morrow, *Rexroth: Complete Poems,* 2003.

*See also* 6 Gallery Reading; Kerouac, Jack; San Francisco; Influences

## Rimbaud, Arthur (1854-1891)

Youthful yet influential French poet; a primary force in French symbolism, a forerunner of surrealism; an innovative poet who applied synesthesia and free verse in a body of work created during his youth; an artist whose turbulent and international experience ended when he died of cancer at age thirty-seven. A writer of interest to many Beat writers because of his visionary approach to poetry, his willingness to derange the senses in pursuit of new perceptions, his world travel, his youthful genius, his lack of concern for refinement in his appearance, and his homosexual passion.

In 1871, Rimbaud, a native of Charleville, arrived in Paris and began a relationship with Paul Verlaine. Their bohemian life together was unstable, and the affair, which included stays in Brussels and England, ended when Verlaine shot Rimbaud, injuring his wrist. Verlaine was prosecuted for the attack, and Rimbaud, reeling from the relationship's stormy end, wrote *A Season in Hell,* which was published in 1873. Apparently setting aside his life as an artist, Rimbaud began a life of international travel and business, including gunrunning in northern Africa. In early 1891, his leg became painful, and returning to Paris, he learned that the swelling was cancerous. Following an amputation, he died in Marseilles. Verlaine published Rimbaud's complete poetry in 1895.

This wildly artistic poet engaged the imagination of many writers who followed him, including Gregory Corso, Allen Ginsberg, Jack Kerouac, and Bob Dylan. Jack Kerouac's "Rimbaud," which is included in *The Portable Jack Kerouac,* ed. Ann Charters (1995), imaginatively discloses the details of Rimbaud's hectic and violent life, his homosexual relationship with Paul Verlaine, Rimbaud's gunrunning, and his desperate and agonizing death. Kerouac ends the poem by converting the biographical information into a cautionary tale: poets should learn from Rimbaud's experience and understand the futility of life.

Gregory Corso in "Marriage," which is included in *The Happy Birthday of Death* (1960), refers comically to Rimbaud, suggesting that Corso's effort to fit into a middle-class community as a married man might involve the display of a picture of Rimbaud on his lawnmower!

—*William Lawlor*

## Bibliographical References

Cecil Hackett, *Rimbaud: A Critical Introduction,* 1981; Graham Robb, *Rimbaud: A Biography,* 2000; Jean-Jacques Lefrere, *Arthur Rimbaud,* 2001.

## Rivers, Larry (1923-2002)

Painter with connections to both abstract expressionism and pop art; sculptor; actor; saxophonist. With Jack Kerouac, Allen Ginsberg, Gregory Corso, Peter Orlovsky, and David Amram, Larry Rivers performed in *Pull My Daisy* (1959), playing the role of Milo in the experimental film produced by Robert Frank and Alfred Leslie.

Born Yitzroch Loiza Grossberg, Larry Rivers began his artistic career as a jazz saxophonist and studied at the Juilliard School. In 1945 he began to paint in a style similar to abstract expressionism. In 1951, Rivers completed a degree in art at New York University. Rivers went on to paint images of family and friends and a series of historical paintings. One of his most famous paintings is *Washington Crossing the Delaware* (1953), a seven-by-nine foot canvas based on the nineteenth-century realistic painting by Emmanuel Leutze. By using softly defined images, Rivers broke from abstract expressionism and moved toward pop art, which is clearly in evidence in his series of paintings based on the image from the Camel cigarette package.

—*William Lawlor*

**Bibliographical References**

*Pull My Daisy,* 1959, is available on video. See also Larry Rivers, with Arnold Weinstein, *What Did I Do? The Unauthorized Autobiography,* 1992; an oversize volume with plates is Sam Hunter, *Larry Rivers,* 1971.

## Rocky Mount, North Carolina

A town of about 57,000 people in northeastern North Carolina; for several years the home of Jack Kerouac's sister, Nin; the location for several key passages in the writings of Jack Kerouac.

In late December 1948, Neal Cassady arrived at Nin's home in a 1949 Hudson Hornet. Neal worked out a plan to move furniture for Jack's mother from Rocky Mount, North Carolina, to Ozone Park, New York. A second trip was planned to drive Jack's mother to Ozone Park.

In 1956, Jack stayed with his sister and family in Rocky Mount. Kerouac enjoyed the early spring, and he meditated, imagining his spirit in previous incarnations. He helped his mother recover from a respiratory ailment by removing from her room some flowers, which a doctor later confirmed had caused an allergic reaction. This wise and perceptive action made Jack think that he might have divine powers. Despite Jack's joy in his spirituality, the down-to-earth neighbors could not accommodate his eccentricity and thought his uncombed, unshaven, barefoot lifestyle was crazy.

These episodes in Rocky Mount are recorded in Kerouac's fiction. In the opening of Part Two of *On the Road,* Sal Paradise speaks of traveling to Testament, Virginia, with his aunt, to visit his brother, Rocco, at Christmastime in 1948. Dean Moriarty arrives in a 1949 Hudson Hornet. The plan is to make two trips to Paterson, New Jersey, to assist Sal's aunt with her moving plans. The parallels to reality are evident, but in the novel the trips also give Kerouac the opportunity to disclose the newly philosophical Dean in contrast to Sal's sensible aunt.

In *The Dharma Bums,* Ray Smith arrives in Rocky Mount, North Carolina, where he visits his mother, sister, and brother-in-law. Ray enjoys the woods and the company of dogs. He savors wine and the television broadcast of midnight mass on Christmas Eve. Through meditation, Ray achieves spiritual transcendence, and even if the neighbors cannot understand, Ray is satisfied.

—*William Lawlor*

**Bibliographical References**

For the biographical background on Rocky Mount in 1948 and 1956, see Dennis McNally, *Desolate Angel,* 1979: 111–112, and 214–215. See the opening section of Part Two of *On the Road,* and pages 131–149 of *The Dharma Bums.*

***See also*** Kerouac, Jack; Cassady, Neal

## Rosenthal, Bob (1950–)

Poet, prose writer, and playwright; Allen Ginsberg's longtime secretary; trustee of the Allen Ginsberg Trust.

—*William Lawlor*

**Bibliographical References**

*Cleaning Up New York,* 1976, developed a cult following in the 1970s. Rosenthal's most recent book of poetry is *Viburnum,* 1994.

## Rosenthal, Irving (1930–)

Born in 1930, active as an author and editor in the fifties and sixties, Rosenthal has been obscure since 1970. He edited the *Chicago Review* before resigning—an obscenity trial occasioned by his publication of parts of Burroughs's *Naked Lunch* led to censorship. He then cofounded *Big Table* with Paul Carroll, continuing to edit and promote innovative Beat works. After spending a year in Morocco, Rosenthal moved to New York, where he wrote his one novel, *Sheeper* (New York: Grove, 1967), ostensibly a "memoir" of Sheeper, a young Jewish male living in New York. In terms of story, or character development, little action actually takes place: Sheeper takes and recovers from taking various drugs, enjoys practicing or thinking about sex with teenage boys, condemns his mother, and attends parties peopled by undisguised Beat figures such as Ginsberg, Huncke, and Trocchi. *Sheeper,* rather than advancing a conventional narrative, celebrates the discombobulated style of Beat literature. On page 69, Sheeper declares that he wanted the reader to always be aware of the printed line and wanted the reader's focus to shift again and again—this desire characterizes *Sheeper:* chapters shift from conventional prose to verse, dramatic dialogue, epistolary passages. One chapter is illustrated only by an engraving. *Sheeper* is self-conscious, profane, unapologetic, sexually explicit, and always compelling. Papers at the University of Delaware Library reveal unpublished sixties writings by Rosenthal: two further chapters of *Sheeper,* a short story, "Pastiche of the Golden Flower," and a translation of his Moroccan friend Mohammed ben Abdullah Yussufi's *First Yarmulkas.*

—*Kevin De Ornellas*

## Bibliographical References
Michael Bronski, *Gay Friction: Uncovering the Golden Age of Gay Male Pulps,* 2003: 367; Fred W. McDarrah, *Kerouac and Friends: A Beat Generation Album,* 1985: 148, 176, 278; Matt Theado, *The Beats: A Literary Reference,* 2003: 6, 103–106, 323; University of Delaware Library, "The Irving Rosenthal Papers," http://www.lib.udel.edu/ud/spec/findaids/rosnthal.htm.

*See also* Censorship; Carroll, Paul; Little Magazines

# Rumaker, Michael (1932–)

Michael Rumaker was born in 1932 in Philadelphia and raised in National Park, New Jersey. In 1952 he enrolled at Black Mountain College and graduated with honors in 1955. In 1956 he hitchhiked to San Francisco, just in time for the Beat movement's West Coast genesis. He moved to New York in 1958 and suffered a breakdown in October, resulting in his hospitalization until 1960. Rumaker went on to earn a master of fine arts degree in creative writing from Columbia University in 1969, and has taught writing at various New York colleges. Rumaker's earliest published works were the stories "The Truck" and "The Pipe," published in *Black Mountain Review* numbers 5 and 6, respectively. He wrote for a variety of periodicals in the late 1950s and early 1960s, and some of his short pieces were collected in *Exit 3 and Other Stories,* republished in the United States as *Gringos and Other Stories.* Most of these works are naturalistic and use a third-person narrator. With the publication of his first novel, *The Butterfly* (1962), Rumaker began to employ a more personal mode. This trend continued throughout the second phase of Rumaker's career, during which he fictionalizes his awakening to his own sexual identity in such novels as *A Day and a Night at the Baths* (1979) and *My First Satyrnalia* (1981). Rumaker also wrote one of the earliest serious reviews of Ginsberg's "Howl" in *Black Mountain Review* 7, and a theory of composition, "The Use of the Unconscious in Writing," in *Measure* 2.

—*Donovan S. Braud*

## Bibliographical References
George F. Butterick, "Michael Rumaker," *Dictionary of Literary Biography* 16, part 2, ed. Ann Charters, 1983; Leverett T. Smith, *Eroticizing the Nation: Michael Rumaker's Fiction,* 1999.

*See also* Black Mountain, North Carolina, and Black Mountain College

# S

## Saint Mark's Poetry Project

St. Mark's Poetry Project, located at Second Avenue and 10th Street in New York's East Village, is a forum for poetry readings, workshops, performance art, and publishing. Funding for the project was secured in 1966 when Reverend Michael Allen and New School professor Harry Silverstein acquired a federal grant for a church-related project intended to promote "creative arts for alienated youth" and the emerging "subculture of the Beat" (cited in Kane 132). Resulting from this initial support and now through private contributions, the project provides New York City's downtown community with four major resources: a film-making program, poetry readings, creative writing and drama workshops, and a publishing center. Historically, the project bridges the beatnik and hippie generations, and its notable featured writers have included Allen Ginsberg, Anne Waldman, Ted Berrigan, and Ed Sanders.

Poet/translator Paul Blackburn shaped the project's identity, recognizing a need for a poetry venue in the tradition of the Tenth Street Coffeehouse, Les Deux Megots, and Café Le Metro. Joel Oppenheimer served as the first director until August 1967. After becoming assistant director in April 1967, Anne Waldman directed the project from 1968 until 1978, while also helping publish *The World*, a mimeo-zine printed and sometimes funded by the project.

Built in 1799, the structure housing the project is the oldest building in the East Village and the second oldest church in Manhattan. Staffed entirely by poets, the project still features Wednesday- and Monday-night poetry readings, three weekly workshops, an annual four-day symposium, and a New Year's Day reading marathon.

—*Brian Gempp*

### Bibliographical Reference

Daniel Kane, *All Poets Welcome: The Lower East Side Poetry Scene in the 1960s*, 2003.

*See also* Waldman, Anne; New York City.

## Sampas, Sebastian (1922–1944)

Jack Kerouac's best friend as Jack came of age in Lowell, Massachusetts; younger brother of Stella Sampas, who married Kerouac in 1969; named Sambatis Sampatacacus at birth.

In "Author's Introduction," which is included in *Lonesome Traveler*, Kerouac says that at age seventeen he decided to become a writer because Sebastian Sampas influenced Kerouac to do so (v). Kerouac adds that Sampas died at Anzio.

In *The Town and the City*, Sebastian is Alexander Panos, and in this novel Kerouac reveals the extreme pain he felt when he learned of Sampas's death by describing the response of Peter to the death of his friend Alex. In *Vanity of Duluoz*, Sebastian is Sabby Savakis.

—*William Lawlor*

**Bibliographical References**

Warren French in *Jack Kerouac: Novelist of the Beat Generation*, 1986, explains the connection between Kerouac and Sebastian Sampas on pages 123–125, exploring both the biographical and fictional details. Ellis Amburn in *Subterranean Kerouac*, 1998, suggests that Kerouac and Sampas were linked homosexually, but the accuracy of Amburn's statements has been questioned.

*See also* Kerouac, Jack; Sampas Kerouac, Stella

## Sampas Kerouac, Stella (1918–1990)

Third wife of Jack Kerouac. In September 1966, Kerouac's mother suffered a stroke, and Kerouac turned to the trusted Sampas family for comfort and assistance. Jack and Stella had known each other for many years and had communicated regularly; she had kept track of his career. They married

on 19 November 1966. Kerouac's *Vanity of Duluoz* (1968) is dedicated to Stella.

**Bibliographical References**

Dennis McNally on pages 322–323 of *Desolate Angel*, 1979, explains the basis for the marriage between Stella Sampas and Jack Kerouac. Tom Clark offers his account of the marriage in *Jack Kerouac*, 1984, on pages 204–205. A picture of the couple appears on page 210 of Clark's biography.

*See also* Kerouac, Jack; Sampas, Sebastian

## San Francisco

San Francisco's North Beach neighborhood, specifically the area around Grant Avenue, Green Street, and Broadway, was the de facto headquarters of the Beat Generation for most of the 1950s. Hipsters often referred to North Beach as simply "the Beach," or "the scene." Adjacent to Chinatown, and

Jack Kerouac's gravestone pays tribute to Stella, his third wife. (Allen Ginsberg/Corbis)

nestled between Russian and Telegraph Hills, North Beach is part of the historic Barbary Coast. In the early 1950s, this area was predominantly ethnic Italian and filled with inexpensive bars, coffee shops, restaurants, and low-rent, cold-water flats. San Francisco's long history as a bohemian outpost attracted those who, by choice or by force, lived on the margins of society. Over the years, this group included a number of writers such as Oscar Wilde, Jack London, and Joaquin Miller. The city's Chinatown and trading ties to the East also allowed its inhabitants access to Eastern cultures and religions, including Zen Buddhism, Taoism, and other alternatives to erstwhile American Puritanism. In the years following World War II, all of these factors united to form a liberal, tolerant city that was a hotbed of innovation, inquiry, collaboration, and radical experimentation in many arts.

In 1952, William Burroughs and Jack Kerouac left New York for San Francisco. Allen Ginsberg followed two years later. They arrived in a city where poets were already a strong presence in the cultural scene. Kenneth Rexroth and Robert Duncan were at the center of two popular weekly salons, whose attendees formed the core of the San Francisco Poetry Renaissance. The Beats' presence energized and galvanized the poetry movement in the city, transforming it from the traditional salon format and more completely engaging it with the spaces of the city, particularly North Beach's bars and restaurants.

The term *beatnik* originated in San Francisco. Herb Caen, longtime columnist for the *San Francisco Examiner*, first printed this amalgam of "Beat" and "Sputnik" as a humorously derogatory name for the legions of disaffected youth flocking to North Beach. During the early decades of the Cold War, adding *-nik* to the ends of words was a popular trend that implied communist associations. "Beatnik" created a noun out of what had previously been an adjective, which allowed for the term to be applied with less rigor and divorced it from its original associations with beatitude and with being "beat"—as in "spent," "exhausted," or "had." This subtle shift also marked a move away from the core literary group and recognized the popularity of a trendy, temporary Beat lifestyle that ballooned in the later years of the 1950s. By 1958, tourists could take bus tours of North Beach that highlighted the Place, City Lights Bookstore, Vesuvio's, and the Co-existence Bagel Shop.

Located at 546 Grant Avenue in North Beach, the Place was a popular Beat restaurant and bar managed by Black Mountain College graduates Knute Stiles and Leo Krikorian. They hosted a weekly "Blabbermouth Night" on Mondays with an open-mike format. Usually there was a designated theme and each participant was given three minutes to improvise. Blabbermouth Nights were well-attended events at which poetry was presented as a public performance. The Co-Existence Bagel Shop, a combination delicatessen and bar located at 1398 Grant, the intersection of Grant and Green, also attracted a following among the Beats. Bob Kaufman's poem *Bagel Shop Jazz* describes the regulars who gathered there. These spaces frequently presented poetry readings featuring their patrons, as did nearby venues the Cellar and the Coffee Gallery.

Vesuvio's bar and 12 Adler Place were owned by Henri Lenoir, who nurtured and cultivated the city's struggling artists, poets, and musicians. Vesuvio's was located on Broadway, across a small alley from City Lights Bookstore. Lenoir decorated his establishments with avant-garde artwork, hosted poetry readings, and featured jazz bands. His bars became popular among the Beats, and Kerouac was practically a fixture at Vesuvio's. In the early 1950s, Lenoir famously employed the artist Wally Hedrick to sit in the window dressed in full beard, turtleneck, and sandals and create improvisational drawings and paintings. Later in the decade, Lenoir capitalized on the popularity of North Beach's Beat scene by selling "beatnik kits" to the tourists. In 1988, Adler Place was renamed Jack Kerouac Alley.

In 1953, City Lights became the country's first all-paperback bookstore and a Beat refuge. Founded by Lawrence Ferlinghetti and Peter Martin, the store specialized in small-press publications, as well as literary and political magazines and newspapers. Two years later, City Lights Publishing was developed. The Pocket Poet Series was launched with a collection of poems by Ferlinghetti titled *Pictures of the*

*Gone World.* Shortly thereafter City Lights published Kenneth Rexroth's *30 Spanish Poems of Love and Exile,* followed by Kenneth Patchen's *Poems of Humor and Protest.* But it was when Ferlinghetti published Allen Ginsberg's *Howl and Other Poems* that the Pocket Poet Series, Ferlinghetti, Ginsberg, and City Lights garnered national attention. The graphic language and sexual imagery of "Howl," including descriptions of homosexual experiences, led to obscenity charges being filed against the publisher, but the book was cleared by the court, and freedom of expression was protected. "Howl" had many ties to San Francisco: Ginsberg wrote the piece while he was living on Montgomery Street in North Beach, and his first performance of it in a local art gallery is legendary.

The 6 Gallery on Fillmore Street was founded in 1954 by artists and poets including Wally Hedrick, Hayward King, Deborah Remington, John Allen Ryan, David Simpson, and Jack Spicer. The space had been converted from a garage by the poets Robert Duncan and Harry Jacobus and the artist Jess who ran the King Ubu Gallery there between 1952 and 1954. In 1955, Ferlinghetti reported to the journal *Arts Digest* that the 6 Gallery was committed to showing painting and poetry together. The small stage in the back of the gallery often was a venue for readings.

On 7 October 1955, Ginsberg shared this stage with five other poets and some plaster sculptures by Fred Martin. Also reading that evening were Michael McClure, Philip Whalen, Philip Lamantia, and Gary Snyder. Ginsberg presented "Howl." Lengthy, rhythmic, unpunctuated lines spilled forth as he spoke while swaying back and forth, often closing his eyes and, by the end, weeping. Throughout the reading, Kerouac, sitting on the edge of the low stage and thus not visible to much of the standing audience, chanted "Go!, Go!, Go!," encouraging Ginsberg and keeping the pace and energy flowing. Kerouac's *The Dharma Bums* includes a thinly disguised fictional account of this night. In *Dharma Lion* (1992), Michael Schumacher notes that the next day, Ferlinghetti wrote to Ginsberg "I greet you at the beginning of a great career. When do I get the manuscript?" The note, a genuine offer for

publication through City Lights, was also an homage to Ginsberg's mentor, Walt Whitman. Exactly a century earlier, Whitman received these words form Ralph Waldo Emerson: "I greet you at the beginning of a great career, which must yet have a long foreground somewhere for such a start" (216). For Ferlinghetti, Ginsberg and the Beat writers were the inheritors of the American poetry tradition. Ginsberg was undoubtedly the highlight of that evening at the 6 Gallery, but the local poets who read their work are often credited with officially launching the San Francisco Poetry Renaissance that night.

By 1957 the attention focused on San Francisco's poets was such that the literary magazine *Evergreen Review* dedicated the entirety of its 169-page second issue to the "San Francisco Scene." This issue featured poems by Ginsberg, Kerouac, Whalen, Ferlinghetti, Snyder, Spicer, Rexroth, and McClure, among others, with additional reportage on the city's artists and jazz musicians. However, by this time, Ginsberg, Kerouac, and Burroughs, along with Neal Cassady and Peter Orlovsky had left the city.

Ferlinghetti's "Dog" appeared in *A Coney Island of the Mind,* published by New Directions in 1958. In this poem, the dog is uninhibited as it walks briskly from San Francisco's Meat Market to Chinatown, past the Romeo Ravioli Factory to Coit Tower. Ferlinghetti follows the animal, an outsider, a being whose presence is acknowledged then forgotten, but whose thoughts are insightful, and at times, sharp and politically focused. The "dog" therefore represents the beatnik. In tracing the path of the dog, Ferlinghetti paints a portrait of the city using vivid imagery and specific landmarks: "Romeo Ravioli Factory" in North Beach, and Coit Tower on Telegraph Hill. Coit Tower is a 210-foot monument to firefighters who helped extinguish the 1906 fires. Erected in 1933, the interior of the tower is decorated with murals painted by artists for the Federal Art Project of the Works Progress Administration. These murals are widely recognized as the prototype for the decade of New Deal art that followed. However, the murals were widely criticized for their content that allegedly included leftist propaganda. Ferlinghetti's juxtaposition within the poem of references to Coit Tower and then Congressman Doyle of the House Un-American Activities Committee is a commentary on the state of American politics and policies.

Gary Snyder, an acclaimed poet of the San Francisco Renaissance, was an early activist in nature conservancy and environmental awareness. A scholar of Chinese and Japanese culture, and later a Zen Buddhist practitioner, avid mountain climber, and advocate for Native Americans, Snyder was responsible for engaging the Beats with Eastern religions. His poetry celebrated the abundance of natural riches in the San Francisco Bay Area, and often included critiques of human effects on the environment. "The Real Work" is written on the occasion of an experience in a rowboat near Alcatraz and Angel Island. The poem is a testament to the abundance of the bay, including sea lions, birds, and sunlight piercing misty air, but the presence of an oil tanker that has delivered its cargo is ominous. Snyder is specific about the setting of the poem, which references Alcatraz and Angel Island and whose histories lend added meaning to the poem. Angel Island was home to the Miwok tribe before the arrival of the Spaniards in California. Following many years of Spanish control of the island, it served as both a U.S. military base and the site of two government facilities, including quarantine and immigration stations. Alcatraz has a similar history of Spanish occupation and, later, American governmental occupation. Alcatraz was the site of the West Coast's first military fort and first lighthouse. During the 1890s, U.S. forces imprisoned several Hopi Indians on the island. From 1934 to 1963, the fort became the infamous prison known as "The Rock." In 1969 the island again was occupied by Native Americans as an act of civil disobedience and an attempt to reclaim from the U.S. government the intertwined history of their people and the island. Snyder's early involvement with issues that we now identify with the grassroots movements of the sixties deeply affected his peers. He was the inspiration for what is considered one of Kerouac's strongest works, *The Dharma Bums.*

Around 1957, San Francisco's artists and poets shifted their attention away from North Beach, which was becoming overrun with poseurs and tourists. They relocated to the Fillmore Street area, a predominantly African American neighborhood that was in the process of being demolished as part of a federal urban renewal project. Lower Fillmore Street was nicknamed "Swing Street" for its profusion of jazz clubs, among them Club Alabam, the Congo, Jimbo's Bop City, and the Long Beat. Billie Holiday and Dinah Washington were frequently featured singers, and the roster of famous musicians who played nightly is extensive. A few blocks to the north, a small apartment complex with four units at 2322 Fillmore Street, owned by the saxophonist Paul Beattie, became home to many artists and poets, including Michael and Joanna McClure, Wally Hedrick and his wife (the painter Jay DeFeo), and the painters Bill and Joan Brown, among others. The nearby 6 Gallery ensured that for the rest of the decade Fillmore joined North Beach as a center for experimental art and poetry.

Starting in the late fifties, San Francisco became known for its assemblage art. Assemblage carried the principles of collage fully into three dimensions, resulting in a sculptural object. Whereas collage consists of glued papers and fabrics, assemblage uses all types of found materials. During the late fifties and early sixties, San Francisco's Fillmore neighborhood, largely in ruins from urban renewal, provided its artists with plenty of free materials from which to create assemblages. Bruce Conner, George Herms, Wallace Berman, and Wally Hedrick were at the forefront of the assemblage movement in San Francisco. Creating art out of the detritus of the city and elevating mundane, cast-off objects to a higher status was not dissimilar to Ginsberg's proclamation in the footnote to "Howl," "The skin is holy! The nose is holy! . . . Everything is holy! everybody's holy! everywhere is holy!" In 1961 the Museum of Modern Art in New York presented an exhibition titled "The Art of Assemblage" featuring the work of these artists.

—*Rebecca Young Schoenthal*

## Bibliographical References
Historical Accounts: James Campbell, *This is the Beat Generation: New York, San Francisco, Paris,*

1999; Richard Cándida-Smith, *Utopia and Dissent: Art, Poetry and Politics in California*, 1995; Michael Davidson, *The San Francisco Renaissance: Poetics and Community at Mid-Century*, 1989; Don Herron, *The Literary World of San Francisco and Its Environs*, 1985; Michael McClure, *Scratching the Beat Surface: Essays on New Vision from Blake to Kerouac*, 1982; John Natsoulas, *The Beat Generation Galleries and Beyond*, 1996; Michael Schumacher, *Dharma Lion*, 1992.

Primary Sources: *Evergreen Review* 2 (1957); Allen Ginsberg, *Howl and Other Poems*, 1956; Jack Kerouac, *The Dharma Bums*, 1958; William C. Seitz, *The Art of Assemblage*, 1968.

**See also** Censorship; San Francisco Renaissance; Kerouac, Jack; Ginsberg, Allen; Burroughs, William Seward; Ferlinghetti, Lawrence; McClure, Michael; Kaufman, Bob; Patchen, Kenneth; Spicer, Jack; Painting; Sculpture

## San Francisco Renaissance

The San Francisco Renaissance refers to the flourishing of literary activity in the Bay Area following World War II and lasting into the 1960s. For many commentators, the San Francisco Renaissance is synonymous with the Beat movement, due to the significant presence of Allen Ginsberg, Jack Kerouac, Lawrence Ferlinghetti, and others who lived in the area at various periods of time. Ginsberg's "Howl" received its first public reading in San Francisco in 1955 and was published the following year by Ferlinghetti's City Lights Books. Several of Kerouac's novels (*The Dharma Bums, On the Road*) were set in the city, and poets who came to San Francisco from elsewhere—Michael McClure, Gary Snyder, Lew Welch, Bob Kaufman, Diane di Prima, Philip Whalen—were usually identified with the Beat movement. But there was a much larger literary community already in place before Ginsberg and company came to San Francisco in the early 1950s. This community included longtime residents such as Robert Duncan, Jack Spicer, Kenneth Patchen, Helen Adam, Kenneth Rexroth, Robin Blaser, Philip Lamantia, William Everson, Josephine Myles, James Broughton, and Madeline Gleason, many of whom had established their literary careers in the 1940s. The confluence of several generations of writers, combined with the city's long history of social iconoclasm, political activism, and bohemian lifestyles helped to create a hospitable climate for innovative writing during the Cold War.

San Francisco had long been a center of artistic innovation and countercultural activities, beginning in the 1880s and 1890s when writers such as Jack London, Frank Norris, Ambrose Bierce, George Sterling, Joaquin Miller, Edwin Markham, and Bret Harte created a Barbary Coast bohemia. Although the earthquake of 1906 put a damper on cultural activity until the 1915 Panama Pacific International Exhibition, the city maintained a buoyant artistic spirit through the roaring twenties and radical 1930s. World War II saw significant demographic changes to the city that were influential in launching an artistic revival that, for the first time, competed with activities in Chicago and New York. The war industry brought factories and housing to the Bay Area, expanding growth in the suburbs and providing new wealth for San Francisco's economy. The relaxing of restrictions on Asian immigration brought waves of new residents from China, and many Latinos and African Americans who had come to the city as part of the war effort stayed on and developed significant enclaves within the city. Soldiers who were stationed in Alameda or the Presidio remained as well, many of them completing their college degrees on the G.I. Bill. The California School of Fine Arts, San Francisco State College, Mills College, the University of California, Berkeley, and many other colleges expanded enrollments and provided an intellectual and creative base within which writers, artists, and academics flourished.

Seeds of a postwar literary renaissance could be seen in the late 1940s when a trio of young poets attending the University of California, Berkeley—Robert Duncan, Robin Blaser, and Jack Spicer—began to formulate a self-conscious literary movement in direct opposition to the English department curriculum. Through a series of readings and lectures, the trio formed a brotherhood of gay poets whose love of modernist art, medievalism, and occult science resulted in a latter-day Pre-

Raphaelite brotherhood. This Berkeley Renaissance, as they called it, was augmented and encouraged by the presence of Kenneth Rexroth, whose home in San Francisco was a gathering place for radicals, Zen monks, poets, and artists unaffiliated with the local academic community. Magazines such as George Leite's *Circle, Goad*, the anarchist journal *Ark*, and the Auerhahn and Bern Porter presses provided significant publishing venues. The libertarian circle, with Rexroth at its center, invigorated a radical political debate, out of which emerged KPFA/Pacifica Radio under the direction of Lewis Hill. Poetry readings at San Francisco State College organized by Robert Duncan and Madeleine Gleason, weekly readings at Duncan's communal house in Berkeley, and the burgeoning arts scene during Douglas MacAgy's tenure at the California School for Fine Arts (now called the San Francisco Art Institute) provided a lively pre-Beat arts environment.

With the arrival of the Beats in the 1950s and through the formation of Ferlinghetti's City Lights books, Donald Allen's Four Seasons Press, and magazines such as the *San Francisco Review, Open Space, Beatitude, Foot*, and the 1957 "San Francisco Scene" issue of *Evergreen Review*, the Renaissance moved into its second, more public phase. North Beach became a bohemian mecca, its nightly revels eagerly documented in local papers (the *San Francisco Chronicle*'s columnist, Herb Caen, coined the term *beatnik*) and national periodicals (*Esquire, Playboy*, the *Nation, Partisan Review*), where the focus was less on literary and more on lifestyle issues. The bars and coffeehouses of Grant Avenue became centers of activity, with jazz concerts, art exhibits, and free-form poetry readings going full time, while tour busses cruised the neighborhood. Not everyone was pleased by the attention, and certain poets—Kenneth Rexroth, Robert Duncan, and Jack Spicer in particular—were openly hostile to what they perceived as a Beat diversion of their hopes for a true literary revival.

With the increase in touristic curiosity about beatniks, several of the poets who were significant to the scene left for Asia (Snyder and Whalen spent long periods of time in Japan) or the East Coast (Ginsberg and Kerouac returned to New York). Robert Duncan maintained closer ties with Black Mountain colleagues Charles Olson, Denise Levertov, and Robert Creeley. William Everson had been a lay brother in the Dominican Brotherhood since 1949 and lived as Brother Antoninus in the priory in Marin County and then at the College of St. Albert the Great in Oakland. But younger poets came to town (Ron Loewinsohn, Richard Brautigan, Stan Persky, David Meltzer) and carried the San Francisco Renaissance forward into the 1960s.

Although the poetics of the San Francisco Renaissance varied from poet to poet, there are certain discernable continuities within the movement. At its base was a romantic revival set in direct opposition to then-current New Critical orthodoxies. Robert Duncan, Allen Ginsberg, and Michael McClure deployed a vatic, at times bardic, idiom that looked back to Shelley, Blake, and Whitman. Gary Snyder, Lew Welch, and Philip Whalen used an economical phrasing influenced by Poundian imagism. Kenneth Rexroth and William Everson wrote long, philosophical landscape poems reminiscent of Jeffers and Wordsworth. Lawrence Ferlinghetti and Bob Kaufman perfected a kind of populist jeremiad that merged Rimbaud and surrealism. Helen Adam, Madeleine Gleason, and James Broughton wrote ballads, masques, and lyrics modeled on Burns and Blake. Surrealism was an influence in many of the poets, most specifically in the work of Philip Lamantia, but manifest as well in early Duncan, Jack Spicer, and Bob Kaufman. What differentiated the neo-Romanticism of the San Francisco poets from their counterparts at Black Mountain or New York was a self-conscious fusion of Romanticism and modernism that had been sundered by New Critical strictures against fallacies of intention and expression. Whereas academic critics of modernism tended to see the work of Eliot, Pound, or Williams as marking a break with Romanticism, poets such as Robert Duncan or Kenneth Rexroth claimed allegiance to a much more eclectic lineage, one that would include Blake and Shelley, Nerval and Whitman, the Dadaists and the objectivists.

The expressivism of San Francisco poets was underwritten by forms of pantheism and numinous presence. Charles Altieri has characterized this trend in postwar poetry as a species of Romantic immanence by which meditative, open-form poems create links between the creative act and generative forces in nature. By testifying to a vital world, by using the poem as a series of responses to the quotidian, the poet participates in a textual sacrament. Allen Ginsberg's ecstatic discovery of a begrimed sunflower in the railroad yards in "Sunflower Sutra," which is included in *Howl and Other Poems* (1956), transforms the flower into a metaphor for redeemed humanity: "We're not our skin of grime, we're not our dread bleak dusty imageless locomotive, we're all beautiful golden sunflowers inside" (38). And Robert Duncan thematicizes this poetics in the first poem of *The Opening of the Field* (1960):

> Often I am Permitted to Return to a Meadow
> as if it were a scene made-up by the mind,
> that is not mine, but is a made place,
> that is mine, it is so near to the heart
> an eternal pasture folded in all thought. (7)

For Duncan and Ginsberg, poetry is not something imposed on an inert world but a form of active testimony to forces and powers immanent in nature. The poet is "permitted" to enter the meadow of the poem where he encounters "an eternal pasture folded in all thought." Jack Spicer's Yeatsian poetics of dictation, William Everson's Jungian archetypalism, or Gary Snyder's shamanistic poetics are all variations on the theme. For these poets, the ideal of spontaneity and immediacy ("first thought, best thought," is Ginsberg's succinct formula) are not ends in themselves but means to greater participation with natural forms.

One of the lasting legacies of this neo-Romantic impulse was the emphasis on the poetry reading—occasionally accompanied by music—as the ultimate forum for poetry. For many commentators, the San Francisco Renaissance *begins* with the 6 Gallery reading of 1955 and continues through North Beach events in bars and coffee houses at the Place, Gino Carlos, the Coffee Gallery, Fugazi's, the Co-Existence Bagel Shop, and other venues. Rexroth, Patchen, Kerouac, and Fer-

linghetti read their poetry to jazz accompaniment. Bob Kaufman read his poems on street corners. Michael McClure roared his "Ghost Tantras" to the lions at the San Francisco Zoo (recorded in a PBS Documentary). Spicer organized "blabbermouth night" at a local bar, the Place, where poets created spontaneous Dada poems for a prize. For San Francisco writers, the poem was a public event, something to be taken off the page and put on the stage. "We must stop sitting on the pot of culture," Spicer advised in the *Occident* (Fall 1949). "There is more of Orpheus in Sophie Tucker than in R. P. Blackmur; we have more to learn from George M. Cohan than from John Crowe Ransom" (43).

This performative poetics can be linked to a strong activist political stance manifest in all of the poets in the Bay region. Kenneth Rexroth had been active as a union organizer and worked extensively with neighborhood community groups. William Everson, Richard Moore, and Lewis Hill were conscientious objectors during World War II, serving in the Waldport CO camp in Oregon. Robert Duncan, James Broughton, Allen Ginsberg, and Jack Spicer were significant figures in the emerging gay rights movement. Michael McClure, Joanne Kyger, Gary Snyder, Diane di Prima, and Philip Whalen were among the most vocal proponents of the early ecology and environmental movement. Many of the poets (Rexroth, Ferlinghetti, Duncan, Lamantia) were anarcho-pacifists who protested the expansion of nuclear weapons throughout their lives. Skeptical critics of the period such as Norman Podhoretz or Irving Howe tended to castigate the Beats for being apolitical, but by "political" they usually meant doctrinaire (whether Democratic or anti-Stalinist) party politics. While it is true that San Francisco poets were not much interested in official political positions, they were hardly apathetic. San Francisco writers were well aware of the region's long history of political activism, beginning with the general strike of 1934, the anti-HUAC demonstrations of the 1940s, the civil rights protests at Mel's Drive-in, and the free speech movement of the early 1960s. Many of the magazines of the period featured political commentary alongside of poetry, and readings throughout the era were often benefits for various social and political causes.

Along with strong political commitments by the poets, one can see a resonant strain of populism that runs through the San Francisco scene. Bob Kaufman was the embodiment of this tendency, composing poems on the spot, reading them on bar tables or getting arrested on Grant Avenue for disorderly conduct. He wrote poems that merged surreal views of midcentury America with savvy observations on local bohemia. For example, in "Bagel Shop Jazz," which is reprinted in *The Outlaw Bible of American Poetry*, ed. Alan Kaufman (1999), he observes

Shadow people, projected on coffee-shop walls,
Memory formed echoes of a generation past
Beating into now.
Nightfall creatures, eating each other
Over a noisy cup of coffee. (65)

Whether through the street poetry of Bob Kaufman, the bop jeremiads of Lawrence Ferlinghetti, or the ballads of Helen Adam, poets in San Francisco maintained a debt to popular traditions that look back to the frontier poetry of Joaquin Miller and the naturalist writing of Bret Harte or Jack London, and that debt continues today in the lively slam, hiphop, and spoken-word scene.

Although the Beats tended to embody a kind of macho, misogynist ethos, the larger San Francisco scene offered a range of alternative identities to the heterosexual, patriarchal family of the Cold War Years. Women poets such as Helen Adam, Joanne Kyger, Josephine Miles, Diane di Prima, and Madeleine Gleason published significant work in a masculinist era, and they often ran poetry readings, published magazines, and participated in the North Beach bar scene. Helen Adam's play, *San Francisco's Burning,* Joanne Kyger's *Tapestry and the Web,* and Diane di Prima's *Dinners and Nightmares* were central documents of the period, the contributions of which are now being recognized in books such as Ronna Johnson's and Nancy Grace's *Girls Who Wore Black* and Brenda Knight's *Women of the Beat Generation.*

The longer tradition of nontraditional lifestyles in the Bay region created a climate for both gay men and women to live, if not out of the closet, at least within a more tolerant urban community, flanked by a nascent homophile movement. The era's McCarthyist paranoia and pervasive homophobia curtailed a good deal of public activity, but there were numerous gay and lesbian bars where alliances could be formed. Among the most important early documents of gay liberation was Robert Duncan's "The Homosexual in Society" (1944), which was published in *Politics* and criticized not only the homophobia of society in general but the closed, isolationist features of homosexual culture. The 1957 obscenity trial of Allen Ginsberg's *Howl and Other Poems* generated a new awareness of openly homosexual lifestyles when Judge Clayton Horn declared that the title poem's depiction of homosexuality was "not without socially redeeming importance." At the end of the era, Judy Grahn's *Common Woman Poems* became a manifesto for feminist and lesbian writers such as Susan Griffen, Ntozake Shange, and Jessica Hagedorn. Many of these literary events in North Beach were followed actively by the early homophile movement such as the Daughters of Bilitis and the Mattachine Society, in whose publications can be found editorials and reviews of Renaissance books and readings. All of these events preceded the Stonewall Revolution of the 1970s but they helped prepare the ground for the later gay and lesbian liberation movement in the Castro district.

The San Francisco Renaissance may have begun as a hoped-for aesthetic revival in the New Critical and Cold War doldrums, but it ended in providing a much larger series of cultural and social alternatives that continued throughout the 1960s and 1970s. To be sure, not all of these later developments were in concert. Significant ideological differences separated the youth culture of the Haight-Ashbury from more militant black and Latino nationalist movements of the late 1960s. But these movements could look back to fruitful coalitions that developed in the late 1940s through the 1950s in which art, politics, and lifestyle coincided. In *The Collected Books of Jack Spicer,* ed. Robin Blaser (1975), Jack Spicer spoke for many of his generation when he celebrated the "city that we create in our bartalk or in our fuss and fury about each other [that] is in an utterly mixed and mirrored way an image of the city. A return from exile" (156). For many writers of the San Francisco Renaissance, the possibility of a redeemed polis was possible, not in the world of intellectual consensus and corporatization, but in the localized "bartalk" and contentions of an oppositional culture.

—*Michael Davidson*

## Bibliographical References

Charles Altieri, *Enlarging the Temple: New Directions in American Poetry during the 1960's*, 1979; Richard Cándida-Smith, *Utopia and Dissent: Art, Poetry, and Politics in California*, 1995; Michael Davidson, *The San Francisco Renaissance: Poetics and Community at Mid-Century*, 1989; Robert Duncan, *The Opening of the Field*, 1960; Lewis Ellingham and Kevin Killian, *Poet, Be Like God: Jack Spicer and the San Francisco Renaissance*, 1998; Lawrence Ferlinghetti and Nancy Peters, *Literary San Francisco*, 1980; Warren French, *The San Francisco Poetry Renaissance, 1955–1960*, 1991; Bob Kaufman, "Bagel Shop Jazz," in *The Outlaw Bible of American Poetry*, ed. Alan Kaufman, 1999; David Meltzer, ed., *San Francisco Beat*, 2001; David Meltzer, *The San Francisco Poets*, 1971.

*See also* Kerouac, Jack; Ginsberg, Allen; Ferlinghetti, Lawrence; San Francisco; Snyder, Gary; Spicer, Jack; Rexroth, Kenneth; Duncan, Robert; Lamantia, Philip; Everson, William; Black Mountain, North Carolina, and Black Mountain College; Music; di Prima, Diane; Patchen, Kenneth; Caen, Herb; Beat and Beatnik; Cold War; Influences; Little Magazines; Publishers; Censorship

## Sanders, Ed (1939–)

One of the most prominent second-generation Beats, Ed Sanders initially caught the attention of the major Beat writers as the editor of *Fuck You/ A Magazine of the Arts* starting in February 1962. This mimeographed journal published W. H. Auden, Norman Mailer, Allen Ginsberg, Gregory Corso, Diane di Prima, Lawrence Ferlinghetti, Michael McClure, Frank O'Hara, Joel Oppenheimer, Gary Snyder, Philip Whalen, John Wieners, Robert Creeley, Charles Olson, Paul Blackburn, Diane Wakoski, and William S. Burroughs. In late 1964, Sanders opened the Peace Eye Bookstore. The bookstore became a haven for the Beats. Seen as a major link between the Beats and the hippie movement, Sanders was tremendously influenced by Ginsberg's "Howl" and Jack Kerouac's *On the Road*. Later in his career, Sanders was heavily influenced by Burroughs and found within the Beat movement a means to express his growing political awareness.

Sanders is a multitalented artist. His book *The Family: The Story of Charles Manson's Dune Buggy Attack Battalion* (1971) is a classic of the true-crime genre. In addition to being a respected writer, he is also one of the founding members (along with Tuli Kupferberg) of the influential folk-rock band the Fugs, who started by playing at places such as di Prima's American Theatre for Poets and recorded six albums from 1965 to 1969. Perhaps most importantly, Sanders has consistently championed moral causes and has remained politically active.

Born James Edward Sanders in Kansas City, Missouri, on 17 August 1939, Sanders was class president in high school and an athlete, playing both basketball and football. Though raised to belong to the suburban masses, Sanders went through dramatic changes after the death of his mother and his discovery of Ginsberg's *Howl and Other Poems*. He left the University of Missouri and hitchhiked to New York City in the spring of 1958, entering New York University and quickly becoming part of the Beat scene. He was arrested for swimming in front of a submarine and for protesting at a Polaris submarine base in 1961. The latter arrest resulted in *Poem from Jail*, his first work of poetry, published by City Lights.

In May 1961 he walked 650 miles from Ohio to New York in the San Francisco-to-Moscow Walk for Peace organized by the Committee for Nonviolent Action. He married Miriam Kittell on 6 October 1961. They have a daughter, Deirdre. In 1962 he participated in the Walk for Peace, which started in Nashville, Tennessee, and ended eight weeks later in Washington, D.C. He received a BA in Greek from New York University in 1963.

It was Sanders's Fuck You Press that published in 1964 Burroughs's *Roosevelt after Inauguration.* In 1965, Sanders was arrested for obscenity by the New York City Police Department and successfully defended himself from the charges with the support of the American Civil Liberties Union, but he eventually lost his magazine and bookstore because of this harassment.

He was an active participant, chanting an exorcism at the 1967 March on the Pentagon to protest the Vietnam War. In 1968, with Jerry Rubin and Abbie Hoffman, Sanders founded the Youth International Party (Yippies). Sanders was present at the Democratic National Convention in Chicago in August 1968 as a representative of the Yippies. In September 1968 he appeared with Kerouac on William F. Buckley's *Firing Line.* Though the drunk Kerouac was verbally abusive to Sanders during the taping, they went out for drinks with Ginsberg after the show and were friendly on what turned out to be Kerouac's last night with Beat writers.

From May to November 1970, Sanders covered the Charles Manson trial for the *Los Angeles Free Press.* In an effort to take the mythical interpretations out of the story of Charles Manson, Sanders conducted numerous interviews and painstaking research that resulted in his book *The Family: The Story of Charles Manson's Dune Buggy Attack Battalion.* In "Ed Sanders," in *The Beats: Literary Bohemians in Postwar America,* ed. Ann Charters (1983), George F. Butterick writes, "He covered the story not to be fashionable or because of its intrinsic sensationalism but to see if his own language and beliefs might not have been co-opted, victimized. In one sense the book was a culmination and a watershed for Sanders, as Manson had shattered illusions about the natural goodness of the new youth and exposed the limitations of Yippie 'Free'" (473–486). After Nixon's reelection in 1972, despite Sanders's efforts to prevent it with a book he wrote with Abbie Hoffman and Jerry Rubin called *Vote!,* Sanders returned to his memories of the Beat era and began working on *Tales of Beatnik Glory.* With the publication of *Investigative Poetry* in 1976, Sanders expanded his conception of poetics. By "investigative poetry" Sanders means poetry that attempts to communicate information, often political, in poetic form while taking back for the poet the responsibility for depicting history. His class on investigative poetry at the Naropa Institute's Jack Kerouac School of Disembodied Poetics in 1977 resulted in the publication of *The Party* in 1980, which focused on the disturbing treatment of W. S. Merwin by Chögyam Trungpa in the fall of 1975. Also in 1980, Sanders published a satirical novel, *Fame & Love in New York.* In 1988 his book *Thirsting for Peace in a Raging Century: Selected Poems, 1961–1985* won the American Book Award. Recently he has been working with "research poetry," such as *Chekhov: A Biography in Verse* and *The Poetry and Life of Allen Ginsberg,* which use Sanders's talent for rigorous research into the lives of influential personalities and combine it with his poetic sensibilities. He currently lives in Woodstock, New York.

*—Kurt Hemmer*

## Principal Works

Poetry: *Poem from Jail,* 1963; *King Lord/Queen Freak,* 1964; *The Toe Queen Poems,* 1964; *Peace Eye,* 1965; *Egyptian Hieroglyphics,* 1973; *20,000 A.D.,* 1976; *The Cutting Prow,* 1981; *Hymn to Maple Syrup and Other Poems,* 1985; *Poems for Robin,* 1987; *Thirsting for Peace in a Raging Century: Selected Poems, 1961–1985,* 1987; *Hymn to the Rebel Café,* 1993; *Chekhov: A Biography in Verse,* 1995; *1968: A History in Verse,* 1997; *America: A History in Verse, Volume I, 1900–1939,* 2000; *America: A History in Verse, Volume II, 1940–1961,* 2000; *The Poetry and Life of Allen Ginsberg: A Narrative Poem,* 2000.

Prose: *The Family: The Story of Charles Manson's Dune Buggy Attack Battalion,* 1971; *Tales of Beatnik Glory,* 1975; *Investigative Poetry,* 1976; *Fame and Love in New York,* 1980; *The Z-D Generation,* 1981; *Tales of Beatnik Glory: Volumes I and II,* 1990.

## Bibliographical References

Anecdotes can be found relating to Sanders in many of the biographies focusing on the major Beat writers, but there has yet to be a major work on this fascinating artist. The *Dictionary of Literary Biography, Volume 16: The Beats: Literary Bohemians in Postwar America,* ed. Ann

Charters, provides a brief biography by George F. Butterick, and the *Dictionary of Literary Biography, Volume 244: American Short-Story Writers since World War II, Fourth Series*, has a brief biography by Brook Horvath, but more scholarly work needs to be done to flesh out this historically significant figure.

*See also* Censorship; Anarchy, Christian

## Scholarship and Critical Appreciation, A Survey of

Critical reception of Beat writing always has been mixed, the early years dominated by sharply (sometimes cruelly) negative reviews, and later, as times and critical appetites have changed, increasingly with insight and respect. Although their work found publishers, in the 1950s, Beat writers were pointedly excluded from anthologies of new writing; women Beats were neglected by editors and reviewers alike for far longer than the men. While some of the female Beats had work published, it was only by obscure presses, and only recently has critical attention turned to their work. Fifty years after the publication of Jack Kerouac's *The Town and the City* (1950) and John Clellon Holmes's *Go* (1952), both of which were negatively reviewed, universities now offer courses in Beat literature, biographies of Beat writers abound, and book-length studies of Beat work are a regular publishing occurrence. Today, the scope of what has been called a movement, a generation, and a phenomenon has expanded beyond a half dozen men in the confines of New York City during the 1950s to include second- and third-generation Beats writing all over the world.

As Beat writing emerged, critics quickly acknowledged the power of the public performances, particularly those of Allen Ginsberg and Lawrence Ferlinghetti, which were a significant departure from the more decorous traditional poetry readings. The energy and unpredictability of Beat readings, beginning with the fabled 6 Gallery reading in 1955 in San Francisco, helped to popularize poetry as literature and as entertainment, and thereby accelerated dissemination of the poetry's radical content. Two foundational Beat texts appeared: Ginsberg's *Howl and Other Poems* in 1956 and Kerouac's *On the Road* in 1957. Fortuitously, *Howl* fell into the hands of the censor, and *On the Road* fell into the hands of Gilbert Millstein. The censor's legal assault on obscenity made Ginsberg a star, and Millstein's effusive praise for the beauty of Kerouac's writing and his book made Kerouac even more noteworthy. . These events did not make the way easy, but they did make it inevitable by alerting a widespread and curious audience to the existence of the Beats. In the introduction to *Beat Down to Your Soul* (2001), Ann Charters explained that the exoneration of *Howl and Other Poems* meant that "outspoken and subversive literary magazines sprung up like wild mushrooms throughout the United States" (xxxiii).

Alongside Millstein's unqualified approval, other reviews of *On the Road* were varied. There were complaints about the book being sociological, reportage, a display of neuroses, instead of being fiction; but there was also some recognition of Kerouac's originality in voice and style. *Howl* was denigrated for its perceived indiscretions, but Ginsberg was praised for his fine ear. More broadly, critics pounded the Beats for being an unthinking, unintelligent, in fact anti-intelligence, bunch of insensitive, undisciplined louts—they did not even dress properly, in the opinion of staid academics. Their lifestyles and their philosophies were as targeted as their writing was. John Tytell has observed that "critics saw them as philistines without a viable literary past, as a species of distasteful and aberrant contemporary anomaly" (*Paradise Outlaws* 24). *Time* magazine in particular—amusingly ironic when seen in light of Ginsberg's remarks in "America"—was unequivocal in its consistent and nasty condemnation of Beat writing. Many critics used the Beats' own remarks regarding their literary forerunners as a way through which to dismiss and denigrate what they wrote. If a Beat admired and emulated Whitman or Rimbaud or Wolfe or Gide, critics gleefully weighed that Beat in the balance and found him wanting, calling him a cheap copy and enlisting negative adjectives to underscore the negative correlation each critic observed. There was occasional praise for evidence of art and talent, but seldom untempered by complaints about the way those talents were being used. What the Beats proclaimed as spontaneous, critics disparaged as messy and lazy. Ann Charters recalled in 2001 the "belittling responses" and the "intolerance" of the "narrowly conservative literary establishment" (xxxvi) when it came to the Beats. This kind of criticism was leveled at what is considered by many to be some of Kerouac's finest work, including *On the Road, The Subterraneans, The Dharma Bums,* and *Doctor Sax.*

However, after the initial shock of the arrival of the Beats, the 1960s opened with the publication of Thomas Parkinson's *A Casebook on the Beat* (1961). The book collected Beat writing and also undertook serious critical examination by a number of scholars and critics, thus acting as a rite of passage into a degree of respectability for the Beats and their work. Parkinson's own essay in that book carefully identified particular strengths and qualities in individual writers: Ginsberg's and Kerouac's "vigor and force"; Corso's and Ferlinghetti's "wit and hilarity"; Snyder's and Whalen's "intelligence, learning, and decency"; McClure's "integrity" (276). Still, in the early years of the decade, the Beat movement was summarily declared dead in a *New Statesman* review, with the prediction that it would be proven to be of little influence. Throughout the 60s *Time* maintained its monotonous condemnation of everything that smacked of Beat, fueled further by the appearance of William S. Burroughs's *Naked Lunch,* which had its own obscenity trial in 1966. Nevertheless, where critics in the 50s used the names of forerunners to dismiss the Beats, some critics in the 60s began to volunteer comparisons and to do so in a positive way. It can never be said that Burroughs's fiction was universally embraced, and there were many complaints that the language was incomprehensible, but nevertheless some critics applauded the experimental nature of his work and wrote with approval of his inventive technique, even recognizing the satirical quality. At the end of the decade, in spite of these signs of progress, writers such as Burroughs, Ginsberg, Kerouac, and Snyder still were struggling against negative reviews in conservative academic publications.

The 1970s are a different critical story altogether. The preceding twenty years had yielded only a few moments of respite during what was a difficult critical apprenticeship for Beat writers collectively. Then, a decade after Parkinson's *Casebook,* Samuel Charters and Bruce Cook both published scholarly books in 1971 and Ann Charters's *Kerouac,* the first Beat biography, appeared in 1973. In the middle of the decade, Snyder's *Turtle Island* met with a very positive reception, and Burroughs's uniqueness was finally being absorbed and appreciated by critics with the stamina to persist. Edited anthologies and collections of Beat writing began to appear, and autobiographical writings such as journals and letters also were published. These kinds of publications demonstrated both an increased interest and a relaxed attitude toward what the Beats did and what they wrote. The last half of the 70s saw the publication of scholarly studies and biographies on Kerouac, Burroughs, Lawrence Ferlinghetti, and Lew Welch, as well as studies of the Beat Generation as a whole. The titles of some of these books took the Beat icon of the angel and integrated it into the critical vocabulary: *Naked Angels* (Tytell 1976), *Genesis Angels* (Saroyan 1979), *Desolate Angel* (McNally 1979).

After the transitional decade of the 1970s, when the Beats had failed to vanish from the critical landscape as predicted, scholars began to build on the comparatively isolated work done earlier to establish the Beats as worthy of study. As with the 60s and 70s, the 80s, too, opened with an important book that took another giant stride in the continuum of Beat scholarship. *The Beats: Essays in Criticism* (Ed. Bartlett 1981) situated the Beat Generation in its literary lineage and drew convincing comparisons between what these writers did and the way they did it, and honored writers and philosophers. The essayists saw the classic quest pattern, Wittgenstein's philosophy, DeQuincey's confession, Jung's visionary artist. They noted the religious and prophetic traditions at work, as well as surrealism, Dadaism, existentialism, and Romanticism. They identified—in utter contradiction of critics in the 50s—Whitman as grandfather, and they pointed to Pound, Jeffers, Williams, Rexroth,

Fitzgerald, and Dickinson as clear influences. By calling thus on the venerable names of American literary tradition, they showed Beat writing to be part of an organic progression in American writing. This collection, along with Michael Davidson's *The San Francisco Renaissance* (1989), combined with the pioneering work of previous decades to make the Beats undeniably an integral part of American letters. The other important contribution to the body of Beat scholarship during the 80s is the abundance of biographies, such as *Memory Babe* (Nicosia 1983), *Lawrence Ferlinghetti* (Smith 1983), *William S. Burroughs* (Skerl 1985), *Jack Kerouac* (French 1986), *Literary Outlaw* (Morgan 1988), and *Ginsberg* (Miles 1989). Kerouac alone had been the subject of four book-length critical biographies within twenty years of his death.

The 1990s began with the publication of Warren French's *The San Francisco Poetry Renaissance* and Gregory Stephenson's *The Daybreak Boys: Essays on the Literature of the Beat Generation* and *Exiled Angel: A Study of the Work of Gregory Corso*, followed soon after by biographies of Kenneth Rexroth (Hamalian 1991), Burroughs (Miles 1992), Ginsberg (Schumacher 1992), Snyder (Murphy 1992), and Frank O'Hara (1993). Most books chose as their subjects those same writers who had been discussed either favorably or unfavorably all along: Kerouac, Ginsberg, Burroughs, Ferlinghetti, Snyder, Corso, and a handful of others. The limited Beat geography initially had included only New York and San Francisco, and while it did begin to expand somewhat, the writers about whom critics and scholars cared continued to be both white and male. This preference has not changed fundamentally, but in the mid-1990s, A. Robert Lee sought to turn some attention to the dependence of Beat literature on African American cultural elements, and Neeli Cherkovski's *Elegy for Bob Kaufman* (1996) appeared. Nevertheless, two more Kerouac biographies, Miles's and Amburn's, were published in 1998, keeping him at the hub of all things Beat.

At the turn of the twenty-first century, where academic journals had once eschewed granting the Beats credibility, an entire issue of *College Literature* has been devoted to teaching Beat literature.

Kostas Myrsiades has edited *The Beat Generation* (2002), a collection of essays that, he writes, seeks to "look beyond the established Beats to argue for a more international Beat canon" (x), including the Beat impact on West German poetry. Where critics earlier identified (positively or negatively) aspects of Beat writing, now whole books are devoted to examinations of those issues: John Lardas's *The Bop Apocalypse: The Religious Visions of Kerouac, Ginsberg, and Burroughs* (2000), Ben Giamo's *Kerouac, the Word and the Way: Prose Artist as Spiritual Quester* (2000), and Jamie Russell's *Queer Burroughs* (2001). Finally, Ronna Johnson and Nancy Grace edited *Girls Who Wore Black* (2002), a volume of essays that engage with the writing of Beat women. Ann Charters's foreword to that volume points out that "many of the Beat males were no more sensitive to the needs of the intellectual women in their midst than many other males of their generation" (x). Johnson and Grace note that the writing of Beat women is different—"technically, stylistically, aesthetically"—from that of the better-known Beat men (2). In their opinion, "the Beat generation incubated feminism and offered women refuge from the stifling silent generation" (7). The essays in their book direct attention, for the first time, to Diane di Prima, Hettie Jones, Elise Cowen, Joyce Johnson, Joanne Kyger, Helen Adam, and Anne Waldman, among others.

—*A. Mary Murphy*

## Bibliographical References

*A Casebook on the Beat* (1961), edited by Thomas Parkinson, includes excerpts from the writing of eight well-known Beats, followed by a dozen pieces of early criticism and commentary, and concludes with a thorough bibliographical section of journals, plus primary and secondary works by and about the Beats; *The Beats: Essays in Criticism* (1981), edited by Lee Bartlett, is a collection of fourteen essays, all focusing on the work of major Beats; Gregory Stephenson's *The Daybreak Boys: Essays on the Literature of the Beat Generation* (1990) devotes individual chapters to nine central figures of the Beat period; John Tytell's *Paradise Outlaws: Remembering the Beats* (1999) is a memoir complemented by photographs taken by Mellon,

Tytell's wife; Ann Charters's *Beat Down to Your Soul,* 2001, is a collection of poems, essays, reviews, and memoirs spanning fifty years of publishing on and by a wide variety of writers and critics, and includes a valuable publishing chronology; likewise, *The Beats: A Literary Reference,* 2001, edited by Matt Theado, brings together essays, interviews, and reviews plus reproductions of manuscript pages, cover art, and photographs; *Girls Who Wore Black: Women Writing the Beat Generation,* 2002, edited by Ronna C. Johnson and Nancy M. Grace, is the first critical collection to focus on the work of the lesser-known women Beats; *The Beat Generation: Critical Essays,* 2002, edited by Kostas Myrsiades, broadens the scope, both geographically and chronologically, of what has thus far been classified as Beat.

**See also** *On the Road, New York Times Review* of; Charters, Ann; Charters, Sam; Tytell, John; Influences

## Sculpture

Sculptors who were contemporaries of the Beats shared with Beat writers an interest in Dadaism, surrealism, French symbolism, spontaneous creativity, and the quotidian life.

Among the sculptors practicing in the 1940s was Joseph Cornell, who is noteworthy for his "boxes." Shaped like a medicine cabinet, and fronted with clear glass rather than a mirror, each box is filled with intriguing and charming items. These items are precious memorabilia, including containers, paper figures, stuffed birds, fragments of printed documents, tableware, and maps. The area within the box may be subdivided with glass shelves or other dividers. As Cornell places these items in unlikely groupings, he invokes the surrealist principle of illogical combinations. Cornell's work with these boxes anticipates the assemblage movement in sculpture, which was closely connected with Beat art on the West Coast in the 1950s.

Another sculptor practicing in the 1940s was Jacques Lipchitz, a Lithuanian who arrived in the United States in 1941 and became a citizen in 1957. While in America, Lipchitz created rounded, muscular figures, some cast in bronze, others carved from stone. These figures were bigger than life-size and expressive of emotion.

Lipchitz's "semiautomatics" sought to draw from the subconscious for creativity; in some cases, Lipchitz worked underwater with clay or plasticine, sightlessly shaping a preliminary version of his work. These semiautomatics bear comparison with the efforts of Beat writers to eliminate conscious control over their writing and to rely on the subconscious.

Marcel Duchamp is well known for works such as *Nude Descending a Staircase* (1912) and is influential because he presented everyday objects, such as a bicycle wheel or a urinal, sometimes with modifications, as art. Duchamp was part of the artistic milieu in New York in the 1940s and 1950s, contributing to exhibitions by other surrealists who had arrived from Europe.

In the 1950s, Robert Morris and his wife, Simone Forti, were dancers in San Francisco, but in 1959 they came to New York City, where they joined the Judson Dance Theater. A need to create props for their dance concerts led Morris to create minimalist sculptures from ordinary wood. Morris continued to experiment with materials as he later sculpted with aluminum, steel mesh, and felt.

Drawing ideas from European predecessors, Wallace Berman became known as the father of the California assemblage movement, which had close ties with Beat culture. He worked at a furniture factory in 1949 and began to produce sculpture with waste and scrap he found at the factory. Starting in 1954, Berman converted the little literary magazine, which was a popular venue for Beat writers, into a work of sculpture. *Semina* departed from the shape and binding of most little magazines and presented hand-printed scraps of paper, drawings, and photographs. *Semina* included contributions from Beat writers such as Michael McClure, Philip Lamantia, and David Meltzer.

Closely associated with Berman is assemblage artist George Herms, whose works often reveal the influence of Cornell. Herms gathers common materials that many people would regard as trash, such as old doorknobs, scraps of cloth, used tools, and worn out shoes, and displays these objects in boxes. In contrast, his sculpture *The Librarian*

(1960) suggests a human form, but it also appears to be a cluttered desk.

Like Herms and Berman, Bruce Conner was part of the assemblage movement, but by using fabrics and cloths, he showed some connection to Robert Morris. *Couch* (1963) is a ragged daybed streaked with paint, but its former elegance and promise of human rest remain. *Portrait of Allen Ginsberg* (1960–1961) is a web of debris, and only the most imaginative viewer can draw a connection with the title.

Along with collage, assemblage art became the key manifestation of sculpture in the Beat era. With gatherings from everyday life, particularly with the reclaiming of items given up for trash, the assemblage artists showed the resourcefulness that World War II had demanded, but also revealed a critical perspective about the postwar focus on material satisfaction.

—*William Lawlor*

## Bibliographical References

*Beat Culture and the New America 1950–1965*, ed. Lisa Phillips, 1995, is an illustrated guide to the exhibition at the Whitney Museum, 1996. Included in this volume is Rebecca Solnit, "Heretical Constellations: Notes on California, 1946–1961," which comments effectively on major artists, including sculptors. Solnit is also the editor of *Secret Exhibitions*, 1990. Availability may be a problem, but one may want to track down George Herms, *George Herms: Then and Now: Fifty Years of Assemblage*, 2003. John Maynard's *Venice West: The Beat Generation in Southern California*, 1991, comments on Berman and other artists.

*See also* Berman, Wallace; Painting; Herms, George; Conner, Bruce; San Francisco

## Sea, The Beats at

The sea and transoceanic travel figured significantly in the lives of several Beat writers, whether they served in the U.S. military, worked in the merchant marine, or sailed the sea to see the world. Lawrence Ferlinghetti served in the navy during World War II, Gary Snyder sailed the Pacific to study Buddhism in Japan, and Jack Kerouac's mar-

itime experiences informed much of his writing. Other writers also found themselves at sea, some sailing to leave the United States after failed sexual relationships or to pursue literary activities.

Lawrence Ferlinghetti joined the U.S. Navy in 1941 and attended midshipmen's school in Chicago before being assigned to New York City's Third Naval District. After patrolling around New York Harbor and New England, Ferlinghetti worked as a signalman aboard the *Ambrose Lightship*, helping ships safely enter the port of New York. After working in 1943 on patrols into the North Atlantic, Ferlinghetti received an assignment that took him to Great Britain, where he worked as a messenger. Ferlinghetti was eventually named skipper of a ship sent to Liverpool to participate in the Normandy invasion of 1944. He eventually found his way back to the United States on his final assignment as a freighter navigator in the Pacific Ocean. It was then that Ferlinghetti witnessed the aftermath of the atomic attack on Nagasaki, just six weeks after the bomb was dropped there. Ferlinghetti was discharged from the navy when his freighter reached Portland, Oregon, a few days later.

Gary Snyder sailed with the Maritime Cooks and Stewards Union in 1948, visiting Colombia and Venezuela. In 1956 he sailed aboard a freighter to Japan, where he studied Zen Buddhism. A year later, in Yokohama, Japan, he boarded the SS *Sappa Creek*, working first as a firefighter and then in the engine room as a wiper. During his year-long assignment, he visited the Persian Gulf, the Mediterranean, Ceylon (now Sri Lanka), and several Pacific ports, before returning to San Francisco in 1958. Snyder wrote of his experiences on the SS *Sappa Creek* in letters to Will Peterson and Philip Whalen. In 1961, Snyder sailed to India with Joanne Kyger; in New Delhi they joined Allen Ginsberg. Ginsberg had sailed to Dakar, Africa, earlier in 1947, after his breakup with Neal Cassady. Snyder's times at sea inform parts of *Earth House Hold* and *Passage through India*, both available in *The Gary Snyder Reader*.

Jack Kerouac also had significant maritime experience before his writing career became a priority to him. He served in the merchant marine in 1942 aboard the SS *Dorchester*, a stint that provided material for the unpublished novel *The Sea Is My Brother*. In May of that year, Kerouac was honorably discharged from the navy after being diagnosed with an "indifferent character." A month later he sailed to Liverpool, England, aboard the *George Weems*. Kerouac wrote about his maritime experiences in *Vanity of Duluoz*, and about the sea itself in *Big Sur*, which concludes with a long sound poem that recreates the rhythm and roar of the Pacific.

Kerouac joined Burroughs in Tangier in 1957, sailing from New York on the SS *Slovenija*. His trip across the North Atlantic included a dangerous storm, which he described in a letter to Joyce Glassman (now published in Jack Kerouac, *Selected Letters 1957–1969*, ed. Ann Charters, 1999: 9–10) as one of the most "awful" experiences he'd ever had at sea. This trip led to one of the largest overseas collaborations of the Beat movement, when in 1957 Kerouac, Ginsberg, Peter Orlovsky, and Alan Ansen traveled to Tangier to work on *Naked Lunch* with William S. Burroughs. Burroughs had settled in Tangier in 1954, after sailing to Europe and Africa late in 1953 when his sexual relationship with Ginsberg ended.

Bob Kaufman also spent time at sea, sailing around the world with the merchant marines. As a cabin boy, Kaufman read books that his supervisor recommended, and later in life Kaufman worked with unions that attended to sailors' issues.

—*Rebecca Devers*

### Bibliographical References

Neeli Cherkovski, *Ferlinghetti: A Biography*, 1979; Jon Halper, ed., *Gary Snyder: Dimensions of a Life*, 1991; Gary Snyder, *The Gary Snyder Reader: Prose, Poetry, and Translations 1952–1998*, 1999; Matt Theado, ed., *The Beats: A Literary Reference*, 2001; Steven Watson, *The Birth of the Beat Generation: Visionaries, Rebels, and Hipsters, 1944–1960*, 1995.

***See also*** Ferlinghetti, Lawrence; Snyder, Gary; Kerouac, Jack; Ginsberg, Allen; Kaufman, Bob

## Selby, Hubert, Jr. (1928–2004)

Novelist Hubert Selby was one of the most drastic explorers and critics of such desolate aspects of modern urban life as violence, addiction, prostitution, and poverty. Like the novels of William Burroughs, Selby's texts indulge in slang-ridden language and portray the unpredictable lives of outsiders and paranoids. Ultraviolent scenes of rape, fighting, and all varieties of humiliation accompany sardonic attacks on the corruption of modern society. Selby's novels of the sixties and seventies are distinguished by a tough moralism; the writer even called one of his books a modern morality play. At times, his work offers an irritating combination of Christian values, social criticism, and neonaturalism, from which Selby emerges as a bleak pornographic moralist.

Born on 23 July 1928 in Brooklyn, New York, the son of a coal miner, Selby left school at fifteen to labor as a dockworker and sailor, joining the merchant marine in 1944. Suffering from tuberculosis and addicted to morphine, Selby was discharged and subsequently held diverse jobs. Following the publication of stories in small journals, his novel *Last Exit to Brooklyn* (1964), a description of existence on the fringes of urban society, made Selby both well known and well censored. But although subject to obscenity charges, the book was praised as a powerful and authentic achievement. Selby's next novel, *The Room* (1971), describes the violent visions of an incarcerated psychopath, while *The Demon* (1976) satirizes the rise of an egotistical Manhattan Casanova. *Requiem for a Dream* (1978) unfolds the struggles of some heroin addicts whose failed dreams of success end in death, prison, and prostitution. Selby also cowrote the screenplay for the cinema adaptation of the book (2000). His final novel, *Waiting Period* (2002), is the inner monologue of a suicidal serial killer.

Until his death of pulmonary disease, Selby taught a writing course at the University of Southern California.

—*Mike W. Malm*

### Principal Works

*Last Exit to Brooklyn*, 1964; *The Room*, 1971; *The Demon*, 1976; *Requiem for a Dream*, 1978; *Song of the Silent Snow*, 1986; *The Willow Tree*, 1998; *Waiting Period*, 2002.

## Bibliographical References

For a collection of critical essays on Selby, see James R. Giles, *Understanding Hubert Selby, Jr.,* 1998; on the aspect of violence, see the chapter on Selby in Patrick W. Shaw, *The Modern American Novel of Violence,* 2000; on obscenity, see Frank Kermode, "'Obscenity' and the 'Public Interest,'" *New American Review* 3 (1968): 229–244; on Selby as a moralist, see Charles D. Peavy, "Hubert Selby and the Tradition of Moral Satire," *Satire Newsletter* 6.2 (1969): 35–39.

# Sexism and Misogyny

The Beat Generation is often considered an "all boys club," and is often charged with being a sexist generation of misogynistic writers. The work of the major Beat authors reflects attitudes that are, at times, sexist. Indeed, in many ways the male writers of the Beat Generation held the same sexist attitudes toward women as did men in mainstream postwar American culture. Throughout postwar culture, women were relegated to the domestic biological roles of mother, wife, and/or sexual plaything. The Beats differed from this dominant view by largely avoiding marriage, or redefining commitment so sexual relationships could be more fluid and open. Also, some Beats were homosexual or experimented with same-sex relationships, which could also foster sexist attitudes. Despite the sexist tendencies, the Beat lifestyle still gave women more freedom than did the mainstream lifestyle. Through their relationships with Beat men, many women writers of the day were exposed to a variety of liberating experiences and enjoyed some of the same sexual freedom as the men.

This range of attitudes about men's and women's roles and relationships is illustrated in the work of Beat writers, both male and female. Jack Kerouac's novels include misogynistic beliefs such as the idea that attractive women stir men into acts of procreation and thereby become pregnant and give birth to children who are doomed to die. Such beliefs indicate a fear and loathing of women. Kerouac's novels also feature a seemingly endless parade of female characters who appear to engage in sexual relationships with the male protagonists and are quickly dismissed after they have fulfilled that role. However, Kerouac's novels also include moments in which the male protagonists realize that they do not understand women and that ultimately the tension is all men's fault. Anecdotes from Kerouac's personal life also illustrate this complex range of attitudes. Kerouac notoriously denied his paternity of daughter Jan Kerouac, failing to take responsibility for his actions. On the other hand, other anecdotes attest to Kerouac's support of women; writer Joyce Johnson, who dated Kerouac during the publication of *On the Road,* has repeatedly said that Kerouac was supportive of her as a writer and urged her to preserve her freedom.

Another example of the complexity of Beat sexism is Beat writer William S. Burroughs. His work *The Job* includes statements that are overtly hostile and misogynistic, indicating that women were a fundamental miscalculation that led to the problems of a twofold reality. Yet as Burroughs's biographer Ted Morgan explains, Burroughs had several close female friends, and was reportedly genuinely in love with his wife, Joan Vollmer, despite his homosexual orientation. That Joan died from an errant gunshot from Burroughs's own hand in an ill-fated game of William Tell is sometimes used as evidence of Burroughs's misogyny. However, such an accusation ignores the complexity of the tragic mishap.

Many scholars of the Beat Generation explain the complex and conflicting sexist attitudes and behaviors of the male Beats through psychoanalytic readings of their texts and their lives. Kerouac's problematic relationship with women and his sexist comments and ambivalence are attributed to the influence of his Catholic upbringing, as well as his intense and close relationship to his mother, Gabrielle. Similarly, scholars speculate about Burroughs's relationship with his mother and his own dis-ease with his feminine characteristics. While Kerouac's and Burroughs's experiences do not necessarily reflect all male Beats' attitudes toward women, they do reflect the complex and often contradictory attitudes found throughout the texts and lives of many male Beats.

With the recent recovery of women writers associated with the male Beats, a more complex picture of the relationships and attitudes between the sexes is forming. Writers Joyce Johnson, Diane di Prima, Joanne Kyger, Janine Pommy Vega, and Hettie Jones, among others, have participated in several discussions on what it means to be affiliated with the Beat Generation. These women have noted that despite the sexism of the male Beats, these men were more liberal in their views of women than mainstream American men.

Many of these women have indicated that the male Beats encouraged their writing. Yet some have indicated that while they were never discouraged from writing, there was never an equal space for the women as writers amongst the male Beats. The women's primary role in Beat relationships tended toward the traditional female roles of care-taking, as well as the new role of "Beat chick." By engaging in sex with men of the Beat Generation, the women were able to join the intellectual and artistic circle of the Beats. Because they felt excluded from the male Beat circle due to sexist attitudes, some of the women writers are wary of being labeled as "Beat." They tend to see the Beat Generation as the mythic "all boys club."

The writing of these women chronicles their encounters and frustrations with the sexism that was rampant in all of American culture. These women defied convention and sexist stereotypes by moving into their own apartments, living independent lives, and exploring their sexuality. The writing by the women of the Beat Generation challenges the stereotypes about sexism by giving voice to the female Beat experience. Works such as Johnson's *Minor Characters* attest to the difficulties and challenges that Beat women faced in going against sexist stereotypes. These works also show the conflict these women felt between wanting the freedom that the Beat lifestyle provided, as well as wanting committed relationships. For all of their challenging of gender roles, many of the female Beats still wanted marriage, which was anathema to many of the male Beats. The general consensus among scholars is that sexism was prevalent in Beat literature and lifestyle, but was perhaps mitigated by the counterculture liberality of the generation. The male Beats, although more supportive of their fe-

male counterparts, still regarded women as muses, sexual playthings, and domestic mavens. The women saw themselves as trying to strike a balance between independence and commitment.

—*Jessica Lyn Van Slooten*

## Bibliographical References

Ann Charters, ed., *Beat Down to Your Soul: What Was the Beat Generation,* 2001; Barbara Ehrenreich, *The Hearts of Men: American Dreams and the Flight from Commitment,* 1983; Ronna Johnson and Nancy M. Grace, eds., *Girls Who Wore Black: Women Writing the Beat Generation,* 2002; Helen McNeil, "The Archeology of Gender in the Beat Movement," in *The Beat Generation Writers,* ed. A. Robert Lee, 1996; Alix Kates Shulman, "The Beat Queens: Boho Chicks Stand by their Men," in *Village Voice Literary Supplement,* 1989.

*See also* Marriage; Sexual Attitudes and Behavior; Kerouac, Jack; Ginsberg, Allen; Burroughs, William Seward; Kerouac, Jan; Vollmer Adams Burroughs, Joan; Johnson, Joyce; di Prima, Diane; Kyger, Joanne; Pommy Vega, Janine; Jones, Hettie

## Sexual Attitudes and Behavior

On the surface, conservative and restrained, but beneath the surface characterized by experimentation and activity that presaged the arrival of the sexual liberation of the 1960s, the sexual attitudes of the Beats, which were shocking in the forties and fifties, became mainstream attitudes in the eighties and nineties.

The superficial sexual conservatism in the mid-twentieth century established the impression that women must not have sex before marriage and should maintain fidelity after marriage. Like most sexual topics, masturbation was unspeakable. These sexual attitudes are revealed in the media of the times. If the bedroom of a married couple was shown on TV, the room had twin beds. Speakers on TV had to restrict their language, and even on late-night TV, the word *virgin* was not appropriate. Programs such as the *Ed Sullivan Show* required performers to adjust the lyrics of songs if suggestions of premarital sex were part of them.

In *Minor Characters*, a memoir about growing up in this restrained environment, Beat writer Joyce Johnson recalls that her mother had difficulty in discussing sexuality and referred euphemistically to "down below."

In 1948, Kinsey's *Sexual Behavior in the Human Male* provoked widespread discussion. Controversial because of survey questions that involved intimacy and sexual conduct, the book suggested, among other things, that homosexuality was not as uncommon as many supposed and that almost all men masturbate. In 1953, *Sexual Behavior in the Human Female* revealed that 50 percent of respondents to the survey had premarital sex, and about one fourth of the surveyed women had extramarital sex as they advanced toward forty years of age. These data contradicted common suppositions, and unwilling to accept such data, writers and commentators refuted Kinsey's investigation and charged that Kinsey was destroying American values. Nevertheless, the results of Kinsey's surveys awakened in Americans a willingness to discuss sex frankly and discover the truth about themselves.

The hallmark of the Beats is candor, and Beat discussions of sex are frank. Allen Ginsberg in describing his 1948 vision of Blake does not hesitate to mention that the vision occurred during an episode of masturbation. In *Visions of Cody*, Jack Kerouac indicates that Cody Pomeray masturbates six times daily, in addition to other sexual activity. In the writings of Ginsberg and William Burroughs, homosexual activity is brought to the fore. Joan Vollmer Adams's four-bedroom apartment near Columbia University in Manhattan became a hub of sexual freedom for the Beats. Perhaps the most famous transgressor of the standards for sexual behavior at midcentury was Dean Moriarty, the character from Jack Kerouac's *On the Road*, who had premarital, marital, extramarital, and bigamous relations. Thus, the writings of the Beats became a factor in the revision of sexual attitudes in the United States at midcentury.

Among these factors was Marilyn Monroe, a sexual icon. When an allegation arose that she had posed in the nude for a popular calendar, she intensified her popularity by frankly admitting that she indeed was the model in question. Hugh Hefner, upstart editor of a new magazine titled *Playboy*, acquired the photos of Monroe and garnered widespread attention for his magazine by publishing them. Soon *Playboy* became an additional factor in bringing sexual openness to the surface of American society.

Books such as *Peyton Place* by Grace Metalious and *Giovanni's Room* by James Baldwin defied conservative standards, but only the most courageous publishers were willing to market such works, and these publishers were rewarded when controversy enhanced sales. Beat writings such as Allen Ginsberg's "Howl" and William Burroughs's *Naked Lunch* faced censorship and legal challenges, but these efforts to stifle the Beats intensified their appeal as public attitudes about sex underwent a transformation.

Perhaps the culminating factor in the transformation of sexual attitudes was Margaret Sanger's effort to provide controlled reproduction for married couples through the birth-control pill. Ironically, women who once seemed maidenly became more open to premarital sex when the fear of pregnancy was removed.

Though not published until 1963, Betty Friedan's *The Feminine Mystique* summarized the changes in sexual attitudes. Women who were once obligated to seek satisfaction and happiness in domesticity and motherhood could declare their dissatisfaction and choose the lifestyles and behaviors that presented attractive alternatives.

—*William Lawlor*

## Bibliographical References

David Halberstam, *The Fifties*, 1993, treats the question of sexual attitudes in detail; the video program that corresponds to Halberstam's book features two episodes that analyze sexual attitudes of the times. Jack Kerouac is frank about sex in *On the Road*, 1957, and *The Dharma Bums*, 1958; Allen Ginsberg's *Howl and Other Poems*, 1956, shocks many readers with its unrestrained references; William Burroughs's *Naked Lunch*, 1959, challenges the limits of propriety even in 2005. A clear review of sexual attitudes and behaviors in Beat writings is Regina Marler,

*Queer Beats: How the Beats Turned America on to Sex*, 2004.

**See also** Sexism and Misogyny; Kinsey Report

## Sexual Freedom

In the Beat lifestyle a central factor leading to uninhibited personal fulfillment; also a legendary part of Beat culture sensationalized in media coverage but not consistently revealed in the actual behavior of the Beats.

Sexual freedom for the Beats arose in contrast to restrictive and prudish attitudes established as public standards. Although the Beats defied societal restrictions, the society that rejected such defiance exaggerated and misrepresented the Beats' sexual freedom. Most Beats accepted heterosexuality, homosexuality, and bisexuality as matters of personal preference; by example, the Beats strove to help society overcome its unnatural rules.

In *Memoirs of a Beatnik* (1969), Diane di Prima reveals both the sexual freedom and the myth of such freedom. She refers to an editor's request for additional sex in a manuscript and explains that in meeting the editor's request she could call on a fellow resident in the apartment for assistance. To verify the possibility of a particular sexual position, di Prima could ask the fellow resident to assume the position. Once the possibility had been verified, the fellow resident would return to his or her previous activity, never thinking of the verification as anything other than routine contact with a friend (137–138).

The contrast between reality and myth appears in *Memoirs of a Beatnik* in two consecutive chapters. In "A Night by the Fire: What You Would Like to Hear," di Prima describes a group of people who spend the night together in bed (106–107). The night develops into a steamy orgy. However, in the next chapter, "A Night By the Fire: What Actually Happened," di Prima describes the multiple persons in the bed again, this time revealing the real version of what happened, a version considerably more innocent (108).

In *The Dharma Bums* by Jack Kerouac (1958), Ray Smith, Japhy Ryder, Princess, and Alvah Goldbook illustrate the struggle to overcome restrictions and establish freedom (27–35). Japhy begins *yabyum* with Princess. Sitting naked and cross-legged on the floor, Japhy calls for Princess, also naked, to sit on him and put her arms around him. In this Tibetan ritual, Japhy is the thunderbolt and Princess is the void. When Japhy loses his balance and tumbles onto the mattress, Alvah joins the naked union and Japhy calls Ray to undress and be part of the activity. However, Ray is living as a celibate, and his instincts make him uncomfortable about being naked in the presence of multiple people. Even so, he joins in *yabyum* fully dressed and kisses Princess's hand, wrist, and body, even as Japhy and Alvah continue their intimacies. Ultimately everyone is naked. Later, Ray and Princess bathe together. Before leaving with Princess, Japhy expresses his lifelong disconnection from the inhibitions of American culture. When Japhy and Princess are gone, Alvah and Ray discuss the value of sensory experience. Alvah wants to enjoy his flesh and know the pleasures of his senses, but Ray rejects the senses and seeks a deeper truth. Alvah goes to sleep, but Ray remains up to reconsider the evening in solitude. He assures himself that the pleasures of the flesh have not overtaken the pleasures of his soul's purification, and in this conclusion he finds sexual freedom.

In *On the Road* (1957), Kerouac again reveals the conflict between sexual freedom and responsibility. Dean Moriarty is involved in numerous relationships, marriages, divorces, reconciliations, and transgressions. He delights in sex as a chief source of satisfaction, and in the midst of involvement, his partners seem to find delight with him. Nevertheless, in Part Three, Chapter 3, women attack Dean for his irresponsibility (193–196). Camille kicks him out and calls him a liar. Galatea berates him for foolishness, selfishness, and irresponsibility. Galatea reminds Dean that he is the father of a child, but he leaves the mother to manage both work and child care. Sal Paradise is unconvinced that Dean is such a devil for pursuing sexual freedom, but as Dean goes through life, more and more people find him insufferable.

In several poems from *Howl and Other Poems* (1956), Allen Ginsberg also favors sexual freedom and questions the society that withholds freedom. In "America," Ginsberg addresses America and asks when America will get undressed (39). In "A Supermarket in California," Ginsberg sympathizes with the circumstances of homosexuals such as Walt Whitman and Federico Garcia Lorca, who endure life in a society that refuses to tolerate their sexual instincts (29–30). In "Song," Ginsberg describes the tenderness and soul-sustaining power of love, but finds that humans carry love as a troublesome load that is not easy to set down (50–53).

Allen Ginsberg, in both his poetry and his life, was an advocate of gay liberation. When he traveled to Cuba, he challenged the Castro government for its refusal to allow sexual freedoms for homosexuals. Ginsberg taunted the communists by announcing that he found Che Guevara to be "cute." Ginsberg spoke often of his homosexuality and wrote about it with great candor, smashing old barriers with regard to that topic.

Various Beat women also showed their advocacy of sexual freedom. In *Tracking the Serpent* (1997), Janine Pommy Vega describes her travels to various continents and refers several times to sexual relationships that reveal the tension between desire and restraint. Joyce Johnson's *Minor Characters* (1983) shows the freedom Joyce wants in contrast to the restrictions her parents would like to impose.

—William Lawlor

**Bibliographical References**

Beyond the discussion of *yabyum*, Jack Kerouac's *The Dharma Bums*, 1958, discusses naked dancing at a wild party at Sean Monahan's house on pages 176–177; in *On the Road*, 1957, in addition to Dean's problems with too much sexual freedom, Kerouac allows Sal Paradise to reveal his freedom with Terry, the Mexican girl, on pages 81–101. Allen Ginsberg's visit to Cuba is described in Michael Schumacher, *Dharma Lion*, 1992: 419–429.

*See also* Reich, Wilhelm; Sexual Attitudes and Behavior; Marriage; News Media and Publicity, The Beats and; Kinsey Report; Nakedness; Kerouac, Jack; Ginsberg, Allen; Johnson, Joyce; di Prima, Diane; Pommy Vega, Janine

## Shearing, George (1919–)

Jazz and bebop pianist; composer; arranger. Born in London, Shearing became famous in Britain when Leonard Feather befriended Shearing and got him airtime on the BBC. Shearing moved to New York in 1947 and produced the highly successful album *September in the Rain*. He solidified his fame in the United States through his performances at Birdland. His composition "Lullaby of Birdland" is a jazz standard. Adopting an accessible jazz style that appealed to a broader audience than just jazz experts, Shearing's quintet achieved enduring popularity.

In *On the Road* (1957), Sal and Dean see the great blind pianist at Birdland in 1949 (127–128). Sal describes this time period as Shearing's peak—a time before his sound became slick and commercial. Dean and Sal enjoy Shearing's rich production of chords and his rocking motion. Dean calls out in support of the performance, and Shearing hears Dean and is motivated. When the show is over, Dean looks at Shearing's empty seat and refers to it as the seat of God.

—William Lawlor

**Bibliographical References**

With Alyn Shipton, George Shearing has written *Lullaby of Birdland: The Autobiography of George Shearing*, 2004; Leonard Feather, *The Jazz Years: Earwitness to an Era*, 1986, includes commentary on Shearing.

## 6 Gallery Reading

In the autumn of 1955, an event took place that triggered the birth of the San Francisco Poetry Renaissance. A group of unknown poets, from both East and West Coasts, gathered in the city to read at a local gallery, and in doing so marked a turning point in the development of the Beat Generation and its subsequent reputation and fame.

The poets were Allen Ginsberg, Gary Snyder, Philip Whalen, Michael McClure, and Philip Lamantia. The master of ceremonies was Kenneth Rexroth, the anarchist elder poet and leading light of the San Francisco literary scene. Rexroth held weekly open evenings at his home, where Ginsberg had first visited soon after his move to San Francisco in the spring of 1954. There he met the surrealist poet Philip Lamantia, whom he had known four years previously in New York, as well as Robert Duncan, Michael McClure, and Lawrence Ferlinghetti. Ginsberg soon became part of their circle.

In the summer of 1955, an artist who ran the 6 Gallery, a cooperative art gallery at 3119 Fillmore Street, suggested to Michael McClure, who had attended previous events there, the idea of holding a poetry reading at the venue. McClure was keen, but family commitments prevented him from devoting time to it. He mentioned the plan to Rexroth, who saw it as a good opportunity to showcase his young poet friends, and gave the task of organization to Allen Ginsberg. Rexroth also suggested Gary Snyder as a participant, and on 8 September Ginsberg met him for the first time and recruited him for the reading. Snyder showed Ginsberg some poems by his fellow student at Reed College, Oregon, and as a result Philip Whalen was added to the roster.

That same month, Jack Kerouac, who had spent the summer in Mexico City, arrived in the Bay Area and met up with Ginsberg, Snyder, and Whalen at Rexroth's house on 23 September, where more plans were drawn up for the forthcoming reading. While in Mexico during August, Kerouac had written his extended poem *Mexico City Blues,* around the same time that Ginsberg had produced the first part of his epic "Howl." Ginsberg invited Kerouac to read at the 6 Gallery, but he refused on the grounds that he was too bashful to perform his work before a large audience.

The date for the readings was fixed at Friday, 7 October, and Ginsberg sent out over a hundred postcards advertising the event: "6 Poets at 6 Gallery . . . all sharp new straightforward writing— remarkable collection of angels on one stage reading their poetry. No charge, small collection for wine and postcards. Charming event."

Proceedings commenced at 8 P.M. To a gathering of around 150 people, Philip Lamantia read some of the poems of his friend, John Hoffman, who had died, aged twenty-one, in Mexico from either peyote poisoning or polio. The symptoms, according to

William Burroughs, were identical. Hoffman, although unpublished, had become an underground legend by that time, and his surviving twenty-nine short poems, collected under the title *Journey to the End,* were similar to Lamantia's own in their surrealism.

Michael McClure was the next to read, and he performed his "Point Lobos: Animism," addressed to Antonin Artaud, as well as the nature poems "Night Words: The Ravishing, Poem," "The Breech," and "The Mystery of the Hunt." He finished with "For the Death of 100 Whales," a protest against the shooting of scores of whales by American soldiers at an arctic naval base the previous year.

In contrast to McClure's stark outcry, Zen poet Philip Whalen then took the stage to perform his semicomic "Plus Ça Change," about a broken-down marriage, followed in similar vein by "The Martyrdom of Two Pagans," and "If You're So Smart, Why Ain't You Rich?" A short interval followed.

It was then Allen Ginsberg's chance to give the first public performance of the long poem, "Howl," that he'd begun writing that summer. Only Part I was considered by Ginsberg to be sufficiently complete at that time, and he read all of it to the assembled audience. Beginning quietly, he gained confidence as he progressed and soon had the crowd transfixed by the power of his performance. Jack Kerouac, who had been passing jugs of wine among the members of the audience, urged on his friend by shouting "Go!" at every line break, much to the irritation of master of ceremonies Rexroth. Neal Cassady, who was there with his girlfriend Natalie Jackson, accompanied Kerouac with shouts of his own. The crowd joined in, inspiring Ginsberg to an even more emotional delivery, which he completed with tears flooding down his face to sustained applause from the audience. Even Rexroth was moved, and he congratulated Ginsberg on an outstanding performance, one that was to launch him on his career as a poet.

But the evening was not yet over, and after the crowd had settled down again, Gary Snyder captivated them once more with his poem about Coyote, the mythical Native American antihero: "A Berry

Feast." Readings from his work-in-progress, *Myths and Texts*, followed.

When the event finished, at around 11:30, the poets and friends dined at nearby Sam Wo's Chinese restaurant before going on to drink at the Place. The following day, Allen Ginsberg received a telegram from Lawrence Ferlinghetti, of City Lights Books, which read: "I greet you at the beginning of a great career. When do I get the manuscript?" (quoted in Michael Schumacher, *Dharma Lion*, 1992: 216).

The manuscript was duly delivered when Ginsberg completed the final parts of "Howl" and was published, together with a selection of his other recent poems, in August 1956, as number four in the City Lights Pocket Poets series. *Howl and Other Poems* became the subject of an obscenity trial, which vindicated the poem, its author, and its publisher. The contacts made between the performing poets just before, during, and after the 6 Gallery event further strengthened the formation and cohesiveness of the Beat Generation writers, and ensured their familiarity and popularity with a wider public during the later 1950s and beyond. This consolidation was further ensured by the eventual publication of Kerouac's *On the Road* in September 1957, and *The Dharma Bums*, in October 1958, the latter including its own account of the 6 Gallery readings.

—*Dave Moore*

### Bibliographical References

A fictional account of the reading appears in Jack Kerouac, *The Dharma Bums,* 1958; Michael McClure discusses the reading in *Scratching the Beat Surface: Essays on New Vision from Blake to Kerouac*, 1982; *Howl, Original Draft Facsimile*, ed. Barry Miles, 1986, includes Appendix 2, which is titled "First Reading at the Six Gallery, October 7, 1955."

*See also* San Francisco; San Francisco Renaissance; Kerouac, Jack; Ginsberg, Allen; Snyder, Gary; Lamantia, Philip; Whalen, Philip; Rexroth, Kenneth

## Snyder, Gary (1930–)

Gary Snyder, poet, essayist, and translator, became identified with the Beat movement as a result of being portrayed as Japhy Ryder in Jack Kerouac's *The Dharma Bums* (1958). Snyder then went on to become one of the premier West Coast Beat poets. He stands apart from his peers due to his deep immersion in Japanese Buddhism and his lifelong commitment to environmental activism, on the one hand. On the other hand, he is also noted for two major and distinct poetic styles. The first is represented by his two book-length poetic sequences, *Myths & Texts* and *Mountains and Rivers without End*, which display complex and frequently esoteric subject matter heavily informed by myth and archetype. This style shows the influence of modernist poetics, especially that of Ezra Pound and William Carlos Williams. The second is represented by his first published collection of poems, *Riprap*, which combines short lines and syntax influenced by Chinese poetry with American working-class vernacular language.

In Kerouac's novel, Snyder is glorified as the utterly cool practitioner of Buddhism, particularly its tantric aspects associated with a high level of wild sexual activity. Snyder is also depicted as a Buddhist sage who dispenses enigmatic words of wisdom. Japhy Ryder's words and actions are as unified as the form and content of Beat poetics. In direct contradiction to T. S. Eliot's modernist notions of a dissociation of sensibility and Prufrock's gap between word and deed, the Beats wrote about immediate sensuous experience and celebrated spontaneity. And unlike the postmodernists, who had concerns with "absence," the Beats were depicted and saw themselves as being filled with "presence." Among the Beat poets, two stand out strongly from the rest in this quest for unity: Gary Snyder and Allen Ginsberg—one on the West Coast and one on the East Coast, and that divide is worth noting.

Over the years, Snyder has both accepted his name and work as being synonymous with the Beats and has sought to distance himself from Japhy Ryder and the Beat image. First, he has pointed out repeatedly that *The Dharma Bums* is a work of fiction with fictional characters. Too often fans and critics have quoted the words of Japhy Ryder and indiscriminately attributed them to Snyder. At the same time, Snyder and others have acknowledged

Gary Snyder made Eastern and Native American cultures significant parts of the Beat movement. (Allen Ginsberg/Corbis)

global turmoil of World War II. Like so many others, his family suffered the poverty of the 1930s and retreated for a while to a semirural lifestyle of raising chickens and cutting up old stumps to make shake shingles, while his father on and off sought work along the West Coast. Growing up, he had ample opportunity to explore the mountains and forests around him, first in Washington State and then in Oregon after his family moved to Portland at the outset of World War II. Snyder graduated from high school in Portland and then attended Reed College. In his teen years he wrote short articles for a mountain-climbing club's magazine, the school newspaper, and then a college literary club. But he himself claims that he did not come into his own as a poet until he overcame imitation and began writing the poems that eventually formed the nucleus of *Riprap,* his first published book. At the same time, his college education laid the basis for much of his poetic work by immersing him in literature and literary debates, exposing him to contemporary poets and fellow aspiring writers, providing the intellectual stimulation of a double major in literature and anthropology, and exposing him to the influence of left-wing professors, whose ideas reiterated and went beyond the anarcho-syndicalist "Wobbly" tradition of Snyder's own family. In fact, the required undergraduate thesis that he wrote at Reed, *He Who Hunted Birds in His Father's Village* (eventually published in 1979) combines his two majors and reveals themes, concepts, and spiritual beliefs that echo throughout his life's work as a writer. He concluded that study by claiming that "Myth is a 'reality lived' and in turn 'Reality is a myth lived'" (109–110). For Snyder, myths and their related religious traditions are very much like poems in that myths are not invented but rather are given to the poet by the world experience of his life and concentrate and articulate key moments of revelation. Likewise, a person's individual actions, path in life, and fundamental physiological reality are not autonomous or even unique but embedded in larger energy flows, including spiritual pathways.

that in many places Kerouac came pretty close to recording actual conversations. Second, Snyder has at times drawn distinctions between the Beats as an East Coast phenomenon and the San Francisco Renaissance as a West Coast phenomenon, while recognizing that the social circumstances giving rise to both, the personalities, and the literary and cultural practices significantly overlap. Clearly both wings of the larger cultural phenomenon can be defined as "hip," with the distinction being more one of the New York scene as frenetic and hot and the San Francisco Bay Area scene as mellow and cool. Interestingly enough, one can even locate differences on the basis of preferences for different variants of Buddhism, Ginsberg being attracted to Tibetan Buddhism and Snyder being attracted to Japanese Zen. Yet for all the differences that one may delineate, the similarities overwhelmingly dominate.

Snyder was born in 1930, a few years later than Ginsberg and some of the other Beats, but earlier than the youngest writers who became identified with the movement. He grew up amid the economic hardships of the Great Depression and the

Almost from the start of his coming into his own as a poet with the "riprap" style poems, he began to receive critical acclaim and notoriety. Both of these resulted in no small part from his sharing the podium at the famous 6 Gallery reading where Allen Ginsberg first read "Howl" to a wildly enthusiastic audience. These two poets established a friendship that endured until Ginsberg's death in 1997. Even though Snyder spent the majority of the years between 1956 and 1968 in Japan, he became a leading poet and activist in the West Coast Beat and hippie movements and, with only a slim production of prose, was widely read and pronounced a worthy successor to Henry David Thoreau.

When Snyder returned to the West Coast permanently after his years in Japan, he brought with him his third wife, Masa Uehara, and their first son, Kai. Soon, another son was born, Gen. Gary and Masa remained married for some twenty years, and he continues to live in the house he designed and helped build, called Kitkitdizze, near Nevada City, California, with his fourth wife. Shortly after his divorce from Masa, he married Carole Koda, who brought two daughters into the marriage. Immediately following this homecoming, Snyder was interviewed by the *Berkeley Barb* and promoted as a counterculture hero. He also published three books in quick succession, two of poetry, *The Back Country* and *Regarding Wave,* and one of prose, *Earth House Hold.* While extremely active throughout the 1970s, giving readings and public lectures, he also established a strong profile as an environmental activist. This profile was codified by the 1974 publication of *Turtle Island,* which won him the Pulitzer Prize for poetry the following year. Toward the end of the decade more prose began to appear, mainly based on his various lectures.

In the 1980s, Snyder accepted a position as a professor of English at the University of California, Davis, and published relatively little. But beginning in 1990, he brought out several major books. Two volumes of prose, *The Practice of the Wild* and *A Place in Space,* established him as a major nature writer, in terms of producing nonfiction prose on environmental themes. He also brought out a large volume of selected and new poems, *No Nature,* and then surprised many of his followers by finally completing and publishing his second poetic sequence, *Mountains and Rivers without End,* on which he had been working for forty years. Regardless of what else he may write, this volume will represent the pinnacle of his poetic career. At the end of the decade, he released a major retrospective volume that did include some new material, *The Gary Snyder Reader: Prose, Poetry, and Translations.* More recently, in 2002, he followed this large volume with a slim collection of prose and poetry culled from the books he published with New Directions between 1968 and 1978. At the age of seventy-two, he retired from his position at U.C. Davis, where he remains professor emeritus.

Snyder's poetics present a variety of styles, from clear, straightforward common speech organized in lyrics with short lines to highly complex field composition relying on mythic allusions and subtle metaphors. These two major styles often appear side by side in the same volume of poetry. Likewise, his poetic themes have tended to remain fairly constant throughout his career, centering on positive and negative human interaction with nature, indigenous and ancient cultural practices contrasted with contemporary mainstream cultural values, and the relationships of the human individual with all other living beings, with community, and with family. Perhaps because of the popular perception of Snyder as an activist and spokesperson for a generation's rejection of American materialism, secularism, and pragmatism, Snyder's poetry has been read and critiqued more for its content than for its form, and yet the two always work together.

With Snyder's first two books of poetry, *Riprap* (1959) and *Myths & Texts* (1960), we see most clearly the polarities of his style, yet it must be noted that the poems in these volumes were written during overlapping time periods—roughly 1954 to 1958 and 1952 to 1956. *Riprap* poems, for many his trademark verse, primarily display short lines, a sparing use of metaphor, an elimination or delay of the presentation of the speaker as an "I," and a meditative quality, even though they usually involve the speaker engaged in participatory activity. This participation takes the form either of work or relaxation from work through engagement with nature. Despite the spare use of language and imagistic style, they narrate or imply a story involving either physical action or a decision about action, such as whether to remain in the United States or travel to Japan, to remain down in the city or take a job as a fire lookout. *Myths & Texts,* presented as a poetic sequence, represents a clear story replete with action, conflict, and meditation, but the story is presented in a fragmented way, displaying the clear rupture with linear narration typical of modernist poetics. Most significant, the growth of the main character is revealed as a spiritual journey toward enlightenment, so that the sequence's climax occurs as a recognition rather than a deed. In this case, true to his claim about the relationship of myth and reality in his undergraduate thesis—completed the same year Snyder started writing this sequence—the poem's conclusion demonstrates the identity of myths and texts, of spiritual beliefs and sensory experience. The difficulty of the sequence lies not so much in the form of the poem, in terms of its fragmentation and the slippery positioning of the speaker, but rather in the heavy use of cultural and religious allusions drawn from a wide variety of Native American cultures and from Buddhist texts and hagiography.

Snyder continued to publish poems while living in Japan on and off throughout the 1960s, but he did not publish a new book of poems until his return to the United States. In 1968 he published *The Back Country,* a large volume with almost ninety of his own poems and eighteen translations of Miyazawa Kenji's poems. The book opens with "A Berry Feast," which he had read at the famous 6 Gallery reading where Ginsberg first performed "Howl." Thus, it contains poems spanning some fifteen years of his writing. They are not arranged chronologically, however, but are organized into a loose sequence with four movements: "Far West," "Far East," "Kali," and "Back." They trace the trajectory of his life from his immersion in the mountains and the Bay Area of the western United States, through his years in Japan. These two sections are followed by "Kali," which records in part his trip to India where he and his wife at the time, Joanne Kyger, traveled with Ginsberg and Peter Orlovsky (some journal entries of this trip are published in *Passage through India*). This section also depicts an inward psychic journey. And the last section, "Back," has poems that can be read as his return to the United States. Interestingly enough, this four-part movement begins and ends with poems about food, and specifically about the possibility of plenitude and satiation. Although scattered throughout the volume, particularly in parts one and two, various poems indicate Snyder's participation in the Beat movement and promote the sense of counterculture community that was fostered. In this searching and reflective volume, Snyder intermixes poems that address ecology, Buddhism, and human relationships with considerable Buddhist attention to the painful aspects of birth, death, and rebirth. The Miyazawa translations mainly reflect depictions of nature and show a striking thematic alignment between the two poets.

Snyder's next two volumes, one of prose and one of poetry, *Earth House Hold* and *Regarding Wave,* have little of the painful introspection found in *The Back Country.* In particular, *Earth House Hold* was received as a Beat/hippie manifesto. Not only do its early selections display Snyder's coming to Buddhism as a spiritual practice, but its later essays suggest a rejection of Western culture and an embrace of Eastern and indigenous values, particularly in "Buddhism and the Coming Revolution," "Why Tribe," and "Dharma Queries." The book ends with a brief description of a subsistence Japanese commune led by Nanao Sakaki in which Snyder participated along with Masa Uehara in 1967. It was there that he and Masa were married on the lip of an active volcano. That island and their marriage became the setting and the moment that govern the bulk of the poems in *Regarding Wave.* While containing some poems criticizing Western culture, the volume primarily contains ecstatic and celebratory poems revolving around Snyder and Masa Uehara's marriage, Masa's pregnancy, and the birth of their first son in the three "Regarding Wave" sections. Also, in the title poem of the volume, which appears at the end of the third section, Snyder unites Buddhism, ecology, and human marriage. All three require commitment, interrelationship, and balanced action. The field composition of this poem, like others similarly formatted, provides readers with detailed directions for the pacing and breathing required to read the poem aloud. In fact, no other volume of Snyder's poetry so clearly appeals to the reader to re-cite the poems aloud rather than read them silently.

The three "Regarding Wave" sections are fol-lowed by two others, "Long Hair" and "Target Prac-tice." Both contain more overtly political poems about American countercultural values, but also, like the rest of the volume, begin to add a concern about "family" that builds on the attention to "tribe" found in *Earth House Hold.* Like *The Back Coun-try, Regarding Wave* consists of short narrative poems and highly symbolic lyrics, again alternating metonymic poems that depict immediate, direct ex-perience, and metaphorical poems that rely heavily on mythical and Eastern allusions for their symbols and images.

Although Snyder had clearly attained a strong counterculture notoriety on the West Coast and was recognized as a preeminent Beat in the New York scene, his reputation remained largely regional and avant-garde until the appearance of *Turtle Island* in 1974. Earning the Pulitzer Prize for Poetry in 1975, *Turtle Island* made Snyder a nationally recognized poet. He not only became increasingly well-known among American readers but also came to the at-tention of English professors and critics, with the first full-length study of his life and work appearing in 1976. No doubt part of the attention directed at *Turtle Island* resulted from the overall growing recognition of the Beats as a literary and cultural force, the sense of victory felt by the antiwar and hippie movements and their beliefs that they were revolutionizing American society, and the political directness with which Snyder's poems treated U.S. imperialism, Native American values, environmen-tal issues, and radical social change. The goal of "reinhabitation" of North America unites these themes to create a unified collection in which Sny-der begins to outline an alternative vision for a bal-anced, noncapitalist way of life on this continent. The first two sections of the book emphasize a neg-ative critique of contemporary industrial societies, as in "Front Lines" and "Mother Earth: Her Whales." The third section, "For the Children," shifts to more upbeat, visionary waters, in which

present-day destruction of nature is placed within the long flow of planetary and human history, as in "Tomorrow's Song." Reiterating the political and vi-sionary elements of *Turtle Island,* Snyder concludes it with "Plain Talk," a set of prose essays, the most famous of which remains "Four Changes." This essay maps out fundamental changes and the steps that need to be taken to realign contemporary American life with the greater flow of nature and world history.

Surprising many of his readers and critics, Snyder let nine years pass before releasing another full-length book. *Axe Handles* appeared in 1983, a slim volume of poetry, with a significantly different tone from *Turtle Island.* Snyder sounds much less apoc-alyptic, although no less political, in this volume, ex-pressing greater confidence in the long cycles of human interaction with the rest of the world. These poems read as if he has realigned his role as a poet and his relationship to society from being a prophet writing jeremiads to becoming a teacher handing down the lessons of experience to forthcoming gen-erations. This volume also contains an entire section devoted to hymns of praise, which have appeared individually in other books, titled "Little Songs for Gaia." Using concepts that can be found in both Buddhism and ecology, Snyder makes use of the imagery of nets and loops in relation to energy flows, balance, and reinhabitation.

Many critics saw the lessening of intensity in *Axe Handles* as a falling off of Snyder's poetic abilities, and this judgment was not dispelled when Snyder published only two volumes of poetry in the fol-lowing decade, ones containing only a smattering of new poems. *Left Out in the Rain,* published in 1986, is subtitled *New Poems 1947–1985* and con-tains all of the poems written during this period but omitted from Snyder's other books, yet only a few were written after the poems of *Axe Handles.* Like-wise, *No Nature: New and Selected Poems,* pub-lished in 1992, contained only fifteen new poems in a volume running to nearly 400 pages. And while these generally display strong artistry, particularly in terms of rhythm and visual imagery, they tend to recycle older Snyder themes often addressed more successfully in earlier poems. In fact in the early

1990s, many younger readers came to know Snyder more as an essayist than as a poet as a result of his publishing first *The Practice of the Wild* in 1990 and then *A Place in Space* in 1995. These volumes defined Snyder as a voice for wilderness and an environmentalist advocate in a way that contrasted with the way his poetry defined him. Not only did he provide a strong critique of contemporary economic and cultural practices, but he also provided a series of corrective recommendations, thereby continuing the kind of analysis solidly established by the prose section of *Turtle Island,* "Plain Talk." Snyder's own concern with situating himself as a "nature writer" can be seen from his including in *A Place in Space* his own essays on the appropriate prosaics of such writing, "Unnatural Writing" and "Language Goes Two Ways." This volume ends with a section titled "Watersheds" and in it Snyder restates and extends his concept of reinhabitation, returning to the image of "Turtle Island" of his 1974 volume and his homestead, "Kitkitdizze," which appears in *Axe Handles.*

For those readers and critics who saw Snyder becoming an essayist at the expense of his poetry, shock, excitement, and celebration marked their response to the appearance in 1996 of the long-awaited and finally completed sequence, *Mountains and Rivers without End.* Although Snyder had been continuing to publish selected pieces of this work in progress, these had mostly appeared in small literary journals and limited edition chapbooks generally out of the public eye. And it is evident from the topics addressed in many sections that he had been writing these throughout the eighties and nineties almost up to the moment of the book's publication. Like his first completed sequence, *Myths & Texts,* this sequence relies on symbols, allusions, myths, and formal elements largely unknown to most American readers. Written over a forty-year period, the thirty-nine poems that this sequence comprises reflect both the multifaceted character of Snyder's life experiences during those decades and the allusions, images, metaphors, and poetic styles that appear in all of his other books. Although a reader need not know it, the volume is organized by means of the tempo-

ral structure of the Japanese Noh play, divided into four acts, with many of the major poems of the sequence also subdividable into such acts. In addition, the poems range across the landscapes in which Snyder has lived and ventured and this spatial dimension is reflected in the controlling image of a Chinese scroll painting, which opens and closes the poem.

In brief, *Mountains and Rivers without End* is written in the service of a culture-building process, rather than with a focus on a hero or a heroic quest. The book emphasizes journeying rather than arriving, and hence the title of the first poem, "Endless Streams and Mountains." Indeed, the final poem emphasizes that the life of the world and the process of human experience and interaction with that world exceed the experience and the lifetime of any given individual. And yet, like the spirits of the Buddhist gods/goddesses, particularly those of wisdom and mercy, that appear throughout the sequence, the spirits of individual human beings leave their marks upon the land and upon the lives of other individuals. In the second part of the sequence, then, Snyder makes clear through its ten poems that compassion provides the starting point for the acquisition of wisdom. And in the third section, such wisdom will enable the traveler, who can be defined not only as the speaker of the sequence but also any human being as a life sojourner, to become one with the world. The fourth part of the sequence, then, ends on a strong note of optimism that the world will continue turning underfoot as people work out their individual paths and their imprints on the planet. The sequence itself in its individual poems mimics the mountains and rivers, the up-and-down nature of life experience. Some poems can be comprehended in an instant, providing guidance for proper behavior, while others remain confusing long after their reading moment has ended, providing food for thought, images for the imagination, and koan-like puzzles for meditation. Key to appreciating this volume is the willingness to flow with the movement of the poems from beginning to end, emotively and sensuously reacting to them rather than too rapidly resorting to logical and critical analysis of their allusions, references, and symbols.

At the beginning of his eighth decade of life, Snyder remains quite active, physically vigorous, and intellectually acute. His traveling has diminished, but he remains an international presence as a poet and a thinker. Readers can anticipate continued publications from him, perhaps more prose than poetry. For one, he has written more essays than poems in recent years. For another, he has a far larger body of unpublished notebooks and journals, which he has meticulously kept throughout his adult years, on which to draw for prose collections that will prove of both historical and contemporaneous intellectual interest. Their publication will in many ways constitute the closest thing to an autobiography that we are ever likely to get from him.

—*Patrick Murphy*

## Principal Works
Poetry: *Riprap*, 1959; *Myths & Texts*, 1960; *Riprap and Cold Mountain Poems*, 1965; *The Back Country*, 1968; *Regarding Wave*, 1970; *Turtle Island*, 1974; *Axe Handles*, 1983; *Left Out in the Rain: New Poems 1947–1985*, 1986; *No Nature: New and Selected Poems*, 1990; *Mountains and Rivers without End*, 1996.

Prose: *Earth House Hold: Technical Notes & Queries to Fellow Dharma Revolutionaries*, 1970; *The Old Ways: Six Essays*, 1977; *He Who Hunted Birds in His Father's Village*, 1979; *Passage through India*, 1983; *The Practice of the Wild*, 1990; *A Place in Space: Ethics, Aesthetics, and Watersheds*, 1995.

Compilations: *The Gary Snyder Reader: Prose, Poetry, and Translations, 1952–1998*, 1999; *Look Out: A Selection of Writings*, 2003.

## Bibliographical References
Full-length studies of Snyder's poetry began with Bob Steuding, *Gary Snyder*, 1976, a literary biography up through *Turtle Island*, followed by Charles Molesworth, *Gary Snyder's Visions: Poetry and the Real Work*, 1983, a narrowly political study of his poetic themes; *Critical Essays on Gary Snyder*, edited by Patrick D. Murphy, 1990, collected significant early critical essays, including the first piece of academic criticism, a 1968 essay by Thomas Parkinson; Murphy then wrote a brief chronological overview of the poetry and prose, *Understanding Gary Snyder*, 1992,

which he revised and expanded into *A Place for Wayfaring: The Poetry and Prose of Gary Snyder*, 2000; Jon Halper edited a collection of reminiscences by others about Snyder's life as *Gary Snyder: Dimensions of a Life*, 1991; Eric Todd Smith provides a brief study of background and context in *Reading Gary Snyder's "Mountains and Rivers without End,"* 1999, while Anthony Hunt's *Genesis, Structure, and Meaning in Gary Snyder's "Mountains and Rivers without End,"* 2004, is an exhaustive study of that poem; additionally Michael Davidson, in *The San Francisco Renaissance: Poetics and Community at Mid-Century*, 1989, treats Snyder within a cultural study of the movement, while Sherman Paul, *In Search of the Primitive: Rereading David Antin, Jerome Rothenberg, and Gary Snyder*, 1986, provides a very personal reading of Snyder's poems; more recently Leonard Scigaj returns to the figure of Japhy Ryder and studies closely several Snyder poems in *Sustainable Poetry: Four American Ecopoets*, 1999.

***See also*** Sea, The Beats at; Kyger, Joanne; Travel: The Beats as Globetrotters; Kerouac, Jack; Ginsberg, Allen; 6 Gallery Reading; San Francisco; Eastern Culture; Environmentalism; Native American Cultures; Mountains, Beats in the

## Sociological Interpretations
Sociologists often view the Beat Generation as a manifestation in the period following World War II of the bohemian lifestyle—an alternative way of living made preferable because the dominant lifestyle is unsatisfying or untenable. In the sociologist's view, the Beats choose deviance rather than conformity, dissidence rather than submission. According to some sociologists, Beat behavior is delinquency, but others recognize a constructive effect in the way of life connected with the Beats.

The Beats, like their bohemian predecessors, are generally Romantic in their outlook. The mood of the Beats may vary from gloominess to silliness. Activities reveal spontaneity, expressiveness, and truthfulness.

David Matza in "Subterranean Tradition of Youth" (1961) associates the Beats primarily with young people. Paul Goodman in *Growing Up Absurd* (1960) seems to agree. However, Mel van Elteren in

"The Culture of the Subterraneans: A Sociological View of the Beats" (1999) qualifies the connection of the Beats to youth by noting that many people over forty were involved in the Beat scene and that the Beat outlook is not strictly for the young.

Sociologists observe the sexual customs of the Beats, noting a pattern of male dominance involving the male "cat" and the female "chick." The males reveal immaturity and unwillingness to make relationships permanent. Van Elteren again qualifies the analysis of the Beat culture by noting that men in general, not just Beat men, may be guilty of immaturity and an unwillingness to establish commitment.

In describing the Beats, van Elteren sees their deviance as lateral rather than vertical. He argues that the Beats opposed the lifestyles of the privileged, but the Beats were not interested in seizing the privileges for themselves; instead, they chose to move to the margins and establish an alternative lifestyle that did not include the trappings of those who remained above.

Ambiguity and contradiction in Beat behavior also concern the sociologist. If the Beats rejected the literary establishment, did they also ultimately want to become a part of it? If the Beats began as a counterculture movement, were they subverted by the forces that moved them into mainstream culture? If the Beats insist on individuality, how do they reconcile such an insistence with their pleasure in communality?

Paul Goodman in *Growing Up Absurd* sees the Beats beginning in middle-class homes, but notes their separation from middle-class values (172). The problem, says Goodman, is that the Beats do not determine a suitable replacement for the middle-class values. The Beats maintain their associations with their parents but do not accept what their parents stand for.

In regard to the principal contribution of the Beats to society, sociologists are divided. Ned Polsky in "The Village Beat Scene: Summer 1960" says that the Beats popularized the use of marijuana, spreading its use far beyond the jazz scene. Acknowledging the influence on drug use, van Elteren observes the Beats' efforts to counteract the imposition of American culture on other societies.

Lawrence Lipton in "The Social Lie," which is the concluding chapter of *The Holy Barbarians* (1959), also sees the Beats rejecting the fraud perpetrated by the dominant American culture, but does not clearly see the Beats as agents of change. In Lipton's analysis, the disaffiliated person rejects society's advertising, militarism, and politics. The Beat refuses to buy the product sold through the lies of advertising, avoids military service because it is founded on lies, and doubts the ballot as a means of shaping society.

—*William Lawlor*

## Bibliographical References

Mel van Elteren's "The Culture of the Subterraneans: A Sociological View of the Beats," which appears on pages 63–92 of *Beat Culture: The 1950's and Beyond*, 1999, is a clear, compact, and thoroughly annotated review of sociological studies of the Beats. To get an impression of sociologists reacting to the Beats at the height of their popularity, one may consult Ned Polsky, "The Village Beat Scene: Summer 1960" in *Hustlers, Beats, and Others*, 1969; Polsky's analysis of the Beats in Greenwich Village is balanced by Lawrence Lipton, *The Holy Barbarians*, 1959, which focuses on Venice West. Francis J. Rigney and L. Douglas Smith in *The Real Bohemia: A Sociological and Psychological Study of the Beats*, 1961, reveal the results of personality tests administered to people at the Grant Avenue Bohemian Colony. Paul Goodman's *Growing Up Absurd* (1960) comments frequently on the Beats as he discusses people coming of age at midcentury, and David Matza focuses on the Beats as a youth movement in "Subterranean Traditions of Youth," which appears in *The Annals of the American Academy of Political and Social Sciences* 338 (November 1961): 102–118.

*See also* Juvenile Delinquency; Sexism and Misogyny; Marriage; Bohemian Movements: Predecessors of the Beats; Venice West; New York City

## Solomon, Carl (1928–1994)

Carl Solomon has a double distinction in Beat history as both the editor who helped get a key "Beat" book into publication and as the dedicatee of Allen Ginsberg's "Howl" (1956).

A sharp student, Solomon completed high school when he was fifteen and enrolled at City College in Manhattan. In 1943, he joined the United States Maritime Service, which enabled him to visit France, where he learned of André Breton, saw a play by Jean Genet, and listened to a poetry presentation by Antonin Artaud. Thus, when Solomon returned to New York, he brought an intensified interest in surrealism and Dada with him.

In 1949, Solomon feared that he was insane and entered the New York Psychiatric Institute for treatment. In this treatment center, Solomon met Allen Ginsberg and over a period of several months had various conversations with him. Ginsberg recorded some of the things that Solomon said when he returned from insulin-shock treatment and later used the selected phrases in "Howl" (1956). Ginsberg's poem is not an accurate record of Solomon's life, but because the poem is dedicated to Solomon and refers to ideas and phrases associated with him, Solomon now has immortal status in Beat literature.

Solomon worked as an editor at Ace Books, the firm of his uncle, A. A. Wynn. Solomon guided William S. Burroughs's *Junky* (1953) into publication but wrangled with Jack Kerouac and eventually rejected *On the Road*.

Between 1956 and 1964, Solomon was an inmate at Pilgrim State Hospital, where he received shock treatment and, as he wrote in *Emergency Messages*, missed out on being part of any social "movement." He died of emphysema in 1994.

Solomon published two collections of essays, *Mishaps, Perhaps* (1966) and *More Mishaps* (1968), and a collection of autobiographical works edited by John Tytell, *Emergency Messages* (1989). Unlike Whitmanesque Ginsberg or "spontaneous" Kerouac, Solomon wrote terse, cryptic essays and poems satirizing his time in Pilgrim, his former associations with the Left and the Beats, and his friend Ginsberg.

—*Matt Stefon*

### Principal Works

Compare Carl Solomon, *Emergency Messages: An Autobiographical Miscellany*, ed. John Tytell, 1989, with Carl Solomon, *Mishaps, Perhaps*, 1966, and Carl Solomon, *More Mishaps*, 1968.

### Bibliographical References

John Tytell, *Paradise Outlaws: Remembering the Beats*, 1999, includes a brief recollection of Solomon; Michael Schumacher, *Dharma Lion*, 1992, offers a summary of Solomon's interaction with Allen Ginsberg: 115–117. In *Howl: Original Draft Facsimile*, ed. Barry Miles, 1995, Solomon contributes to the extensive notes that clarify the poem; in *The Portable Beat Reader*, ed. Ann Charters, 1992, one finds a short biographical sketch and two short selections of Solomon's writings.

***See also*** Ginsberg, Allen

## Sommerville, Ian (1941–1976)

Mathematician; artist; actor; collaborator with Brion Gysin, Antony Balch, and William S. Burroughs.

With Brion Gysin and William Burroughs, Ian Sommerville worked on cut-ups and produced a collaborative book entitled *Brion Gysin Let the Mice In* (1973). These cut-ups involve the cutting of a page of text and the rearrangement of the parts of the page to form a new text, which may be scrambled language but which may also create special results in the language. The trio collaborated again to produce an audio recording *Break Through in Grey Room* (1986), which presents cut-ups as spoken-word performances. Sommerville teamed with Antony Balch and William S. Burroughs to produce various short films in the 1960s. These experimental films are now available on the video *Towers Open Fire* (1995).

Sommerville also combined with Brion Gysin to produce the Dreamachine, a work of kinetic art. This work consists of a perforated cylinder that rotates around a bright light. The light flickers in a manner similar to the flickering of a strobe light, and if one faces the Dreamachine with his or her eyes closed, one is induced to see images and forms on the eyelids.

—*William Lawlor*

## Bibliographical References

Michael Schumacher gives a brief description of Ian Sommerville on pages 357–358 of *Dharma Lion*, 1992; Ted Morgan refers briefly to Sommerville various times in *Literary Outlaw*, 1988; in Barry Miles, *Beat Hotel*, 2000, one finds a description of Sommerville's personality and his connection to William S. Burroughs: 183–187.

*See also* Gysin, Brion; Burroughs, William Seward

## Spicer, Jack (1925–1965)

Poet; playwright; lecturer; leader on the poetry scene during the San Francisco Renaissance; close associate of Robert Duncan and Robin Blaser.

Although born in Los Angeles, Spicer established his writing career in San Francisco shortly after World War II. He studied at the University of California, Berkeley, where he became friends with Duncan and Blaser. Spicer subsequently taught at the University of Minnesota and the California School of Fine Arts.

In 1954, he was the cofounder of the 6 Gallery in San Francisco, the location for the famous 6 Gallery reading.

In 1957, at the San Francisco Public Library, Spicer led a workshop titled Poetry as Magic. Among others, Helen Adam and Robert Duncan participated. The magic in the workshop had little to do with prestidigitation; instead, Spicer sought to find the factors that affected souls and emotions. To enroll, participants had to complete a questionnaire that asked about worldviews, personal desires, and wildlife. Spicer set up a large roundtable, and participants in the workshop sat facing everyone else. Meetings were intended to be private sessions for members only.

During the 1950s, Spicer was a key organizer of the popular Blabbermouth Night at the Place, a bar in San Francisco. A microphone was available for volunteers ready and willing to babble. Some people in the audience applauded; others shouted out their criticisms. The best babbler won a small prize.

Spicer's Imaginary Elegies were included in Donald Allen's landmark anthology *The New American Poetry* (1960); in *The Poetics of the New American Poetry*, eds. Donald Allen and Warren Tallman (1973), one finds "Jack Spicer to Federico Garcia Lorca" and "Excerpts from the Vancouver Lectures." These publications are a clear sign of the quality and importance of Spicer's work, but usually he did not seek or accept publication. He preferred to publish his work in small editions that did not circulate very much beyond the San Francisco area.

Spicer shared the Beats' enthusiasm for public presentation of poetry, but his theory of poetry was not typically Beat. In fact, he doubted the Beats, and he and the loyal members of his circle wrote parodies of writings by Beats, distributing the parodies with author credits given to the authors being mocked, as if the poems were actually written by Beat authors.

Unlike the Beats, who saw poetry as the product of a particular person's experience, Spicer saw the poet as a channel for an outside force that passes through the poet but retains control over the outcome of the poem. Rather than write individual poems, Spicer preferred to write a series of poems or a full collection.

Spicer sometimes is referred to as a deep image poet, perhaps because of his affinity for the imagistic power of the poetry of Federico Garcia Lorca. Others see Spicer as a forerunner of Language Poetry.

He died of alcoholism in 1965.

—*William Lawlor*

## Principal Works

Although most of Spicer's publications were small editions published through White Rabbit Press, his works are now available in *The Collected Books of Jack Spicer*, ed. Robin Blaser, 1975; Spicer's poetics are made clear in *The House That Jack Built: The Collected Lectures of Jack Spicer*, ed. Peter Gizzi, 1998.

## Bibliographical References

Michael Davidson includes a chapter "'The City Redefined': Community and Dialogue in Jack Spicer" in *The San Francisco Renaissance*, 1989: 150–171. Michael McClure includes "An Empire of Signs: Jack Spicer" in *Lighting the Corners*, 1993: 113–127; Edward Halsey Foster provides compact coverage of Spicer's life and work in *Jack*

*Spicer,* 1991; a full biography is Lewis Ellingham and Kevin Killian, *Poet Be Like God: Jack Spicer and the San Francisco Renaissance,* 1998.

**See also** San Francisco Renaissance; San Francisco; Duncan, Robert; 6 Gallery Reading.

## Spontaneity, The Beat Generation and the Culture of

Both in literature and in life, the Beat Generation championed spontaneity as one of its central defining values. Wanting to experience and express life as directly as possible, the Beats promoted numerous spontaneous art forms and social behaviors, ranging from stream-of-consciousness confessional writing and improvised jazz poetry performances to spur-of-the-moment road trips and uninhibited sexual and drug experimentation. Spontaneity played a particularly prominent role in the Beats' new cultural sensibilities because the Beats saw spontaneity as a kind of master key that would enable them to unlock doors and escape from the prevailing social and cultural conventions that prevented them from experiencing life to the fullest. Ultimately, the Beats promoted spontaneity as part of a two-pronged aesthetic and political attack on the "square" culture of 1950s *Leave-it-to-Beaver* America. Aesthetically, the Beats advocated a more spontaneous literary style to challenge the New Critical academic formalism that had dominated literary studies since the modernist innovations of T. S. Eliot. In addition, the Beats celebrated both spontaneous art and spontaneous behavior as a form of political protest that opposed the emerging ideology of post-WWII corporate America. Rebelling against the dominant culture's values of emotional sobriety, social conformity, and political apathy, the Beats advocated greater spontaneity—in both literature and life—to advance alternative countercultural values such as uninhibited personal self-expression, manic emotional intensity, and a sense of at least cultural, if not exactly political, rebellion.

In both their cultural manifestos and their literary works, the Beats repeatedly articulated a spontaneous vision of life and literature. In particular,

Kerouac's most famous literary manifestos, "Essentials of Spontaneous Prose" and "Belief & Technique for Modern Prose," identify spontaneity as the essence of great art. Rejecting traditional notions of discipline, craft, and even grammatical correctness, Kerouac advocates instead an alternative sense of writing as the wild and undisciplined expression of an artist's most intimate and uninhibited thoughts. While writing *On the Road,* Kerouac put this spontaneous ideal into practice, typing the entire manuscript on a continuous roll of paper during a three-week marathon writing session. Even though his editor made him revise the original manuscript, the published version still reflects the spontaneous energy of Kerouac's initial composition process. Moreover, the novel itself chronicles and celebrates the Beat Generation's emerging sense of life and art as a series of spontaneous improvisations. Not only does the novel's hero, Dean Moriarty, move from road trip to jazz club to sexual liaison in a seemingly endless and largely improvised quest for continually escalating kicks, but the artistic challenge taken up by Kerouac's narrator, Sal Paradise, is to find a way to narrate Dean's tale without getting hung up on literary and grammatical conventions. In short, *On the Road* established itself as the testament of the Beat Generation largely because it developed a new aesthetic strategy for expressing the spontaneous, uninhibited adventures of Dean (Neal Cassady) in the spontaneous, uninhibited narrative voice of Sal (Kerouac). In this sense, Kerouac turned to spontaneity both to articulate the Beat Generation's alternative countercultural worldview and to develop its new spontaneous literary style.

While Kerouac's *On the Road* provides the most widely known example of Beat spontaneity, a similar interest in spontaneity extends throughout the work of both major and minor Beat writers. Much like *On the Road,* the first section of Ginsberg's "Howl" both celebrates a subterranean world of urban hipsters passing through an endless series of surreptitious adventures—ranging from listening to jazz on rooftops and engaging in seventy-hour intellectual conversations to experiencing furtive sexual encounters and drug trips—and articulates a new poetic voice that can better capture the irregular and unpredictable rhythm of the Beats' alternative lifestyles. In effect, the tradition-breaking style of Ginsberg's fragmented, eccentric, and antipoetic vernacular poetry mirrors, at the level of style, the unconventional social behaviors that Ginsberg describes in his poem. Like Kerouac, Ginsberg infuses his poetry with a sense of spontaneity that simultaneously functions on both thematic and formal levels, so that the unconventional aesthetic strategies employed in the text create an artistic double for the unorthodox social behaviors espoused by the Beat counterculture. Similar attempts to develop spontaneous artistic strategies for articulating counterhegemonic Beat values can be found in William Burroughs's cut-up method, Bob Kaufman's jazz poetry, Ted Joans's Afro-American surrealism, and Anne Waldman's improvised poetic chants. Each of these Beat writers developed his or her own variation on spontaneous prosody, but all shared a common goal of exploring new ways to enliven literary discourse with a more uninhibited and spontaneous style.

To develop this more spontaneous style, the Beats drew on an eclectic combination of literary precedents, ranging from William Carlos Williams's imagism and the Lost Generation's bohemianism to Walt Whitman's vernacular poetics and William Blake's radical mysticism. Even more important, the Beats modeled their sense of spontaneity on nonliterary sources such as the improvisational energy of bebop jazz, the radical contingency of abstract expressionist art, and the complex and chaotic rhythms of everyday urban life. In addition to being jazz aficionados, Kerouac, Ferlinghetti, Joans, Kaufman, and other Beat writers collaborated with jazz musicians on jazz poetry performances. Many Beat writers also explicitly defined their aesthetic ideals by analogy to jazz. The introduction to Kerouac's *Book of Blues*, the "Oral Messages" section of Ferlinghetti's *A Coney Island of the Mind*, and Ginsberg's "Notes for *Howl and Other Poems*" all describe Beat writing as an attempt to approximate the spontaneity, creativity, and complexity of improvisational jazz. In fact, it is hard to find a Beat writer or Beat text that does not return repeat-

edly—if not obsessively—to jazz both as a theme and as an aesthetic model. Beat literature is overflowing with descriptions of jazz clubs, jazz records, jazz musicians, and jazz performances, and they are almost invariably described in a style that imitates, more or less successfully, the dynamic energy of bebop jazz.

In addition, Beat writers also emulated the spontaneity of abstract expressionist art. Beat writers such as Ferlinghetti, Joans, and Michael McClure were also visual artists, and they made frequent comparisons between their work and the abstract expressionist style of painters such as Jackson Pollock and Clyfford Styll. Excellent examples of this interrelationship between Beat writing and the visual arts can be seen in Ferlinghetti's *A Coney Island of the Mind* and Joans's *All of Ted Joans and No More*, both of which include frequent references to modern art.

The dynamic energy of urban environments, especially subterranean and bohemian urban neighborhoods such as Times Square and Greenwich Village, also provided the Beats with another inspiration for their emerging sense of spontaneity. In almost every Beat description of urban life, from Ginsberg's "Howl" and John Clellon Holmes's *Go* to Kaufman's "On," one recognizes the Beats' sense of cities as spaces alive with an unpredictable and dynamic vital energy. Whether it was the beat-down lifestyle of urban junkies such as Herbert Huncke or the vital energy of urban cultural centers like the Five Spot, the Beats repeatedly found inspiration for their spontaneous art in the urban environments that surrounded them.

Initially, critics such as Norman Podhoretz and Irving Howe dismissed the Beats' spontaneous literary style as adolescent, narcissistic, and anti-intellectual, but more recent critics have reinterpreted Beat literature as a significant and effective kind of cultural discourse. In particular, Daniel Belgrad's *The Culture of Spontaneity: Improvisation and the Arts in Postwar America*, argues that the Beats were part of a much larger cultural movement that used spontaneous art to challenge the ideology of corporate liberalism. Trying to find some method to the Beats' madness, Belgrad connects Beat literature with a wide range of spontaneous art forms that pervaded post-WWII American culture, including bebop jazz, abstract expressionist art, modern dance, and performance art. In addition, Belgrad argues that this emerging culture of spontaneity aspired to do much more than simply experiment with new aesthetic styles. Focusing instead on the cultural and political work performed by these new spontaneous art forms, Belgrad reinterprets Beat writing and other spontaneous cultural discourses as politically engaged artistic practices that may not have promoted any explicit political agenda, but they still used spontaneous aesthetic forms to encourage new modes of perception and oppositional cultural values. In one of the most persuasive explanations of the social and political significance of the Beat Generation, Belgrad argues that Beat literature functioned like a cultural Trojan horse, disguising its political agenda beneath an aesthetic mask of spontaneity.

Ultimately, the Beat Generation's sense of spontaneity dramatically influenced the historical evolution of post-WWII American culture. As one of the primary movements shaping the emergence of what Donald Allen described as the New American Poetry, the Beats worked alongside African American modernist, Black Mountain, and New York School poets to redirect the course of American poetry, turning it away from the formalistic modernism of T. S. Eliot toward more open and vernacular poetic forms. In addition, the Beats' sense of spontaneity also carried over into nonliterary media, influencing cultural traditions as diverse as rock-and-roll music, performance art, and the avant-garde cinematic techniques of experimental filmmakers such as John Cassavetes and Al Leslie. In addition, the Beat movement also powerfully influenced the emerging counterculture of the 1960s by providing an early avenue for social protest and experimentation with alternative lifestyles. Today, however, the legacy of Beat spontaneity is probably felt most strongly in the slam poetry movement, which, like its Beat predecessors, values the emotional intensity of oral performance and improvisation over the precision of formal craft.

—*Robert Bennett*

## Bibliographical References

The most comprehensive discussion of the Beat Generation's use of spontaneity can be found in Daniel Belgrad, *The Culture of Spontaneity: Improvisation and the Arts in Postwar America*, 1998; a more focused discussion of Kerouac's spontaneous aesthetic is developed in Regina Weinreich, *Kerouac's Spontaneous Poetics: A Study of the Fiction*, 2002; Kerouac describes his views on spontaneous art in Jack Kerouac, "Essentials of Spontaneous Prose" and "Belief & Technique for Modern Prose," reprinted in *A Casebook on the Beat*, edited by Thomas Parkinson, 1961; Allen Ginsberg offers his ideas on spontaneity in "On Improvised Poetics," "Notes for *Howl and Other Poems*," and "When the Mode of Music Changes the Walls of the City Shake," in *Poetics of the New American Poetry*, edited by Donald Allen and Warren Tallman, 1973; see also Allen Ginsberg, *Spontaneous Mind: Selected Interviews, 1958–1996*, ed. David Carter, 2001.

*See also* Kerouac, Jack; *On the Road*, Sale of the Scroll of; Ginsberg, Allen; Kaufman, Bob; Music; Joans; Ted; Burroughs, William Seward; Waldman, Anne; Williams, William Carlos; Painting; New York City; Dance; Performance Humor; Black Mountain, North Carolina, and Black Mountain College; Film

## Styles of Dress, The Beats and

The 1950s, an era in which white Americans fled to the suburbs to raise families and to escape the sufferings and sacrifices World War II had imposed on them, remains known for its conservative ideals and fear of communism. Men headed downtown in business suits to work at their nine-to-five jobs, while women worked at home—wearing dresses and aprons—where they raised children, cooked, and cleaned. This era was marked by bobby socks, the poodle skirt, and stereotypical gender roles. Men were clean cut, wore their hair short, and enjoyed sports. Women spent time fixing their hair into elaborate beehives, wearing dresses, and reading housekeeping magazines. Men worked to bring home meat for the table and televisions for the house. It was a decade of acquiring material goods that constituted a life of prosperity, happiness, and contentment—in short, an "ideal" life. Any attempt to cross this ideal border, whether exemplified by deliberate actions or through passive forms of actions, such as dress—specifically dressing counter to the suburban norm—was often construed as deviant or communist behavior.

The Beats stood counter to the suburban image of the typical American, and magazines, television, and film were quick to create a stereotypical caricature of the Beats. Magazines such as *Life* (November 1959) depicted the Beats as rebels, developing a false portrait of the Beat: a long-haired, thin man (with a beard or goatee) or a long-haired, waif-like Beat woman in the streets, dressed in all black, wearing sunglasses, and beating bongo drums. This image also appeared on television in the form of the character Maynard G. Krebs, played by Bob Denver, on *The Many Loves of Dobie Gillis.* Maynard complained about going to work, sported a goatee, and did scat singing while wearing torn sweatshirts. In the movie *Hairspray,* a Beat couple appears in a short scene—they are seen wearing all black, ironing their hair straight (opposite to the main character who wears her hair in elaborate updos, which represent sixties trends). The Beat couple appears manic and paints, sings, and plays the bongos sporadically, using terms such as "cool cat." The woman beatnik in the film wears black stockings instead of bright-colored clothes and pumps, and the man wears a beret and lace-up boots. The Beats were portrayed as existential, deviant, and unpredictable in movies—opposites to the clean-cut suburban ideal.

This stereotype of the beatnik pervaded popular culture, despite individual Beats, such as Jack Kerouac, the founder of the Beat Movement, who appeared in the public eye dressed in flannel jackets, khakis, and loafers—looking as if he had just come from the rails. The early Beats did not wear suits, did not have jobs downtown, and did not have wives in the suburbs. Kerouac's casual dress projected the image of a vagabond riding the rails or a working 1940s American tired after a day of labor. The Beat look was inspired by Depression-era photographs by James Agee and songs by Woody Guthrie that indicate the American identity of the individual suffering but rising to meet his destiny.

This vision of America resonates in Ginsberg's poems and Kerouac's novels; heroes of the Depression, artistic loners, and survivors influenced the Beats and inspired them. Their very definition of themselves, as "Beat"—beat down, downtrodden—reflects those heroes, who are beat, exhausted, and, in the end, beatific. An image of Kerouac as a Dharma bum, a man in traveling clothes with his backpack at his side hitching a ride, comes readily to the mind of someone who has read *On the Road* or *Dharma Bums.* This image supports the definition of Beat, echoes the image of riding the rails, and provides a timeless image of Kerouac in our heads—an image of the origins of Beat.

Into the sixties, the Beats grew closer to Buddhism, adopting it as their own way or following elements of it to whatever degree they felt was right for them as individuals. Philip Whalen wore the robes of a Zen monk, and Allen Ginsberg visited India in the early sixties to practice meditation and yoga. He adopted the dress and fashion of the place—the Indian prints. Ginsberg's wild hair, beard and moustache, and baggy clothes influenced the hippie generation of artists and youth who became known for wearing or adopting this style of dress as a part of their own costumes of rebellion. The hippies also dressed this way as they adopted the practices of meditation, lobbied for peace in Vietnam, and challenged government and suburban responses to civil rights and foreign policy.

Ginsberg continued to influence trends and attitudes; he always seemed on the cusp of cultural change, and his dress in the seventies again reflected an evolution in the Beat movement. He appeared trim and clean cut, wearing jackets and ties purchased from Good Will—a more conservative look—when he made public readings. He seriously studied Buddhism and wrote and read poetry at literary functions. For him, the focus of a revolution turned inward.

Because the Beats inspired casual dress and behavior, counter to the strict fifties mentality, many women were also attracted to the movement. Many of the core women Beats found freedom in their personal and professional relationships. Hettie

343

Jones, author of *How I Became Hettie Jones* (1990), was in the forefront of this movement and paved the way for the sixties feminists by serving as an example that ran counter to the traditional housewife image. She became a writer—a woman with a job outside the traditional role of wife to a Beat writer. She helped support her husband's career and promoted the idea of casual dress—freeing women from restrictive clothes, first from corsets and later from bras. Straight hair and no makeup meant less time primping and more time for writing, thinking, and living.

Dress and fashion changed because courageous men and women wore what they wanted to wear instead of wearing what their culture indicated they ought to wear. The Beat movement served as the impetus for that change, and today the ideals of individuality that the Beats initiated continue.

—Lisa Wellinghoff

## Bibliographic References

Holly George-Warren, ed., *The Rolling Stone Book of the Beats: The Beat Generation and American Culture,* 1999, includes various references to style and dress; see a satirical photographic impression of Beat dress in Paul O'Neil, "The Only Rebellion Around," *Life* 30 November 1959: 114–116.

## Suffering

A universal problem; a problem of aggravated proportions for many members of the Beat Generation; a problem to be addressed frankly and fully through religion and reflection; a problem to be solved, as much as possible, through art.

Buddhism, the religion studied and adopted by many members of the Beat Generation, has a fundamental connection to suffering. In the Four Noble Truths of Buddhism, the first Noble truth is that all life is suffering. The cause of such suffering, according to the second Noble Truth, is inappropriate desire. The third Noble Truth indicates that suffering can be abated, and the fourth Noble Truth is that the Eight-Fold Path can lead the Buddhist away from troublesome desires and thereby reduce suffering. Beats such as Gary Snyder, Allen Ginsberg, Lenore Kandel, and Jack Kerouac are familiar with these Buddhist truths and use them to face suffering.

Christianity, like Buddhism, has suffering at its center. Christ suffered so that humankind might be redeemed. The Stations of the Cross, especially the crucifixion, make Christ's suffering clear, and Kerouac's devotion in the spirit of Christ's suffering is so strong that his example is a lesson for many other Beats, even if they do not otherwise accept Christianity.

Kerouac's life was filled with suffering. In his childhood, he endured the loss of his brother, Gerard, who died an agonizing death because of rheumatic fever. As a young adult, Kerouac lost his inspiring friend, Sebastian Sampas, who died in battle in World War II. The death of Kerouac's father followed, and later in life, Kerouac lost his sister. This suffering compelled Kerouac to confront the cruel reality of death and to reconcile the blessings of life with the power of death. To deal with this issue, Kerouac accepted a post as fire lookout on Desolation Peak and endured more than sixty days of isolation.

Allen Ginsberg's life was similarly plagued with suffering. In his childhood, he witnessed his mother's struggle with insanity. As a young man he saw her lobotomized, and as a mature man he dealt with her death. Throughout his own life he struggled to face his homosexuality in an era that viewed such behavior as perversion. Ginsberg and his friends faced agonizing challenges to their sanity in a world bent on violence and hatred. In travels to nations such as India, Ginsberg was witness to daily examples of suffering that overwhelmed him.

Both Kerouac and Ginsberg created a personal and flexible religious approach to suffering. Kerouac responded to the suffering of his brother and the problem of suffering in general in *Visions of Gerard* (1963), which explains Gerard's saintly endurance of pain and death and reveals the family's bewilderment at the apparent injustice of God.

When Ginsberg's mother died, he wrote "Kaddish," chronicling her difficulties, confessing his anguish, and honoring her memory. He faced his homosexuality (and his father's reaction to it) as honestly as possible. Troubled by the daily miseries in the Eastern world, he turned to Eastern belief systems and meditation to clarify his thinking.

William S. Burroughs, although he came from a family environment that provided many advantages, found that material things provide no escape from suffering. Addicted to drugs, he faced the agony of withdrawal. Affected by drugs and alcohol, he shot his wife, Joan Vollmer Adams Burroughs, by accident. Driven by homosexual passions, he pursued gratification in brief encounters. He saw his only son lose his life in a battle with substance abuse.

Unlike Kerouac or Ginsberg, Burroughs did not construct a personal religion in response to suffering. In contrast, he maintained a profound distrust of seemingly religious people, whether they followed Eastern or Western belief systems. Burroughs, however, like Ginsberg and Kerouac, used art to solve the problem of suffering. As Burroughs says in *Last Words*, ed. James Grauerholz (2000), love is the surest relief for pain, and the expression of that theme through his writing is soothing to both Burroughs and his readers (253). In "Memory Gardens," which is included in *Collected Poems* (1984), Ginsberg states that the writer has a key responsibility—to make the pain of life more bearable (534).

Ginsberg's poetry serves as a relief for suffering. Finally, Kerouac probes the inevitability and universality of suffering. In *Visions of Gerard* (1963), Kerouac admits that suffering is beyond human understanding.

—*William Lawlor*

## Bibliographical References

Kerouac describes the Four Noble Truths of Buddhism in *Some of the Dharma*, 1997; Kerouac's description of his brother's suffering (and the suffering of those who saw Gerard suffer) is in *Visions of Gerard*, 1963; Kerouac's isolation on Desolation Peak is described in *The Dharma Bums*, 1958, and *Desolation Angels*, 1965; he refers to the death of Sebastian Sampas in "Author's Introduction," which opens *Lonesome Traveler*, 1960; Allen Ginsberg's "Kaddish" appears in *Kaddish and Other Poems*, 1961, and "Memory Gardens" is in *The Fall of America*, 1972, but both poems are in *Collected Poems*, 1984; *Last Words*, ed. James Grauerholz, 2000, reveals the many losses Burroughs suffered in his final months.

***See also*** Kerouac, Jack; Ginsberg, Allen; Burroughs, William Seward; Sampas, Sebastian; Vollmer Adams Burroughs, Joan; Desolation Peak; Eastern Culture; Mental Illness

# T

## Tangier

A port city in northwestern Africa with the Atlantic Ocean to the west, the Mediterranean Sea to the east, and the Strait of Gibraltar to the north; an international zone that in the years following World War II offered an inexpensive and uninhibited lifestyle for foreigners who had an external source of income; after 1956, a city in the newly independent Morocco.

In 1954, William Burroughs arrived in Tangier and found the city pleasingly permissive. Law enforcement did not interfere with the sale of drugs, hashish was smoked in public, and young men could be paid to provide sexual pleasure. Blessed with a Mediterranean climate, Tangier was a refuge for Burroughs after his arrests on drug charges in the United States and his accidental shooting of his wife, Joan Vollmer Adams Burroughs, in Mexico.

Unfortunately, the permissiveness of Tangier allowed Burroughs to slip into a heavy drug habit, and although he met Kiki, a Spanish boy who satisfied Burroughs's sexual desires, Burroughs found no intellectual companionship with the young man. Burroughs tried various times to rid himself of addiction, and he began to write a novel titled *Interzone* about Tangier.

In 1957, Jack Kerouac visited Burroughs in Tangier. He assisted Burroughs with the typing of the scrambled materials he had produced and took some pleasures in the freedoms Tangier afforded, but disenchanted by the food and poor sanitation, he left in about a month. Kerouac describes his visit to Tangier in "Big Trip to Europe," which is included in *Lonesome Traveler* (1960).

Shortly before Kerouac's departure from Tangier, Allen Ginsberg arrived with Peter Orlovsky. Soon Alan Ansen arrived from Venice. Although some animosity arose between Burroughs and Orlovsky, the four worked steadily for about eight weeks on converting Burroughs's material into the novel *Naked Lunch* (1959).

In *Naked Lunch,* which was published in the United States in 1962 and then faced a censorship trial, Burroughs creates Interzone, sometimes referred to as the Zone, and he apparently takes Tangier as the basis for surrealistic description of a nightmare world. At Interzone University, the classes are chaotic, violent, and ugly. The political factions include the Divisionists, Liquefactionists, Senders, and Factualists, and these groups are engaged in competition for control. According to the narrator, the Zone is one huge edifice in which people lose consciousness, pass through walls, go from bed to bed, and conduct all business in bed. Paperwork makes business unbearably slow. In *Naked Lunch,* the Zone is a horrifying metaphor of politics and business.

Other important figures associated with the Beats and Tangier are Paul and Jane Bowles. With Aaron Copland, Bowles visited Tangier in 1931 but did not establish lasting residence there until 1947. Jane joined him there a year later. Bowles's most popular novel, *The Sheltering Sky* (1949), tells the story of a young married couple's journey into the

In this 1961 gathering in Tangier, Morocco, Peter Orlovsky (seated left) and Paul Bowles (seated right) accompany (standing left to right) William Burroughs, Allen Ginsberg, Alan Ansen, Gregory Corso, and Ian Sommerville. (Allen Ginsberg/Corbis)

desert of northwestern Africa and the effect the foreign culture has on their souls.

—*William Lawlor*

### Bibliographical References

Ted Morgan provides information on Tangier and Burroughs's life in Tangier in *Literary Outlaw*, 1988: 234–271; on pages 253–254 of *Dharma Lion*, 1992, Michael Schumacher adds Ginsberg's perspective to the account. Kerouac's visit to Tangier appears in "Big Trip to Europe," which is a section of *Lonesome Traveler*, 1960: 135–171. Greg Mullins describes expatriate writers in Tangier, especially Burroughs and Paul Bowles, in *Colonial Affairs: Bowles, Burroughs, and Chester in Tangier*, 2002.

***See also*** Burroughs, William Seward; Ginsberg, Allen; Kerouac, Jack; Bowles, Paul; Bowles, Jane; Vollmer Adams Burroughs, Jane

## Teachers, Beats as

For some members of the Beat Generation, teaching is a natural and satisfying occupation; for others, the activity is only rewarding if it can be done outside of the normal academic context; for some Beats, teaching is an unacceptable distraction from artistic devotion.

Allen Ginsberg is perhaps the Beat writer who falls most naturally into the role of teacher. His father, Louis Ginsberg, was a high school teacher in Paterson, New Jersey, and in a subtle way served as a model for Allen, who became distinguished professor of English at Brooklyn College of the City University of New York. Ginsberg also taught at the Naropa Institute, where he and Anne Waldman cofounded the Jack Kerouac School of Disembodied Poetics. Naropa University is now an accredited institution.

Ginsberg frequently called on his many friends and associates to assist him in teaching. He arranged panels so that students could hear a variety of opinions. He also encouraged his students to assemble bibliographies—in some cases each student in a class took a section of a bibliography as his or her responsibility and the consolidation of the work of all students created the total bibliography as an outcome of the class. Ginsberg also encouraged his students to investigate the bibliographies of little-known or emerging writers. Although not popular with all his students, he was generous with his grades, almost always giving A's and B's. In the Ginsberg archives held at Stanford University, videos of Ginsberg's classes are available, as well as many of his teaching materials.

Other Beats have taught at schools and universities but have found special satisfaction in teaching at prisons. Janine Pommy Vega has taught in prisons in New York, California, and Peru for more than twenty-five years and has served on the Prison Writing Committee for PEN America. She began her teaching in prisons in connection with Incisions/Arts, a nonprofit organization led by George Dickenson. In 1987, Pommy Vega became the director of Incisions/Arts. She has edited numerous anthologies of works written by inmates at correctional institutions.

Hettie Jones has served as the chair of the Prison Writing Committee for PEN America and for ten years has run a workshop at Bedford Hills Correctional Facility in New York State. In 1997, she edited *Aliens at the Border,* a collection of poetry written by female prisoners at the Bedford Hills Correctional Facility. Together Pommy Vega and Jones have written *Words over Walls: Starting a Writing Workshop in Prison* (1999).

Numerous others connected with the Beat Generation have established teaching as a major part of their lives. Timothy Leary, before becoming in-

volved in the Psychedelic Revolution, lectured on psychology at Harvard. Gary Snyder taught at the University of California, Davis. Robert Creeley teaches at the State University of New York in Buffalo. David Meltzer teaches at the New College of California. Ad Reinhardt was well known for his lectures on art, and both Stan Kenton and Gene Krupa dedicated themselves to teaching later in their careers.

Other Beat writers did not find that teaching could be combined with the life of a full-time writer. Although Jack Kerouac delivered a few lectures, he never pursued an academic career. Similarly, Burroughs taught briefly at City College in New York, and in the early days of the Beats, he was an informal tutor for Ginsberg and Kerouac, but Burroughs did not try to earn a living as a teacher.

—*William Lawlor*

## Bibliographical References
William Lawlor, *The Beat Generation: A Bibliographical Teaching Guide,* 1998, discusses various approaches to teaching the Beats; Lawlor's "A Compact Guide to Teaching the Beats," which appeared in *College Literature* 27.1 (Winter 2000): 232–255, is an updating of the book-length bibliography.

***See also*** Naropa Institute; Ginsberg, Allen; Waldman, Anne; Jones, Hettie; Pommy Vega, Janine; Creeley, Robert; Meltzer, David; Snyder, Gary; Reinhardt, Ad; Kenton, Stan; Krupa, Gene; Curriculum, Beats in the; New York City

## Technology, Beats and
Beat writing depicts and employs a variety of technologies, including the car, tape recorder, typewriter, television, and record player. The Beats' portrayal of technology, as well as their use of it in the production of their work, is particularly significant given the pervading culture of mechanization, surveillance, and mass culture in postwar America. Their relationship to technology thus gives a sense of their engagement with the dominant culture.

Technology is often presented in terms of consumerism and set in contrast to the natural in Beat writing. Allen Ginsberg's "Sunflower Sutra" (1956) for example depicts a desolate cityscape littered with the detritus of consumer culture, with a single sunflower placed in stark relief. Jack Kerouac's *On the Road* (1957) takes the car as a central focus of the text, with its characters seeking escape from the consumer culture of the fifties by appropriating one of its most symbolic products. Kerouac's *Dharma Bums* (1958) is also often used to demonstrate the Beat attitude toward consumerism and mass culture. In its critique of numerous domestic technologies, the text portrays the television as a medium that silences and isolates people from one another—Kerouac himself sat in front of his television set when his fatal esophageal hemorrhage began. Kitchen machinery is also presented in a grotesque parody in William Burroughs's *Naked Lunch* (1959).

Although many Beat writers engage with technology in various ways, the work of Jack Kerouac and William Burroughs exemplifies the most sustained response. They explore a variety of technologies within their work, as well as making use of technology in their experimental writing techniques. Both writers also demonstrate highly contrasting attitudes toward technology, and this contrast is particularly borne out in their experiments with audiotape.

Burroughs discusses tape experiments in "The Invisible Generation" section of *The Ticket That Exploded* (1964). He explores the possibility of using the tape recorder as a powerful weapon in undermining systems of social control and investigates this possibility further in his later works *Electronic Revolution* (1971) and *The Third Mind* (1979). Some of the results of Burroughs's use of the editing facilities of audiotape are also presented in *The Third Mind*. These include his experiments with techniques such as splicing, along with some of his early computer experiments.

Experimentation with tape is central to Kerouac's *Visions of Cody* (1972), which presents transcripts of unrehearsed recorded dialogue between Kerouac and Neal Cassady, along with other figures of the Beat Generation. Technology is, of course, integral to Kerouac's process of textual production through his use of the typewriter. Adapting the technology by using a continuous-feed of paper instead of single sheets, Kerouac famously typed *On the Road* onto a single scroll of paper, leading Truman Capote to quip, "That's not writing, that's typing." The very centrality of the typewriter to Kerouac's quest for new methods and forms of expression highlights the complex and contradictory relationship of the Beats to technology.

—*Catherine Nash*

## Bibliographical References

In "Technologies of Presence: Orality and the Tapevoice of Contemporary Poetics," which is included in *Sound States: Innovative Poetics and Acoustical Technologies*, ed. Adalaide Morris, 1997, Michael Davidson links Beat tape experiments to a tradition of sound poetry and places them within a wider context of surveillance culture; N. Katherine Hayles, "The Materiality of Informatics," in *How We Became Posthuman: Virtual Bodies in Cybernetics, Literature, and Informatics*, 1999, is a chapter (192–221) on Burroughs's tape experiments with specific reference to *The Ticket That Exploded*.

*See also* Kerouac, Jack; Burroughs, William Seward

## Theater

During 1950s and 1960s, mainstream theater apparently was in decline as fewer Broadway shows were produced and attendance numbers dropped, but growth in alternative theaters and performance was exceptionally strong. The growth in alternative theater was stimulated by philosophies and views of art similar to those that influenced the Beat writers, and some Beat poets, such as Michael McClure and Diane di Prima, also wrote plays. The most important and lasting group that shared Beat goals and philosophies was the Living Theatre, which experimented with language and unconventional dramatic structures in ways similar to the methods of Beat writers, such as Kerouac and Ginsberg, in poetry and prose.

Mainstream Broadway theater of the fifties and early sixties was characterized by landmark musicals such as *The Threepenny Opera* (1954), *West Side Story* (1957), *The Sound of Music* (1959), *Gypsy* (1959), and *Fiddler on the Roof* (1964) and

*The Nervous Set* was a musical satire of the Beats.

ical new way. In its early years, the Living Theatre produced plays characterized by experiments in poetic language, reflecting the belief that language was a tool that reached directly to the subconscious, and in dramatic structures that called spectators' attention to the artificiality of dramatic conventions, to alienate spectators from the characters in the drama; in other words, the spectators were led not to feel empathy for the characters.

The Living Theatre presented drama by established playwrights such as Luigi Pirandello, whose plays questioning dramatic structure matched Beck and Malina's philosophy, and radical interpretations of classic works such as *Antigone* and *Frankenstein.* The Living Theatre is best remembered, however, for its presentation of original works, especially Jack Gelber's *The Connection* and Kenneth Brown's *The Brig,* its most critically successful play. *The Connection,* which opened on 15 June 1959, in a former department store in New York and won an Obie in 1960, depicted a group of heroin addicts waiting in an apartment for their drug dealer, "the connection" of the title, to arrive. In the second act, their connection, Cowboy, arrives, and the addicts use the drugs he brings. Although the topic of the play is close to the gritty reality of subject matter that characterized Beat writing and shocked audiences, the dramatic structure made the play particularly significant theatrically. Framed as the production of a documentary, the addict story represented a play-within-a-play introduced by actors who presented themselves as the "producer" and "playwright," and at the intermission, the actors mingled with the audience still in character as addicts asking for a fix. These illusions made the audience unsure which were the "real" elements of play and which were the planned elements of the drama, so confusing audience members that some fainted when one of the characters "shot up" during Act 2. In addition, throughout the play there were points when the action stopped and jazz music played for minutes at a time, leading the audience to believe that the production had fallen apart. Judith Malina saw the play as moving between the two "liberating forces" of jazz and drugs, just as the production sought to liberate drama from preconceptions about dramatic

dramas by Tennessee Williams, Arthur Miller, and Eugene O'Neill, but factors such as the rise of television and the popularity of rock music led to decreased audience interest in mainstream theater. Increased production costs led to fewer productions and drove up the cost of tickets, further reducing attendance at Broadway plays. In conjunction with Broadway's decline, however, regional (or resident nonprofit theater) and other alternative theater groups flowered during this period.

The Living Theatre was founded in 1948 by Julian Beck and Judith Malina and produced its first plays in 1951. Influenced by Bertolt Brecht and Antonin Artaud's theories of drama and Jackson Pollock's practice of art, the Living Theatre saw theater as a force for social change and political action. This troupe sought to generate a nonempathic reaction in their audience by removing the fourth wall of the theater (the invisible divider through which the spectator witnesses the stage action, symbolic of the traditional distance established between the audience and the play) so that the audience would connect in a visceral way to the performance and thus see traditional social order and hierarchies in a rad-

structure and the reality of the spectators and actors' interactions.

*The Brig* (1963) took this deconstruction of what constituted drama even further. Set in a military prison, a "brig," on a base in Okinawa, the play's characters are eleven prisoners representing a cross-section of normal society. Modeled after Artaud's "theatre of cruelty," *The Brig* depicts the brutality of the confined prison society over the course of a single day. Malina prepared the actors to present the dehumanizing subject matter by seeking to replicate the abnormal social relationships in the prison by instituting a depersonalizing set of rules the actors agreed to abide by during rehearsals. This set up the improvisations within the play to draw the spectators into a drama that was marked by what some critics called "nondialogue" and "noncharacters." The anarchist message of the play reflected Malina and Beck's belief that all authoritarian structures within society must be broken down and reformed along more communal lines.

After the company's theater was seized by the IRS for nonpayment of taxes—and the subsequent sit-in protest and trial—the Living Theatre left for Europe, where its members lived, performed, and created collectively until 1968. They returned to tour the United States in 1968, when they performed their last major production, a staging of *Frankenstein,* that included yoga, nonverbal elements, multiple stages, representations of bombing in Vietnam, and other nontraditional dramatic elements. After Beck died in 1985, the Living Theatre continued to create new political dramas, including *Not in My Name,* a play in protest of the death penalty. Directed by Judith Malina, the play is currently performed in Times Square in New York and in Italy on or near the dates of executions.

The outgrowths of the Living Theatre were many, including the New York Poets Theatre, formed by Beat poet Diane di Prima with her husband at the time, Alan Marlowe, after her stint as a stage manager and performer for the Living Theatre. A number of her plays were also performed by the Living Theatre, including *Murder Cake* (1960) and *Paideuma* (1960). The New York Poets Theatre produced plays by di Prima, Robert Duncan, James Schuyler, John Wieners, and others. Di Prima is also known for her *Memoirs of a Beatnik* and the poetry newsletter *The Floating Bear,* started with LeRoi Jones, which published writing by many of the other Beat writers. Another influential offshoot of the Living Theatre was the Open Theatre. Formed by Joseph Chaikin, an actor who had played the role of Leach in *The Connection,* the Open Theatre centered on workshop exercises that pioneered an acting method that changed the actor's focus from "becoming" a character to embodying a character in gestures and sound; this method left a lasting impact on dramatic conventions in the American theater.

Not all theater relating to the Beats was avant-garde, however; one play that originated in Saint Louis then made it to Broadway was a musical satire of the Beats, *The Nervous Set,* which ran for only twenty-three performances, but contributed lasting jazz standards such as "The Ballad of the Sad Young Men." The gap between mainstream theater and a youth culture dissatisfied with established ideas and culture continued to exist until the late 1960s when counterculture ideas again made it to Broadway in the musical *Hair* (1967).

On the West Coast, innovations in theater came from the San Francisco Mime Troupe, created by R. G. Davis, and the Actors Workshop of San Francisco, under producing directors Herbert Blau and Jules Irving. The Actors Workshop originally produced one of the key dramas in relation to the Beats, poet Michael McClure's *The Beard* (1965). Containing only the characters Jean Harlow and Billy the Kid, archetypes of the sex symbol and the outlaw, the play embodied Ginsberg's "liberation of the word" through repetitious obscenities. This language and the simulated sex scenes in the play led the Berkeley police to charge the actors with "lewd and dissolute conduct in a public place" (McClure, "Afterword," 95). The American Civil Liberties Union eventually succeeded in getting the charges dropped, and the play was performed again in California and on Off-Off-Broadway in New York.

Happenings were another radical form of drama unique to this era. Happenings originated from Allan Kaprow's *18 Happenings in 6 Parts,* performed at the Rueben Gallery in Manhattan in 1959. Orchestrated by performers, physical layout, and specific objects in the gallery space, spectators participated in the play by following instructions written on cards. Michael Kirby in his book *Happenings* (1965) is generally credited with coining the definitive meaning of the term: "a purposely composed form of theatre in which diverse alogical elements, including nonmatrixed performing, are organized in a compartmented structure" (21). Although this definition and Kaprow's original happening are highly structured, happenings later came out of the galleries and theaters into the streets and other public spaces and eventually the term came to mean an unusual event based on art and improvisation, often with a political edge.

The experimental theater of this era not only extended and gave expression to the ideas of the Beats, it also left a lasting impact on contemporary American drama. Happenings were a precursor to today's performance artists and postmodern theater, while the existence of Off- and Off-Off-Broadway theaters, the range of language, spaces, staging methods, and relationships between actor and spectator have all been influenced by the drama of the Beat period.

—*Rebecca Stephens*

## Principal Works

Kenneth H. Brown, *The Brig: A Concept for Theatre or Film,* 1965; Michael McClure, *The Beard,* 1965; Jack Gelber, *The Connection,* 1960 (also reprinted in *The Obie Winners: The Best of Off-Broadway,* ed. Ross Wetzsteon, 1980); Tommy Wolfe, Fran Landesman, and Richard Hayes, *The Nervous Set,* 1959 (original cast recording reissued DRG, 2002).

## Bibliographical References

Useful overviews of the various theater groups are included in Felicia Hardison Londre and Daniel J. Watermeier, *The History of North American Theater,* 1998, and *The Cambridge History of American Theatre,* Volume Three, ed. Don B. Wilmeth and Christopher Bigsby, includes "The Beats, Avant-Garde and Rock'n'Roll" by Arnold Aronson. More in-depth discussions of the avant-garde nature of the performance groups are James Roose-Evans, *Experimental Theatre: From Stanislavsky to Peter Brook,* 1996, specifically chapter 12, "Further Experiments Today—In America"; Arnold Aronson's *American Avant-Garde Theatre: A History,* 2000, contains extensive material on "happenings," the Living Theatre, and the Open Theatre, as does Margaret Croyden, *Lunatics, Lovers and Poets: The Contemporary Experimental Theatre,* 1974. Book-length studies of the Living Theatre are Pierre Biner's *The Living Theatre,* 1972, Robert Sanford Brustein's *Revolution as Theatre,*1971, and John Tytell's more recent *The Living Theatre: Art, Exile, and Outrage,* 1997. We, *The Living Theatre,* 1970, by Gianfranco Mantegna, includes fascinating pictures of Living Theatre performances and text of discussions about their political and theatrical goals with Julian Beck and Judith Malina. More on the Living Theatre's philosophy and Beck's notes on drama are available in his *The Life of the Theatre: The Relation of the Artist to the Struggle of the People,* 1972; *The Diaries of Judith Malina 1947–1957,* 1984, provides helpful background material for understanding the Living Theatre and its cultural context. Current activities of the Living Theatre are posted on its website at *http://www. livingtheatre.org/index.html.* Valuable recent articles on the Living Theatre's productions include Cindy Rosenthal, "Antigone's Example: A View of the Living Theatre's Production, Process, and Praxis," *Theatrical Survey* 41.1 (May 2000): 69–87, and Mike Sell, "Jazz, Drama, and Drug War: The Living Theatre's Production of *The Connection,*" *On Stage Studies* 20 (1997): 28–47. Richard Gilman's "With Harlow in Hell," in *Common and Uncommon Masks: Writings on Theatre 1961–1970,* presents a substantial analysis of McClure's *The Beard,* and the play and other materials about McClure are also available on the Michael McClure Home Page (*http://www.thing.net/ ~grist/l&d/mcclure/mclure.htm*), which McClure helps curate.

*See also* McClure, Michael; Spontaneity; di Prima, Diane; New York City; Landesman, Jay, and Fran Landesman

# Thompson, Hunter Stockton (1937–2005)

Journalist, satirist, firearms enthusiast, and would-be politician, Hunter S. Thompson is known as the founder of "Gonzo Journalism," a style of reporting that emphasizes immediacy and the intimate involvement of the journalist in the event being reported. Often linked to the New Journalism because of its foregrounded subjectivity, and to the tradition of the Beat writers because of its spontaneity and because it often involves the use of intoxicants to alter or expand the consciousness of the reporter, Gonzo Journalism is exemplified in works such as *Hell's Angels* (1967), Thompson's first book. A cultural-anthropological examination of the biker subculture, *Hell's Angels* offers not only a critique of "square" society, but sometimes-disturbing revelations about the journalist himself, who runs, he claims, considerable risk in becoming so intimate with the outlaw motorcycle gang.

Although his book on the 1972 presidential campaign, *Fear and Loathing on the Campaign Trail* (1973), is widely regarded as the best piece of campaign reportage ever written, Thompson is probably best known for his 1971 work *Fear and Loathing in Las Vegas*, a semifactual account of his attempts to cover a motorcycle race in Las Vegas that expands into a social critique of and elegy for the sixties.

Thompson has published numerous articles in magazines such as *Esquire* and *Sports Illustrated* and has worked as a columnist for the San Francisco *Examiner.* For many years, he held two positions on the *Rolling Stone* masthead, one as foreign affairs editor under his own name, and one as a sports reporter under the name Raoul Duke.

In Woody Creek, Colorado, on February 20, 2005, Thompson shot himself and died in his home. He was 67.

—*David Arnold*

## Bibliographical References

Jean E. Carroll, *Hunter,* 1993; Paul Perry, *Fear and Loathing: The Strange and Terrible Saga of Hunter S. Thompson,* 1993; Hunter S. Thompson, *Kingdom of Fear: Loathsome Secrets of a Star-Crossed Child in the Final Days of the American Century,* 2003.

## Travel: The Beats as Globetrotters

The major Beat writers traveled extensively throughout their lives, both within the United States and internationally. These travels began early in their careers, either while studying or soon after graduating, and took them to Central and South America, Africa, Asia, and Europe. If they all eventually settled in the United States—Jack Kerouac in Florida, Allen Ginsberg in New York, and William Burroughs in Kansas—it was not without the opportunity to make that choice consciously, with a perspective perhaps made possible by distance.

Burroughs, in June 1936, was the first to leave, traveling around Europe for over a year after graduation from Harvard. He returned with a taste for the sexual and intellectual freedoms seen in central European artistic circles. Although he did not return to Europe for twenty years—traveling in 1956 from his home in Tangier to London for drug treatment—the possibilities Burroughs found in this first trip abroad set up a pattern for much of the rest of his travels. Whether moving from New York to a ranch in Texas in 1947, from Texas to Louisiana the following year, or from there to Mexico City in 1950, Burroughs was searching for a place where he could live his life without external control. That he moved on so frequently, eventually leaving Mexico City in December 1952 to avoid possible consequences for the accidental shooting of his wife and to spend six months searching for *yagé* in South America, is proof that even the most laissez-faire of places can become precarious if one is on the wrong side of the law. From 1954 to 1965, Burroughs alternated between Tangier (where Kerouac, Ginsberg, and others visited him and where *Naked Lunch* took shape), Paris, and London, close to where his lover, Ian Sommerville, worked. In 1973, after living the last eight years mostly in England, he returned to New York.

Compared with Burroughs, Ginsberg, and Snyder, Kerouac spent much less time traveling and living abroad. His first major trip was to England, crossing the Atlantic in 1943 as a merchant marine delivering ammunition to Liverpool. Further travels to Europe followed, most notably in 1957 on a Yugoslavian freighter bound for Tangier where Burroughs was then residing, and then on to Paris where Gregory Corso was living. After three months abroad, however, he shipped back from England to New York. Although he had many plans to travel further afield—to China and India in particular—he traveled again only to Europe, once to Brittany in 1965 to research his ancestry and to Portugal, Spain, and Germany in 1968 with Tony and Nicky Sampas. The majority of his travels outside the United States were in Mexico. The first of these, with a departure from Denver with Neal Cassady and Frank Jeffries in May 1950, is recounted in the fourth part of *On the Road*. On the many occasions he was in Mexico, he most often stayed with Burroughs (up until 1952), smoked easily-available marijuana, and either worked on his writing, especially *Doctor Sax* and *Visions of Cody*, or found material for his writing, as in his meetings with Esperanza in Autumn 1956, a relationship later recreated in *Tristessa*. His final trip to Mexico City was in July 1957; after discovering that Bill Garver had died only a month before and witnessing the destruction caused by an earthquake, Kerouac stayed alone in his hotel room, unable to work on *Desolation Angels* as he had planned.

Certainly the most itinerant of the Beats, Ginsberg began his travels much as Kerouac did, raising money in the U.S. Maritime Service. In 1947, after a trip to see Cassady in Denver and Burroughs in Texas, Ginsberg left the United States for the first time, shipping out for fifty days to Dakar, Africa. For the next forty years, Ginsberg traveled extensively around the world, visiting friends, giving readings, promoting numerous political causes, and exploring a huge range of cultures. His first main travels were to the south, to Cuba and Mexico in 1953–1954 and then again to Mexico in 1956 to visit Kerouac. In March 1957, he set sail with Peter Orlovsky to Tangier. After some time with Burroughs, they then headed north into Europe, moving through Spain to Italy, through Austria and Germany to Paris, where Ginsberg stayed, with side trips to England, for the next ten months. In 1960, Ginsberg traveled from a literary conference in Chile into the jungles of Peru, searching for *yagé*, much as Burroughs had done seven years earlier. In February 1962, after touring Europe and the Middle East with Orlovsky, Ginsberg and Orlovsky landed in Bombay. For the next year, they traveled in India, meeting up with Snyder and his wife in Delhi and visiting a range of gurus together, including the Dalai Lama in Dharmsala. Heading from India to Vancouver in spring 1963 for a summer of teaching, Ginsberg visited Thailand, Vietnam, and Cambodia and then stayed with Snyder in Japan, experiencing there the vision later written up as "The Change." As Ginsberg's fame grew, his travels continued, but none was as long as those of the early sixties: in 1965, he went to Cuba, the Soviet Union, and Prague, where he was crowned May King; in 1967, he went to London again, and then traveled to Venice, where he spent time with Ezra Pound; in 1971, he toured Australia giving readings; in the 1980s, he visited Eastern and Western Europe, Mexico, Nicaragua, and Israel. By the time of his death in 1997, he had traveled to every continent in the world.

Other figures associated with the Beat Generation also traveled widely. Cassady went south on a number of occasions to Mexico City, with Kerouac in 1950 and again in 1952, and died there in 1968. Gregory Corso spent two weeks in Mexico City with Ginsberg, Orlovsky, and Kerouac in 1956 before leaving for Paris in 1957. Although Corso made several trips back to the States, he also spent time in Greece and traveled to England with Ginsberg. Seemingly taking the place of Kerouac, he was in Tangier in 1961 for the tense reunion of the New York Beats.

Gary Snyder, after studying Japanese and Chinese at the University of California, Berkeley (UCB), went to Japan in 1956 on a grant from the First Zen Institute of Japan. In 1957, he boarded a freighter in Yokohama, working in the engine room as it toured the Persian Gulf, the Pacific, and the Mediterranean. He was back in San Francisco briefly in 1958 before returning to Japan between 1959 and 1964, studying Zen in Kyoto under Oda Sesso Roshi. With his wife, Joanne Kyger, he visited Ginsberg in India in 1962 and, after a brief period lecturing at UCB, again returned to Japan to study from 1965 to 1968.

*—Andrew Elliott*

## Bibliographic References

Information on Beat travels can be found in the main biographies of each writer, including *William Burroughs: El Hombre Invisible, a Portrait*, 1993, and *Ginsberg: A Biography*, revised edition, 2001, both by Barry Miles; *Memory Babe: A Critical Biography of Jack Kerouac*, 1983, by Gerald Nicosia; and *Gary Snyder*, 1979, by Bert Almon. A photographic history of 9 rue Git-le-Coeur, the residence of many of the Beats when in Paris, can be found in *The Beat Hotel*, 1984, by Howard Chapman; *The Beat Hotel: Ginsberg, Burroughs, and Corso in Paris, 1958–1963*, 2000, by Barry Miles, describes the scene in more detail. Joanne Kyger writes about her time with Snyder in Japan and their Indian meeting with Ginsberg in *The Japan and India Journals: 1960–1964*, 1981.

*See also* Ginsberg, Allen; Burroughs, William Seward; Kerouac, Jack; Snyder, Gary; Kyger, Joanne; Tangier; Mexico City

# Trungpa, Chögyam (1939–1987)

Tibetan Buddhist spiritual leader; founder of Naropa Institute in Boulder, Colorado; advisor of Allen Ginsberg.

Chögyam Trungpa, Rinpoche, was born in Geja, a village in eastern Tibet, and when he was a little more than a year old, he became a spiritual leader upon certification that he was the Tenth Trungpa Tulku. After the Chinese domination of Tibet restricted Buddhism, Trungpa fled in 1959. He spent time in India, studied at Oxford in England, and established a monastery in Scotland. He was not an ascetic monk, but his taste for "wild wisdom" won him a following. In 1969, an auto accident left him paralyzed on his left side. He later married Diana Phybus and moved to the United States, where in Vermont he founded the Tail of the Tiger, the first Tibetan Buddhist meditation center in the United States. He bought land in eight states, and despite a lifestyle that seemed more appropriate for a playboy than a monk, he won acceptance.

In 1971, he met Allen Ginsberg and in a short time transformed Ginsberg's outlook on his life and art. Ginsberg complained of weariness with his reading schedule, and Trungpa challenged Ginsberg to trust in his own mind, to create poetry spontaneously during performances, and to shave his beard.

By 1975, Trungpa had successfully combined countercultural literary forces with his Tibetan Buddhism, and at the Naropa Institute Anne Waldman, Allen Ginsberg, Gregory Corso, Philip Whalen, and Gary Snyder were all on hand. William S. Burroughs never was fully confident in Trungpa, referring to him as the "Whiskey Lama" because of his steady drinking. Trungpa's royal lifestyle, including guards and chauffeured car, seemed inconsistent with the life of a monk.

In November 1975, the "wild wisdom" of Trungpa reached unfortunate proportions at a Buddhist retreat at the Snowmass ski resort in Colorado. At a party, Trungpa disrobed, and he ordered others to do the same. W. S. Merwin and his companion Dana Naone preferred not to participate in the nudity and retreated to their room, but Trungpa refused to accept such behavior and dispatched his guards, who forcibly compelled Merwin and Naone to be part of the party. The incident prompted bad publicity for the Naropa Institute, led to the failure of a grant application at the National Endowment for the Humanities, and put Allen Ginsberg on the defensive for a long time.

With the passage of time and with extended diplomatic efforts by Ginsberg, the problems raised by Trungpa at Snowmass faded. Trungpa's health declined, however, and in his final months he slipped into a coma. He died on 4 April 1987 and was cremated and commemorated with full Tibetan Buddhist rites at his meditation center in Vermont.

—*William Lawlor*

## Bibliographic References

Michael Schumacher compactly describes Trungpa's life and his relationship with Ginsberg in *Dharma Lion*, 1992: 549–551, 685; Ted Morgan in *Literary Outlaw*, 1988, explains Burroughs's view of Trungpa on pages 486–490. The controversy about the incident involving Merwin and Naone is given elaborate discussion in Tom Clark, *The*

*Great Naropa Poetry Wars,* 1980, and in *The Party: A Chronological Perspective on a Confrontation at a Buddhist Seminary,* 1977, prepared by the Investigative Poetry Group under the direction of Ed Sanders.

***See also*** Ginsberg, Allen; Eastern Culture; Naropa Institute; Party, The Beat

## Tytell, John (1939–)

Pioneer in literary criticism about the lives and literature of the Beat Generation, including not only the works of Jack Kerouac, Allen Ginsberg, and William S. Burroughs, but also the writings of Carl Solomon and the activities of the Living Theatre.

### Bibliographical References

*Naked Angels,* 1976, opened the door for many subsequent discussions of the Beats; *Living Theatre: Art, Exile, and Outrage,* 1995, is an in-depth study of Judith Malina, Julian Beck, and their circle; *Paradise Outlaws,* 1999, includes photos by Mellon and is Tytell's memoir about Beat lives; *Reading New York,* 2003, combines memoir with an account of New York as a literary locale.

***See also*** Scholarship and Critical Appreciation, A Survey of; Solomon, Carl

# U

## Upton, Charles (1948–)

Although born after the Beat literary movement began, Charles Upton is connected to the Beats because of his writing style, which recalls the long line of Walt Whitman and Allen Ginsberg. *Panic Grass* (1968), a poem inspired by a cross-country trip in 1967 and published with the aid of Lew Welch, combines the spiritual energy of Ginsberg's "Howl" (1956) with the zeal for travel in Jack Kerouac's *On the Road* (1957). When the nineteen-year-old Upton read his poem in San Francisco in 1968, he was received with enthusiasm and viewed as a young visionary; however, Upton soon withdrew from the poetry scene and was unsatisfied with subsequent writings. He now writes mainly on Sufism.

### Bibliographical References

*Panic Grass*, 1968, is a City Lights publication. *Time Raid*, 1969, is published by Donald Allen's Four Seasons Foundation.

# V

## Vancouver Poetry Conference (1963)

Organized by Warren Tallman, a teacher at the University of British Columbia, the 1963 Vancouver Poetry Conference brought together some of the most important figures of twentieth-century poetic innovation. The conference featured important poets such as Allen Ginsberg, Phillip Whalen, Robert Duncan, Charles Olson, Robert Creeley, Denise Levertov, and Margaret Avison. Over a period of three weeks, the conference included seminars, writing workshops, lectures, and poetry readings, which were meant to augment a summer program at the university. The conference was a watershed moment in the interaction of key figures of postwar North American poetry, bringing together poets of disparate and often conflicting formal and creative styles.

The participants often appeared on the same stage together, and this mixture resulted in many wonderful exchanges, which both delighted and challenged the audience. Each of the poets conducted lengthy readings that featured detailed explanations about the influences and formal properties of their work while integrating questions and requests from listeners. The conference is also important in that it is an early example of the social and political temperament that led to later musical festivals, such as the Monterey Pop Festival, and the "Be-Ins" of the late sixties.

Along with its sister conference in Berkeley in 1965, the Vancouver conference captured many of its innovative poetic participants in their prime, introducing and helping to define the formal and creative movements that would develop throughout the 1960s.

Fred Wah made recordings of the conference, which have been digitized, along with other lectures and readings from the conference participants, by the Slought Foundation and are available online at http://slought.org/.

—David N. Wright

### Bibliographical Reference

There is, as of yet, no comprehensive published material relating directly to the Vancouver Poetry Conference, but Libbie Rifkin's "Making It/ New: Institutionalizing Postwar Avant-Gardes" in *Poetics Today* 21:1 (Spring 2000): 129–150, offers an overview and connects it with the Berkeley conference.

*See also* Ginsberg, Allen; Whalen, Philip; Duncan, Robert; Olson, Charles; Creeley, Robert

## Venice West

A small but effusive community of poets, artists, and assorted free spirits who gathered in an economically depressed beach town of Los Angeles from the mid-fifties through the early sixties. The proclivity of these people for drugs matched their ambivalence about profiting from their notoriety as outsider artists, and much of their writing until recently has been out of print. Although often perceived as an isolated outpost of Beat culture, the primary writers of Venice Beach were in contact with a wide range of better-known poets, ranging from Robert Creeley to Gary Snyder. According to Stuart Perkoff, the name "Venice West" was first used in a poem by Saul White to describe a loose assemblage of artists. The core membership never seems to have comprised more than several dozen people, a count that includes spouses, children, and lovers. Its most prominent visibility in the mass media occurred in a *Life* magazine article, which had a picture of poet and pulp writer Lawrence Lipton reading a poem to the accompaniment of jazz musicians in his living room. Six months later, Lipton published his barely disguised account of Venice West, *The Holy Barbarians*, which the artists whom it depicted thoroughly despised for its publicity-hungry distortions. The poets who constituted the core of Venice West were Perkoff, White, Bruce Boyd, Frankie Rios, Tony Scibella, Maurice Lacy, Charley Newman, and John Thomas. Other writers who spent time there included Charles Foster and Alexander Trochii. Its members eventually scattered to San Francisco and Denver, although both Thomas and Perkoff returned and lived their last years there, and Rios and Scibella have read in Venice in recent years.

—*Bill Mohr*

## Bibliographical References

*Life* magazine, 21 September 1959, includes various photos; Lawrence Lipton, *The Holy Barbarians*, 1959, presents a stylized account; John Arthur Maynard provides an historical account of the community in *Venice West: The Beat Generation in Southern California*, 1991; a thorough biographical investigation of its central figures can be found in *Beach and Temple: Outsider Poets and Artists of Western America 1953–1995* by David B. Griffith, 1998; Warren French gives Venice West a brief survey in *The San Francisco Poetry Renaissance*, 1991. Philomene Long's film, *The Beats: An Existential Comedy*, splices together rare visual documentation; see also John Thomas and Philomene Long, *The Ghosts of Venice West*, 1998.

**See also** Creeley, Robert; Snyder, Gary; Perkoff, Stuart Z.; Lipton, Lawrence

## Vollmer Adams Burroughs, Joan (1924–1951)

Common-law wife of William S. Burroughs and the mother of his only child, William S. Burroughs, Jr.; with Edie Parker, renter of apartments at 421 West 118th Street and later 419 West 115th Street in Manhattan where many members of the Beat Generation gathered; victim of accidental shooting by William S. Burroughs in Mexico City on 6 September 1951.

Joan Vollmer was born in Loudonville, a community near Albany, New York. Her father, David W. Vollmer, the successful manager of a plant, provided well for his family, but seeking to escape from the lifestyle of her parents, Joan chose to attend Barnard in New York City.

Joan married Paul Adams and gave birth to Julie Adams in August 1944. In the summer of 1945, Joan asked Adams, who was then in the military, if he would consent to a divorce.

Frequenting the Manhattan apartments were Jack Kerouac, Hal Chase, Lucien Carr, Allen Ginsberg, and William Burroughs. As Burroughs became involved with addictive drugs, the crowd at the apartment came to include Herbert Huncke, Bob Brandenburg, Phil White, and Vickie Russell. With these hustlers and petty thieves as instructors, Joan Vollmer Adams and William Burroughs learned to abuse nasal inhalers to experience the effects of Benzedrine. The couple's relationship progressed to cohabitation, but in April 1946 William Burroughs was arrested for forging medical prescriptions, and the jailing that ensued divided the couple. Joan contacted Burroughs's analyst, who contacted his parents; they helped settle the legal problems, with the proviso that Burroughs return to the family home in St. Louis. Joan faced financial difficulties, and the criminals sharing her apartment faced pressures from the police. Finally, Joan lost the apartment, and because of her abuse of Benzedrine, temporarily lost her mind as well. She entered the mental ward at Bellevue Hospital.

By the end of October, Joan was released from Bellevue, and she reunited with Burroughs, conceiving William S. Burroughs, Jr. With financial support from Burroughs's family, the couple left New York for a farm in New Waverly, Texas, where Vollmer and Burroughs, who now considered themselves Mr. and Mrs. William Burroughs, lived in 1947.

The plan was to grow marijuana, and Herbert Huncke became an assistant. William S. Burroughs, Jr., was born on 21 July 1947. Allen Ginsberg and Neal Cassady visited the Texas family in August, but disappointed that Cassady would not commit to homosexual love, Ginsberg shipped out to Dakar, Africa, and Cassady drove Burroughs and Huncke back to New York, where Burroughs hoped to raise money through sales of marijuana. However, the quality of the marijuana was dubious, and sales were poor.

The couple tried to return to Texas, but Burroughs had relapsed into addiction while in New York and decided to take the cure at the U.S. Public Service Hospital in Lexington, Kentucky. In February 1948, the couple was back in east Texas, and Burroughs was off addictive drugs, but both he and Joan were indulging in liquor. Convinced that the marijuana farming in New Waverly could not work out, Burroughs sold out and made preparations for a move to New Orleans. After living in a boarding house for a while, Burroughs acquired a home in Algiers, Louisiana, just across the river from New Orleans. This home became the location for a visit from Jack Kerouac, Neal Cassady, and others in January 1949, a visit famously recorded in *On the Road.* Although Burroughs made some efforts to be a family man, the homosexual bars and drug scene in New Orleans proved unavoidable. In the presence of known drug users, Burroughs was spotted in a car in New Orleans and was picked up. With the help of Joan and attorney Robert S. Link, Jr., Burroughs, sick with withdrawal symptoms, was released on bond and taken to De Paul Sanitarium.

On 15 April 1949, Burroughs signed out of the sanitarium, and on the advice of his attorney, he left town. He and Joan began life in Pharr, Texas, just a short distance from the legal sanctuary available in Mexico. The trial came up in New Orleans on 27 October 1949, but Burroughs did not make an appearance. He and Joan moved to Mexico City,

contracting the attorney Bernabe Jurado to protect Burroughs against extradition.

In Mexico City, Joan could not get her Benzedrine inhalers, and she turned to tequila. Burroughs enrolled in Mexico City College on the G.I. Bill but soon renewed his involvement in homosexuality and drug addiction. Disappointed by Bill's behavior, Joan expressed her objections, especially to the addiction, and the couple fought.

In June 1950, Neal Cassady, Jack Kerouac, and Frank Jeffries visited Joan and Bill in Mexico City. In August, Lucien Carr paid a visit. When these guests were gone, Joan filed for a legal termination of the common-law marriage with Burroughs.

With Lewis Marker, for whom Burroughs had a homosexual passion, Burroughs embarked on a quest through several South American nations for *yagé*, a hallucinogen known to natives. Lucien Carr and Allen Ginsberg arrived in Mexico City in August 1951. Joan and Lucien drove drunk to Guadalajara, frightening Allen Ginsberg and Joan's two children, but the recklessness led to no harm.

Burroughs and Marker returned to Mexico City on 3 September 1951. On 6 September 1951, with both Joan and William confused and intoxicated, William Burroughs shot Joan in the forehead, killing her. Some contradictions exist in the testimony from the eye witnesses and in the statements of Burroughs himself about whether Burroughs called for Joan to take part in a William Tell routine, in which Burroughs would shoot something, such as a glass or piece of fruit, off of Joan's head, and about whether Joan and Burroughs had previously carried out such a routine. Moreover, speculations have arisen about bribes paid to legal authorities to secure impunity for Burroughs.

—*William Lawlor*

## Bibliographical References

Ted Morgan, *Literary Outlaw,* 1988, reviews the circumstances of Joan Vollmer's life, her relationship with William S. Burroughs, and her death; Brenda Knight, "Joan Vollmer Adams Burroughs," in *Women of the Beat Generation,* 1996, celebrates Joan Vollmer's personality and her contribution to the rise of the Beats; James

Grauerholz, "The Death of Joan Vollmer Burroughs: What Really Happened?" is an address given at the Fifth Congress of the Americas at Universidad de las Americas in Puebla, Mexico, on 18 October 2001, and the essay on which the address is based offers in-depth treatment of the circumstances leading to Vollmer's death.

*See also* Burroughs, William Seward; Algiers, Louisiana; New York City; Parker, Edie; Burroughs, William Seward, Jr.; New Waverly, Texas

# W

## Waldman, Anne (1945–)

Anne Waldman, attracted to the poetic energy of the Beat Generation as early as 1965, forged mentorships and friendships with Beat poets and writers such as Allen Ginsberg, Robert Duncan, Michael McClure, Brenda Frazer, Lew Welch, and Philip Whalen. Although she represents a younger Beat Generation, she has become an energetic and spiritual poet, editor, critic, and teacher, propelling Beat poetics forward and keeping poetry a vital genre in America. She edited numerous magazines, served as the director of the Poetry Project at St. Mark's in New York, embraced Buddhism, and cofounded the Jack Kerouac School for Disembodied Poetics at Naropa in Boulder, Colorado, where she also taught. Her poetry elegantly integrates elements of Buddhism, chants, and feminism, and she is known as a dynamic reader of her own poetry and the work of others.

Waldman grew up in Greenwich Village after WWII. Her parents and her environment supported her bohemian-artistic desire to become a poet. Her father wanted to write novels, and he played the piano, and her mother translated for her ex-husband, a Greek poet. Her childhood associations with exiled artists and poets allowed her to experience diversity firsthand and taught her to work hard to achieve her own artistic dreams. While very young, Anne Waldman performed in the Greenwich Village Children's Theatre, and in the 1950s she saw Gary Snyder read and met Diane di Prima, who also influenced Waldman's poetic path. Waldman became interested in Buddhism, which various members of the Beat generation had been studying. She studied at Bennington College under influential teachers and traveled abroad to Greece and Egypt. In 1965, she attended the Berkeley Poetry Festival, where Allen Ginsberg, Robert Duncan, Charles Olsen, Lenore Kandel, and other influential poets read their work. Her early experiences with the Beats ignited her desire to become a poet and motivated her to work in the writing field in her own backyard. When she returned to New York, she coedited *Angel Hair* with Lewis Warsh (and later *Full Court Press*) and continued to write her own poetry, which was published in *City Magazine*.

She also directed the Poetry Project at St. Mark's Church-in-the-Bowery from 1968 to 1978, continuing to support and promote poetry and the artistic environment in which she grew up and in which she found herself a community leader. From 1970 to 1973 she practiced Buddhism, attending a retreat led by Chögyam Trungpa in 1970. She concentrated on meditation, breath, and chant—all elements integrated into the music of her own poetry. During that period, she published books of poetry, including *Baby Breakdown, Up through the Years, No Hassles,* and *Life Notes,* and in 1971 she edited *Another World.* In 1974, Trungpa asked her and Allen Ginsberg to create a poetics department at the Buddhist-inspired Naropa Institute in Boulder, Colorado. Waldman and Ginsberg cofounded the Jack Kerouac School for Disembodied Poetics. At

Poet Anne Waldman, along with Allen Ginsberg, founded the Jack Kerouac School of Disembodied Poetics, at the Naropa Institute in Boulder, Colorado. (Allen Ginsberg/Corbis)

Naropa, Waldman continued to lead artists by accepting the role of teacher to future writers who, like her, found a community of intellectuals seeking their own artistic desires through spontaneity, experience, and Buddhist ideals. In 1975, Lawrence Ferlinghetti's City Lights published *Fast Speaking Woman, and Other Chants,* which asserted her role as the instructive poet interested in the role of the artist woman. Her best-known volume of work, *Fast Speaking Woman,* revealed a bright poet interested in the roles women play, and she expertly depicted women's strength.

Waldman continued her own role as a writer instructing writers by coediting volumes one and two of *Talking Poetics from Naropa Institute* in 1978–1979. Teaching form and theory of poetry while publishing her own poetry deepened her own poetic interests, and two significant books of poetry,

*Skin Meat Bones Poems* and *Makeup on Empty Spaces,* were published. *Skin Meat Bones Poems,* published in 1985, combines her political and musical interests, and *Makeup On Empty Spaces,* published in 1984, explores her religious and feminist interests. Both serve as insights into Waldman's own theories on the performative act of poetry. Her next significant book of poetry, *Iovis: All Is Full of Jove* (1993–1997), asserts the male dominance of the epic genre and attempts to reconcile or balance the male and female energies that have up until now been male dominated in literature, language, and politics. Written in postmodern fragmented form, it combines the traditional myth of the epic with the ordinary, everyday event. *Iovis* is also divided into two books, Book I and Book II, ending respectively with a divorce and an illness; however, Waldman's two-book epic counters despair by pleading for understanding and compassion in order for reconciliation and healing to occur. Her epic reveals an underlying Buddhist vision corresponding to her own religious beliefs.

As Waldman wrote *Iovis,* she continued as a coeditor of *Disembodied Poetics, Annals of the Jack Kerouac School* (1994), editor of *The Beat Book* (1996), and editor of *Out of This World: An Anthology of Writing from Saint Mark's Poetry Project 1966–1991* (1992). She published *Kill or Cure* in 1994, *Kin* in 1997, *Polemics* (with Anselm Hollo and Jack Collon) in 1998, and *Marriage: A Sentence* in 2000. She has participated in conferences on the Beats and on poetry, and she also participates in readings of Beat poetry to music, including her own. Some of those readings have been videotaped. Naropa has tapes of her lectures and conferences, as do the Berg Collections at the New York Public Library and the Bancroft Library at the University of California at Berkeley. A prolific and hardworking woman, Anne Waldman continues to write poetry today to bring hope and understanding to her audience. She also continues to live the ideals set forth in her poetry. Her work in the roles of editor, teacher, critic, and poet support her revolutionary and Beat spirit, and such work continues to propel original and experimental poets into the ears of the public.

—Lisa A. Wellinghoff

**Primary Works**

*On the Wing,* 1967; *Giant Night,* 1968; *Baby Breakdown,* 1970; *No Hassles: An Unhinged Book in Parts,* 1971; *Life Notes,* 1973; *Memorial Day* (with Ted Berrigan), 1971; *Life Notes: Selected Poems,* 1973; *Fast Speaking Woman and Other Chants,* 1975 (expanded edition, 1996); *Journals and Dreams,* 1976; *Talking Poetics from Naropa Institute,* Volumes 1 & 2, 1978–1979; *Cabin,* 1982; *Makeup on Empty Space Poems,* 1984; *Skin Meat Bones Poems,* 1985; *Helping the Dreamer: Selected Poems, 1966–1988,* 1989; *Ivois: All Is Full of Jove,* 1993–1997; *Kill or Cure,* 1994; *Kin,* 1997; *Marriage: A Sentence,* 2000.

**Bibliographical References**

Two of Waldman's poems and a biographical note appear in *The Postmoderns: The New American*

*Poetry Revised,* 1982; a short biographical account is in *The Beats: Literary Bohemians in Postwar America,* ed. Ann Charters, 1983; in *The Portable Beat Reader,* ed. Ann Charters, 1992, one finds a biographical note and the poem "Our Past"; selections of Walman's writing and biographical information can also be found in *Big Sky Mind,* ed. Carole Tonkinson, 1995; *Beat Voices,* ed. David Kherdian, 1995; *Women of the Beat Generation,* ed. Brenda Knight, 1996; and *"We Who Love to Be Astonished": Experimental Feminist Poetics and Performance Art,* ed. Laura Hinton and Cynthia Houge, 2001; videos include *Anne Waldman,* 1991, a production of the Lannan Foundation, which includes a reading and an interview; *The New York Beat Generation Show, Vol. 2: Women and the Beats,* from Thin Air Video, 1995; and *Recent Readings/New York, Vol. 2: Waldman-Vicuna,* also a Thin Air Video, 1996; Edward Foster interviews Anne Waldman in *Talisman* 13 (Winter 1995); Alice Notley reviews *Iovis,* Books I and II, in *Chicago Review* 44.1 (1998).

*See also* Naropa Institute; Eastern Culture; Saint Mark's Poetry Project; New York City; Trungpa, Chögyam

## Warhol, Andy (1928–1987)

Commercial artist, painter, and filmmaker; a major producer of Pop Art who is generally recognized as the founder of the movement.

Born Andrew Warhola in Pittsburgh, Pennsylvania, Warhol completed his studies at the Carnegie Institute of Technology in 1949. He began a career as a commercial artist in New York City by working for magazines such as *Vogue* and *Harper's Bazaar.* In the 1960s he began to paint images of figures from comics, such as Popeye and Superman. He progressed to his famous Pop images, such as the Campbell's soup can, Coca-Cola bottles, and the faces of famous people, such as Elizabeth Taylor, Chairman Mao, and Marilyn Monroe. These Pop productions were silk screens of enlarged photos. His numerous films, which proved daringly experimental, include *Sleep* (1963), *Empire* (1964), and *The Chelsea Girls* (1966).

A socialite as well as an artist, Warhol was known for the flamboyant company he kept, including Mick Jagger, Lou Reed, and Truman Capote, who gathered at the Factory on Union Square in New York City. On 3 June 1968, Valerie Solanas made an unsuccessful attempt to assassinate Warhol at the Factory; Warhol suffered a gunshot wound and felt its effects the rest of his life. Warhol died during gall bladder surgery in 1987.

—William Lawlor

## Bibliographical References

Steven Watson, *Factory Made: Warhol and the Sixties,* 2003, examines Warhol's milieu; a biographical study is Victor Bockris, *Warhol,* 1997; Gerard Malanga, *Archiving Warhol,* 2002, is an illustrated history of Warhol's career.

*See also* Painting

## Watts, Alan (1915–1973)

Alan Watts introduced Eastern thought to many members of the Beat Generation and the hippies. Although his career spanned many decades, he reached the height of his influence during the sixties when his lively (and often spontaneous) lectures packed campus halls around the country.

Watts was born in England in 1915. He later attended King's College and eventually received a master's degree. He emigrated to the United States in 1938 and then settled in California, where he died 16 November 1973.

Watts became widely recognized for his Zen writings (*The Way of Zen* in 1958 and "Beat Zen, Square Zen & Zen" in 1959 being perhaps the two most influential on the Beats) and for *The Book on the Taboo against Knowing Who You Are.* Over his career, Watts wrote dozens of books and recorded hundreds of lectures and seminars that entranced millions of people. He presented Eastern philosophies to the Western masses and interpreted them in ways that marked him a serious philosopher in his own right. His philosophy stresses self-expression and individuality, helping to make his thought popular among bohemians, Beats, and hippies.

Watts was also a lifelong scholar and held fellowships from Harvard University and the Bollingen Foundation. He later was professor and dean of the American Academy of Asian Studies in San Fran-

Alan Watts made Zen accessible to many Americans. (Pictorial Parade/Getty Images)

cisco and led students on trips to the Far East, where his own work was less known than in the West.

—John M. Carey

## Principal Works

*The Way of Zen,* 1957; *The Book on the Taboo against Knowing Who You Are,* 1966; *The Essential Alan Watts,* 1978; *Zen and the Beat Way,* 1999; *What Is Zen?* (compilation of lectures), 2000. A number of audio-visual recordings are also available featuring Watts's lectures. "Beat Zen, Square Zen & Zen" (1959) is available in Ann Charters, ed., *The Portable Beat Reader,* 1992.

## Bibliographic References

Dan McLeod: "Alan Watts" in *The Beats: Literary Bohemians in Postwar America,* 1983, remains the best reference for the link between the Beats and Watts. Biographical studies include Monica Furlong, *The Life of Alan Watts,* 1986, and David Stuart, *Alan Watts,* 1976.

*See also* Eastern Culture

## Wavy Gravy (Hugh Romney) (1936–)

Noted hippie activist, involved in the Beat movement in the 1950s in the Greenwich Village section of New York City, a onetime member of Ken Kesey's Merry Pranksters, and a founder of the famous "Hog Farm" commune, Wavy Gravy is perhaps best known for his announcement from the stage on the morning of the third day of the 1969 Woodstock Music and Arts Fair, "What we have in mind is breakfast in bed for 400,000." At Woodstock, he and the other "Hog Farmers" billed themselves as the "Please Force" and were responsible for security and for administering the free kitchen and the bad trip/"freak-out" tent. Wavy's concern for the welfare of others continued to mark his contributions to society, as he later became a founder of the Seva Foundation, which attempts to provide culturally sustainable solutions to problems throughout the world, and he also founded Camp Winnarainbow, a summer camp for children.

Born Hugh Romney on 15 May 1936, in East Greenbush, New York, he became better known as Wavy Gravy after B. B. King bestowed the nickname on him during the 1969 Texas Pop Festival. He was graduated from the Neighborhood Playhouse School of the Theater in New York City in 1961. While a student at the school, he worked nights as poetry and entertainment director at the Gaslight Café in Greenwich Village. During this time, he associated with Lenny Bruce, Bob Dylan (a onetime roommate), and Paul Krassner before moving to California in 1962.

Once in California, he connected with other like-minded hippies, set up the Hog Farm, and became involved in psychedelics, music, and social activism. For a while, he was a member of the Committee, an improvisational theater company in San Francisco. In 1964, he and his second wife, Bonnie Jean Beecher (who later adopted the Sufi name "Jahanara"), cofounded the Hog Farm commune on the site of an actual hog farm where the owner of the farm allowed the commune residents to live for free in exchange for taking care of the hogs. The Hog Farm Commune later moved from the Los Angeles area to a location in northern New Mexico. Following Woodstock, Wavy Gravy and the Hog Farmers continued to be socially and politically active. A clown as well as an activist, Wavy Gravy ran unsuccessfully for City Council of Berkeley, California, in 1990 on the slogan, "Let's elect a real clown for a change." Wavy Gravy also coordinated the "Nobody for President" campaigns in the 1970s and 80s. In 1978, he worked with the World Health Organization to found the Seva Foundation.

At one time Ben and Jerry's Ice Cream named a flavor after him.

—*Timothy D. Ray*

### Principal Works

*The Hog Farm and Friends,* 1974; *Something Good for a Change: Random Notes on Peace through Living,* 1992.

### Bibliographical References

Dennis McNally, "Bethel to Sears Point (8/16/69–12/4/69)" and "Hollywood and Home Again (2/6/66–5/1/66)," in *A Long Strange Trip: The Inside History of the Grateful Dead,* 2002; Timothy Miller, "Communes Begin to Spread, 1965–1967," in *The 60s Communes: Hippies and Beyond,* 1999; Sarah Satterlee, "How I Became a Clown," *Whole Earth Review* 70 (Spring 1991); "Seva Foundation" at <http://www.seva.org>; "Wavy Gravy's Homepage" at <http://www. wavygravy.net>; *Woodstock: Three Days of Peace & Music,* 1997.

*See also* Kesey, Ken Elton; Merry Pranksters

## Welch, Lew (1926–1971)

An underappreciated West Coast innovator, Lew Welch produced what Samuel Charters has termed "a group of poems that are among the purest and most precise of all the Beat creations" (quoted in

Phillips, 71). A contemporary and undergraduate roommate of Gary Snyder and Philip Whalen at Reed College in the late 1940s, Welch spent much of the 1950s in conventional academic and professional pursuits. His late entry into the San Francisco Beat milieu in 1959 and scant publication of his work during his lifetime ensured little notoriety outside of a circle of fellow artists, but within this small circle, Welch's mastery was widely recognized. Anne Waldman states in *The Beat Book* (1996), "It has been said that in the sixties you gauged a poet's seriousness by the distance Lew Welch's poetry lay from his or her bed" (260). Perhaps better known as the figure David Wain in Kerouac's *Big Sur* than for his substantial body of work, Welch's poetry, essays, prose, and correspondence compare favorably with the work of any Beat contemporary.

Born in 1926 in Phoenix, Arizona, Welch grew up with his mother and sister in various California towns following his parents' early separation. In a 1969 interview with David Meltzer, Welch claimed the dubious honor of having the earliest psychiatric hospitalization of any Beat figure, at the age of fourteen months. A track star in high school, Welch graduated in Palo Alto, enlisted in the U.S. Air Force, and was discharged shortly thereafter as WWII ended. Transferring from Stockton Junior College to Reed in Portland, Oregon, in 1948, Welch began his apprenticeship in earnest in the company of Whalen and Snyder. Welch was deeply influenced at the time by William Carlos Williams, who spoke at Reed the summer of Welch's 1950 graduation, praising Welch's thesis on Gertrude Stein later published as *How I Read Gertrude Stein* (San Francisco: Grey Fox, 1993). Williams's American poetic voice, stripped of what Welch perceived as the literary pretensions of T. S. Eliot and others, later served Welch as a model for the remainder of his life's work. At Williams's invitation, Welch visited the older poet in New Jersey several times in the following year, during which time Welch lived and worked in New York City.

In 1951, Welch enrolled in a graduate program in philosophy at the University of Chicago, switching to English shortly thereafter and studying with linguist James Sledd, who further influenced Welch's vision

of an American vernacular poetic speech. After suffering a breakdown and undergoing psychoanalysis, Welch took a job in 1953 as an ad copywriter at Montgomery Ward, married, and remained in Chicago. While successfully writing ad copy for the next five years and supervising dozens of fellow employees, Welch's voluminous correspondence with Whalen and Snyder, collected in *I Remain, Volume 1* ( 1980), indicates Welch's increasing sense of vocation as a poet. Welch's position with Montgomery Ward (and his marriage) dissolved shortly after a transfer to Oakland in 1958. For the remaining thirteen years of his life, Welch worked as a cab driver, a commercial fisherman, a longshoreman's clerk, and an academic lecturer, devoting long stretches of time exclusively to writing and, increasingly, to drinking.

Welch's first chapbook, *Wobbly Rock*, a single extended poem appearing in 1960, exemplifies Welch's credo that "the artist is only interested in what's what" (*How I Work*, 95). As Welch explained in a lucid lecture delivered at Reed, less than two months prior to his disappearance in 1971, "*It* [Wobbly Rock] *is a real rock*" (*How I Work*, 77). Welch's concern and attention to the "what" rather than the "why" of what is connects his work not only to West Coast peers Snyder and Whalen, but to Kerouac, with whom Welch shared a cross-country drive (Welch at the wheel) in 1959 and the coauthorship with fellow traveler Albert Saijo of *Trip Trap: Haiku on the Road* (1973). The combined influences of Zen, Williams, Kerouac, Han Shan, and Li Po came to a head in two short collections composed between 1960 and 1964, *Hermit Poems* and *The Way Back*. These compressed, dense, but plainly stated poems resulted largely from a period of self-imposed isolation in an abandoned Civilian Conservation Corps cabin in Northern California and yielded Welch's widely anthologized "I Saw Myself," from which the title of his comprehensive posthumous work *Ring of Bone, Collected Poems 1950–1971* is drawn.

Although not prolific as a poet, Welch nonetheless steadily wrote after his return to the Bay Area, despite and because of his engagement with the burgeoning counterculture of mid-60s San Francisco and the debilitations of his self-admitted alcoholism. Welch's one attempt at extended fiction, *I, Leo* (1977), remained unfinished. Also posthumously released, *How I Work As a Poet and Other Essays*, collected from miscellaneous sources including transcriptions of lectures, is a minor and witty masterpiece, an extended reflection on craft and the distinguishing features of an American poetic language grounded in American speech.

Shortly after delivering the lecture central to *How I Work* at Reed in March 1971, Welch disappeared into the Sierra foothills close to the home of Gary Snyder, leaving a note that left little to the imagination regarding his intentions, a note lent further gravity and prescience by one of Welch's final poems, "Song of the Turkey Buzzard," describing in graphic terms Welch's integration into the food chain. The note designated Donald Allen as Welch's literary executor, a task Allen has since attended to with great energy as editor of Welch's Grey Fox publications, almost single-handedly keeping Welch in the public eye to the extent he has remained. Aside from the aforementioned collections and work, Grey Fox has also published a second volume of Welch's letters (*I Remain, Volume II*, 1980) and a collaborative work authored by Welch, Snyder, Whalen, and Allen, *On Bread and Poetry* (1977). The only extended examination of Welch's life and work thus far remains Aram Saroyan's *Genesis Angels: The Saga of Lew Welch and the Beat Generation* (1979). Welch's long-time companion Magda Cregg has recently edited a collection of reflections on Welch, *Hey Lew: An Homage to Lew Welch* (2001).

—*Tracy Santa*

## Principal Works

*How I Work As a Poet and Other Essays*, 1973; *Ring of Bone: Collected Poems 1950–1971*, 1991.

## Bibliographic References

Rod Phillips, *"Forest Beatniks" and "Urban Thoreaus": Gary Snyder, Jack Kerouac, Lew Welch, and Michael McClure*, 2000; Aram Saroyan, *Genesis Angels: The Saga of Lew Welch and the Beat Generation*, 1979.

*See also* Snyder, Gary; Whalen, Philip; Kerouac, Jack; Williams, William Carlos; Upton, Charles

# Whalen, Philip (1923-2002)

Philip Whalen is considered the most serious Buddhist and scholar among the Beats as well as perhaps the most perennially underrated Beat poet. His interest in Buddhism continued to grow unchecked from its early roots, and he eventually favored his Buddhist practices over his poetry, becoming a full-fledged monk and later an abbot after years of practice and study. His poetic input dropped off over time, but he nevertheless left behind a large outpouring of Buddhist-influenced poetry that successfully blends Eastern and Western impulses. He also shares with most of the Beats an interest in experimenting with static forms and a drive for liberated self-expression that has endeared him to many of today's Language poets.

Philip Whalen was born on 20 October 1923 in Portland, Oregon. Most of his childhood was spent in The Dalles, a small town down the Columbia River from Portland. He first discovered Buddhism in the library of his hometown as a high school student while in pursuit of alternatives to Christianity. His interest was put on hold when World War II broke out, and he opted to serve in the U.S. Army Air Corps. Upon release, he planned to study Oriental languages at University of California, Berkeley, but money trouble forced him to return to the Pacific Northwest to attend Reed College in Oregon. This decision proved fortuitous as he became roommates with Lew Welch and Gary Snyder, striking up strong, lifelong friendships with both.

The three future poets shared their discoveries and interests with one another, making it hard to trace who actually introduced what to whom. The three shared a fondness for haiku (particularly the translations of R. H. Blyth) and interest in the writings of D. T. Suzuki. When William Carlos Williams visited the college, the three enterprising writers offered him poems to critique; Whalen often cited this moment as an early inspiration for his poetic career.

Whalen later moved to the San Francisco area, where he worked a number of odd jobs and was soon introduced via Gary Snyder into the circle of writers that included Jack Kerouac and Allen Ginsberg. Many accounts suggest that Whalen did not plan to pursue a career in poetry but only hoped to

Philip Whalen is flanked by Allen Ginsberg (left) and William Burroughs (right) at the swimming pool at the Varsity Apartments in Boulder, Colorado, in 1976. (Photo by Gordon Ball)

dabble in it. This level of interest changed when, while a fire lookout on Sourdough Mountain, he received a letter from Snyder inviting him to participate in the famous 6 Gallery reading of 7 October 1955 (along with Ginsberg, Snyder, Lamantia, and Michael McClure). Whalen agreed to participate, and after the reading, he suddenly found himself at the forefront of the San Francisco Renaissance. His poetry began to appear in a number of journals, such as the *Evergreen Review,* and he was featured in Donald Allen's groundbreaking *New American Poetry* anthology of 1960. His first full-length collection, *Like I Say,* appeared in 1960 and featured open references to many of his contemporaries. Whalen published continuously throughout his long career; and while his poetry remained his most well-known work, he was also the author of two novels (*You Didn't Even Try* and *Imaginary*

*Speeches for a Brazen Head*) and published various works of nonfiction, including assemblages of letters he wrote to other Beat figures. His early poetry was collected in 1967 in *On Bear's Head* and most later volumes of his work cover a span of years. More recently, he has published *The Kindness of Strangers* and *Canoeing up Cabarga Creek* (a collection of Buddhist poems from 1955 to 1986).

Whalen's poetry is marked by his serious interest in Buddhism (contradicting the mass culture's assertion that the Beat-Buddhist axis was just a passing fad). Like his fellow Buddhist devotees, Snyder and Kerouac, Whalen also sought enlightenment by working the solitary life of a fire lookout in the Cascade Mountains. These early solitary times may have helped propel him into his decision to later join the monastic life. In the mid-sixties, he followed Snyder to Kyoto and finally took up extended residence there from 1969 to 1971, studying and practicing Buddhism. Upon returning to the States, he was invited by the abbot to live at the San Francisco Zen Center. A year later, he was ordained a monk, and three years later, he became the head monk of the Zen Mountain Center in Tassajara Springs. In the 1970s and 1980s, he was also a periodic lecturer and teacher at the Naropa Institute in Boulder, Colorado. In 1991, he became abbot of San Francisco's Hartford Street Zen Center, where he lived and worked until his death on 26 June 2002.

Whalen's poetry is marked by his linguistic turns of phrase and the unique way in which he seamlessly incorporates Western and Eastern styles, influences, and allusions into one unified vision. Although he is not an overtly political poet, as are many of the other Beat writers, Whalen shares their interest in opening formerly closed worlds and forms and emphasizing self-actualization and expression. His experiments with language stem from a lifelong love of languages and a desire to improve his own communication abilities.

Whalen is featured in Kerouac's *Dharma Bums* as Warren Coughlin, who is described as "180 pounds of poet meat." Kerouac also used him as the model for Ben Fagen in *Big Sur*. In fact, Kerouac greatly admired Whalen and considered him one of the better writers in their circle.

Whalen's reputation is stronger among other writers than it is in the general public. Snyder, Kerouac, and Ginsberg all publicly sang his praises, but mainstream fame continues to elude him. Many in the contemporary schools of Language poetry consider him a forefather, as do post-Beat writers—he is largely responsible for the emergence of American Zen poetry. Many critics also consider him to be the most "scholarly" of the Beats, and his lifelong love affair with reading every book he could is strong support for this claim. Even in his later years as his eyesight faded and he became partially blind, he remained an avid reader.

—*John M. Carey*

## Principal Works

Whalen's books include *Like I Say*, 1960; *Three Mornings*, 1964; *Every Day*, 1965; *On Bear's Head*, 1969; *Severance Pay*, 1970; *The Kindness of Strangers*, 1976; *Enough Said*, 1980; *Heavy Breathing*, 1983; *Canoeing up Cabarga Creek*, 1996; *Overtime*, 1999. His poems can also be found in Carole Tonkinson, ed., *Big Sky Mind*, 1995; Ann Charters, ed., *The Portable Beat Reader*, 1992; David Kherdian, ed., *Beat Voices*, 1995; Anne Waldman, ed., *The Beat Book*, 1996.

## Bibliographic References

Michael Davidson, *The San Francisco Renaissance*, 1989; Warren French, *The San Francisco Poetry Renaissance, 1955–1960*, 1991; Carole Tonkinson, ed., *Big Sky Mind*, 1995; Ann Charters, ed., *The Portable Beat Reader*, 1992; David Kherdian, ed., *Beat Voices*, 1995; Anne Waldman, ed., *The Beat Book*, 1996.

*See also* Eastern Culture; Snyder, Gary; Welch, Lew; Mountains, Beats in the; Kerouac, Jack; Williams, William Carlos; 6 Gallery Reading

## White, Josh (1915–1969)

Singer of blues, gospel, folk, and political music; guitarist. In the 1920s, White was a blues singer in the South who made recordings on labels associated with black performers. By the 1930s, he was a significant figure on the blues scene, influencing many other Southern blues musicians. In the 1940s, white audiences in New York discovered him. White played folk music with Pete Seeger, Woody Guthrie, and Leadbelly. With Paul Robeson, he appeared on Broadway in *John Henry*. His big folk-pop hit was "One Meat Ball." In the 1950s, he found success in Europe but was hampered in the United States by the Red Scare because of his identification with communism.

—*William Lawlor*

## Bibliographic References

Elijah Wald, *Josh White: Society Blues*, 2002, is a lively account of White's diverse talents and performances. Josh White's "One Meat Ball" is included on the CD *Josh White Sings the Blues and Sings Volume 1 and 2*, 1995.

*See also* Music; Red Scares

# Whitney Museum Exhibition: Beat Culture and the New America 1950–1965

Curated by Lisa Philips in the mid-nineties, this touring exhibition of Beat culture attempted to situate the legacy of the Beat Generation within the context of the wider social and artistic upheavals of the period. As well as displaying items belonging to Beat writers, such as the teletype-scroll of Jack Kerouac's *On the Road* (1951) and the manuscript of Allen Ginsberg's "Howl" (1956), the exhibition juxtaposed obscure ephemera, historical documents, film and audio recordings and artwork.

Loosely divided into East and West Coast exhibits, *Beat Culture* investigated constellations of influence both within and beyond the Beat canon. Among the wealth of artwork on display were paintings by Wally Hedrick, Robert Rauschenberg, Larry Rivers, Jackson Pollock, and Robert LaVigne; sculpture and assemblage by Bruce Connor, Edward Kienholz, George Herms, and Fred Mason; photographs by Robert Frank, Fred W. McDarrah, Larry Keenan, and Allen Ginsberg; and screenings of experimental films by Shirley Clarke, Harry Smith, and John Cassavettes. An interactive console played jazz and audio samples of Beat poets reading their work as visitors traversed the galleries.

One of the most significant exhibits was the newly restored painting *The Rose* (1958–1965) by the late Jay DeFeo (1929–1989). A monumental structure, encrusted with masses of white-lead paint, DeFeo's masterpiece remains a key work of the postwar San Francisco art scene. Currently weighing around 2,600 pounds, *The Rose* was restored and attached to a new backing specifically for the show, with the help of aeronautical engineers and fabricators from Industrial Light and Magic

Reactions to *Beat Culture* were mixed. While it attempted to clarify the subtler crosscurrents and exchanges of the period—between Beat subculture and the emergent identity politics of the sixties and seventies, for instance—it was characterized by some commentators as an attempt to elevate Beat above its class. Writing in *Art and America,* Carter Ratcliff lamented what he termed the amount of "exhilarated amateurism" in the show, questioning why high-modernist figures such as Pollock, Rauschenberg, Franz Kline, and other "heavy-weight New Yorkers" jostled alongside the "wonderfully inept" canvases of Jack Kerouac (Ratcliff, 64–65). Certainly the exhibition made no claim to enforce aesthetic standards or rigid definitions—an impossible task given its scope and eclecticism. Rather, it attempted a fascinating exercise in historical, cultural, and artistic retrieval.

After its residence at the Whitney (9 November 1995–4 February 1996) *Beat Culture* toured the United States, visiting the Walker Art Center, Minneapolis (2 June–15 September 1996) and finally the M. H. de Young Memorial Museum/The Fine Arts Museums of San Francisco (5 October–29 December 1996).

—*Ben Moderate*

## Bibliographical References

For the catalog of the exhibition, reproductions of the exhibits and various essays, see Lisa Philips, *Beat Culture and the New America,* 1995; a CD-ROM, *The Beat Experience,* 1995, was produced in association with the show, and contains audio and video files of the exhibits. Reviews of the show include Carter Radcliff, "And the Beats Go On," *Art in America,* March 1996: 63–65; and Michael Kimmelman, "At the Whitney, A Celebration of Beat Culture (Sandals and All)" *New York Times,* 10 November 1995: C1.

*See also* Painting; Sculpture; Film; Rauschenberg, Robert; Rivers, Larry; Frank, Robert; Kerouac, Jack; DeFeo, Jay; Pollock, Jackson; Kline, Franz; Herms, George; Conner, Bruce.

# Wieners, John (1934–2002)

Political gadfly and homosexual activist, Beat fellow traveler and poet of a singular, melancholy humanism, John Wieners traced a notable—if inconsistent—literary career in postwar America, from the dynamism of Black Mountain College in the mid-1950s, to the heady dawn of San Francisco's sexual revolution, to the bohemian retreats of Greenwich Village. Born in Boston, Massachusetts, Wieners graduated from Boston College with a B.A. in English and subsequently enrolled from 1955 to 1956 at Black Mountain College, where he studied with the poets Robert Creeley and Robert Duncan. The college had already become an outpost of notable American avant-gardists—now canonized in certain accounts as late modernist "masters," such as the musician John Cage and the artist Robert Rauschenberg, in addition to Wieners's more immediate literary mentors, Creeley, Duncan, and Charles Olson, the school's director.

In the late 1960s, Wieners moved to San Francisco, where, after a conservative Irish Catholic upbringing, he reveled in the social and literary permissiveness of West Coast life. Wieners's bald treatment of homosexuality—both his own and that of urban counterculture at large—found expression in impenitent titles such as "A Poem for Cocksuckers." Many of his works incorporate aspects of his own transgressive sexuality as well as intimate elegies to lovers. Wieners was also a notable activist involved in civil-rights movements for homosexuals, women, and blacks, and his poetry often reflects these social and political commitments.

Wieners's poetic style is conversational and anecdotal. He does not strain to edit either the rhythms and improvisations of casual speech, or the mundane details of an event or encounter, but rather makes these the very marrow of his poetry. The vocative address is also a frequent characteristic of his verse: "Rise, shining martyrs" ("With Meaning"); "Oh Johnny, women in the night moan yr. name" ("Act 2, for Marlene Dietrich"); "Oh come back" ("A Poem for Painters"); "Oh poetry, visit this house often" ("Supplication"). These invocations, along with the staccato lilt of his verse, make the reader feel directly addressed.

Like many writers of his generation, Wieners struggled with both mental illness and drug and alcohol addiction and incorporated such compulsions into his poetic world. Wieners's poem "With Meaning," for example, suggests a compendium of his (and his generation's) travels and experiences; what Wieners calls "imagination's park" in this poem is a parade of short, sharp images unfurling in various locations across the country, ebbing and flowing between hope and abjection: LSD trips and speeding cars, "Berkeley and motorcycles," pajamas and prisons, movie matinees and graves. The mix of bright-eyed excitement and seedy misery is perhaps typical of Beat literary circles, but the particular alchemy of brooding and faith in social (and literary) redemption—as the poem's positivist title would suggest—is unique to Wieners. This combination stayed with the writer as he struggled with both addiction and poetic form late in his career.

Throughout his prolific, although mercurial, career, Wieners wrote three plays and nearly thirty volumes of poetry and prose; not all of these remain in print, however. Wieners eventually returned to his native Boston, playing a prominent role in both the local literary scene and local activist causes.

—*Ara H. Merjian*

## Principal Works

Wieners's poetry includes *The Hotel Wentley Poems,* 1958; *Ace of Pentacles,* 1964; *The Asylum Poets (for My Father),* 1969; *Nerves,* 1970; *Select Poems,* 1971; *Cultural Affairs in Boston: Poetry and Prose 1956–1985; Selected Poems: 1958–1984,* 1986; and *The Journal of John Wieners Is to Be Called 707 Scott Street for Billie Holiday, 1959,* 1996. Wieners's papers are at the Special Collections Department of the University of Delaware Library.

## Bibliographical References

See Raymond Foye, "John Wieners," in *The Beats: Literary Bohemians in Postwar America,* ed. Ann Charters, 1983; Wieners appears in *Word of Mouth: An Anthology of Gay Poetry,* ed. Timothy Liu, 2000; a collection of writings in tribute to Wieners is *The Blind See Only This World: Poems for John Wieners,* ed. William Corbett, Michael Gizzi, and Joseph Torra, 2000; Pamela Petro, "The Hipster of Joy Street: An Introduction to the Life and Work of John Wieners" appears in *Jacket* 21, February 2003, which is available at *http://jacketmagazine.com/21/wien-petro.html.* In Neeli Cherkovski's *Whitman's Wild Children,* 1988, one finds a chapter on Wieners titled "Memory of Love: John Wieners."

# Williams, Charles Melvin ("Cootie") (1911–1985)

Jazz trumpeter and bandleader of the swing era known for his range of expressive tones, including the "growl" and effects created with the plunger mute. In 1929, he joined the Duke Ellington Orchestra and became a highlight of performances as Ellington designed elaborate solo opportunities for Williams. In 1940, he played with Benny Goodman's band, and subsequently he included such notables as Thelonious Monk and Charlie Parker in a new big band. Williams's band accompanied Ella Fitzgerald, with Williams demonstrating his flair for combining his trumpet stylings with the performance of jazz vocalists. In small-group arrangements, Williams played with Lionel Hampton and Billie Holiday.

## Bibliographical References

An obituary for Cootie Williams appears in the *New York Times,* 16 September 1985; in *What to Listen for in Jazz,* 1995, Barry Kernfeld describes Cootie Williams.

# Williams, William Carlos (1883–1963)

A modernist poet who influenced the Beats, William Carlos Williams was born in Rutherford, New Jersey, where he established a lifelong medical practice and also became a prolific writer, publishing fiction, criticism, and poetry. Playing an active role in avant-garde poetic movements in New York City, he experimented with tones of voice and rhythmical sequences of actual talk. Steeped in the Imagist movement and the American idiom, he focused on immediacy, which for him was "no ideas but in things," and he wrote what came to be known as the triadic verse form.

Major works include *Kora in Hell* (1920), *Spring and All* (1923), and *Autobiography* (1951). Williams received, posthumously, the Pulitzer Prize for *Pictures of Brueghel* (1962). All the while, William Carlos Williams remained a practicing physician, writing poetry in between delivering more than two thousand babies.

Mentoring Allen Ginsberg led to Williams's writing of the prologue to *Howl and Other Poems* (1956) and the publishing of Ginsberg's letters in the five-volume epic, *Paterson* (1963). Williams's influence on the younger and more experimental

William Carlos Williams made natural speech and imagism important influences on Beat writing. (Library of Congress)

poets, specifically the Beats, continued as Lawrence Ferlinghetti, in 1957, reissued *Kora in Hell* in his Pocket Poets Series.

Also, in 1957, Ginsberg introduced Williams to Kerouac, Corso, and Orlovsky in a visit to Williams's home, where the young poets took turns reading their poetry aloud and drinking wine. Recreating this historic meeting with the elder Williams in *Desolation Angels,* Kerouac includes Williams's response to solicited advice. Williams replies, "There's lots of bastards out there" to which Kerouac writes, "I've wondered about that ever since" (*Desolation Angels,* 324).

The aspiring poets of the San Francisco Renaissance, including Philip Whalen, Gary Snyder, and Lew Welch, were drawn to the poetry of the modernists and read much Williams. In 1950, as undergraduates, they attended his poetry reading at Reed College, where Williams called them poets and encouraged them to use their own language.

The San Francisco Renaissance not only brought Williams to the public forum, but also it gave him a sense of satisfaction. In 1959, Williams wrote "Contribution to the Symposium on the Beats," confirming not only "beatnik" poetry but his own idea that form as a process develops with the contemporary. In a 1996 interview, Ginsberg mused on the importance of the intergenerational exchange: "I learned a lot from William Carlos Williams." Ginsberg added, "At the same time, Williams learned from his connection with myself and [Peter] Orlovsky—renewed his lease so to speak . . . he became the sage that he was" (quoted in Holly George-Warren, *The Rolling Stone Book of the Beats*, 268).

—Patricia Hillen

## Principal Works

*In the American Grain*, 1925; *Collected Poems, 1921–1931*, 1934; *The Complete Collected Poems of William Carlos Williams*, 1938; *Selected Essays of William Carlos Williams*, 1954; *Paterson*, 1946–1958.

## Bibliographical References

John Lowney, *The American Avant-Garde Tradition: William Carlos Williams, Post-Modern Poetry, and the Politics of Cultural Memory*, 1997; Holly George-Warren, ed., *The Rolling Stone Book of the Beats*, 1999; Jack Kerouac, *Desolation Angels*, 1960; J. Hillis Miller, ed., *William Carlos Williams: A Collection of Critical Essays*, 1966.

***See also*** Ginsberg, Allen; Influences; Ferlinghetti, Lawrence; Snyder, Gary; Whalen, Philip; Welch, Lew

## Wobblies

A popular reference to the Industrial Workers of the World (IWW), a union founded in Chicago in 1905 to organize unskilled workers, including immigrants, minorities, and women in a massive coalition to carry out a large-scale strike and thereby bring down the corrupt capitalist system. The Wob-

blies—who got their name from Harris Gray, the owner of the *Los Angeles Times* who opposed unions—stood in contrast to Samuel Gompers's American Federation of Labor (AFL), which represented skilled workers, such as carpenters and machinists, and offered membership only to white men.

The Wobblies themselves became divided into factions: on one hand, Eugene Debs led a group favoring involvement in the political process and elections; on the other hand, an anarchist group had little faith in such procedures and favored strikes, protests, and even violence. The division was resolved when the groups agreed to pursue both the political process and activism, provided that the IWW did not align with a particular political party.

In 1907, Bill Haywood, a leader of the Wobblies, was tried for the murder of the governor of Idaho but was successfully defended by Clarence Darrow. In 1915, Joe Hill, another leader of the Wobblies, was put to death after his controversial conviction on charges of murder and robbery.

The Wobblies were advocates of the rights to free speech and assembly, and they sought to use these freedoms to express the grievances of workers; in response, police and vigilantes took forceful action to silence the Wobblies.

In 1912, factory workers in Lawrence, Massachusetts, went on strike to win better hours and wages, but police used fire hoses to deter the picketers. When the strike persisted and wives and children of the workers took trains to New York to seek food and shelter, even these hungry and poorly clothed people met forceful resistance. Public outrage forced concessions to the workers.

This gain in public favor was largely lost as World War I began in Europe, as the Russian Revolution developed, and as the United States was drawn into the war. The Wobblies opposed the war and the draft and in 1918 faced charges of conspiracy to obstruct the war. Convicted, Bill Haywood fled to Russia, and the IWW lost unity and strength.

For the Beats, the Wobblies represented the struggle of the poor against a cold and hostile society. In "America," which is included in *Howl and Other Poems* (40), Allen Ginsberg says that he has sweet memories of the Wobblies. Ginsberg's brother, Eugene, was named in honor of Eugene Debs. Gary Snyder sympathized with the labor struggles in the Pacific Northwest, and he later was blacklisted because of those sympathies.

Although the Wobblies did not achieve the goal of overturning the capitalist system, they did show that unskilled workers could organize, as is shown in the Congress of Industrial Organizations.

—*William Lawlor*

## Bibliographical References

The most current review of the Wobblies is Paul Buhle, *Wobblies! A Graphic History*, 2005; the broad background of the movement is unfolded in Paul Renshaw, *The Wobblies: The Story of the IWW and Syndicalism in the United States*, 1999, and Len De Caux, *Labor Radical: From the Wobblies to the CIO*, 1970.

*See also* Brooks, Eugene; Communism and the Workers' Movement; Music; Ginsberg, Allen

## Wolfe, Tom (1931–)

Wolfe was among the most innovative journalists who explored sixties culture. His jazzy style and ear for the jargon and manners of an exuberant era made him one of the founding fathers of New Journalism. Exploring the subcultures of the "Me Decade," as he termed the late sixties and seven-

ties, Wolfe's articles anatomized a time of prosperity, individuality, and enjoyment. He was particularly interested in new trends, the concept of social status, and the attempt of subcultures to bypass traditional class distinctions.

Born in Richmond, Virginia, on 2 March 1931, Wolfe graduated from Washington and Lee University (1951), received a doctorate in American Studies from Yale in 1956, and began a career as a journalist, critic, and novelist.

—*Mike W. Malm*

## Principal Works

Prose: *The Kandy-Kolored Tangerine-Flake Streamline Baby*, 1965; *The Electric Kool-Aid Acid Test*, 1968; *Radical Chic & Mau-Mauing the Flak-Catchers*, 1970; (with E. W. Johnson) *The New Journalism*, 1973; *Mauve Gloves & Madmen, Clutter & Vine*, 1976; *The Right Stuff*, 1979; *The Bonfire of the Vanities*, 1987; *A Man in Full*, 1998.

## Bibliographical References

For a relatively comprehensive study of Wolfe's life and work, see William McKeen, *Tom Wolfe*, 1995; critical essays on Wolfe's work are collected in Harold Bloom, ed., *Tom Wolfe: Modern Critical Views*, 2000; and in Brian Abel Ragen, *Tom Wolfe: A Critical Companion*, 2002; reviews on Wolfe are found in Doug Shomette, ed., *The Critical Response to Tom Wolfe*, 1992.

*See also* Kesey, Ken Elton; Merry Pranksters

# Y

## Young, Lester (1909–1959)

Lester Young was a tenor saxophonist noted for a cool, smooth sound. Young started his career backing such jazz innovators as Count Basie and Coleman Hawkins. His instrumental and improvisational prowess was recognized by Billie Holiday, who gave him the moniker "Prez." Young is instantly recognizable as the calm, sultry tone on many albums of the bebop era. He often played in bands backing the popular female singers of bebop jazz, his style ideally suited to interplay with the melodies of the voice. Allen Ginsberg refers to Young in *Composed on the Tongue*, remarking, "Lester Young is what I was thinking about. . . . 'Howl' is all 'Lester Leaps In'" (43).

—*David N. Wright*

### Bibliographical References

See Allen Ginsberg, *Composed on the Tongue*, 1980; and Steven Paul Scher, ed., *Music and Text: Critical Inquiries*, 1992.

***See also*** Ginsberg, Allen; Music; Kerouac, Jack; Holiday, Billie; Hawkins, Coleman

# Index

*Note: page numbers in **bold** font indicate primary entries in the Encyclopedia*